IMAGES
of America

CERES

I0807617

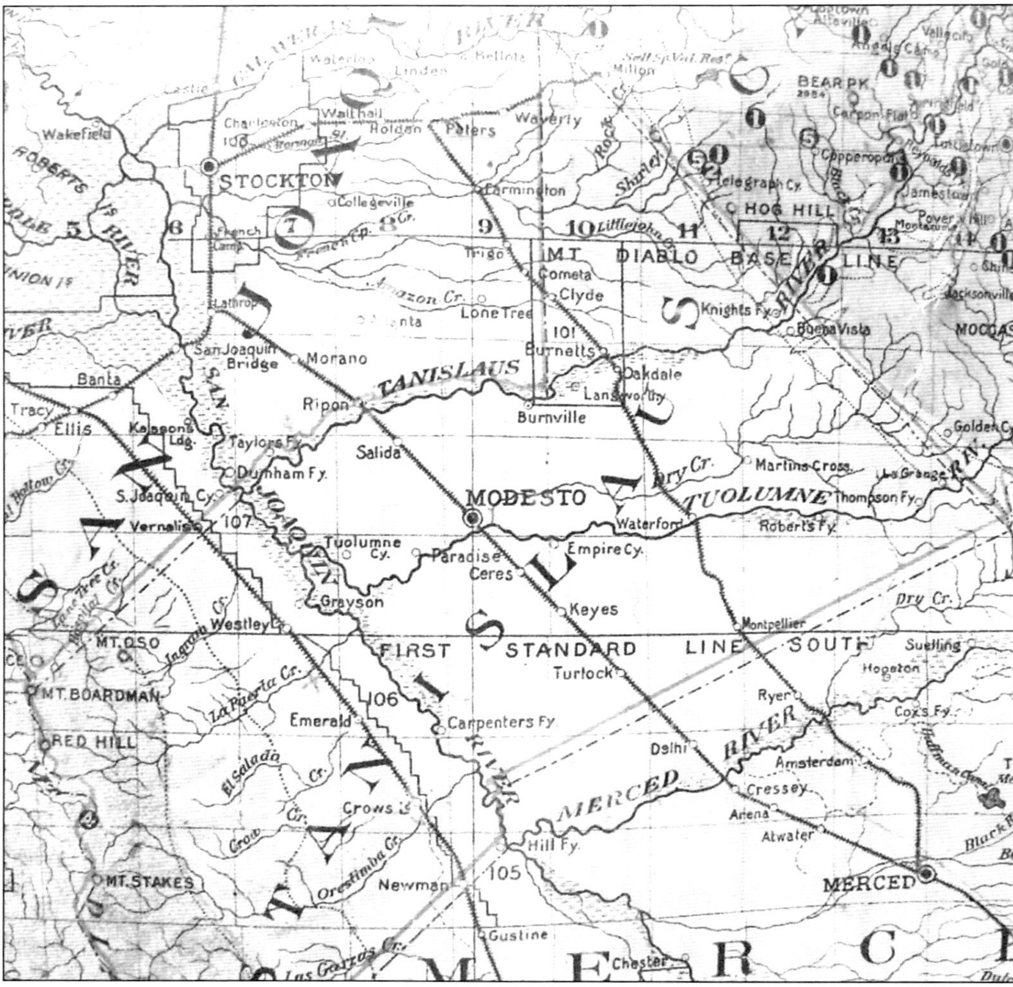

This 1870s map shows the tiny settlement of Ceres along the Central Pacific Railroad tracks cutting through the center of Stanislaus County. A number of towns on this map no longer exist, including Tuolumne City, Paradise, and Empire City. Burnville (or Burneyville) became Riverbank. Since its founding, Ceres has remained a healthy and thriving community. (Author's collection.)

On The Cover: The Ceres Drive-In, or Burger 19, was a popular burger joint in the 1950s operated by Bob and Ruth Simpson. The building was first used as Wayne Hosmer's service station, then as a fruit stand, and then a nine-stool cafe operated by L. R. Cooper. In April 1955, the Simpsons opened Burger 19 on a $25 per month lease. The eatery was located at the present-day drainage basin at the eastern approach of the Pine Street overpass. (Ruth Simpson.)

IMAGES
of America

CERES

Jeff Benziger

ARCADIA
PUBLISHING

ISBN 978-0-7385-8101-9

Published by Arcadia Publishing
Charleston, South Carolina

Printed in the United States of America

Library of Congress Control Number: 2010921990

For all general information contact Arcadia Publishing at:
Telephone 843-853-2070
Fax 843-853-0044
E-mail sales@arcadiapublishing.com
For customer service and orders:
Toll-Free 1-888-313-2665

Visit us on the Internet at www.arcadiapublishing.com

This book is dedicated to Phil Reynders, who was instrumental in establishing the Ceres Museum, and to Mildred Lucas—one of the sweetest souls on God's green earth—whose research in the 1970s captured important details about this history-rich California city.

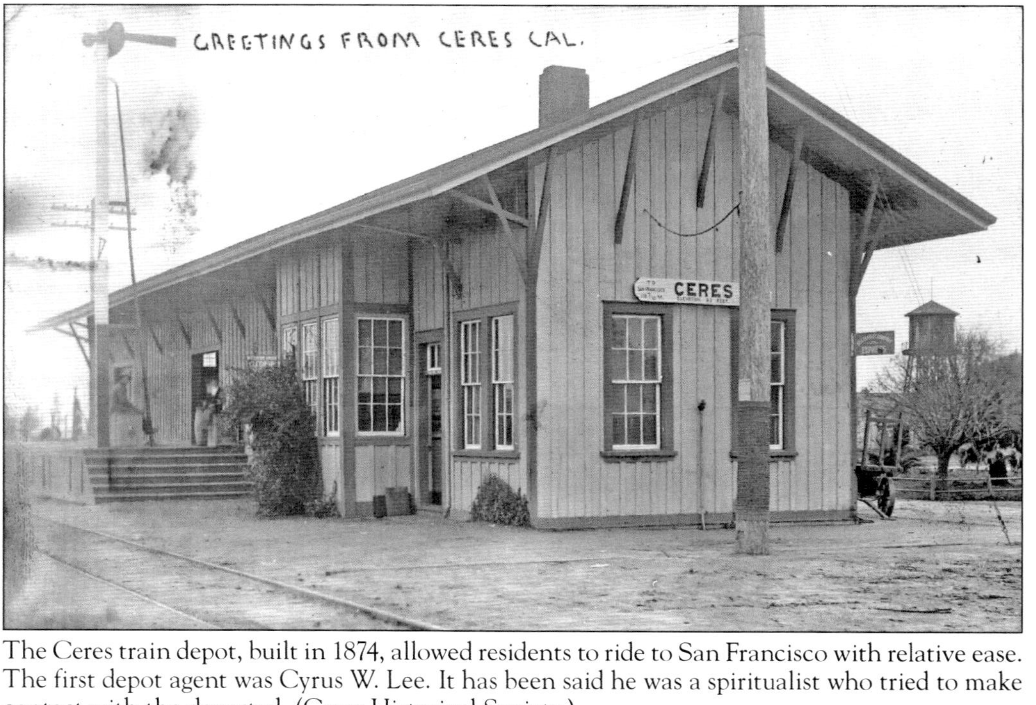

The Ceres train depot, built in 1874, allowed residents to ride to San Francisco with relative ease. The first depot agent was Cyrus W. Lee. It has been said he was a spiritualist who tried to make contact with the departed. (Ceres Historical Society.)

Contents

Acknowledgments

Ceres was long overdue for a book of this nature. Never before has there been such a collection of historic images of Ceres in one volume. This work would not have been possible without the assistance of the good folks of Ceres. Mildred Lucas eagerly rushed to assist in this endeavor and delved into her personal collection of photographs and historical materials. To her I offer my profound appreciation. The book was greatly enhanced by Phil Reynders and Sheryl Trout of the Ceres Historical Society. Thanks are also due to Grant Lucas, Ruth Simpson, Marion Gondring Sanders, Claudia Grubeck, Jan Vilas Conway, Verna Nelson, the Pallios family, Jean Mouton, Dennis Barbour, Phil Reynders, Diana Wilson, Shirley Ollar, Pat Cousins, and Betty Ham. Jason Coley of the Ceres Police Department and Cindy Heidorn of Ceres City Hall also provided photographs and deserve praise. Brian Weber, Bryan Nicholes, Carissa Higginbotham, and Brian Hunt at the Ceres Fire Department also provided great assistance. Sid Long was of immense help when it came to understanding the role of Superior Fruit Ranch as well as providing images of the construction of the Don Pedro Dam in the 1920s. A number of people contributed to my knowledge of Ceres' rich past during my years of editing the *Ceres Courier*, and I have appreciated how they, in a way, assisted in this work. These people include Ruth Jorgensen, Caryl Fowler, Mae Hensley, and Merle Fountain.

In keeping with Ceres' slogan, "Together We Achieve," I'm proud of this work we have accomplished together.

INTRODUCTION

Most California towns sprang up as the result of the massive influx of immigrants stemming from the gold rush of 1849. While Ceres is far from the gold fields, it can trace its foundation to the lust for gold. Word of James Marshall's January 24, 1848, gold discovery in Coloma was the single greatest catalyst for the development of California. Many Easterners sought out the Gold Country on a dangerous wagon trail trek over land or by a treacherous sea route to San Francisco. Sierra Nevada communities like Auburn, Placerville, Jackson, Columbia, Angels Camp, Jamestown, and Sonora boomed, but many souls quickly grew disillusioned. Hunting for gold was a backbreaking and slow endeavor. Many turned to more traditional jobs, such as running mercantiles, supplying freight, blacksmithing, and farming. They came down out of the hills to squat on the flat land of the San Joaquin Valley where soil was perfect for farming wheat and alfalfa.

Many who settled in Ceres did so out of indifference to gold striking. Daniel Whitmore knew the life of an Atlantic sea captain and packed up with wife and children from Michigan for California in 1854. He arrived in Stockton to grow wheat and soon would be the first one to build a home in Ceres, which has preserved it to this day. James Warner, born in England, came to California in 1852 by sea in search for gold. He eventually found his way to Ceres as a businessman. John Service left Auburn for Ceres in the fall of 1867. Along with Warner, Service first laid his eyes on the Stockton area in December 1864. Vermont-born Ephraim Hatch ran away from Boston to escape an abusive father and ended up in San Francisco at age 19 with $1 in his pocket. He walked from Stockton to the gold fields. He eventually became a huge landowner in the area that is Hatch Road up to the Tuolumne River and over to South Modesto. These were the men who ended up in the region that was to become Ceres.

In the shadow of Modesto, Ceres has a fascinating past well worth celebrating.

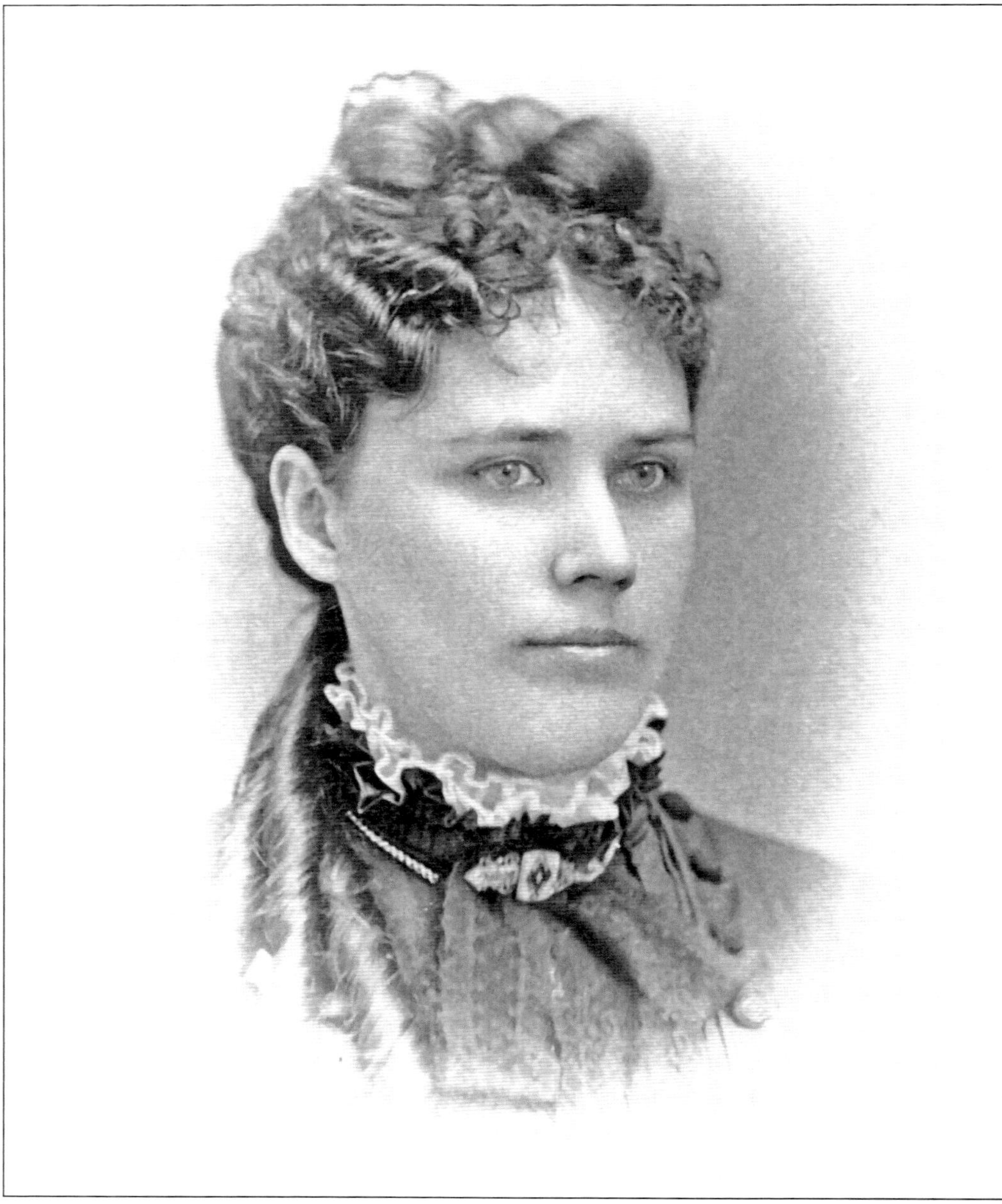

Elma J. Carter was responsible for giving Ceres its name in 1871. Elma was the pretty daughter of Levi and Fanna Carter, the first settlers in the Ceres-Keyes region. Because the region was planted in wheat, the schoolteacher believed that Ceres, the Roman goddess of agriculture, was a fitting name for her father's granary and warehouses along the new Central Pacific Railroad tracks south of the settlement. The name Ceres was picked up for the town after Levi Carter sold a section of his real estate holdings to Daniel Whitmore. Curiously, the area's horse-watering stop was near the Carter house and was named Esmar by taking the first letters of the names of the Carter children—Elma, Stanton, Melbourne, Aletha, and Roscoe. In 1889, 47-year-old Elma married Edward H. Hills and lived out the rest of her life in Modesto. She died May 30, 1902. (Jan Vilas Conway.)

One

Rooted in the Land

The abundantly rich soil drew farmers who had a vision for a new town for raising families. Like many after the gold rush of 1849, Ohio-born Daniel Whitmore, who had learned sailing in Massachusetts, decided to head for California. He and his wife, Lucy, left Pittsford, Michigan, in the spring of 1854 in a wagon train bound for California. Five months later, the Whitmores arrived in the Stockton area and settled in the Cherokee Lane vicinity until 1857. He farmed wheat and later moved into Stanislaus County, purchasing 10,000 acres in 1867 south of the river at present-day Ceres. Arriving with the Whitmores were John and Julia Service. Daniel's brother, Richard K. Whitmore, showed up in 1869 at about the time Daniel was building a house that stands today on Fifth Street. The first buildings constructed in the Ceres area, however, were Levi Carter's granary and warehouse on his 2,400 acres south of town. From Stockton, Carter snatched up land in Stanislaus County from 1863 to 1865 and named his new establishment where horses were watered Esmar Station. In 1871, introduction of the railroad near Whitmore's town resulted in a Ceres depot. In 1872, Carter sold Daniel Whitmore a block of land for $9,000 that extended from Tenth Street to Central Avenue and from Whitmore Avenue to Service Road. Ceres was built within that block. In 1875, Daniel Whitmore filed the first town plot and offered lots to anyone who pledged to refrain from selling alcoholic beverages. With its mild climate (except for some blisteringly hot summer days), Ceres blossomed as a town. Wheat remained the primary crop grown in the area until irrigation was made available from the La Grange Dam in 1900. An availability of year-round water allowed other crops to be grown, including figs, peaches, walnuts, almonds, and vegetables. Dairy cattle provided milk for the Ceres Creamery, which produced Ceres Butter.

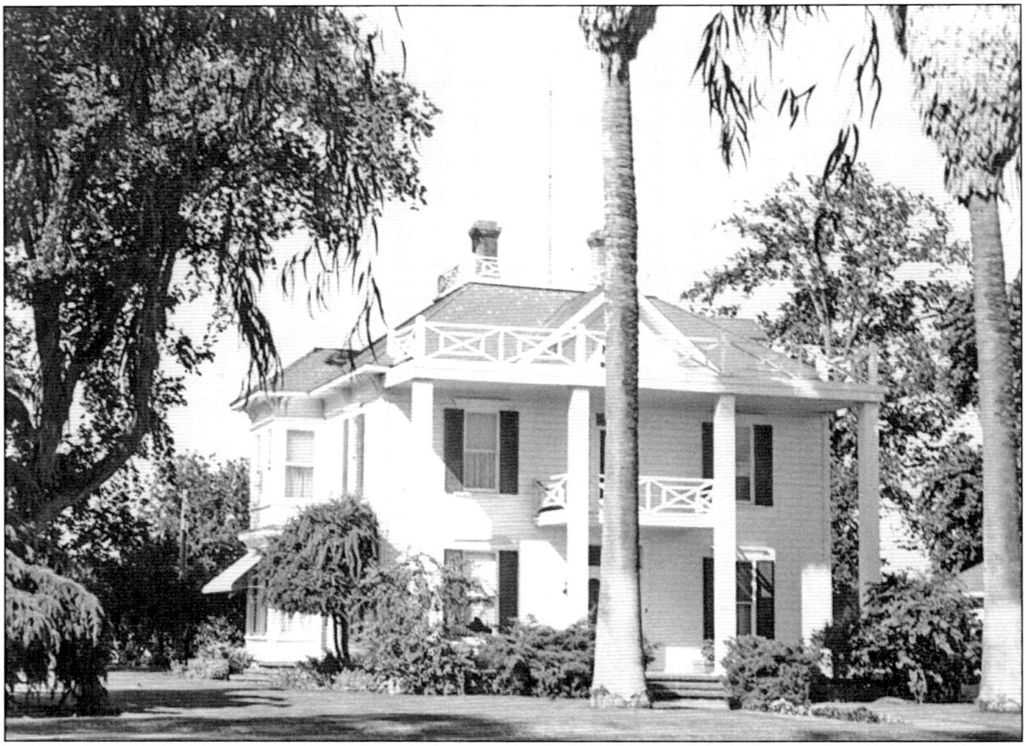

The Carter-Vilas home was the first in the Ceres region. Levi Carter built the house south of the future Ceres town site in 1865. At the time Carter farmed 2,400 acres in the area that would become Ceres and Keyes. Carter has been called the "first citizen of Ceres" as his house was built before Daniel Whitmore's 1870 residence. After the Central Pacific Railroad laid its tracks in 1870, the first railroad crossing was near the Carter house and named Esmar. The spacious 112-acre estate was sold in 1905 to Marcellus Vilas, a New York native who came to Ceres from Shasta County. The house was enlarged in 1892 and has remained in the Vilas family. (Mildred Lucas.)

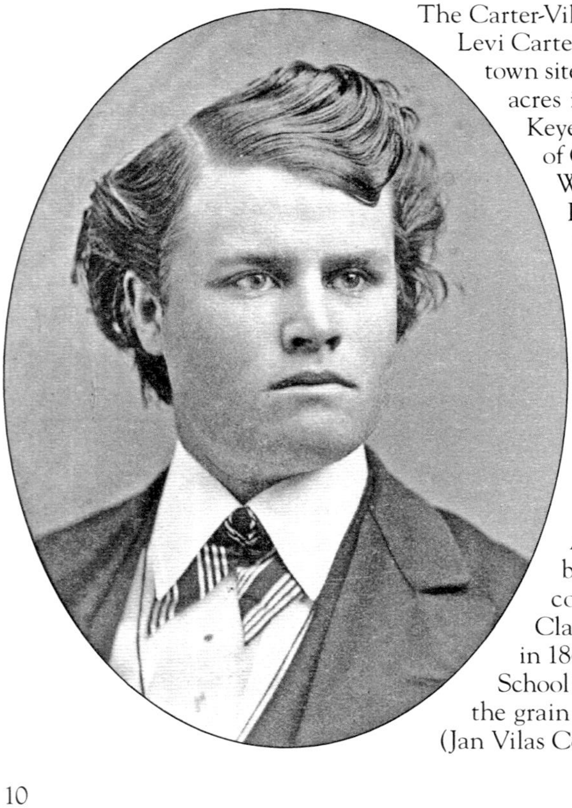

A son of Levi Carter, Stanton L. Carter became an attorney and judge of the superior court in Fresno. He was born in 1853 in Clayton, New York, and arrived in California in 1862. Stanton graduated from Stockton High School in 1871 and then worked summers managing the grain warehouse in Ceres. He later studied law. (Jan Vilas Conway.)

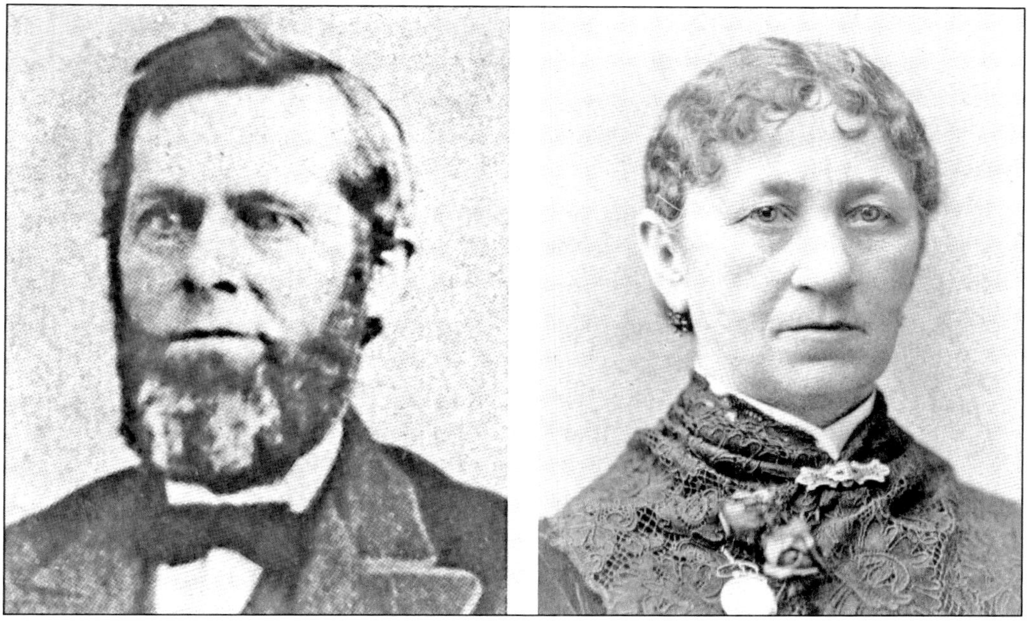

Daniel Whitmore (1816–1893) and Lucy J. Whitmore (1826–1898) (above) were among the first settlers and are credited with establishing Ceres. Daniel recorded the first town map in 1875, and Lucy was known as a wonderful mother to sons Eugene W. (1860–1870) and Leonard H. (1847–1873). In 1870, Daniel Whitmore completed this first home (below) in Ceres on Fifth Street. It was purchased by the city in the late 1980s and restored. It is listed on the National Register of Historic Places. (Ceres Historical Society.)

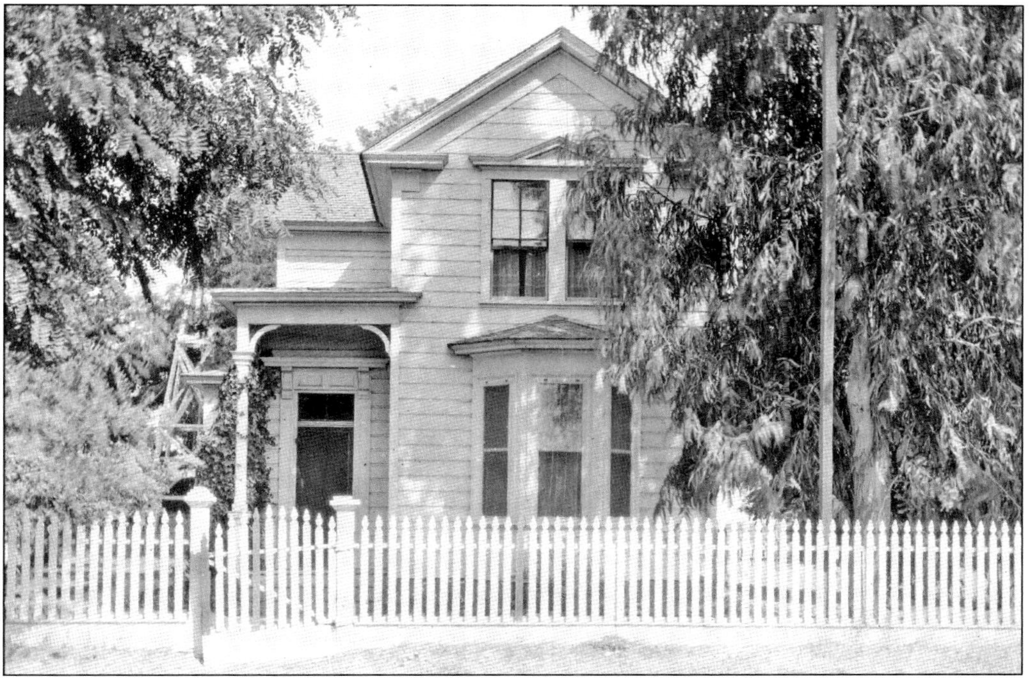

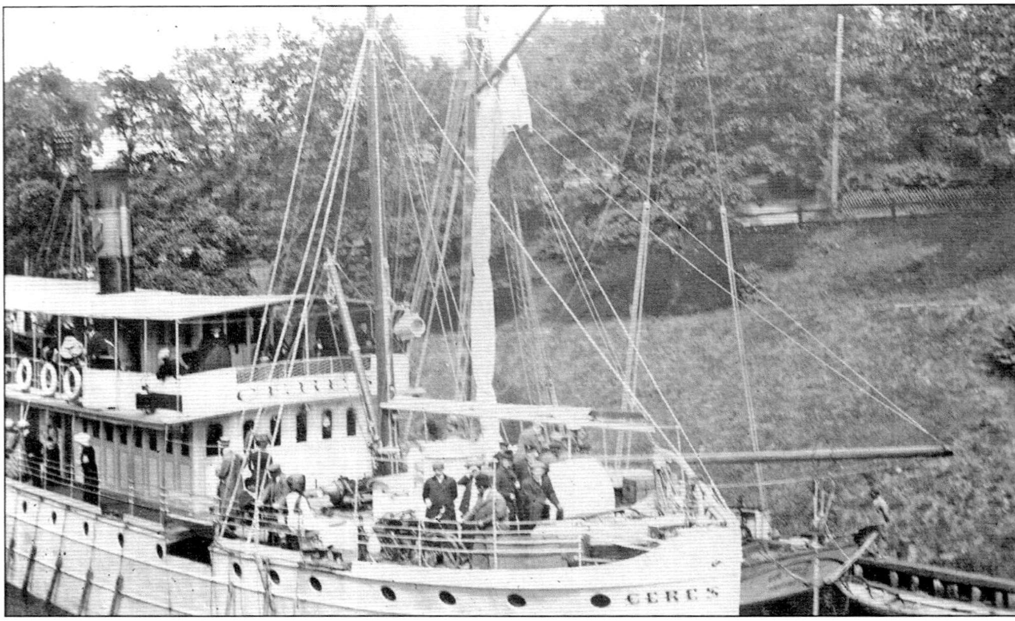

Wheat was the primary crop grown in Ceres from the 1860s through the 1890s, before irrigation water arrived. Crops were shipped out on the "river highways" via barges pulled by steamships from Whitmore's Ferry on the Tuolumne River. Grain was also loaded up at Sand Hill on the Tuolumne River near present-day River Oaks Golf Course. Wheat was hauled up the San Joaquin River to Stockton. The steamer *Ceres* was owned by Cornwall, Peters, and Company and was in use as of 1878. (Author's collection.)

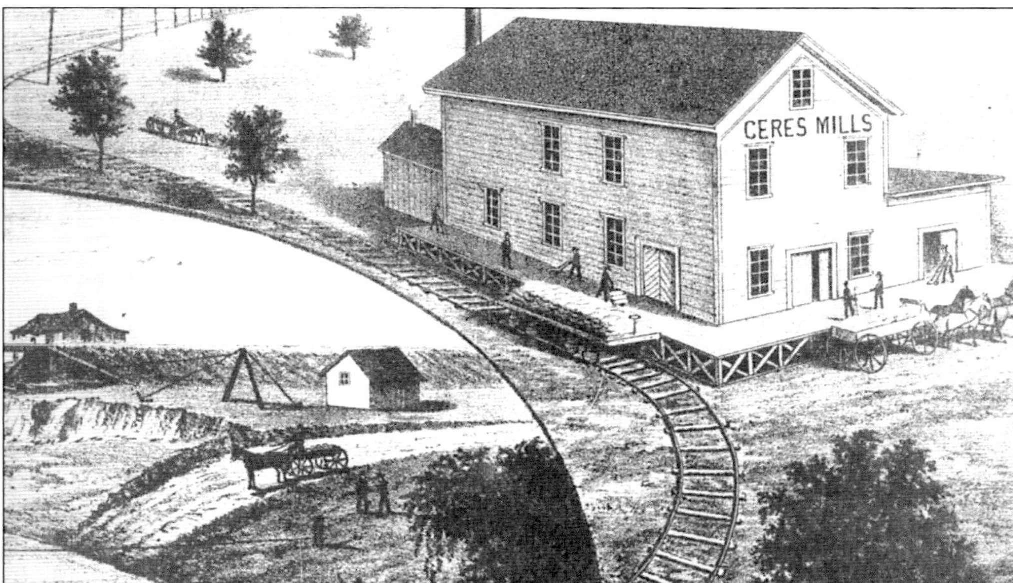

This is a 19th-century artist's rendering of the Ceres Mills belonging to Daniel Whitmore. The inset at left depicts Whitmore's Ferry crossing on the Tuolumne River at a location between today's Seventh Street and Ninth Street bridges. The ferry operated between 1877 and 1883. (Author's collection.)

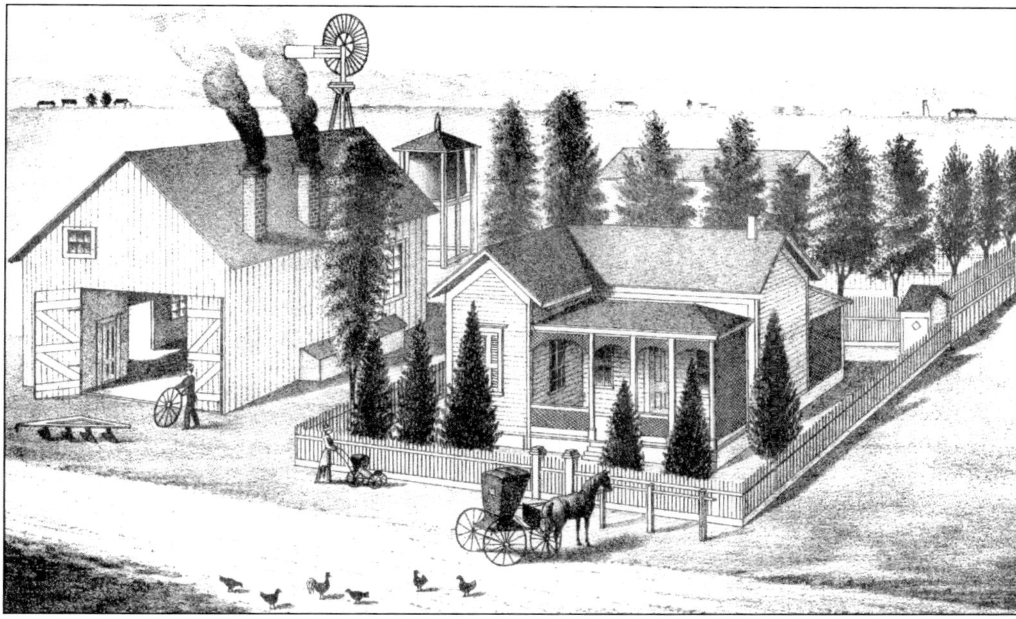

John Greany Annear built this blacksmith shop and home in Ceres as depicted in L. C. Branch's *History of Stanislaus County* published in 1881. Annear was born in England in 1843 and came to Ceres with wife Tabitha in 1872. Ceres' first blacksmith was so successful that he was able to purchase 300 acres of land from Levi Carter south of town in 1874. Annear resided on Fifth Street until his death on January 7, 1928. (*History of Stanislaus County.*)

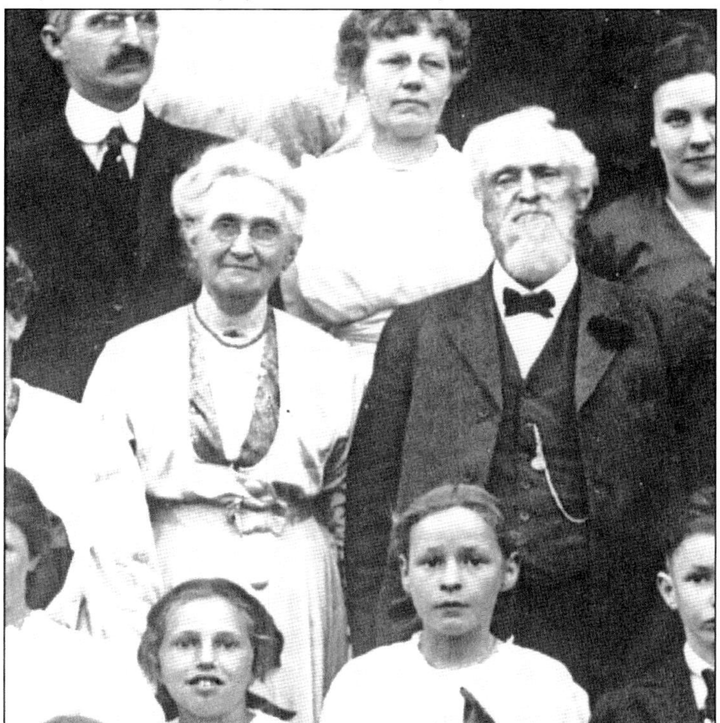

Along with the Whitmores and the Warners, New York native John Service was one of the first to settle in Ceres. He and his wife, Julia Hall Warner Service (seen here on their 50th wedding anniversary), came to Ceres in 1867 from Auburn with the Warner family. They purchased 640 acres to the south of the future town site, paying just $1.25 per acre. Service also bought land between Snelling and La Grange. Ill health forced him to retire in 1899 and move to Berkeley. The father of 11 children, John Service died during a 1920 visit to Ceres. (Ceres Historical Society.)

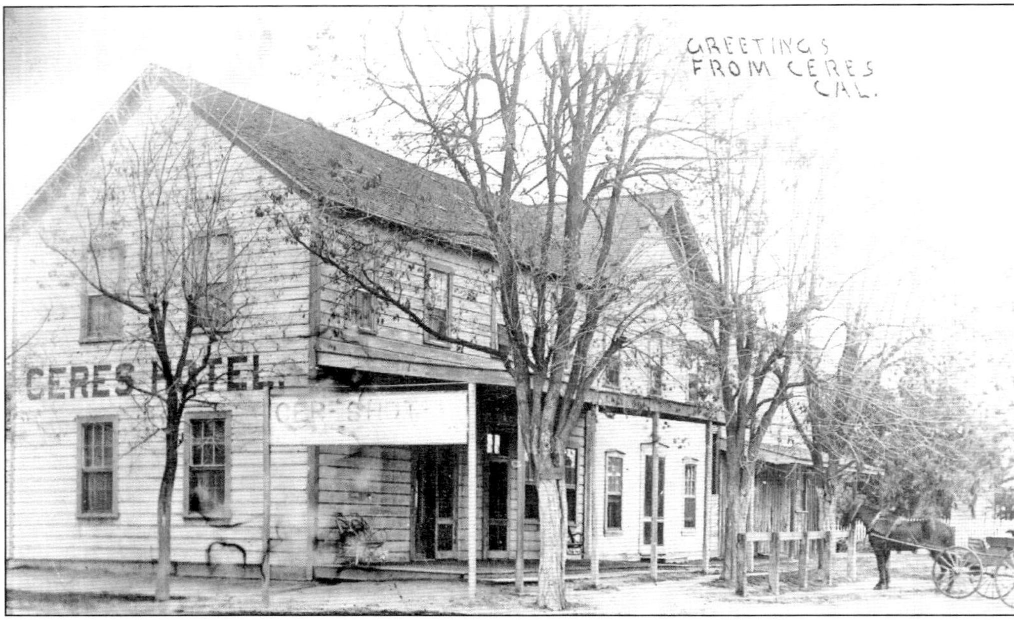

This two-story wooden Ceres Hotel was an important asset for the town's growing business climate. It was located between Fourth and Fifth Streets on the highway. (Ceres Historical Society.)

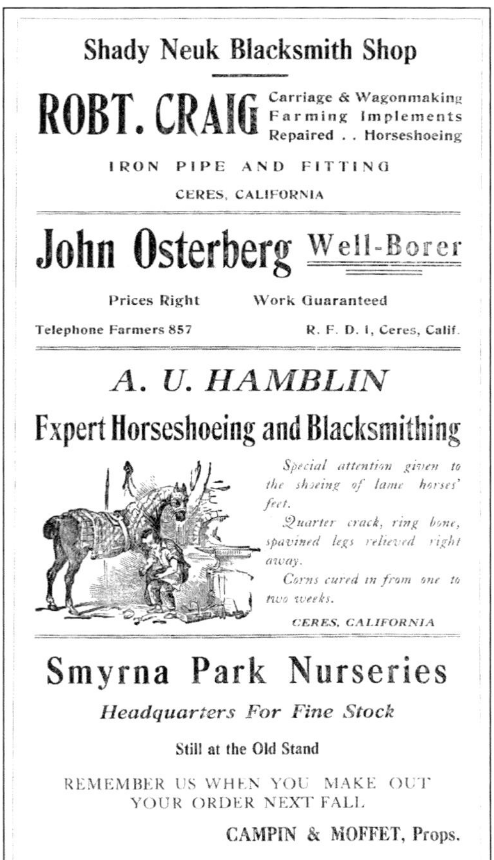

These advertisements for local businesses appear in the 1911 Ceres High School yearbook, the *Cereal*. They included blacksmiths Robert Craig and A. U. Hamblin, well-driller John Osterberg, and Smyrna Park Nurseries operated by Fred Moffet and Daniel Campin. (Mildred Lucas.)

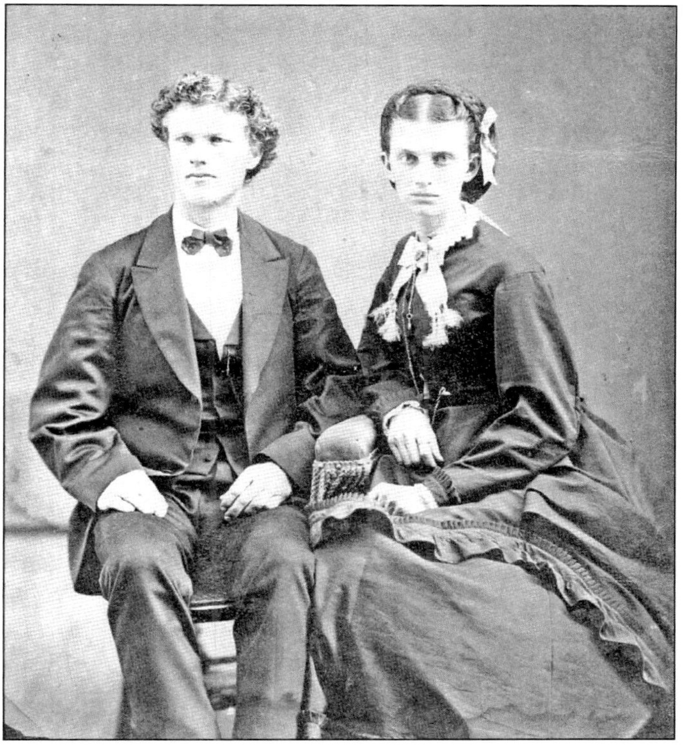

Thomas and Mary Caswell (right) were early Ceres settlers and farmers. Caswell Avenue and Thomas Street were both named after Thomas Caswell (1843–1927), who farmed 320 acres near present-day Caswell School beginning in 1901. His ranch extended from Whitmore Avenue to Hatch Road. The family of the Irish immigrant (also below) is perhaps best known for granting to the state 640 acres on the Stanislaus River west of Ripon in San Joaquin County for Caswell Memorial State Park. Mary Avenue was named for Mary Orinda Andrews Caswell (1844–1928). (Mark Perra.)

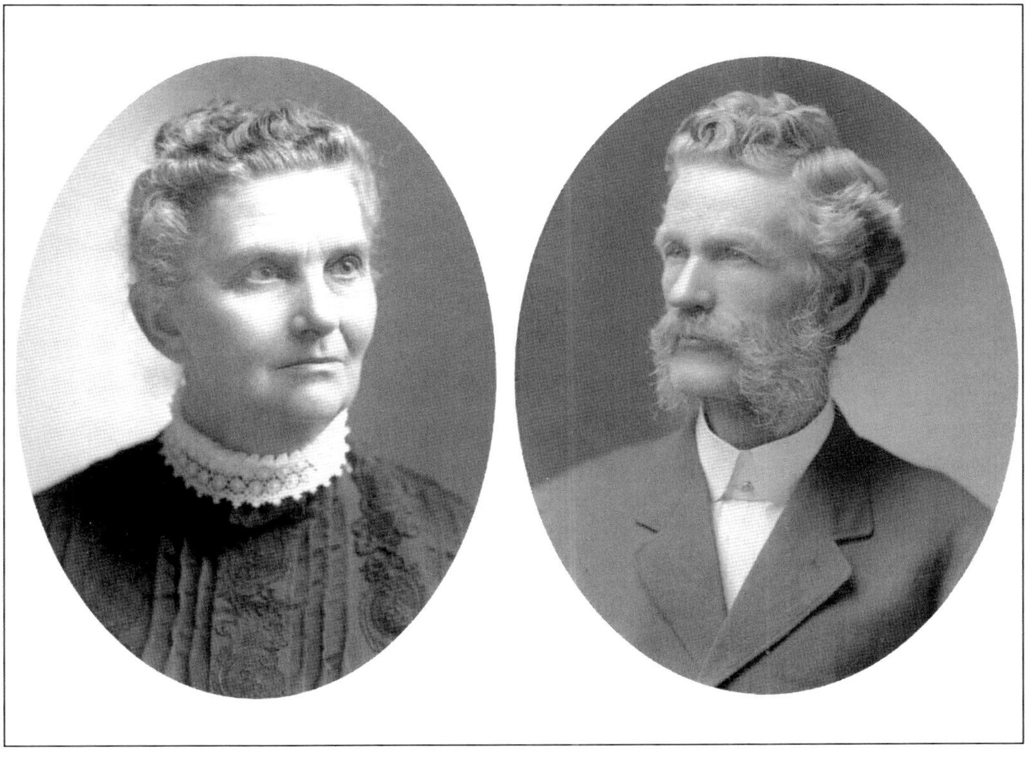

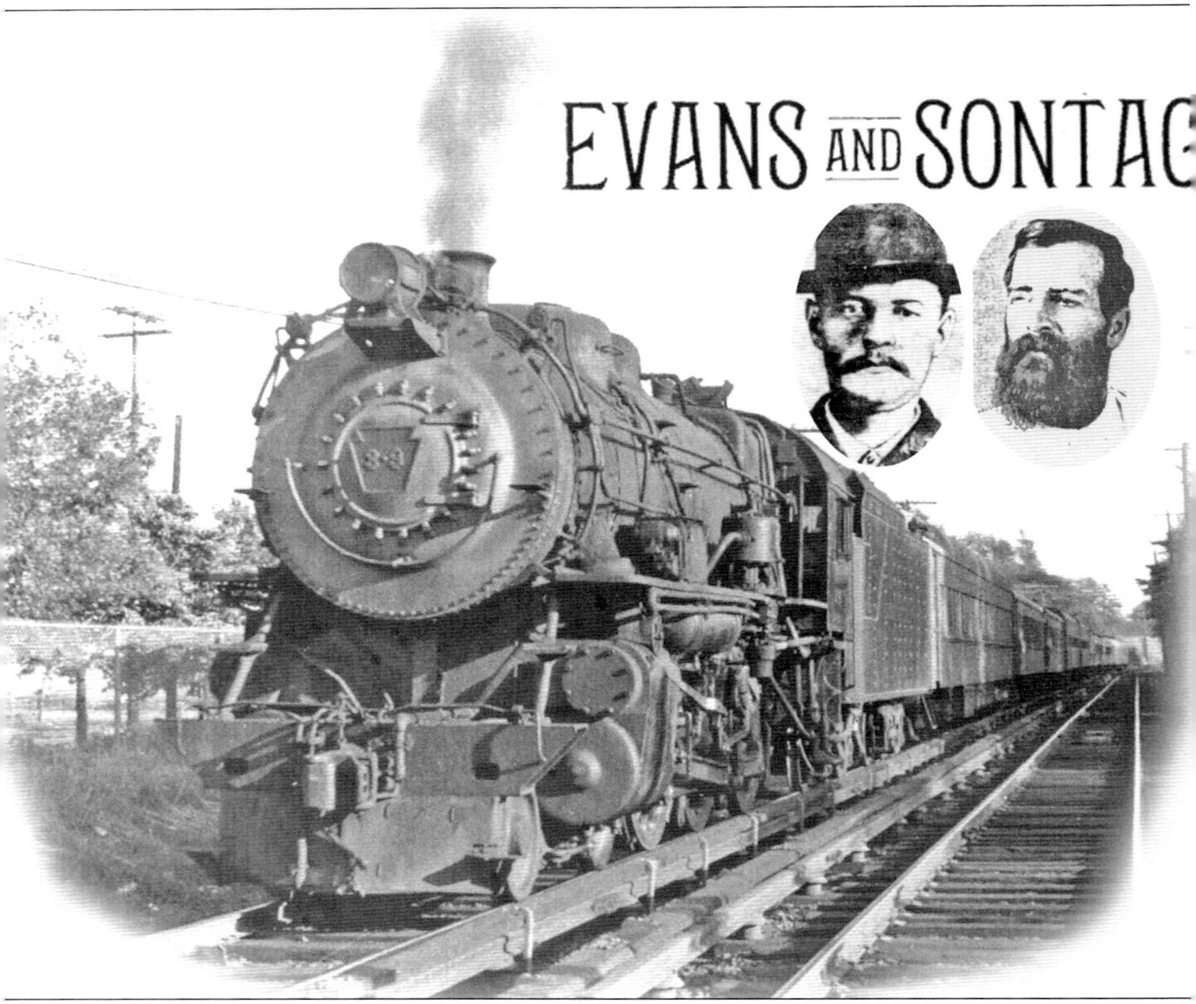

Ceres was the scene of a train robbery likely staged by famous robbers John Sontag and Chris Evans. Two bandits waited for the September 3, 1891, southbound no. 19 train at Ceres and hopped on it as its water tank was being filled. About a mile south of town, the masked gunmen burst into the engineer's cabin and ordered conductor Andrew Neff to stop the train. Neff and the train's fireman were directed back to the express coach. The robbers barked for messenger U. W. Reed to open up the car, but he refused, so the outlaws lobbed a lit stick of dynamite at the door to blow it open. After the gunmen ordered the fireman through the hole, Reed told him to stop. Another stick was tossed in to kill the agent, but it was extinguished. The thieves made off with valuables and jumped from the train but were fired on by two train detectives. A gun battle ensued, with detective Len Harris struck in the neck. The outlaws took off on a horse that had been tied to a post near the Carter mansion. They left a coat that bore a cleaner's mark traced to Visalia, where Evans lived. The Ceres robbery was the last for Sontag and Evans. Lawmen tracked them to a cabin near Sequoia National Park where a gun battle ensued in June 1893. Sontag died from his injuries, and Evans lost his eye and was jailed; he was pardoned in 1917 by Gov. Hiram Johnson but died that same year. (Author's collection.)

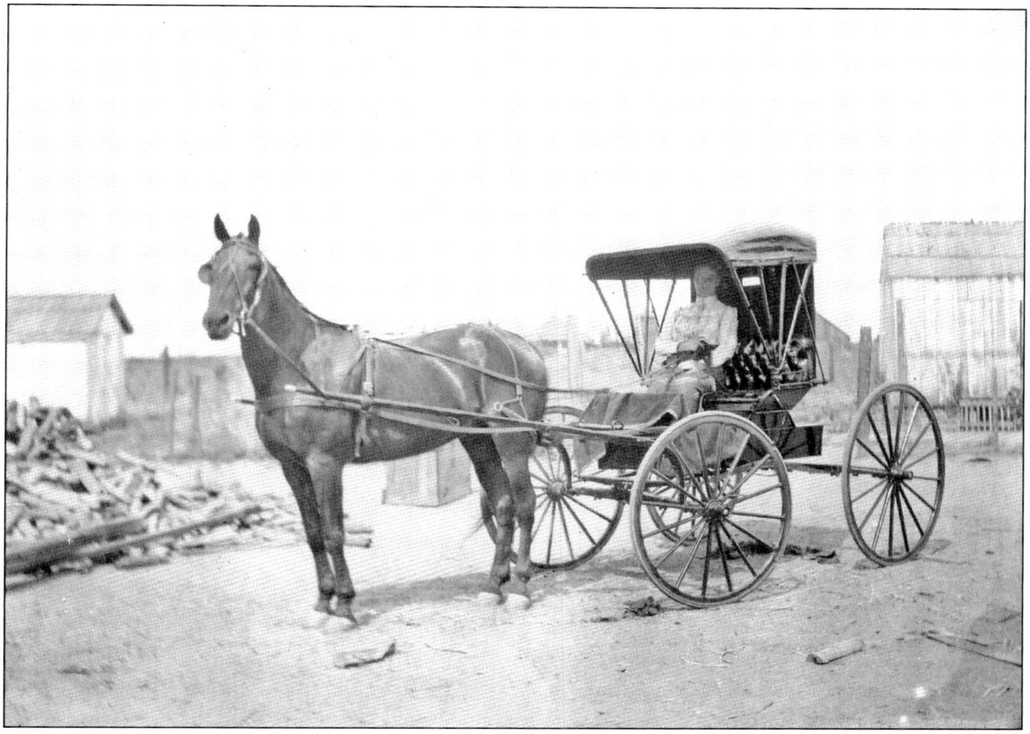

Since her husband Robert Craig was a blacksmith and wagon outfitter, Viola Averill Craig rode around Ceres in style and comfort (above). She came to Ceres in 1880 to be with brothers George William "Will" Averill (right) and Jesse Averill. After arriving in 1879, Will set up a blacksmith shop with brother-in-law George B. Hall where the Valero station is today in downtown Ceres. Will had served in the Civil War before heading to California and was assigned to the Army of the Potomac. During a nine-month hospital stay, Will met Pres. Abraham Lincoln. Lincoln, he recounted, sized him up and asked him to stand back-to-back to see who was taller; Will was two inches shorter than Abe. On another occasion, Mary Todd Lincoln gave the ailing Will an orange. It was said that Will delighted in bringing the first Christmas tree to Ceres, setting it up inside the First Baptist Church. He died in 1929 as one of the most loved men in town. (Ceres Historical Society.)

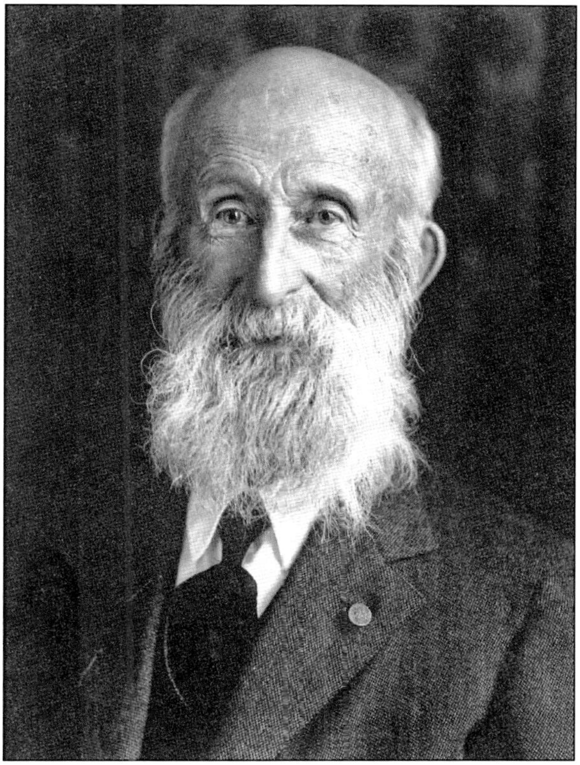

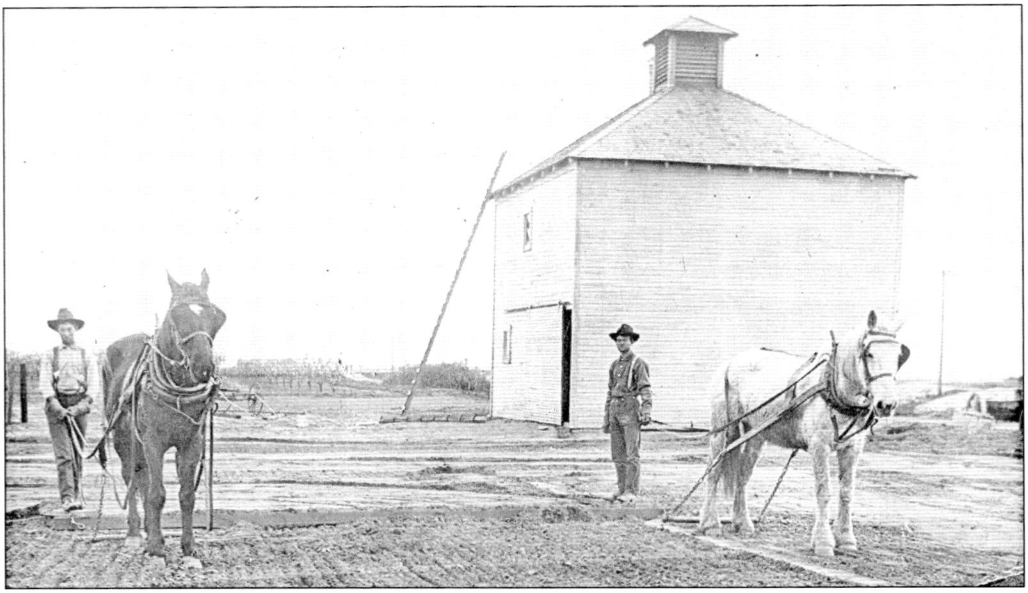

G. T. Lucas (right) and brother Newel Crane Lucas prepare to drag the ground on the Reed Ranch on Whitmore Avenue, later to become the Norman La Rosa Ranch. This 1909 scene was photographed north of Whitmore Avenue east of the Ceres Main Canal in an area now filled with houses. The horses were named Babe and Belle. (Grant Lucas.)

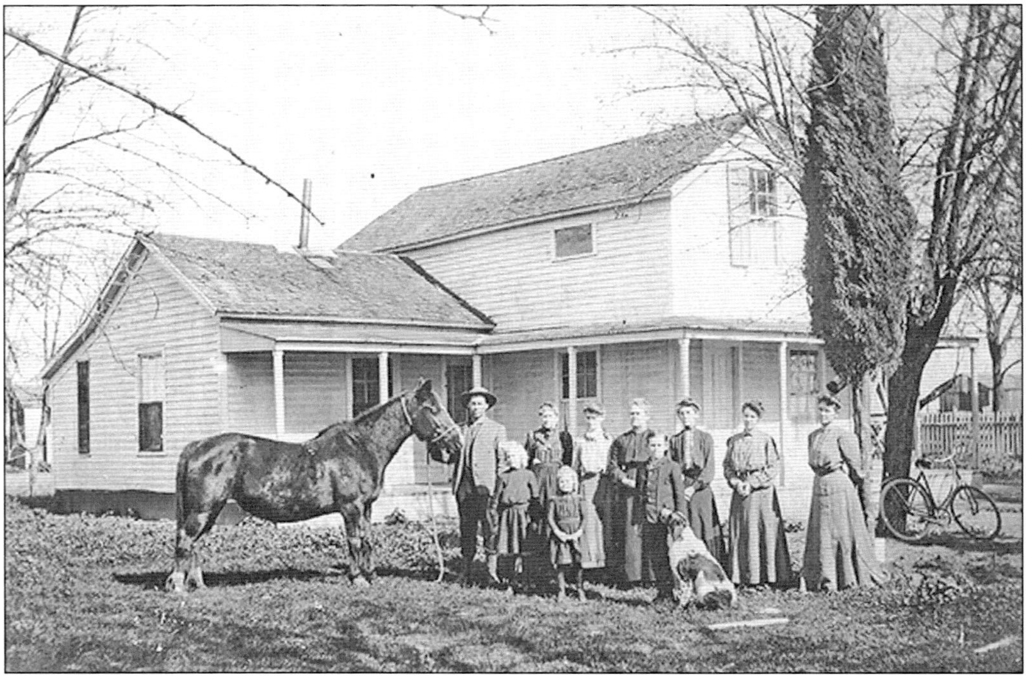

The Richard K. Whitmore family stands in front of the homestead, located at the northeast corner of Whitmore Avenue and Mitchell Road, where today's Carl's Jr. sits. Richard came to Ceres in 1869 after brother Daniel Whitmore settled here. He farmed 1,280 acres purchased from Levi Carter. He is credited with laying out the town site in 1875. (*Ceres Courier*.)

Er Barbour came to Ceres in 1916 and began farming 25 acres in the area of Mitchell Road between Fowler and Hatch Roads. In the days before it crossed the Tuolumne River, Mitchell Road was known as Barbour Road. Born in 1861 in Bowling Green, Ohio, Barbour lived in a home where the present-day entrance to Las Casitas Mobile Home Park is located. This is how he appeared in 1892 in Pasadena before his move to Ceres. Barbour died June 29, 1954. The oldest of his 10 children was William "Homer" Barbour, who opened a Ceres service station. (Dennis Barbour.)

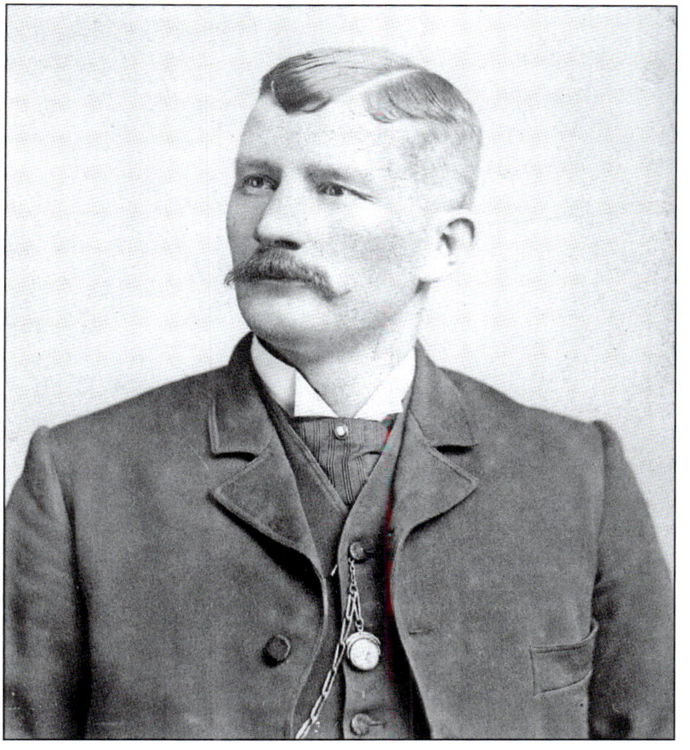

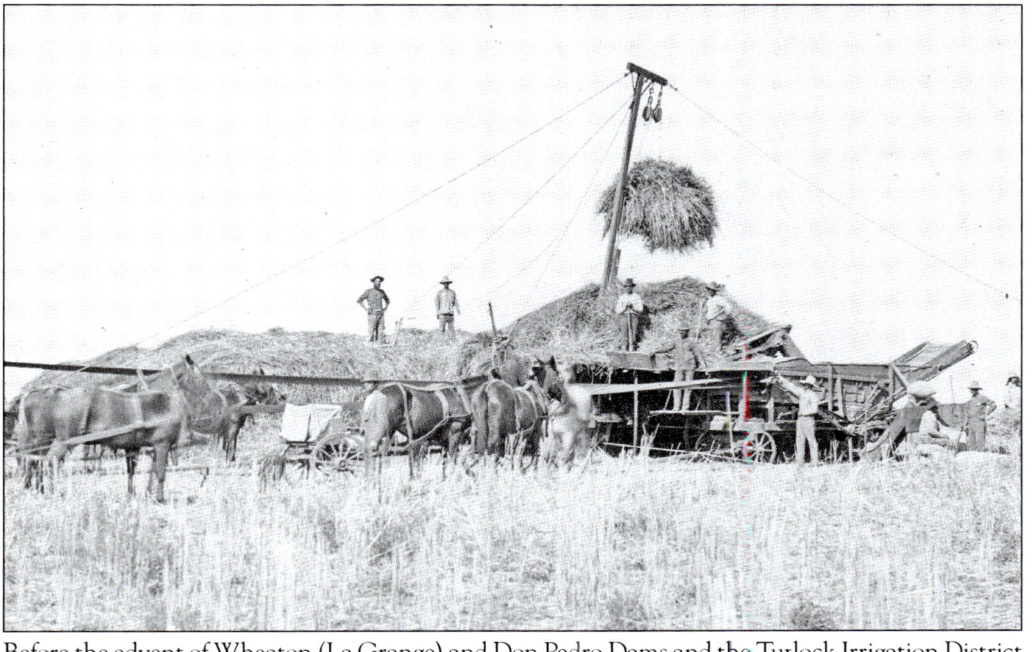

Before the advent of Wheaton (La Grange) and Don Pedro Dams and the Turlock Irrigation District canal system, the rich soil of Ceres was used to grow wheat. It was gathered into piles through the use of mule and machine. From wagons, the wheat was loaded onto barges before the railroads arrived in 1871. As water became available, land was used for more diverse crops. (Sid Long.)

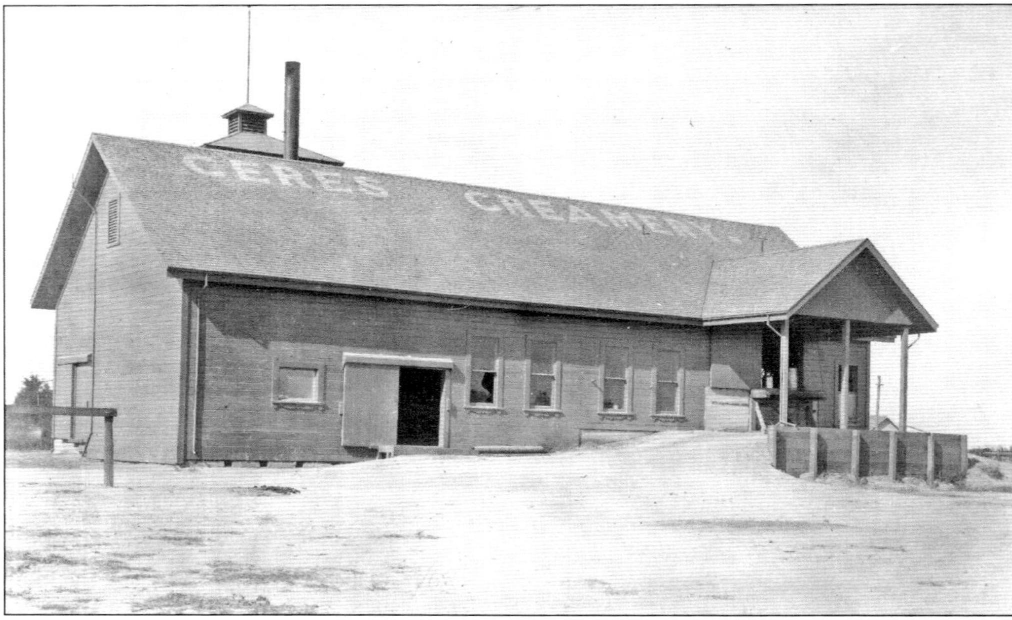

Located near the Central Pacific Railroad tracks, the Ceres Creamery was an economic engine in Ceres. The plant was churning out 1,500 pounds of butter each day under its own label (below) and employing a number of Ceres area workers. The product was shipped to such California cities as San Francisco. It remained successful for two years before disaster struck. Late in the evening on September 16, 1905, the $16,000 business was destroyed by fire for the second time. The firm was managed by E. C. Barnes and its officers were President S. J. Irvin of Modesto, Vice President Dan Baldwin of Ceres, and Secretary J. U. Gartin of Ceres. (Ceres Historical Society.)

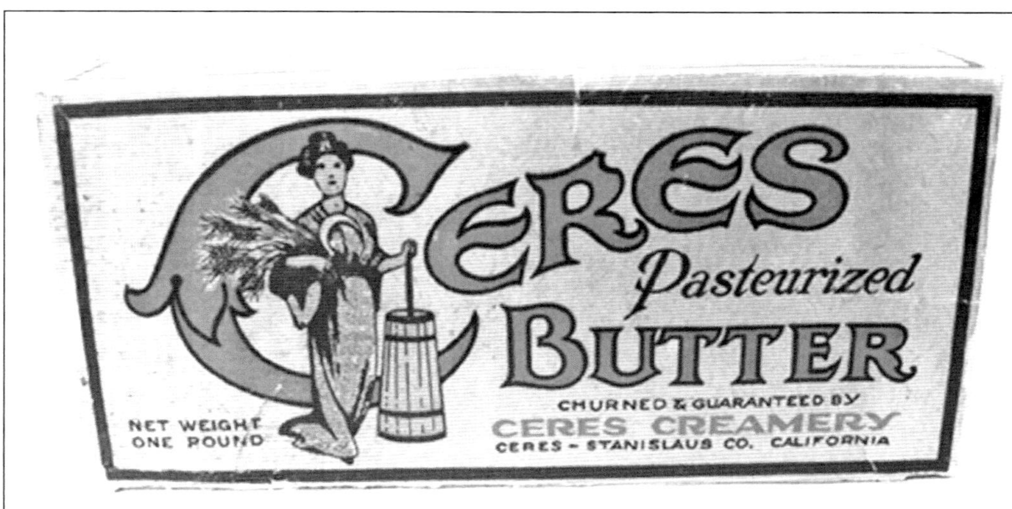

A sooty-faced Robert Craig and his men were busy blacksmithing in his shop in downtown Ceres when this photograph was taken. Craig was born in Scotland in 1859 and arrived in Ceres in 1889, retaining his thick brogue. He opened his blacksmith shop in 1905. (Ceres Historical Society.)

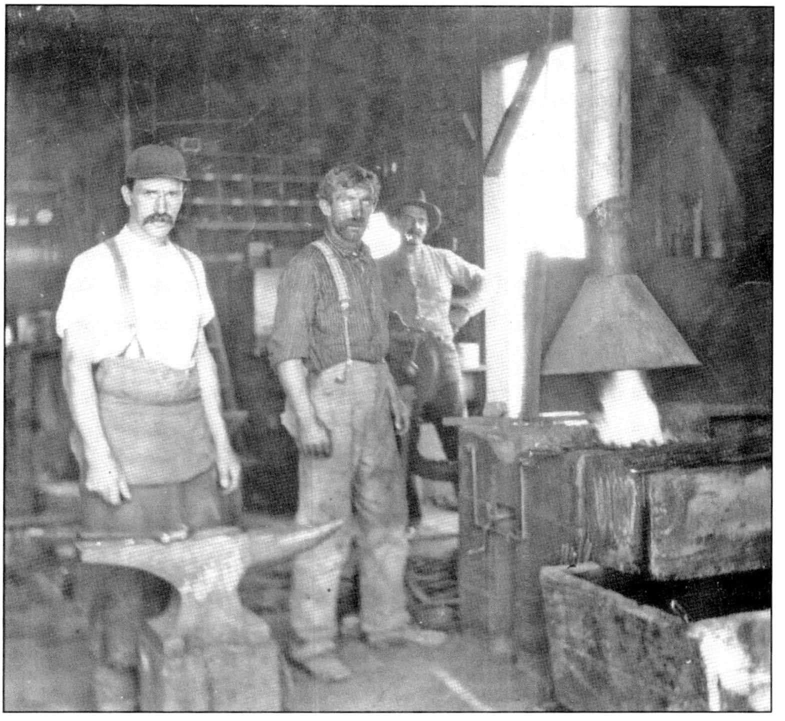

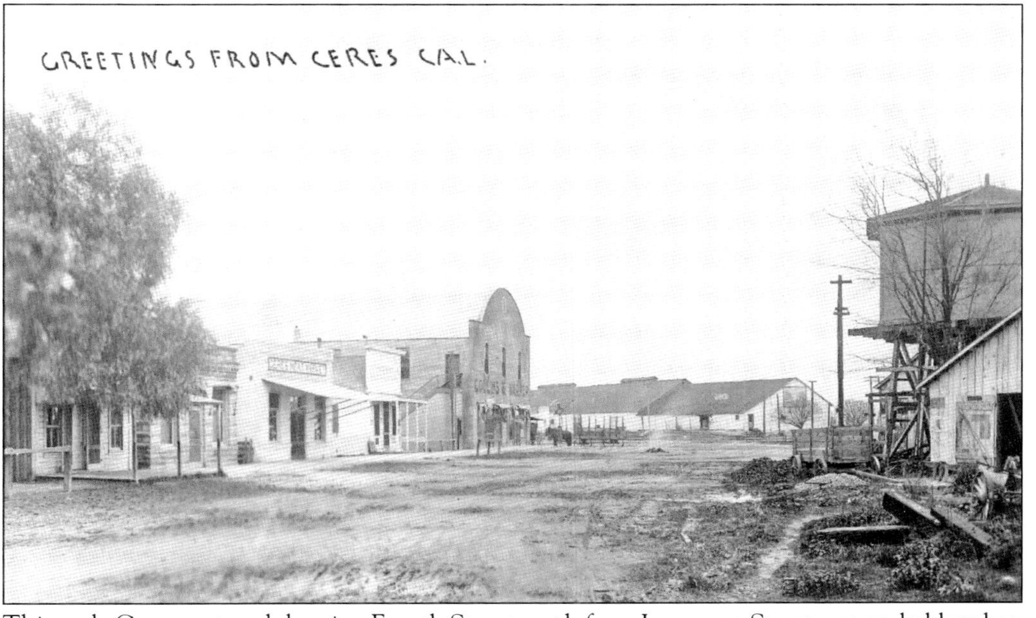

This early Ceres postcard showing Fourth Street south from Lawrence Street was probably taken around 1908. The white 1905 Turlock Irrigation District building is visible, but the most prominent landmark is the round-topped Collins & Warner Hall (at center). Beyond Fourth Street are grain warehouses along the Central Pacific tracks. A wooden water tower (at right) was located on the west side of Fourth Street near Lawrence. A warming fire is burning in the middle of Fourth Street. (Ceres Historical Society.)

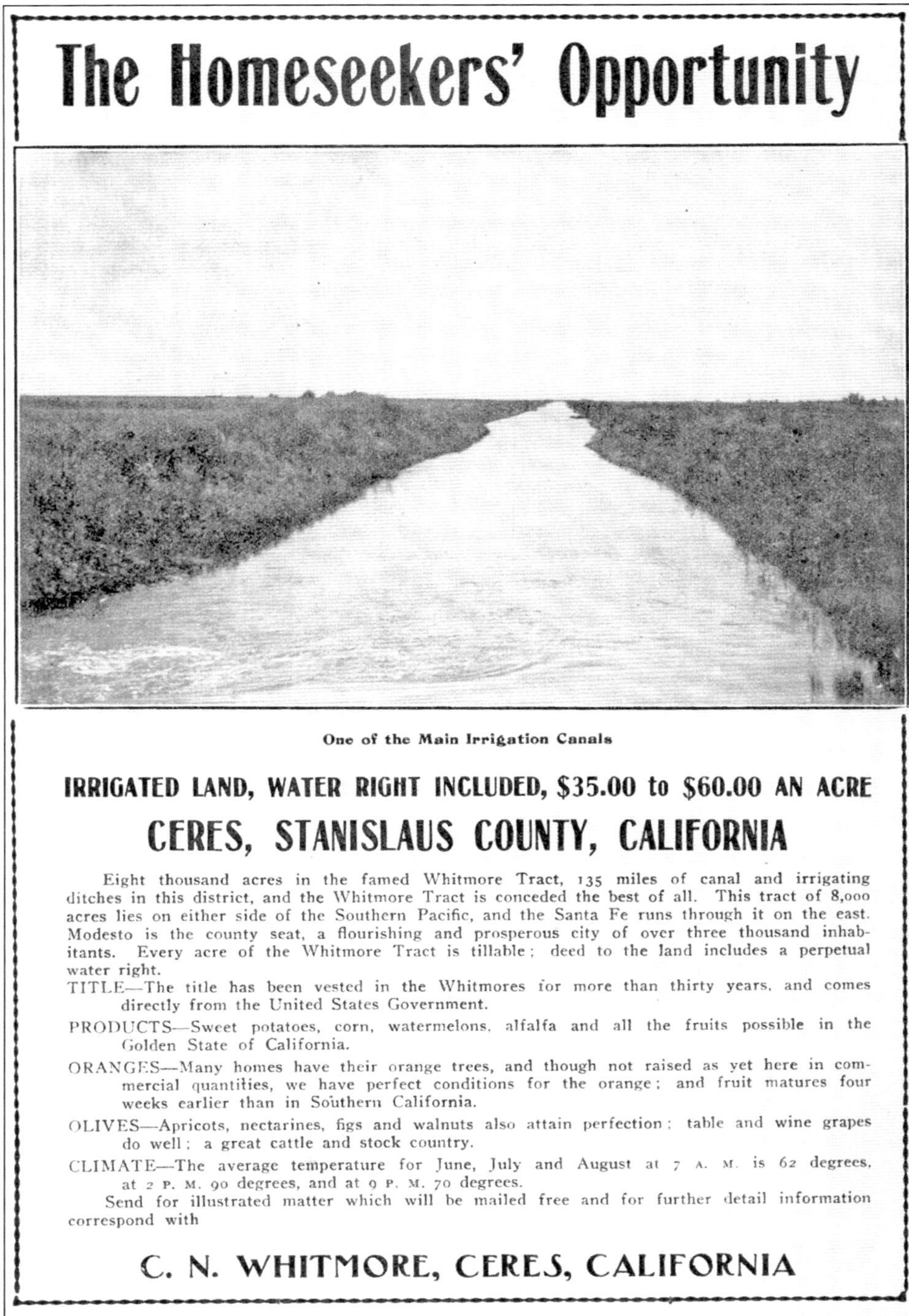

Clinton Whitmore placed this advertisement in *Sunset* magazine to entice growers to the area. Whitmore was selling off 8,000 acres and mentions that the good soil yields sweet potatoes, corn, watermelons, alfalfa, fruits, oranges, olives, and grapes. The selling price of land was a bargain rate of $35 to $60 an acre. (Ceres Historical Society.)

Clinton N. Whitmore was an influential member of the Ceres community for many years. Born in Michigan on August 20, 1845, he was the son of Ceres founder Daniel Whitmore. He served as the Sunday school superintendent at First Baptist Church for 21 years. He not only helped to manage his father's 10,000-acre wheat farm around Ceres but was instrumental in leading Turlock Irrigation District (TID) to build its irrigation system. He served as treasurer of TID for 16 years and assisted in the building of the TID office on Fourth Street (below). Clinton Whitmore died on August 6, 1912. His Fifth Street mansion went to his widow, Maria E. Clinton (1857–1939). Upon her death the mansion went to daughter Jennie Whitmore Caswell and son-in-law Wallace Caswell. (Author's collection.)

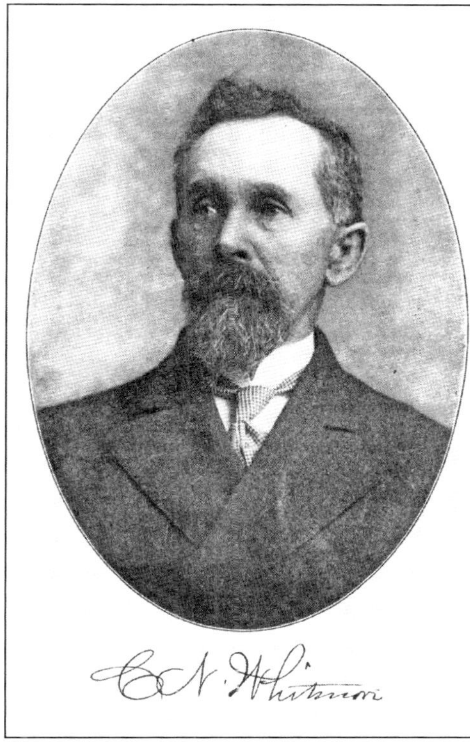

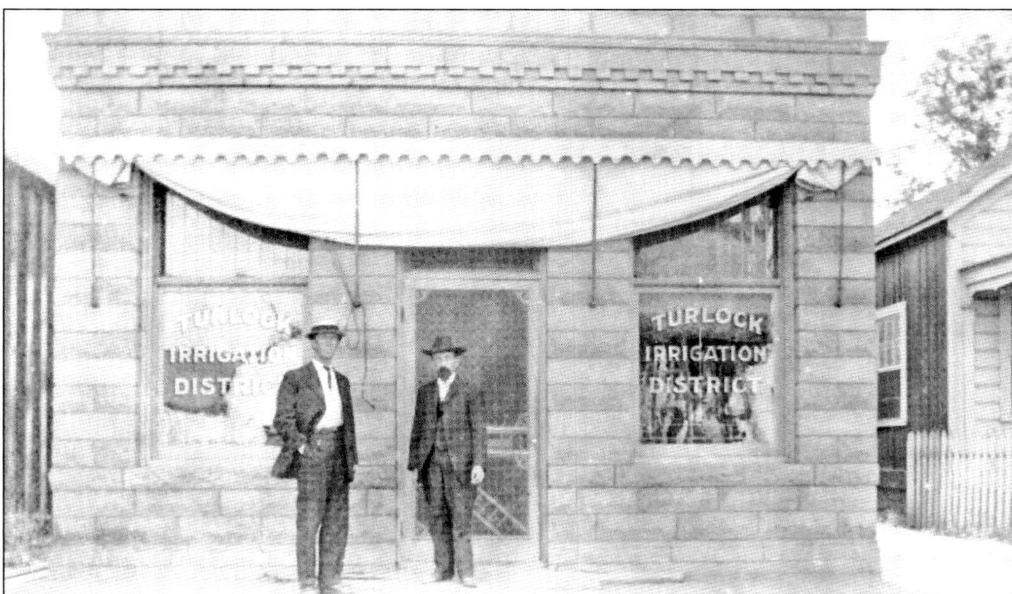

Ceres was the site of the first Turlock Irrigation District office. This brick building, pictured here after its opening in 1905, stands today on Fourth Street. Ceres first received irrigation water from the La Grange Dam in March 1900, as evidenced by an article that appeared in the Modesto *Daily Evening News*. The first area of Ceres to be irrigated was a parcel owned by Henry Stirring north of Hatch Road near the present-day Ceres Marketplace Shopping Center. (Mildred Lucas.)

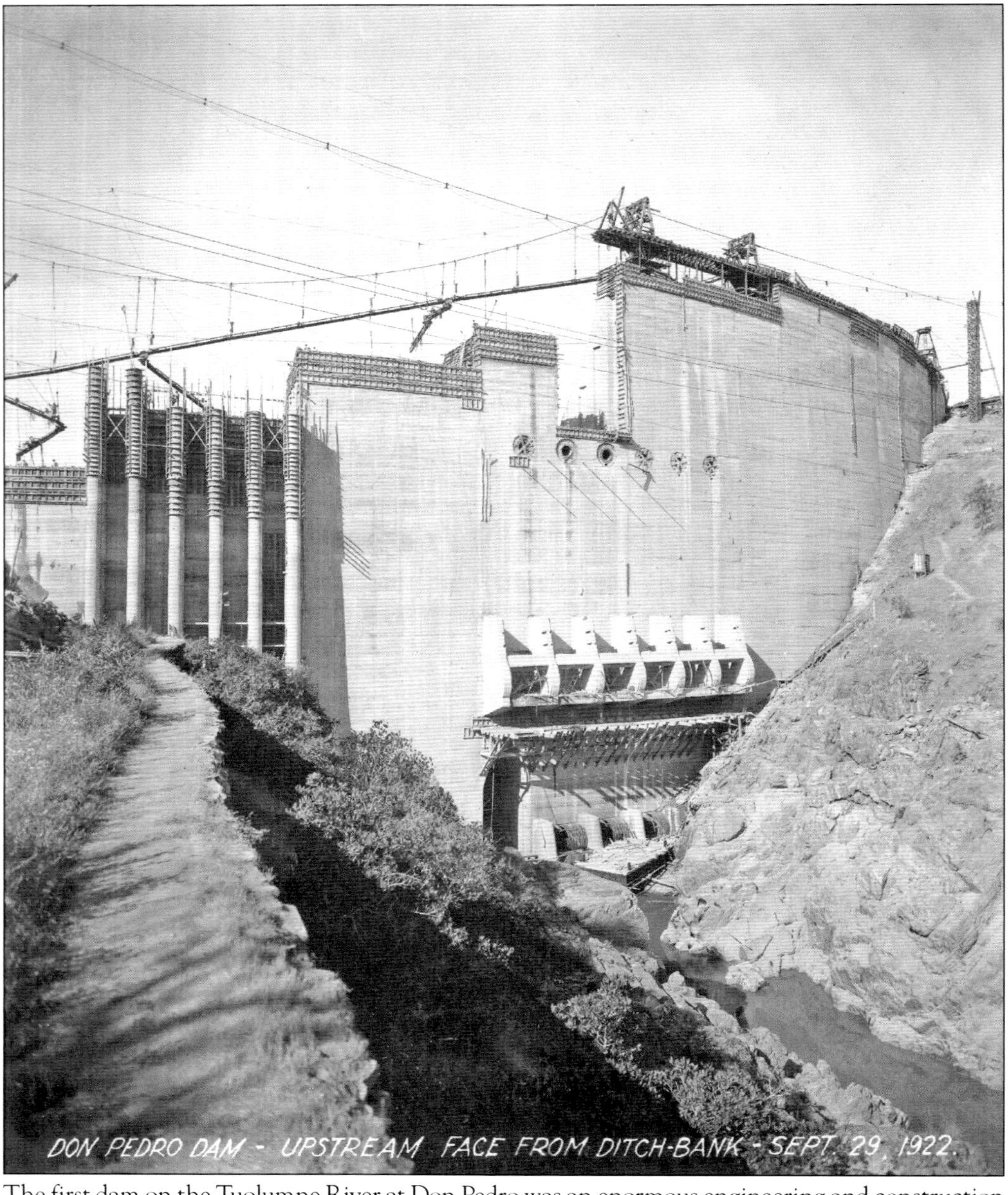

The first dam on the Tuolumne River at Don Pedro was an enormous engineering and construction task that baffles the mind even today. The dam, formed by the pouring of an estimated 296,552 cubic yards of concrete to a height of 284 feet, was operational in 1922 and opened up farming opportunities in the Ceres area. Behind the dam was a storage capacity of 289,000 acre-feet, or enough water to cover 289,000 acres at a foot deep. At the time, it was the largest manmade structure in the world. (Sid Long.)

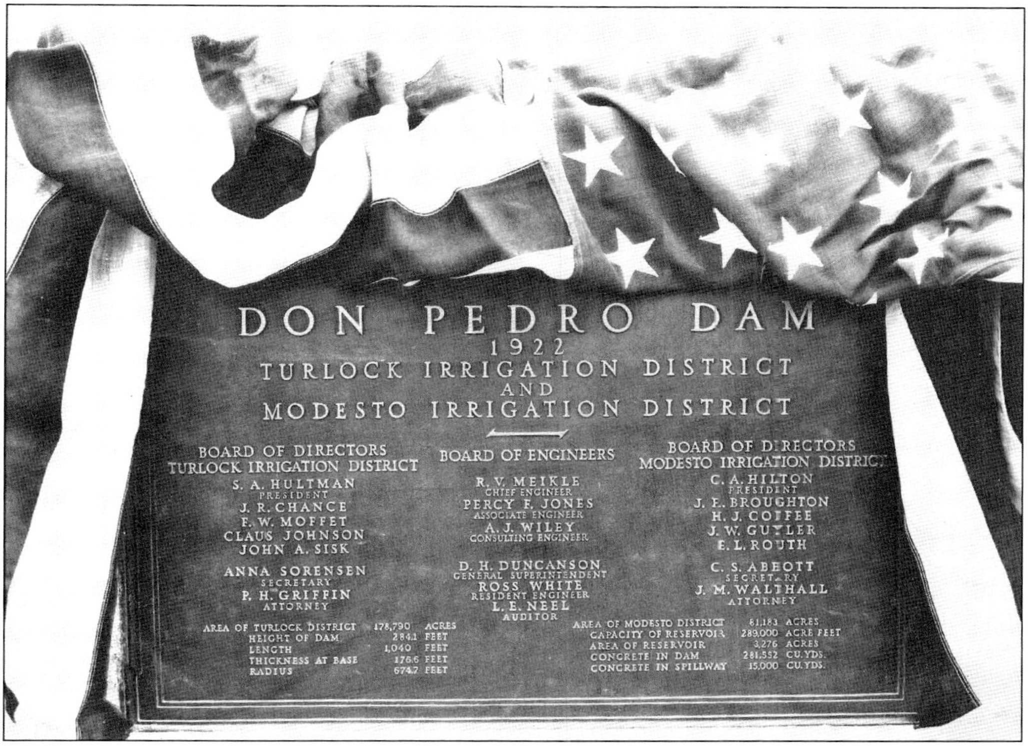

The first Don Pedro Dam in 1922 bears a plaque with the name of Ceres farmer Fred W. Moffet (right) who served on the Turlock Irrigation District (TID) board. A visionary, Moffet knew that a plentiful supply of water would mean prosperity for farmers in the Ceres area. The dam was a joint project of both the Modesto and Turlock irrigation districts. Moffet's grandson, Sid Long, would later serve on the TID board. (Sid Long.)

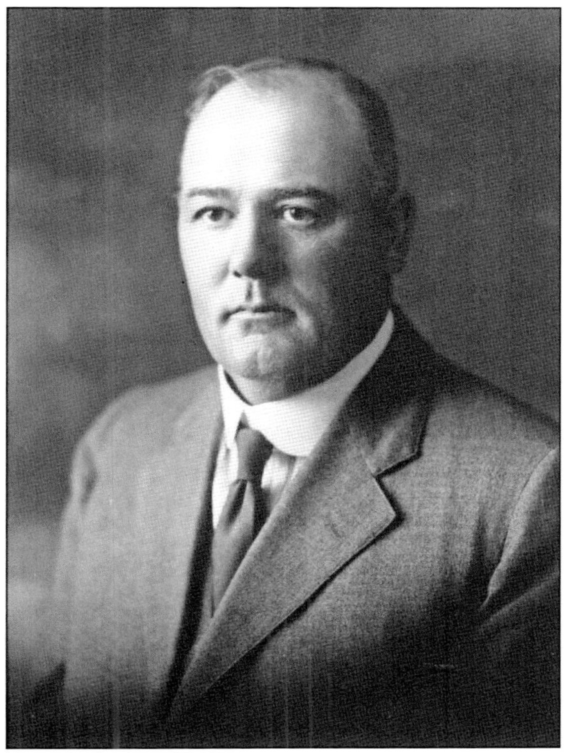

Fred Moffet started Superior Fruit Ranch in 1904 with partners E. S. Welch and Dan Campin on 320 acres between Ceres and Hughson. He lived in a house that sat at the corner of Whitmore Avenue and Moffet Road. As a member of the Turlock Irrigation District board, Moffet helped guide the construction of the first Don Pedro Dam from 1921 to 1923. After suffering a stroke in 1955, he turned ranching operations over to grandson Sid Long. (Sid Long.)

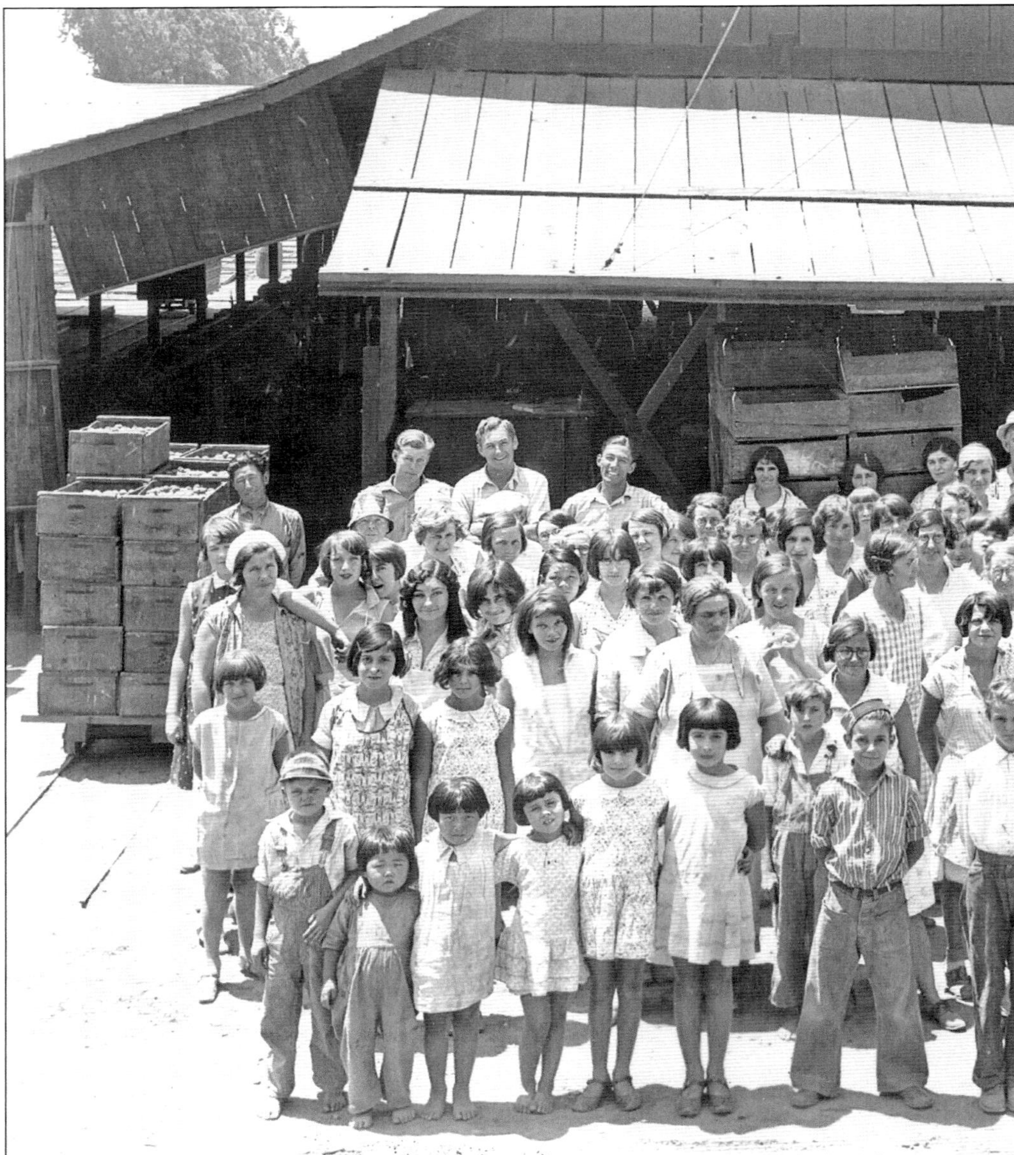

At peak summer harvest season, Superior Fruit Ranch required a large local labor force. Men picked the fruit while the ladies cut the fruit in halves inside a shed before it was carried out into the sun where it dried. Dried fruit was used for K-rations during World War II. This image was taken in the 1930s near the cutting shed. The only person identified is George Cabral, the boy standing in the front row wearing a beanie, a smile, and bell-bottom trousers. (Sid Long.)

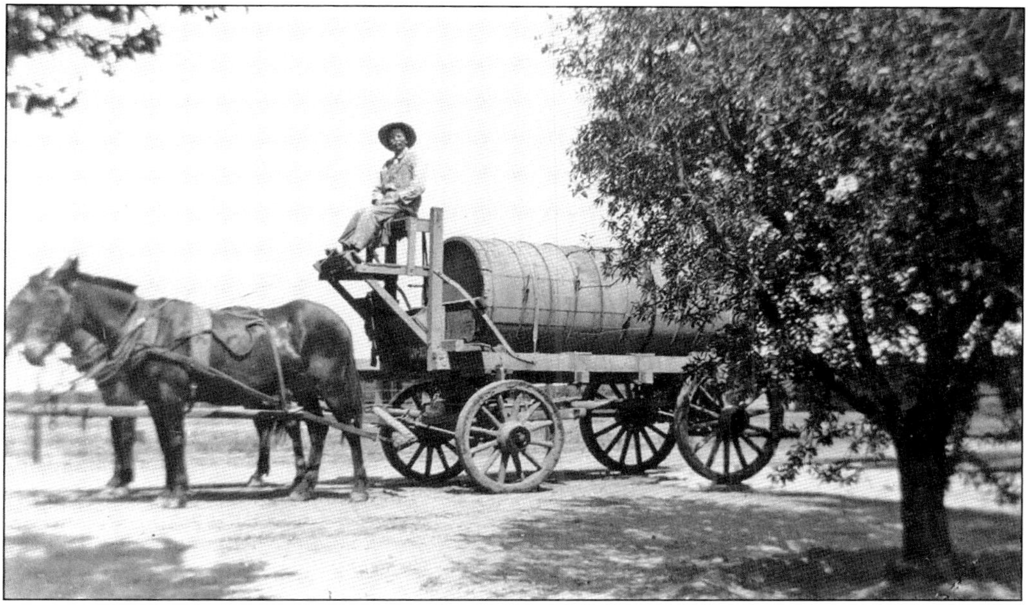

This water wagon, pulled by a pair of strong mules, kept down the summer dust on Superior Fruit Ranch around the turn of the century. The ranch, located between Ceres and Hughson on Whitmore Avenue, is still in operation today. (Sid Long.)

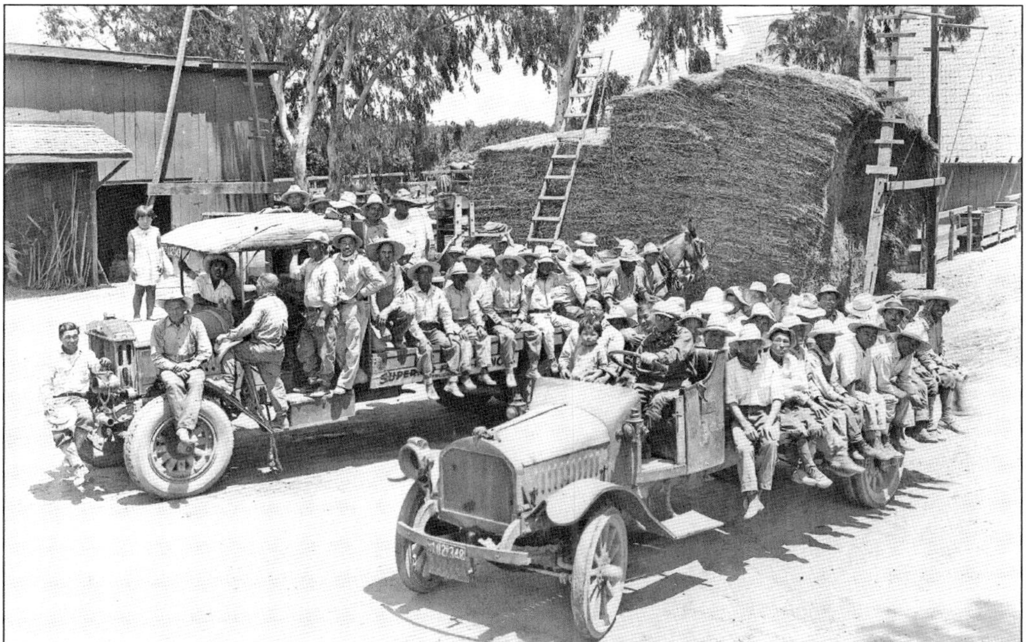

Japanese workers came to the valley in the 1910s and 1920s to work in agriculture. During the 1930s, Superior Fruit Ranch employed a work crew of Japanese men. When the attack on Pearl Harbor stirred anti-Japanese sentiments, ranch owner Fred Moffet resorted to hiring guards to keep the crew and families from being assaulted and harassed. Later Pres. Franklin Roosevelt had Japanese-Americans interned at camps throughout the West. (Sid Long.)

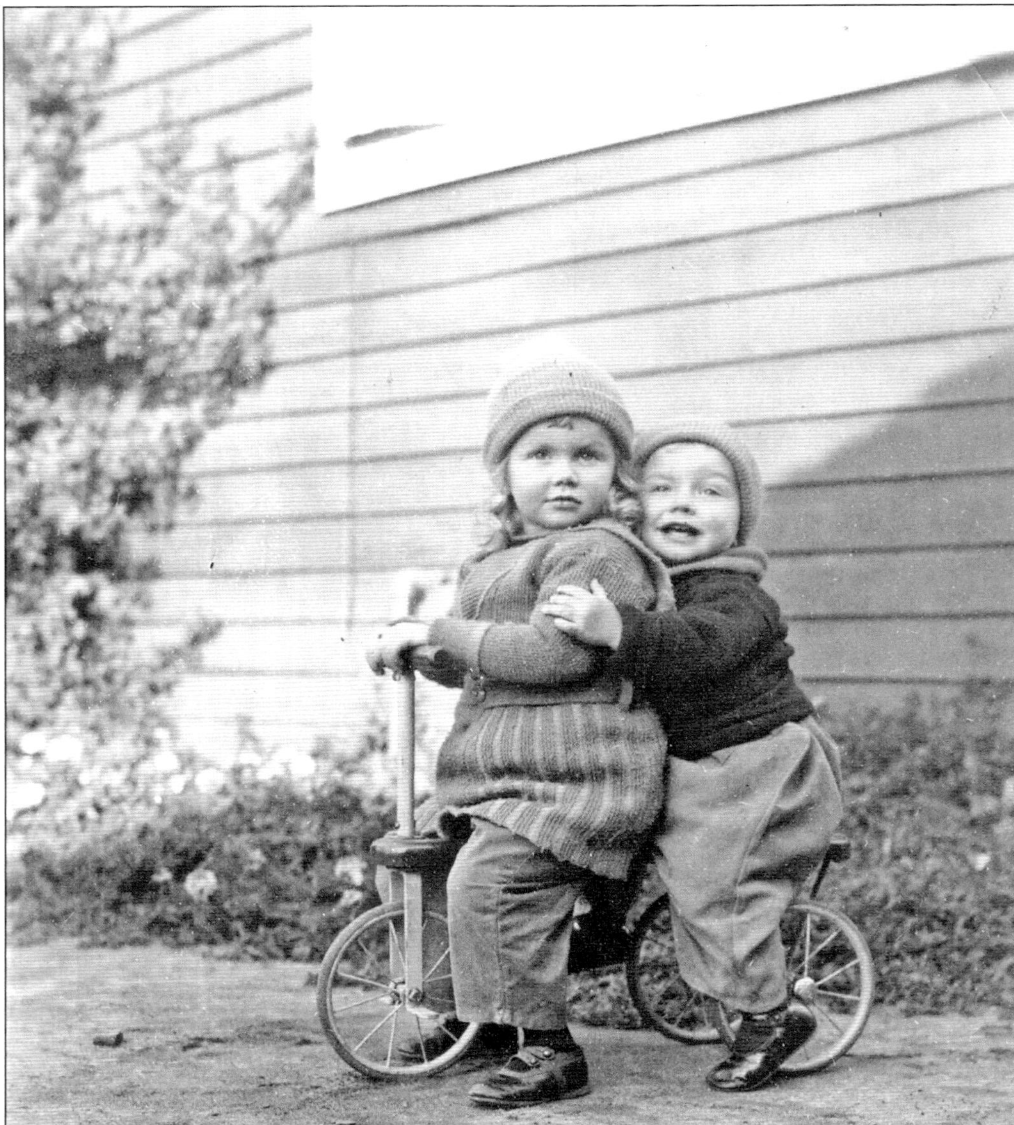

Siblings Wanda and Bruce Hosmer stop from their fun on a tricycle for a pose (c. 1924) outside their home at 2545 Fourth Street just north of the Castle, the unique landmark residence at Fourth and Magnolia. Wanda (born in 1920), and Bruce (born in 1922) were the children of Wayne and Petra West Hosmer. Wanda, a blue-eyed blonde, was quite a looker when she became a young woman and always had the attention of the young men of Ceres. Two other children came along later; Loren Hosmer in 1925 and Dale in 1936. The Hosmers were typical of Ceres families: good, honest, hard working, and industrious people. At the time of this photo, the Hosmer house was located in an orchard at the northern edge of Ceres, and the property had a barn in back of the residence. Ceres was a solid family town and home to only about 650 residents at the time of the Calvin Coolidge presidency. The Hosmer children buried their father in 1966. Petra, an immigrant from Denmark, passed away in 1984. Wanda died in Arizona in 2009. (Loren Hosmer.)

Two

A Community Develops

Ceres and its neighboring city to the north, Modesto, were established at about the same time, but it was the latter that boomed. Ceres incorporated as a city in 1918, and it continued to grow at a small but steady rate from the early 20th century to the beginning of World War II. After around 1900, prosperity came to the region when irrigation channeled water to farmers in Waterford, Hughson, Ceres, and Turlock. Ceres, however, remained a sleepy town compared to Modesto, the county seat, and by 1920 had just 637 citizens. A decade later, Ceres grew to 981 residents. By 1940, the town was home to 1,332 people. Businesses grew. A number of stores provided immediate goods, while Modesto and Turlock establishments offered what wasn't available in Ceres. Modesto Lumber opened a lumberyard on the west side for the building needs in Ceres. Between 1901 and 1903, the town's happenings were published in a newssheet called *The Ceres Scraper.* Clarence Bronough started an official newspaper, the *Ceres Courier*, in 1910. Dr. S. W. Cartwright, the town's first mayor, opened Ceres Drug Store in 1907. The Bank of Ceres began in 1911, but bank manager Arthur Harris was notoriously stingy with loans. The thrift, however, remained financially solvent during the Great Depression. When things got tough during the 1930s, Ceres housed a number of migrant workers. Lizzie Nail opened Nailtown on the west side of the tracks, renting out pads for tents for migrants in the Collins Road area.

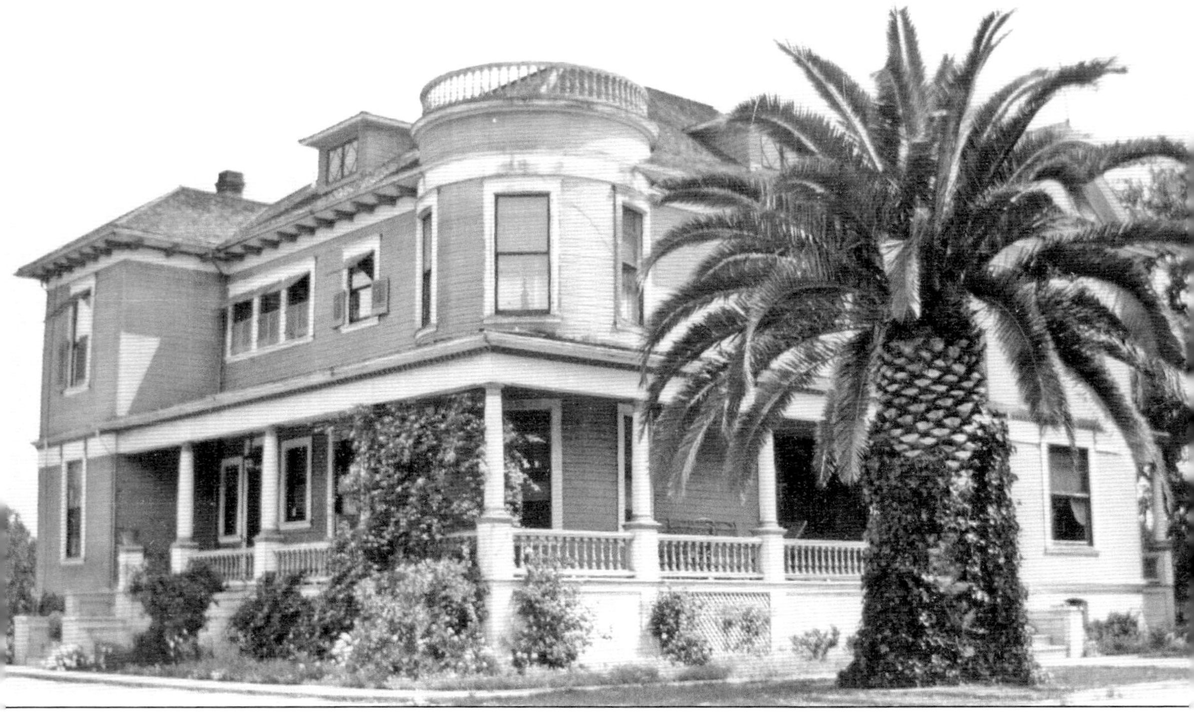

In 1903 Clinton N. Whitmore constructed this majestic home between Fifth Street and Sixth Street. It was a focal point of social life in Ceres. After he died on August 6, 1912, the house went to his widow, Maria E. Whitmore. When Maria passed in 1939, daughter Jennie Whitmore Caswell and her husband Wallace Caswell owned the house. The last Whitmore to own it was Robert Whitmore and his wife Edna. The sprawling mansion stayed in the Whitmore family until 2005 when it was purchased by Cary and Nancy Pope. Many private and public functions are held here, including concerts, parties, and weddings. (Ceres Historical Society.)

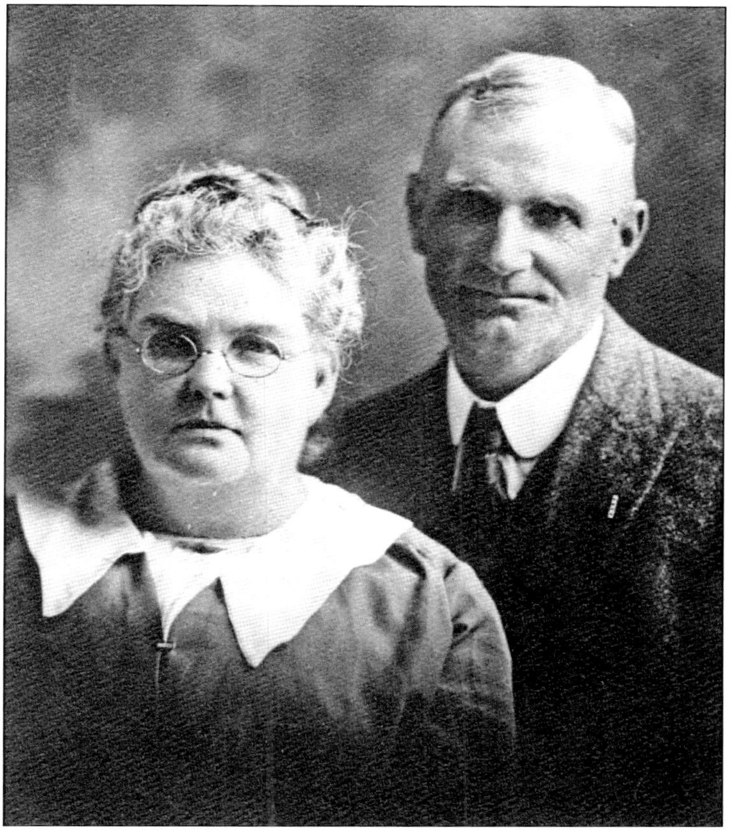

Evangeline and Charles Baldridge came to Ceres by covered wagon from Hollister in 1902. Their daughter was Myrtle Baldridge, who later married constable Will Ham. Charles immediately found work on the Clinton Whitmore Ranch, his place of employment until 1929. The Baldridges lived on Whitmore's experimental fruit garden at the intersection of Service Road and Highway 99. Their son, Wayne Baldridge, was mayor in the 1930s. (Betty Ham.)

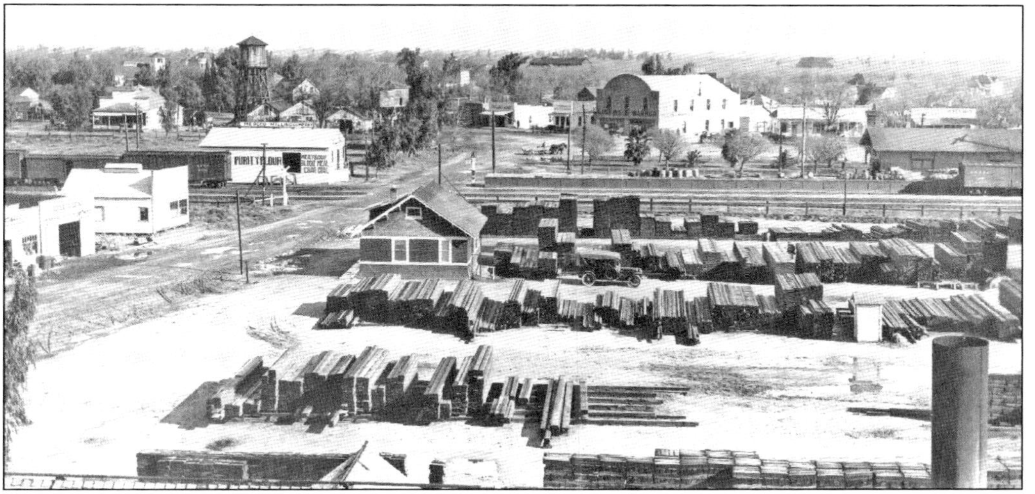

This panoramic view of early Ceres was taken some time between 1908 and 1910 from atop the Modesto Lumber Yard building, now the city corporation yard on Railroad Avenue. The photograph, which was taken looking northeast into Ceres, shows the train depot and dock at right, the Collins and Warner building on Fourth Street, and the water tower. Far in the background are the top of the Clinton Whitmore Mansion and the bell tower of First Baptist Church, at upper left. (Mildred Lucas.)

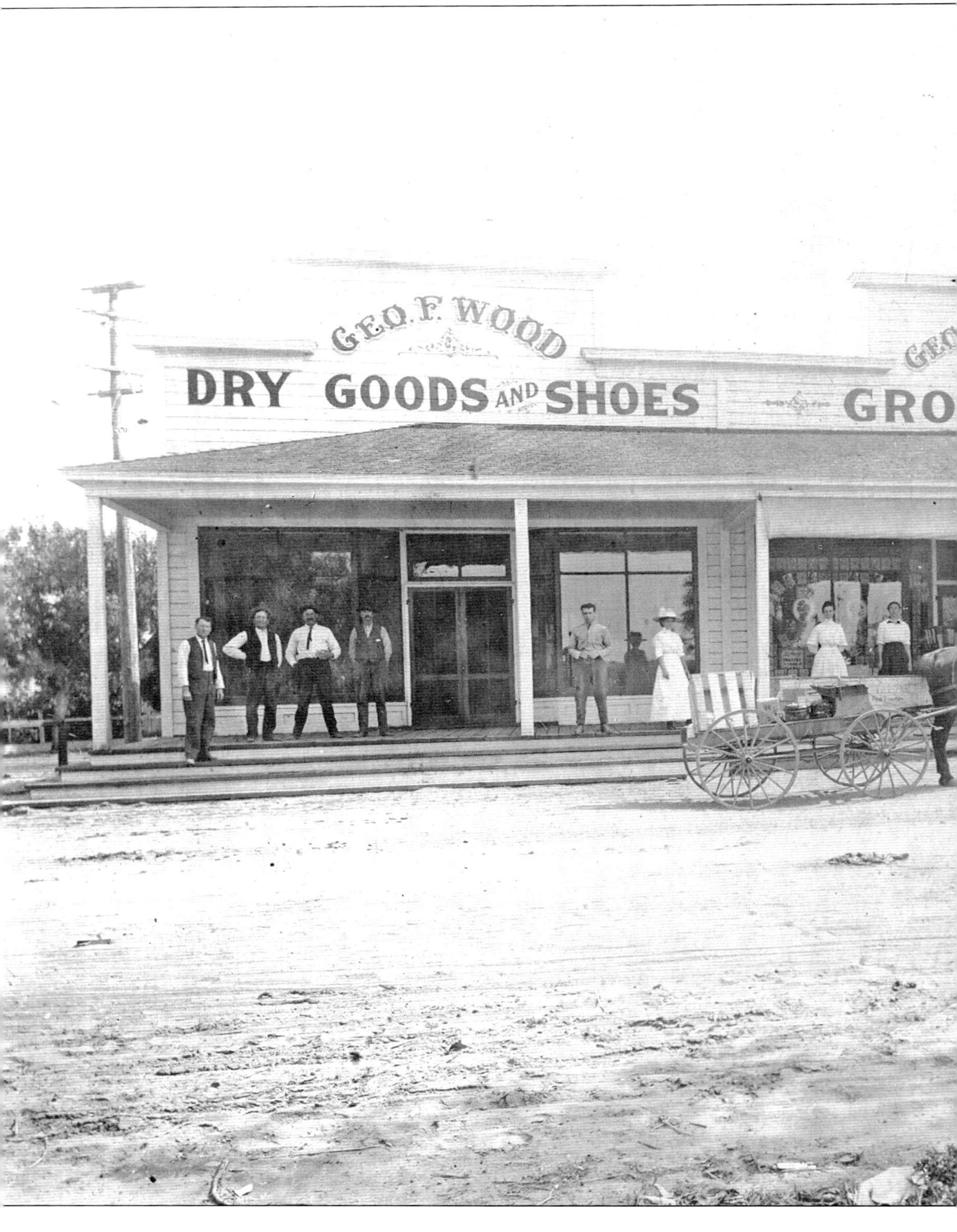
GEO. F. WOOD
DRY GOODS AND SHOES
GRO

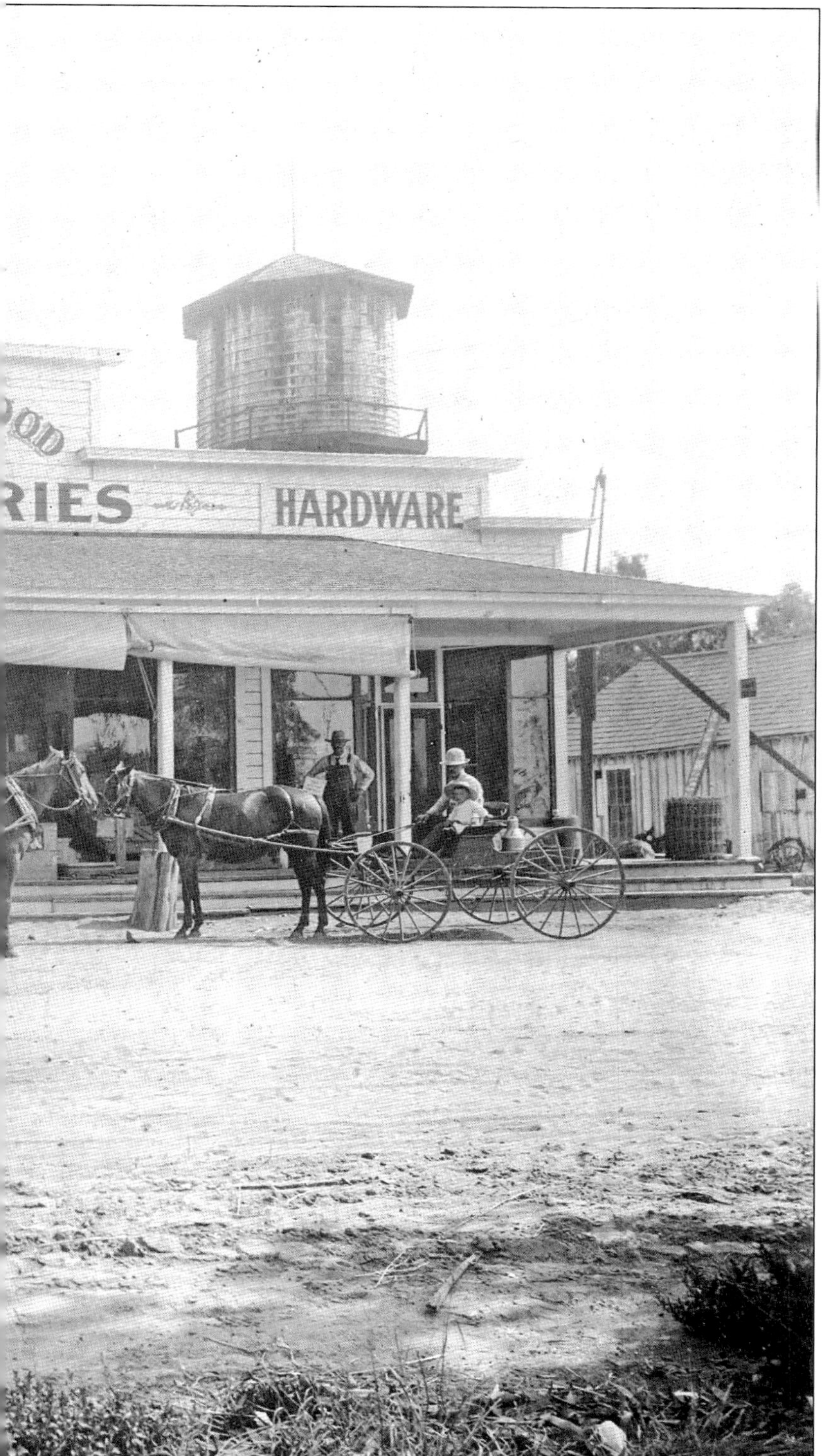

The George F. Wood Mercantile was an important place where Ceres residents could purchase food items and everyday goods. The store was located on the highway just south of Lawrence Street and faced the southwest. It sold food, dry goods, and shoes as well as hardware. Interior pictures from the 1920s showed Wood selling such products as baking powder, Kellogg's Corn Flakes, bananas, Hills Brothers coffee, Japan Tree Tea, Blue Can Brand Coffee, Wesson oil, and fresh bread. Wood operated this store until 1928. He died in 1939, just a few years before Mert's Cash Store opened on the spot sporting a drive-through grocery experience. Today Jackpot Gas and a Valero station sit on the spot once occupied by this pioneer mercantile. (Betty Ham.)

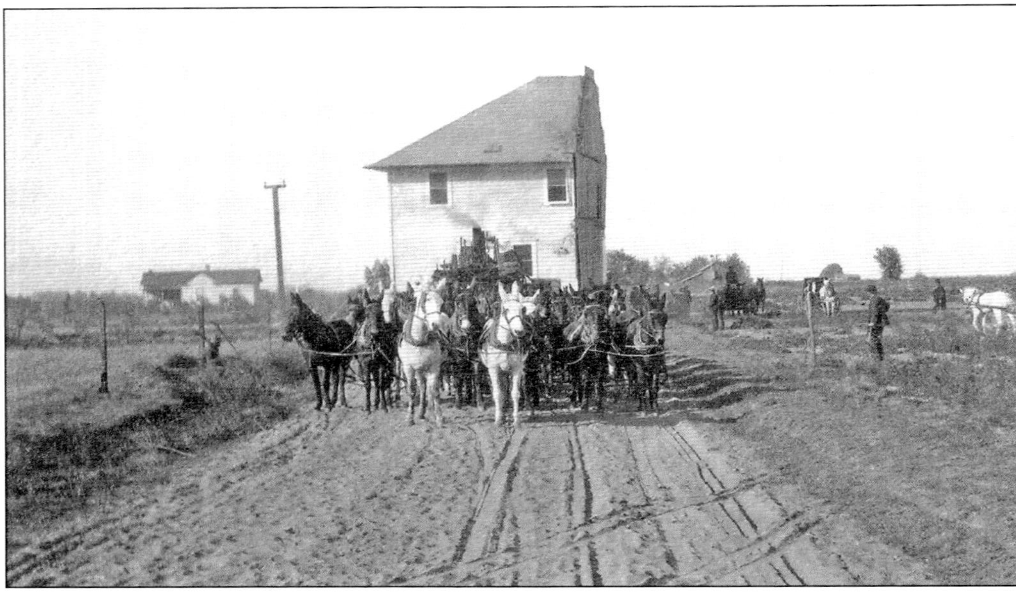

It was a fair and square deal when Hughson took the Gillette Hotel from Ceres. For two years the hotel, built in 1905, graced Fourth Street in Ceres. Hughson town founders Charles Flack and C. W. Minniear realized the hotel's value to visitors and workers in their fledging village. In 1907, they purchased the structure for $25,000 and relocated it to Hughson in halves hauled down Whitmore Avenue by mule teams. It was actually moved on logs placed beneath it to act as giant rollers. The process took three weeks for the first half and employed a 65-horsepower steam engine that later proved unnecessary. Moving the second half took only a week. A reported dispute about a lease caused a Mr. and Mrs. M. L. Coward to remain in their living quarters as the hotel was being moved. (Hughson Historical Society.)

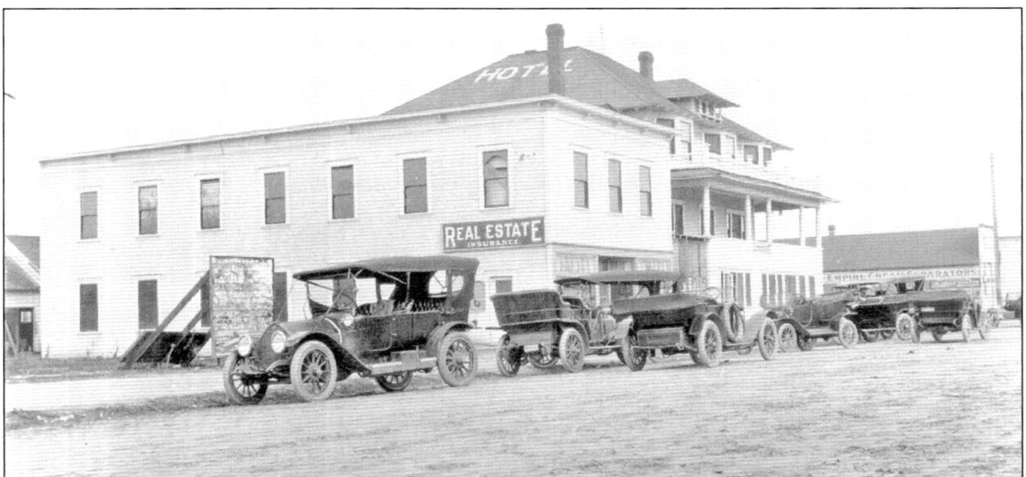

The former Gillette Hotel became the Hughson Hotel, pictured here in 1918. The original building was set in place on top of a first floor at the northwest corner of Hughson Avenue and Charles Street in Hughson. In 1912, an annex was attached to the west side of the now three-story building. Since 1935, the historic Gillette Hotel has been known as the Independent Order of Odd Fellows Hall. (Hughson Historical Society.)

Ezra Frank Hosmer was a farmer in Mill Town, South Dakota, before he uprooted his wife Margaret and his children first to Utah, then to Ceres in 1912. Hosmer farmed in the area of Central Avenue and Service Road. His children included Wayne and Harry. Tragedy struck when Harry was killed during a storm after climbing up a windmill to make repairs and was fatally struck in the head by a moving part, knocking him to the ground. Ezra is buried in the Ceres Memorial Park. (Loren Hosmer.)

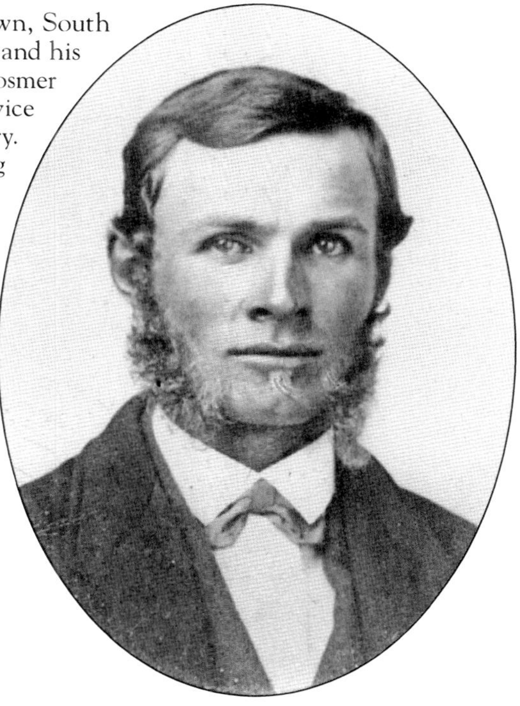

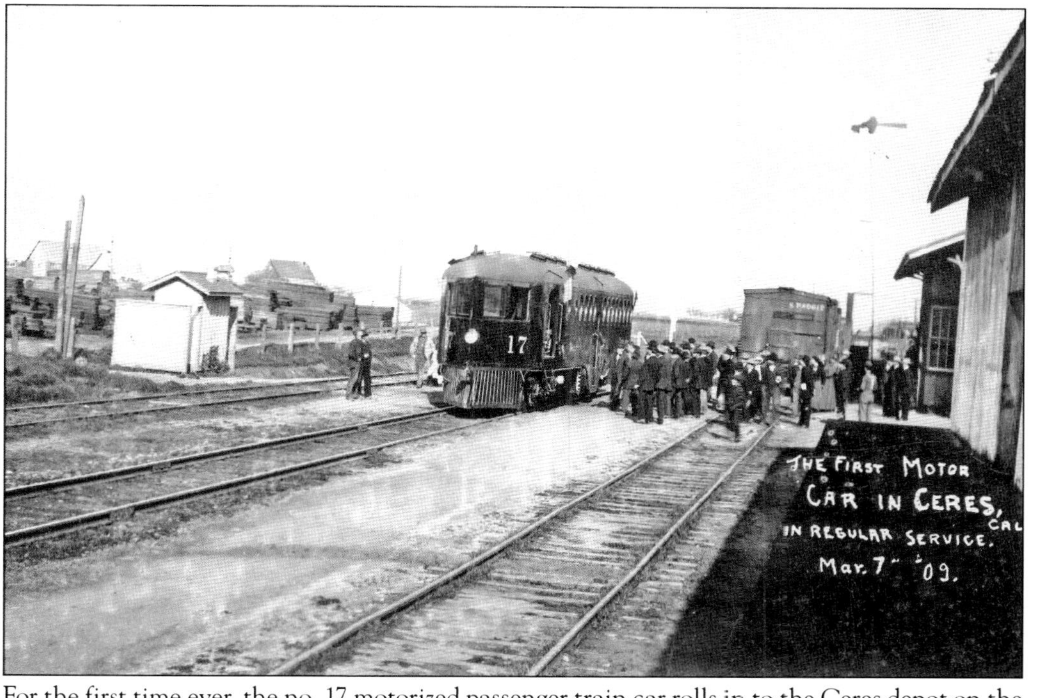

For the first time ever, the no. 17 motorized passenger train car rolls in to the Ceres depot on the morning of March 7, 1909. A small crowd has awaited its historic arrival and no doubt a few of them climbed aboard to take a ride down the Southern Pacific tracks. This car is believed to be one from Stockton. The white building at left is an outhouse. (Ceres Historical Society.)

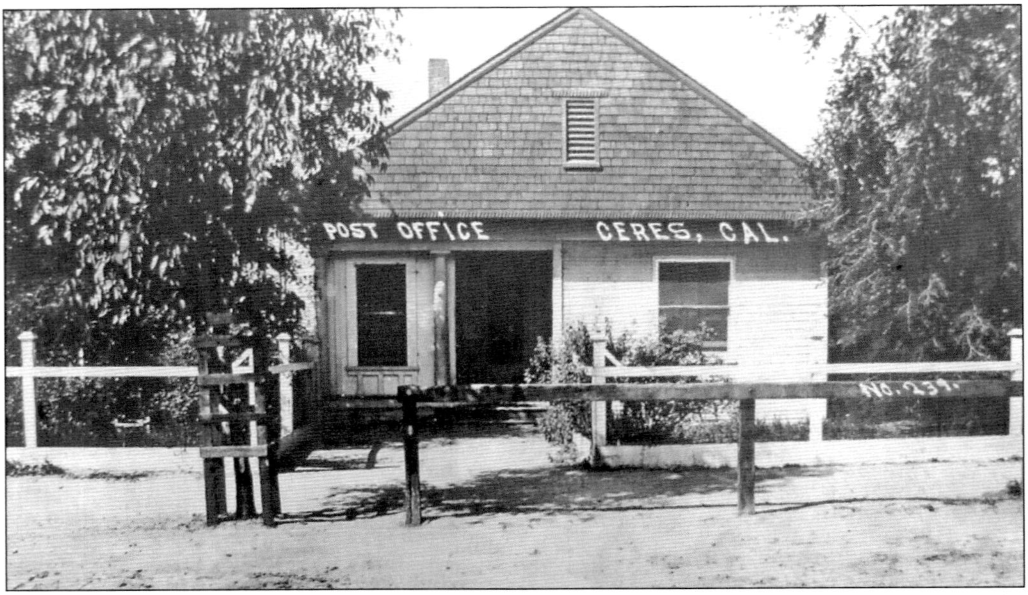

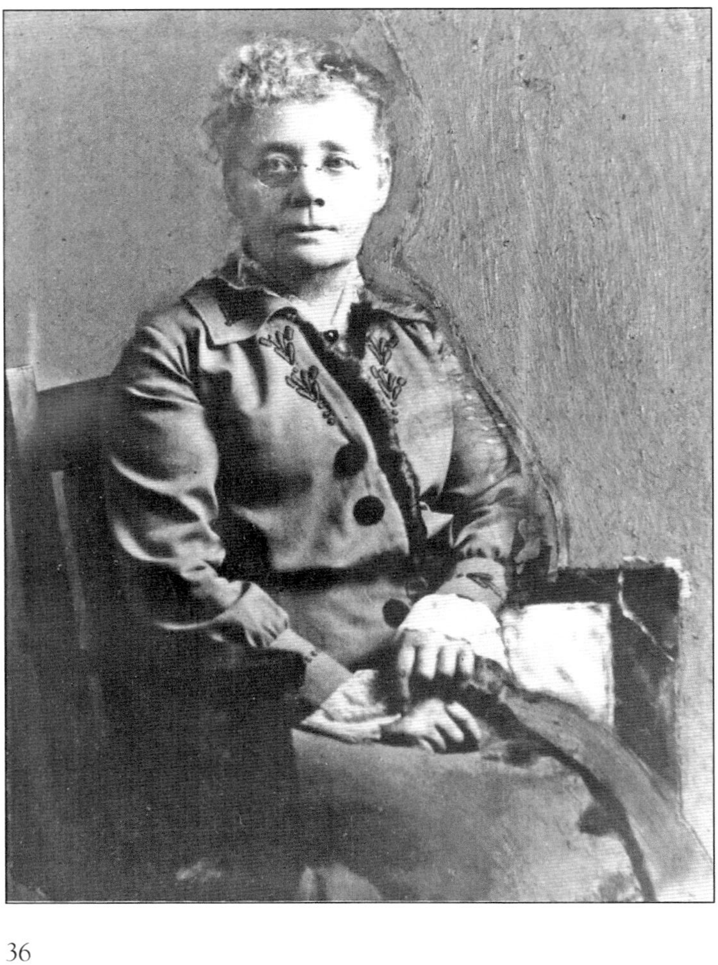

Allura Ulch (1852–1936) came to Ceres in 1880 and worked as a journalist and reporter for the *Modesto Journal*, *The Ceres Scraper*, and later the *Ceres Courier*. She lived at the northwest corner of Fourth and Lawrence Streets (above). The widow had a rental library and charged 10¢ to rent a book to supplement her income. In 1900, Ulch was the first appointed Ceres postmistress (by Pres. William McKinley). She continued to report the news in Ceres up until her death in 1936. Ulch spent the rest of her years in the house, also once the post office, after it was moved to the northwest corner of Sixth and Lawrence Streets. She became the clerk of the Ceres Baptist Church in 1888 and held that position for 35 years. (Mildred Lucas.)

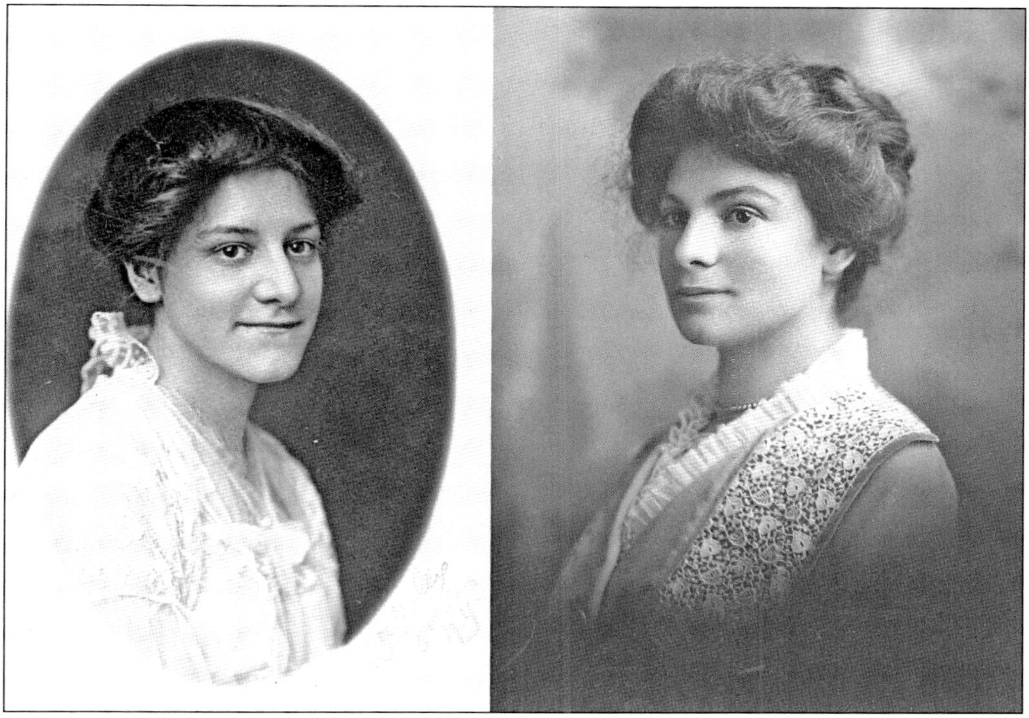

The library in Ceres is named for Florence Gondring (left). This c. 1906 portrait was taken during her days as a student at Columbia University in New York City. She had previously graduated from San Jose State University. Florence settled in Stockton, where she was a schoolteacher. When both Florence and sister Frances Gondring (right) retired, they came back to Ceres to take care of the family farming interests. Frances seeded the money for the Ceres library and dedicated the building in memory of Florence. (Marian Sanders.)

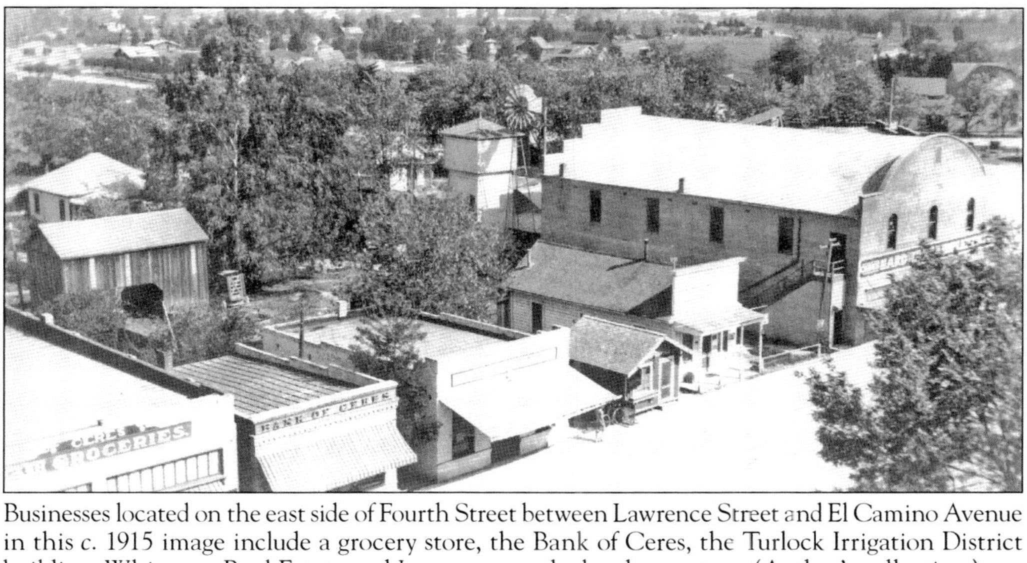

Businesses located on the east side of Fourth Street between Lawrence Street and El Camino Avenue in this c. 1915 image include a grocery store, the Bank of Ceres, the Turlock Irrigation District building, Whitmore Real Estate and Insurance, and a hardware store. (Author's collection.)

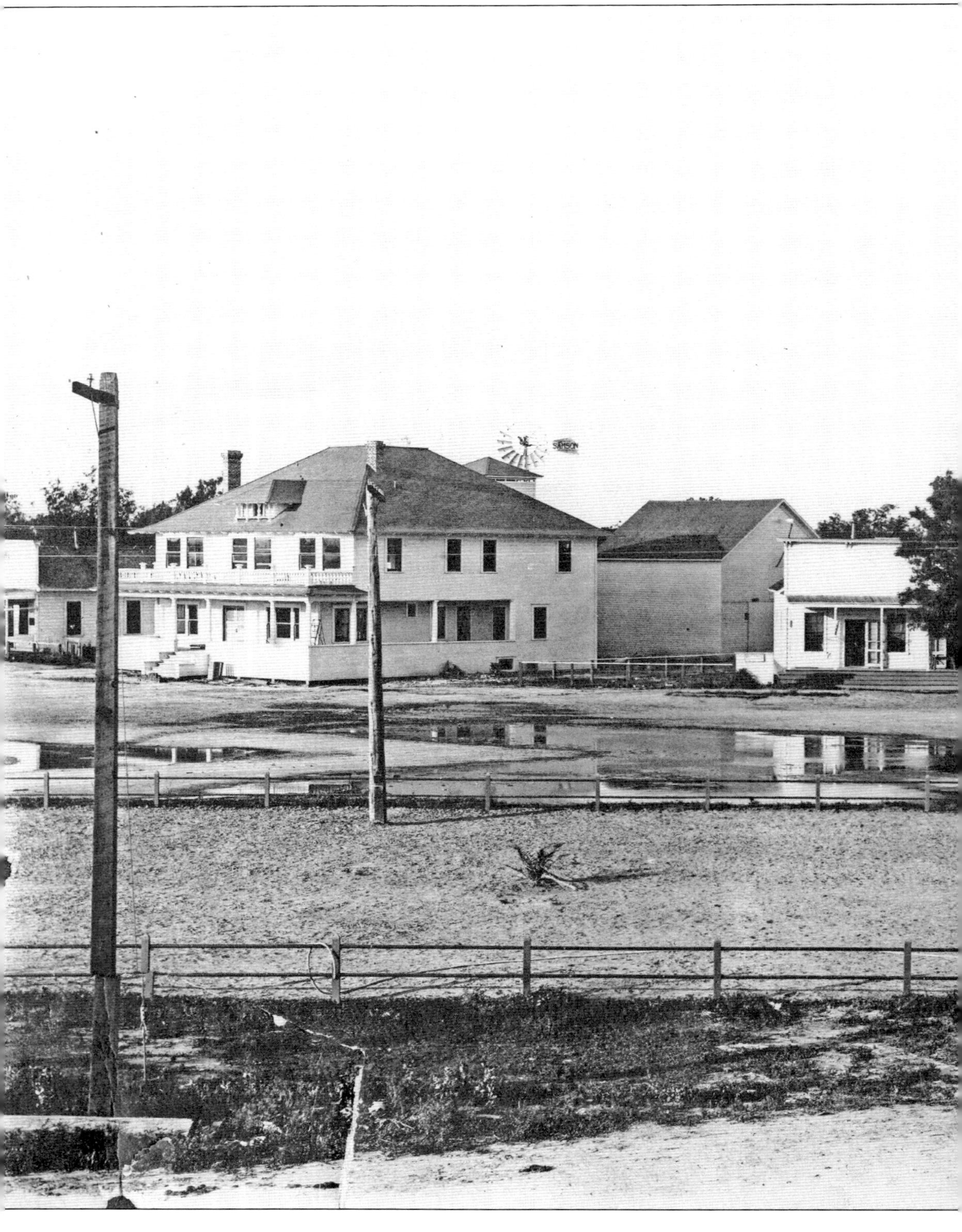
SAMSON

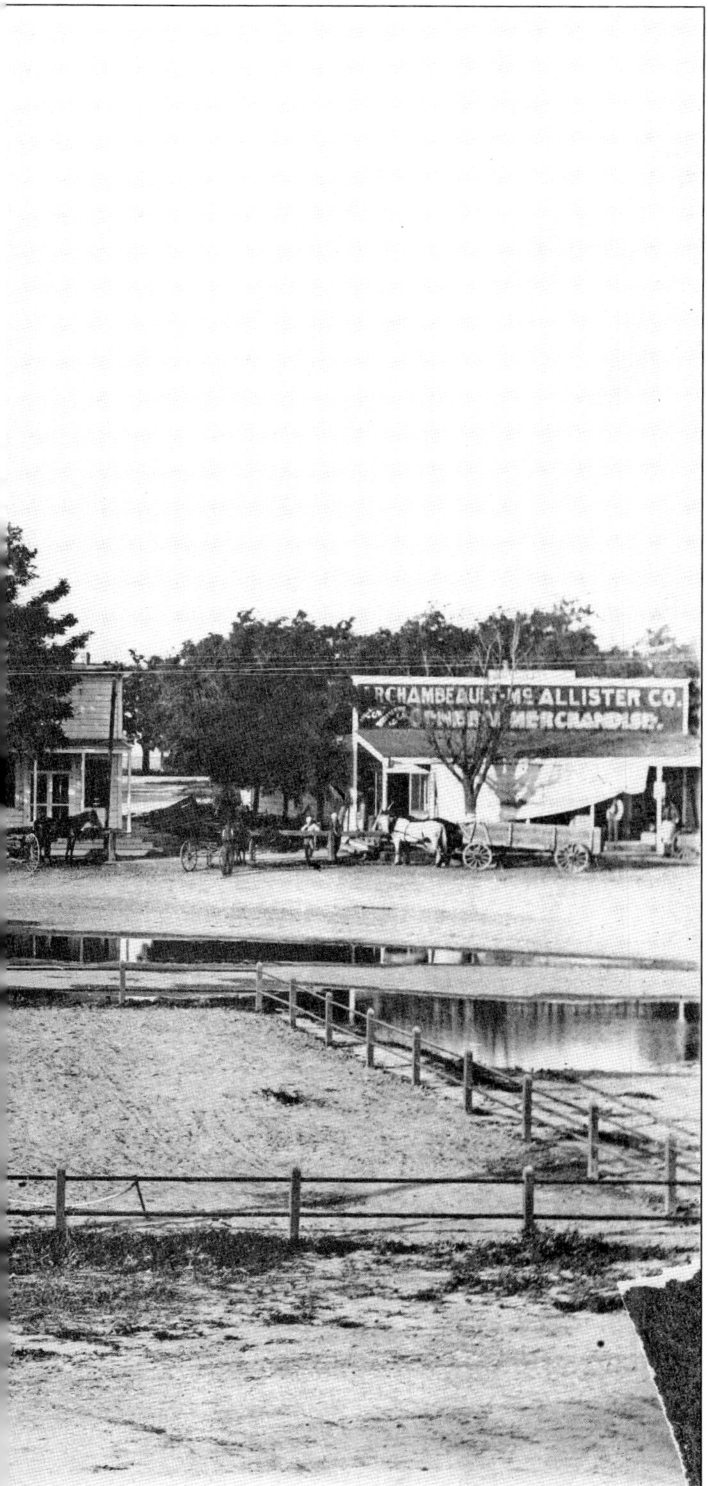

Around the beginning of the 20th century, downtown Ceres stretches along what is now El Camino Avenue, north of the Pine Street overpass. At left, the large white building is the Gillette Hotel, moved to Hughson in 1907. It was replaced by the large Collins and Warner Hall, which later became Ceres Hardware Store. On the right, commercial structures include the Chambeault and McAllister Company Mercantile (Mildred Lucas.)

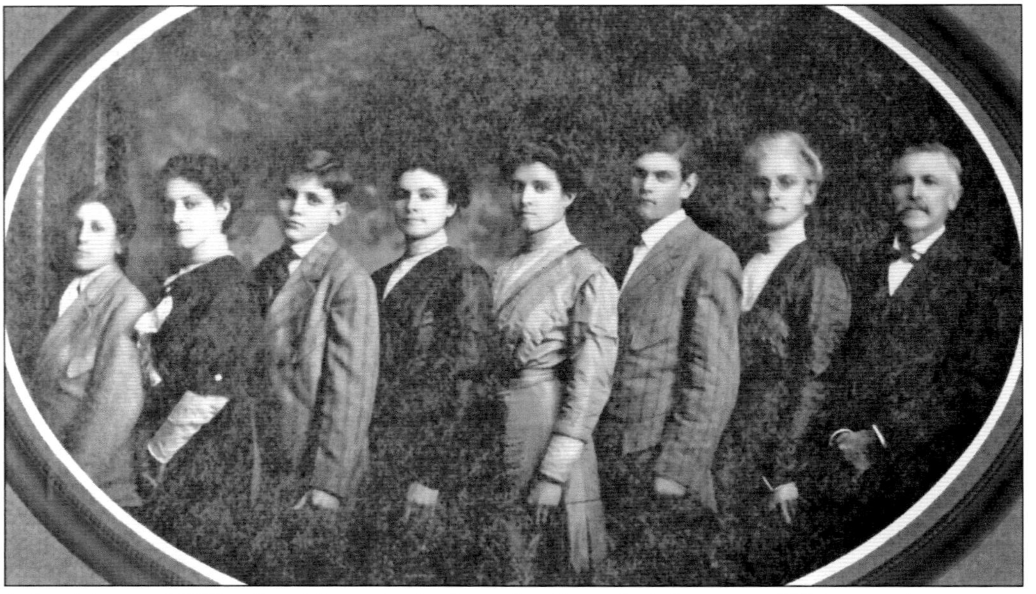

Judge John and Dillie Gondring raised a large family at their home on Whitmore Avenue, on land now occupied by the Richland Shopping Center. In this December 1910 photograph, from left to right, are Alfred (a 1917 graduate of Ceres High School), Florence, Augustus "Gus" (who died in 1924 after being kicked in the head by a mule), Frances, Nettie (Hansen), John "Jack" Jr. (who became Ceres postmaster in 1933), Dillie, and Judge John. They came to San Jose from Nebraska in 1906 and then moved to Ceres. (Marian Sanders.)

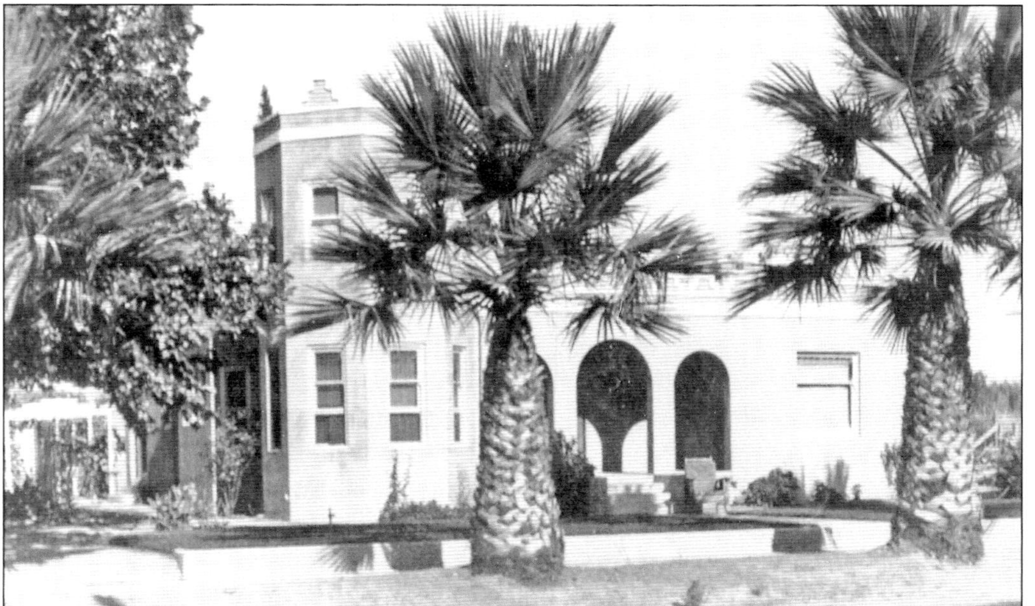

A most unusual home, the Castle at Fourth and Magnolia Streets was constructed around 1903 by Ceres school principal John A. Wagener. He borrowed the idea for the Mexican-Aztec architecture after seeing buildings like this during a trip to Oaxaca, Mexico. (Ceres Historical Society.)

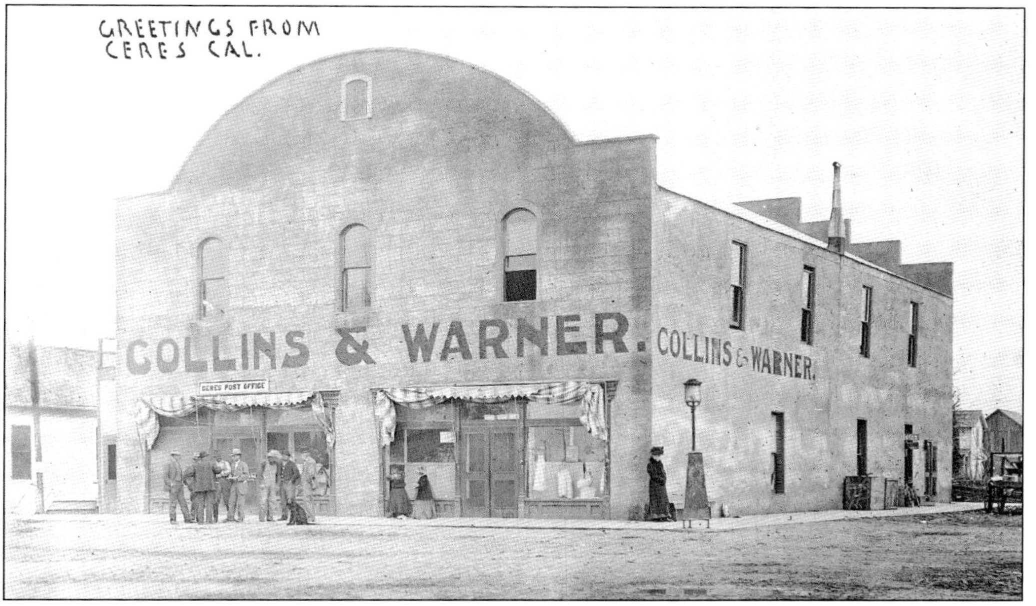

Collins and Warner Hall, at Fourth and El Camino, housed the Ceres post office at the time of this photograph. The upper floor was used for community gatherings and dances. Frank Lander opened Ceres Hardware in the building. In 1925, Lander sold the business to Guy Aspinall, who ran Ceres Hardware with son Wendell until the 1960s. Many today recall this site being where Youngdale's operated. (Marian Gondring Sanders.)

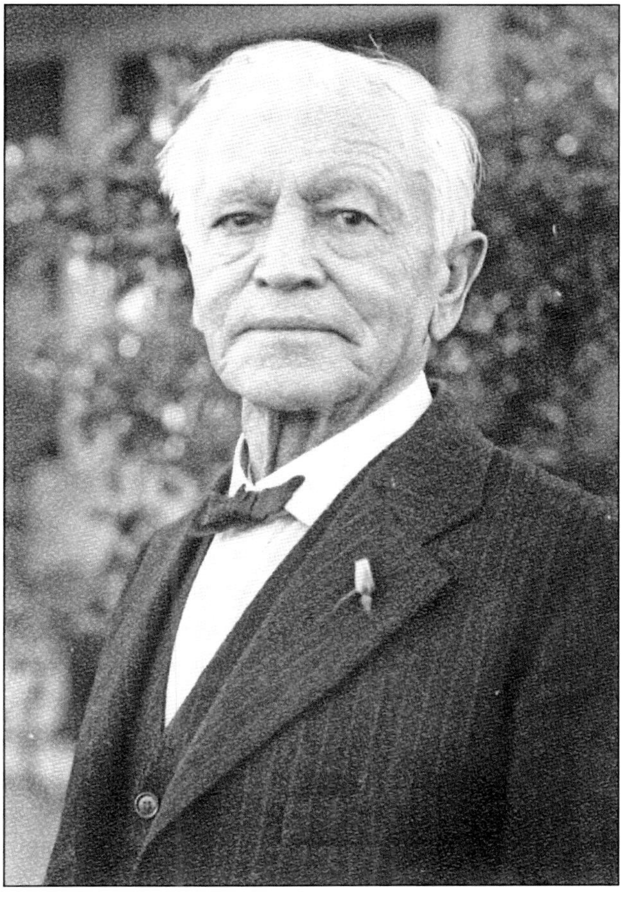

Always sporting a rose on his lapel, Judge John M. Gondring would walk from his home on Whitmore Avenue to the court building on Fourth Street in downtown Ceres. Born in Chicago in 1856, the Democrat was elected to the Nebraska state senate in 1896. In 1905, he moved his family to San Jose and then on to Ceres in 1910. Gondring died in March 1933 at age 77 after being stricken in the courtroom. (Marian Sanders.)

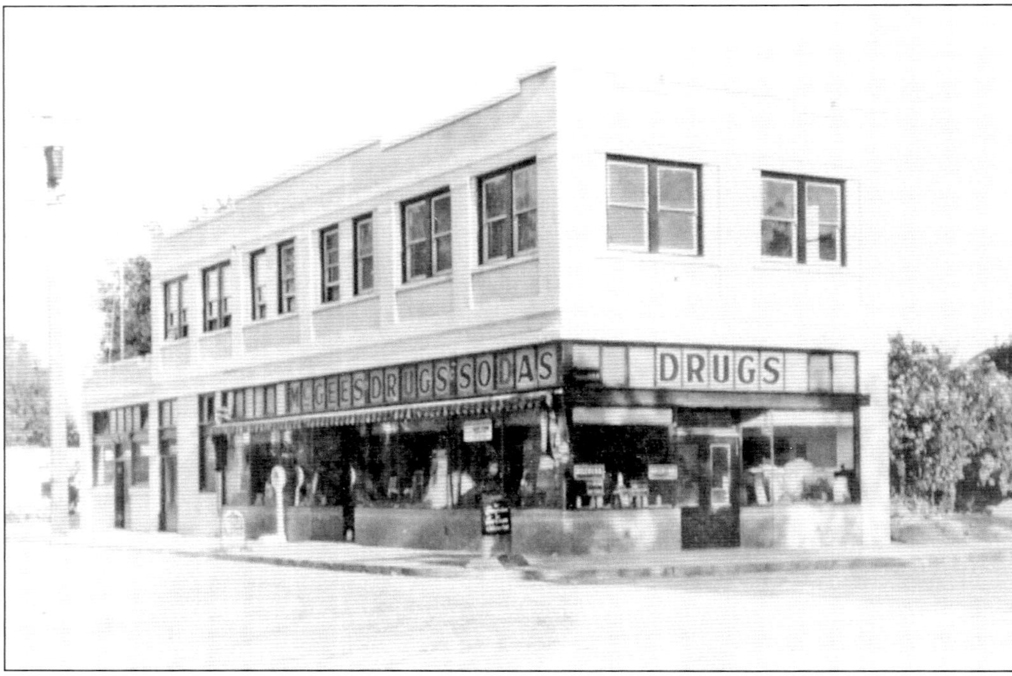

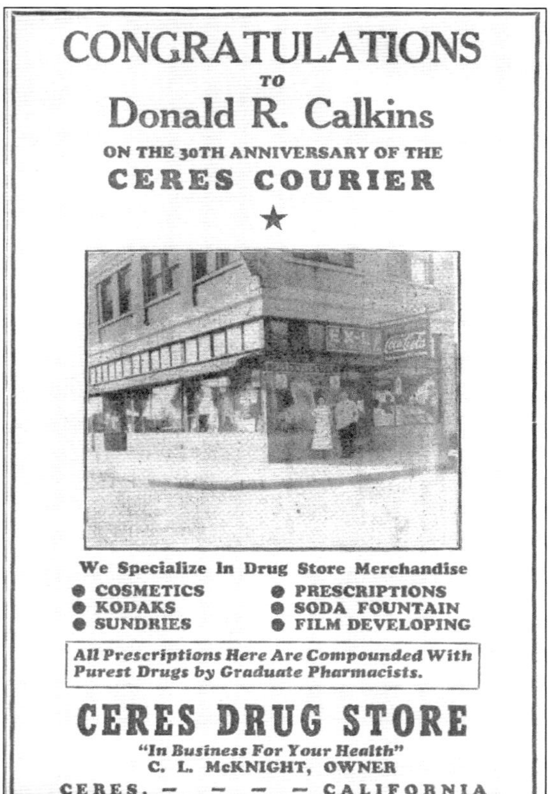

McGee's Drug Store was not just a place to get prescriptions filled; kids spent pennies and nickels for soda pop and candy. Located at the northwest corner of Fourth and Lawrence Streets, the store was constructed by Loren E. McGee after Allura Ulch moved her house in 1927. In 1929, the business was sold to J. D. Anderson. In 1939, Claude McKnight, a soda jerk turned pharmacy college graduate, took over the drugstore. (Ceres Historical Society.)

This quarter-page advertisement appeared in a 1941 commemorative issue of the *Ceres Courier* celebrating the 30th anniversary of the founding of the newspaper. Druggist Claude McKnight, who later became mayor, ran this congratulatory notice. The drugstore was located in the building standing at the northwest corner of Fourth and Lawrence Streets. (*Ceres Courier.*)

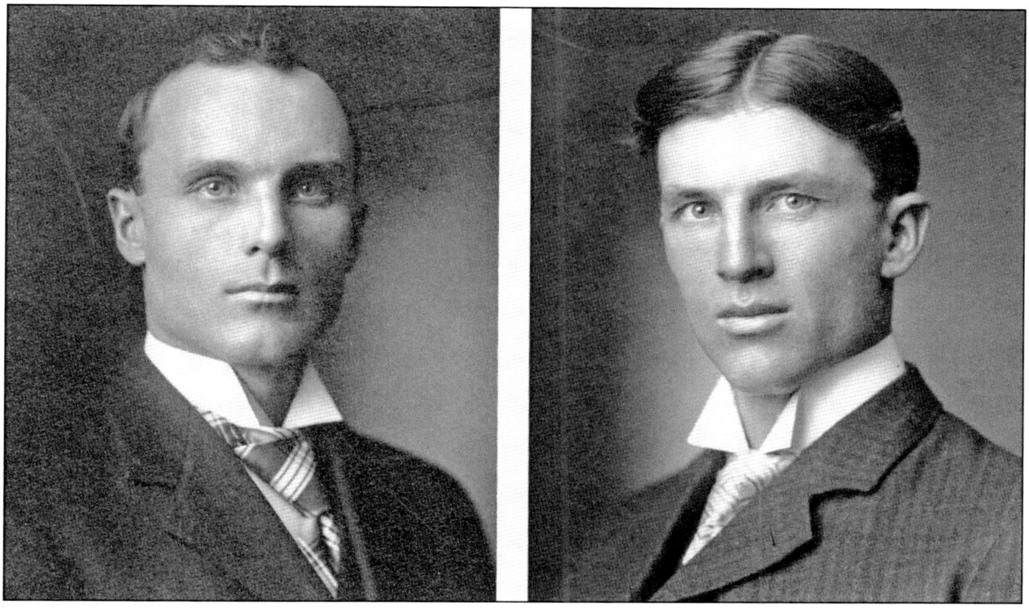

Brothers Wallace (left) and Henry Caswell were key developers of the Ceres community. Wallace (1875–1950) and Henry (1876–1949) were the sons of Thomas and Mary Caswell. Wallace, a graduate of the University of Michigan, married Jennie Whitmore. Wallace spent time in Iowa as an attorney before settling in Ceres in 1933. Henry attended Vista College in Iowa before settling in Ceres in 1905, where he served on the first library board. Henry married Helen Cross, the church organist at the Methodist church, and they owned a ranch in the Westport area. Two streets in Ceres—Wallace Avenue and Henry Avenue—were named after the two brothers. (Mark Perra.)

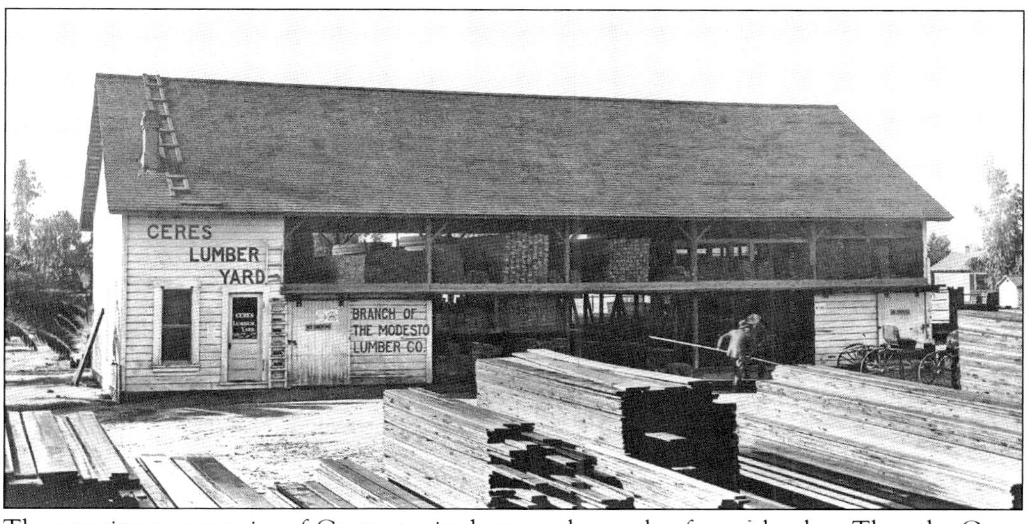

The growing community of Ceres required an ample supply of good lumber. Thus the Ceres Lumber Company was opened west of the railroad tracks on what would later be known as Railroad Avenue. James Gartin organized the Ceres yard of the Modesto Lumber Company in 1903. Gartin served on the first Ceres city council. (Mildred Lucas.)

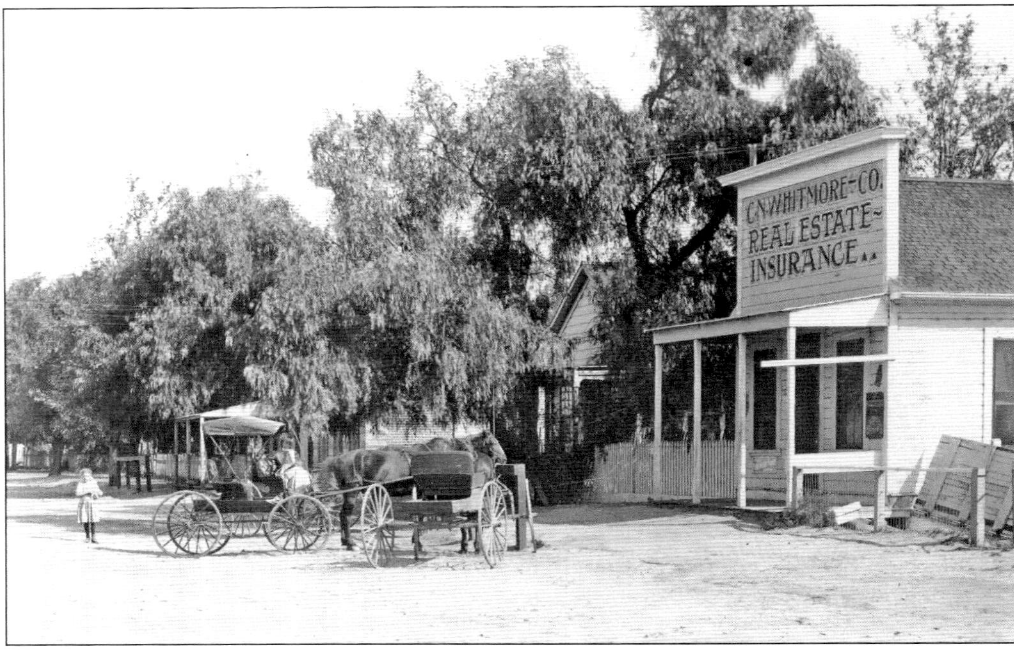

Horse-drawn buggies are parked in front of Clinton Whitmore's Real Estate and Insurance office on Fourth Street (above). The simple building was located south of the old brick TID office that remains standing today. Just north of the TID office was a very similar building (below) that housed the Ceres Meat Market. (Ceres Historical Society.)

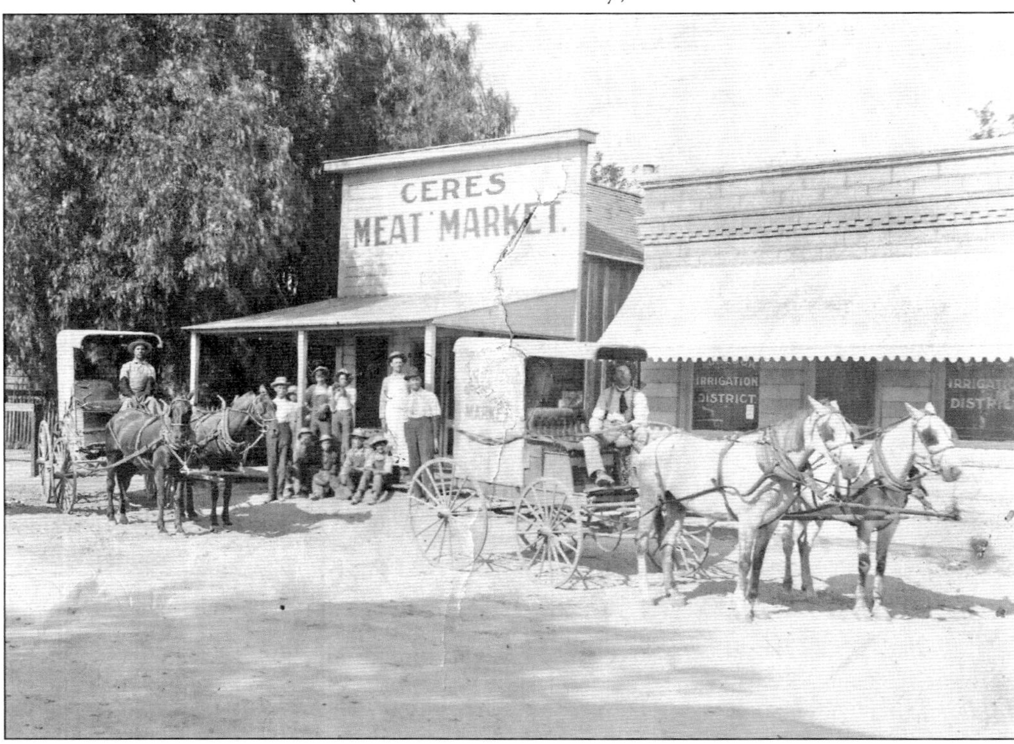

These two ads appeared in early Ceres High School yearbooks in the 1910s. The top notice was placed by R. C. Doolittle for his confectionery store at Lawrence at Third Streets. The bottom promotion is for J. M. Vincent, blacksmith. Joseph Vincent came to Ceres from Sonora in 1904 and bought the Averill blacksmith shop. In 1919, Vincent sold the establishment and started a water business, converting the windmill process over to electric pumps. (Mildred Lucas.)

The

Ceres Confectionery

For Everything Refreshing

Ice Cream, Ice Cream Sodas

and all kinds of Summer Drinks

Special Rates for

PARTIES AND ENTERTAINMENTS

R. C DOOLITTLE, Prop.

For Skillful Repair of Farm or Other Machinery or Millwork, go to

J. M. VINCENT

THE BLACKSMITH

Horses don't go lame When They're Shod by Vincent

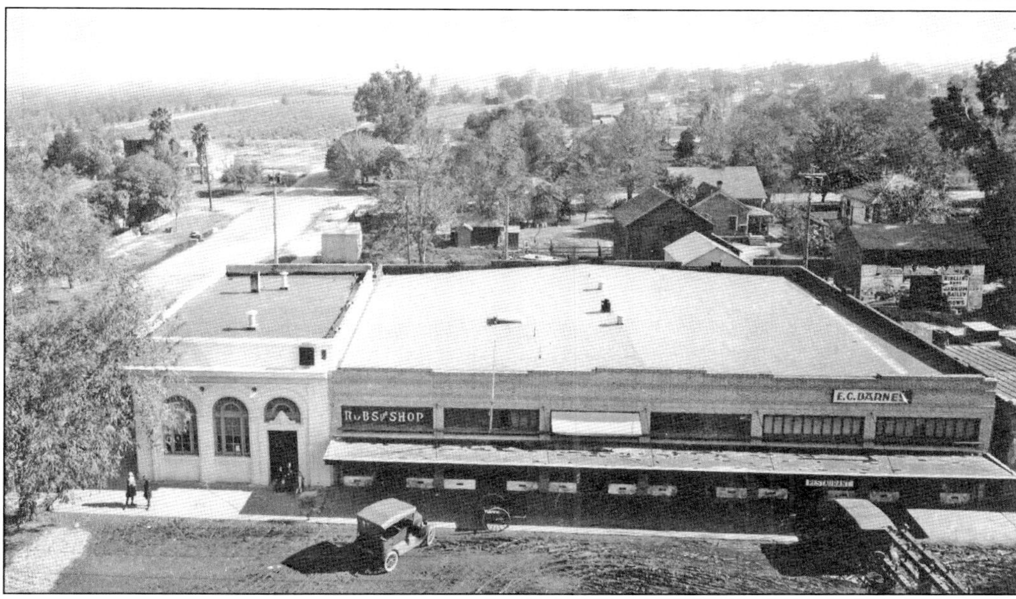

This view of Ceres (c. 1915) was taken from the roof of the IOOF Hall and shows a Fourth Street block and lands beyond. The white building at left is the Bank of Ceres. Lawrence Street is at left, pictured before Whitmore Elementary School was constructed. (Ceres Historical Society.)

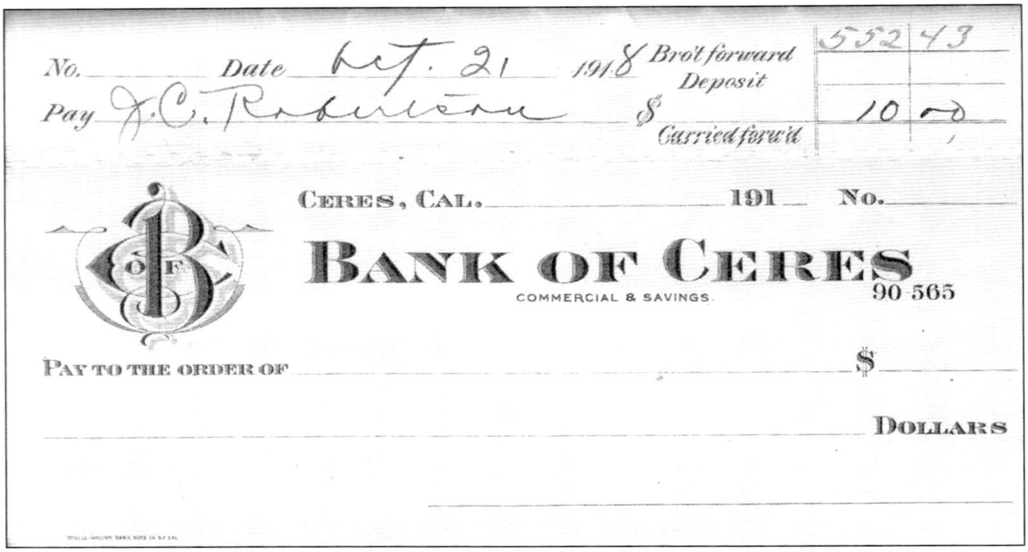

This 1918 checkbook (above) belonged to L. Stokes. The Bank of Ceres (below) opened its doors on April 11, 1911, and first operated on the east side of Fourth Street until moving into a larger building on the southeast corner of Fourth and Lawrence Streets. That building is still standing. The bank's first directors were Vaughn D. Whitmore, L. M. MacDonald, Antony Morgan, C. S. Grandi, G. R. Stoddard, Myron Warner, and W. P. Clarke. (Mildred Lucas.)

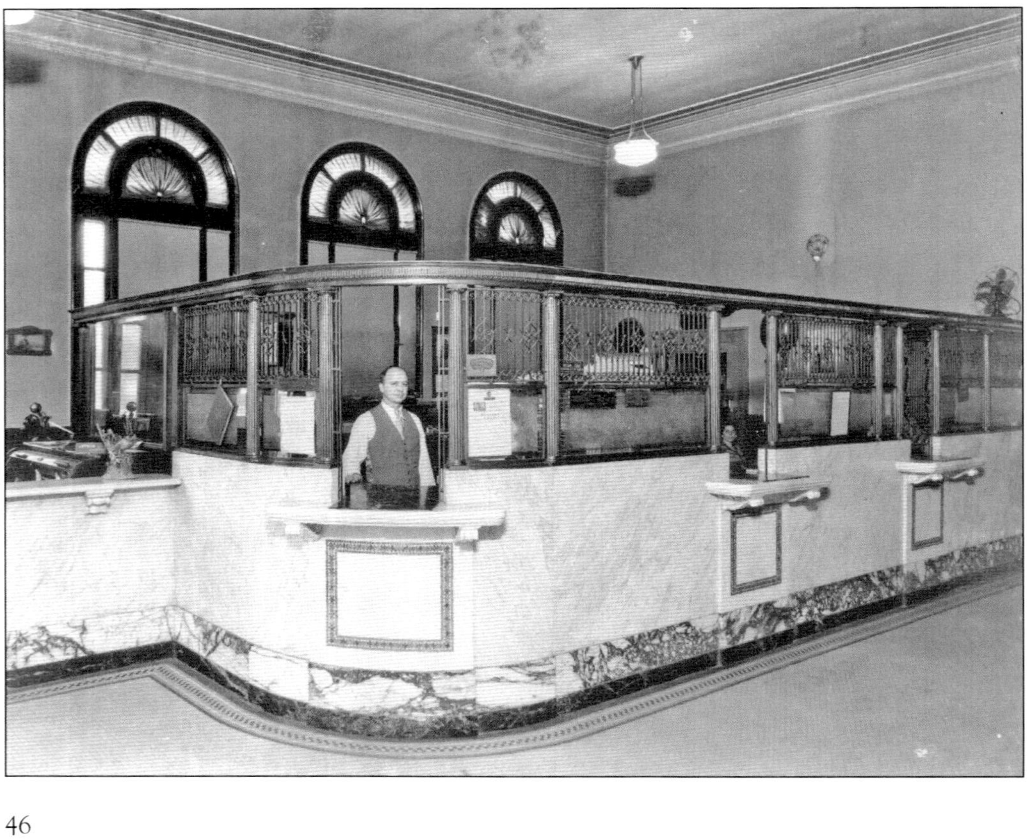

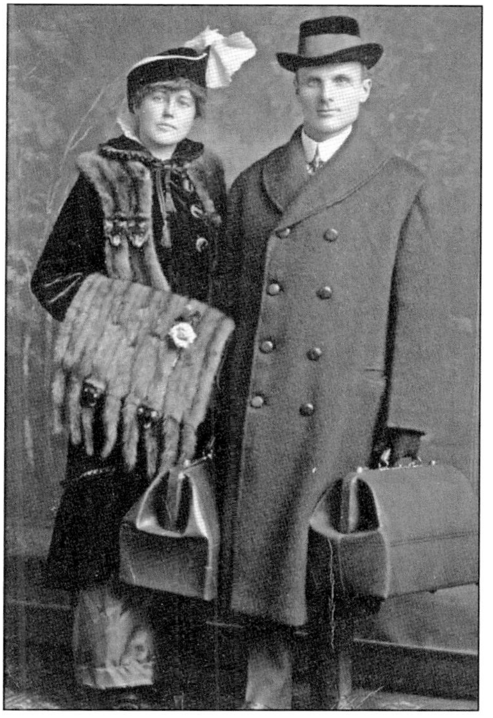

Wallace and Jennie Whitmore Caswell were wealthy by Ceres standards and enjoyed traveling, as shown here with travel bags in hand. They met in Ceres, were married in 1910, and lived in Iowa for 23 years. They returned to Ceres in 1933 and were very much a part of the Ceres social scene. Jennie was five years younger than her husband but survived him by 16 years after his 1950 death. (Ceres Historical Society.)

One of the earliest documents relating to the incorporation of Ceres as a city is this declaration of the results of the first city council election. On February 25, 1918, the city incorporated, with Dr. S. W. Cartwright as mayor until April 13. He served only a month and nine days until an April 15 election decided on Vaughn D. Whitmore. The first serving on the city council were C. H. Sikes, J. U. Gartin, C. T. Haynes, City Clerk J. A. Wagener and City Treasurer E.C. Baird. (City of Ceres.)

City Treasurer

E. C. Baird 27 votes.

It is hereby adjudged, ordered and declared that the following named persons have been and are duly elected to the offices set down after their respective names.

G. C. Whitmore	Trustee
S. W. Cartright	Trustee
C. T. Haynes	Trustee
J. U. Gartin	Trustee
C. H. Sikes	Trustee
J. A. Wagener	Clerk
E. C. Baird	Treasurer

And the Clerk is hereby further ordered to send certificates of election to the above named persons.

On motion of V. D. Whitmore, duly seconded and passed, the Clerk was authorized to purchase the necessary books and stationery for the records of the City of Ceres as required by statute.

Meeting adjourned.

Attest V. D. Whitmore

J. A. Wagener
Clerk

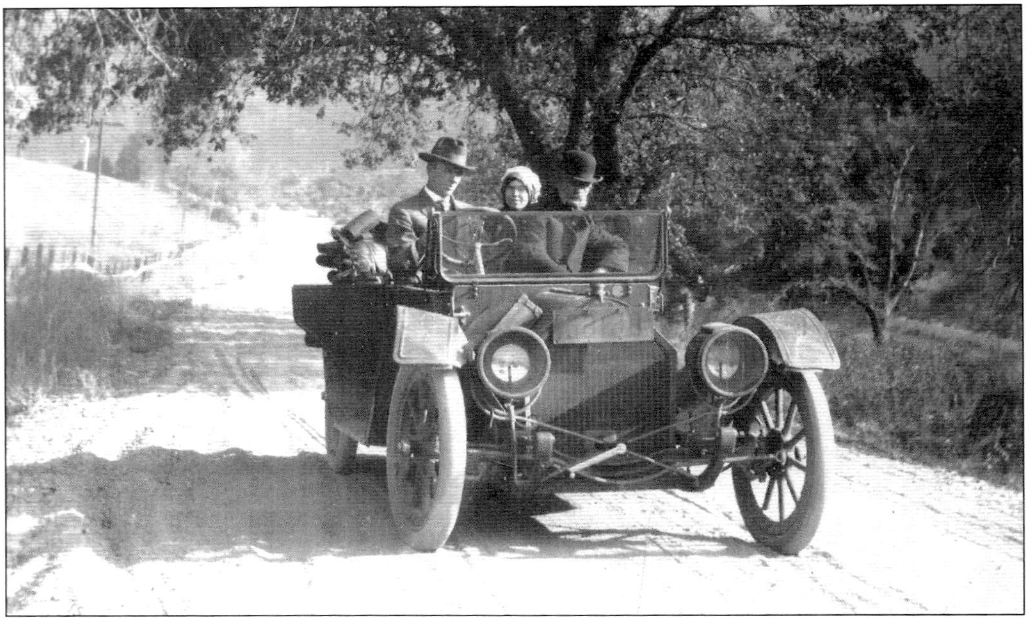

The Caswell family takes a leisurely drive in the foothills near La Grange. In the front seat of this vintage automobile are Wallace Caswell and his father, Thomas. The lady in the backseat may be Jennie Whitmore Caswell, Wallace's wife. (Mark Perra.)

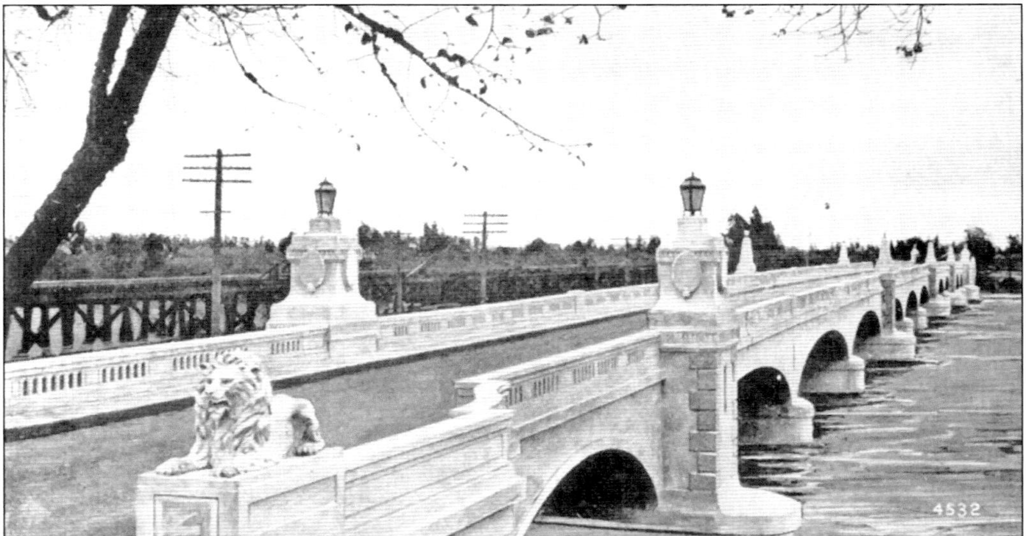

After it opened on March 17, 1917, the Seventh Street Bridge was the primary way Ceres residents accessed Modesto. The street was then Highway 99, known as the Golden State Highway. The two-lane bridge, with majestic concrete lions guarding both ends, proved too narrow for growing auto traffic volume. The southern approach at Hatch Crossing had a dangerous curve to access River Road. A new bridge was needed, thus the Ninth Street Bridge was hurried as a relief measure during the Depression. The Ninth Street Bridge cost $350,000 in federal funds and was dedicated by Gov. James Rolph in June 1933. Later Ceres and Modesto were connected east of the Modesto Airport via the Mitchell Road Bridge. (*Ceres Courier.*)

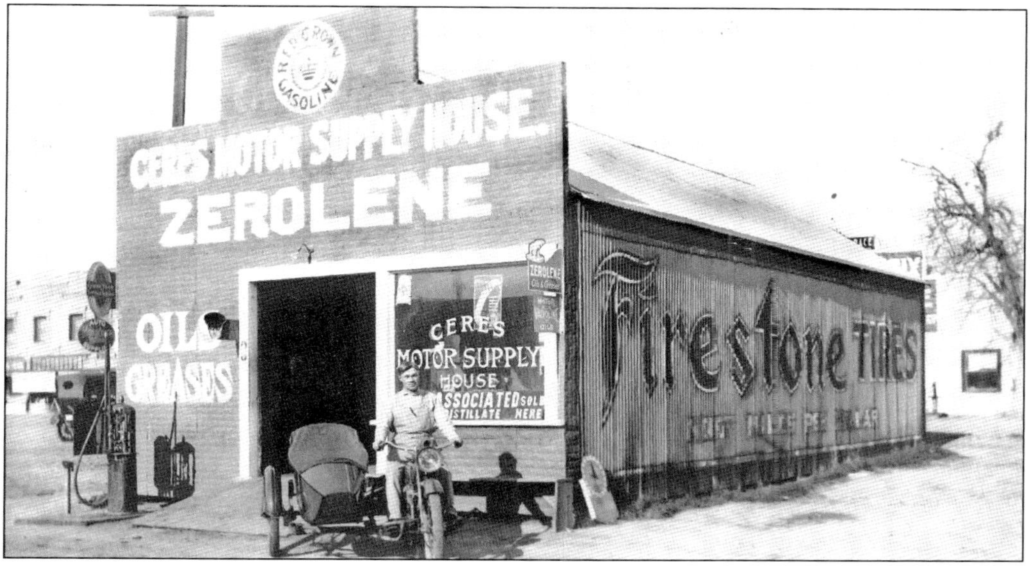

Wayne Alfred Hosmer sits on his Harley with a sidecar (above), which often held his wife Petra for rides. He operated this service station on the corner of Third and Pine Streets. The son of early Ceres resident Ezra Hosmer, Wayne (also below) was a cutting-edge motorcycle enthusiast who mixed a love for Harley Davidson cycles with business sense to open the Ceres Motor Supply House. This building (c. 1917) was located where Fifth Street intersects with Highway 99 at the present-day Pine Street overpass. Hosmer's shop sold oil, greases, tires, parts, and gasoline. The business operated for 35 years and moved three times for various expansions of Highway 99. Wayne Hosmer was born in Mill Town, South Dakota, in 1891; he died in 1966. (Loren Hosmer.)

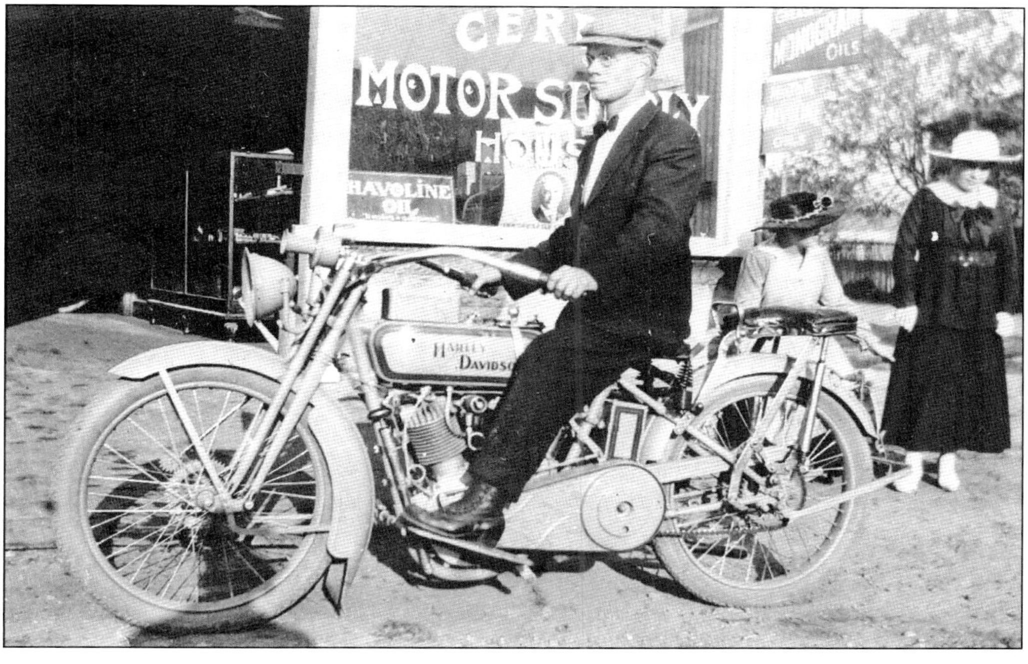

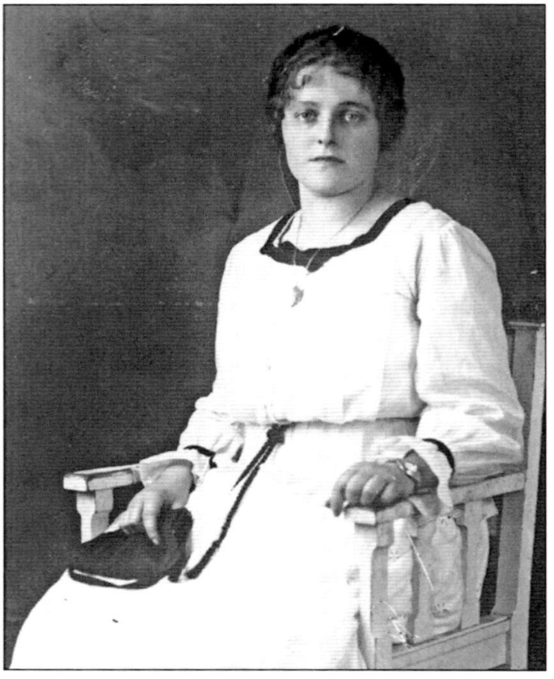

Henrietta "Frenchie" Trion Dillon came to Ceres as a World War I bride after she met doughboy Jack Dillon in 1919 while in France as a Red Cross nurse. Dillon brought her home aboard a troop ship to Missouri, then Kansas, then Keyes, California, in 1926. In 1934, the couple moved to Fifth Street, where Frenchie managed a boardinghouse and worked the soda fountain in Claude McKnight's drugstore. Jack, the first town marshal in Ceres, died in 1943, just a year after winning the election for Ceres constable. Frenchie also operated Frenchie's Cafe. (Jake Dillon.)

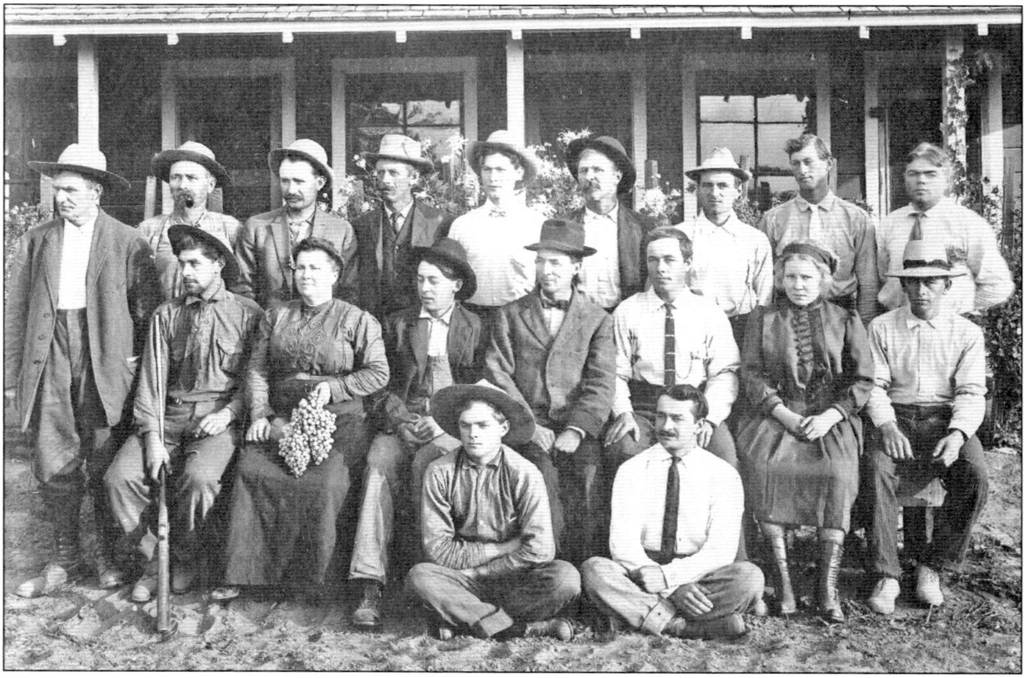

This was the harvest crew at the Whitmore Ranch (*c.* 1910). The building was located at Ninth and Whitmore Streets. The women in this picture, Lydia Wilson (second row, third from left) and daughter Lizzie Wilson (Nail) (second row, second from right), cooked for the workers. Lydia lived on Fifth Street near the ranch. Lizzie later opened her own boardinghouse west of the railroad tracks in Ceres. A bunch of grapes rests in Lydia's lap. (Shirley Ollar.)

Ed Wilson, pictured here gripping a bat, helped organize the Ceres Baseball Association in March 1911. Other baseball-loving men who formed the group were Frank Roberts, Frank Mitchell, Earl Neal, Vaughn Lee, C. Neal, Fred Mitchell, Floyd Pendergrass, and Bob Root. Wilson, who came to Ceres in 1904, also served as a constable and member of the city council. He helped lay the forms for the first strip of concrete highway through Ceres. (Shirley Ollar.)

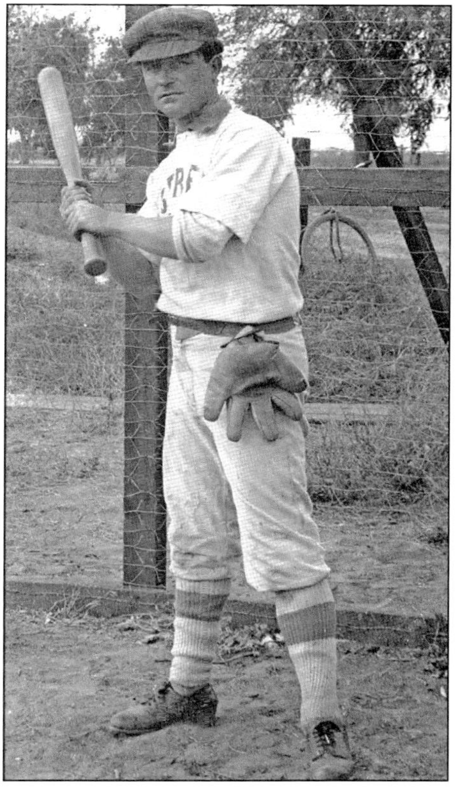

The Caulkins family poses for this photograph in 1911 on the front porch of their Smyrna Park area home on Roeding Road near Faith Home Road. They are, from left to right, (first row) Wendell Forney, Mary Forney, Alice Dora Caulkins, and Charles Crawford; (second row) Glen Forney and Nelly Caulkins; (third row) Ellis Caulkins, Frank Forney, Grace Caulkins Forney, Mary Faye Caulkins, Dewey Crawford, and Asa Caulkins; (fourth row) Mary Emma Whittier Caulkins, William Caulkins, Nellie Crawford, and Parker Crawford (on lap); (fifth row) Alice Whittier, Fred Caulkins, and Nelson Davis. (Pat Cousins.)

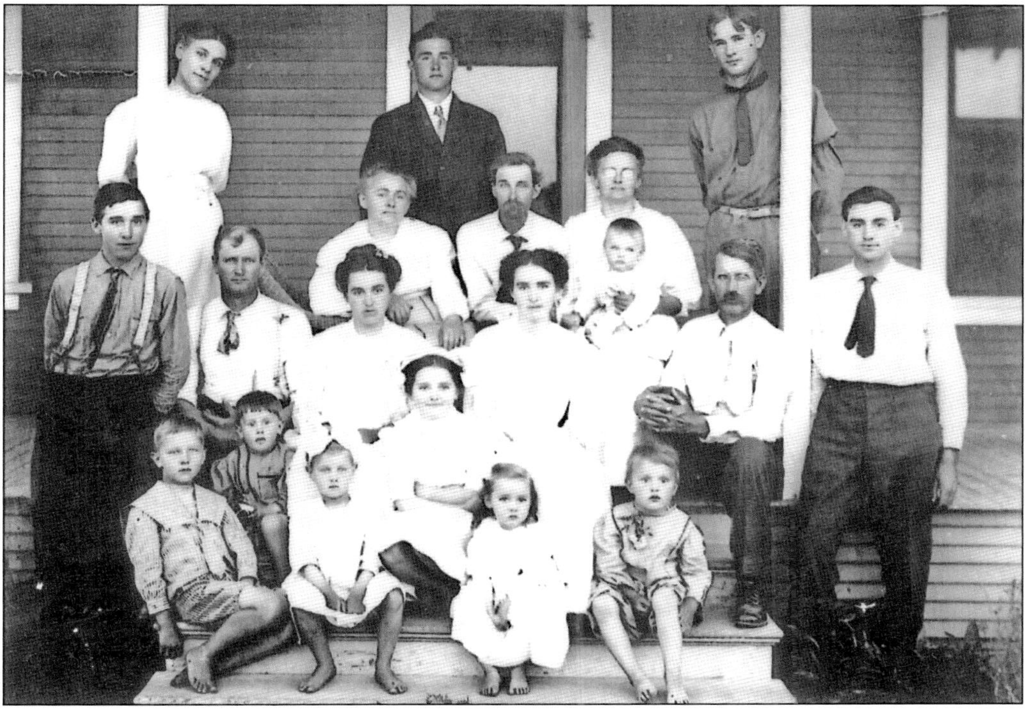

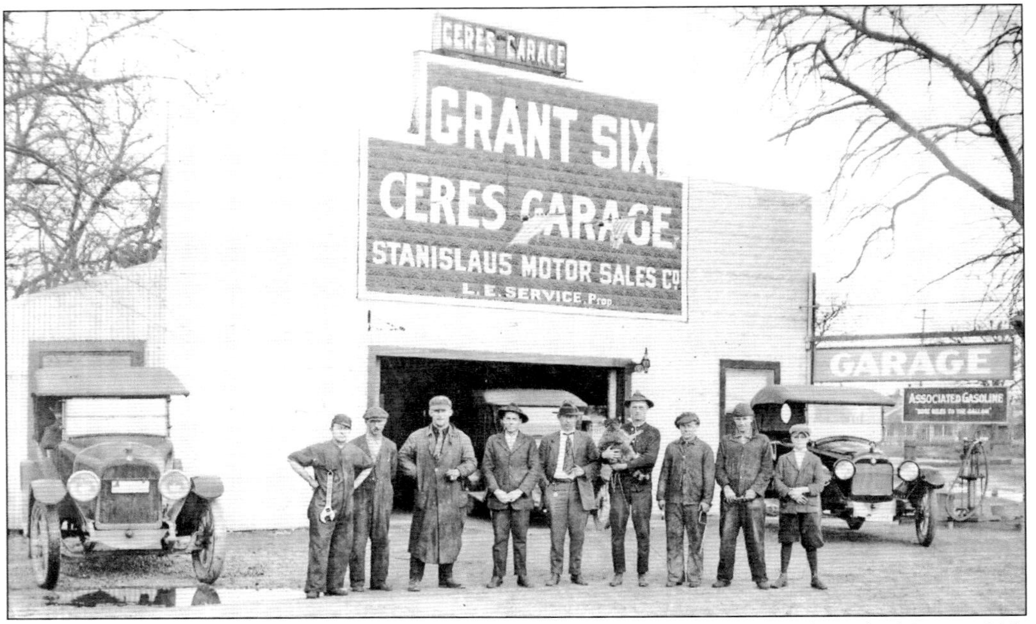

Lawrence Edward Service's Grant Six Ceres Garage was located at the south end of Ceres. Old-timers remember this structure being on the west side of Fifth Street, facing east, approximately opposite the Fifth Street Plaza. Service, at far left, sports a rather large-sized crescent wrench. L. E. "Scottie" Service was a descendent of John and Julia Service. (*Ceres Courier.*)

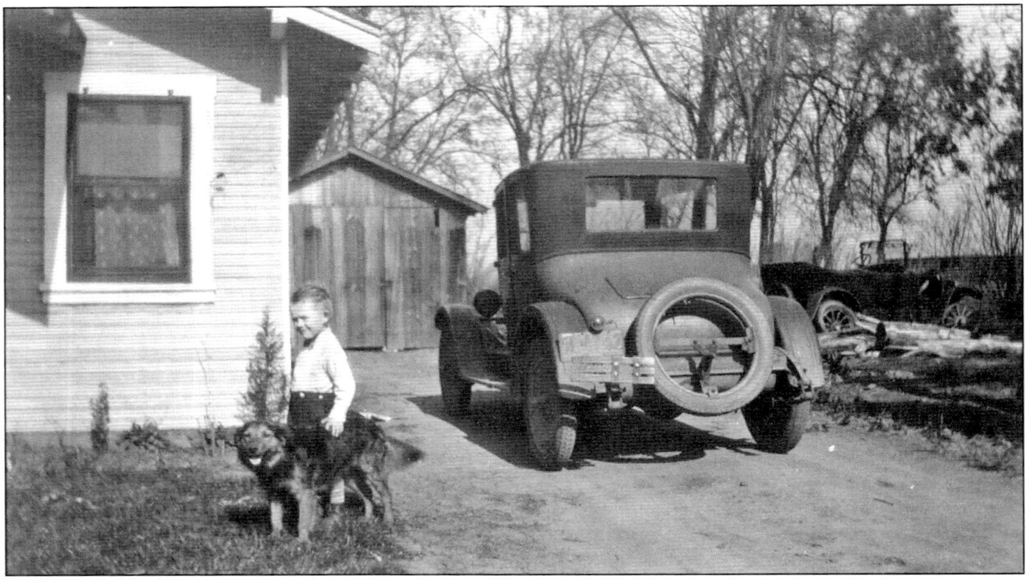

Leroy "Lee" Barbour, pictured here as a little boy with his dog, grew up in this ranch home on Fowler Road near the present-day entrance to the Las Casitas Mobile Home Park. He returned to Ceres from World War II to operate his father's gas station. Lee was a charter member of the Ceres Lions Club in 1948, served on the planning commission for 13 years, and spent two decades as a volunteer fireman. Barbour was named citizen of the year in 1988 and died in 1994. His son Dennis took over the family business. (Dennis Barbour.)

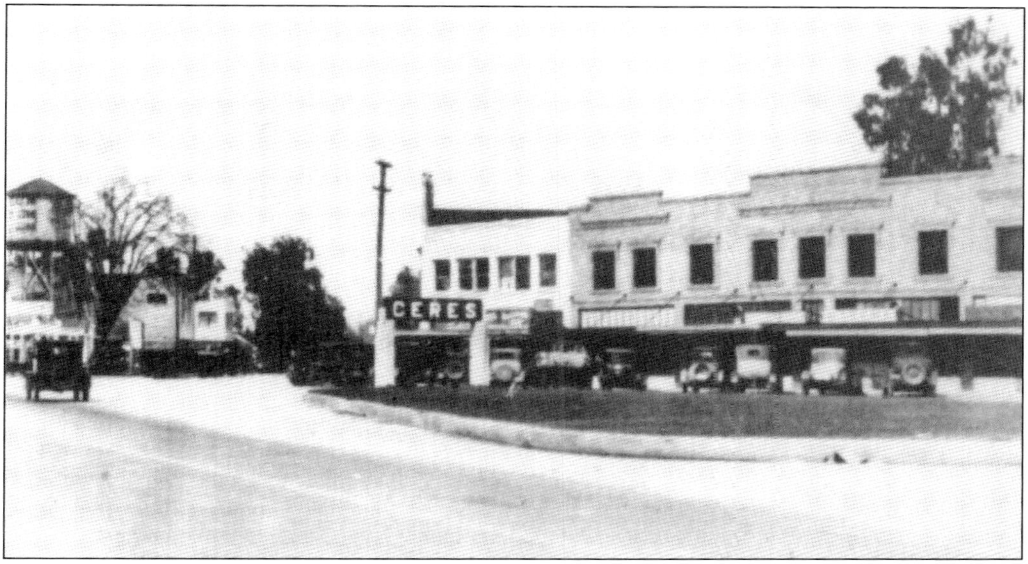

During the 1930s, a small island on the old Highway 99 through Ceres just south and east of Fourth Street served as a park posted with a community sign. The row of two-story commercial buildings was leveled in the 1960s when Highway 99 was turned into a freeway. (Mildred Lucas.)

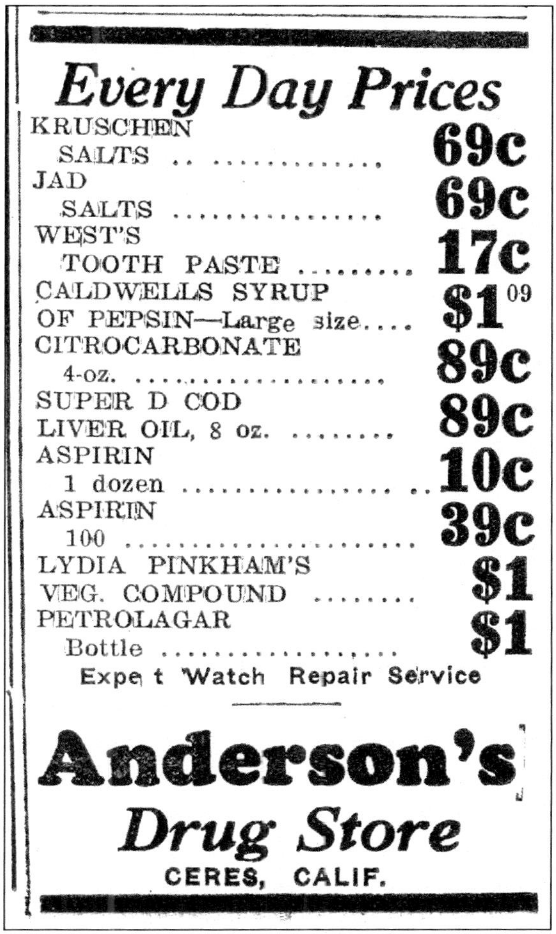

Anderson's Drug Store ran this advertisement in a *Courier* edition in March 1933. The ad indicates the offering of expert watch repair. Lydia Pinkham's Vegetable Compound, used to relieve menstrual and menopausal pains, cost a mere $1. (*Ceres Courier.*)

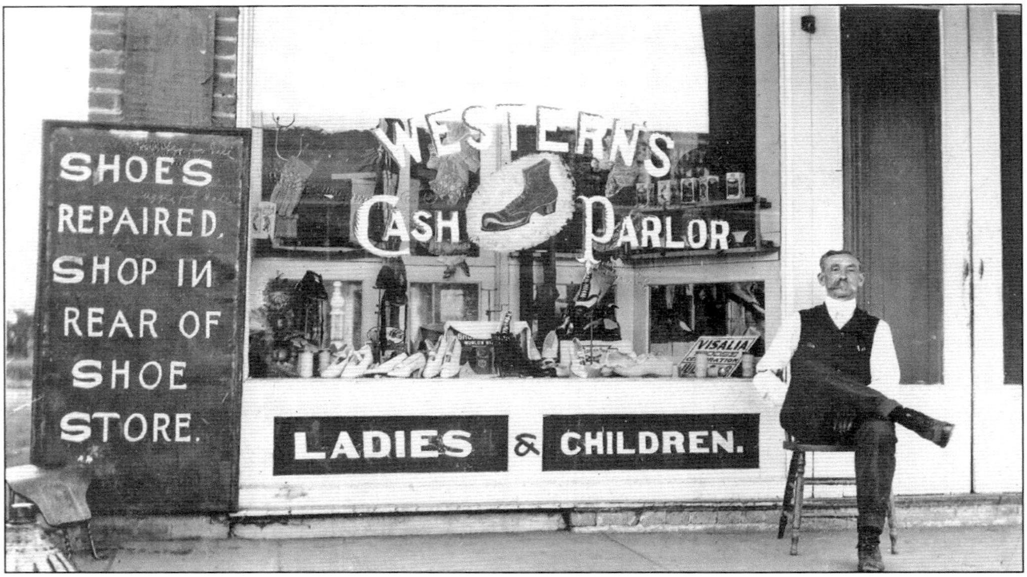

Business was slow the day Pina Western sat outside his Western's Cash Parlor (c. 1922). This store was located in the bottom floor of the Odd Fellows Hall on Fourth Street and primarily sold shoes. Western came to Ceres in 1919. The store was later taken over by a Mr. Lowery. (Claudia Grubeck.)

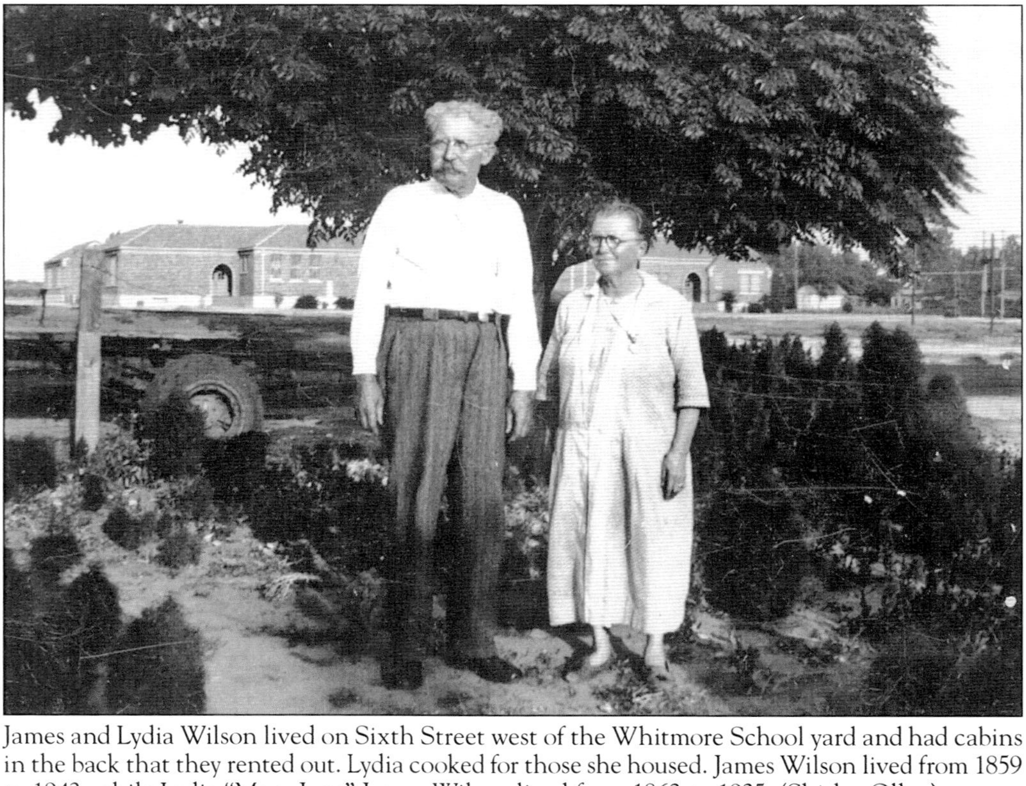

James and Lydia Wilson lived on Sixth Street west of the Whitmore School yard and had cabins in the back that they rented out. Lydia cooked for those she housed. James Wilson lived from 1859 to 1942, while Lydia "Mary Jane" Jasper Wilson lived from 1862 to 1935. (Shirley Ollar.)

Siblings Rachel and Bill Noble shared a strong bond, visible here in 1927. The death of their mother, Vida Noble, drew them even closer when Rachel was 18 and Bill was 10. The family lived on Creamery Road (now Central Avenue). In 1935, Rachel became the harvest queen at the first Ceres Harvest Festival, held on Third Street between North and Magnolia Streets where city hall is today. In his last five years, Bill wrote a history column published in the *Courier*. (Polly Noble.)

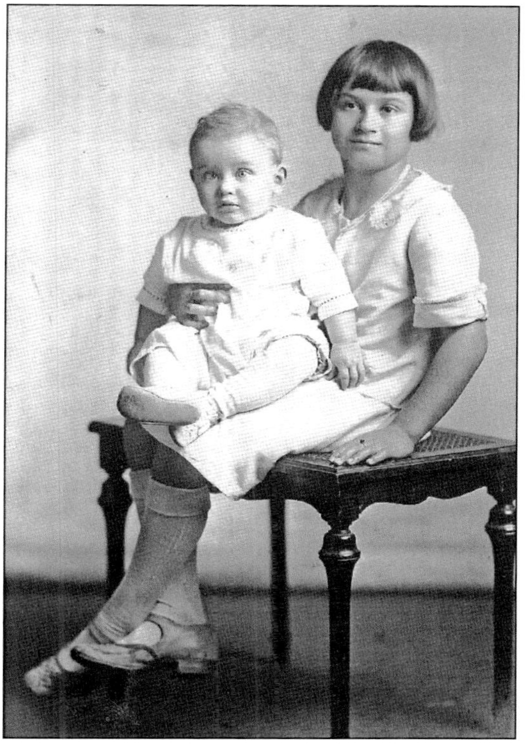

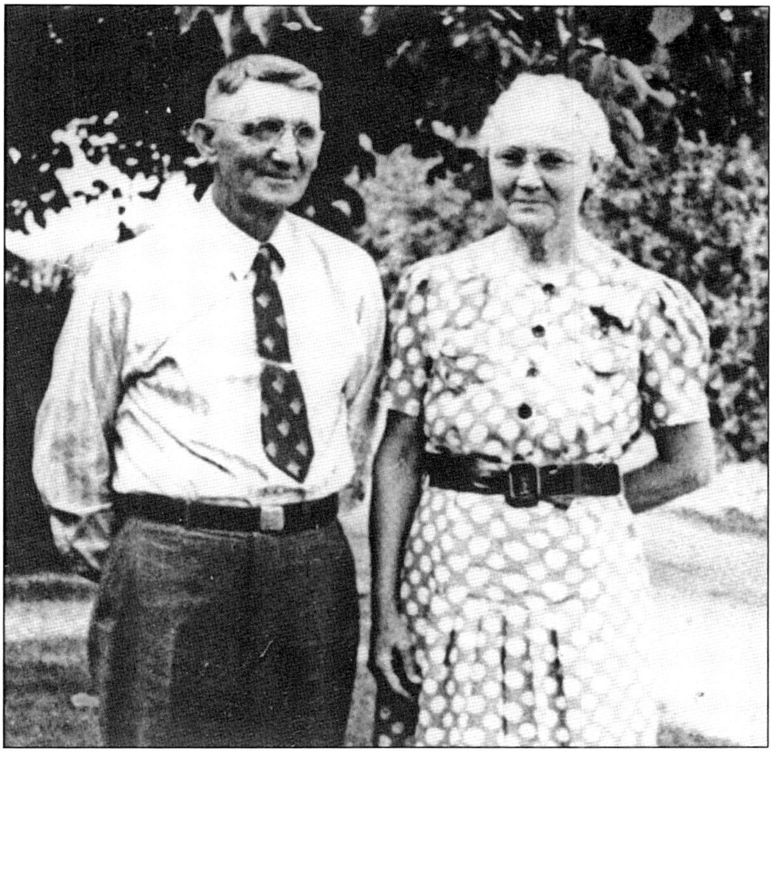

Frederick David Salter and wife Annie Blacklock Salter came to Ceres in 1902 from Hollister, California, purchasing land at Service and Faith Home Roads from Clinton Whitmore for $35 an acre. Annie said that in those days from her porch she could see her husband leaving Ceres over two miles away since there were no trees in view. (Claudia Grubeck.)

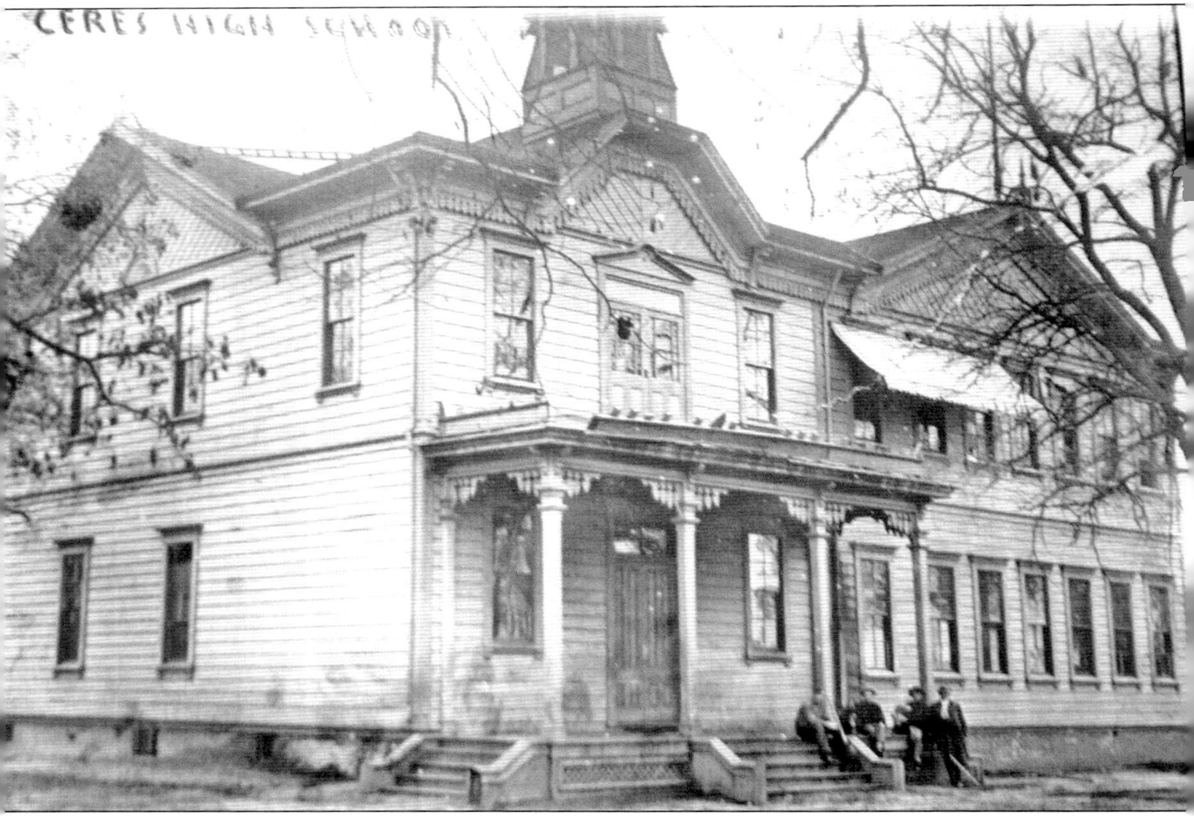

In 1887, this two-story school building opened in what is now Whitmore Park, then Triangle Park. In 1908, a need for a high school led students to meet in the Grange Hall located in another section of the park. Ceres High School officially opened for the first time on August 31, 1908, with 25 eager students and Principal J. E. Williams at the helm. Students came from the Tuolumne River to the north, Hughson to the east, Keyes to the south, and Westport to the west. The next year 55 students were enrolled, with H. H. Tracy as principal. (Ceres Unified School District.)

Three

School Days

The first known school in Ceres, Davis School, was a small structure built on a farm owned by M. M. Williams on Hatch Road at Highway 99. Harvey Bates Davis organized the Davis School District on January 27, 1859. In 1870, a one-room schoolhouse replaced the original building. In 1886, residents taxed themselves to build a two-story school in what is now Whitmore Park. It opened in 1887 and was enlarged in 1898, after Ceres residents approved a tax by a vote of 15 to 6 on September 3. In 1908, high school students needed a separate school and began to meet in the Grange Hall. John A. Wagener, principal of Ceres Grammar School, was instrumental in starting the high school. The first graduating class in 1912 received diplomas in the upstairs of the Collins and Warner Hall on Fourth Street. A brick high school was completed in 1915 on Whitmore Avenue, immediately west of what is now the old gymnasium. The 1915 school building was razed in 1965 to make way for a new administration building, classrooms, and the Doghouse. Ceres Grammar School was built in 1909 on North Street. Its first principal was John Andrew Wagener, who served until 1920. The facility was located where present-day Ceres Fire Station no. 1 sits and was replaced by Whitmore School on Lawrence Street in 1930. After World War II, more schools were needed. Caswell Elementary opened in 1948, and Don Pedro followed in 1949. In 1957, Carroll Fowler Elementary School and Walter White Junior High School were added. When Mae Hensley Junior High School opened in 1972, Walter White became an elementary school. Argus Continuation School opened in 1968. Other schools that opened were Virginia Parks Elementary, 1998; Sam Vaughn Elementary and Blaker Kinser Junior High in 1994; Adkison and Sinclear elementaries and Central Valley High School in 2005; Joel Hidahl and La Rosa Elementary Schools in 2006; and Whitmore Charter on the Berryhill Campus in 2007. In 1965, Ceres merged with the Westport district, with a rural school that was built in 1948.

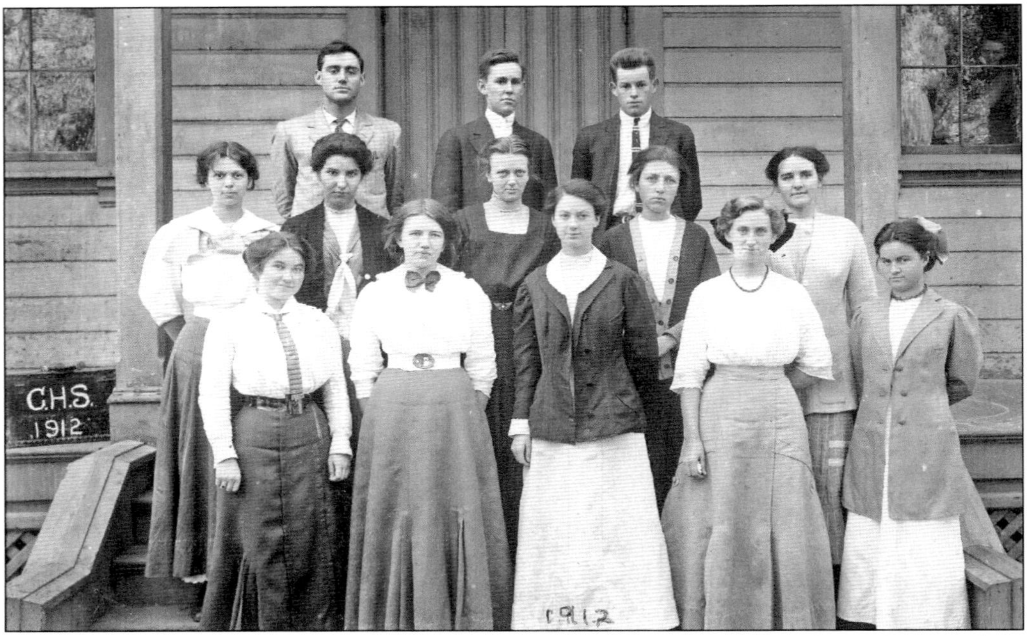

The 1912 senior class of Ceres High School stands outside the schoolhouse door. They are, from left to right, (first row) Anita Fulton, Rowena Parsons, and three unidentified; (second row) Alice Brown, Mabel Norton, Catherine Brown, unidentified, and Faye Caulkins; (third row) Asa Caulkins, Alan Stout, and Allan Ham. Classmates not pictured are Richard Whitmore, Eulalie Chute, Lorena Moon, Emma Fleener, Winifred Wagener, and Hildred White. (Ceres Historical Society.)

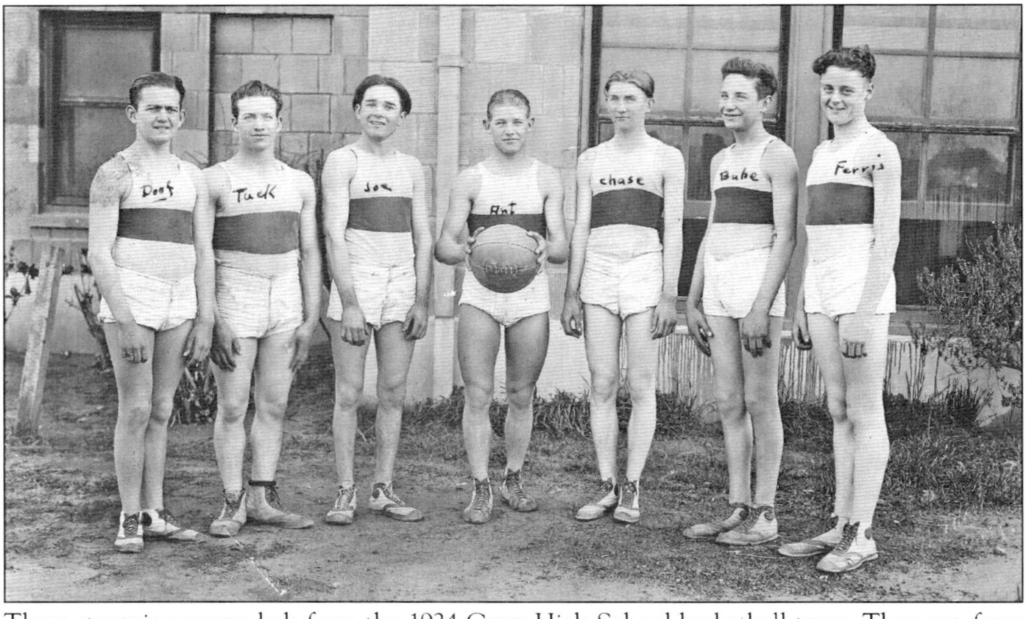

These strapping young lads form the 1924 Ceres High School basketball team. They are, from left to right, Weston "Doof" Barnes, Clarence "Tuck" Colbert, Joe Vierra, Arendt "Art" Rohde, Weston Chase, Chester "Babe" Besecker, and Farris Hartman. Rohde was considered one of the best ever all-around CHS athletes. (*Ceres Courier.*)

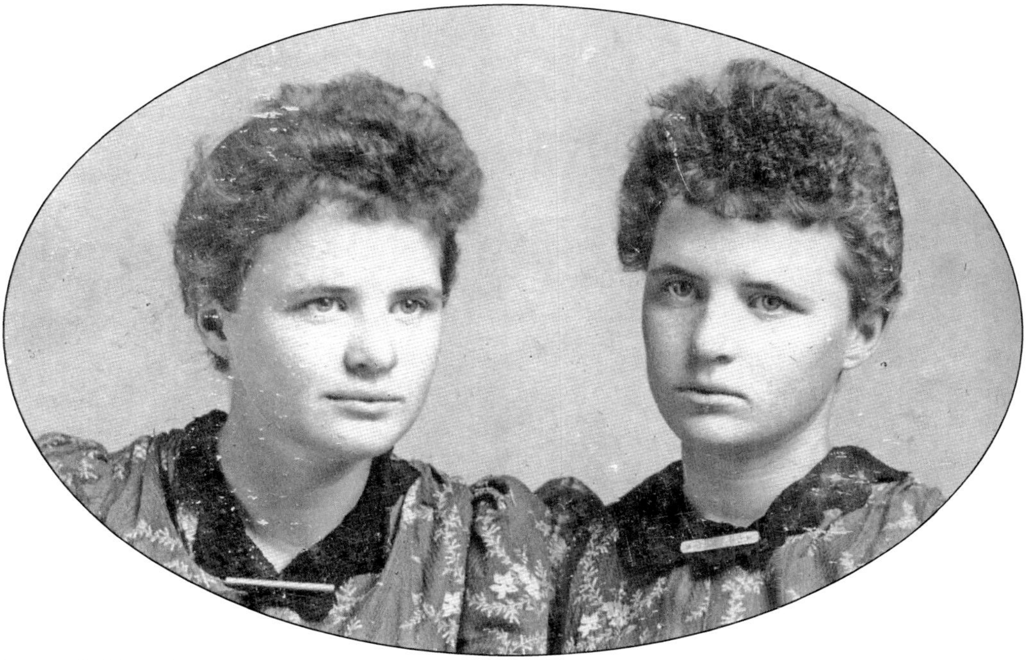

Bessie (left) and Jessie Wood were the twin sisters of merchant George F. Wood. George named his own daughter, Jessie Wood Crombie, after his sister Jessie. Jessie Wood Crombie (not pictured) graduated from Stanford University in 1917. She later married James Crombie, with whom she developed the Crombie Rose. Jessie Crombie died in 1962. (Ceres Historical Society.)

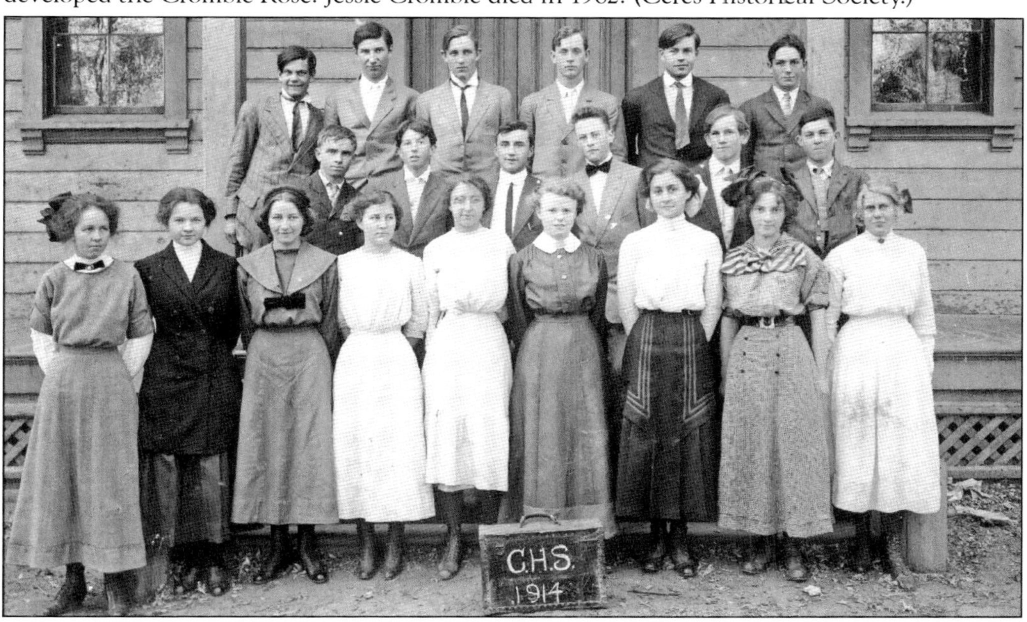

Ceres High School seniors pose for a class picture in 1914. While the specific identities of these students are not known, a list of graduates that year includes Nelson Davis, Edna Ellis, Anna Fleenor, Mabel Magladry, Roy Owen, Howard L. Rowe, Esther Winnie Rowe, Stanley Triplett, Willis Wagener, Alma Lowry, Oryl Wing, Charles N. Whitmore, and Doris Whitmore. (Ceres Historical Society.)

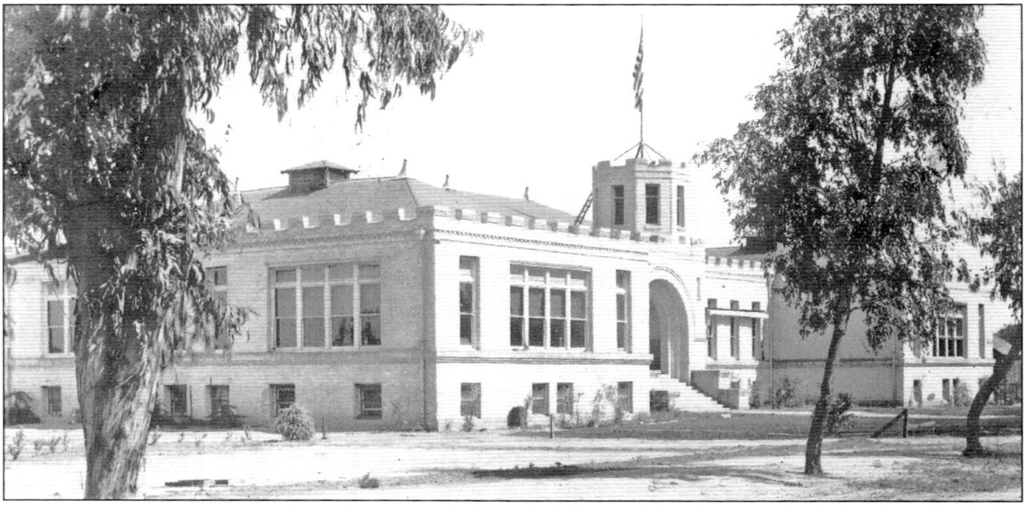

The "White Brick" Ceres Grammar School was built in 1909 on North Street between Second and Third Streets, facing south toward Whitmore Park (then Triangle Park). The main building was made of brick and covered in a material in which students could etch their names. Two wooden buildings were later brought in for classrooms. Students called the brick building the Big Building because it housed fourth through eighth grade. Ceres built the new Whitmore School on Lawrence Street east of Sixth Street in 1930. On moving day, students walked four blocks to the new school with books in hand. The old school remained standing for a while but was then leveled to make way for the Ceres Police Station, now the site of Ceres Fire Station no. 1. (Ceres Historical Society.)

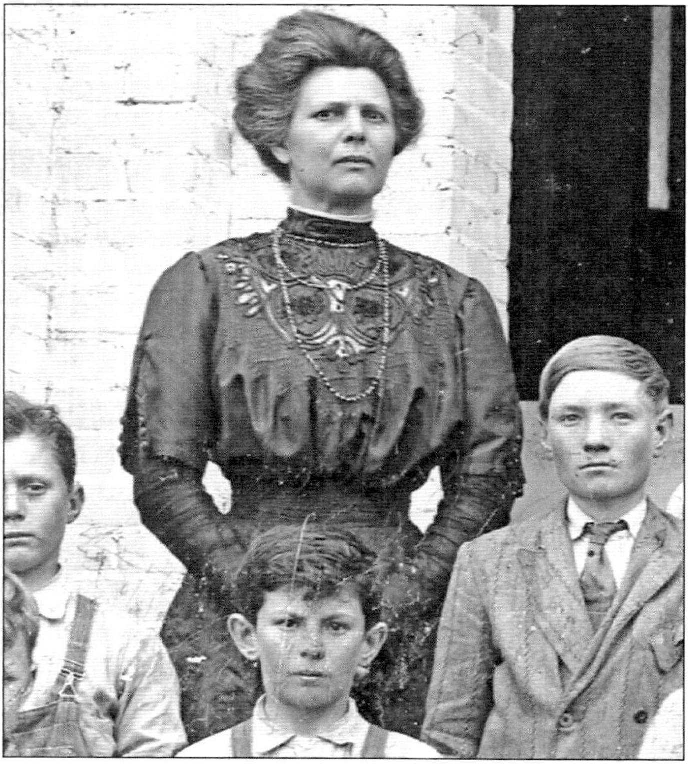

The identity of this rather stern-looking schoolmarm, posing with her students on the steps of the White Brick School in the 1910s, is unknown. However, she likely ran a tight classroom. Most of the boys showed up for school in overalls but some, like the lad at right, could afford suits for such occasions. (Ceres Historical Society.)

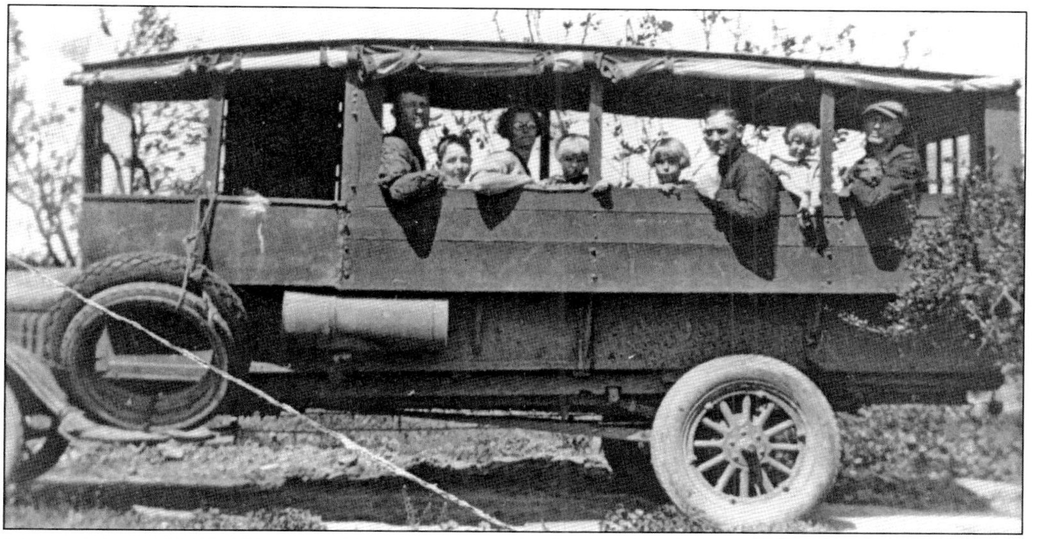

Henry Edward "Ed" Wilson and brother-in-law Wylie Cox built this early school bus using the chassis of a Model T truck. Ed owned and drove the bus but was paid by the state for its use and his services. This 1910 image shows him sitting inside his bus, which sported gray paint not easily visible on foggy days. Wilson drove the bus in Ceres for 25 years. (Shirley Ollar.)

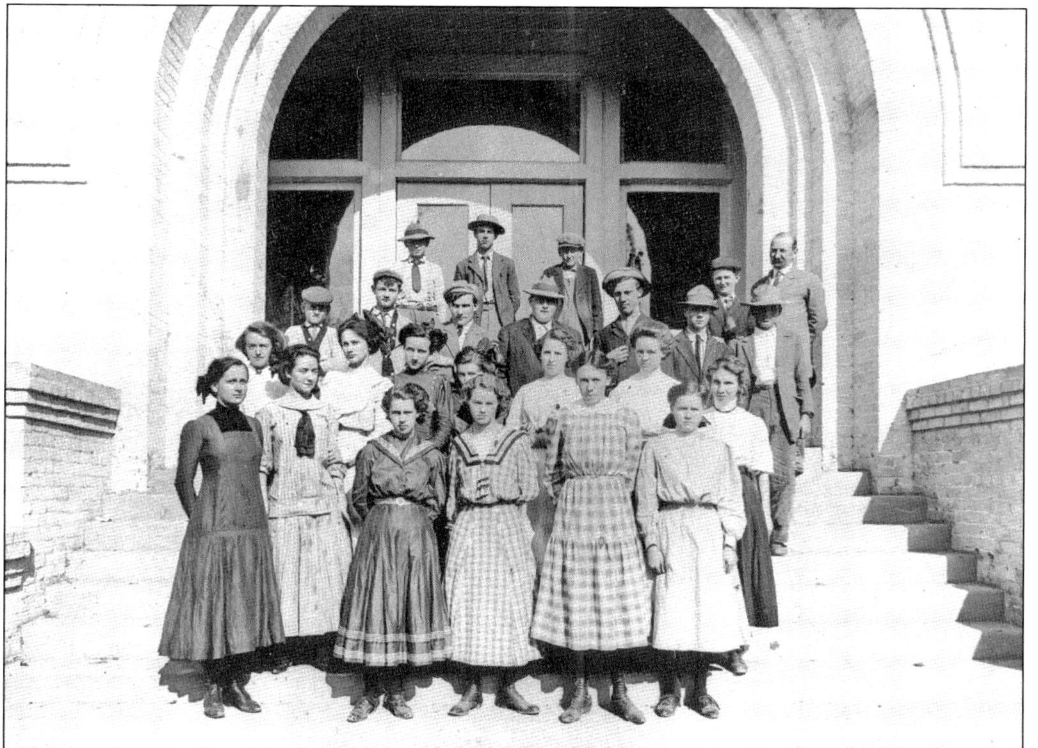

Standing on the steps of the Ceres Grammar School on North Street is the class of 1911. Principal John Andrew Wagener is seen at upper right. He served from 1905 to 1920. The only student identified is Nita Lucas, standing in front center. (Mildred Lucas.)

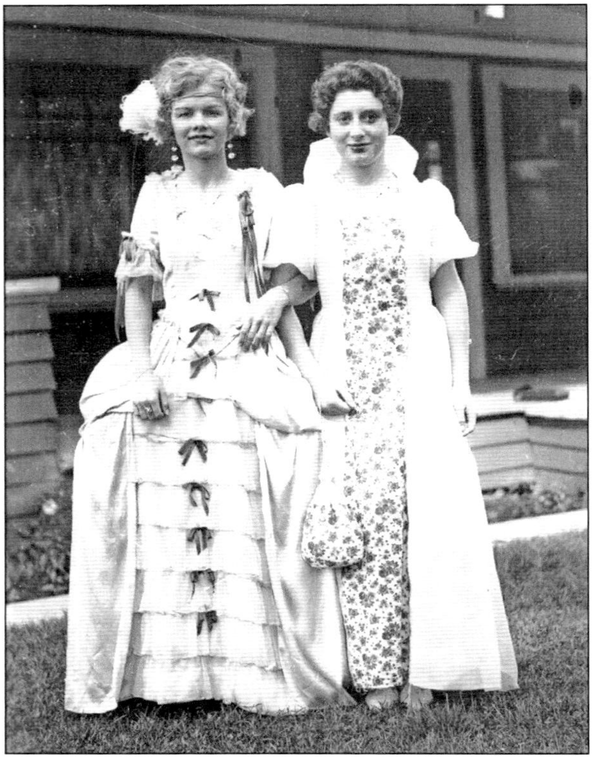

Wanda Hosmer (left) and classmate and friend Betty Lee Taylor (later Baker) pose in fancy dress, probably for a Ceres High School play. This photograph was taken in the front yard of the Hosmer home, still standing at 2545 Fourth Street. (Loren Hosmer.)

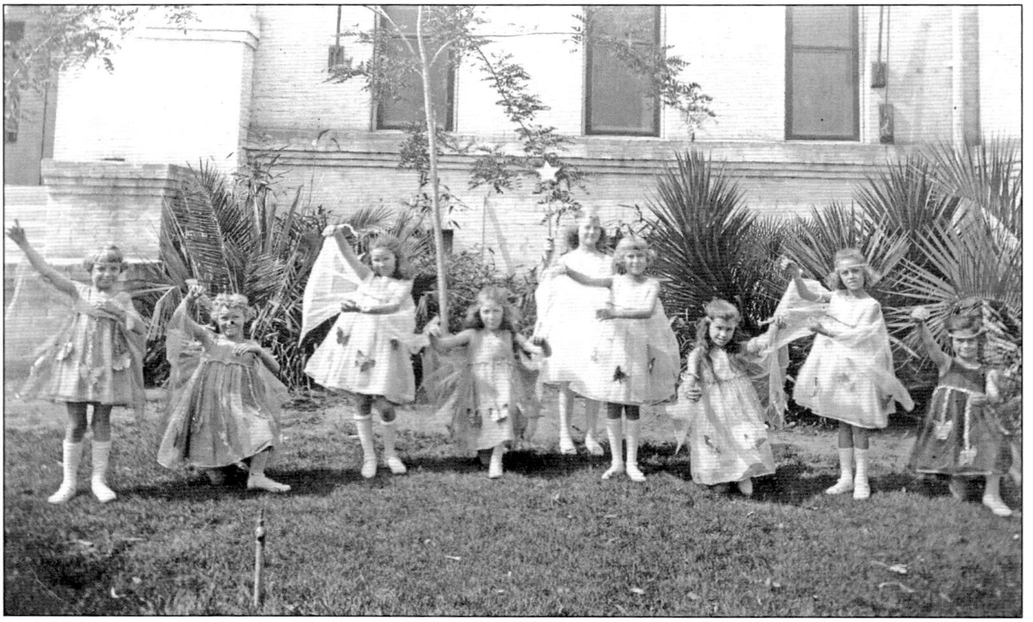

These Ceres girls were charmingly dressed for a school celebration—probably for a May Day celebration in or around 1928—in front of the "White Brick" Ceres Grammar School. The only girl identified is Wanda Hosmer (fourth from right). The school was located where present-day Ceres Fire Station No. 1 sits. (Loren Hosmer.)

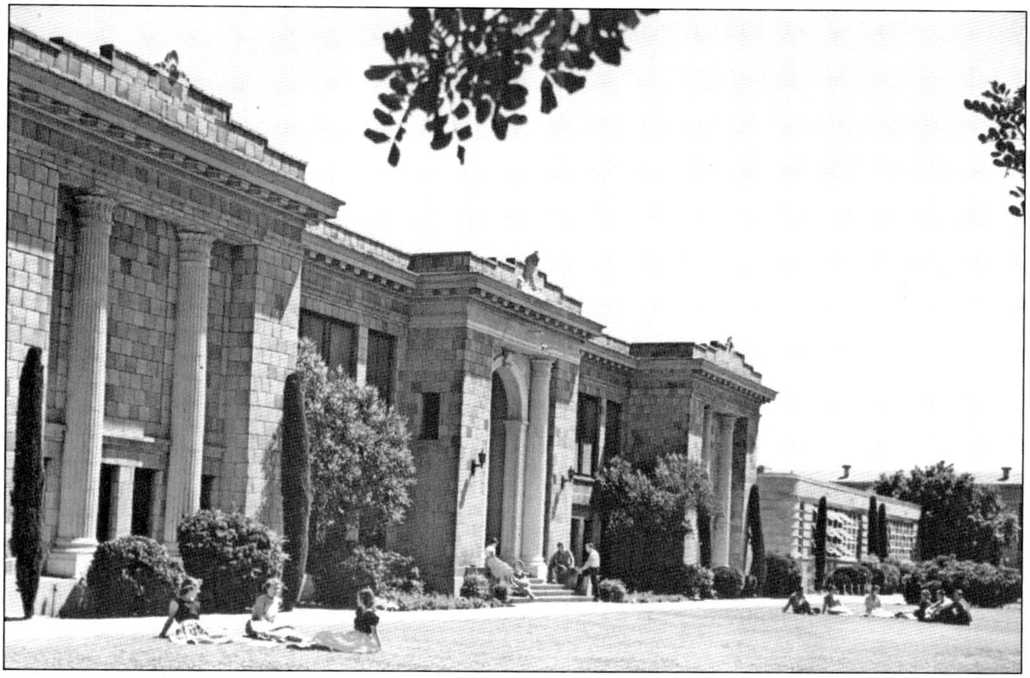

Ceres High School was opened in 1908 and produced its first graduating class in 1912. In 1915, this structure was built for Ceres High School and faced south on Whitmore Avenue immediately west of what is now the old gymnasium. The building cost $31,000 and furnishings ran $3,000—a bargain by today's dollar value. Debate was the most popular class in 1918. This building was razed in 1965 to make way for new construction. (Ceres High School.)

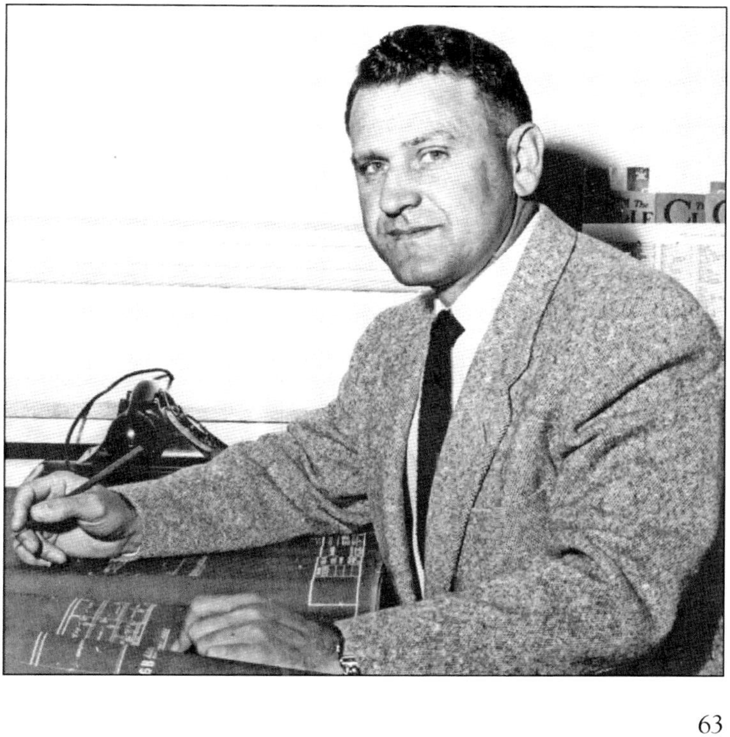

Fleming E. Haas gave 37 years of his life to students. Haas lived in Ceres for over 60 years and became a Ceres High School science teacher in 1944. He also coached football and basketball. Haas later became a counselor, vice principal, and principal. He resigned in February 1968 to oversee continuation education and the opening of Argus Continuation High School. For 11 years, Haas was Ceres Unified School District's business manager, a post he enjoyed until retirement in 1981. (Ceres High School.)

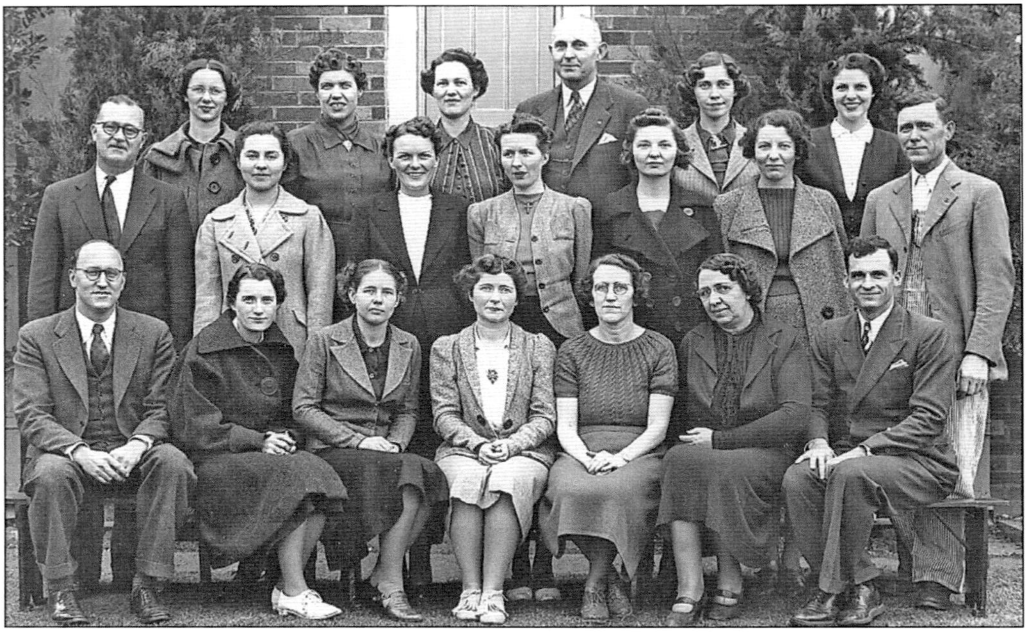

Ceres Grammar School teachers gathered for this 1938 photograph. The teachers are, from left to right (first row) Charles Isenhut, Maude Smith, Imogene Western, Lena Belle Turner Coover, Emma Krohn, Geneva Klinke, and Boyce Ashford (brother of Mae Hensley); (second row) Hugh "Pop" Cavanaugh, Mary Vierra Music, Marie McDonald, ?, Louise Kuzensa, Dorothy Vivian, and school custodian Cliff Landreth; (third row) Clair Mall, Elizabeth Corson, Agnes Norcross, Principal Walter White, Nell Smith and Grace Bertelson. (Mae Hensley photo courtesy the *Ceres Courier.*)

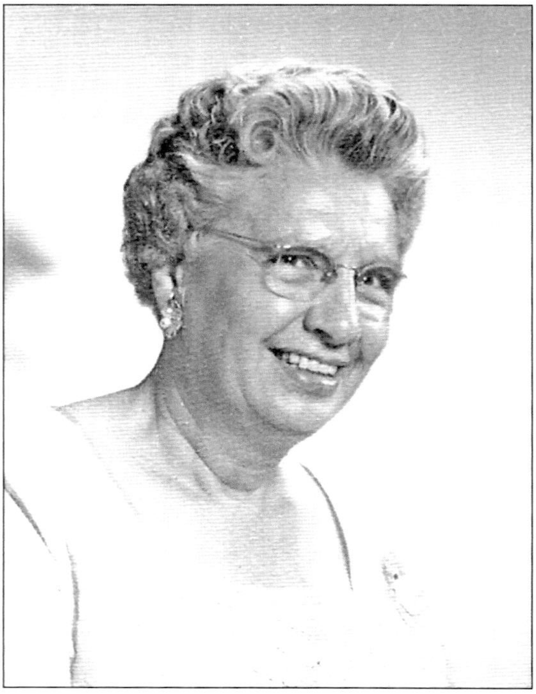

For eight decades, Mae Hensley was one of Ceres' most well-known and loved residents. Born in 1903 in Oklahoma, she became a teacher in Utica before coming to California in 1925 to attend the State Teachers College at San Jose. On the way to apply for a Hughson teaching position, Hensley inquired about a job in Ceres. She was placed in charge of a 66-student eighth grade class. Hensley left teaching to raise her children but returned in 1939. She was the attendance officer from 1947 to 1964. The junior high school in Ceres bears her name. Mae Hensley died in 2004. (*Ceres Courier.*)

Walter White was an endearing figure in Ceres. Pictured with his wife Geneva, White was a congenial and respected disciplinarian. He was principal of Ceres Elementary School beginning in 1923 and became superintendent in the 1930s. Even the children he paddled at school revered the man. White served as mayor from 1956 to 1964. Geneva White taught school in Ceres. The couple lived in the large two-story home at the southwest corner of Fifth and North Streets. (Marian Sanders.)

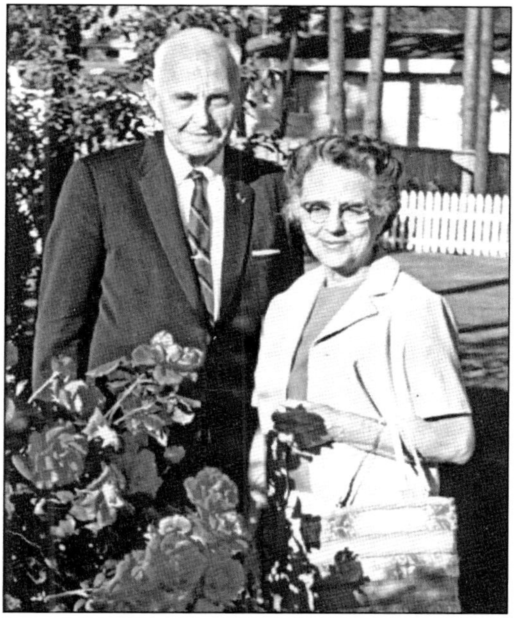

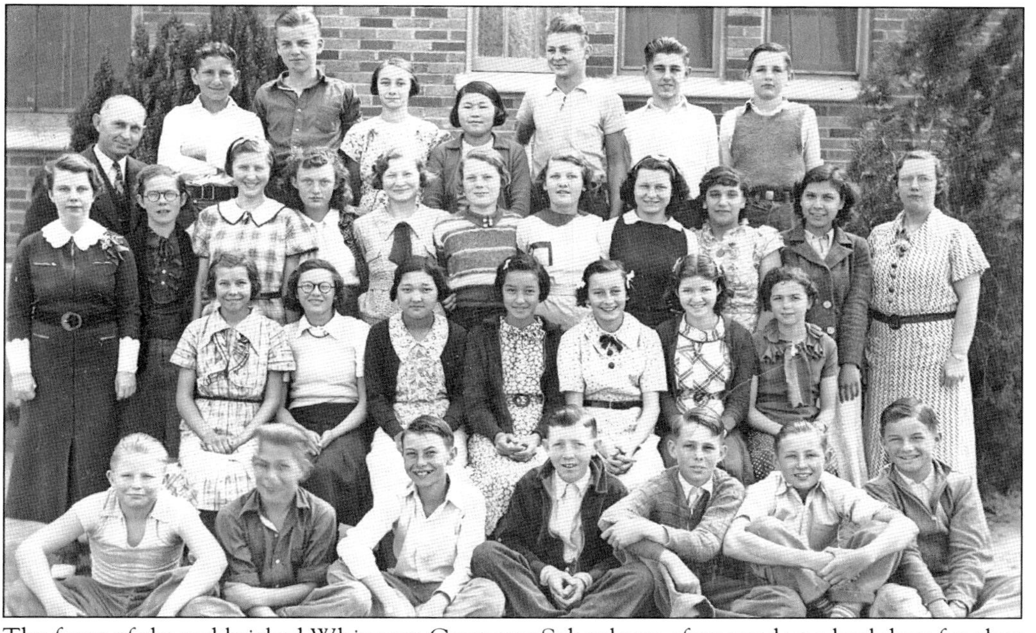

The front of the red-bricked Whitmore Grammar School was often used as a backdrop for class photographs, such as for this eighth grade class. The back of the photograph is signed by everyone pictured. They are (alphabetically, but not in order of position) Marvin Anderson, Alonzo Bacon, Mary Bailey, Ronald Berryhill, Cecil Ann Bilson, Lorraine Chapman, Marjorie Craig, Alice Davis, Stanley Davis, Margaret Dunn, Gladys Francis, Shizue Fukui, Gordon Ham, Nannadee Hensley, Virginia Hodges, Donald Jepsen, Virginia Knox, Dorothy Lemos, Charlotte A. Leonhardt, Joe Machado, Thornton McCurry, Olive Mall, Joyce Masin, Ruby Perrin, Kathleen Santa Cruz, Rosemary Service, Kathryn Simms, Vivienne Sisk, Dale D. Smith, Bobby Stonum, Ruth Thompson, Billy Warner, Ruby Webster, Walter White, and Misao Yamauchi. (Betty Ham.)

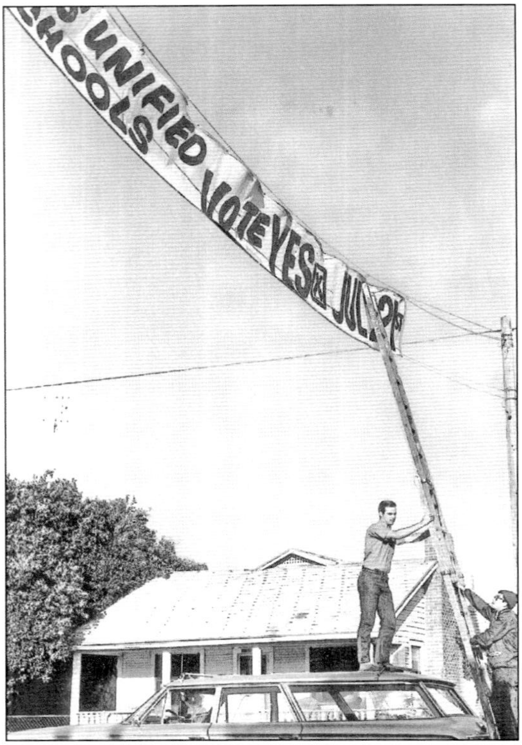

In July 1970, Ceres Unified School District sought passage of a bond to build Mae Hensley Junior High School. Here college students Patrick Lucas and Alan Fujii place a banner high over Fourth Street in front of the Vincent family home. The bond passed. (Mildred Lucas.)

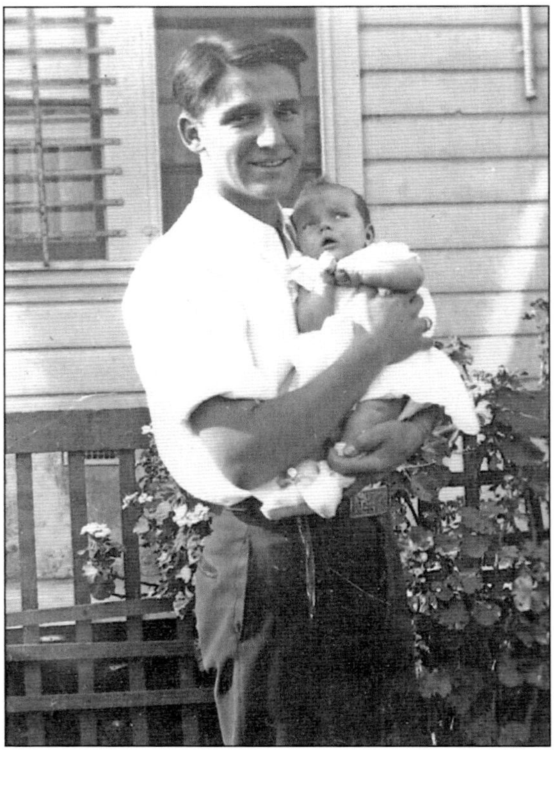

Wayne Salter, a doting father holding his daughter Claudia in 1937, was a devoted community and church servant. Born in 1912, Salter graduated from Ceres High School in 1930 and was a farmer. He later served on the Ceres School Board for 12 years, retiring in 1961. Salter was also an elder, treasurer, and Bible teacher at Ceres Christian Church. He was named the 1993 Ceres Agribusiness Man of the Year. (Claudia Grubeck.)

Alice Dora Caulkins Melugin was a schoolteacher who lived all of her 100 years in Ceres. She lived on a Roeding Road farm from her birth on November 22, 1909, in Smyrna Park, a colony east of Ceres. She was the seventh and last child of William O. and Mary Emma Whittier Caulkins, who had moved from Nebraska by train to rural Ceres in 1903 to buy a farm. She attended Ceres schools and was the 1928 Ceres High School class valedictorian. She graduated from Modesto Junior College in 1930, attended Moody Bible Institute in Chicago for a year, and then graduated from the University of California, Berkeley in 1934. In the 1930s she taught schools in Ceres, Denair, and Gratton until her 1941 marriage. After raising four daughters, Mrs. Melugin served as a substitute teacher from 1960 to 1970, then taught at MJC for 20 years. She died in 2009. (Pat Cousins.)

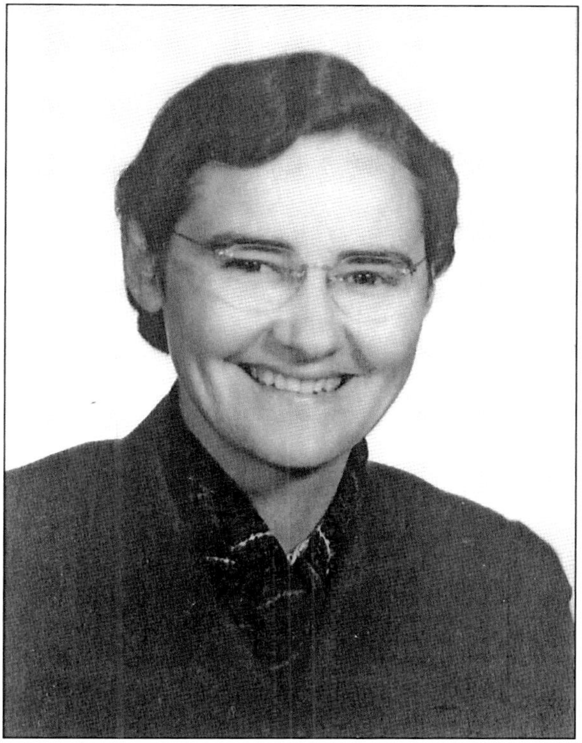

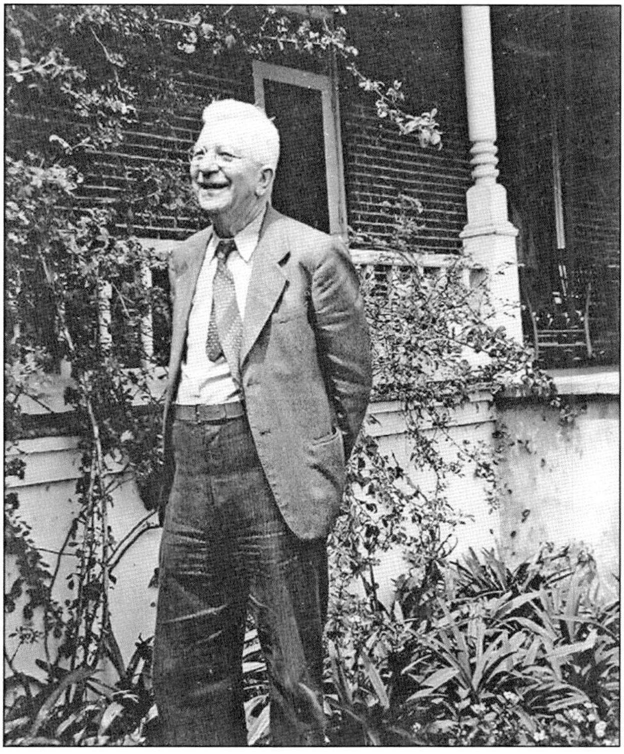

Carroll Fowler Elementary School opened in 1957 with the name of this early-day Ceres resident. Raised in Duarte, California, but visiting Ceres as early as 1903, Fowler taught at the University of California. In 1906, he married Aurelia Whitmore, daughter of Richard K. Whitmore. In 1913, Fowler and his wife moved to Duarte to manage orange groves owned by his family. He commuted to Ceres once the Ceres ranch in the Smyrna Park/ Mae Hensley Junior High area converted to peaches. Fowler was president of the Ceres Library Association when it was formed in 1905. (Dr. Mary Fowler.)

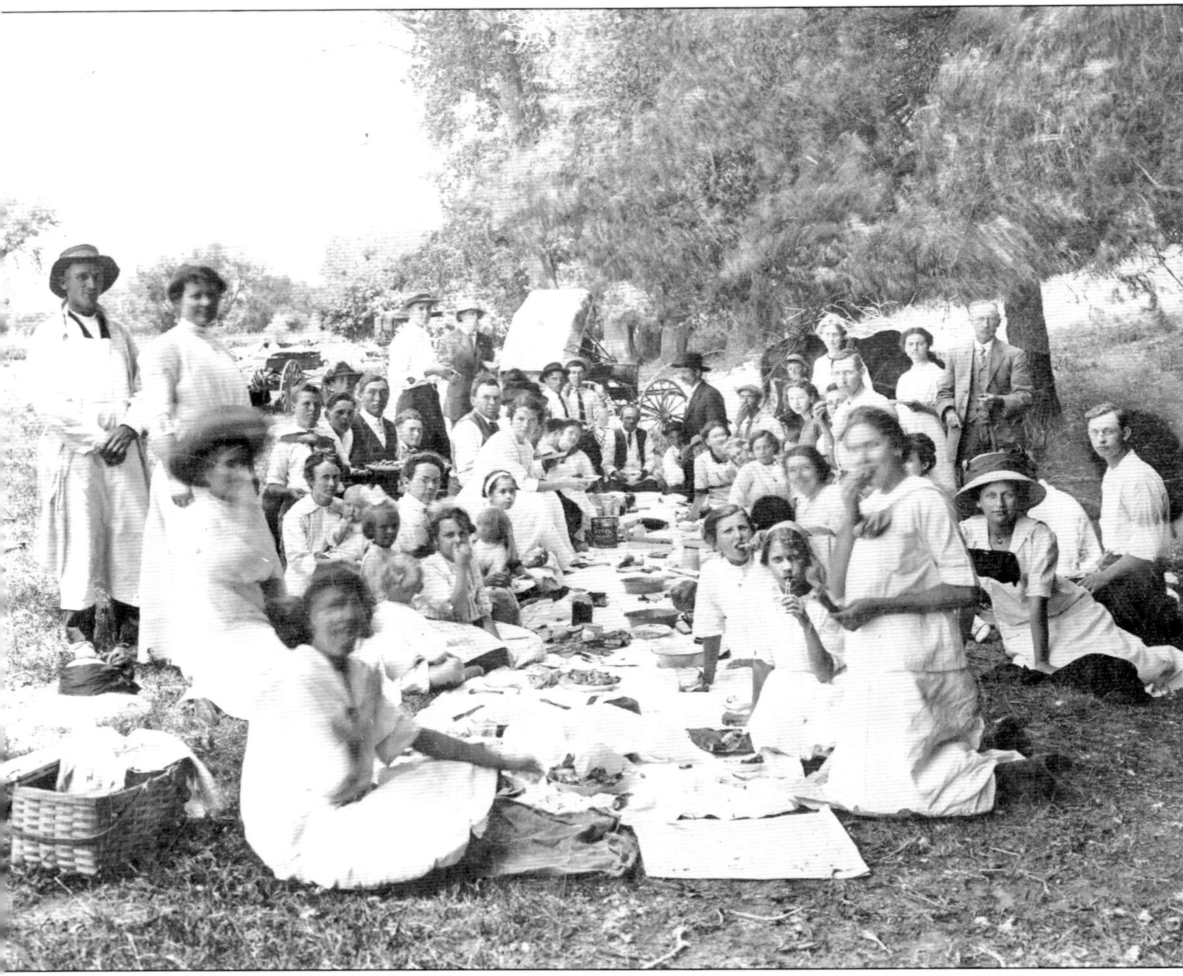

First Baptist Church members found their social life steeped in church activities, such as this picnic probably along the banks of the Tuolumne River. The Ceres church attracted both young and old. (Ceres Historical Society.)

Four

Church Life

Faith played an important role in the development of Ceres. The church community provided a spiritual underpinning for early families as well as a social connection with others. The Methodists were the first to start ministering to Ceres. A circuit-riding pastor from Stockton held services in Ceres as early as 1869, the year Daniel Whitmore built the first home. The first family in Ceres used its financial resources to establish a Baptist church, organized in 1879 with 12 members. The Baptists erected the first church building in town on land donated by Whitmore at the northwest corner of Fifth and North Streets. Built at a cost of $7,000, it was dedicated in 1882. J. M. Helsley was the first pastor. Tragically the grand building burned to the ground on November 12, 1899—after the church had allowed its insurance policy to lapse—but was rebuilt. The Baptists also built a two-story parsonage at the corner of Fourth and North Streets that stands today. The Methodist church was constructed at Sixth and Lawrence Streets. Harold Persing, a graduate of the Glad Tidings Bible School in San Francisco, established a Pentecostal church in 1919. The church building was erected on North Street, west of Second Street. Today it is Valley Christian Center. The Congregational Church of Ceres was organized May 17, 1903, mostly by transplants from Nebraska and Iowa. At first, they built a small chapel on Roeding Road and later changed their name to the Smyrna Park Congregational Church and moved to Park and Sixth Streets in 1908. Tent revival meetings were often held in Ceres during summer months, and a favorite spot was in the park area near the first elementary school. The First Church of Christ, or the Christian Church, was organized in 1908 at the home of C. H. Edison. Member Nancy Conner gave the lot at Third and North Streets where a new building was dedicated in 1909. The congregation moved a block north in 1951. The Ceres Christian Church is now located on Roeding Road.

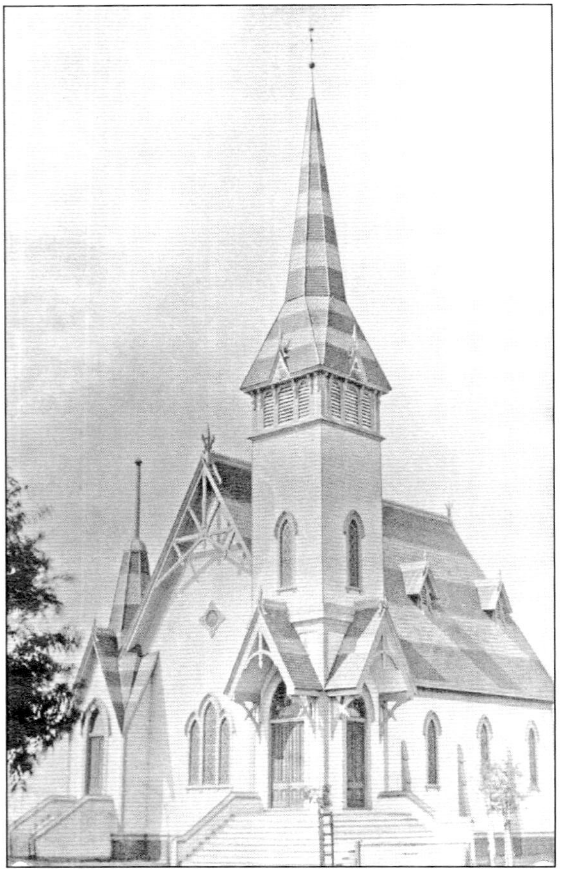

First Baptist Church was built in 1879 at the northwest corner of Fifth and North Streets. This structure burned but was rebuilt. The congregation added on to this church in 1950. (Ceres Historical Society.)

This postcard view of First Baptist Church was taken looking west on North Street. The building in the center is the parsonage, finished in 1908. The house at far left was located at the northwest corner of Fourth and North Streets but is gone today. (Ceres Historical Society.)

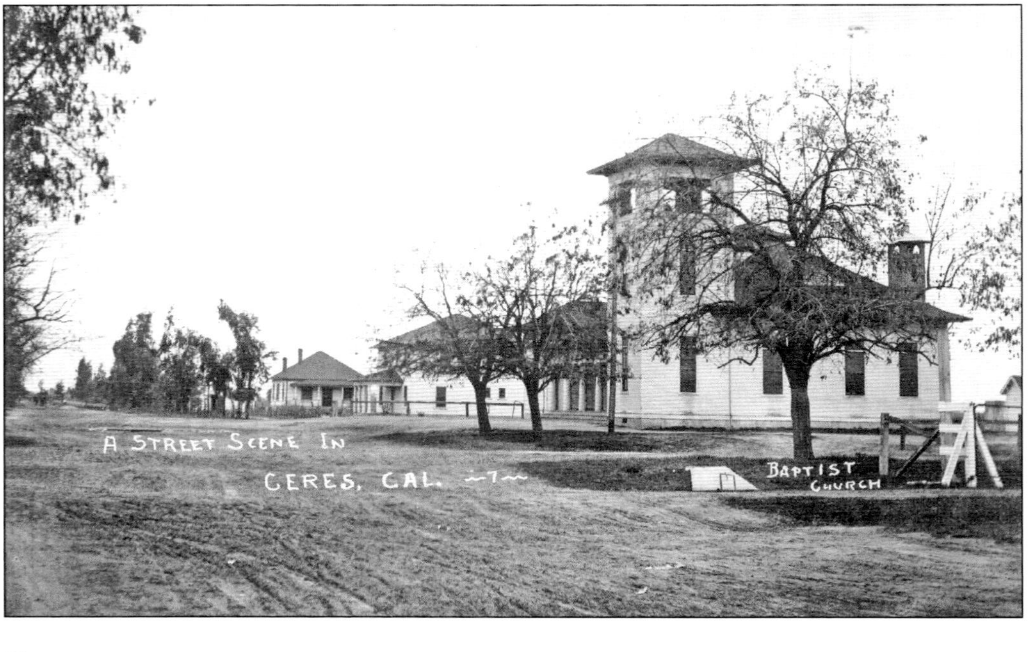

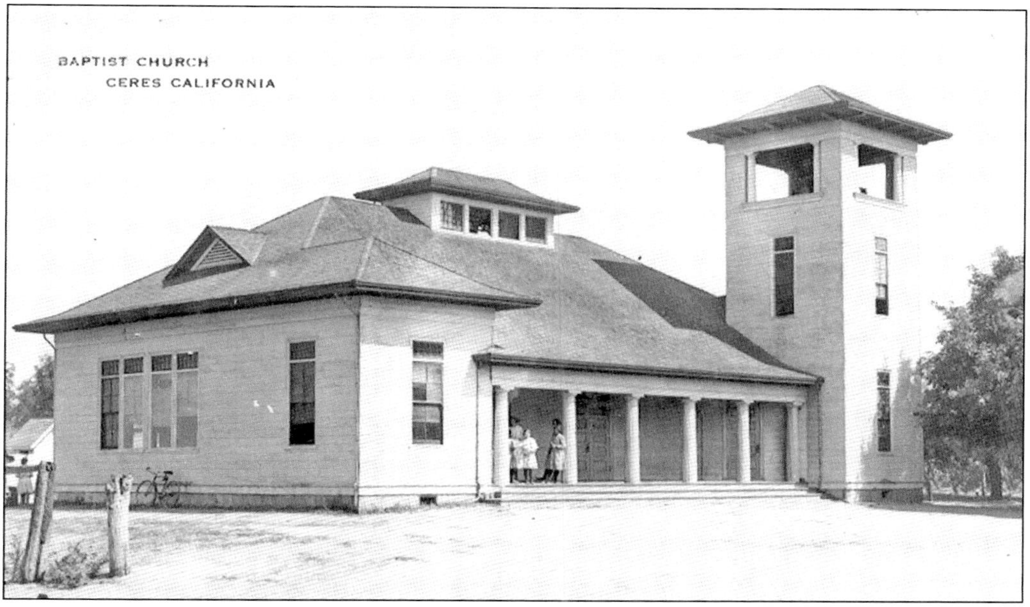

At the northwest corner of Fifth and North Streets, this was the second version of the First Baptist Church building. It is pictured in the 1920s. (Ceres Historical Society.)

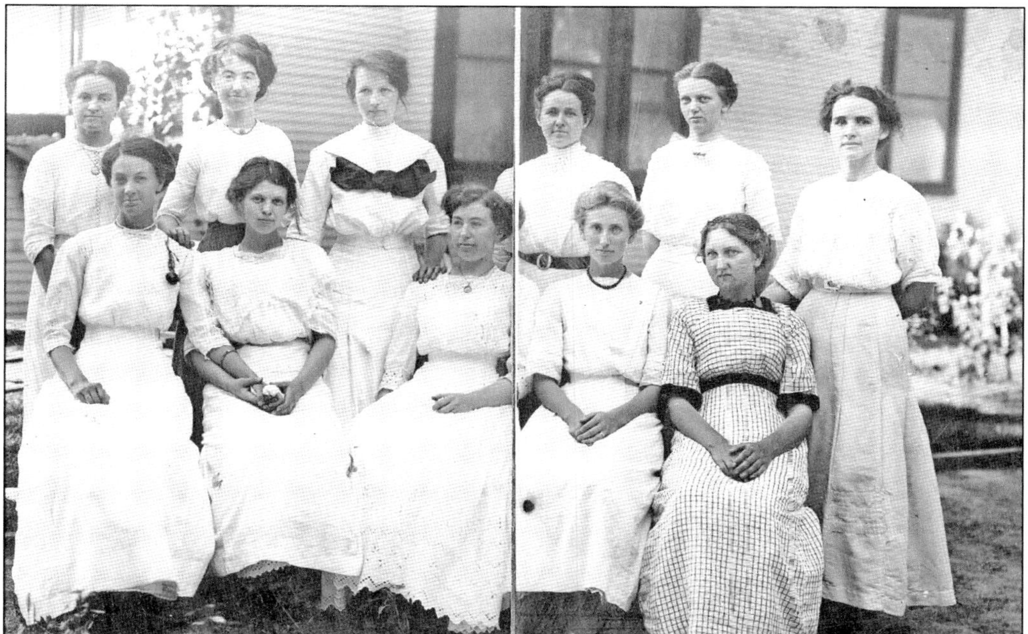
These 11 young ladies were part of First Baptist Church's Young Ladies group around 1913. They are gathered on the east side of Newell A. Lucas's home on what is now Don Pedro Road east of Highway 99. The women are identified as, from left to right, (sitting) Hildred White Willett, Alice Brown, Cora Lucas Taylor, Lorena Moon Caulkins, and Emma ?; (standing) Eulalie Chute, Jettie Lucas Thomason, Anna Carlson Sikes, Mamie Smith Griggs, Catherine Brown Wilson, and Mary Fay Caulkins. (Mildred Lucas.)

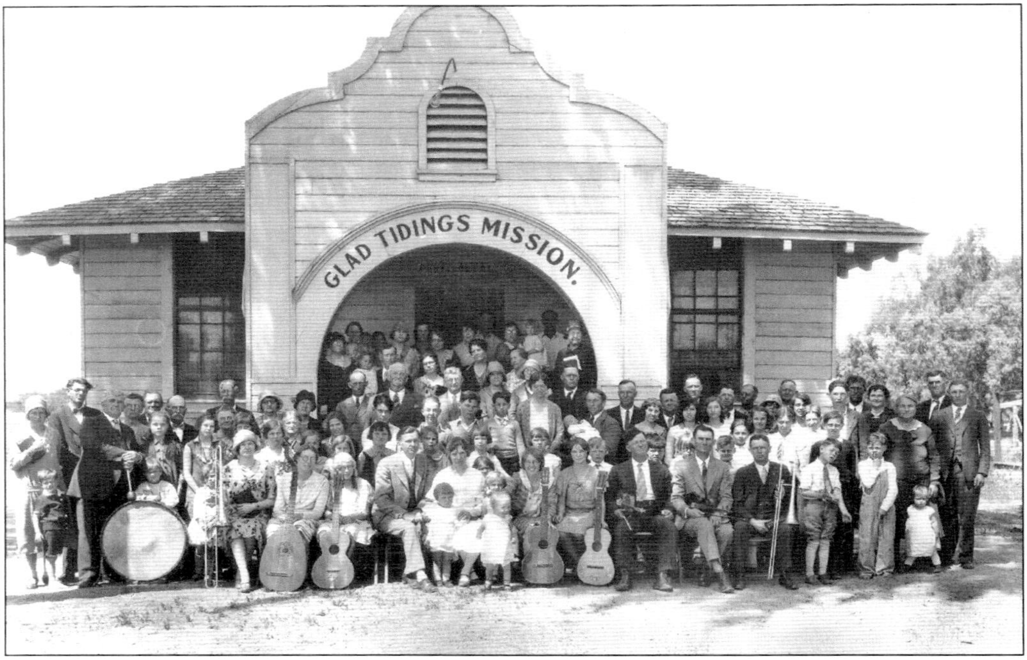

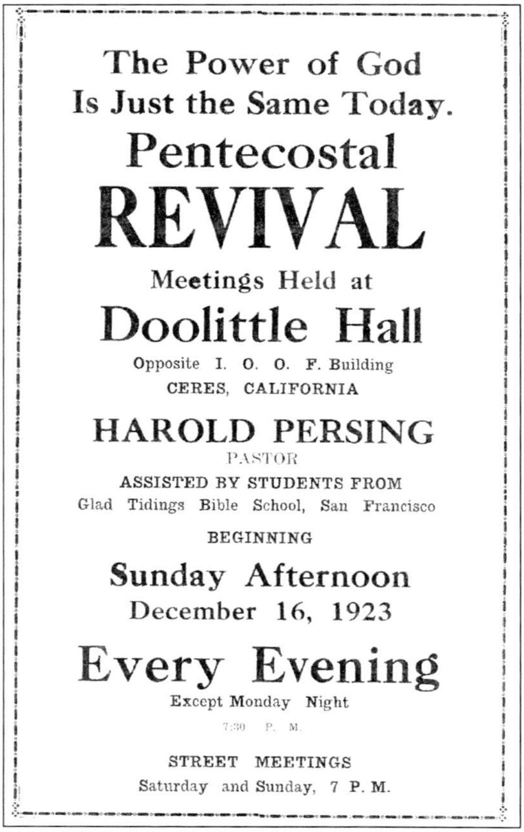

The Power of God
Is Just the Same Today.

Pentecostal

REVIVAL

Meetings Held at

Doolittle Hall

Opposite I. O. O. F. Building
CERES, CALIFORNIA

HAROLD PERSING

PASTOR

ASSISTED BY STUDENTS FROM
Glad Tidings Bible School, San Francisco

BEGINNING

Sunday Afternoon
December 16, 1923

Every Evening

Except Monday Night

7:30 P. M.

STREET MEETINGS
Saturday and Sunday, 7 P. M.

The congregation of Glad Tidings Mission Assembly of God Church (now Valley Christian Church) on North Street west of Second Street gathered for this 1931 photograph. This original building still stands, but its facade was changed in the 1940s. A fellowship hall and kitchen were added in 1955. Glad Tidings was established in 1919 as the Ceres Pentecostal Church by Harold Persing, a Ceres native who graduated from the Glad Tidings Bible Institute in San Francisco and became the church's first pastor. The first meetings were held in a private home on Roeding Road. Members would play instruments while riding in a hay wagon as a way of drawing new people to services. Prior to this structure being constructed in 1925, the small congregation met in Doolittle's pool hall and confectionery at Third and Lawrence Streets. (Shirley Ollar.)

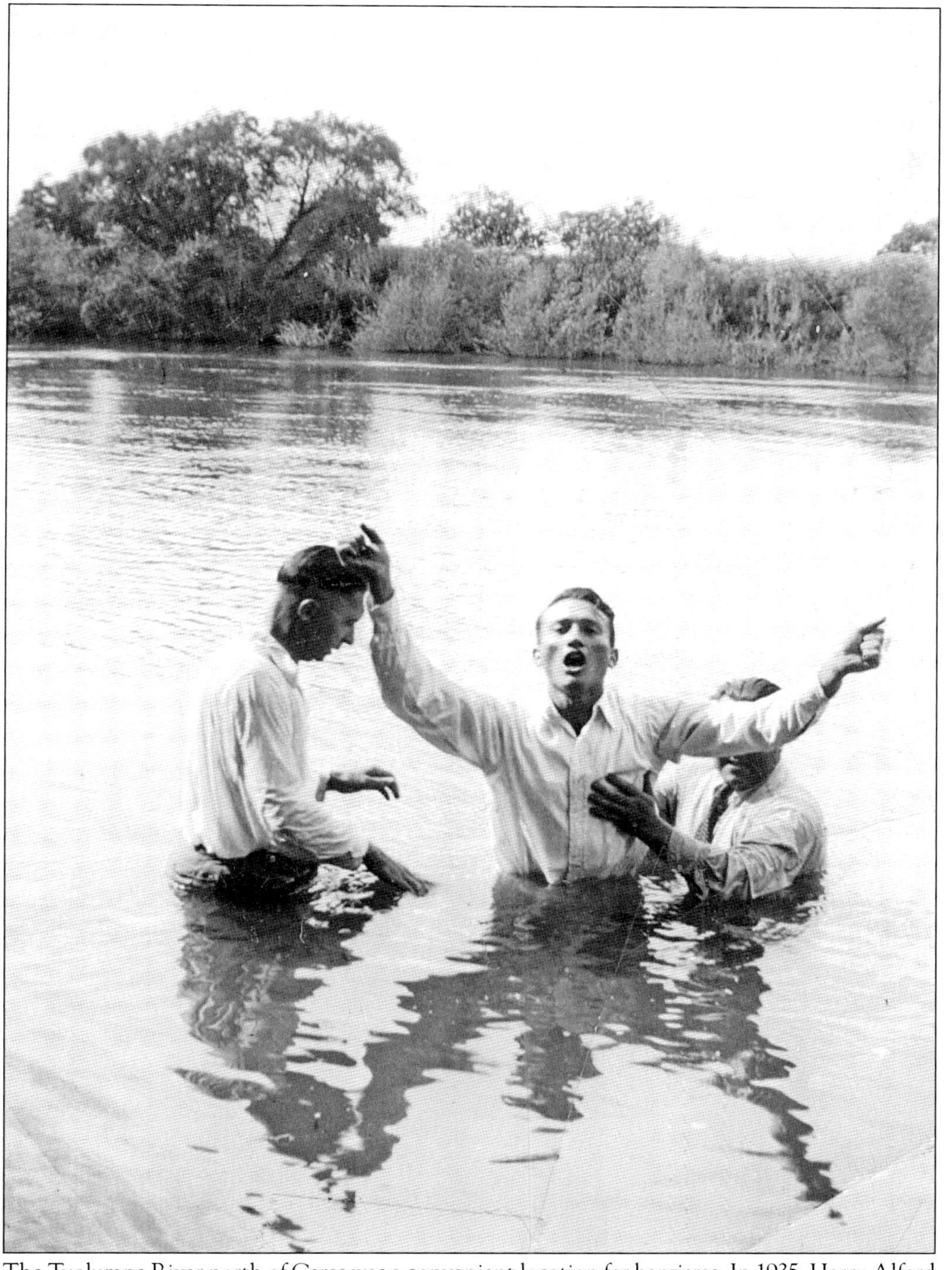

The Tuolumne River north of Ceres was a convenient location for baptisms. In 1935, Harry Alford Oeth of Ceres holds up his hands in declaration of his faith and is baptized by Pastor Morrison in an Assembly of God ceremony. Oeth (1910–1960) served as pastor of the Glad Tidings Mission Assembly of God Church from 1941 to 1943. (Shirley Ollar.)

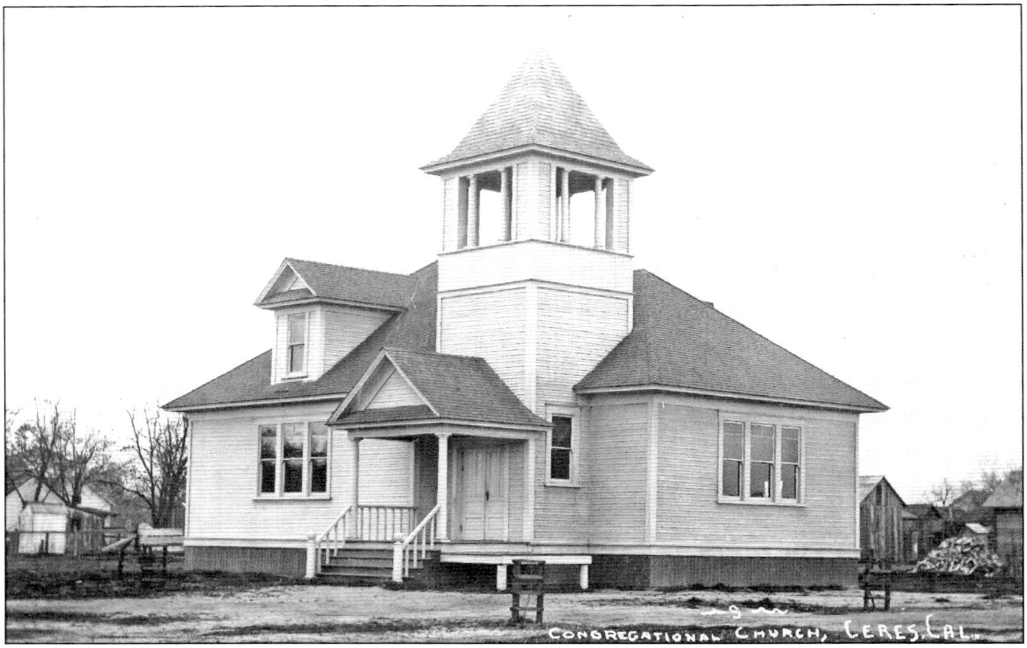

In this August 11, 1909, image, the Congregational Church of Ceres stands at Pine Street and El Camino. (Ceres Historical Society.)

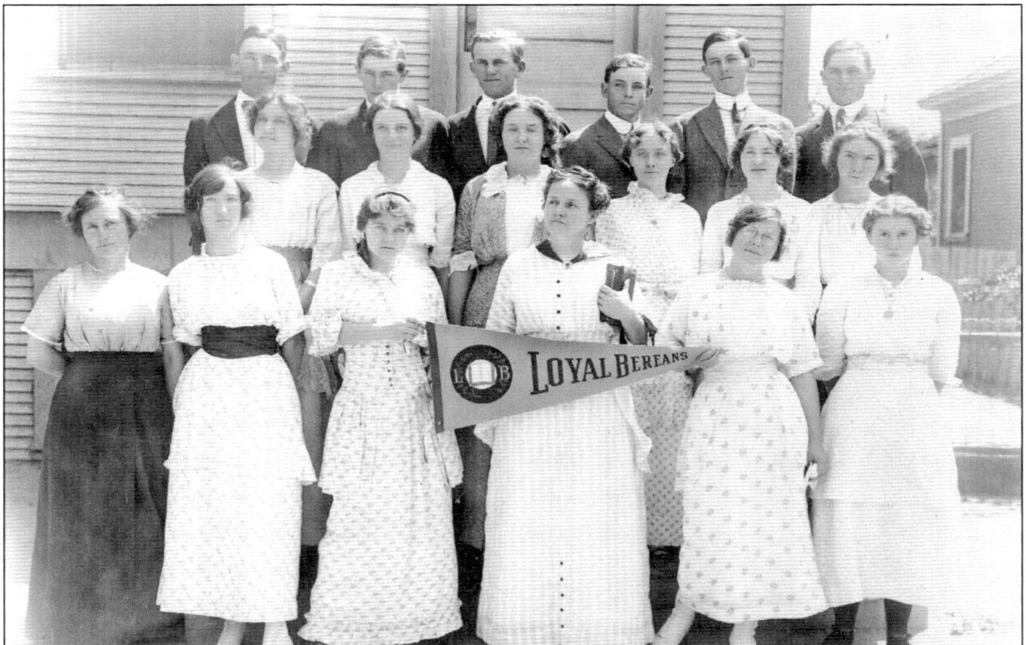

The young people of First Baptist Church in Ceres formed a Sunday school group called the Loyal Bereans. They studied the Bible and offered members a social network. (Ceres Historical Society.)

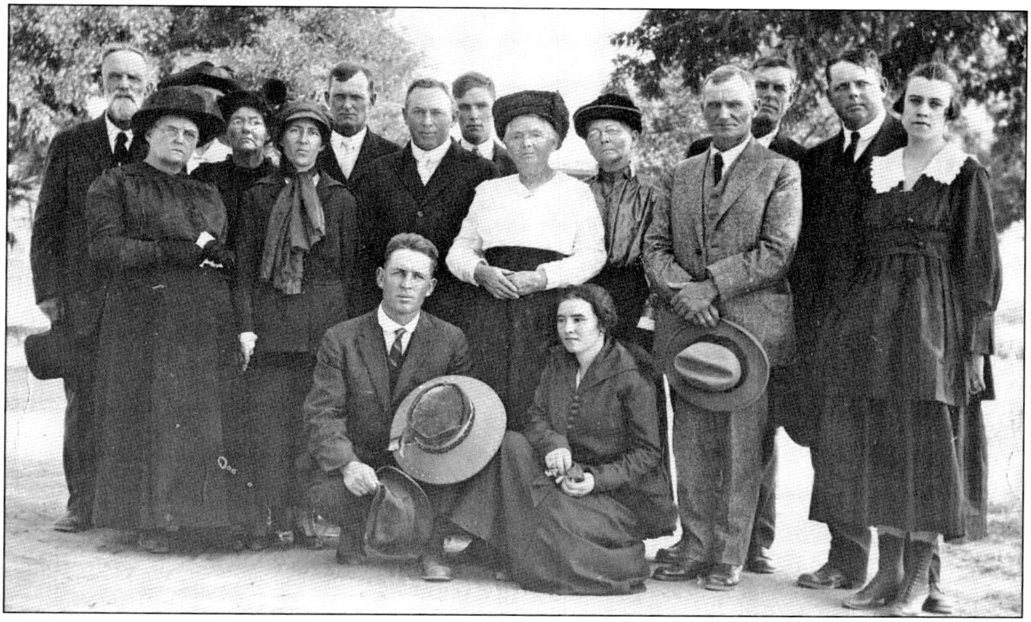

The Meek and Baldridge families pose in their Sunday-go-to-meeting attire sometime in the 1920s or 1930s. Art Meek is kneeling in front with an unidentified woman. Other family members, from left to right, are Grandpa Meek, Grandma Baldridge, ? Corum, Myrtle Meek, Sydney Meek, ? Corum, Wayne Baldridge, ? Corum-Jones, ? Corum, Charles Baldridge, Allen Meek, Albert Meek, and Edith Meek. The Meeks and Baldridges met in 1886 in Newhall when a Meek daughter married C. F. Baldridge. (Betty Ham.)

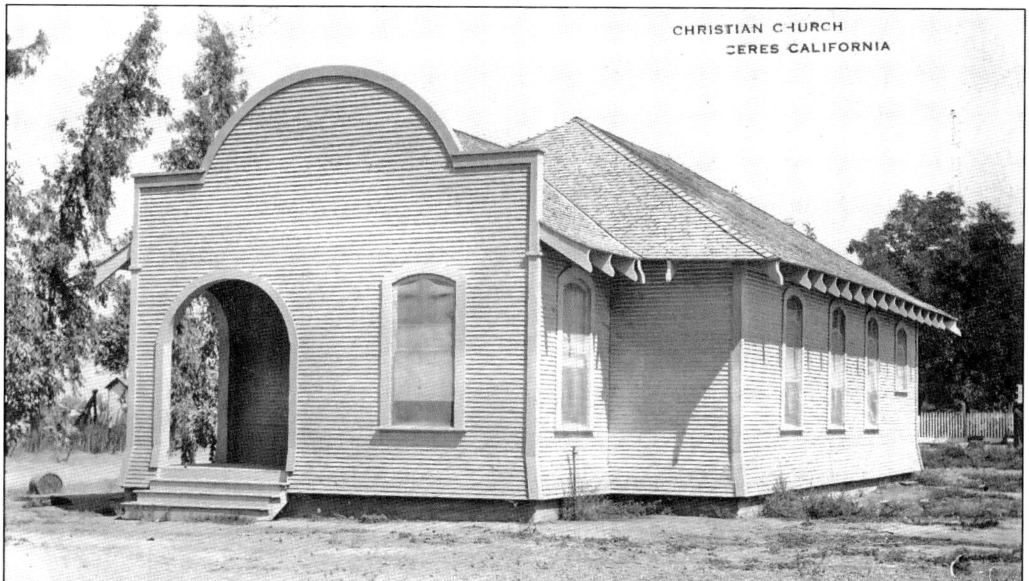

The Christian Church of Ceres was located at the southeast corner of Third and North Streets. It moved north one block to the site of the present-day Ceres Community Center. This original building became the Masonic Lodge. Today the church is thriving on Roeding Road east of Ceres. (Ceres Historical Society.)

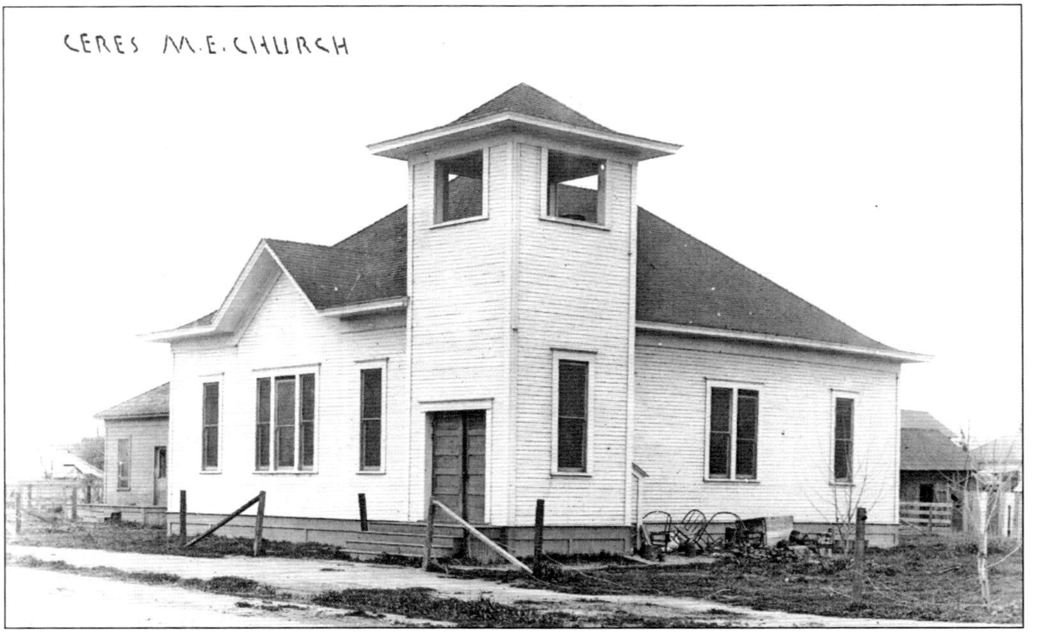

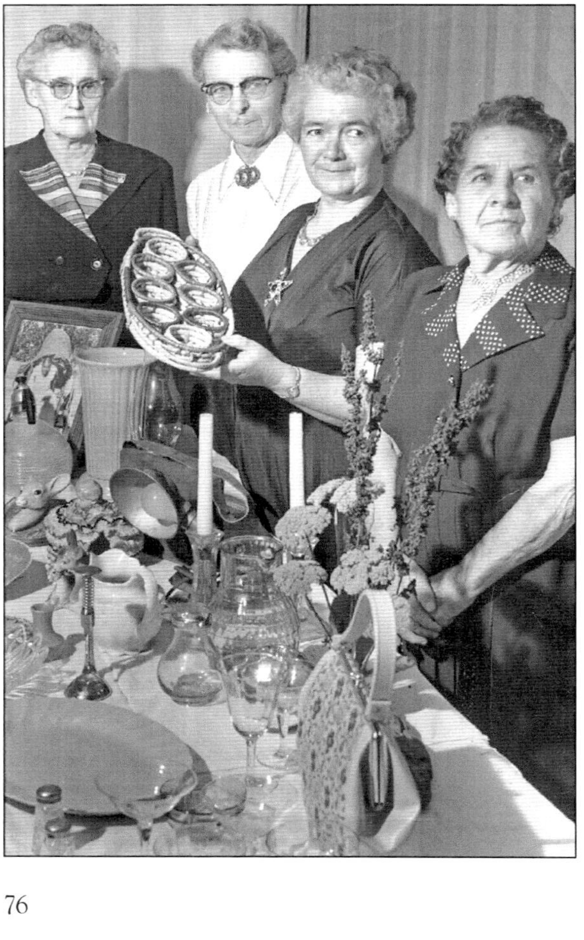

As early as 1869, a circuit-riding pastor from the Methodist church stopped in Ceres on his Stockton territory. The Methodists eventually built this church from 1906 to 1907 at Sixth and Lawrence Streets. Its 1889 parsonage burned in 1893 despite the valiant attempt of a bucket brigade to fight the flames. A new sanctuary was added in 1923. (Ceres Historical Society.)

The Ceres Methodist Church was vibrant and active in the 1960s, and these ladies were integral church servants. They are, from left to right, Mae Buoy, Bess Wilson, Mary Service, and Della Service. The church closed its doors in 2007 to merge with the Hughson Methodist Church. (Mildred Lucas.)

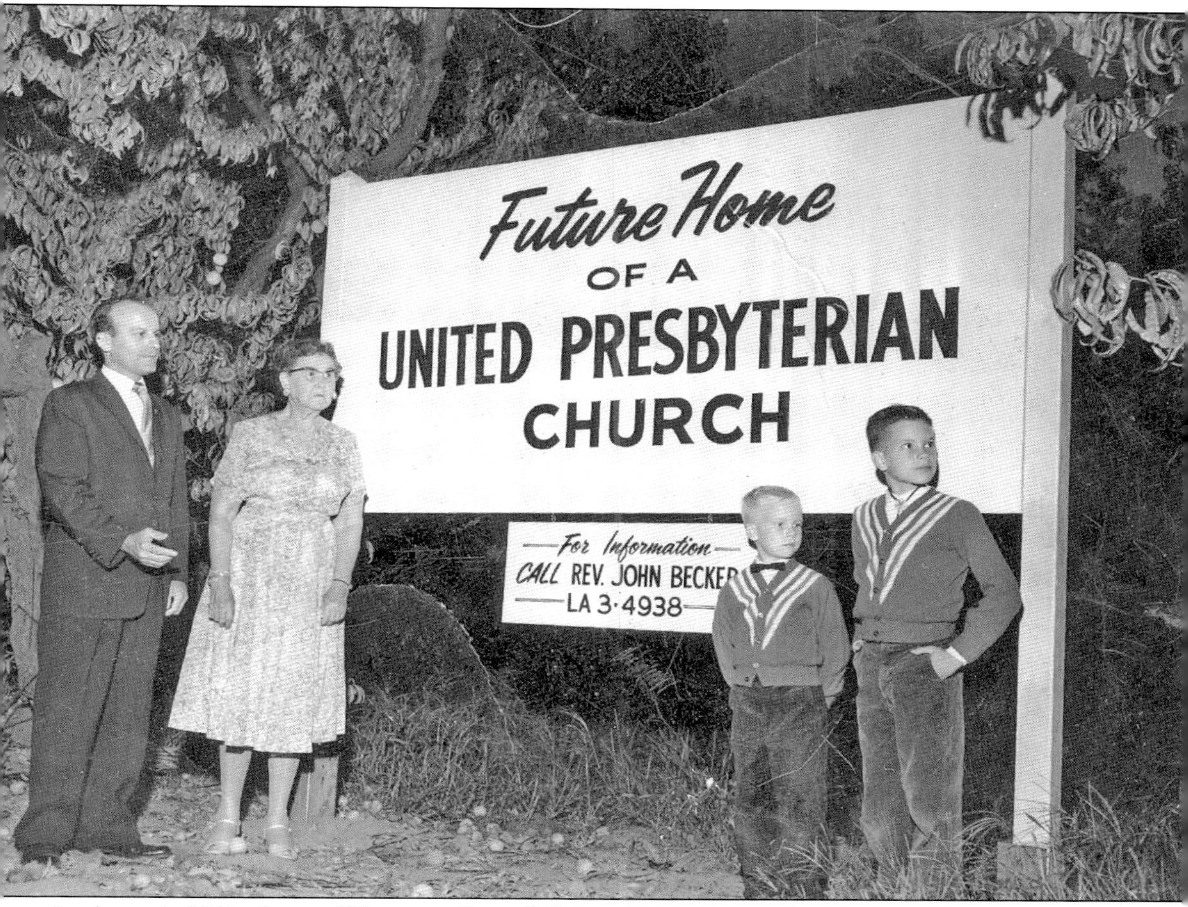

In the early 1960s, Jennie Whitmore Caswell donated a 10-acre peach orchard on Moffet Road for construction of United Presbyterian Church, now Harvest Presbyterian Church. Pictured in this promotional photograph are Rev. Jack Becker of Geneva Presbyterian Church in Modesto, Jennie Whitmore Caswell, and Timothy and Patrick Lucas. The organizing committee consisted of Jack Becker, Grant Lucas, Mildred Lucas, and Bertha Veneman. (Mildred Lucas.)

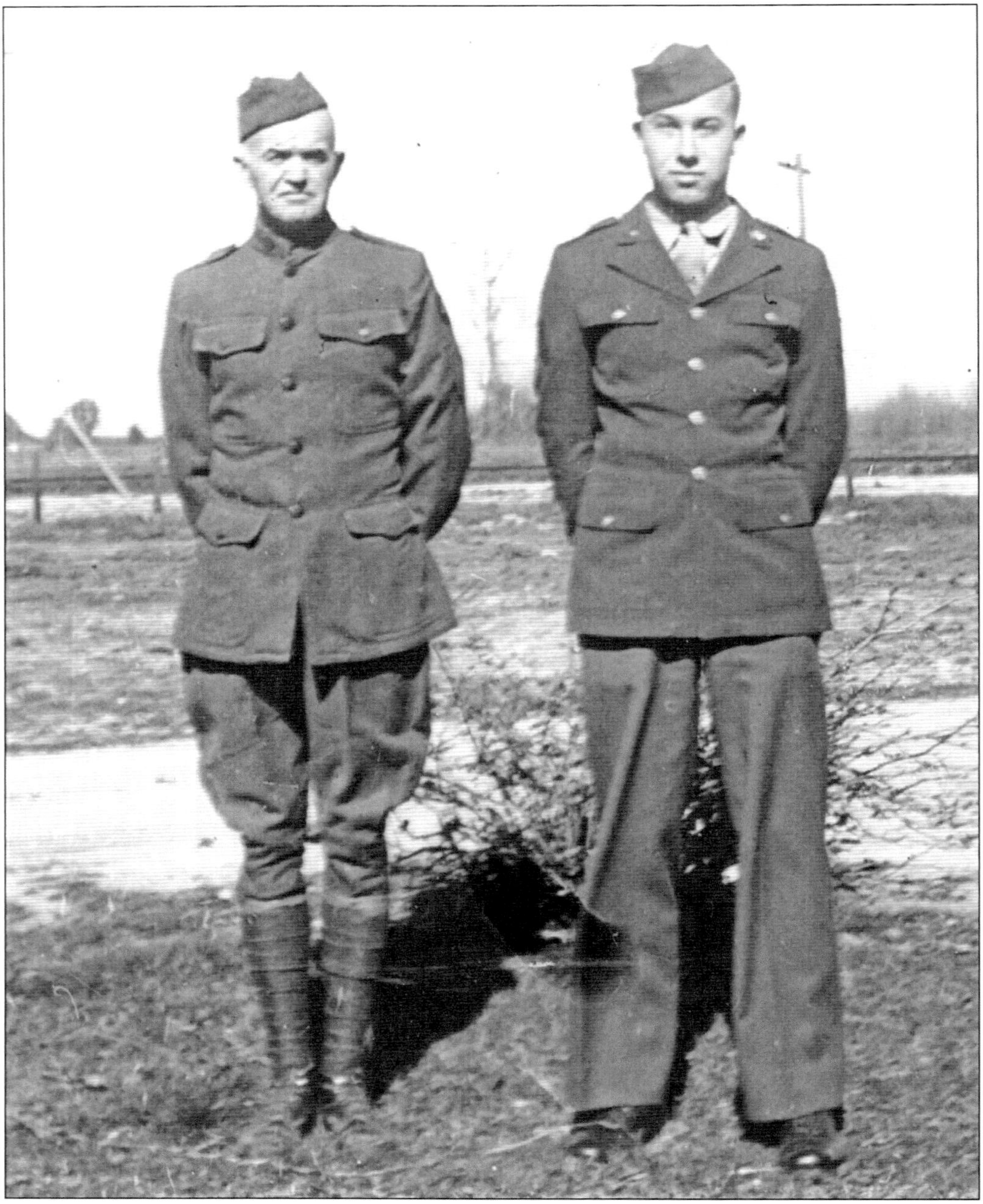

Garland G. T. "Doc" Lucas and son Grant served in World Wars I and II, respectively, and wore their uniforms for this August 1943 photograph. Doc Lucas lived from 1890 to 1970. Grant was a 1940 Ceres High School graduate and was drafted into the Army in 1942. He later learned that his grandmother, Lizzie Shrider, was responsible for sending him off to war as she served on the local draft board. A chemistry major, Grant was sent to Utah to experiment with instruments of chemical warfare before deployment to Europe as a paratrooper. (Grant Lucas.)

Five

The Protectors

From its inception, Ceres needed protection from fires as well as criminals. Wooden structures were most susceptible to fires, a fact of which Ceres was painfully aware as Daniel Whitmore's Ceres Flour Mill, constructed in 1882 to mill wheat farmed in Ceres, burned after a year of operation. Another heartbreaking fire occurred on November 12, 1899, when the First Baptist Church was charred by an inferno. The majestic building had only been a part of the Ceres landscape since 1882. Because the congregation allowed an insurance policy to lapse, a replacement structure was not finished until 1900. Fire also claimed the Ceres Creamery at 11:00 p.m. on September 16, 1905. The new structure's loss was estimated at $16,000, a whopping sum at that time. The economic impact was staggering as the plant was churning out 1,500 pounds of butter each day and employing many Ceres workers. Losses prompted Ceres to organize a volunteer fire department in June 1911. Storekeeper George F. Wood was elected the first chief, a post he held until 1921 when the department was reorganized. Clifford Strait succeeded him. In those early days, volunteers were summoned to fires through the sounding of a dinner bell hanging from the Fourth Street water tank within earshot of most residents. When the iron triangle broke, Ceres purchased a bell from Turlock. The last great fire was the 1991 blaze that razed the brick Whitmore School then used by the Ceres Unified School District as its headquarters. After the city's 1918 incorporation, T. F. Perrin became Ceres' first marshal at $5 per month. By 1920, Albert Rich, his replacement, earned $20 per month. In 1934, Jack Dillon was Ceres' first police chief. In 1942, he was elected Ceres constable but died from a heart attack months later. Louis Garl succeeded him. In 1943, A. R. White became chief but deferred to S. M. Christiansen in 1944. Ceres demanded a night officer, so J. M. McGuffey was hired. He reportedly fired shots at a car that ran through a blockade. Other chiefs were Henry Triplett (1946), Kenneth Foster (1951), Leroy Cunningham (1952), Pete Peterson (1983), and Art deWerk (1999).

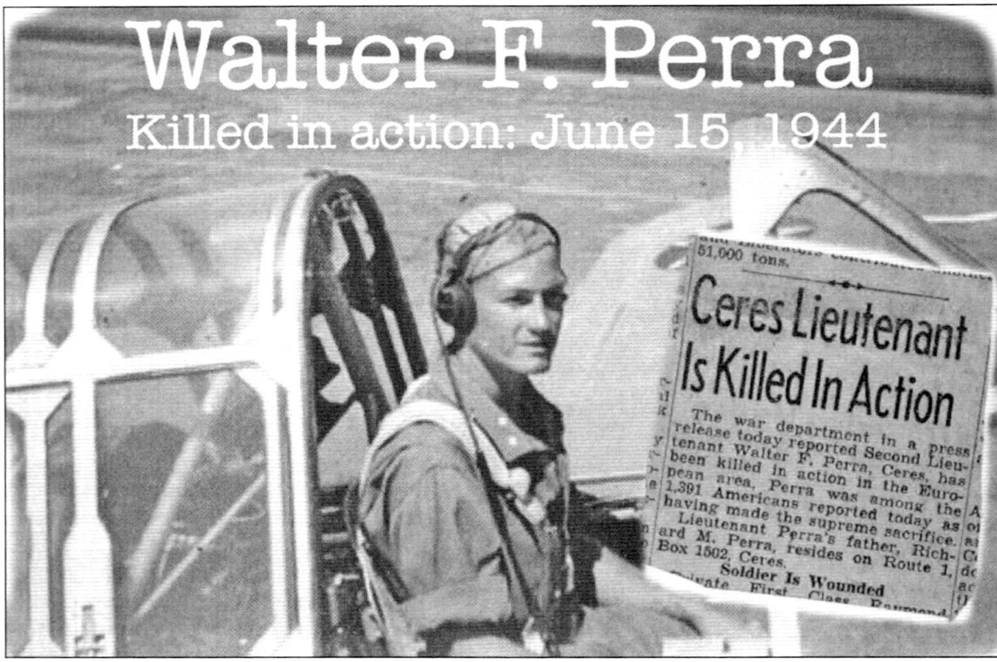

Country boy Walter Perra went off to war, never to return. The Ceres man died at age 24 on June 15, 1944, when his plane was shot down in France. Perra, a Minnesota native born in 1919 to Richard and Ida E. Perra, moved to Ceres in 1931. He and brother Medrick Perra built model airplanes as youngsters, the first indication that Walter was interested in aviation. In the war, Walter flew a P-38 on numerous missions over enemy territory, disabling railroads and supply lines and clearing the way for advancing Allied forces. In 2008, Perra was featured in a documentary about five Americans killed during the Normandy campaign. The American Battle Monuments Commission authorized the film. (Mark Perra.)

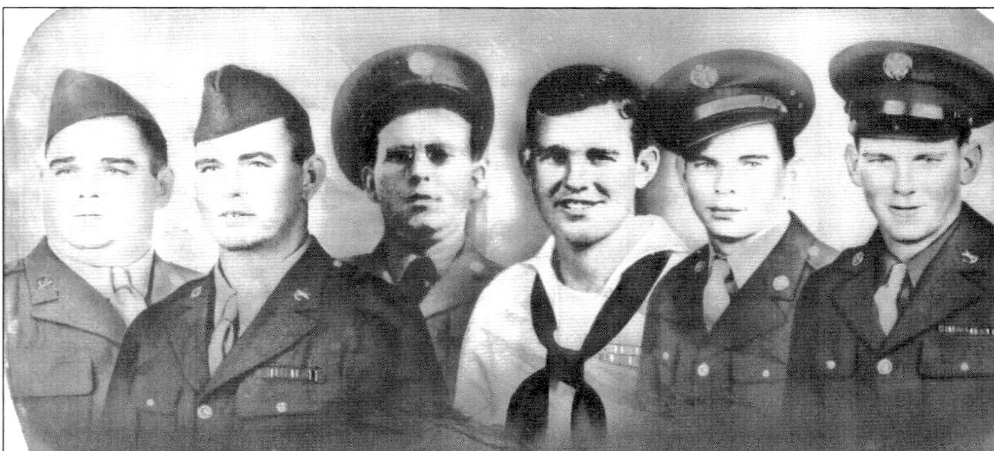

World War II prompted the six sons of Aria and Eliza Young of Ceres to enlist in the military. They are, from left to right, Arlis, Connie, Otho "Boag", Hershel "Trent", Orville, and Ezell "Easy." Ezell was wounded by shrapnel, and Hershel's ship was hit, but all six came back alive. A Modesto photographer made this composite photograph after he spotted six stars in the window of the Young house and learned that all six sons were serving. (Diana Wilson.)

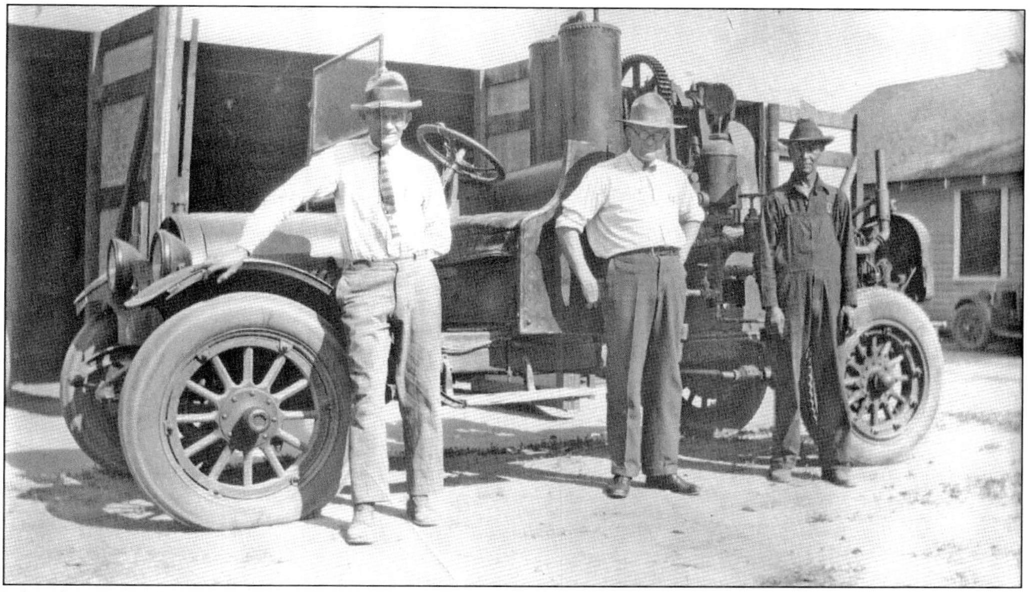

This homemade fire engine with two front ends was the laughingstock of Ceres until its power was demonstrated. Ray McMillan (left) and Lee Gill (right) pose with Will Ham (center), who constructed the fire engine from a Ford Model T. On one mutual aid call, Modesto firefighters saw the contraption and laughed until Ham directed a stream of water at them to show how much water pressure would blast them. The Ceres Fire Department was located on Fourth Street where the *Courier* offices are today. (Betty Ham.)

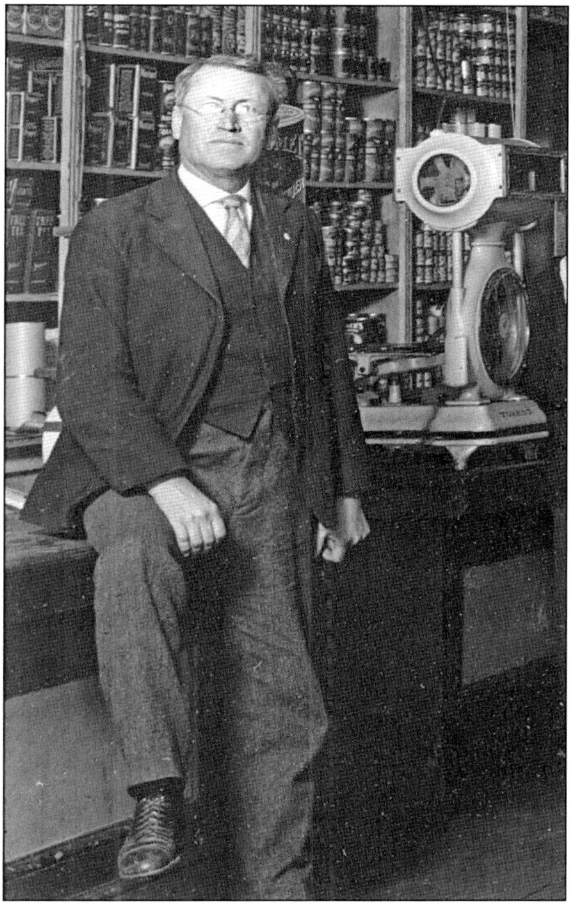

George F. Wood was an important man in developing Ceres. He was the owner and operator of the largest mercantile store in the early part of the 20th century. On Feb. 29, 1921, he posed for this photograph inside his store. He served as Ceres' first fire chief from 1911 to 1921. Born in Kansas, Wood came to Modesto in 1885 and served as postmaster there from 1898 to 1902. His opened his store in 1902 and ran it until 1928. Wood lived in a house at Fourth and North Streets, where the Wells Fargo Bank is located. His daughter, Jessie Wood Crombie, was well-known in Ceres social circles. (Betty Ham.)

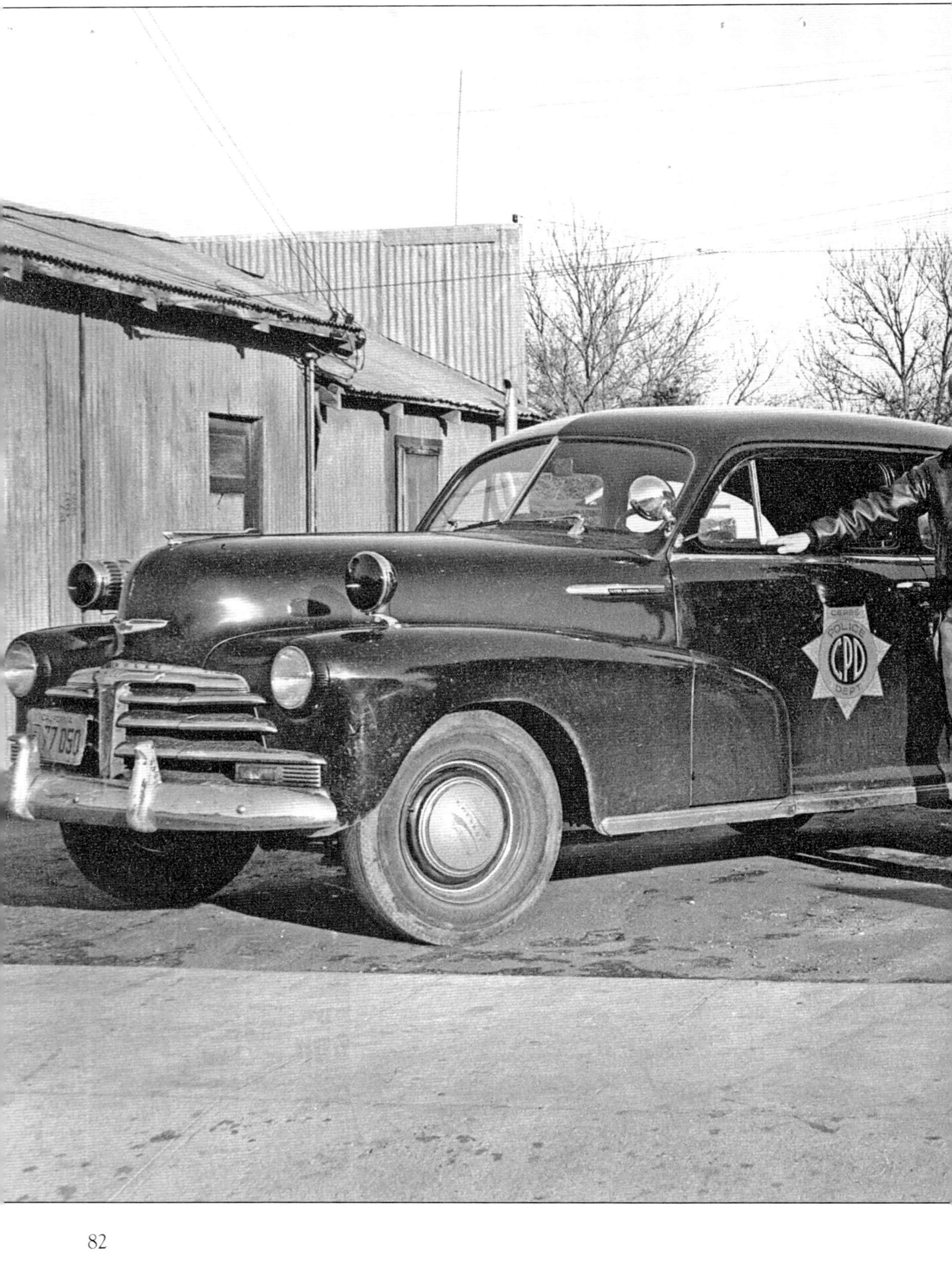
POLICE
CPD
DEPT

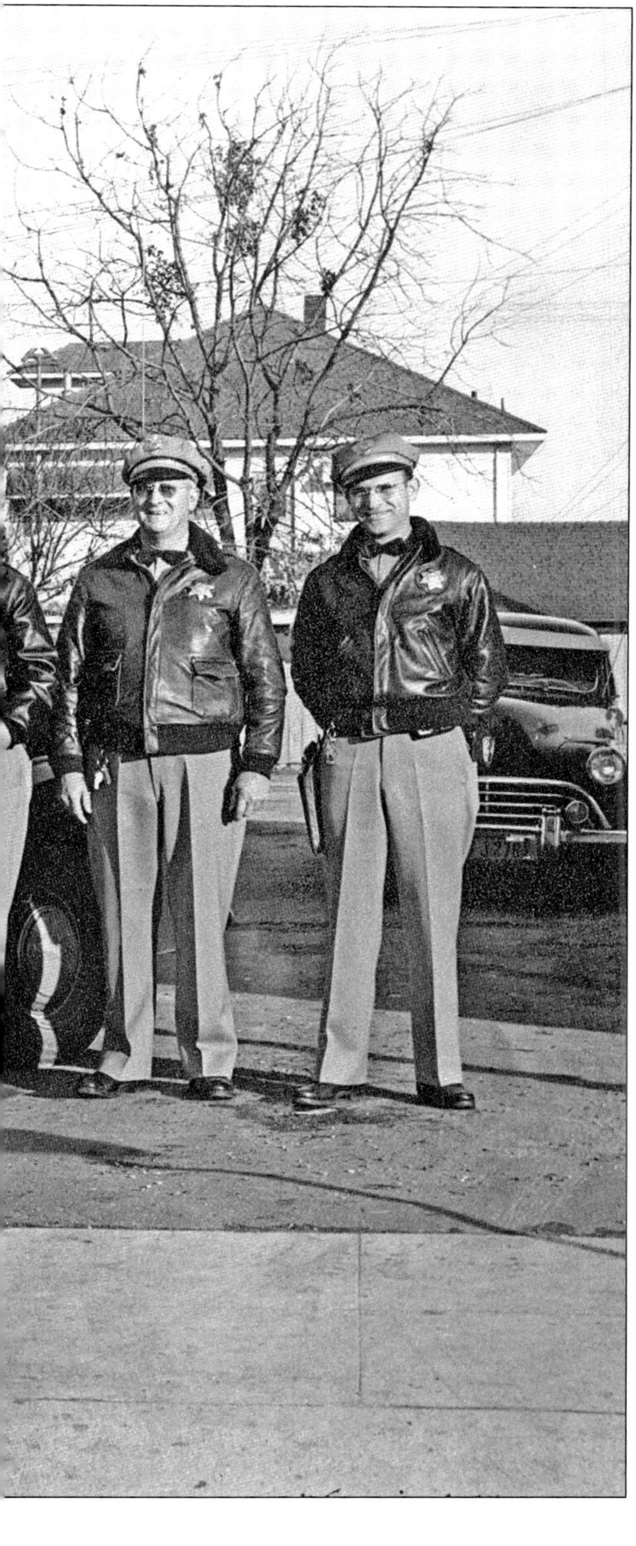

Ceres police chief Henry Triplett and officers Floyd Randal and Kenneth Foster stand in the police department's Fourth Street parking lot in the late 1940s. Today the office of the *Ceres Courier* sits on this exact spot. The police department and city hall were located in a house that today houses Sole Saver Shoe Repair. To the north, a metal building served as the fire department. A jail cell located inside the fire department featured steel bars in the front and quarter-inch steel plates for walls, but the ceiling was made of lightweight tin roofing material and prisoners were able to escape. (Ceres Police Department.)

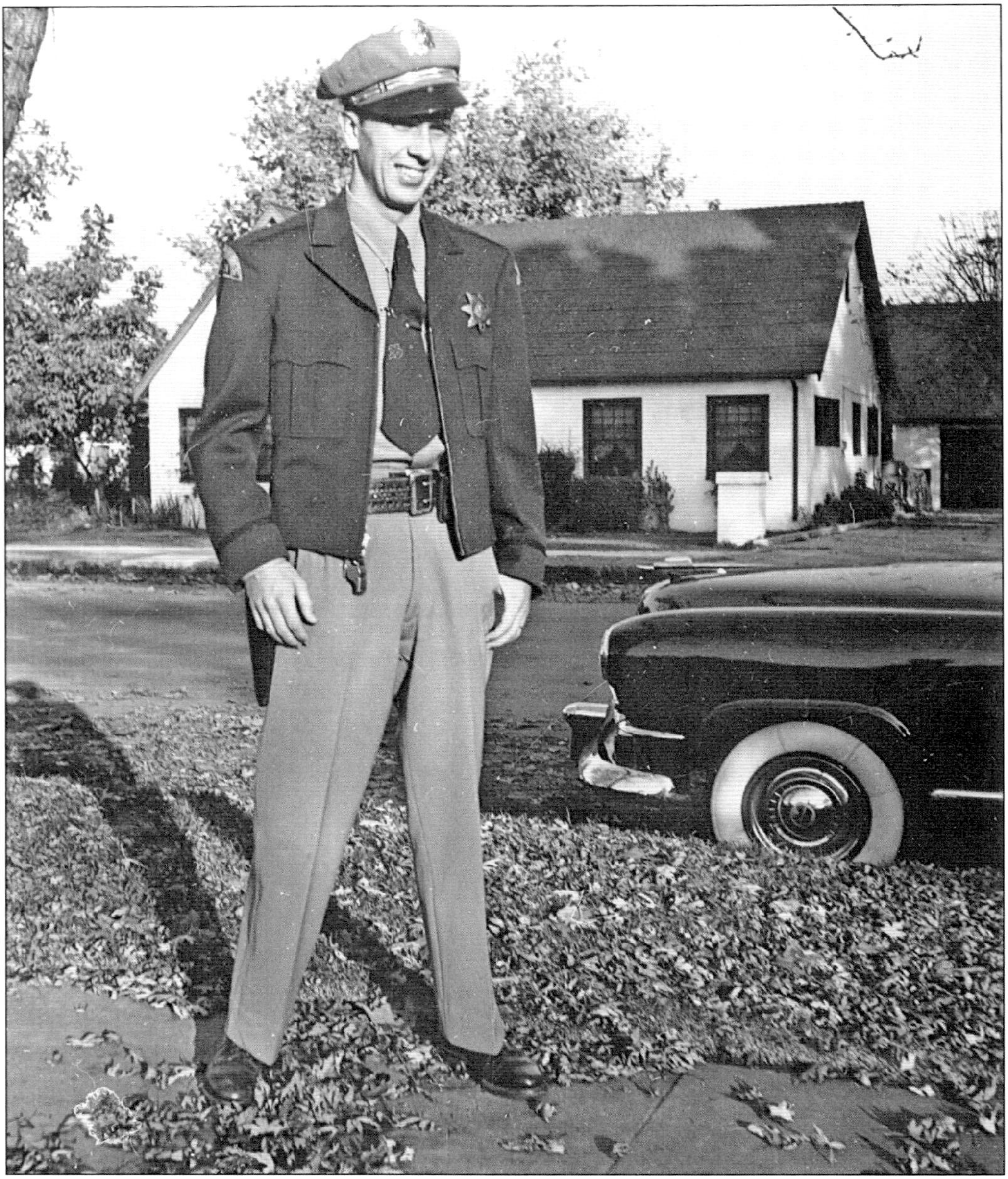

Leroy Brian Cunningham ran the Ceres Police Department as chief for 26 years, from 1956 to 1983. Cunningham was first hired as a relief policeman on August 1, 1949, with absolutely no training. He once told the *Courier*, "I weighed 130 pounds wringing wet. I needed the gun to hold me to the ground. There I was, 21 years old, scared stiff, and carrying a gun. I was out there all night, by myself, patrolling this town. That was a terrible thing to do to the citizens of this community." He relied heavily on local officers for pointers. In 1950, Cunningham was drafted to serve in the army during the Korean Conflict but returned to Ceres two years later. He died in 2005. (Ceres Police Department.)

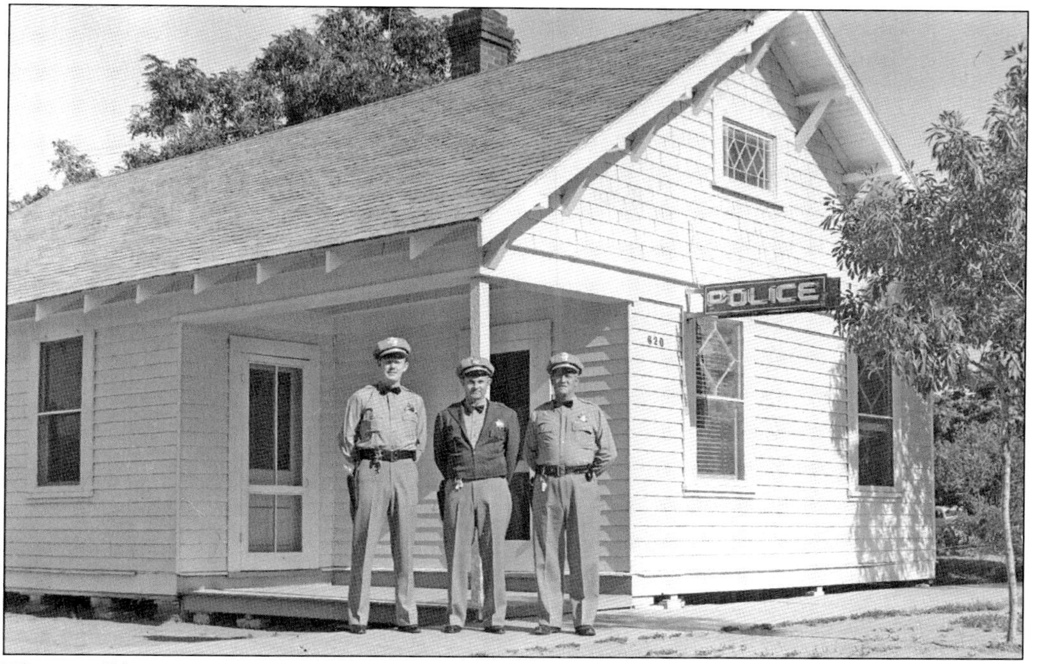

This small house on Fourth Street served as the Ceres Police Station in the late 1940s and early 1950s. The building's number is 620 but later the streets were renumbered. The building is now 2948 Fourth Street, where Sole Saver Boot and Shoe Repair operates. A large single window replaced the two smaller windows seen here. The building started out as the first office of the *Ceres Courier* established by publisher Clarence Bronaugh. (Ceres Police Department.)

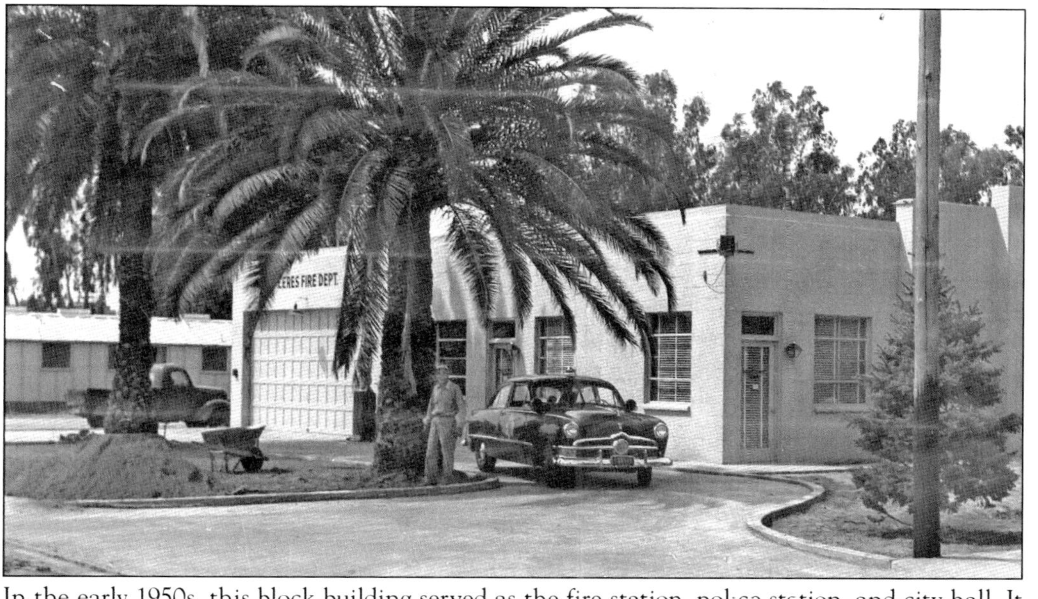

In the early 1950s, this block building served as the fire station, police station, and city hall. It was removed from North Street just north of Whitmore Park to make way for Ceres Fire Station No. 1. The palm tree seen in front was one of two planted when the site contained the first Ceres Grammar School. The trees remained until they were uprooted in 1970. (City of Ceres.)

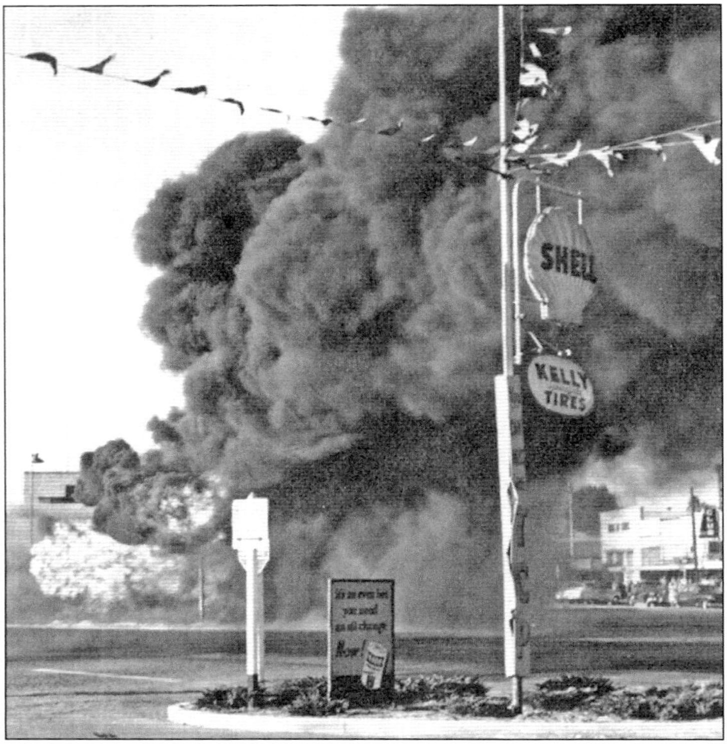

On October 1, 1958, downtown Ceres witnessed this horrendous explosion and fire. A gasoline tanker truck carrying 7,500 gallons of fuel was being driven southbound on two-lane Highway 99. The inexperienced truck driver locked up his wheels to avoid striking a passenger car that ran a red light at the intersection at Fourth Street and El Camino, and the trailer jackknifed and overturned. Sparks ignited the entire fuel tank, causing a massive explosion and inferno. The driver died after being badly burned trying to escape the flames. (City of Ceres.)

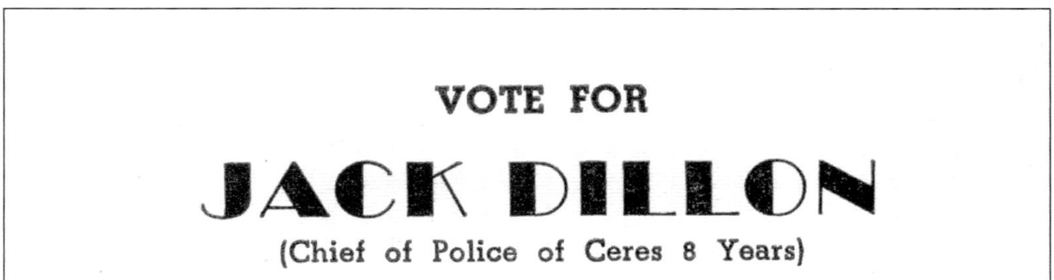

VOTE FOR

JACK DILLON

(Chief of Police of Ceres 8 Years)

FOR

CONSTABLE

Ceres Township

PRIMARIES AUGUST 25, 1942

Jack Dillon, the first town marshal in Ceres, handed out these campaign cards for the August 1942 election. He prevailed in the polls and became Ceres constable, but died in 1943. (City of Ceres.)

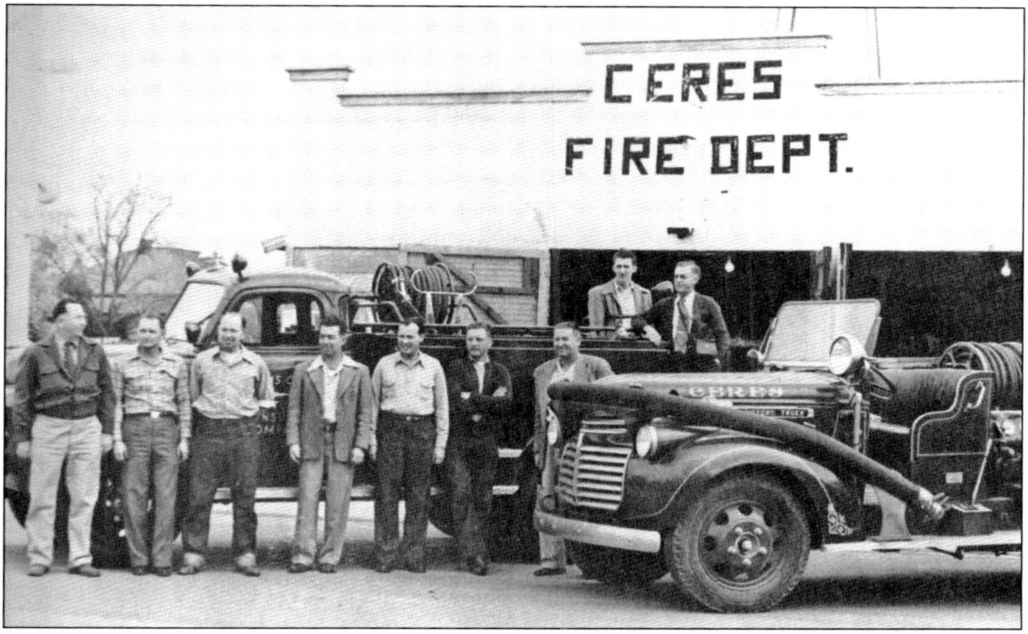

Ceres fire officials gathered for this photograph in the 1940s in front of the fire station, which was then located on the east side of Fourth Street between North and Lawrence Streets. (City of Ceres.)

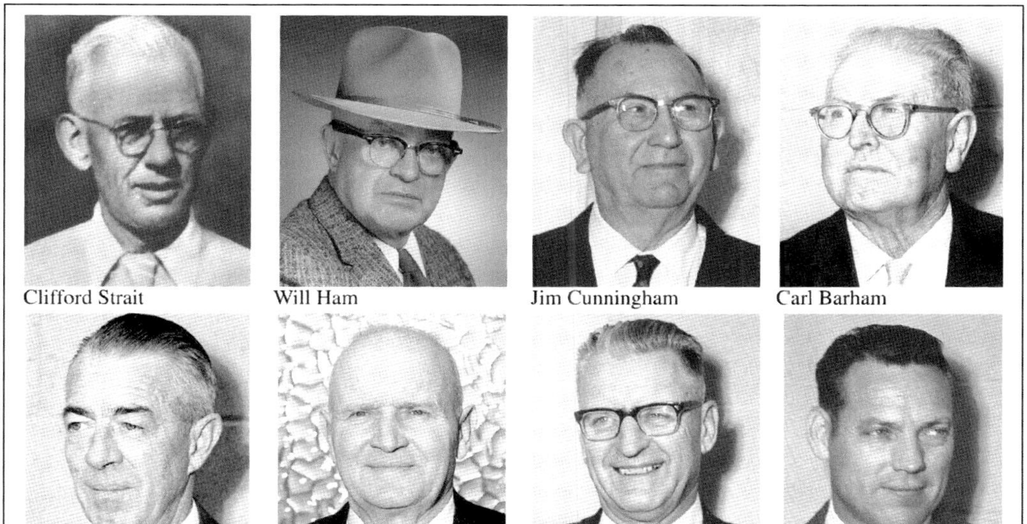

Eight men supervised firefighting in Ceres for a collective 63 years. They succeeded the first fire chief, George F. Wood. Clifford Strait served from 1921 to 1926; Will Ham, 1926 to 1935; Jim Cunningham, 1935 to 1946; Carl Barham, 1946 to 1949; Kenneth E. Wilson, 1949 to 1951; June L. Barnes, 1951 to 1961; Chesley Ludden, 1961 to 1967; and Truman Showen became the first full-time chief in 1968 and served until 1984. In the 1980s, the city merged fire and police departments into a Department of Public Safety. Others placed in charge of firefighting were Brian Weber, Dan Davis, Bryan Nicholes, and directors Pete Peterson and Art deWerk. (City of Ceres.)

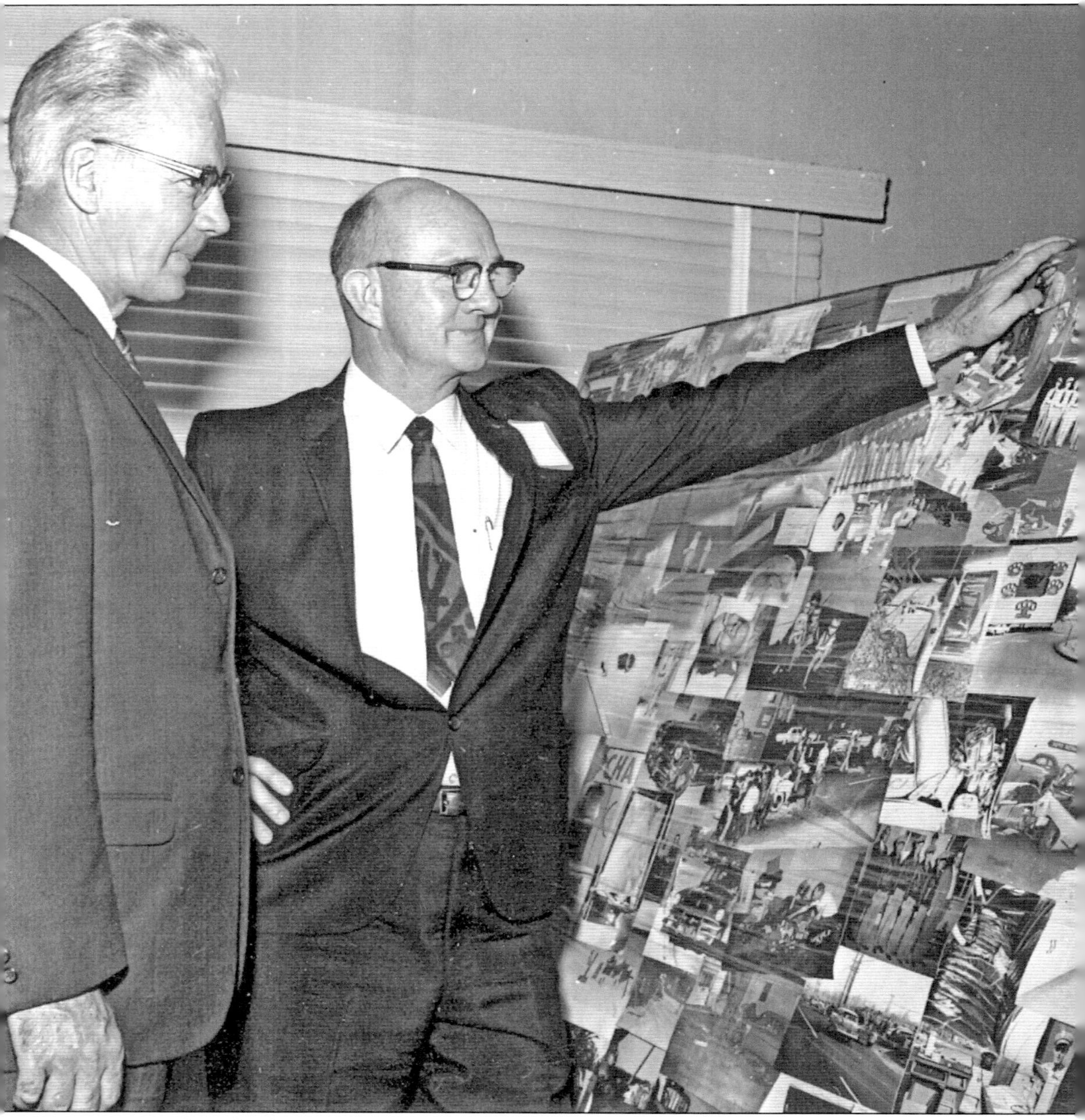

Ceres police chief Henry Triplett (left) and fire chief June Barnes take a look at a collection of photographs on a special occasion in 1951. Barnes was fire chief from 1951 to 1961. Triplett was police chief from 1946 to 1951 and was elected to the Ceres city council in 1956. (City of Ceres.)

Loren Hartman had a close call with a burglary suspect on January 2, 1979, at a Mitchell Road store. Hartman was shot with his own service revolver, which was taken from him during the arrest. He was wounded despite wearing a bulletproof vest and was saved when Officer Louis Arrollo (below) opened fire and killed the suspect. Hartman grew up in Southern California, and it was said his fast draw earned him a spot in a shootout on *Gunsmoke*. Hartman came to Ceres in 1964 and became a Ceres officer in 1970, promoted to sergeant in 1980. He was killed in an August 25, 1985, motorcycle accident near Oakdale. (*Ceres Courier*.)

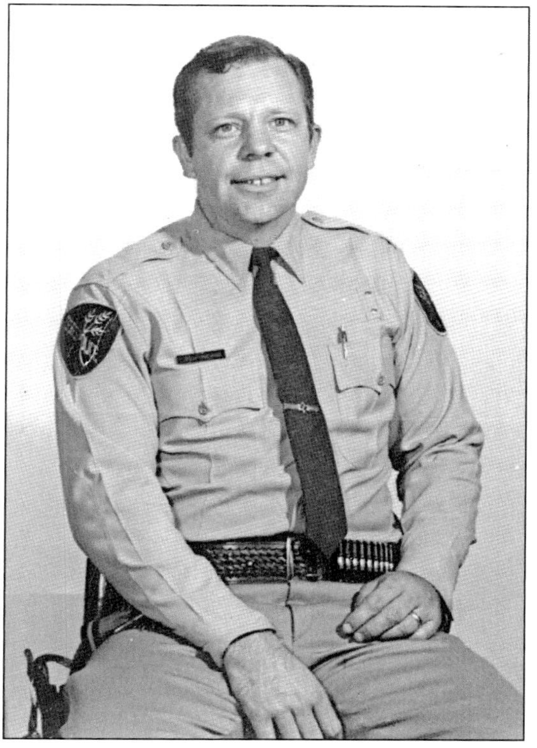

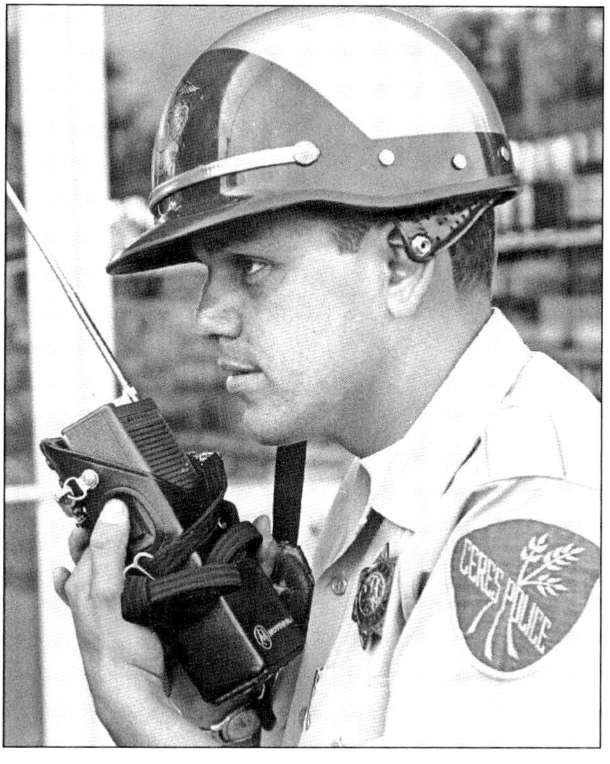

Officer Louie Arrollo, talking on his radio in the 1970s, is a well-known Ceres figure. He served twice as mayor, from 1987 to 1990 and again from 1999 to 2001. Arrollo was hired as a Ceres reserve officer in 1963 and became a sworn officer in 1965, working his way up to sergeant, lieutenant, and police commander. (*Ceres Courier*.)

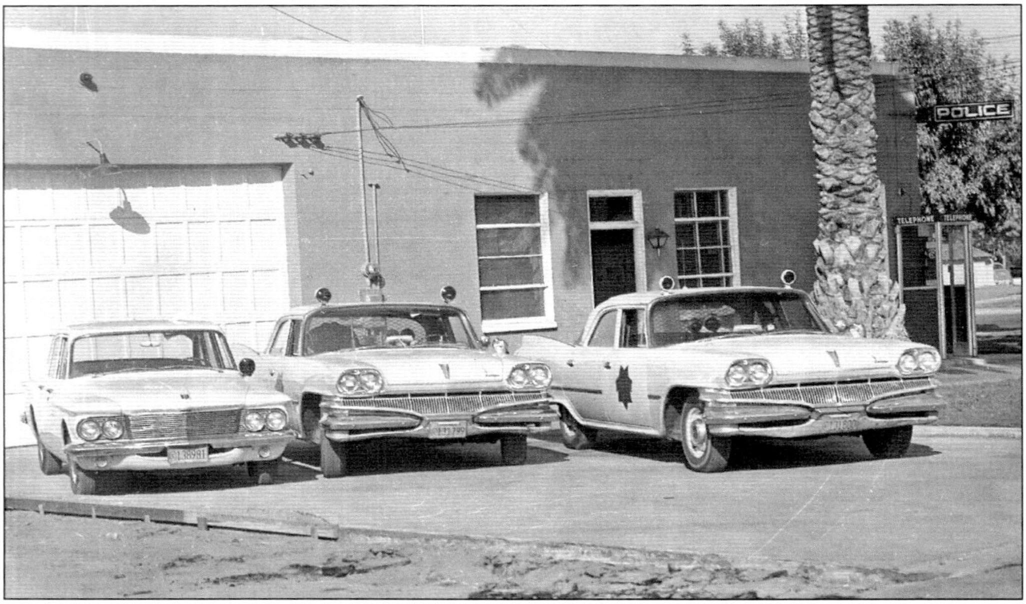

These Ceres police cars look like something out of Mayberry because they were the model-of-choice for law enforcement vehicles at about the same time as the popular television series *The Andy Griffith Show.* The squad cars are parked in front of the police station on North Street. (City of Ceres.)

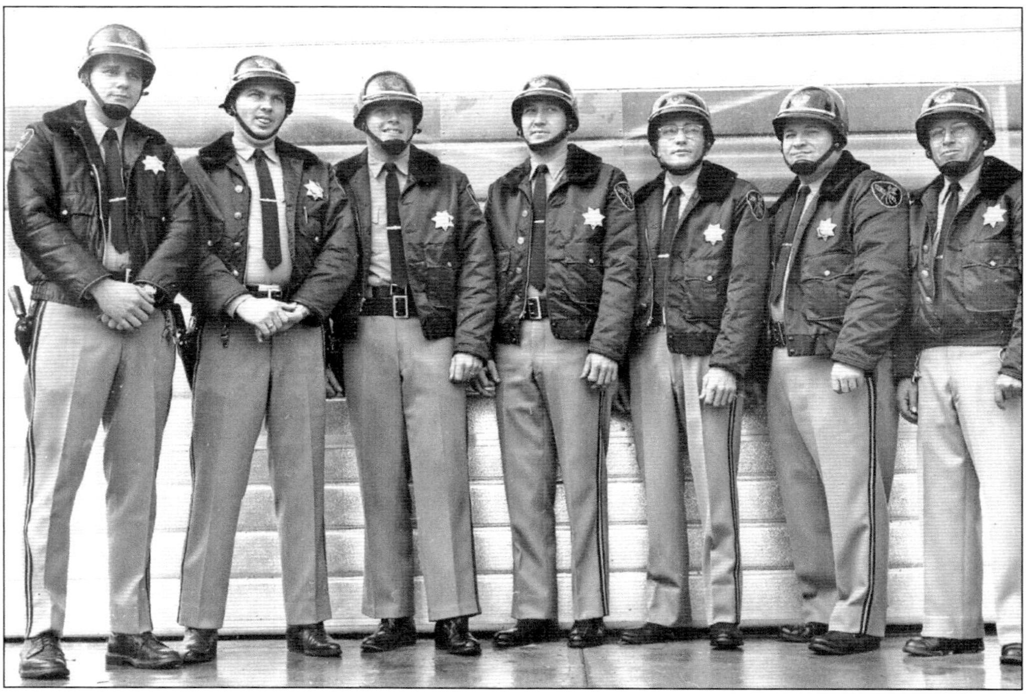

Ceres attracted a number of reserve officers. In this early-1970s photograph are, from left to right, Dave Racher, ? White, Ron Trimble, J. D. Michael (a full-time officer assigned as liaison officer to the reserve unit), Irvin Park, William F. "Bill" Battles, and Louie Rogers, captain of the police reserve unit. (City of Ceres.)

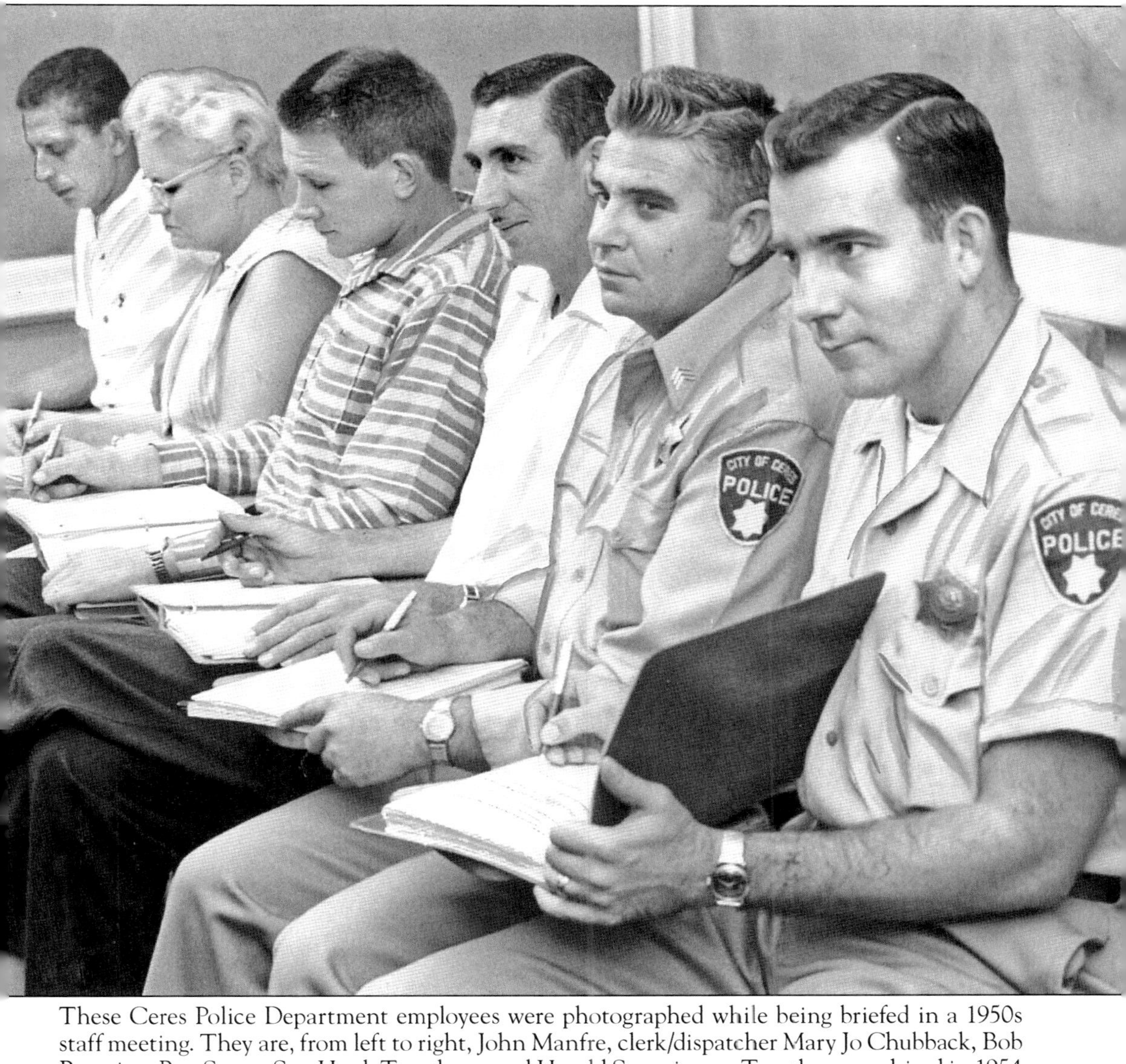

These Ceres Police Department employees were photographed while being briefed in a 1950s staff meeting. They are, from left to right, John Manfre, clerk/dispatcher Mary Jo Chubback, Bob Bunning, Ray Stane, Sgt. Hank Trantham, and Harold Swearingen. Trantham was hired in 1954 as an officer and became the city's first lieutenant in August 1962. He retired in 1980 and died in 1991. (Ceres Police Department.)

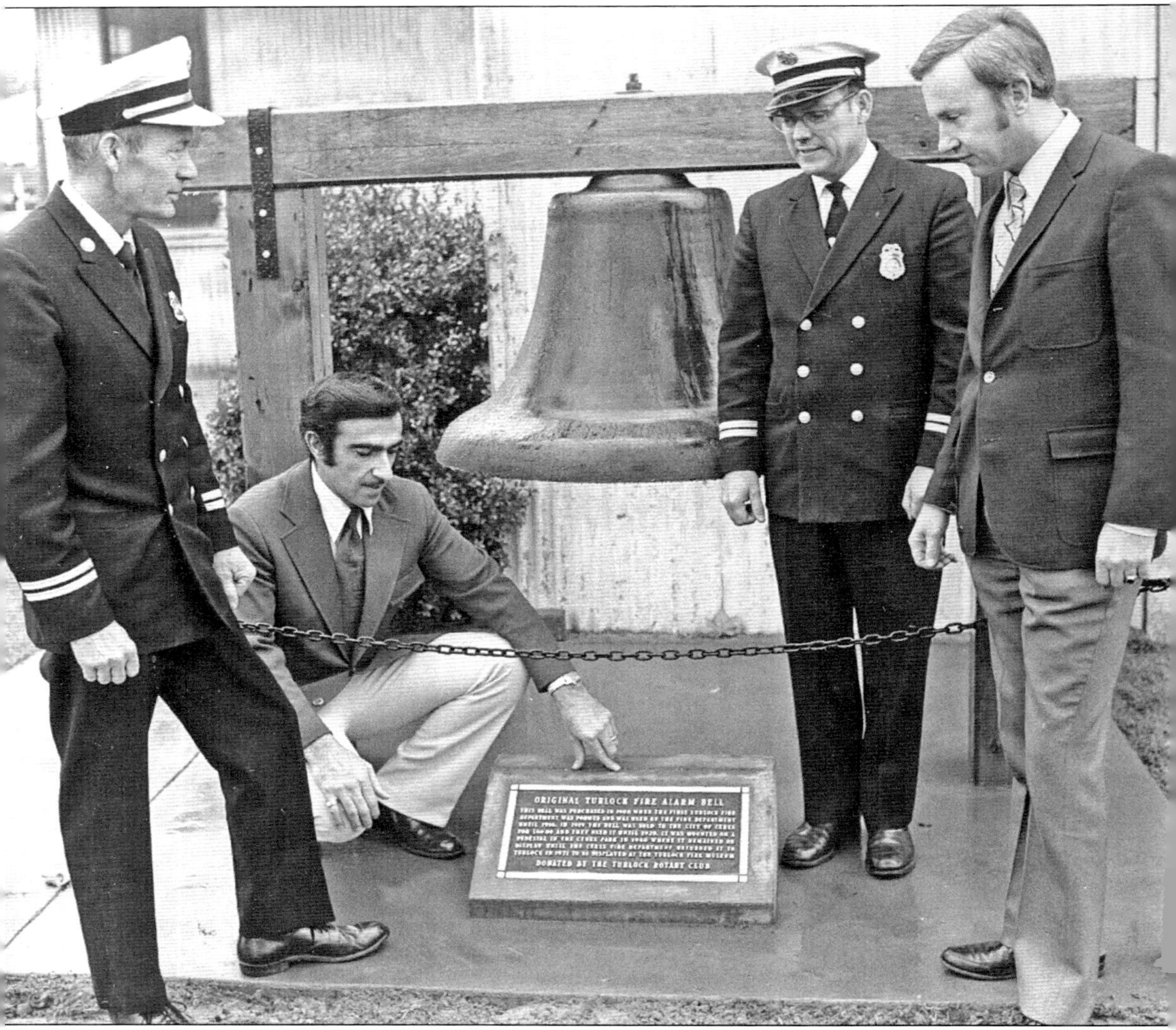

Some Ceres residents were unhappy at the exchange of the Ceres fire bell in the 1970s. The bell was originally used by Turlock Fire Department to summon firefighters from 1908 to 1916. In 1919 Turlock sold the bell to the city of Ceres for $60 and it was struck for Ceres fires from 1919 to 1928. When the bell was retired from service it was mounted on a pedestal at Whitmore Park in 1940. In 1971 Turlock asked if they could put the bell into a Turlock museum and Ceres obliged. A concrete replica sits in place of the metal bell. Here Ceres fire chief Truman Showen (standing just to the right of the bell) makes the presentation. (City of Ceres.)

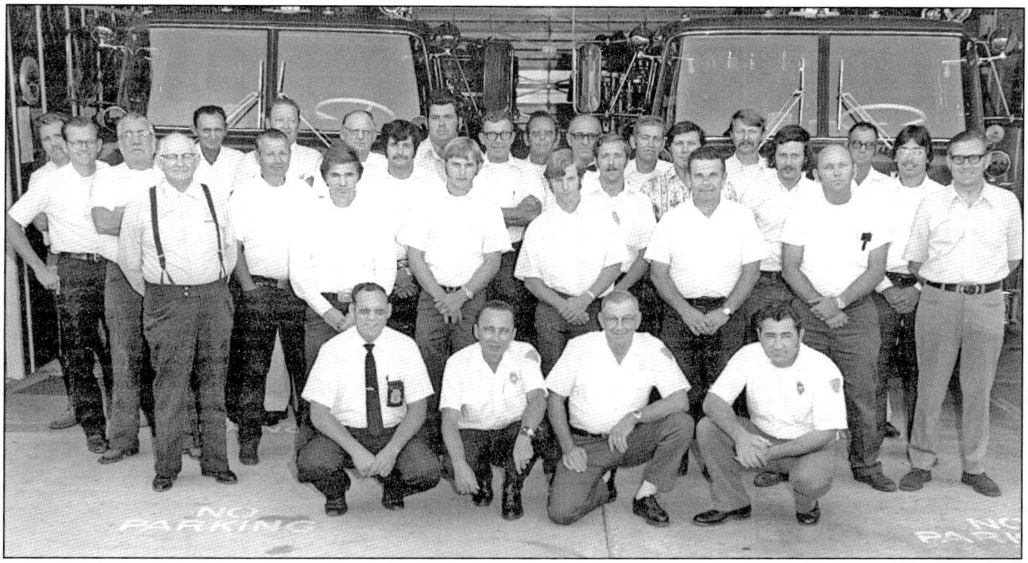

This was Ceres' volunteer firefighting force in June 1974. Pictured are, from left to right (first row) Fire Chief Truman Showen, Assistant Chief Darwin Borges, Captain Johnny Marks, and Captain Gene Silvey; (second row), Jerry Freeman, Jay Weber, Leo Henson, Commissioner Charlie Hanson, Howard Haverly, George Edgerly, John King, Vernon Emerald, Gene Carrol, Bruce Smith, Robert Trotter, Richard Erickson, Paul Tanner, Lloyd Kee, Walt Butler, Al Mattice, Paul Wilson, Danny Kirk, Boyd Byous, Walt Butler Jr., Frank Hoefert, Danny Davis, Roy Larson, Jack Bowser, Gary Sexton, and Mayor Ted Humphries. The photograph was taken in the station that was razed for Ceres Fire Station no. 1 at the corner of North and Third Streets. (City of Ceres.)

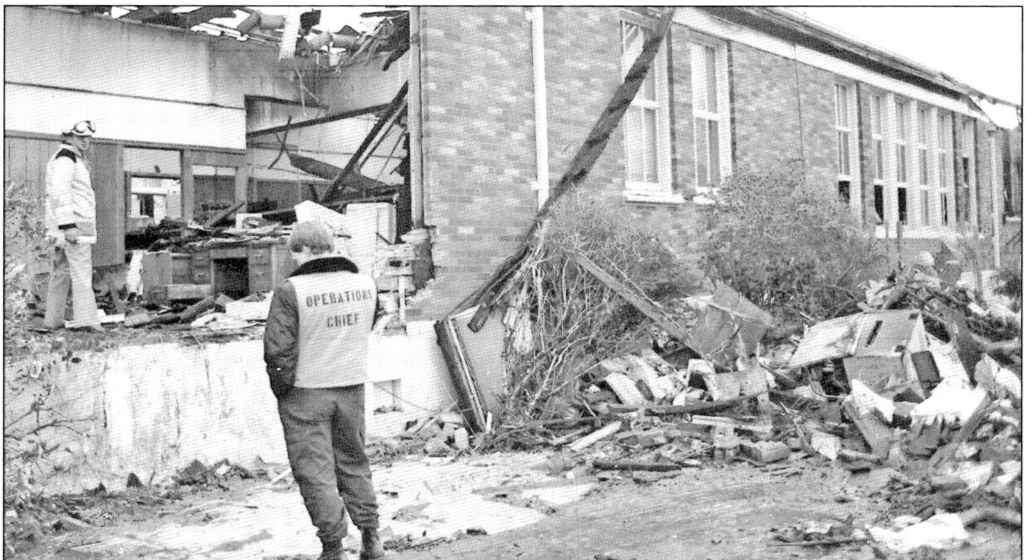

On the night of January 11, 1991, the historic brick Whitmore Elementary School on Lawrence Street, then used as the Ceres Unified School District (CUSD) headquarters, was destroyed by fire. Jack Rudd, business manager of CUSD, sifts through the charred remains while Fire Chief Bryan Nicholes watches. (Marc Paulus, *Ceres Courier*.)

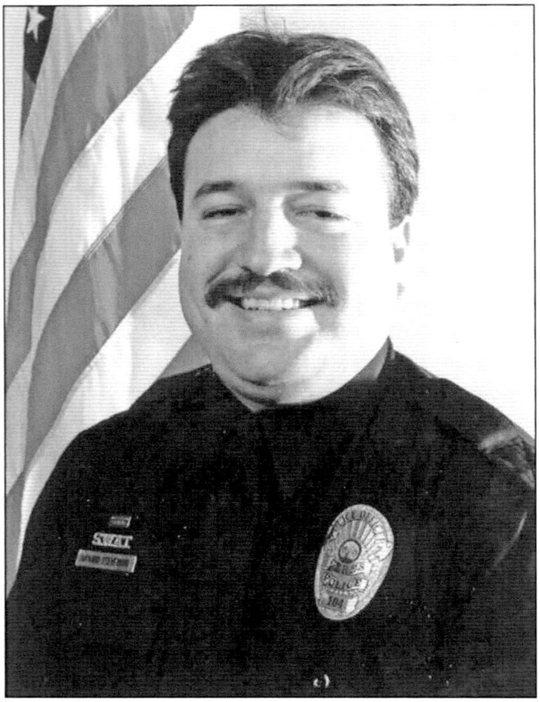

Ceres grieved its first on-duty police officer death on January 9, 2005, when AWOL Marine Andres Raya murdered Sgt. Howard "Howie" Stevenson in a senseless act of violence. Raya stood in front of George's Liquors on Caswell Avenue, holding an automatic rifle under a rain poncho. He fired some rounds, then had the clerk call 911 to bait officers into a trap. Sam Ryno (opposite page at top) was seriously wounded and pulled to safety by Officer Chris Melton. Stevenson approached from the east and was fatally shot. Raya was later killed after charging officers in a nearby alley. (*Ceres Courier.*)

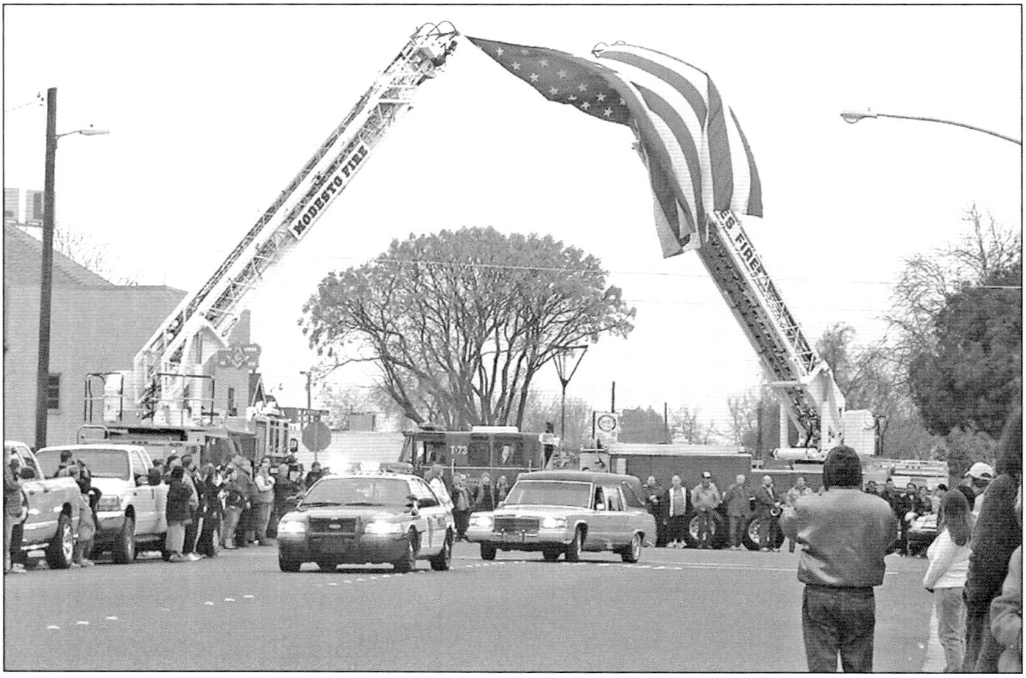

On one of the saddest days in Ceres history, the funeral procession of Sgt. Howard Stevenson passes beneath a giant American flag draped between two fire truck ladders at the intersection of Third and North Streets (above). Many mourners along the route broke down with silent sobs. (*Ceres Courier.*)

Sam Ryno was elevated to the rank of sergeant after he was seriously wounded in the January 9, 2005, attack on officers outside of George's Liquors. While he overcame his serious injuries with the help of his devoted wife, Lynda, Sergeant Ryno never returned to duty. A park on the west side of Ceres at Brown Avenue and Stone Springs Drive was named after Ryno in 2007 as a way of honoring his 24 years of service with the Ceres Police Department. (City of Ceres.)

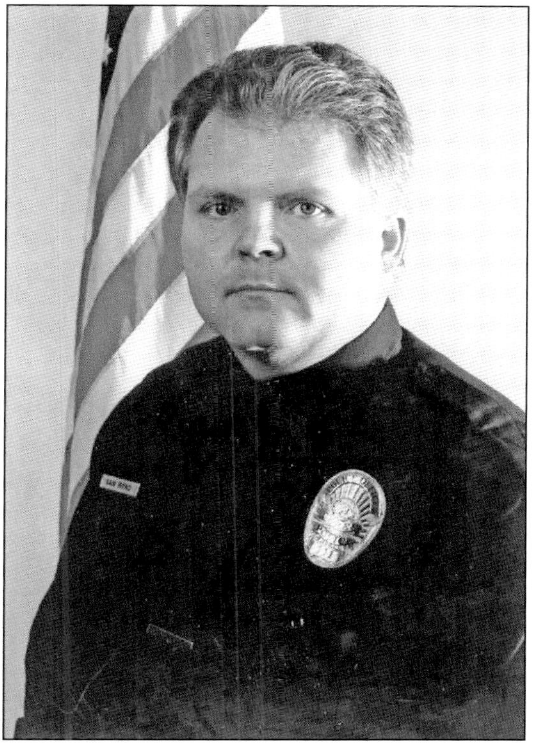

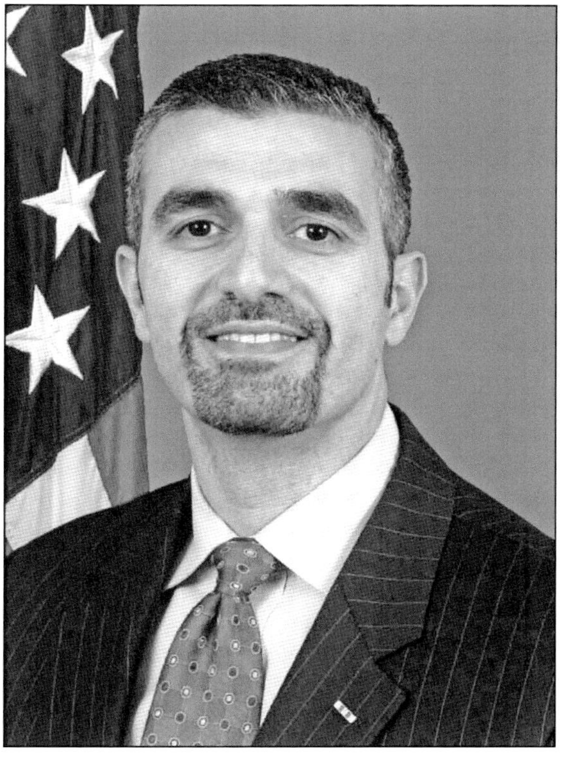

Former Ceres police officer George Piro became a special FBI agent who, in December 2003, became the FBI team leader responsible for interrogating Saddam Hussein, former president of Iraq. Piro spent nearly seven months interrogating Hussein and other key figures within the former Iraq regime. Piro appeared on the CBS program *60 Minutes* to relate his experiences with the Iraq president, who was executed for crimes against humanity. Born and raised in Lebanon, Piro is a fluent Arabic and Assyrian speaker. Piro was with Ceres Police from 1989 to 1997. (FBI.)

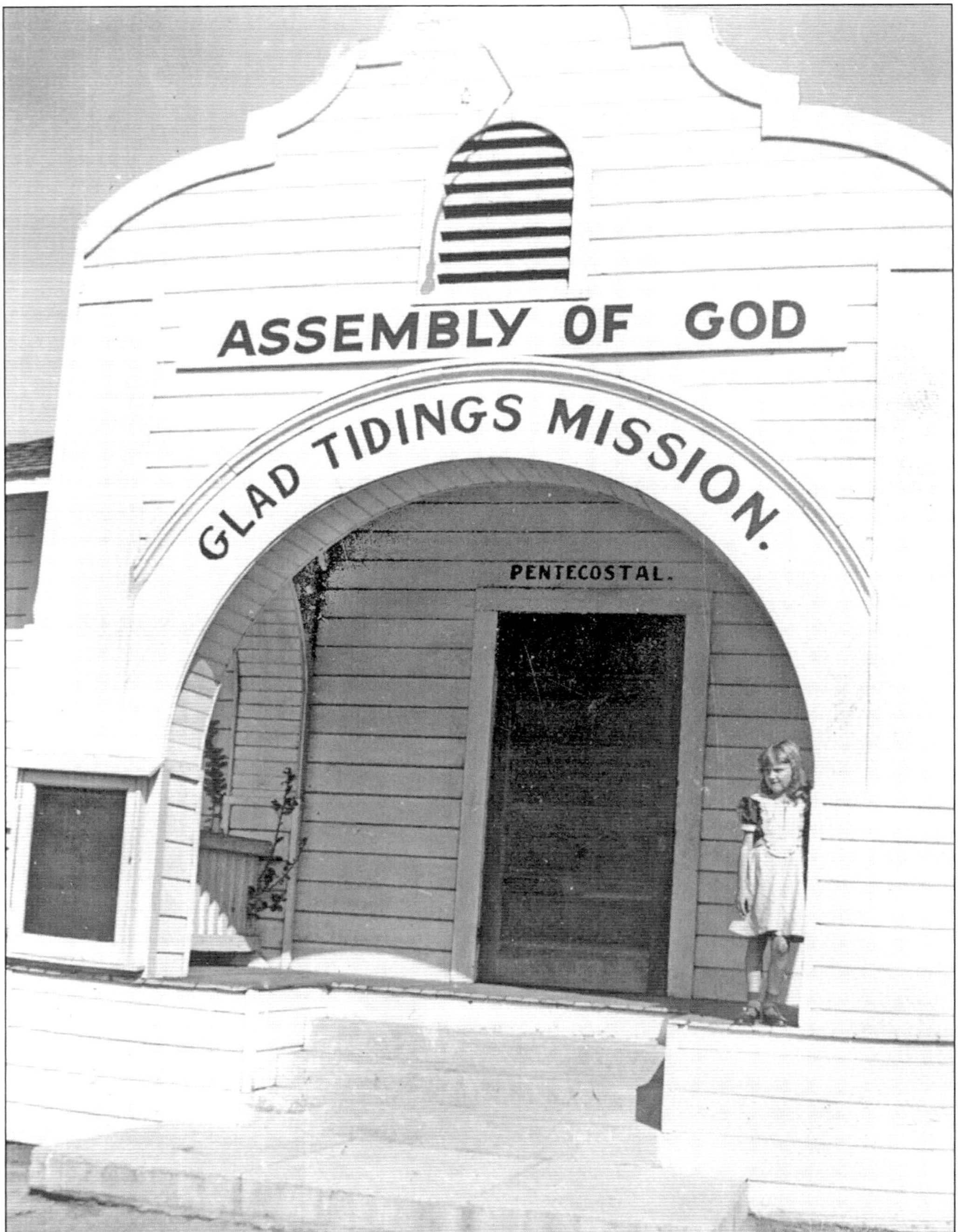

After Americans defeated enemies in two global theatres and GIs came home to raise their families, Ceres was a safe all-American town. For many, the successful raising of good kids in Ceres included faithful attendance at one of the many churches in town. Little Shirley Oeth stands outside the Glad Tidings Mission Assembly of God Church (now Valley Christian Church) where her parents worshiped. (Shirley Ollar.)

Six

Ceres after World War II

World War II interrupted the plans of many Ceres High School graduates who had different ideas for work or careers. But like millions of Americans, they rose to the call. One family in particular, the Youngs, gave it their all. Six brothers decided to enlist in the military. After the war ended, they returned to Ceres and started families. Before the war, Ceres had a population of 1,332 residents, but postwar numbers rose. Residential developments popped up, like the Caswell tract in 1946 and then Morrow Village. By 1950, the town had nearly doubled in size to 2,351 residents; by 1960, Ceres' population reached 4,406. Peaches were the crop of choice in the 1940s and 1950s, with the Ceres Dehydrator Plant on Whitmore becoming a key employer. More residents meant a need for more schools, specifically Don Pedro Elementary and Caswell Elementary in 1947 and 1948, respectively. Walter White Elementary was added in 1956; Carroll Fowler, in 1960. Civic groups took root, including the Lions Club in 1947. Growth as a bedroom community for Modesto changed Ceres and Stanislaus County. Downtown was altered significantly when the state widened Highway 99 into a four-lane freeway in the 1960s. In 1961, the community received national attention when citizens spruced up Ceres with help from the Fuller Paint Company. Murals were painted on downtown buildings, and the *Saturday Evening Post* took notice. A debated General Plan of 1965 hammered out a proposal to grow Ceres all the way to the Tuolumne River and both west and east. On September 17, 1951, the 78-bed Memorial Hospital opened north of town. By 1956, the hospital had seen its 5,000th birth. But after a larger hospital was constructed in Modesto in 1970, the Ceres facility was in less demand and closed in 1993 despite huge community concerns about a lack of acute care. In the 1970s and 1980s, Ceres developed commercially along Central and Whitmore Avenues and Hatch Road.

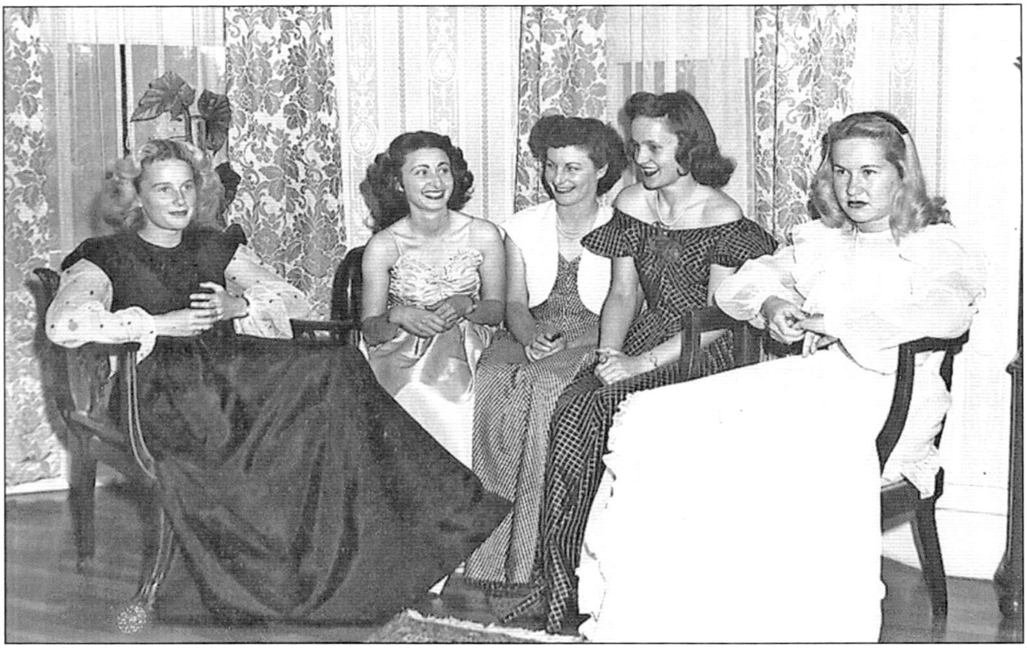

High school senior girls were treated to tea parties at the Clinton Whitmore Mansion as an important part of the social life in Ceres. Pictured here in 1946 are, from left to right, Carleen Lewis Goodrich, Ann Bollakis Johnson, Erma Schroeder Bartles, Jackie Morgan Higbee, and Martha Ghormley Meyers. (*The Courier.*)

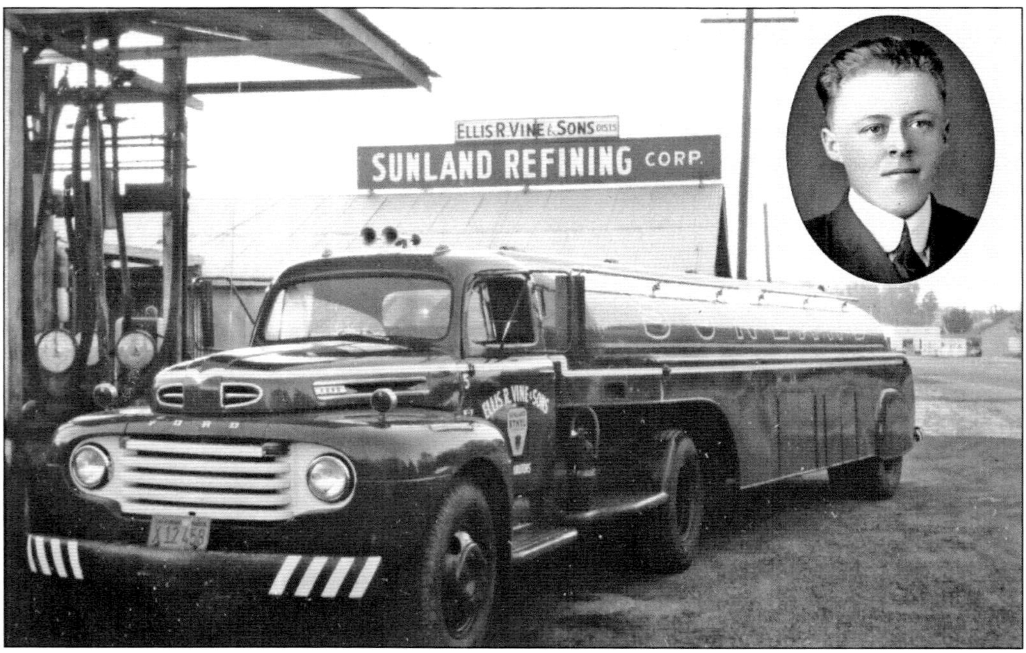

E. R. Vine and Sons Petroleum Distributorship started in 1933 on Railroad Avenue. Ellis R. "E. R." Vine (insert) served in the Canadian Air Force before he came to Ceres from Minnesota. He died at age 71 on March 6, 1970. (Risse Keys.)

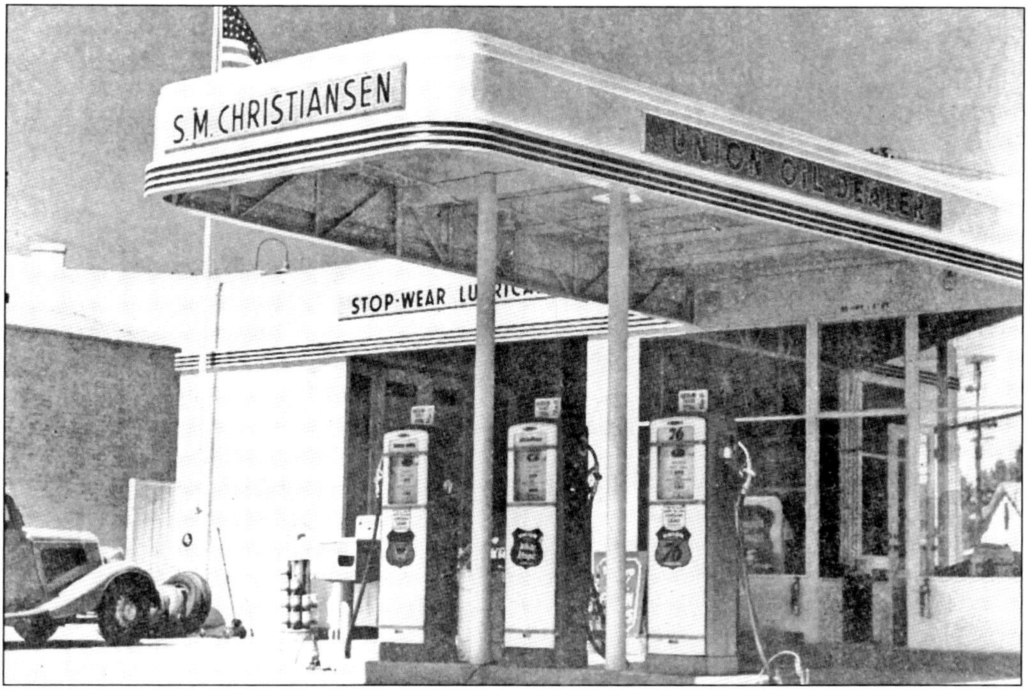

S. M. "Scottie" Christiansen ran this small service station during World War II and after. It was located at the corner of Highway 99 and Fourth Street on the site that later held a Shell station. It was just south of Mert's Grocery. Christiansen was an influential member of the community and served as mayor from 1939 to 1942. (*Ceres Courier.*)

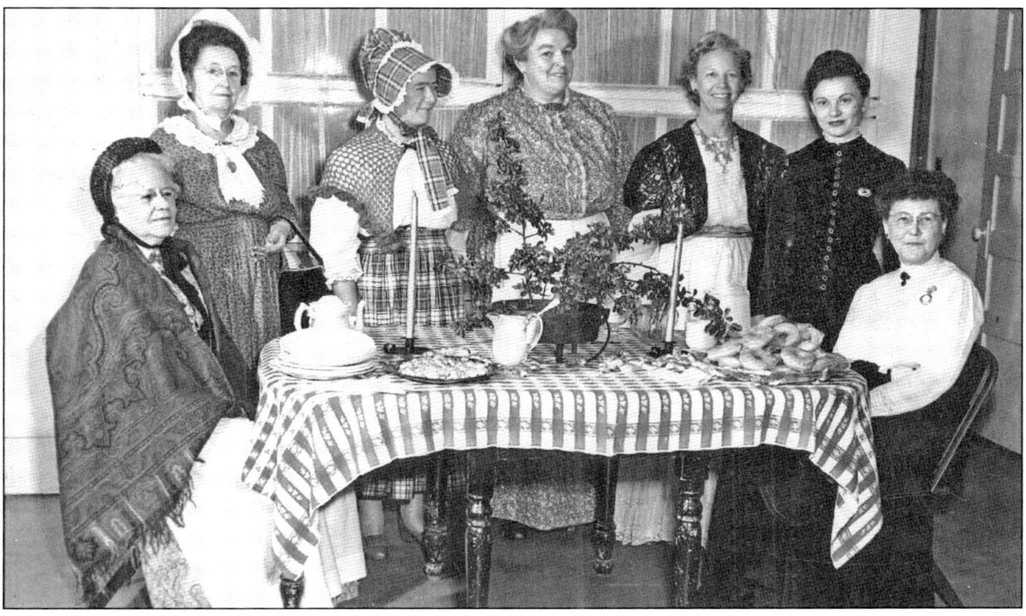

The Ceres Garden Club ladies gathered for this 1948 photograph. Club members, from left to right, are Byrdelia Moffet, Flora Aspinall, Mary Helen Turner Service, Marguerite Graham, Florence Woodworth, ? Norwood, and Jennie Whitmore Caswell. (Mildred Lucas.)

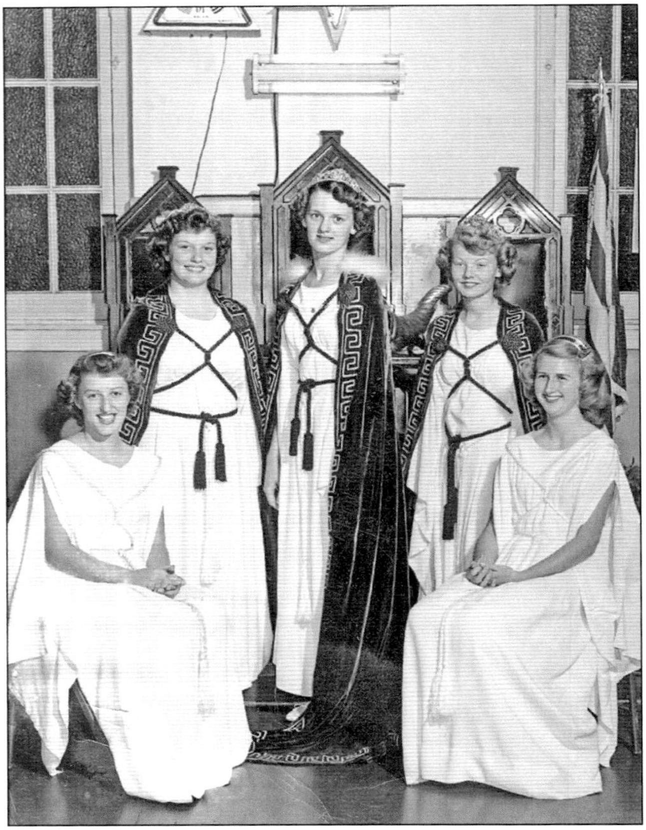

These five young Ceres ladies were installed as officers in the Ceres Bethel 171 of Job's Daughters at the Ceres Masonic Lodge *c.* 1950. The lodge is part of Eastern Star, which is affiliated with the Masons. (*Ceres Courier.*)

Gus and John Pallios opened Richland Market at the corner of Evans and Richland in 1951. The brothers built their business through a guiding principal that customers were more important than any potential profit. On the first day of business, the store reaped $75 in receipts; the next day, $110. It later expanded, as shown here in 1957. In October 1960, the brothers moved the market to Whitmore and Moffet Roads in the building housing Richland Ace Hardware. The Pallioses constructed Richland Shopping Center in 1967 but did not move the store to its current location until 1971. (Richland Market.)

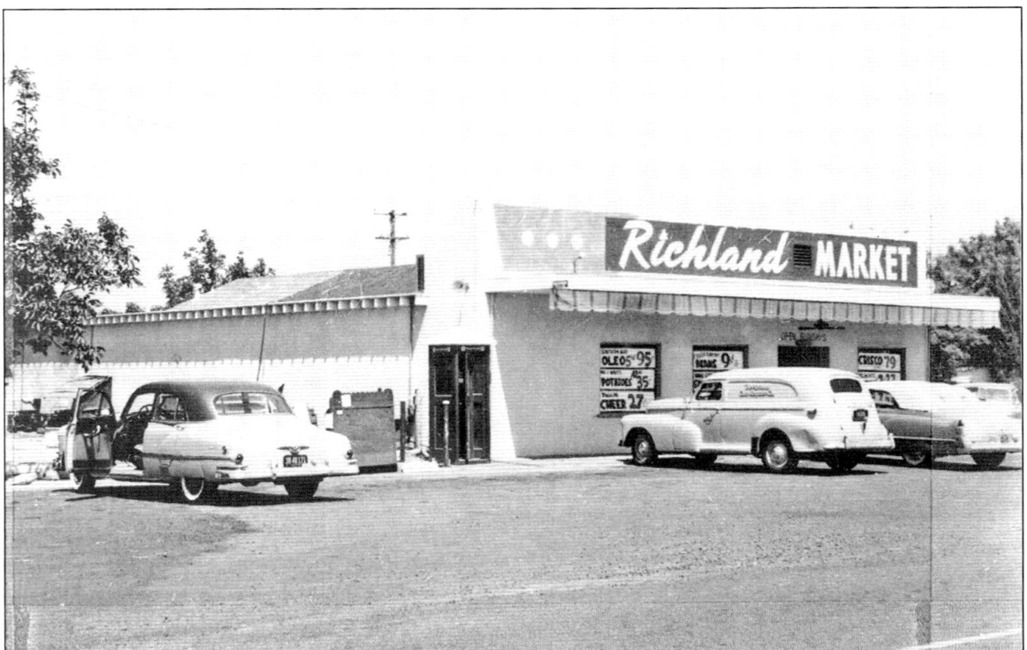

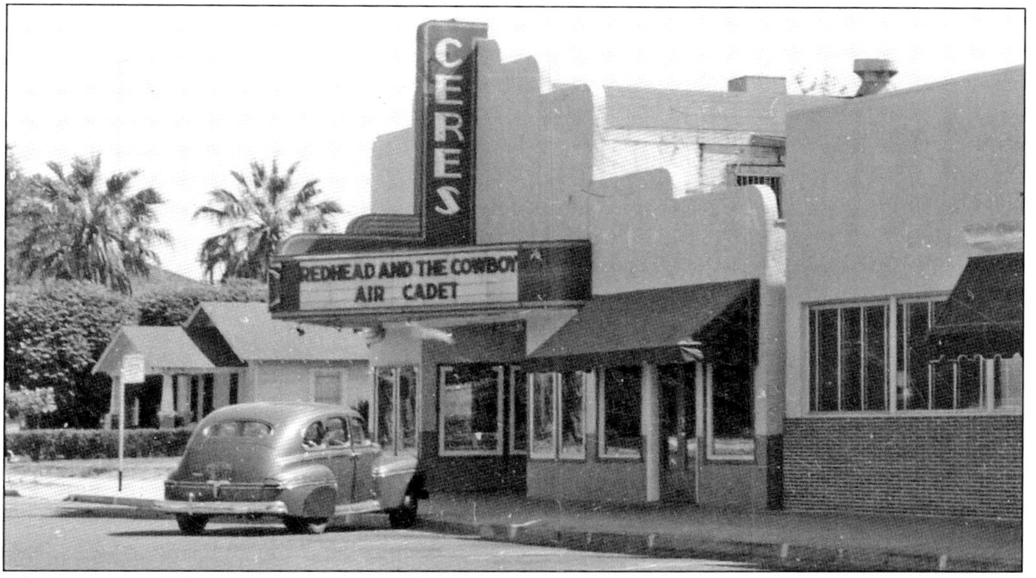

The marquee of the one-screen Ceres Theater on Fourth Street advertises the showing of *Redhead and the Cowboy* and *Ace Cadet*, both released in 1951. The building opposite Wells Fargo Bank is used today as a church. The Ceres post office was located at right. (Ceres Historical Society.)

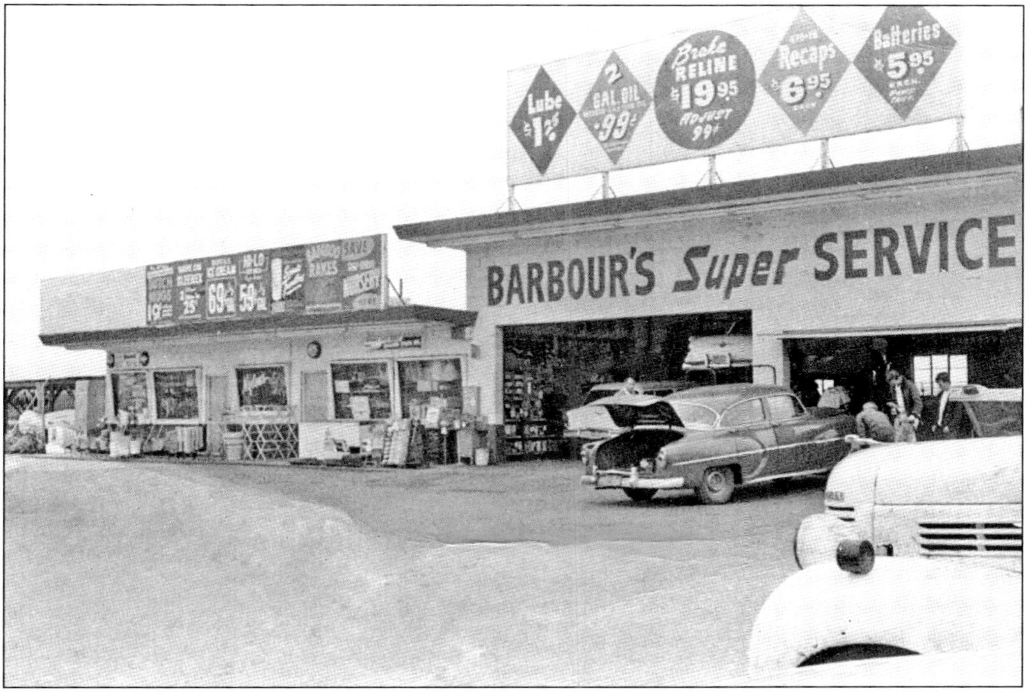

Ceres residents have found Barbour's Save Center, at the corner of Whitmore Avenue and Mitchell Road, to be a great place to pick up grocery items. In early 1960, a person could have his or her car fixed here as well as pick up a half-gallon of ice cream for 69¢ or two boxes of Kleenex for 25¢. Today Boyette's Petroleum operates the station, with the old auto shop now closed and used as the entrance to the store. (Dennis Barbour.)

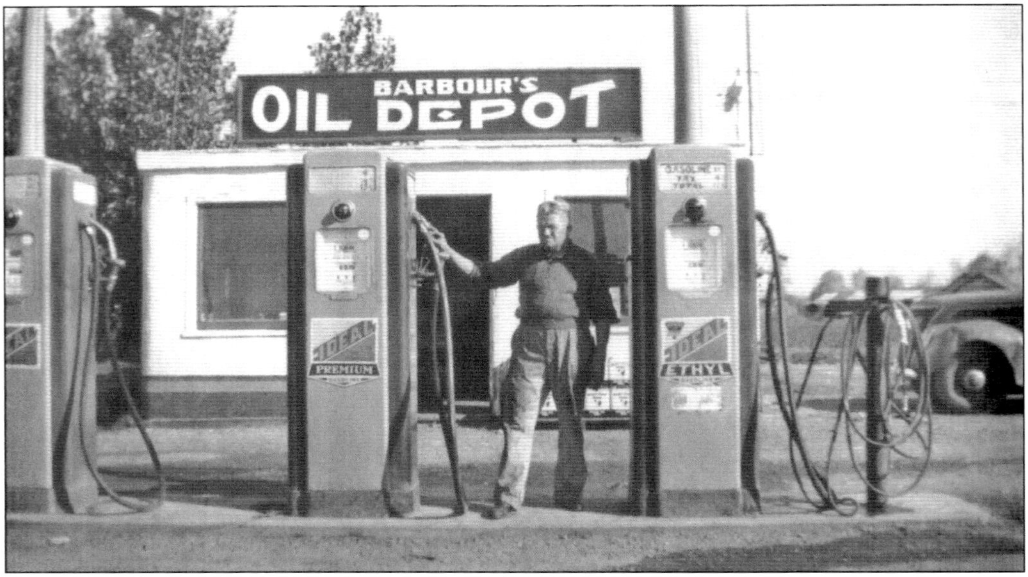

Homer Barbour (1897–1966) opened Barbour's Oil Depot on Highway 99 north of Whitmore Avenue and south of Richland Avenue. Widening of Highway 99 meant the station had to go, so he relocated the business to the southwest corner of Mitchell Road and Whitmore Avenue. (Dennis Barbour.)

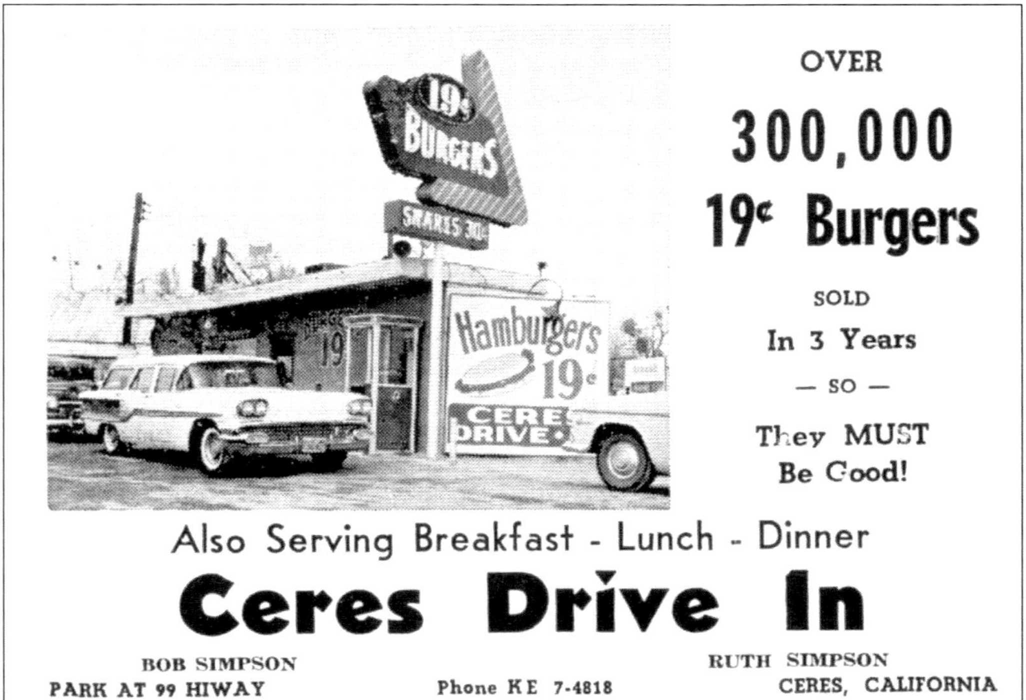

Bob and Ruth Simpson served 76,680 hamburgers in 1955 at the Ceres Drive-In, or Burger 19, at the bargain rate of six for $1. By their third year, they had served 107,268 burgers. The hangout closed December 1, 1962, when the building and land were needed for right-of-way for the Highway 99 expansion. This is an advertisement placed in the *Courier.* (Ruth Simpson.)

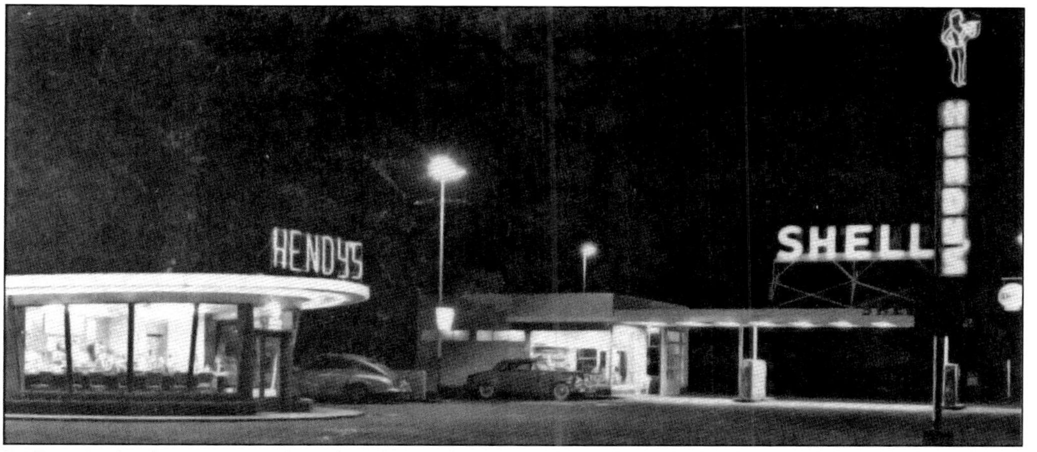

Before the highway was widened in the early 1960s, this combination of businesses served the west side near the railroad tracks at Highway 99 and Hackett Road—Hendy's Drive-In and Doerksen's Shell station. Hendy's was owned by Bill Henderson and featured carhops. Bill Doerksen owned the filling station. The buildings came down when the freeway was widened. This image appeared in an ad in the 1952 Ceres High School yearbook, the *Cereal.* (Ruth Simpson.)

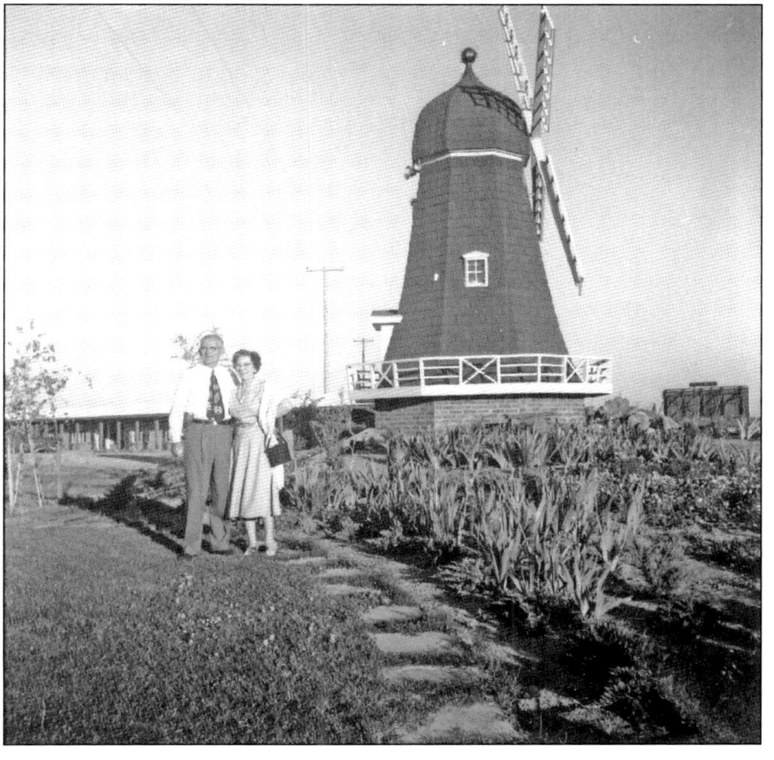

Park and Jeanette Stokes were the creators of the Blue Mill Motel, seen here in 1954. Park was a native of Denmark and wanted to build something different after they came to the Ceres-Modesto area from Pennsylvania in the early 1950s. They also constructed a restaurant, Alberti's, next door. The building is now used as offices for the California Canning Peach Advisory Council. (Ceres Historical Society.)

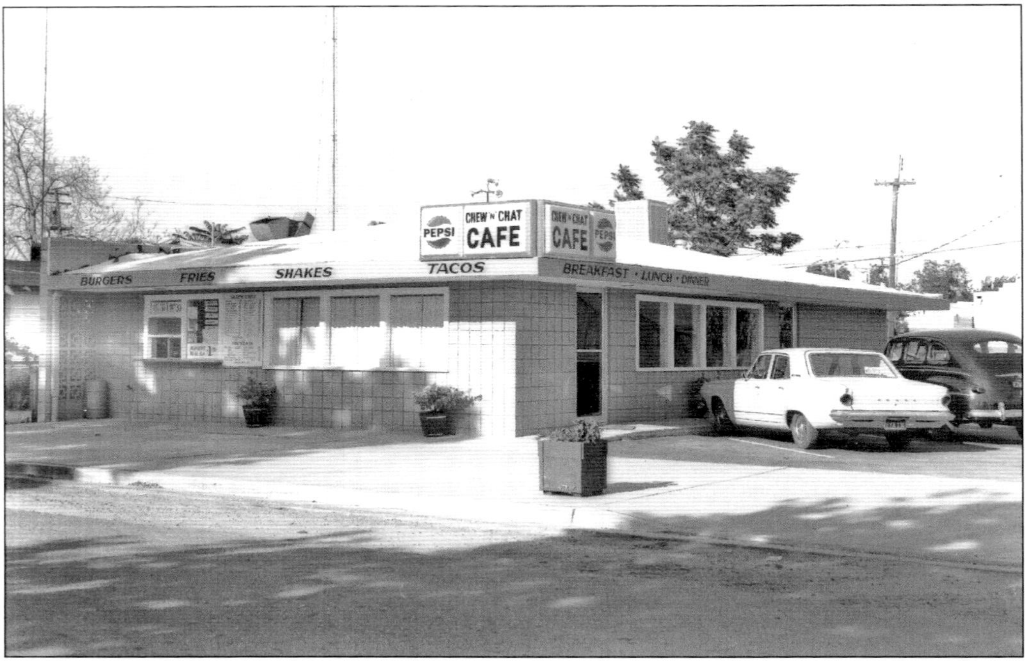

When Bob and Ruth Simpson were forced to abandon Burger 19 in 1962, they built the Chew 'N Chat on Third Street east of Whitmore Park. The site was the home of George and Lizzie Shrider from the 1910s to the 1940s. After the Shriders' deaths, the house was rented out for a few years but then razed because of deteriorating condition. The Chew 'N Chat operated from April 1963 to November 1, 1977. The building later became a Chinese restaurant and then Silva's Family Restaurant until a fire gutted the building. The Turlock Irrigation District office now sits on the lot. (Ruth Simpson.)

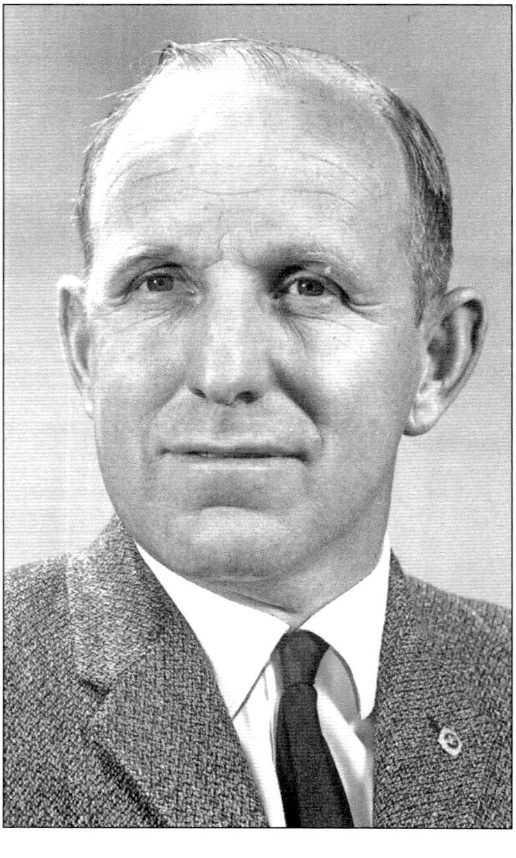

Homer Vilas, a 1938 Ceres High School graduate, served on the Ceres Union High School board. He is credited with the idea of a school swimming pool and was instrumental in its fundraising. Business partner Earl Brown also assisted in the endeavor. Both also contributed the manual labor and loaned equipment for the construction. (Steve Vilas.)

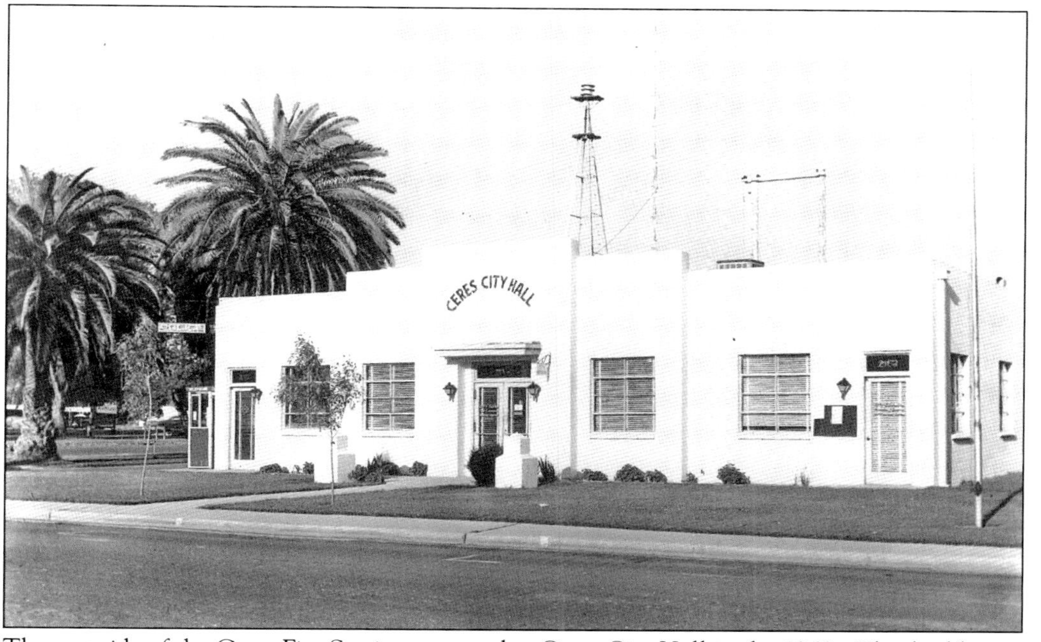

The east side of the Ceres Fire Station was used as Ceres City Hall in the 1960s. This building is gone now and in its place is Ceres Fire Station no. 1 at the northwest corner of Third and North Streets. (City of Ceres.)

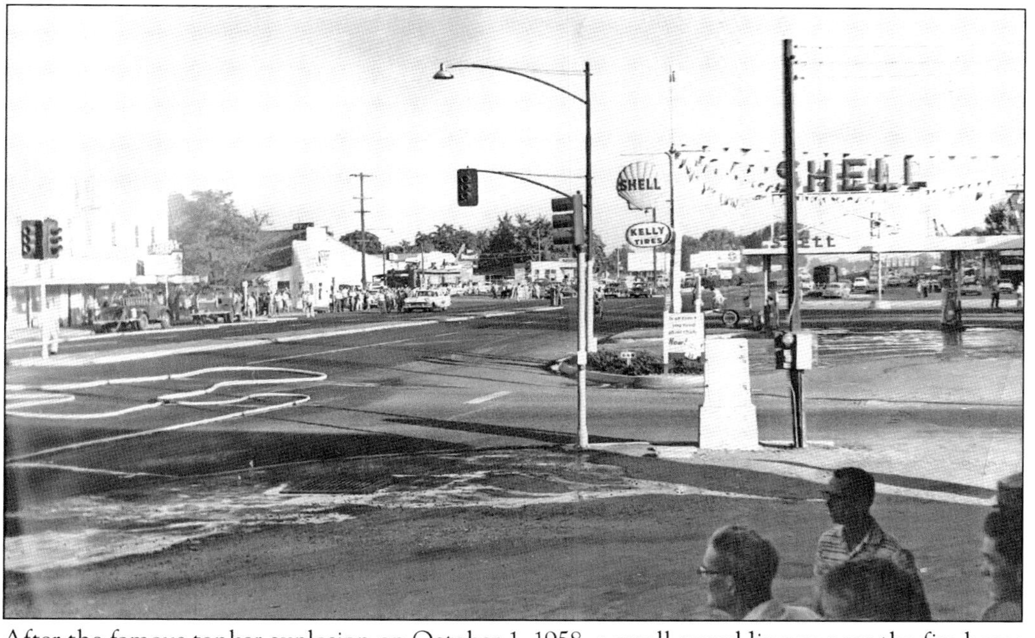

After the famous tanker explosion on October 1, 1958, a small crowd lingers near the fire hoses and water on Highway 99 looking south toward Keyes. The buildings at left sit immediately south of Fourth Street. On the right, Hendy's Shell station sits between Hackett Road and Central Avenue. Ceres Drive-In (Burger 19) is visible beneath the extended traffic signal. This vista was wiped away when the state widened Highway 99 in the early 1960s. (City of Ceres.)

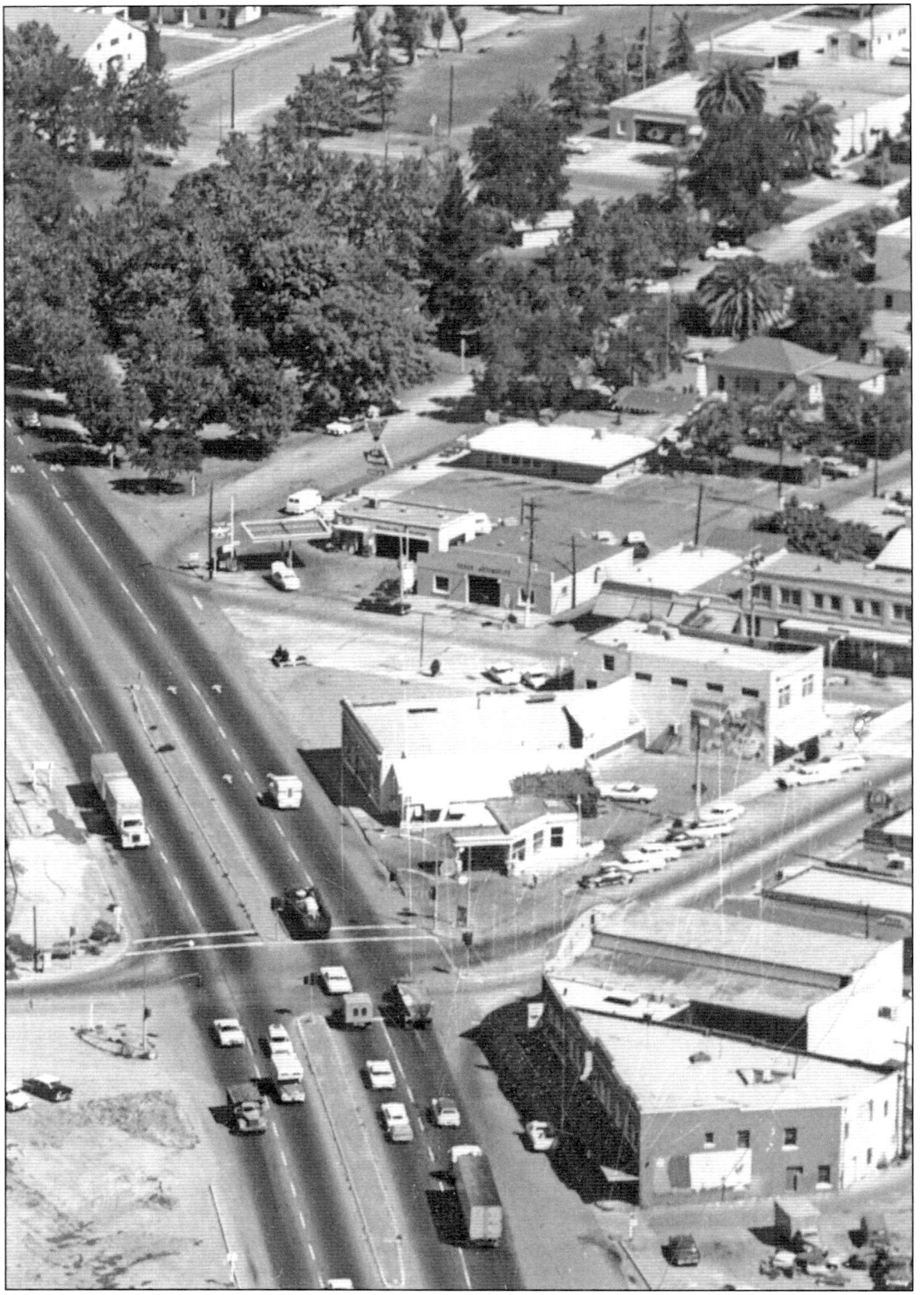

This aerial photograph shows downtown Ceres and Highway 99 in 1962. The intersection of Highway 99 and Fourth Street was controlled by traffic signals. A mural on the two-story IOOF Hall is visible in the middle right. Whitmore Park is the tree-covered lot at upper left. Another city park at the top of picture was later replaced by city hall. The small service station at the corner of Fourth Street and Highway 99 as well as the grocery store behind it were removed and replaced by Shell and Terrible Herbst gas stations. (City of Ceres.)

Ceres has always enjoyed its parades and this one in 1965 had Fire Chief Truman Showen and Bob Bowman pulling an antique fire hose cart. Bowman was a building inspector and member of the Ceres city council. Riding behind them in the antique car are Art Phillips and Les Siebright. Al Stohler is riding on a trailer. The retail buildings in the background on Lawrence Street were individual businesses but were later connected to become Alfonso's Mexican Restaurant. (Truman Showen.)

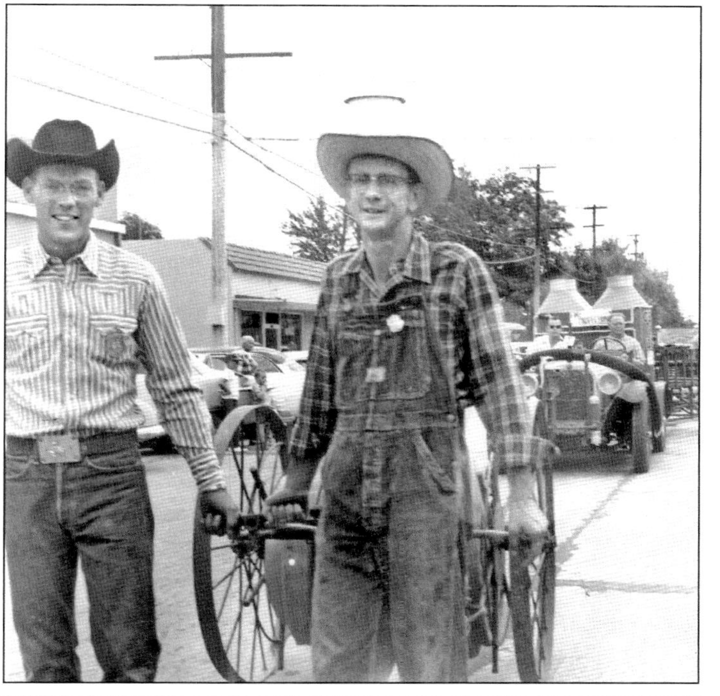

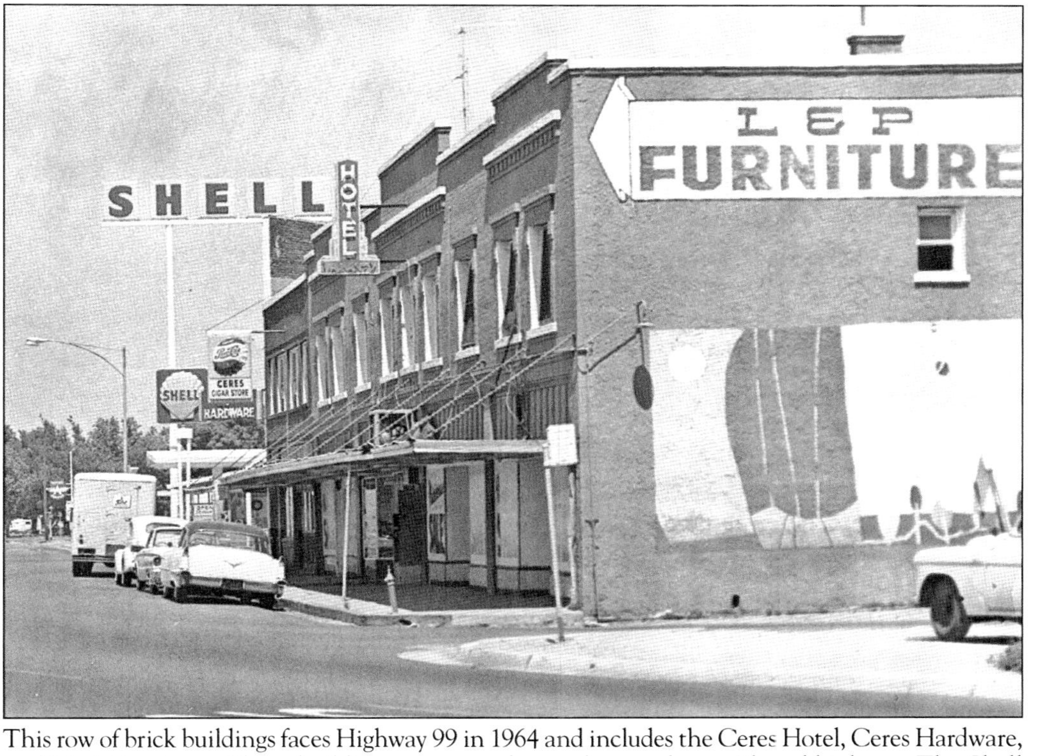

This row of brick buildings faces Highway 99 in 1964 and includes the Ceres Hotel, Ceres Hardware, and L&P Furniture. These buildings were razed to make way for a widened highway. The Shell station sign in the background was changed a few years ago to Valero. (City of Ceres.)

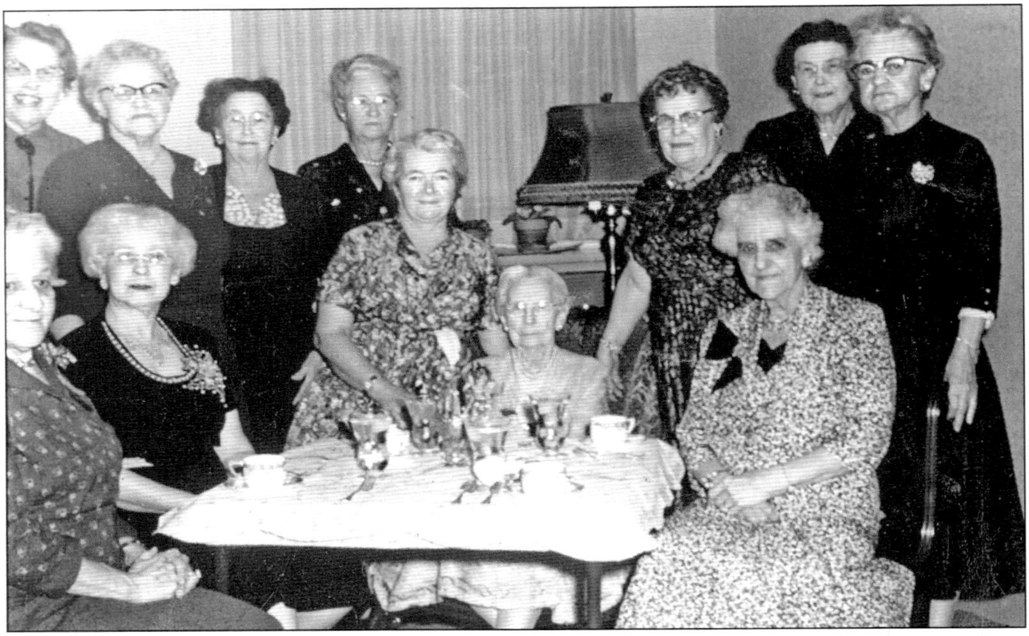

Several important ladies from Ceres gather in this December 1957 photograph. They are, from left to right (seated) Florence Gondring, Lynda Sperry, Mary Turner Service, Flora Service, and Mrs. Collins (mother-in-law of Hollywood director Frank Capra); (standing) unidentified, Mrs. Arthur Harris, Mrs. Aspinall, Mollie Lander, unidentified, Jennie Whitmore Caswell, and Sylvia Malin. (Marian Sanders.)

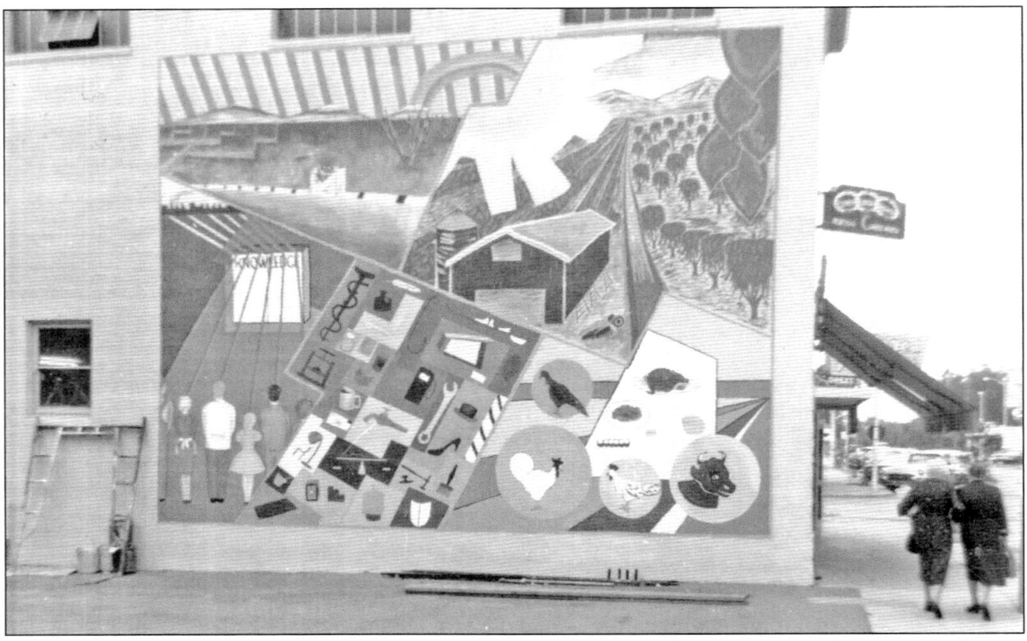

The south wall of the Odd Fellows building is decorated with a large mural depicting Ceres' agricultural roots during the Paint Up Festival in May 1961. A crowd of about 500 volunteers painted other businesses. This mural remains to this date. (Ceres Historical Society.)

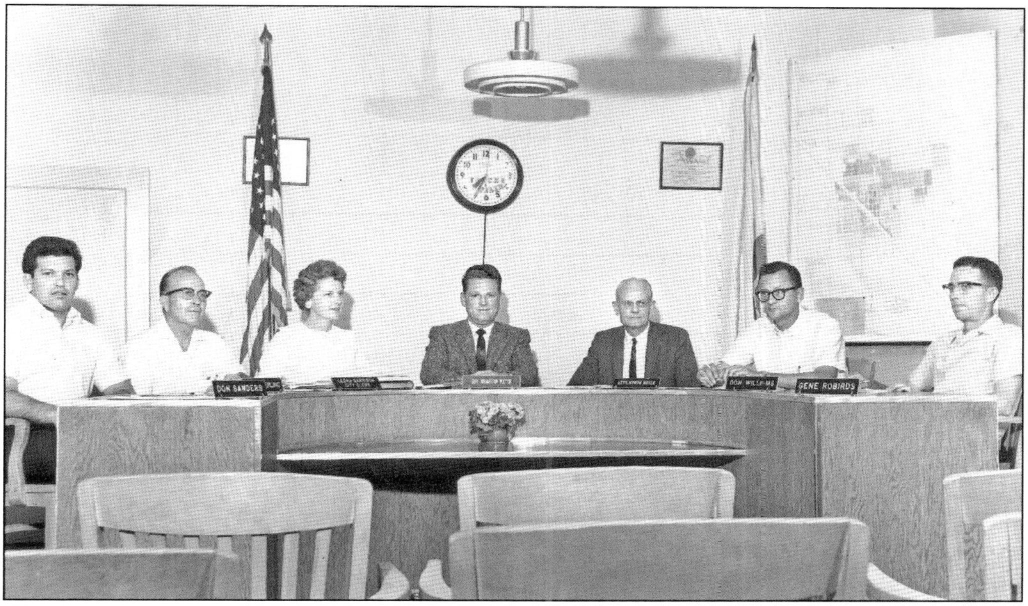

The Ceres city council in the 1960s includes, from left to right, Councilmen Don Sanders and Chub Sterling, City Clerk Leona Garrison, Mayor Guy Wharton, City Attorney Myron Moyles, and Councilmen Don Williams and Gene Robirds. (City of Ceres.)

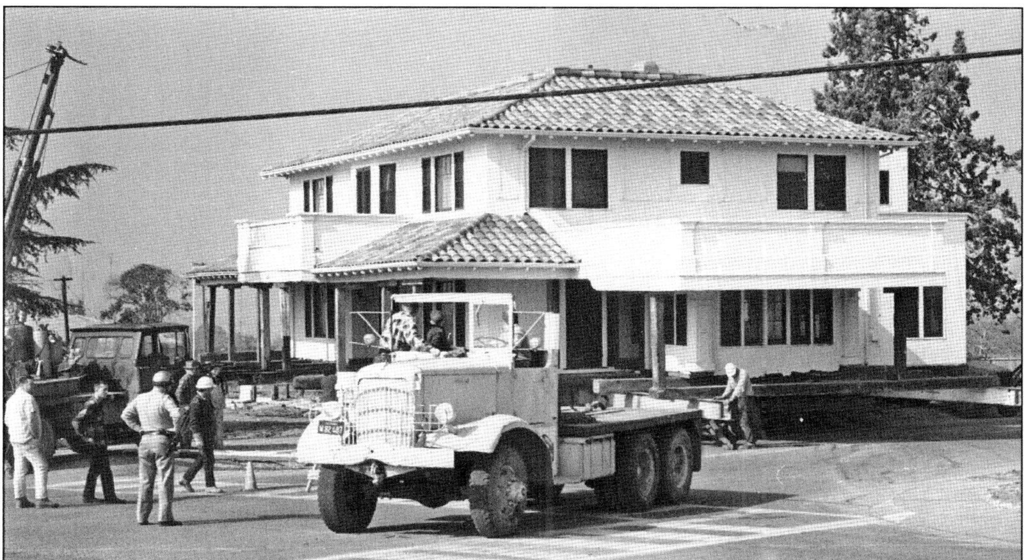

The two-story Fred W. Moffet residence was built in 1919 at the northwest corner of Whitmore Avenue and Moffet Road. On February 5, 1964, the landmark residence of the founder of Superior Fruit Ranch was moved from its perch to 2704 Mitchell Road, where it was converted to the Missourian Restaurant by Bill and Verda Brumley. Today the house is home to La Cascada Mexican Restaurant. The vacated spot was filled by the Peach Tree Restaurant, now the My Garden Cafe. (Ceres Historical Society.)

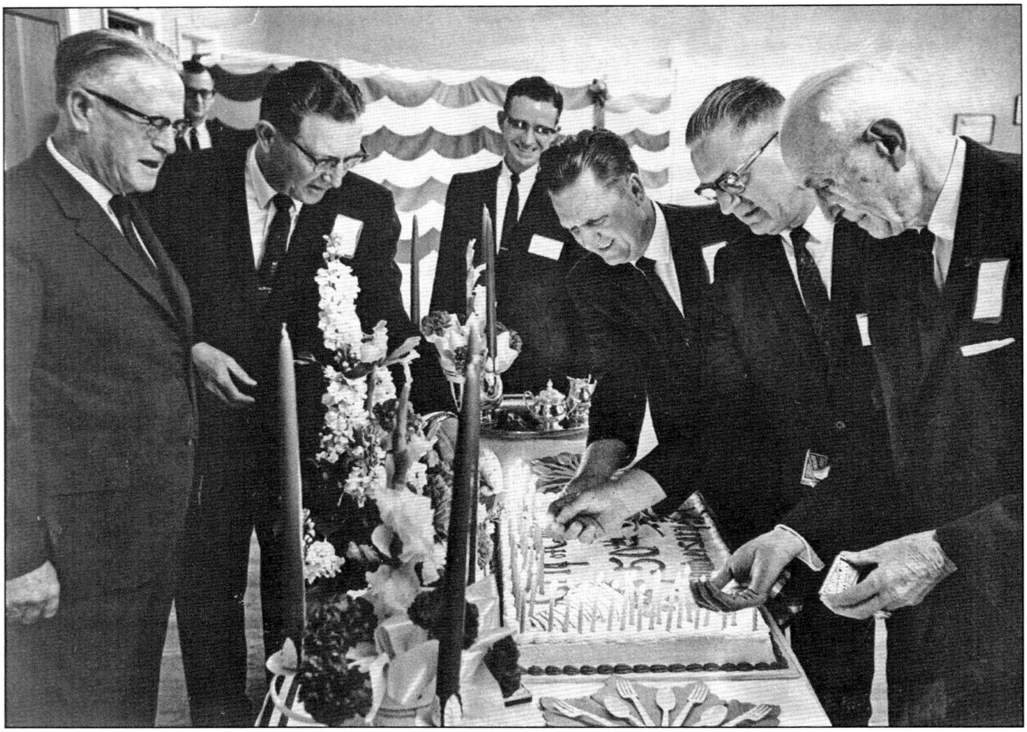

On February 24, 1968, Ceres city council members and past mayors light candles on a cake celebrating the 50th anniversary of the incorporation of the city of Ceres. They are, from left to right, Charles Whitmore, former mayor Claude McKnight, Mayor Gene Robirds, former mayor Guy Wharton, and former mayors Ches Ludden and Walter White. (City of Ceres.)

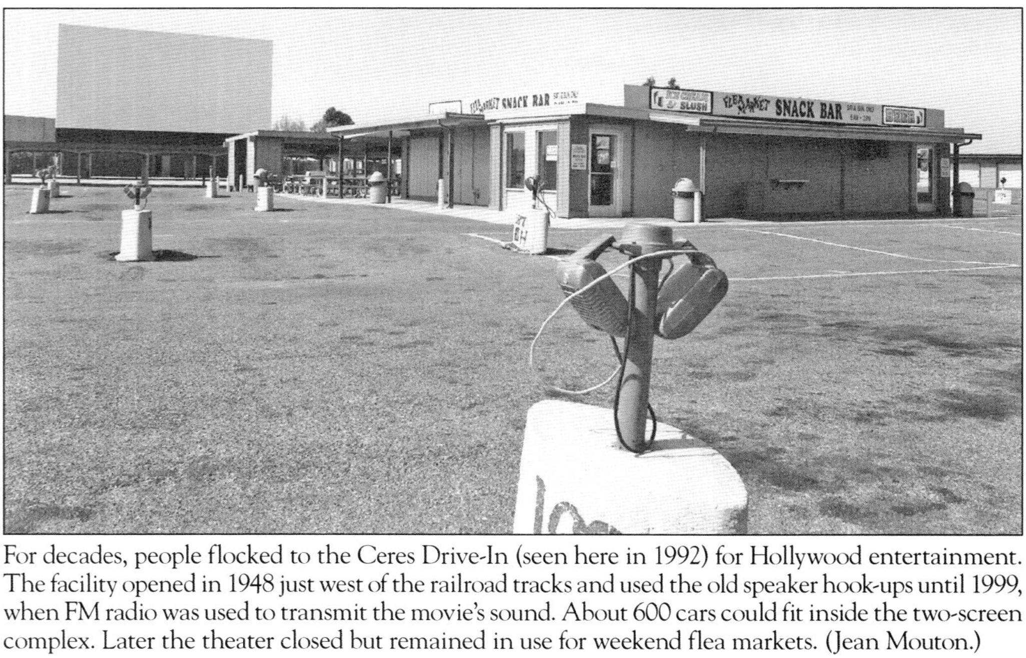

For decades, people flocked to the Ceres Drive-In (seen here in 1992) for Hollywood entertainment. The facility opened in 1948 just west of the railroad tracks and used the old speaker hook-ups until 1999, when FM radio was used to transmit the movie's sound. About 600 cars could fit inside the two-screen complex. Later the theater closed but remained in use for weekend flea markets. (Jean Mouton.)

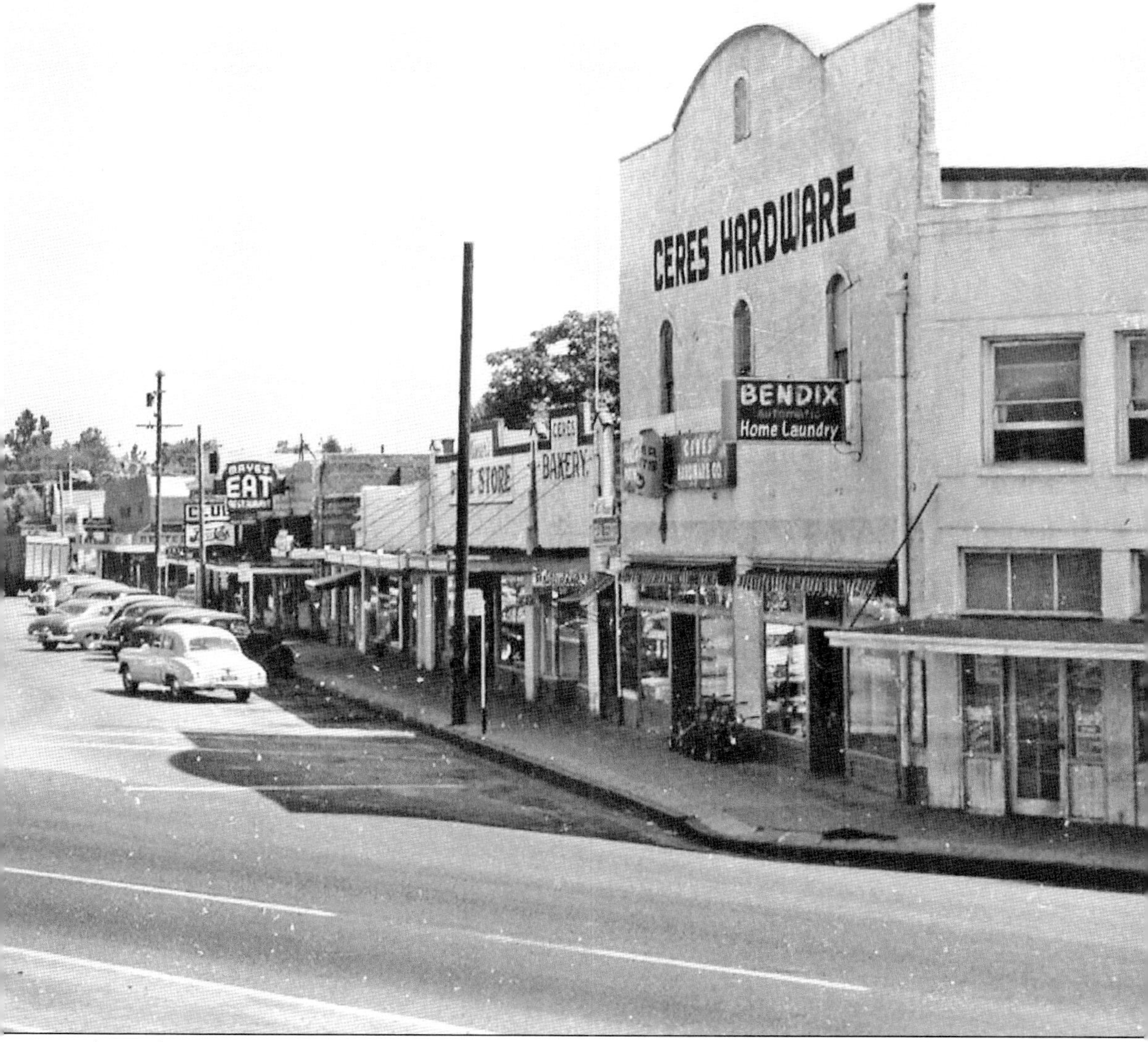

In the mid-1960s, Ceres Hardware dominates the intersection of Fourth Street and old Highway 99. The store facade closely resembles its former self, the Collins and Warner hall. (Ceres Historical Society.)

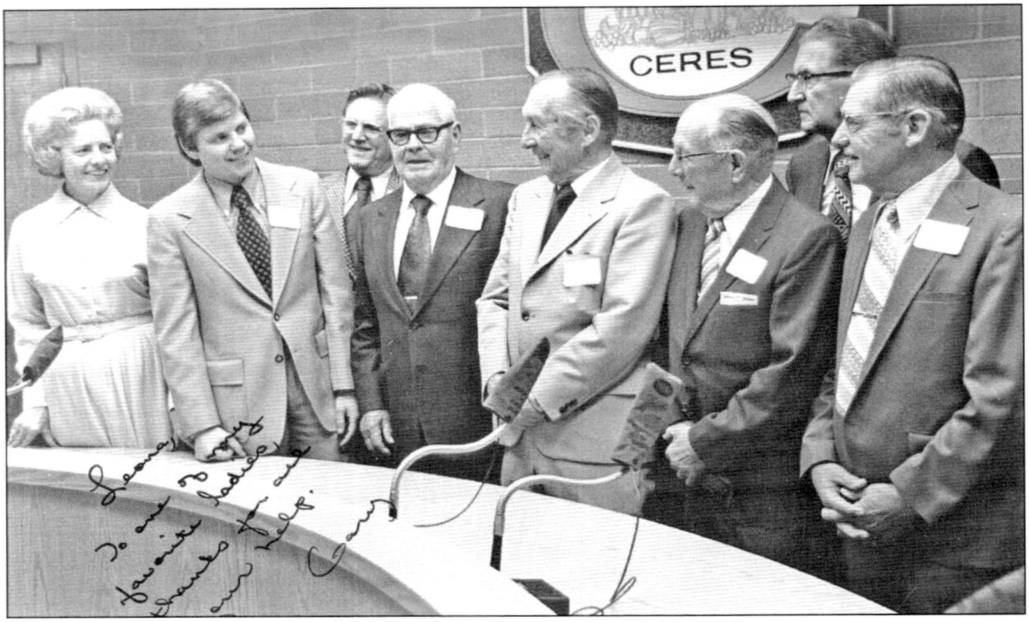

The dedication of the new Ceres City Hall in 1976 brought together former and current city leaders. A youthful Mayor Gary Condit (second from left) posed with City Clerk Leona Garrison, ex-mayor Guy Wharton (in back), ex-mayor Henry Kline, Councilman Anthony Vincent (who also owned the Vincent Water Company), former city clerk Floyd "Shorty" Johnson, ex-mayor Claude McKnight, and City Councilman Art Rohde. (City of Ceres.)

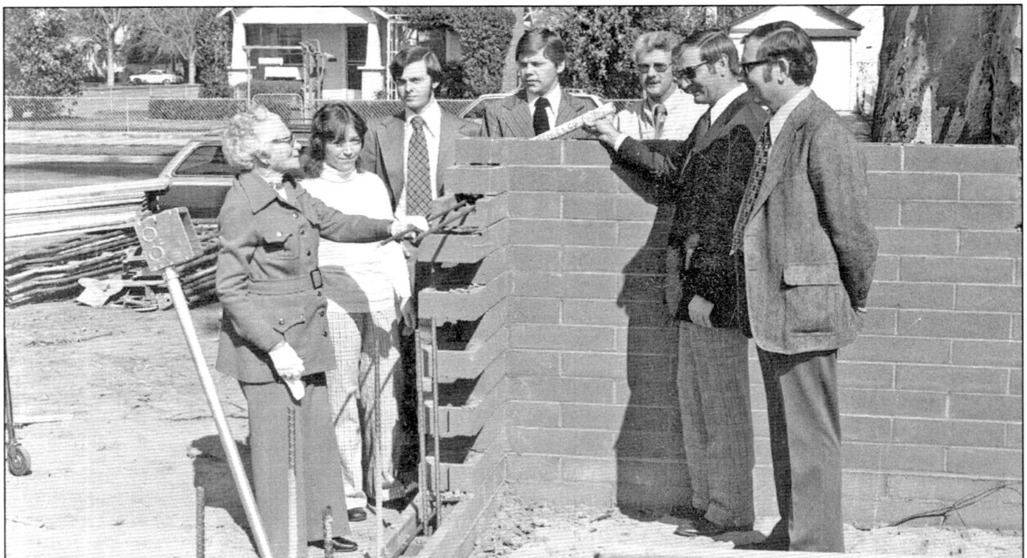

On February 25, 1974, city officials gathered with Frances Gondring to conduct a cornerstone ceremony for a new $455,900 city hall/library complex. Frances donated $27,000 in the name of sister Florence Gondring to build a larger library. Gathered here were Gondring, Ceres librarian Linda Rowland, Councilmen Steve Wright, Gary Condit, and Robert Bowman, Mayor Michael Scates, and Vice-Mayor Ted Humphries. (Verna Nelson.)

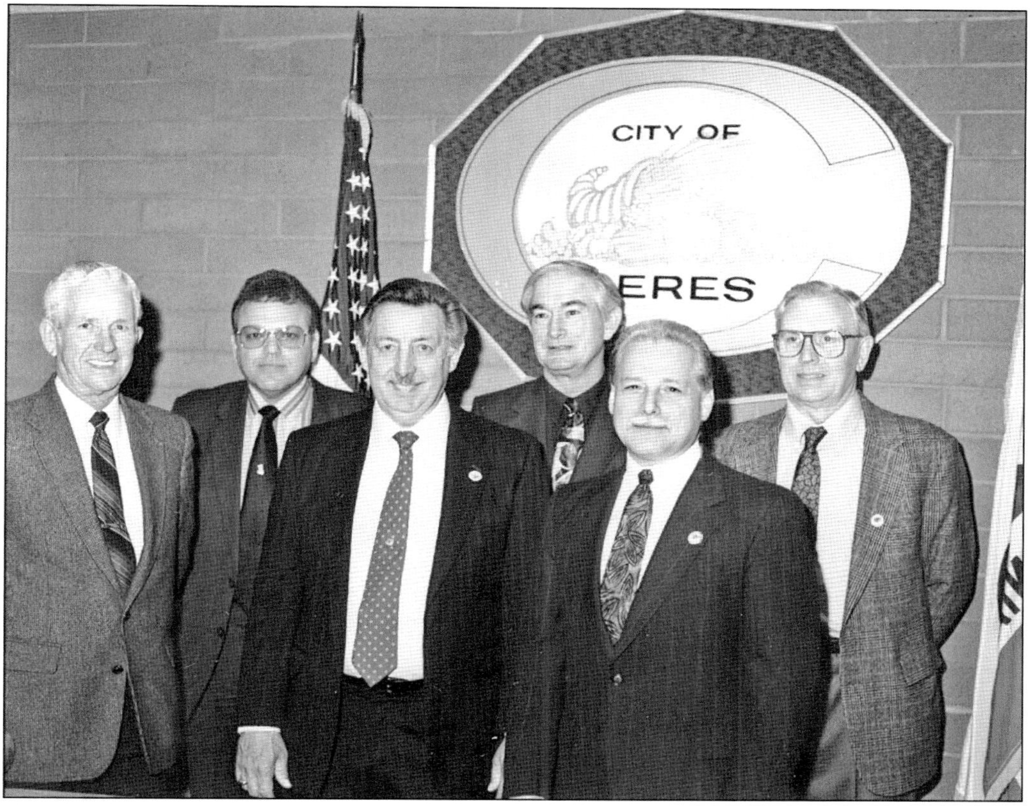

The 75th anniversary of the city of Ceres in 1993 drew together these six men who all served as mayor. They are, from left to right, Gene Robirds, Louie Arrollo, Richard McBride, Jim Delhart, Sal Cannella, and Ted Humphreys. McBride was the current mayor. (City of Ceres.)

Mayors of Ceres & Terms of Office

1). Dr. S.W. Cartwright	1918	15). Ted Humphries	1976-80
2). Vaughn D. Whitmore	1918-30	16). Sal Cannella	1980-83
3). J. Wayne Baldridge	1930-38	17). Brian Carlin	1983-85
4). Claude McKnight	1938-39	18). James "Jim" Delhart	1985-87
5). S.M. Christiansen	1939-42	19). Louis Arrollo	1987-90
6). John A. Moffet	1942-46	20). Richard G. McBride	1990-93
7). Henry Kline	1946-50	21). Barbara Hinton	1993-97
8). Carl Barham	1950-54	22). Leo Havener	1997-98
9). Chesley D. Ludden	1954-56	23). Eric Ingwerson	1998-99
10). Walter White	1956-64	24). Louie Arrollo	1999-2001
11). Guy D. Wharton	1964-66	25). Eric Ingwerson	2001-03
12). Gene Robirds	1966-70	26). DeLinda Moore	2003-05
13). Michael Scates	1970-74	27). Anthony Cannella	2005-
14). Gary A. Condit	1974-76		

Since incorporation, 25 residents of Ceres have served as mayor, but there were 27 terms because Eric Ingwerson and Louie Arrollo each served two non-consecutive terms. (*Ceres Courier.*)

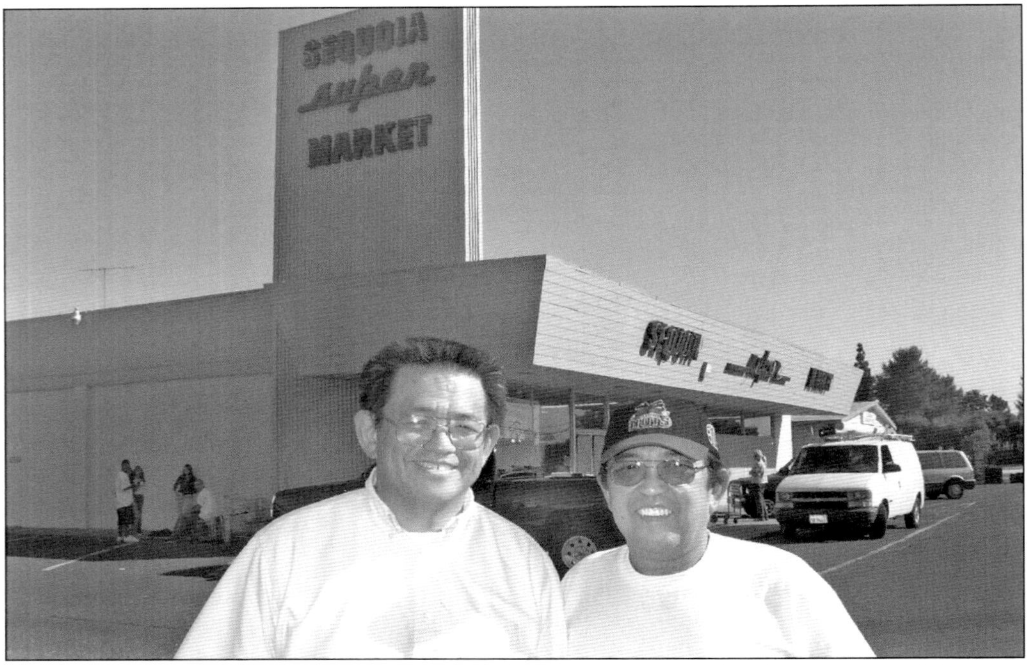

Brothers Frank and Dickie Chong ended an era in Ceres when they closed their Sequoia Market in September 2005 after 50 years of continuous operation. The store was built in 1955 by their parents, Frank and Mable Chong, and served a population of about 3,100 people. Truly a hometown business, Sequoia Market delivered food purchases to shut-ins and gave many Ceres High School students their first jobs. The Chongs also went out of their way to support community causes. (*Ceres Courier.*)

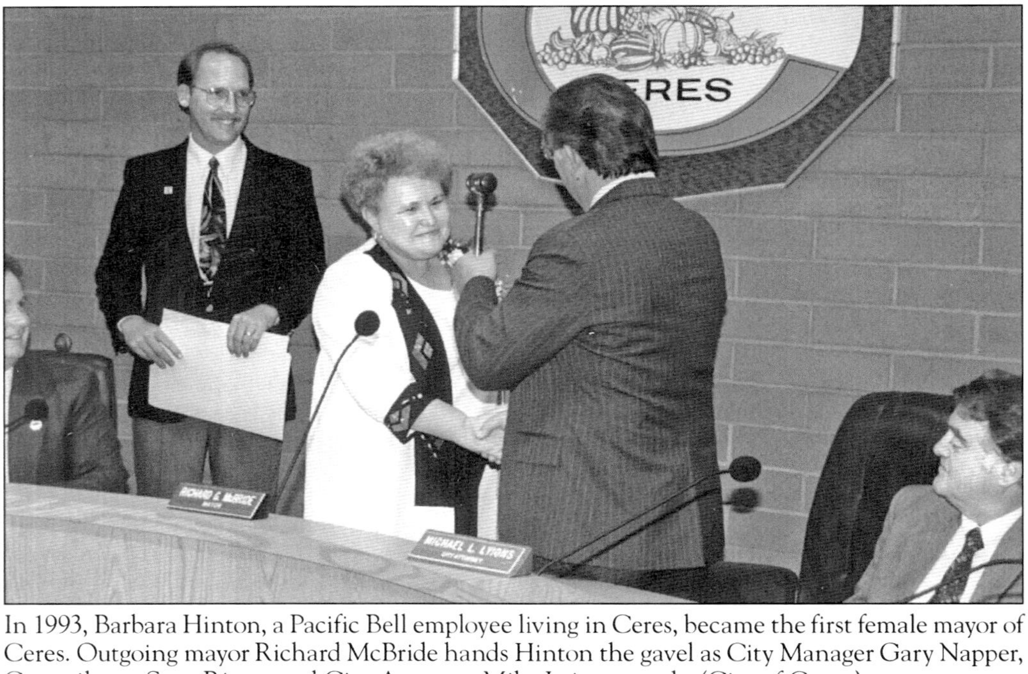

In 1993, Barbara Hinton, a Pacific Bell employee living in Ceres, became the first female mayor of Ceres. Outgoing mayor Richard McBride hands Hinton the gavel as City Manager Gary Napper, Councilman Stan Risen, and City Attorney Mike Lyions watch. (City of Ceres.)

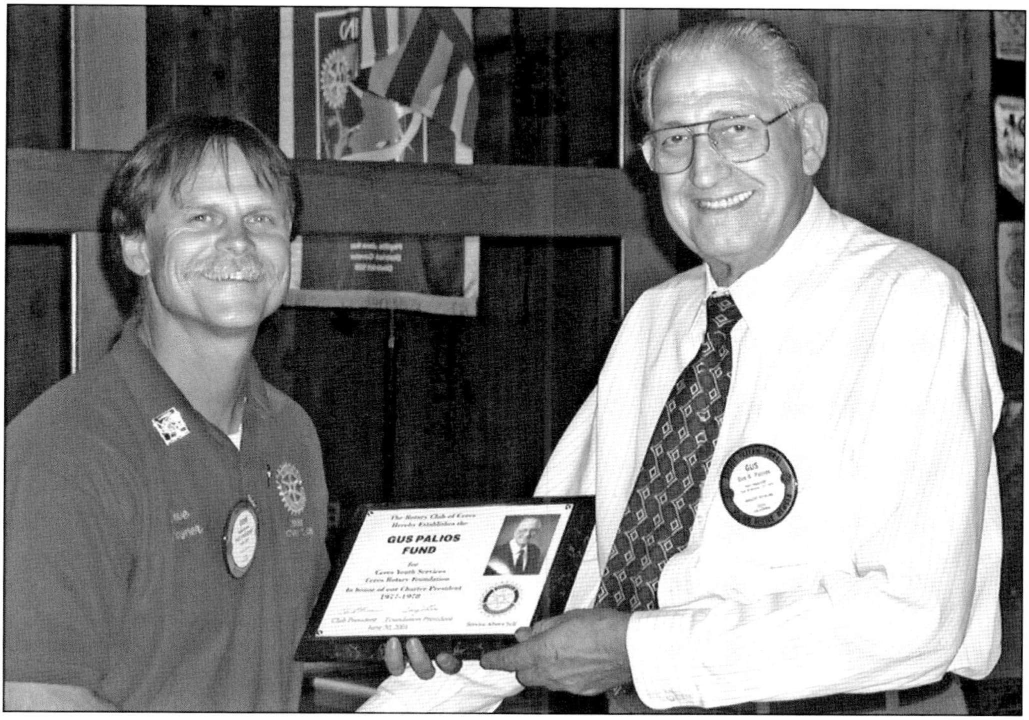

Businessman Gus Pallios (right) was a key figure in the community. Pallios, the charter president of the Ceres Rotary Club (1977–1978), was honored in 2007 with the naming of the Gus Pallios Fund for Ceres Youth Services. Handing him a commemorative plaque is club president Dave Hosmer. (*Ceres Courier.*)

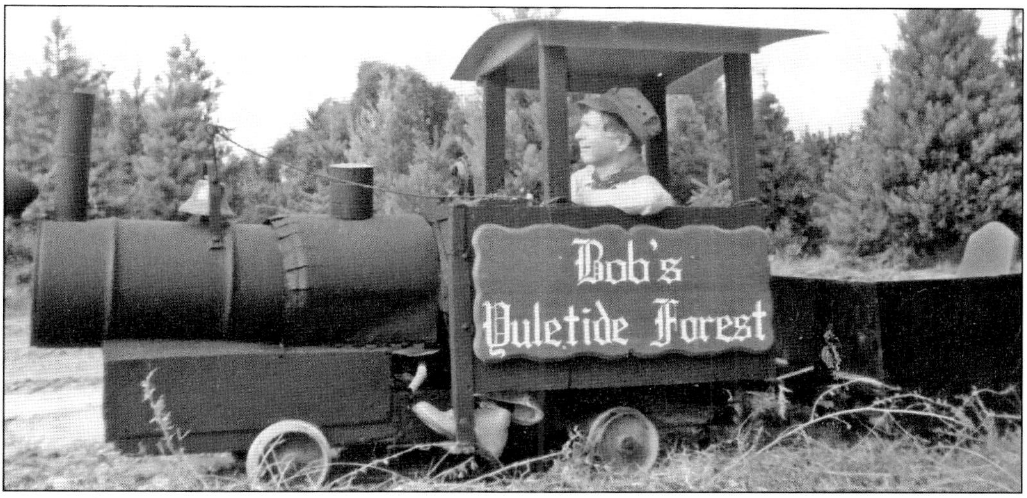

During the 1960s, 1970s, and 1980s, Bob Jorgensen enjoyed treating children to rides on this small homemade train at Bob's Yuletide Forest on the Mitchell Road property of his parents, Homer and Ruth Jorgensen. Bob suffered from cerebral palsy and the tree farm was a way for him to remain active. In 1962, the Jorgensens planted 7,000 Christmas trees shortly after Bob graduated from high school. Bob devoted half of his life to the farm until the disease slowed him down and led to his death at age 45 in 1990. The tree farm closed in 1995. (Mark Perra.)

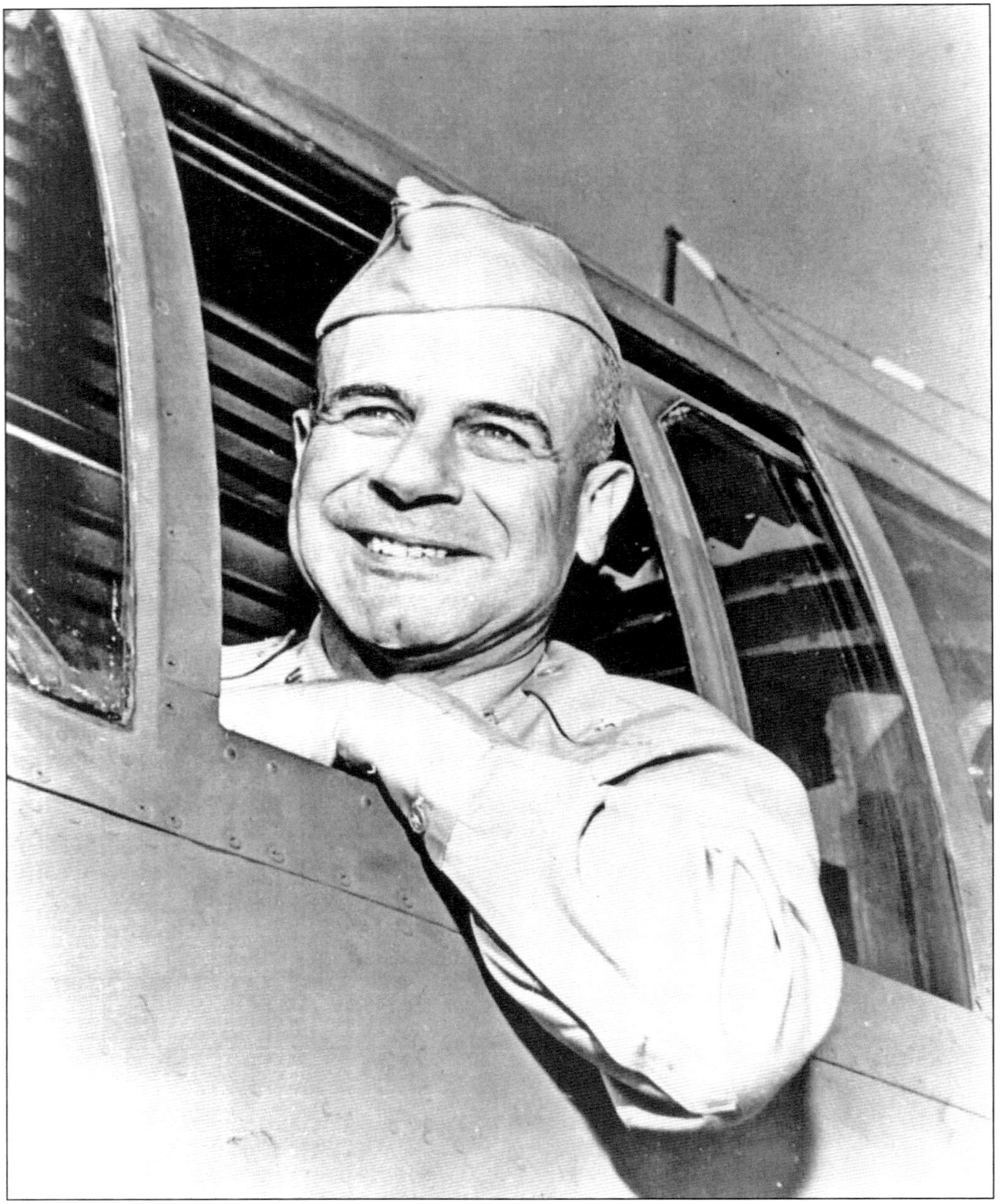

Jimmy Doolittle, the World War II hero who led a daring bombing raid on Tokyo after Pearl Harbor was attacked, was intimately acquainted with Ceres. Prior to World War I, the Bay Area native spent summers working at his uncle Ralph's candy shop on Lawrence Street. Ralph C. Doolittle came to Ceres from Oakland after the 1906 San Francisco earthquake. He operated a 22-acre dairy farm and in 1909 built a confectionery on the corner of Lawrence and Third Streets (where Jack's Texaco sits today). He later sold novelty items, books, stationery, and toys. Jimmy spent time working in the store and became known among the townsfolk. His April 18, 1942, raid won him national fame as a war hero. (Author's collection.)

Seven

THE FAMOUS AND THE POLITICAL

Extraordinary people have come from Ceres and some very important people have dropped by from time to time. Ceres gave song leader Cliff Barrows—the internationally famous emcee of Billy Graham's televised Christian broadcasts since the 1950s—his spiritual upbringing. In preparation for the 1948 Modesto Crusade, Graham visited the Barrows homestead in rural Ceres where the Modesto Manifesto was hammered out with Barrows and George Beverly Shea. The compact provided the moral structure to keep Graham's ministry free from sexual and financial corruption. Also raised in First Baptist Church of Ceres was Ed Hayes, who became president of Denver Theological Seminary.

In 1967, Medrick and Ruth Perra opened their home to student Zalmay Khalilzad of Afghanistan and taught him about American values and politics as he attended Ceres High School. Khalilzad served as the U.S. ambassador to Afghanistan, to Iraq, and to the United Nations under Pres. George W. Bush. His knowledge of Iraq helped President Bush deal with Saddam Hussein during the Iraq War. Also, former Ceres police officer George Piro interrogated Hussein for the FBI after his capture. Fresh from Oklahoma, Gary A. Condit made Ceres home in 1967. While attending college in 1973, Condit became mayor of Ceres, years before he became a popular congressman. Condit's congressional career came to a grinding halt when national media linked him romantically to missing intern Chandra Levy of Modesto. The scandal brought droves of national TV reporters to Ceres and was the biggest cable TV news story of 2001 until the September 11 terrorist attacks. Other notable politicians from Ceres included two state Food and Agriculture directors in Clare Berryhill and Henry Voss. Clare's sons, Tom and Bill, made history in 2007 as the first brothers to serve in the California State Assembly in over 60 years. Sal Cannella became assemblyman in 1990. Numerous U.S. presidents came through Ceres. Former vice president Richard Nixon stopped in 1961 to campaign for governor. Two sitting presidents rode through Ceres—Theodore Roosevelt in 1903 and Harry Truman in 1948—as did two future presidents—John F. Kennedy in 1960 and George H. W. Bush in 1988.

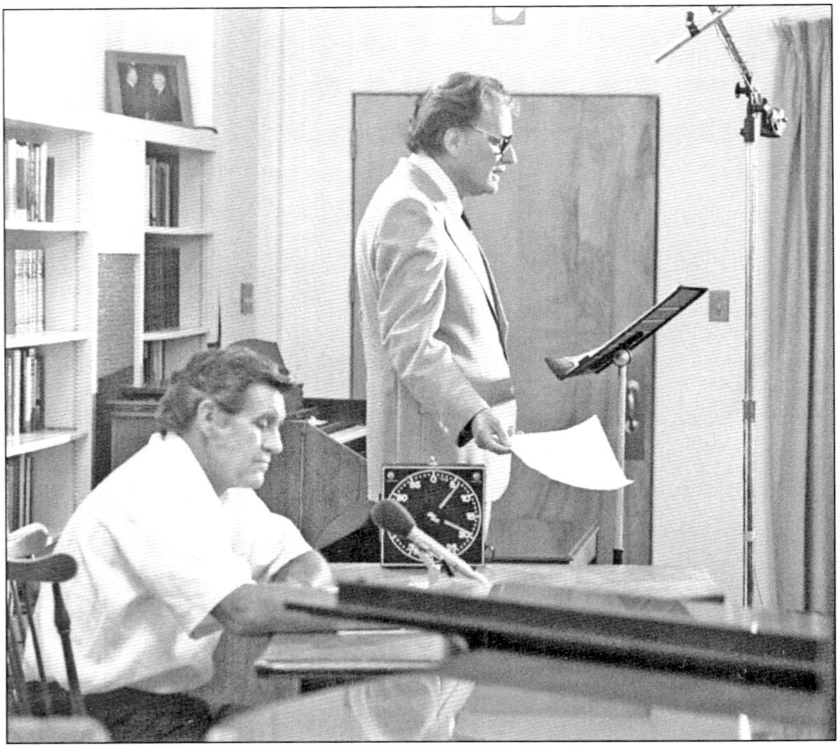

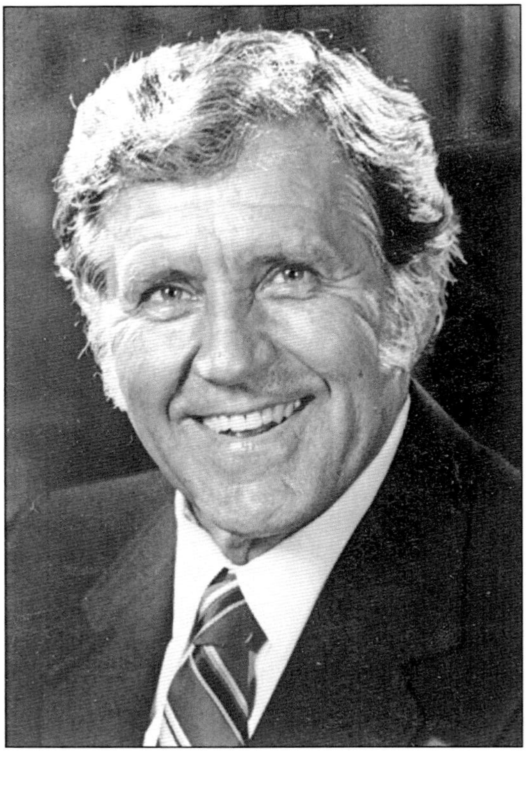

Cliff Barrows, a 1940 Ceres High School graduate (seated, above), became internationally famous with evangelist Billy Graham. Barrows announced at Graham's televised crusades. Barrows met Graham at a Youth for Christ rally in Asheville, North Carolina, during his honeymoon with his bride Wilma. Graham's worship leader was sick, so Barrows was asked to fill in, and it was the start of a lifelong friendship. Barrows became president of World Wide Pictures and directed Graham's *Hour of Decision* radio program in 1950. The Barrows family hosted Graham in 1948 when he conducted his Modesto crusade. In 1988, Barrows was inducted into the Gospel Music Hall of Fame. Cliff's father, Charles Barrows, came to Ceres in 1907. His marriage to Harriet Griggs was announced on the June 8, 1922, front page of the *Courier*. Cliff was born on Service Road in 1923, the first of five children. He accepted Jesus Christ as his Lord and Savior at 10, after being influenced by two pastors at First Baptist Church, Paul Jackson and Carl Dearfelt. (Billy Graham Evangelistic Crusade.)

Singer Chester Smith had strong connections to Ceres. The Oklahoman came to California in 1936 to work in the fields. His parents got Smith into his first radio gig as a child in Fresno. He walked into the studios of KTRB in 1947 as a high school dropout. He told the *Ceres Courier* in 2000, "I could be a cotton picker, a peach picker, or a guitar picker." His band performed in Ceres and South Modesto, and in 1954 Smith recorded a Capitol Records hit in "Wait A Little Longer, Please, Jesus." Smith was turned down by the Bank of Ceres for an $80,000 loan to start KLOC radio in 1963. He used Ceres as the station's city of license. Smith became a millionaire with numerous other TV and radio stations. (Author's collection.)

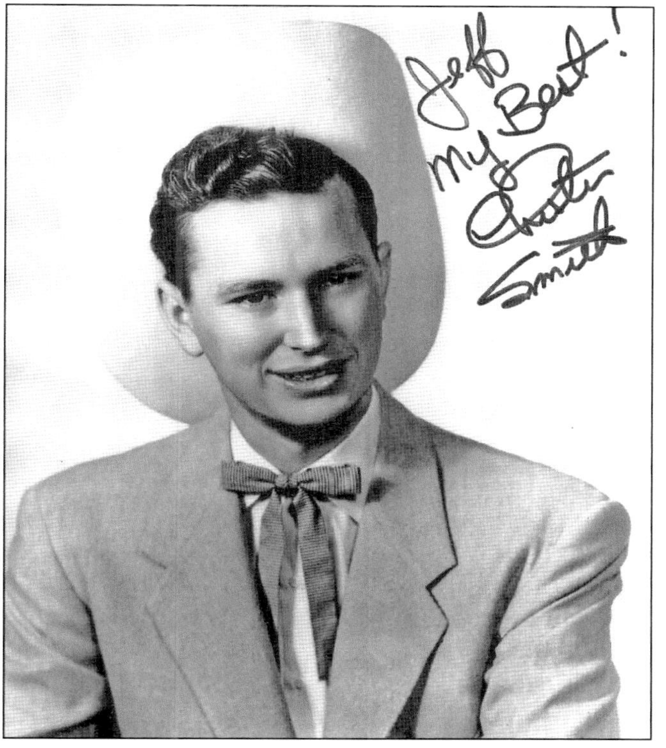

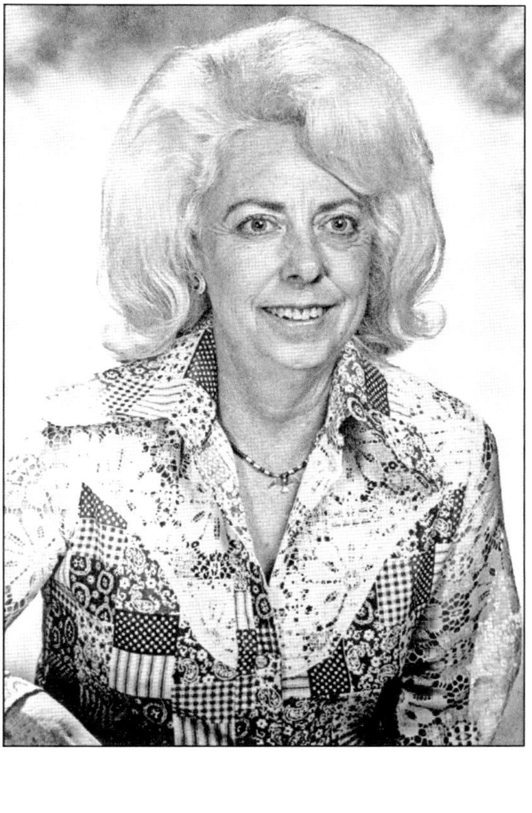

Rose Maddox, the first woman elected to the Country Music Hall of Fame, had roots in Ceres. Maddox Brothers and Rose played in the area of Smyrna Park early in their work. Her sister, Alma Truxel, lived in Ceres. Rose's career started after arriving in the valley during the Dust Bowl. Brother Fred grew tired of picking fruit in 1937 and turned to music. Rice's Furniture Store agreed to sponsor them on KTRB as "The Alabama Outlaws." Fred played slap bass, Cal played harmonica and rhythm guitar, and 11-year-old Rose sang. Her nicknames were "The Original Hillbilly Filly" and "The Grandmother of Rockabilly." (*Ceres Courier*.)

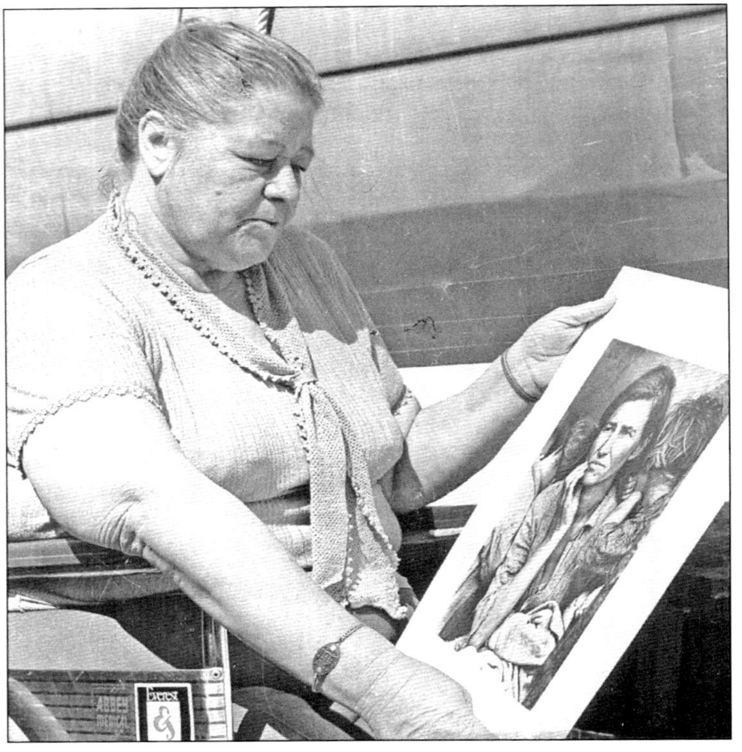

Ruby Sprague, who lived on Holm Avenue in Ceres before her death in 1990, became part of Depression era history. Dorothea Lange took a famous 1936 photograph of a destitute and unable-to-work (because a pea crop was frozen) Florence Hill Thompson and her small daughters in a migrant camp near Nipomo, California. Ruby's head is at the right side of the famous Migrant Mother photo, now an iconic image of the Depression later used on a U.S. postage stamp. Ruby's mother lived in south Modesto before her death in 1983. (Jeff Benziger.)

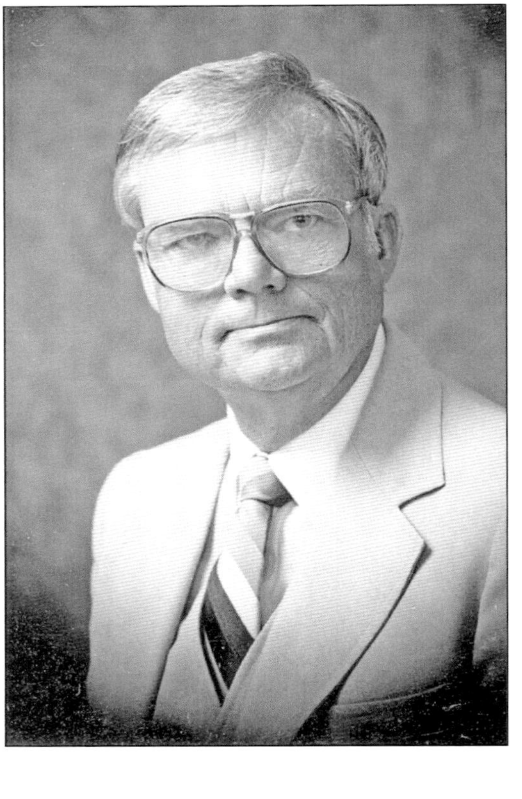

Lee Roddy was editor and publisher of the *Ceres Courier* in the 1970s. Before coming to Ceres, Roddy worked at KTRB from 1947 to 1955. He penned over 50 books, including *The Life and Times of Grizzly Adams*, the basis for a TV series with Dan Haggerty; and *The Lincoln Conspiracy*, a *New York Times* best seller made into a motion picture. Roddy insists he wrote both books and that movie producers Charles E. Sellier Jr. and David Balsiger put their names on the covers. Roddy also authored the D.J. Dillon Adventures series and 15 Ladd Family Adventures. (*Ceres Courier*.)

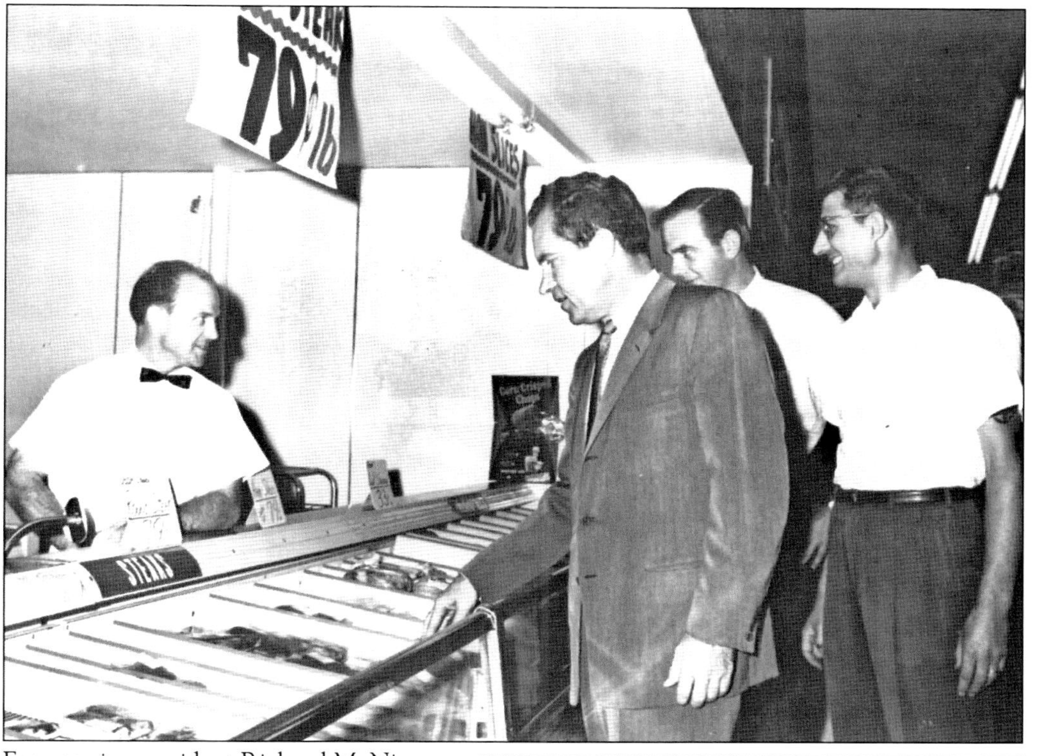

Former vice president Richard M. Nixon checks out the steaks at Richland Market in Ceres on a 1961 campaign stop. Behind him is store co-owner Gus Pallios. Nixon ran for governor of California that year but lost a year later to Edmund G. "Pat" Brown. Eight years later Nixon became president. The Whitmore Avenue store had only been open at its new location a year. Today the building is Richland Ace Hardware. (Pallios family.)

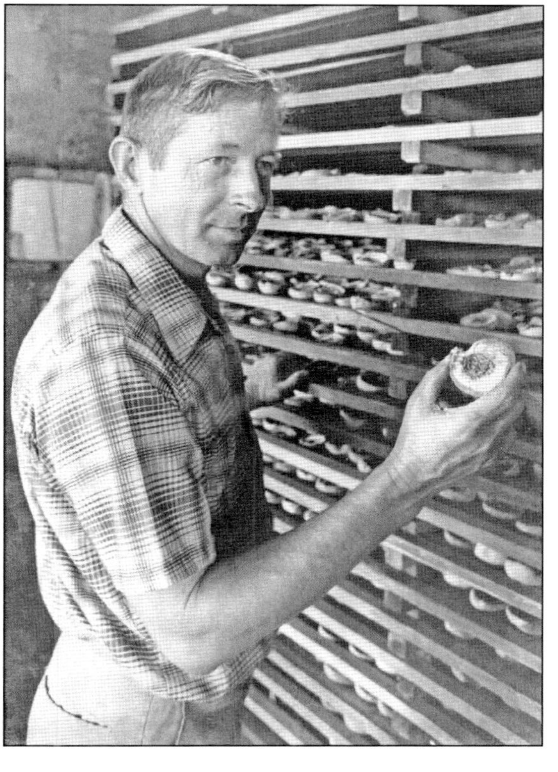

Holding cut peaches at the Ceres Dehydrator, Clare Berryhill (1926–96) had a political future ahead of him. He was on the Ceres school board before serving in the state assembly from 1969 to 1970. Berryhill was a California state senator from 1972 and 1974 and was director of the California Department of Food and Agriculture from 1983 to 1987. He lost to Gary Condit in a special congressional election to replace Tony Coelho in 1989. Cancer claimed Berryhill in 1996. (*Ceres Courier.*)

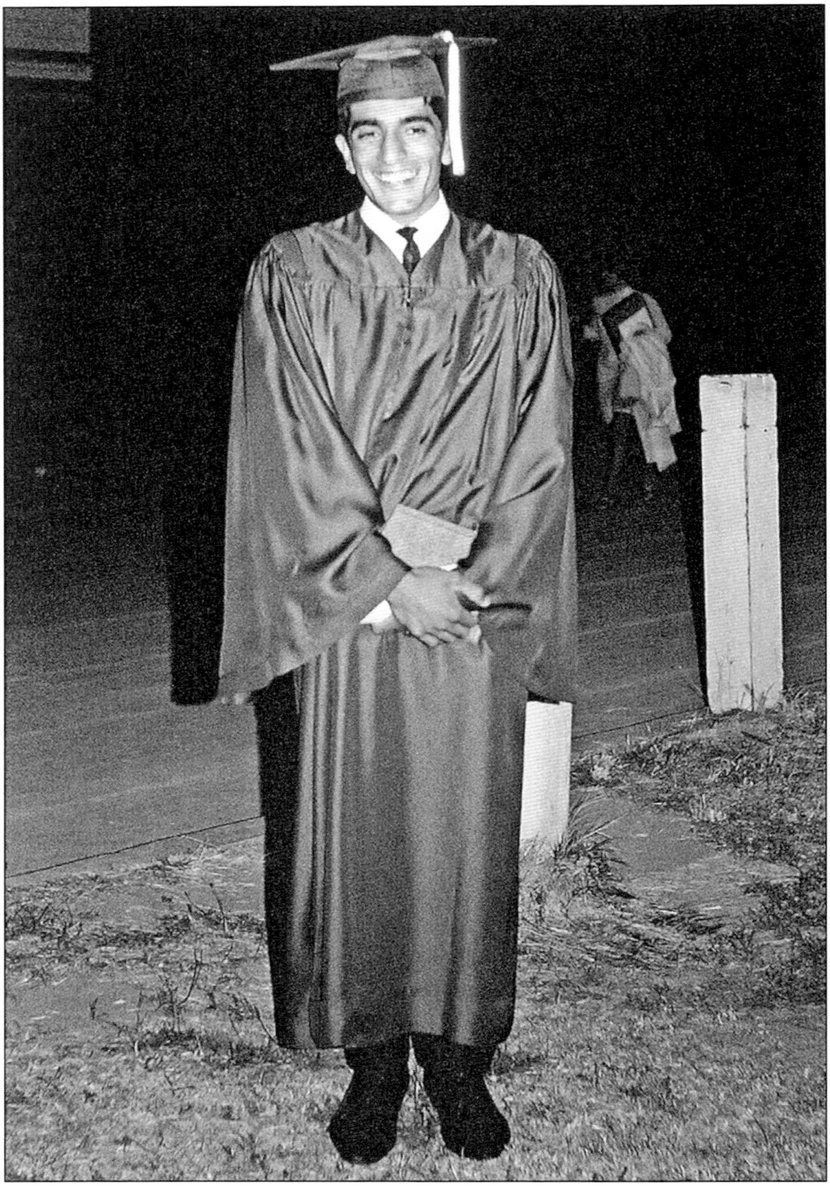

Ceres played a pivotal role in the life of this young man, a Ceres High graduate of 1967 named Zalmay Khalilzad. He later became the U.S. ambassador to the United Nations. The diplomat was born in Afghanistan and came to Ceres in 1966 as an exchange student living with Medrick and Ruth Perra. Khalilzad said his time in Ceres was an "eye-opening experience and really made me start thinking about what I wanted to do in the world." Perra suggested that Khalilzad go into politics. As an Afghan, Khalilzad recalls being a novelty in Central California speaking to service clubs and churches. He said it was before the Rotary Club, the Lions, and city meetings, "that I saw this unique democratic spirit. I saw a society open to all people . . . institutions in which power was based not on birth but merit . . . opportunity for all to succeed through hard work and civic society—neighbor helping neighbor—that was inspiring." In 2003, Secretary of State Colin Powell swore him in as U.S. ambassador to Afghanistan. (Mark Perra.)

Gary A. Condit (right) became a household name in 2001 when the 18th Congressional District representative became the subject of intense media attention after an alleged romantic link to missing Washington, D.C., intern Chandra Levy. The scandal eroded Condit's popularity, and he was defeated by Dennis Cardoza in 2002. Condit was born and raised in Oklahoma but followed his family (below) to Ceres in 1967. The Condit children, from left to right, are Burl (later a police officer and Ceres school board member), Gary, Darrell, and Dovie. Behind them stand their parents, Pastor Adrian and Jean Condit. While attending college in 1973, Gary became mayor of Ceres. He was later elected to the Stanislaus County Board of Supervisors and, in 1982, to the California State Assembly, where he made news as a member of the Gang of Five. In 1989, the Democrat succeeded Tony Coelho in Congress. (Author's collection.)

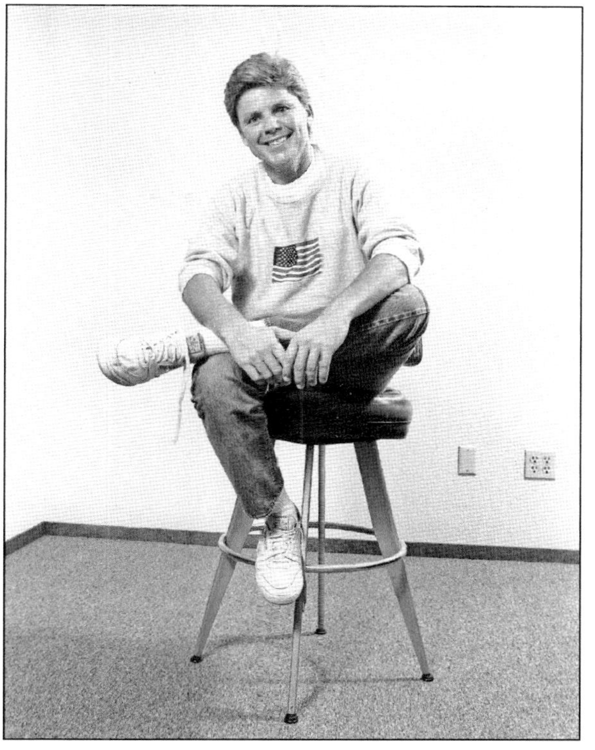

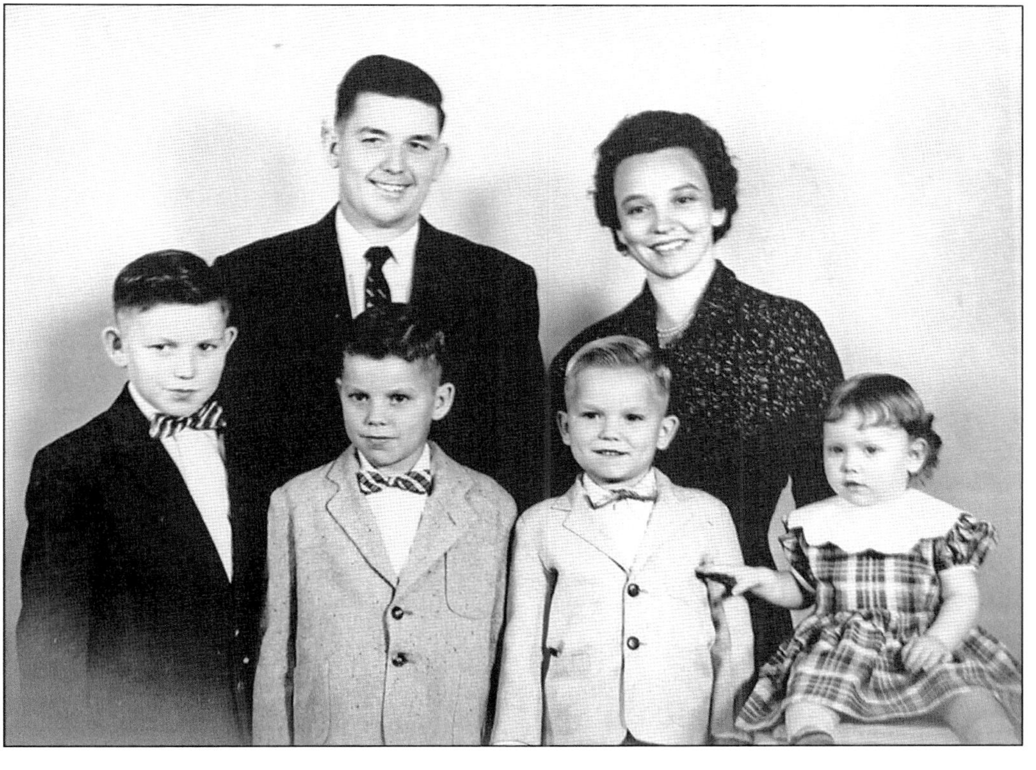

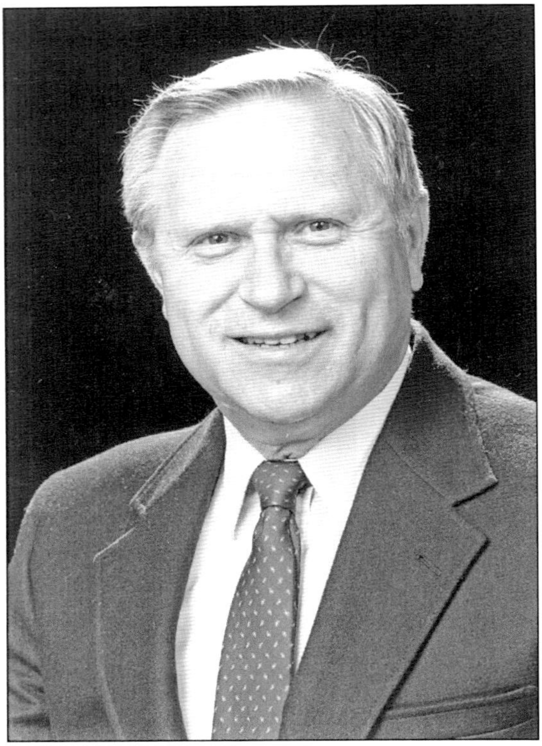

Dr. Edward L. Hayes, fourth president of the Denver Seminary in Denver, Colorado, grew up in Ceres, where he attended First Baptist Church. He also was executive director of the Mount Hermon Association in Santa Cruz from 1979 to 1993. Dr. Hayes previously served the seminary as academic dean and professor of Christian education. He retired in 1996, having served Denver Seminary for 23 years. (*Ceres Courier.*)

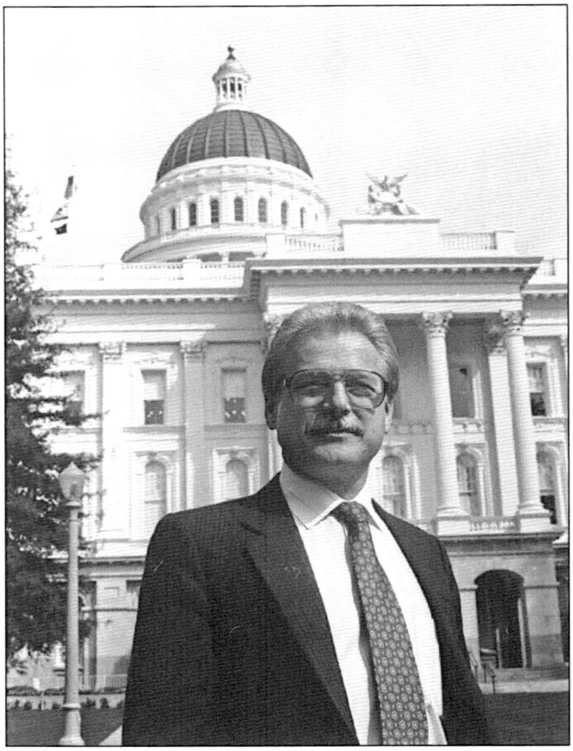

Sal Cannella got involved in politics as a Ceres planning commissioner. He was elected to the city council in 1976 and served as mayor from 1980 to 1983. Cannella then became a Stanislaus County supervisor. In 1990, he ran in a special election for the 27th California State Assembly district vacated by Gary Condit, who had been elected to Congress. Cannella was reelected in 1990, 1992, and 1994. (*Ceres Courier.*)

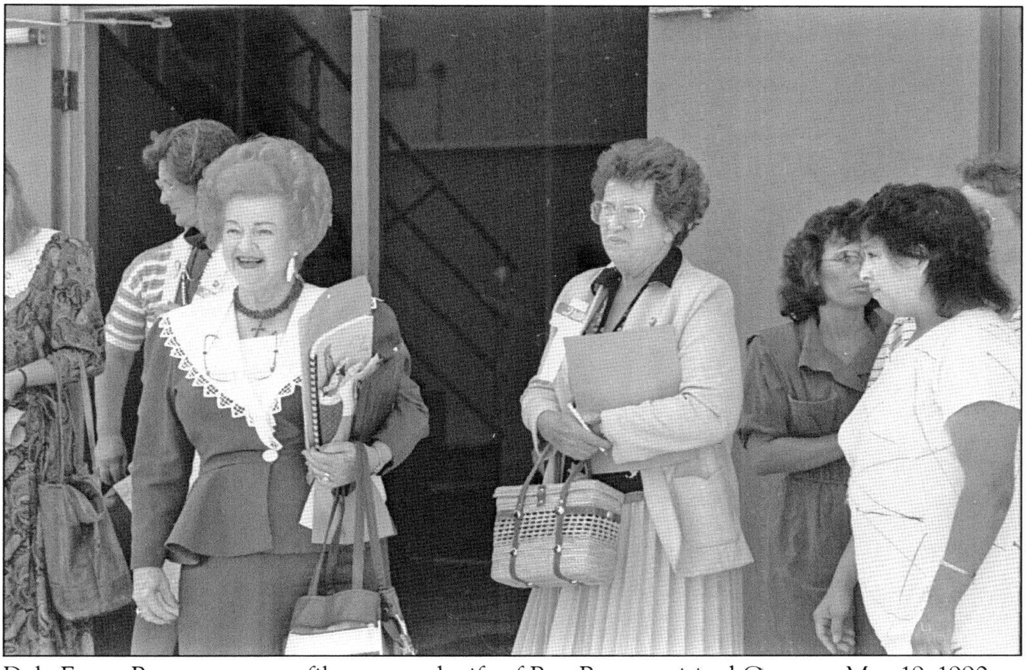

Dale Evans Rogers, western film star and wife of Roy Rogers, visited Ceres on May 19, 1990, at the invitation of the Soroptimist International of Ceres. She is seen here leaving a Women's Awareness Day talk at the Mae Hensley Junior High School gymnasium. (*Ceres Courier.*)

The Herb Henry family is well known among southern gospel music circles in Central California. Henry is pastor of Richland Faith Assembly of God Church in Ceres. With his wife, Nancy, and children—Amanda, Chris and Angela, the group has participated in gospel music concerts throughout California. Herb serves as president of the Western States Gospel Music Association, a group he helped form in 1990. (Herb Henry.)

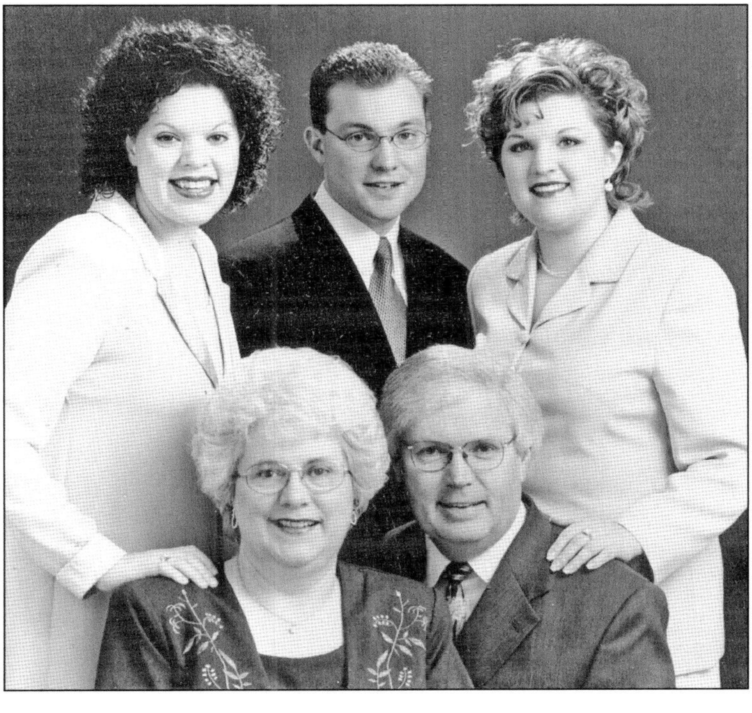

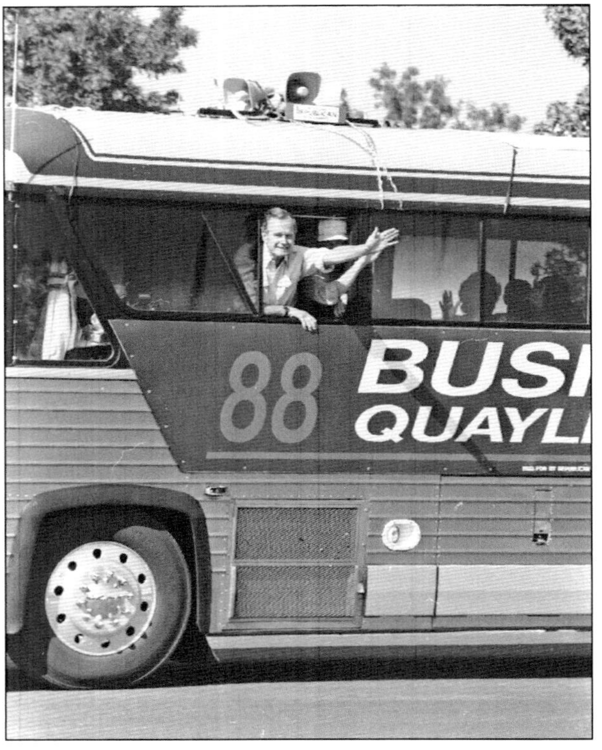

Ceres police helped the Secret Service cordon off traffic from Mitchell Road traffic for the motorcade of Vice President George H. W. Bush rolling through Ceres during an October 15, 1988, campaign trip. Bush spoke at Beyer Park in Modesto, then boarded a bus down Oakdale Road, past the Modesto Airport, and across the Mitchell Road bridge into Ceres. Bush bypassed Ceres eateries for a lunch stop at Latif's in Turlock. Mike Love of the Beach Boys is waving through the window with Bush. Also aboard are Bruce Johnston of the Beach Boys, Jeb Bush, Gov. George Deukmejian, and Barbara Bush. In February 2000, Jeb's son, George P. Bush, came to the *Ceres Courier* offices to stump for his uncle, George W. Bush. (Jeff Benziger.)

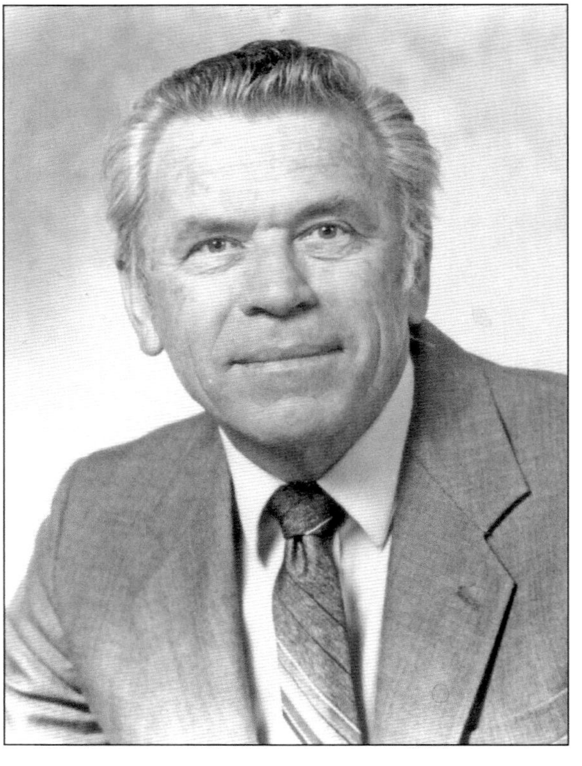

Ceres farmer Henry J. Voss was appointed director of the California Department of Food and Agriculture in 1989 by Gov. George Deukmejian. Voss previously served as president of the California Farm Bureau from 1981 to 1989. Voss moved from San Jose to Ceres in 1960, farming 500 acres of peaches, prunes, walnuts, almonds, grapes, and cherries. He left office in 1995 and died July 6, 1996. Mourners at his Hughson funeral included Gov. Pete Wilson. (*Ceres Courier.*)

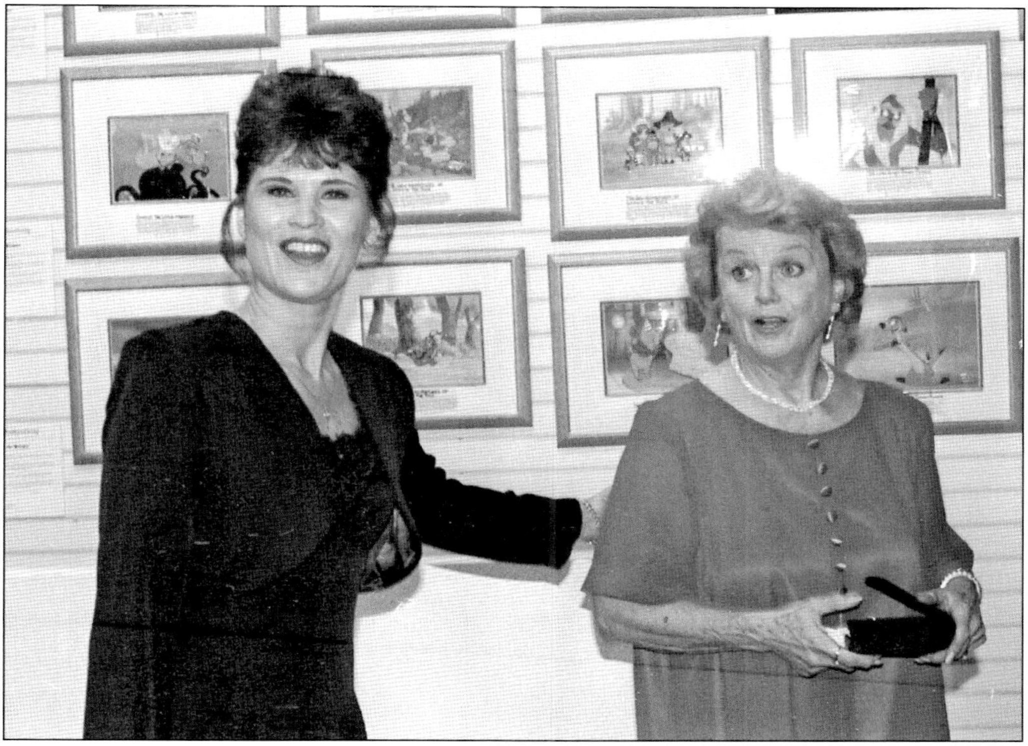

Ilene Woods, the voice of Cinderella in Walt Disney's 1950 animated feature film, visited a Ceres Disneyana shop Sept. 21–22, 1996. Woods (right) was shown around the Enchanted Castle shop located in the Taylor Shopping Center, at the corner of Mitchell and Whitmore, by owner Tina Olson. Woods signed autographs for store customers. Mary Costa, voice of Disney's Sleeping Beauty, also visited the store. (Jeff Benziger.)

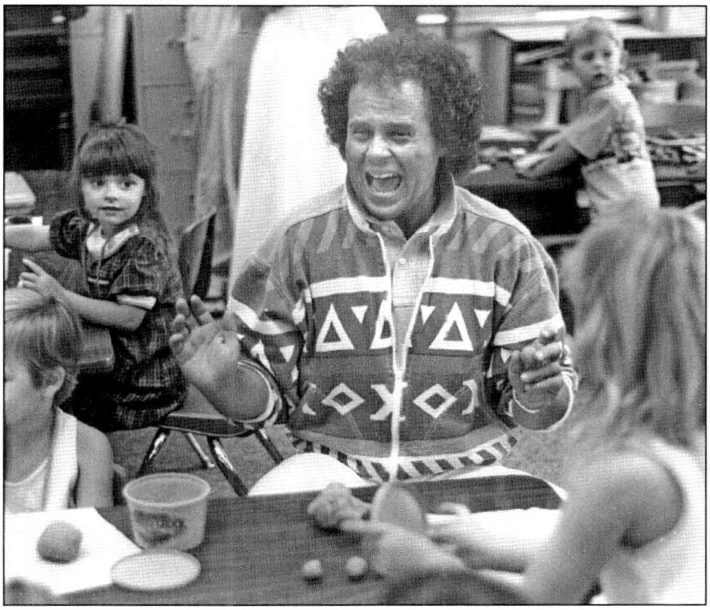

Fitness guru Richard Simmons let out a series of shrieks as he played in the kindergarten classroom of Anne Aubert during his surprise visit to Walter White Elementary School on July 10, 1991. The happy-go-lucky TV personality flew to Stockton and then drove to Ceres to film an infomercial spot with Aubert after she lost 125 pounds on his weight loss plan. (*Ceres Courier.*)

IMAGES
of America

CLAXTON-HEPBURN MEDICAL CENTER

I0807668

On the Cover: This photograph was taken around 1902 in the new operating room that was furnished by Dr. Grant C. Madill, chief surgeon from 1890 to 1943. For additional information, please see page 11. (Courtesy of Claxton-Hepburn Archives.)

IMAGES
of America

CLAXTON-HEPBURN MEDICAL CENTER

Claxton-Hepburn Archives

ARCADIA
PUBLISHING

ISBN 978-0-7385-7639-8

Published by Arcadia Publishing
Charleston, South Carolina

Printed in the United States of America

Library of Congress Control Number: 2011926065

For all general information, please contact Arcadia Publishing:
Telephone 843-853-2070
Fax 843-853-0044
E-mail sales@arcadiapublishing.com
For customer service and orders:
Toll-Free 1-888-313-2665

Visit us on the Internet at www.arcadiapublishing.com

Contents

ACKNOWLEDGMENTS

The production of this book was inspired by the celebration of Claxton-Hepburn Medical Center's 125th anniversary in 2010. The project would not have been possible without the efforts of a small committee of staff and volunteers who worked together to sort and organize the medical center's historical photographs. Laura Shea, Michele Catlin, both from the Community Relations Office, and Cindy Clusen, of the Claxton-Hepburn Medical Center Foundation, spent many hours over several months, with volunteers Therese Kelly (A. Barton Hepburn Hospital Nursing School graduate from 1959) and Frances Van Horne (A. Barton Hepburn Hospital Nursing School graduate from 1947) sorting, organizing, and identifying photographs. In the fall of 2010, Kelsey Redpath, a senior at St. Lawrence University, joined the group as an intern to help continue the process of organizing and cataloguing photographs. Kelsey worked closely with Cindy Clusen during her spring 2011 semester to select photographs, format them in the book, and write captions. The group was also fortunate during this time for the efforts of David E. Martin, an author of several other books published by Arcadia, who provided invaluable assistance by scanning hundreds of photographs and providing advice along the way. Chuck Kelly, retired publisher of the *Ogdensburg Journal* and *Sunday Advance News*, reviewed photographs and manuscripts, greatly improving accuracy and completeness of the information. Likewise, many longtime employees of the hospital, such as Roberta Morrison, Charlotte Paro, and Vicky Sharpe, pitched in with information that was indispensable.

Although the photographs in this book came primarily from the Claxton-Hepburn Archives, credit is given where appropriate for the use of materials from the St. Lawrence University Special Collections, the St. Lawrence County Historical Association, and the private collections of community members.

We are also grateful to the many members of the medical center staff, board members, and community members who reviewed and contributed photographs, helped to identify people and events in the pictures, and provided great moral support throughout the process.

INTRODUCTION

In 1885, the Grey Nuns of Ottawa opened a refuge in Ogdensburg, New York, for the sick, aged, poor, and orphaned, called the Ogdensburg City Hospital and Orphan Asylum. This institution grew out of the nuns' passion for providing for those in need. These simple and sacrificial beginnings remain today in the form of bedrock values of caring and compassion. Even as the hospital has grown in size and specialization and received state and national recognition for the quality of care it provides, today's Claxton-Hepburn continues to be devoted to the day-to-day medical needs of the North Country community.

The first hospital in St. Lawrence County, the Ogdensburg City Hospital and Orphan Asylum was founded in the post–Civil War era when medical facilities emerged with further urbanization and industrialization of the United States. Prior to this period, most medical care was provided in the home—whether childbirth or surgery. However, in the 1880s, the process of sterilization came into practice, which helped to professionalize modern medicine and encourage the development of more hospitals.

The Ogdensburg City Hospital and Orphan Asylum was originally housed in the old Ford Mansion, located across King Street from the hospital's current front entrance. In 1902, a new building was constructed across the street in the block that the hospital continues to occupy today. A west wing was added to this building a few years later, and then an east wing was added in 1918. Ultimately, a new building was opened in front of the original 1902 building on King Street in 1960, and a new west wing was constructed in the early 1970s. Buildings on Rensselaer Avenue and Mansion Avenue, originally constructed for the nursing school, were converted to doctors' offices in the late 1960s and to administrative offices later.

Philanthropy has driven the history and growth of the hospital. A. Barton Hepburn, one of its primary benefactors, grew up in the foothills of the Adirondacks in Colton, New York, about 30 miles from the hospital, in the 1840s and 1850s. Hepburn made his way through careers as a teacher in a local school, a rural lawyer, and a surveyor. He made his first fortune logging local forested lands and eventually became an assemblyman in Albany representing seven towns across St. Lawrence County. His career track culminated with his appointment as comptroller of the currency by Pres. Benjamin Harrison and, later, when he served as president of Chase National Bank. His friends and associates included many historic figures, such as Theodore Roosevelt, J.P. Morgan, and others, but his heart never left northern New York.

Hepburn made his first gift to the hospital in 1910 in memory of his brother Hawley Hepburn. By his passing in 1922, Hepburn had given over a million dollars to the hospital, which helped to fund new facilities and establish a nursing school that would supply nursing staff to both the hospital and other local medical facilities, from 1902 until 1968. In 1918, the hospital was renamed A. Barton Hepburn Hospital to recognize the generosity of this North Country native.

Although the hospital was overseen by a nonsectarian group of community board members, it was managed by the Grey Nuns until 1976, when the first lay administrator was appointed.

In 1983, a hospital foundation was formed for the purpose of soliciting, holding, and investing funds for the support of the facility. From the 1990s on, modernization and specialization of the hospital accelerated. This growth and development was marshaled by the efforts of a group of foundation and hospital donors and volunteers.

From the early 1990s through 2008, five major capital campaigns brought in over $21 million, which helped to establish the county's first full-service cancer center, the Richard E. Winter Cancer Center, in 1994. Shortly thereafter, the Helen and Stanley McCadam Medical Office Building was constructed for doctors' offices. In 1999, the Dr. Ravinder N. Agarwal Renal Center, a stand-alone renal center, opened. In 2000, new or renovated facilities for the main entrance, lobby, cafeteria, physical therapy, cardiology, cardiopulmonary rehabilitation, pharmacy, chapel, emergency room, medical surgical floor, and radiology were added. In 2004–2005, the Richard E. Winter Cancer Center was expanded, adding space for infusion treatments as well as the Barbara Cuthbert Welch Garden. Finally, from 2006 to 2008, new and renovated facilities for ambulatory surgery, radiology, mental health, wound healing, and obstetrics were constructed.

Dr. E. Garfield Claxton was a key part of this advancement. Born in Ottawa, Dr. Claxton formed his practice in Ogdensburg in 1932 and devoted his career to caring for women and babies. Numerous editorials from the *Ogdensburg Journal* praise the doctor's deep compassion for his patients. When he left the community to move to Florida in his later years, it would have been easy for Claxton to forget his roots in Ogdensburg; yet in 2001, he made a $7.5-million gift—the largest gift by a living donor in the region's history up to that point. This exceptional contribution further fueled growth of the medical center and allowed for a flexible savings at the foundation that is managed for the benefit of the medical center. At the time of this gift, the name of the hospital was changed once more, to Claxton-Hepburn Medical Center, to recognize Dr. Claxton's significant impact on the hospital.

Claxton-Hepburn has always been on the cutting edge, tailoring service offerings to fit the diverse health needs of this rural community, and this continues today. Claxton-Hepburn offered hemodialysis as far back as 1968, long before many urban hospitals. As the largest community hospital in the county, Claxton-Hepburn was also the first hospital in St. Lawrence County to offer cancer care.

Today, the medical center continues to serve as a regional referral center for acute psychiatric services, radiation and medical oncology, chronic dialysis treatment, and wound healing. It is also a leading provider of primary care in the community, with six clinics in the rural area surrounding the hospital, and serves as a regional, and even national, leader in quality initiatives. Claxton-Hepburn has received two awards from the Institute for Health Care Improvement (IHI) and one from the Voluntary Hospitals of America (VHA). In addition, Claxton-Hepburn was featured in a 2011 article in *Scientific American* on curbing hospital-acquired infections.

All of this success has been possible because of the dedication and enthusiasm of the community. Today, Claxton-Hepburn benefits from the dedication of 80 members of the active medical staff and over 800 employees. They are joined by approximately 35 board members, 42 regular hospital volunteers, over 165 members of the auxiliary, and 6,118 donors. Together, this community of caregivers is taking the medical center into its next 125 years and continuing to strive for excellence.

One

Ogdensburg City Hospital and Orphan Asylum

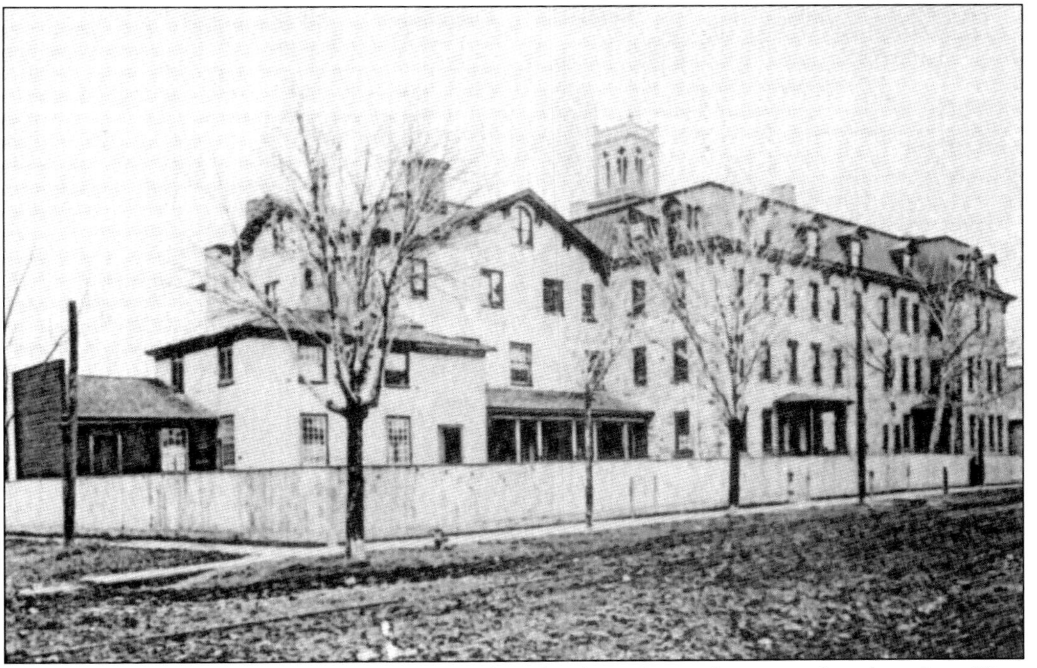

In 1885, the Grey Nuns of Ottawa open "a refuge for the sick, aged, poor and orphans" on King Street in Ogdensburg, in a complex of buildings constructed around the Ford Mansion. In 1886, the Ogdensburg City Hospital and Orphan Asylum was incorporated. On the left in this image is the Judge Nathan Ford home, built in 1805. Next door on the right is Our Lady of Victory Convent Boarding and Day School for Girls. The picture was taken just prior to the 1885 start of renovations to the Ford Mansion, which created the Ogdensburg City Hospital and Orphan Asylum. The tower of the Notre Dame Church can be seen above the convent. This site is now the parking lot across from the King Street entrance to the hospital.

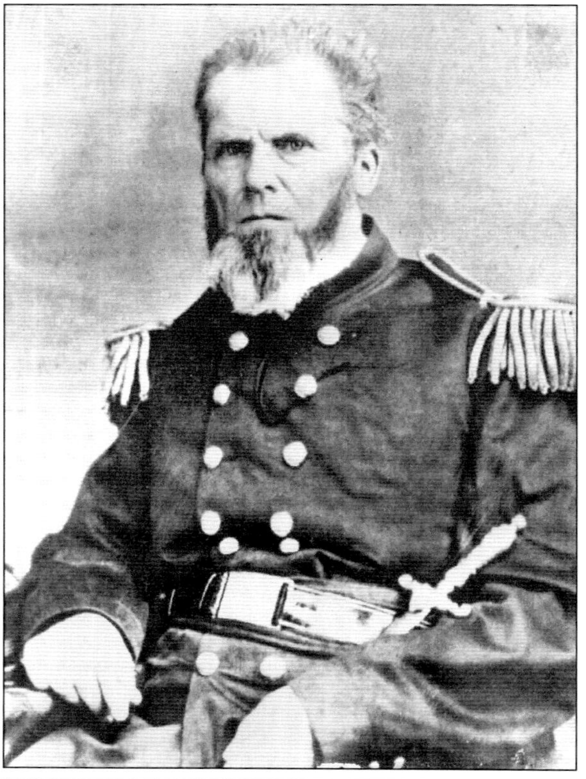

Dr. Socrates Norton Sherman was an Ogdensburg pioneer physician who lived from 1801 to 1873.

This is believed to be an early picture of the Ogdensburg City Hospital medical staff around 1890.

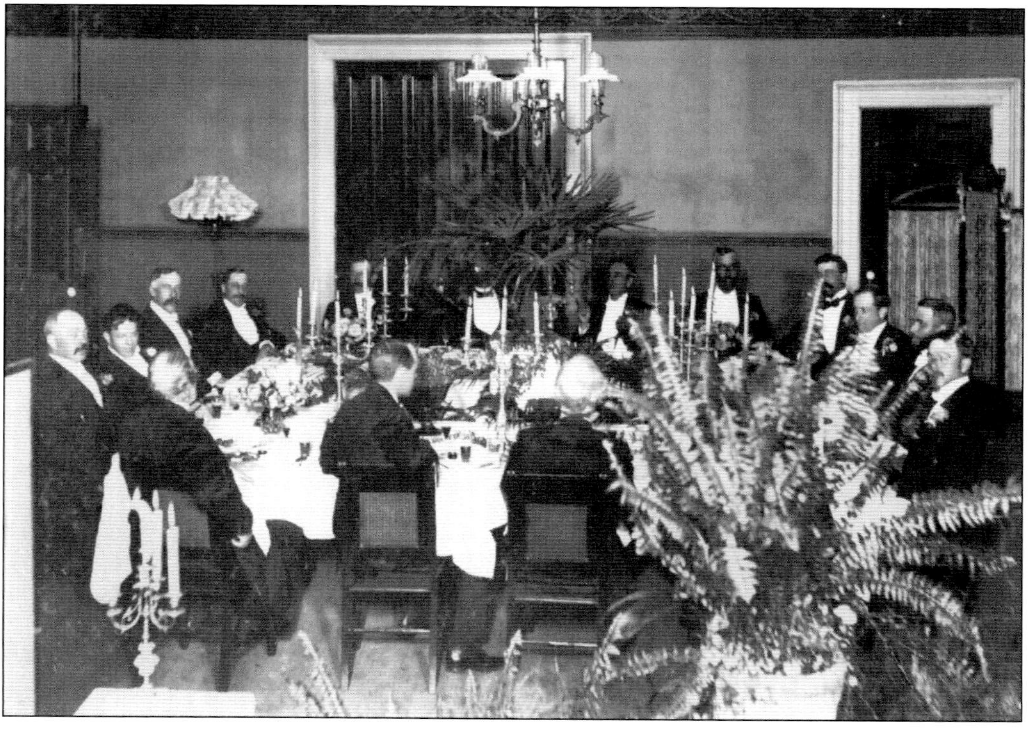

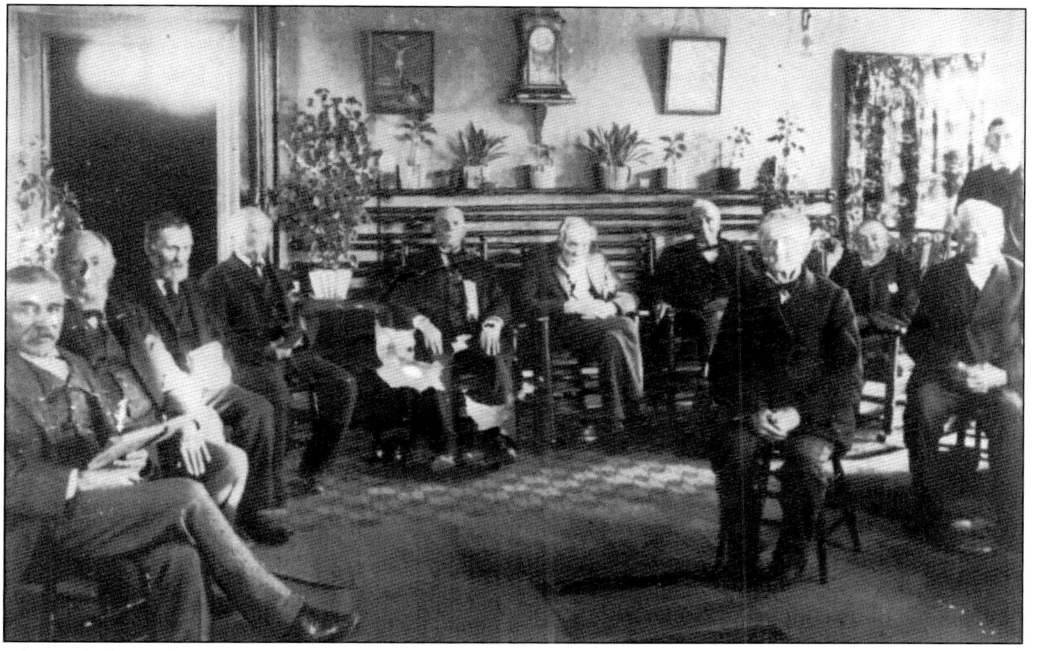

This is believed to be a photograph, taken perhaps around 1900, of the Old Men's Ward at the Ogdensburg City Hospital and Orphan Asylum.

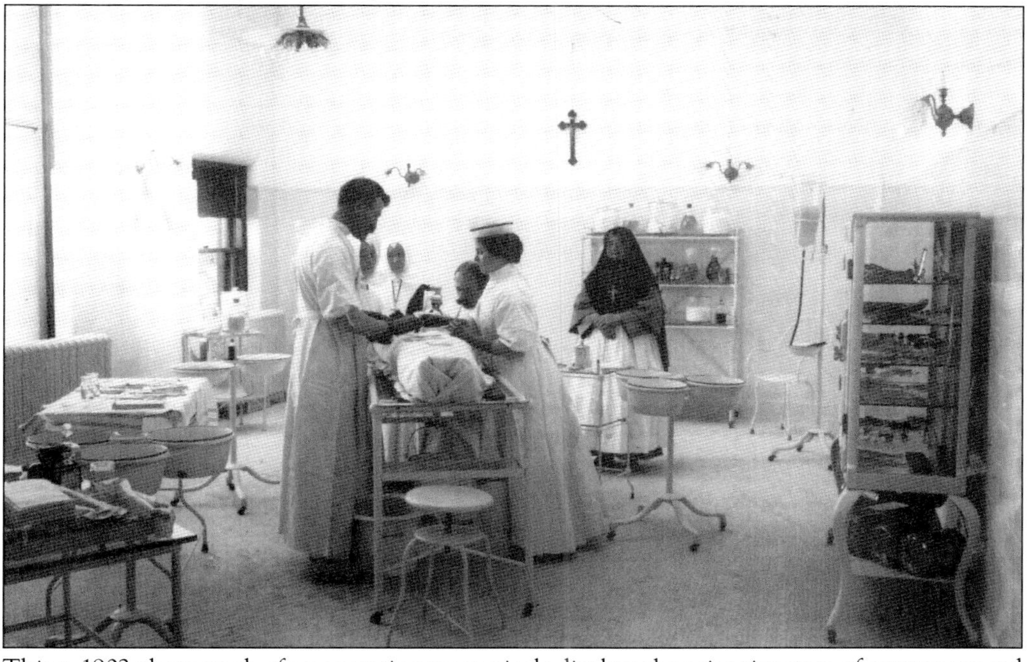

This c. 1902 photograph of an operating room nicely displays the primitive state of surgery around 1900. There were gloves, but no masks or caps and no draping of the table. The patient has no IV, but there is a big bottle, tubing, and stand in the corner, available if needed. The three nuns and three crosses highlight the hospital's rich religious history. This operating room in the new, 60-bed, 1902 hospital building was furnished by Dr. Grant C. Madill, chief surgeon from 1890 to 1943.

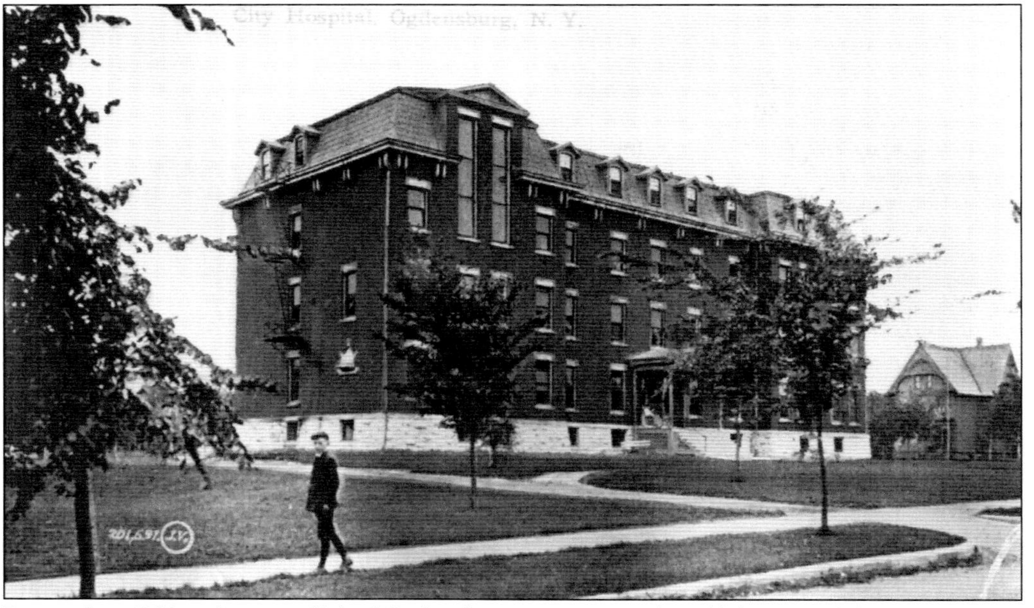

Pictured in 1902 is the new, 60-bed Ogdensburg City Hospital. Half the cost of the new hospital was donated by Ogdensburg mayor and businessman George Hall. It opened across King Street from the Ford Mansion. The mansion continued to serve as a nursing home and orphanage, operated under the Ogdensburg City Hospital and Orphan Asylum charter until the name was formally changed in 1960 to St. Joseph's Home.

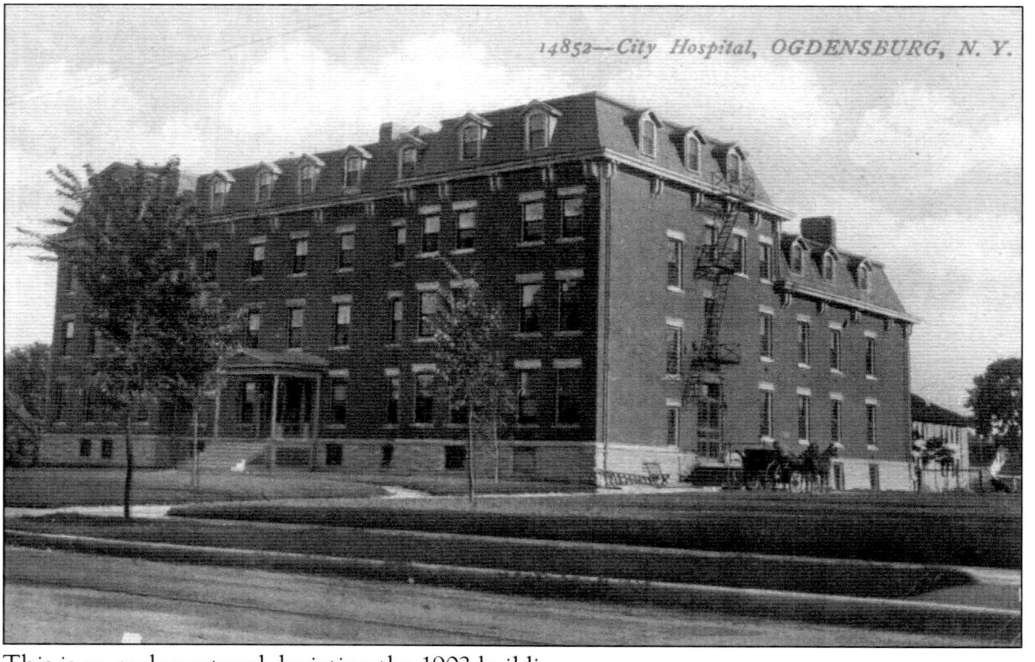

This is an early postcard depicting the 1902 building.

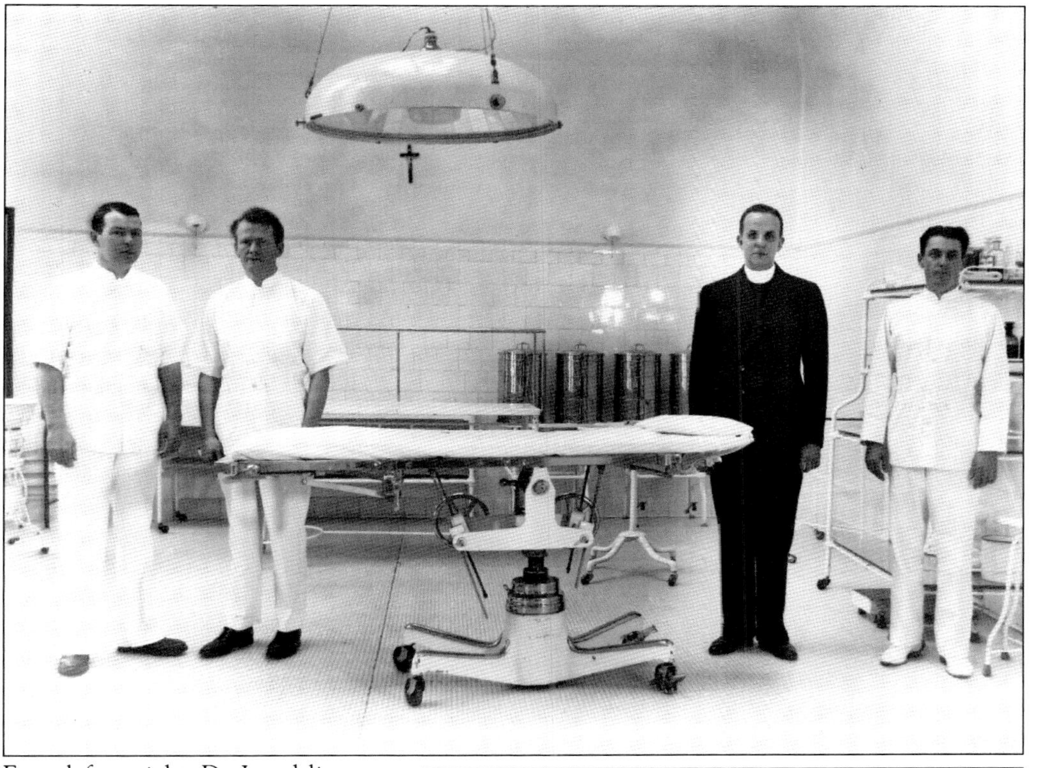

From left to right, Dr. Lauchlin J. Baker, Dr. John Free, an unidentified clergyman, and Dr. Rutherford D. Rodger are shown in the operating room in the 1930s.

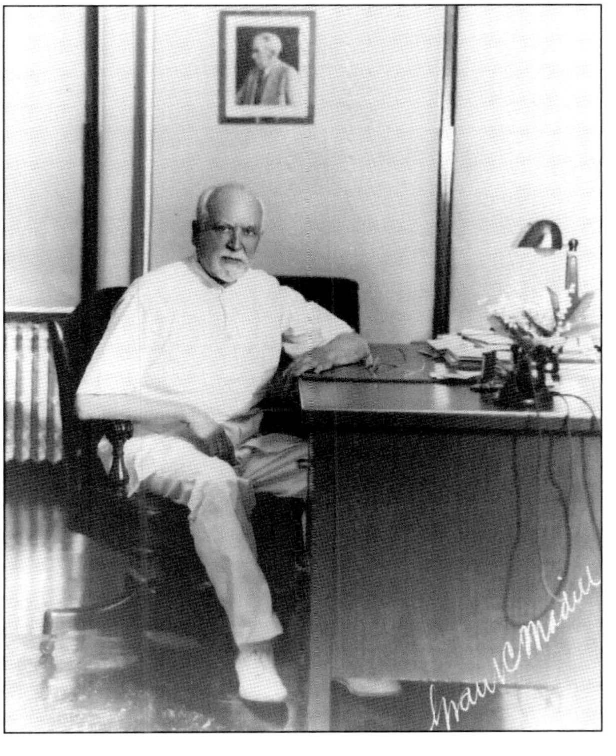

This is a portrait of Dr. Grant C. Madill, chief surgeon from 1890 to 1943.

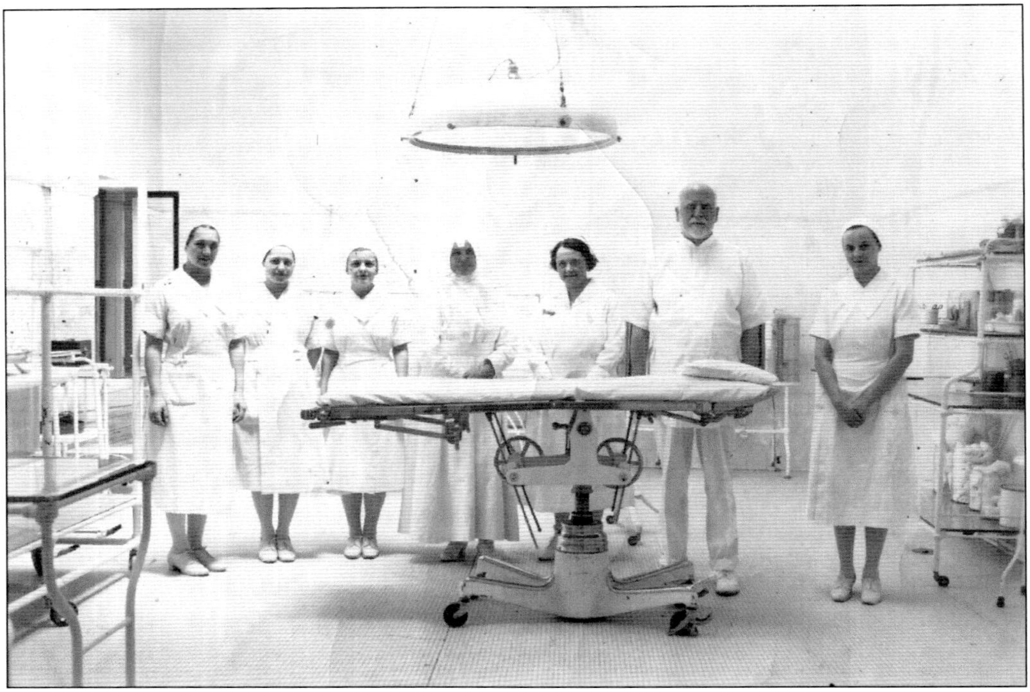

Dr. Grant C. Madill poses with the operating room staff. The nun is Sister Dunstan. On the far right is nurse Alice Miller, who later married Dr. Rutherford D. Rodger. The others are unidentified.

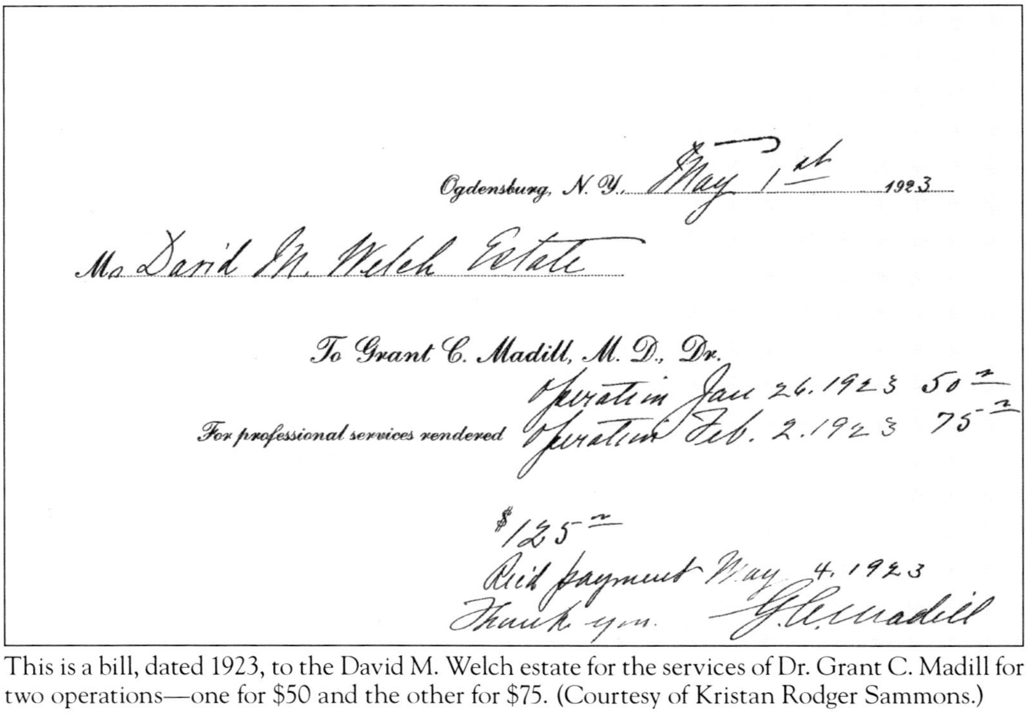

Ogdensburg, N. Y. May 1st 1923

Mr David M. Welch Estate

To Grant C. Madill, M. D., Dr.

For professional services rendered Operation Jan 26. 1923 50.00
Operation Feb. 2. 1923 75.00

$125.00

Rec'd payment May 4. 1923
Thank you. G. C. Madill

This is a bill, dated 1923, to the David M. Welch estate for the services of Dr. Grant C. Madill for two operations—one for $50 and the other for $75. (Courtesy of Kristan Rodger Sammons.)

Two

A. Barton Hepburn

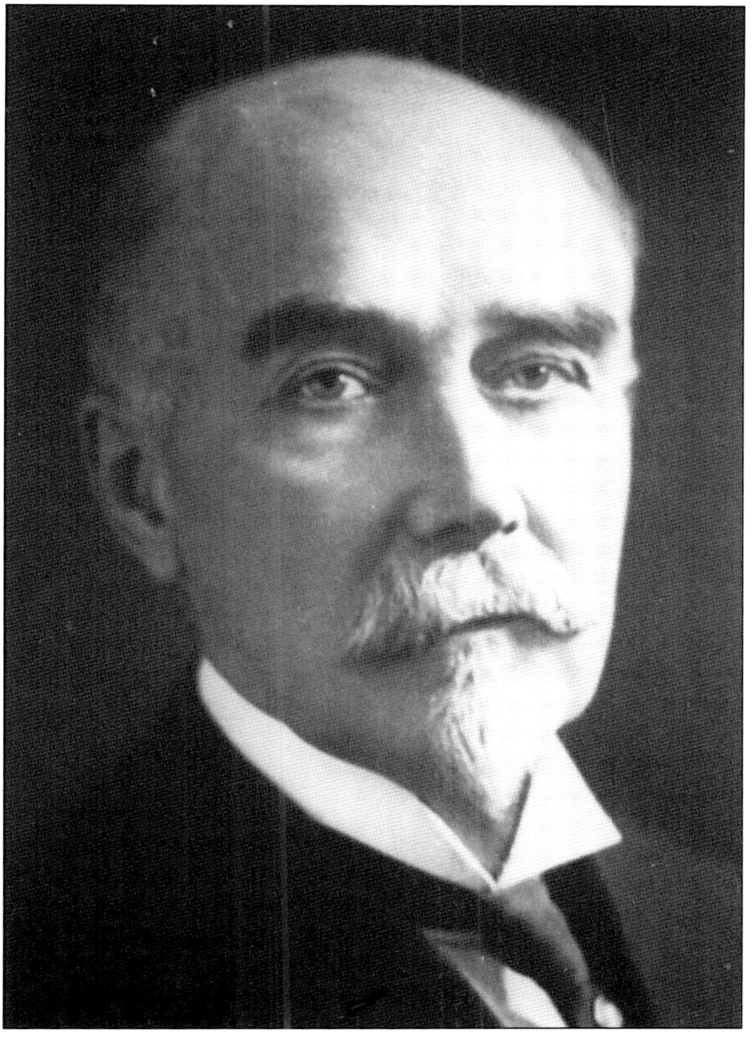

A. Barton Hepburn, one of the hospital's major benefactors, was born on July 24, 1846. Hepburn, born in Colton, made his way as a rural teacher and forester early in his career. He later became a New York state assemblyman and was appointed comptroller of the currency by Pres. Benjamin Harrison. Finally, he became president of Chase National Bank.

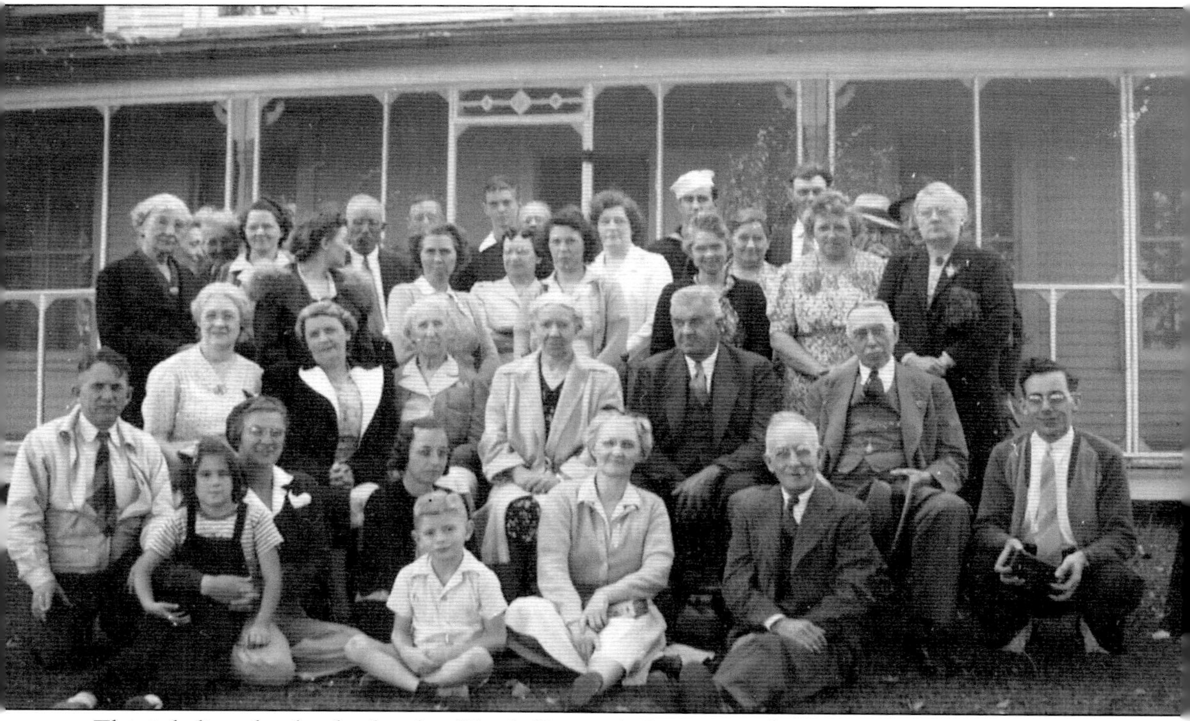

This is believed to be the family of Emily Eaton, A. Barton Hepburn's second wife, in the 1930s. Hepburn and Eaton met in Canton while Eaton attended St. Lawrence University, and they were married in 1887. The Hepburns were active philanthropists. In 1910, Hepburn made his first gift to the hospital—$1,000 in memory of his brother Hawley. In 1915, Hepburn gave $50,000 for an endowment fund and $80,000 for a new wing on the east end of the hospital. The hospital board changed the name of the facility to the A. Barton Hepburn Hospital in honor of Hepburn in 1917. During the next few years, before his death in 1922, Hepburn gave $100,000 for a new residence for the nursing school and $345,000 for another building. Finally, Hepburn left the hospital $500,000 upon his death. In addition to their work with the hospital, the Hepburns also funded a number of libraries in St. Lawrence County and made donations to Middlebury College and St. Lawrence University. (Courtesy of the A. Barton Hepburn Collection, Special Collections, St. Lawrence University Libraries, Canton, New York.)

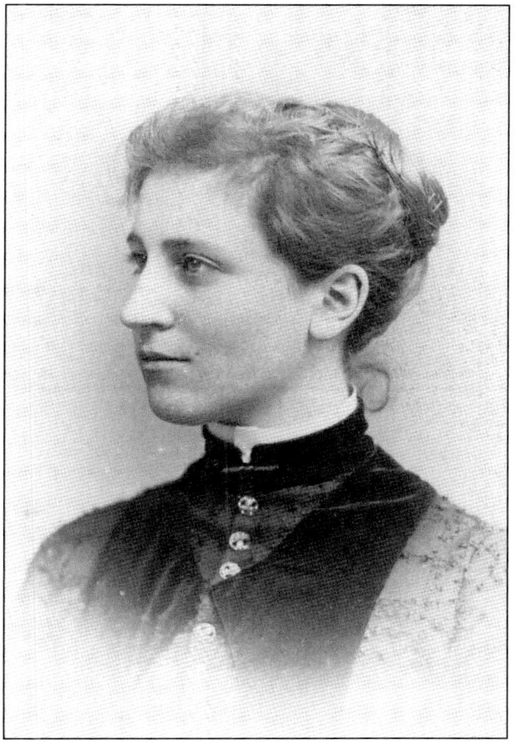

Emily Eaton was born on September 7, 1865, in Middlesex, Vermont. She graduated from St. Lawrence University in 1886. After marrying A. Barton Hepburn, Emily served as a longtime board member for St. Lawrence University. In the photograph below, she attends Charter Day at St. Lawrence University in 1931. The Hepburns supported construction of Hepburn Hall, a science building at the university. Later, Emily and her friend Cora Dean, from Gouverneur, made significant contributions for the construction of Dean-Eaton Hall, a women's residence. (Both, courtesy of the A. Barton Hepburn Collection, Special Collections, St. Lawrence University Libraries, Canton, New York).

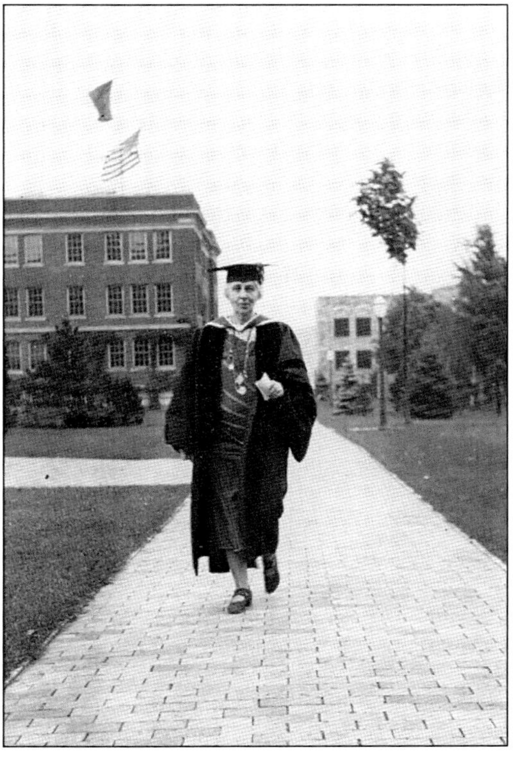

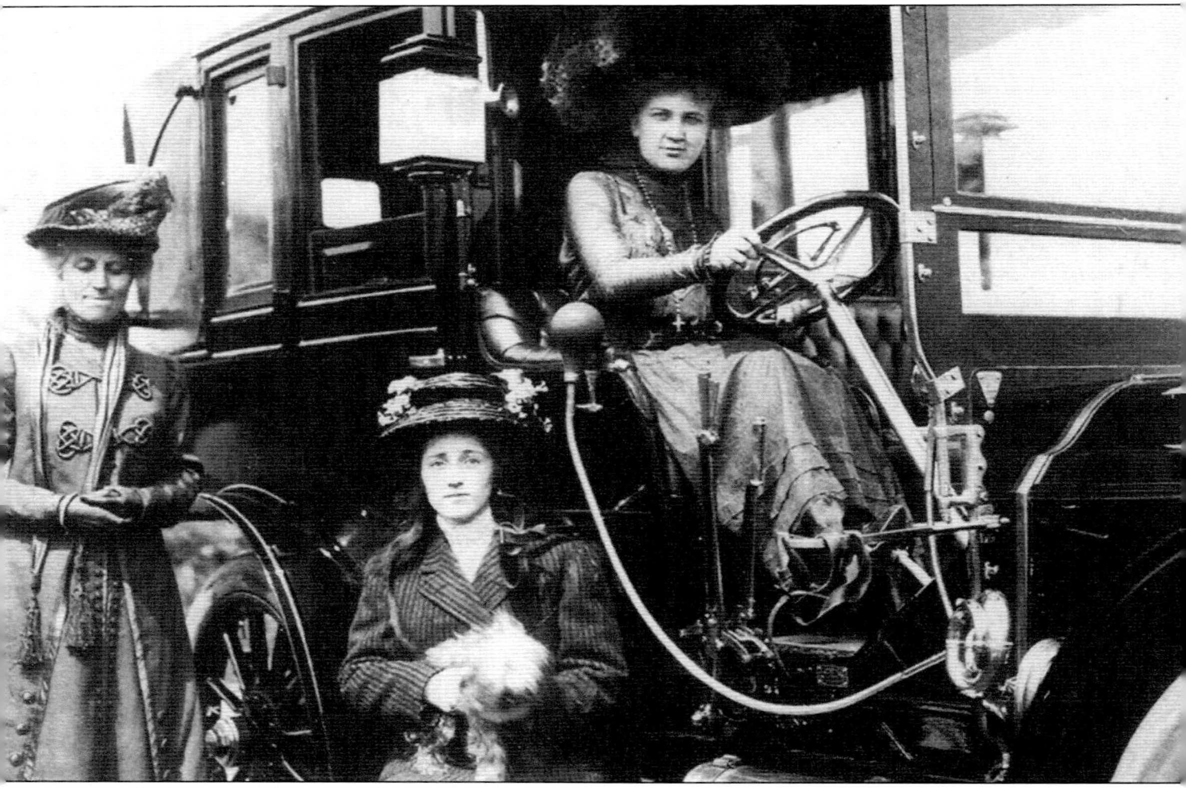

Emily Eaton Hepburn and her two daughters are posing with their first Packard. Beulah, the elder daughter, is in the driver's seat. Cordelia, the younger daughter, is holding the dog. (Courtesy of the St. Lawrence County Historical Association, Canton, New York.)

Three

A. Barton Hepburn Hospital School of Nursing

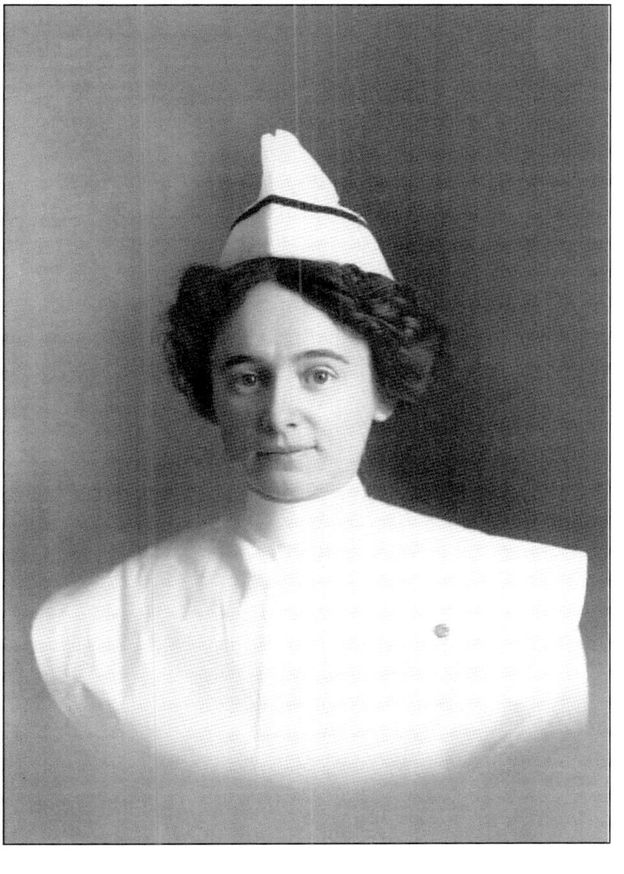

This is a portrait of Helen Cunningham. She was a member of the first graduating class from Hepburn School of Nursing in 1905. On May 22, 1902, the A. Barton Hepburn Hospital School of Nursing commenced as the Ogdensburg City Hospital School of Nursing. Students learned nursing skills under the supervision of the nuns. They also made beds, gave baths, cleaned, swept, and dusted.

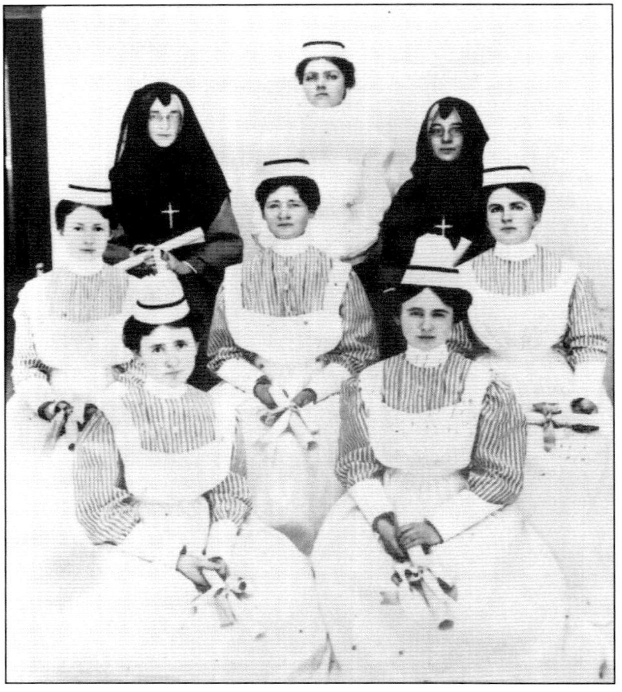

Pictured are member of the nursing school's first graduating class in 1905. They are, from left to right, (first row) Agnes Paro and Helen Cunningham; (second row) Mary LeClair, Winnifred Webb, and A. Grace Merry; (third row) Sister Barnabas, superintendent of nurses Josephine Callahan, and Sister Saint John.

In this picture are members of the class of 1920. From left to right are (first row) Ruby Raycroft, Myrtle Davidson, Stella Duchesneau, Anna Reynolds, Katherine Jackson, and Irene Legary; (second row) Nellie Jones, Thelma Brothers, Elizabeth Hand, Frances Murphy, Olive Newvine, and Theresa Fitzpatrick; (third row) Mary Marshall, Helen Pierce, and Ruth McDonald.

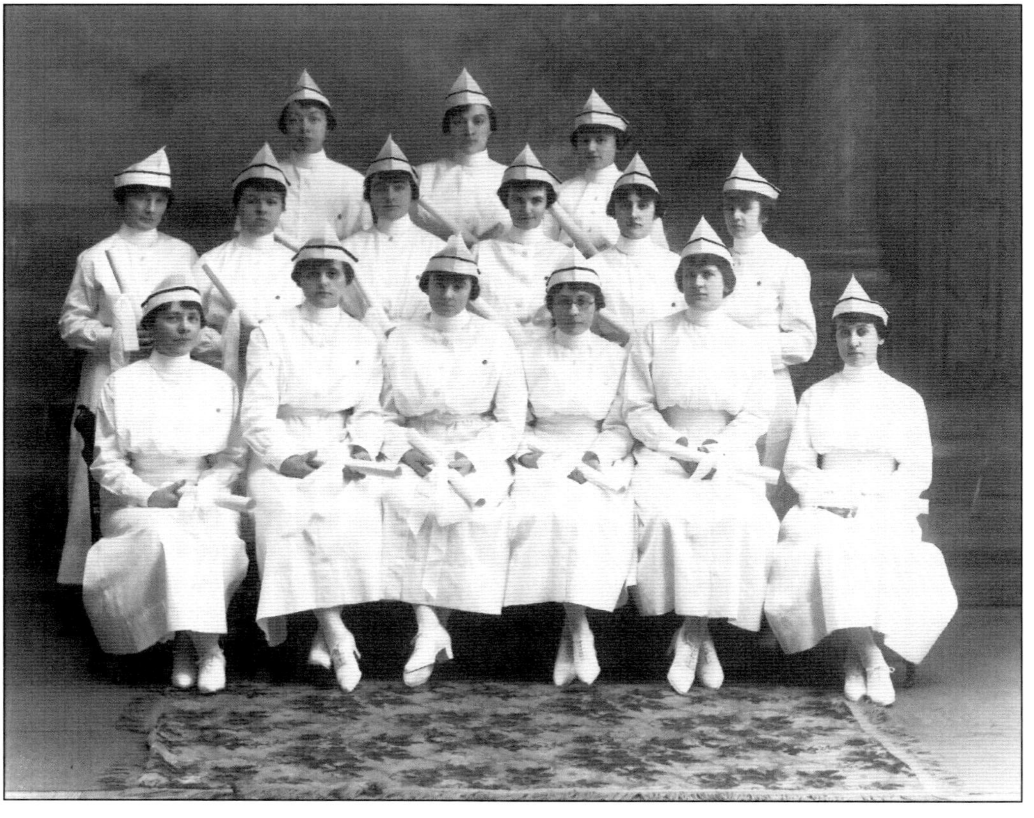

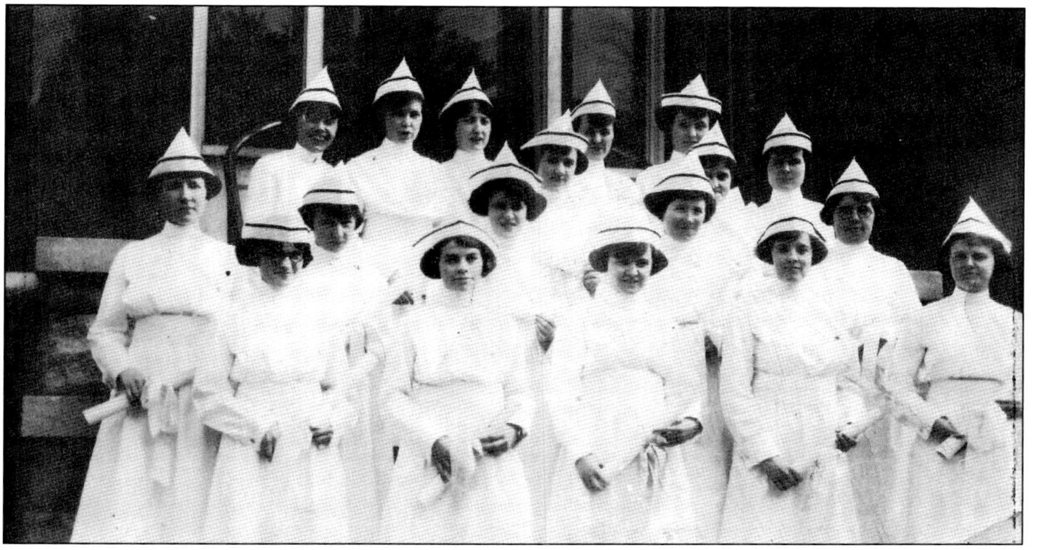

Pictured here is the class of 1923. They are, from left to right, (first row) Mabel Drake, Gertrude Doyle, Viola Wagner, Margaret Sullivan, Kathleen Higgins, and Marion Breen; (second row) Marion Hocknell, Florence McGowan, Helen Keegan, Mildred Wilson, Margaret Lynch, Catherine Sullivan, and Kathleen McEvoy; (third row) Lillian Kiah, Clio Bourke, Bernadette Contway, Elva Brown, and Thelma Allen. (Courtesy of Cathy Ramie.)

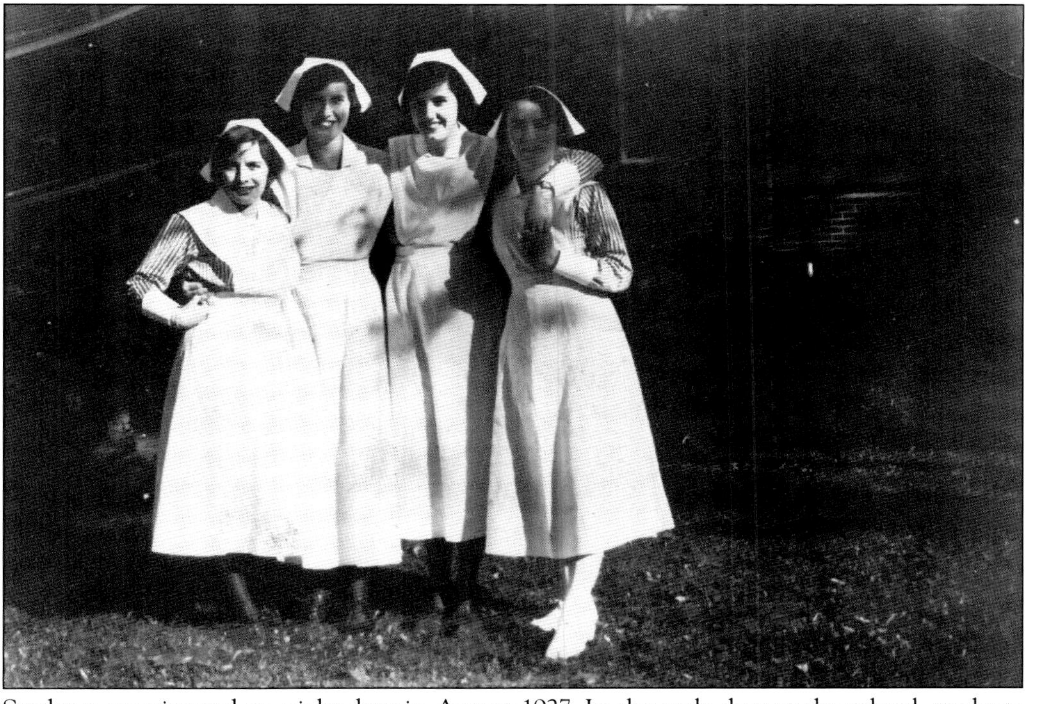

Students are pictured on night duty in August 1927. In the early days at the school, students worked 72 hours a week, all seven days, from 7:00 a.m. to 7:00 p.m., or night duty, from 7:00 p.m. to 7:00 a.m. They had one hour off every day. Once a week, they had time off from 2:00 p.m. until 9:30 p.m. Each student was given an annual vacation of two weeks.

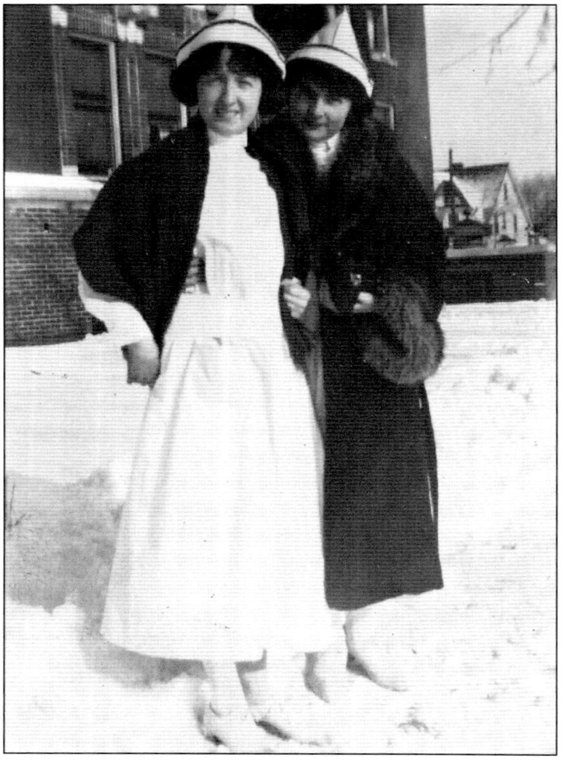

Unidentified members of the class of 1923 pose outside the nurses' residence in the winter. (Courtesy of Cathy Ramie.)

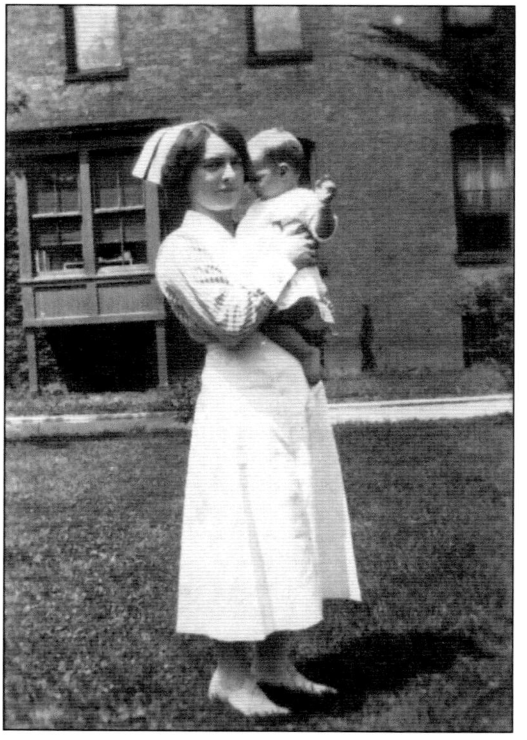

Marion Hurley, a member of the class of 1927, poses with "Baby" Cusick in 1926.

Marion Hurley is pictured with three unidentified classmates in Clifton Springs, New York, in 1927.

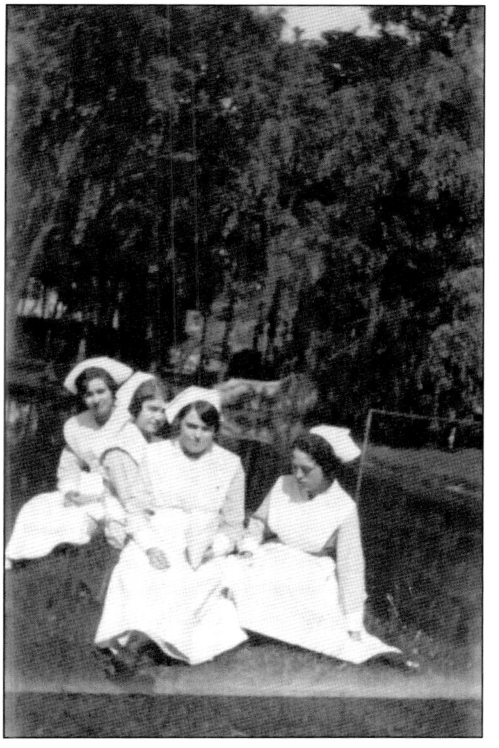

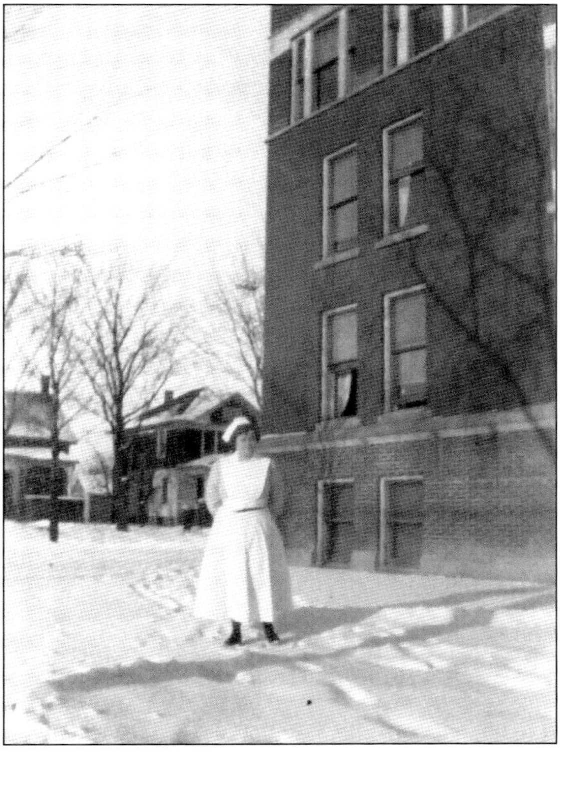

Marion Wallace, a member of the class of 1927, is pictured outside of the nurses' residence on March 3, 1925.

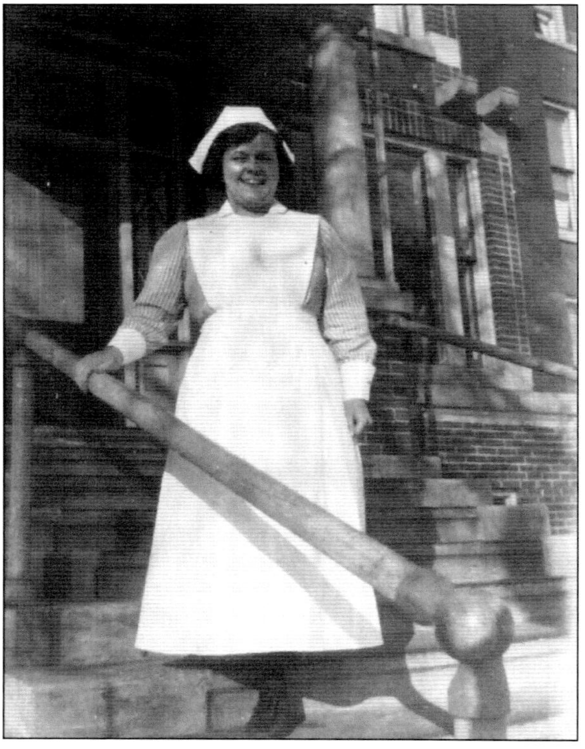

Here, Marion Wallace poses on the stairs of the nurses' residence.

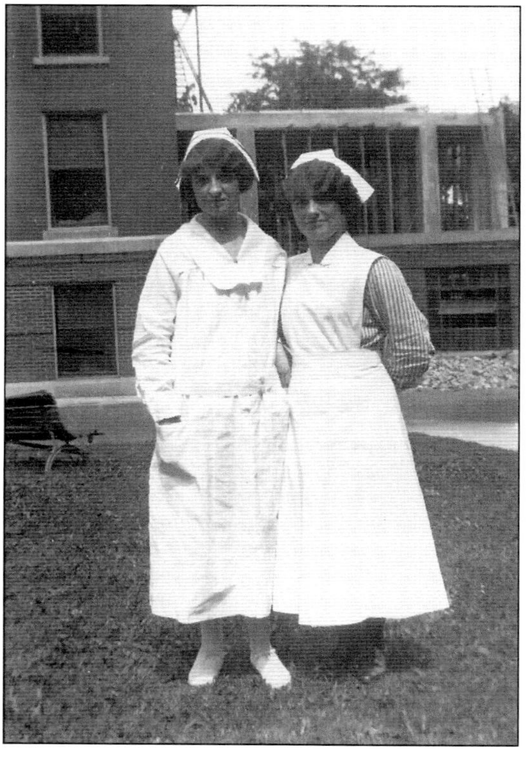

Two unidentified members of the class of 1923 pose in front of the construction site for an addition to the nurses' residence. (Courtesy of Cathy Ramie.)

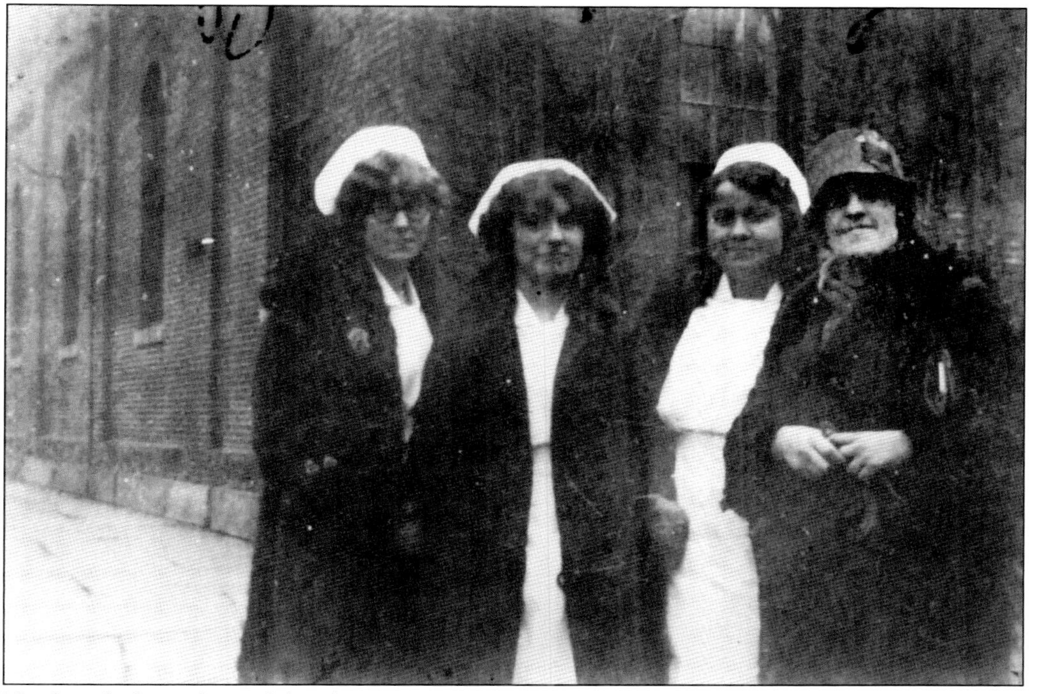

Unidentified members of the class of 1927 pose for a photograph in Clifton Springs, New York.

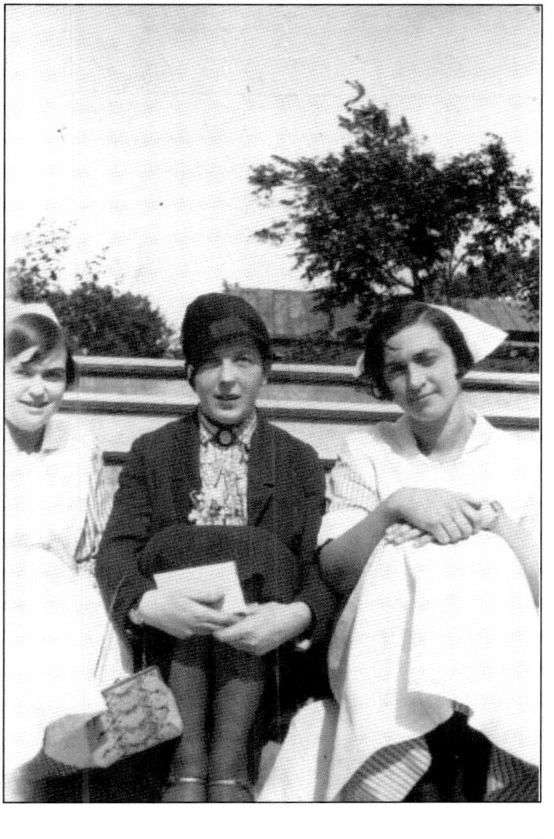

Three unidentified members of the class of 1927 are pictured on June 7, 1927, in Clifton Springs, New York.

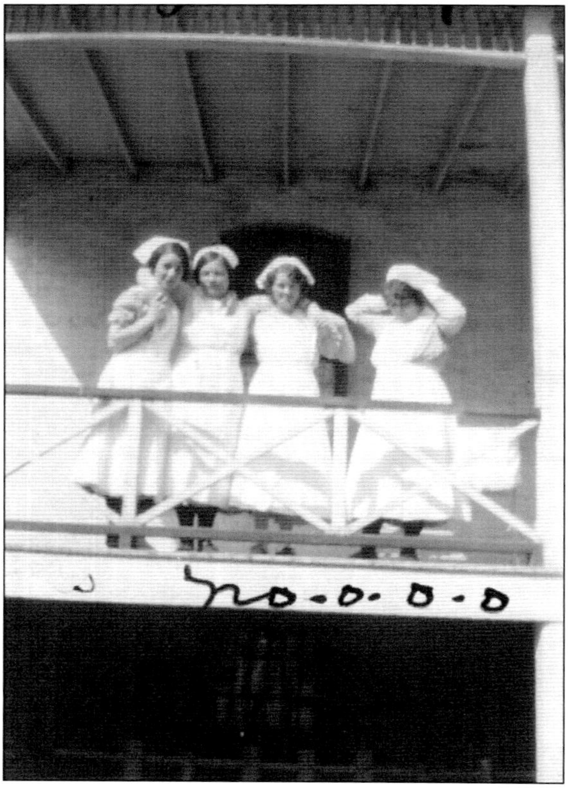

These members of the class of 1927 are pictured on a balcony. The writing on the picture says, "No-o-o-o." Below, members of the class of 1927 are joking around outside the nurses' residence. The picture is captioned "Surprised."

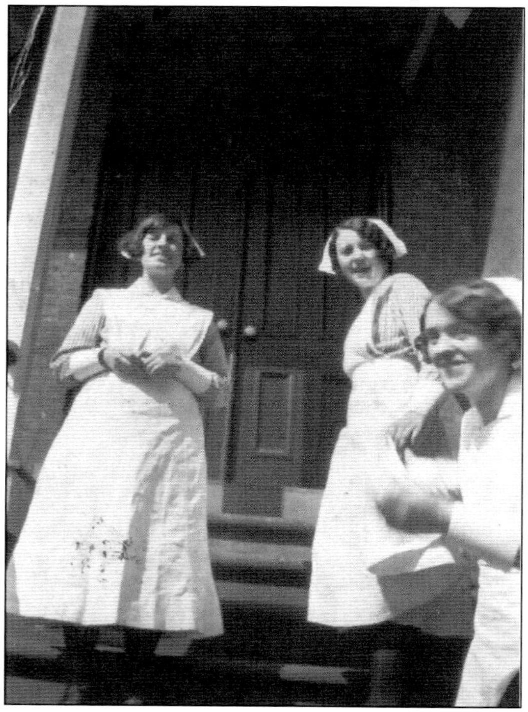

This is a portrait of Marion Wallace. She later married and became Mrs. Hubert Silver.

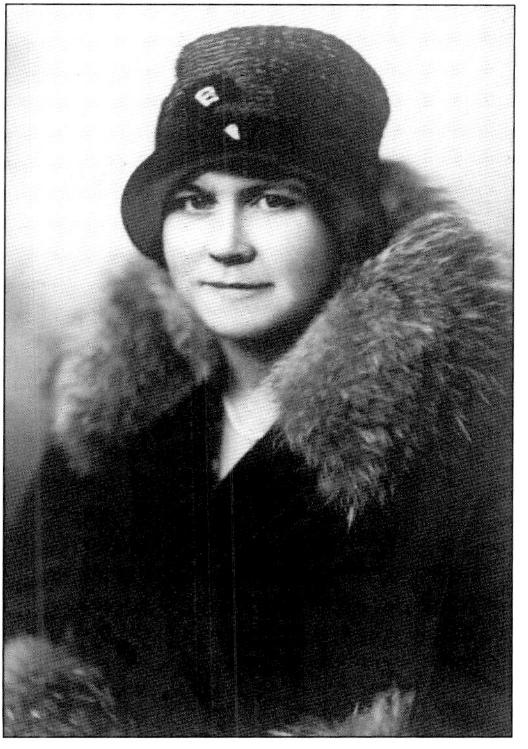

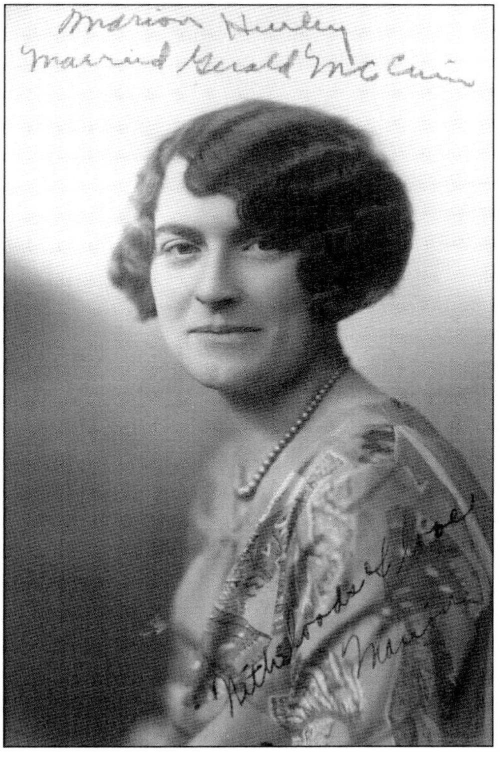

This is a portrait of Marion Hurley, who married Gerald McCain. Marion signed the picture, "With Loads of Love, Marion."

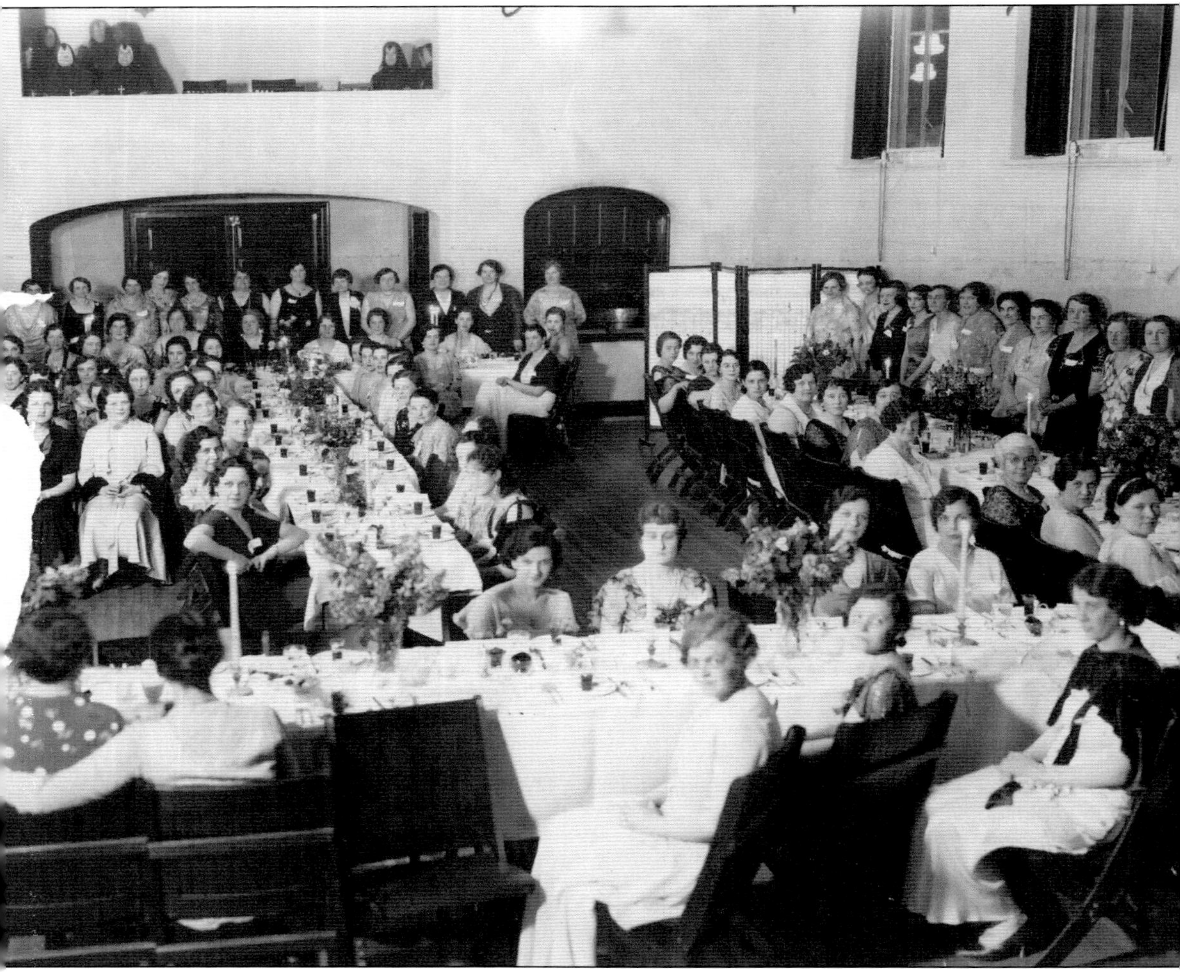

An alumnae banquet in 1933 was held in the auditorium at Hepburn Hospital Nursing School. Nuns are observing from the balcony as the alumnae enjoy the event.

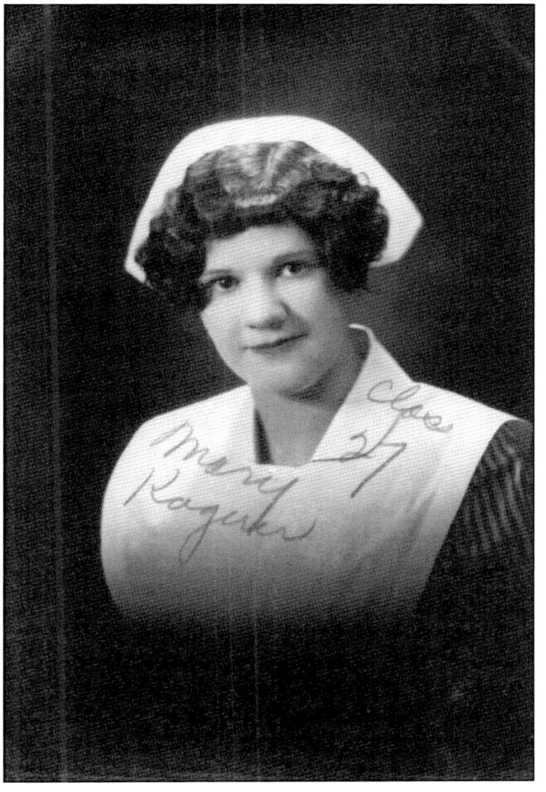

Mary Kagerer, pictured on the right, was a member of the class of 1927. Frances Callan, pictured below, was also member of the class of 1927, and she later served as the alumnae association president from 1940 to 1942.

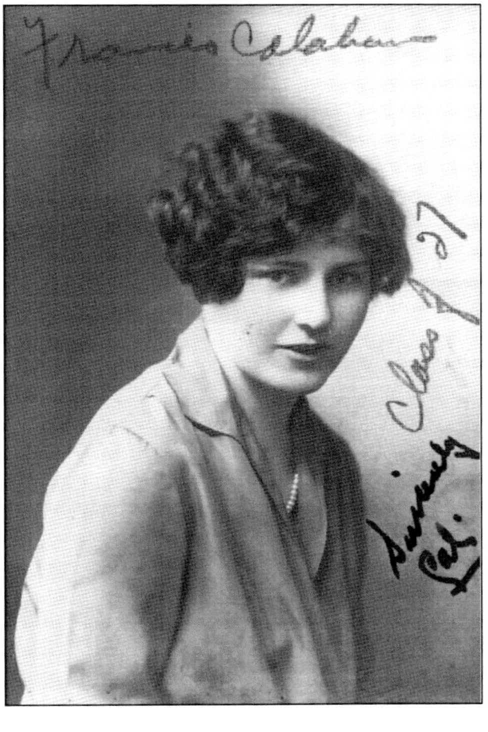

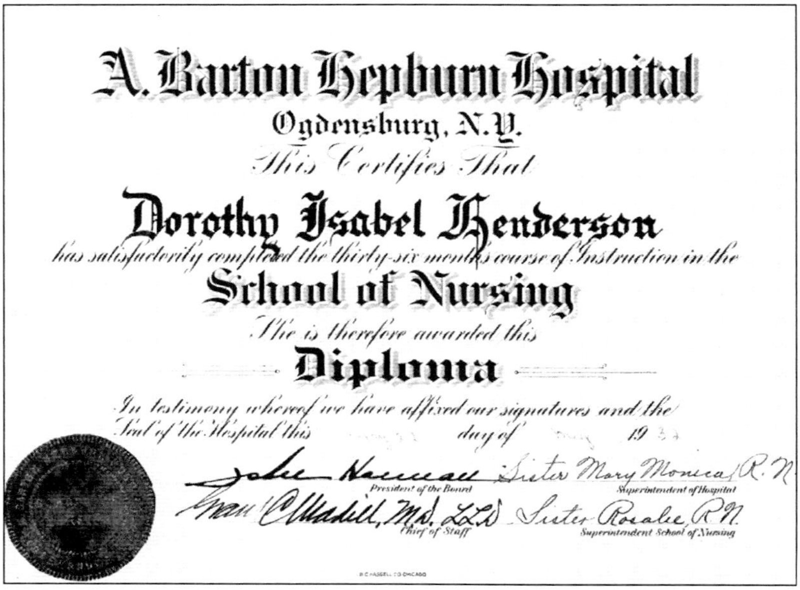

A. Barton Hepburn Hospital

Ogdensburg, N.Y.

This Certifies That

Dorothy Isabel Henderson

has satisfactorily completed the thirty-six months course of Instruction in the

School of Nursing

She is therefore awarded this

Diploma

In testimony whereof we have affixed our signatures and the Seal of the Hospital this day of 19

Sister Mary Monica R.N.

President of the Board — Superintendent of Hospital

Sister Rosalie R.N.

Chief of Staff — Superintendent School of Nursing

Pictured is the A. Barton Hepburn Hospital School of Nursing diploma issued to Dorothy Isabel Henderson in 1932. (Courtesy of Jennifer Shaver.)

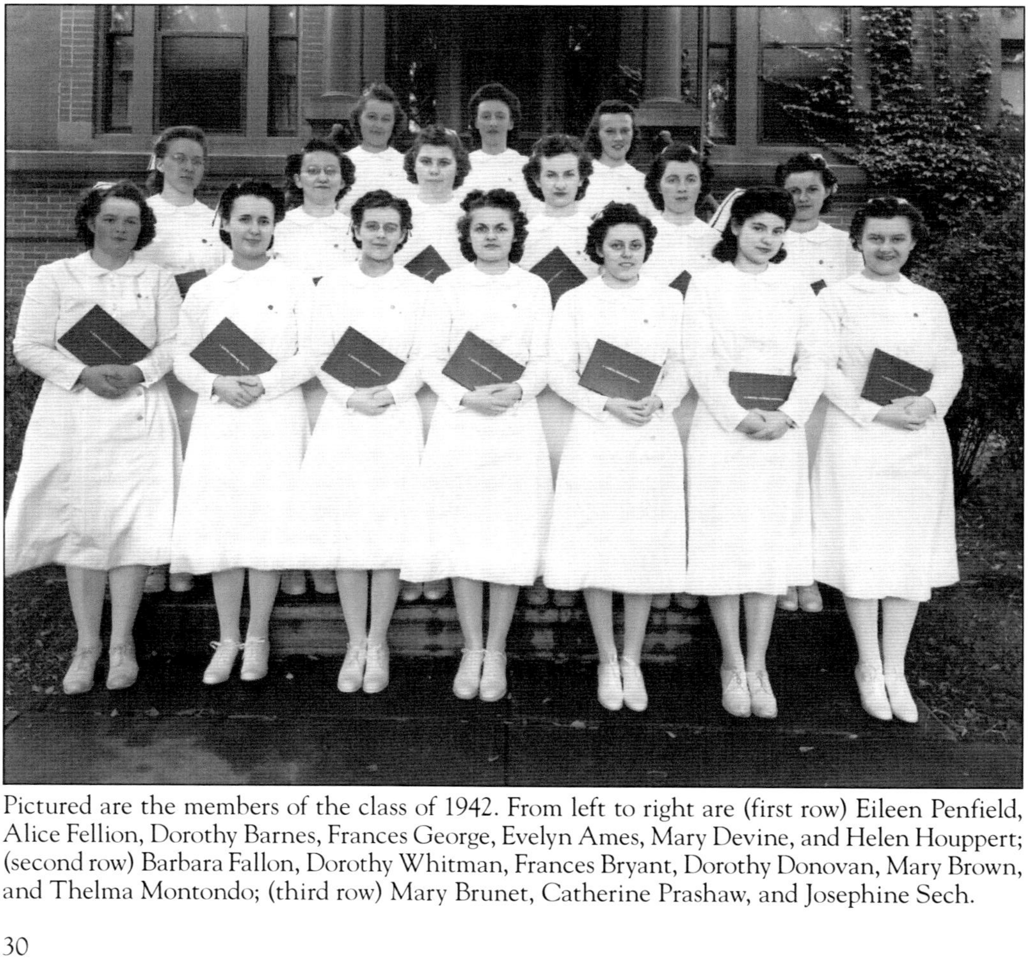

Pictured are the members of the class of 1942. From left to right are (first row) Eileen Penfield, Alice Fellion, Dorothy Barnes, Frances George, Evelyn Ames, Mary Devine, and Helen Houppert; (second row) Barbara Fallon, Dorothy Whitman, Frances Bryant, Dorothy Donovan, Mary Brown, and Thelma Montondo; (third row) Mary Brunet, Catherine Prashaw, and Josephine Sech.

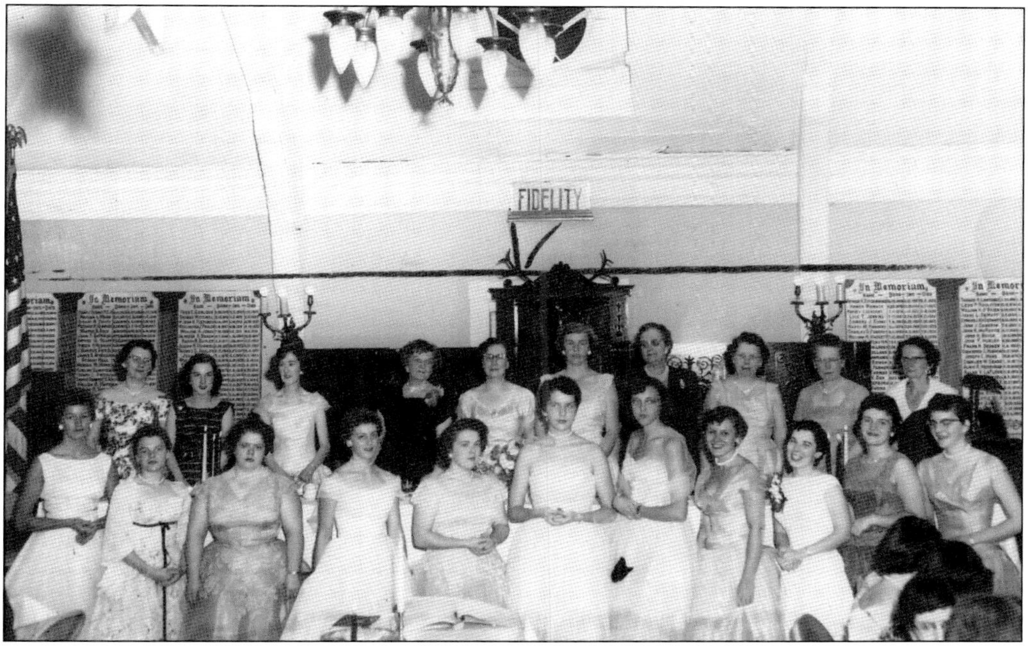

This is a c. 1954 photograph of the Florence Nightingale Induction at the Elks Club. Some of those in the first row are Bev Bessette Ashlaw, Yvonne Densmore McGill, Ann Grant Clinton, Geraldine Hillborne Montroy, Carol Hughto, Pauline Lashomb Donahue, Ann Sholette Dillon, and Carol Tierney. Among those in the second row are Carol Ann Wilcox Yando, Carolyn Kelly, Iona Rumble Singh, Wava Earle, Grace Schermerhorn Barr, Bessie Brown Lavigne, Lillian Kiah, Helen Brown Ward, and Ann Finney. The Florence Nightingale Induction was a capping ceremony at the end of the first year when students made a Florence Nightingale pledge to service.

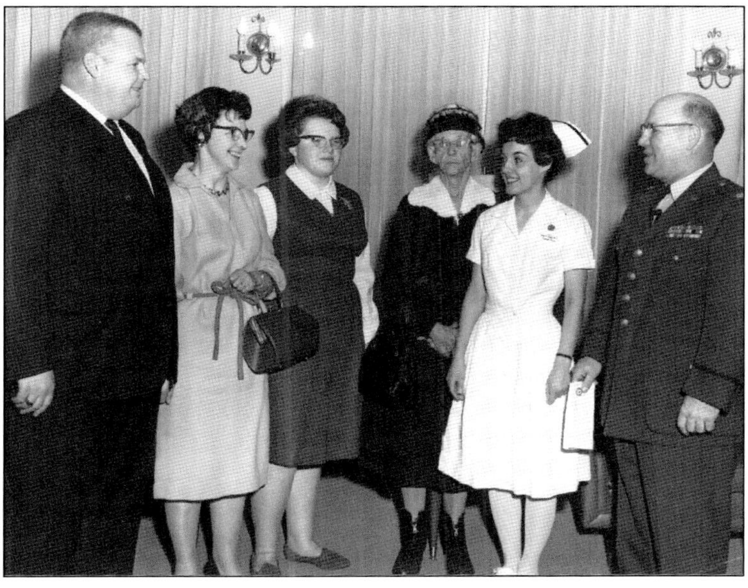

This picture was taken at the hospital at a reception for Elaine C. Doyle, class of 1962, before she left to enter the US Air Force. Pictured from left to right are Joseph Doyle (Elaine's father), Frances Doyle (Elaine's mother), Anita Doyle, Elaine's Grandmother Woodside, Elaine, and Lawrence Bouchard (the officer of the Air Force who inducted Elaine). (Courtesy of Frances Doyle.)

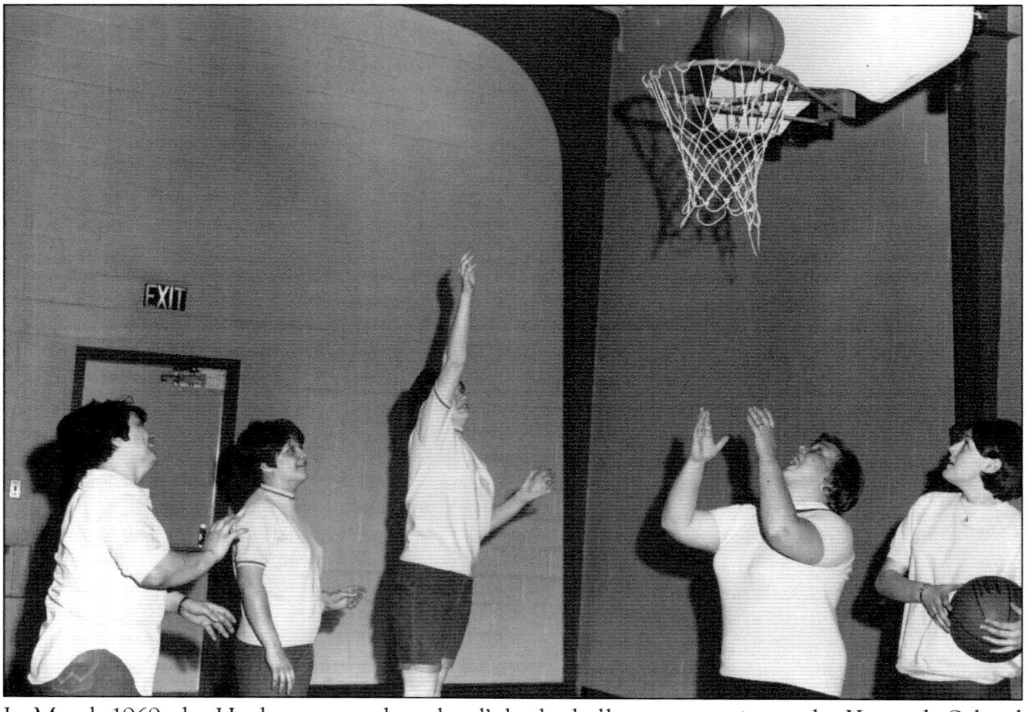

In March 1969, the Hepburnettes, the school's basketball team, practice at the Kennedy School gymnasium. Pictured are Cassie Donnelly, Emily Hooper, Shirley Beaulieu, Carol Sharlow, and Mary Morley.

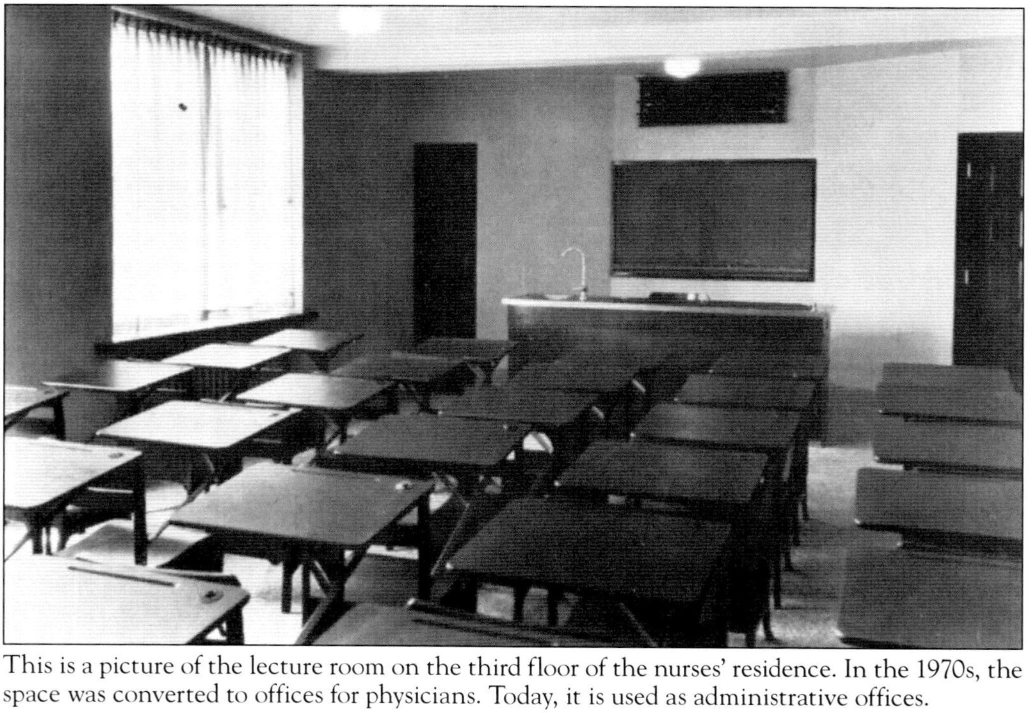

This is a picture of the lecture room on the third floor of the nurses' residence. In the 1970s, the space was converted to offices for physicians. Today, it is used as administrative offices.

This photograph captures a graduation ceremony held in June 1968. Recessing down the aisle, from front to back, are Sandra Anderson Lyons, Cassie Donnelly, Frances Hart, and Jean Hepburn Cappecino. On stage are, from the left to the right, Barbara Mallette Kirby, Ann MacCaull, Mary Sargent Spooner, Mary Yerdon Caratsole, Patricia Ibey, Carol Smith Kilroy, Eileen McCormick Elwood, and Elizabeth Loucks Chapman.

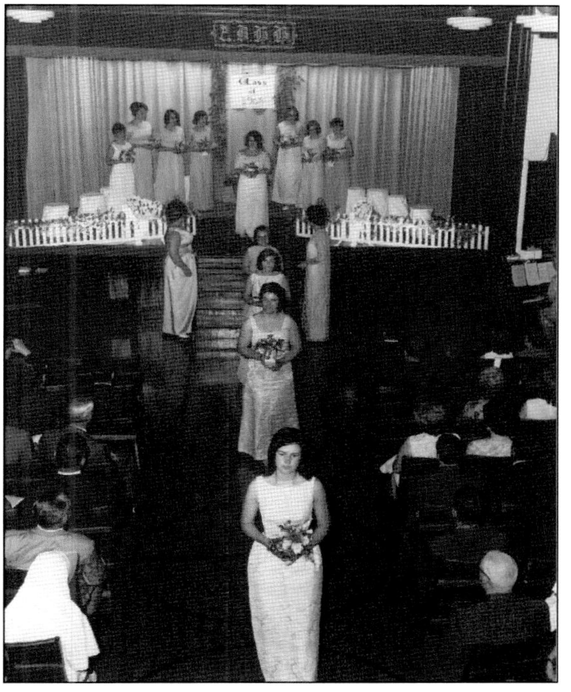

This picture was taken at the May 1965 senior class formal. Shown from left to right are Sr. Mary Loretta (faculty), John Gutlman (escort), Janet Perry (senior), Michael Langstaff (escort), Patricia Durant (senior), and Sr. Madeleine William (teaching director).

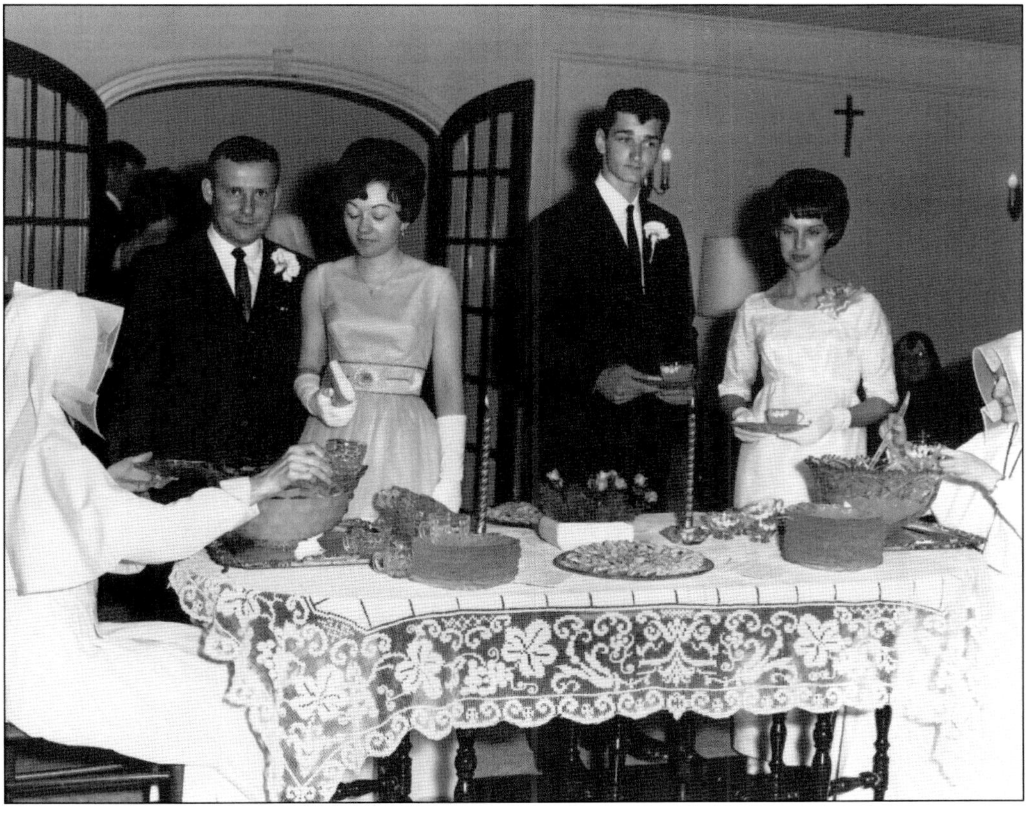

SCHOOL OF NURSING

A. BARTON HEPBURN HOSPITAL

Ogdensburg, New York

PRE-ADMISSION		
Psychometric Test	$ 8.00	
Physical Examination Fee	12.00	
Total		$ 20.00
FIRST YEAR (Payable in two installments—on admission and the following January)		
Tuition	$200.00	
(Includes $20.00 acceptance fee)		
*Textbooks	100.00	
Health Service Fee	15.00	
Library Fee	20.00	
Laboratory Fee	20.00	
Social and Recreation Fee	10.00	
Total		$365.00
SECOND YEAR (Payable in September)		
Tuition	$110.00	
*Textbooks	45.00	
Achievement Test Fee	5.00	
Health Service Fee	12.00	
Library Fee	15.00	
Social and Recreation Fee	10.00	
Total		$197.00
THIRD YEAR (Payable in September)		
Tuition	$ 75.00	
*Textbooks	15.00	
Achievement Test Fee	3.00	
Library Fee	15.00	
Social and Recreation Fee	10.00	
Graduation Expenses	35.00	
Total		$165.00
Grand Total		$747.00

*ADDITIONAL EXPENSES

1) Hospital, Medical-Surgical Insurance coverage required, group plan available. Approximate cost, $62.40 per year. Payable semi-annually—September and March.
2) Uniforms and cape $90.00
3) Bus transportation to Mater Dei College (freshman year only) $50.00
4) Cancer Nursing - Affiliation Maintenance Fee (Junior or Senior Year) $50.00

* Subject to change

NO REFUNDS WILL BE MADE AFTER ADMISSION TO THE SCHOOL

1964-66

This is a copy of the tuition schedule for the school of nursing from 1964 to 1966. The grand total for three years was $747.

RATES FOR REGISTERED NURSES

AS APPROVED BY

A. Barton Hepburn Hospital Alumnae Association

Shall Not Exceed

IN HOSPITAL

Medical, Surgical, Obstetrical, Communicable:
- 8 hour duty...... $4.00
- 12 hour duty...... $6.00

Mental, Alcoholic:
- 8 hour duty...... $4.65
- 12 hour duty...... $7.00

While caring for two patients—12 hour duty, each $4.50

Above prices include $1.00 *for board*

IN PRIVATE HOME

Medical, Obstetrical, Communicable:
- 12 hour duty...... $5.00
- 20 hour duty...... $6.00

Mental and Alcoholic:
- 12 hour duty...... $6.00
- 20 hour duty...... $7.00

While caring for two patients....
- 12 hr duty, each $4.00
- 20 hr duty, each $5.00

Above prices do not include $1.00 *for board*

HOURLY NURSING IN HOME OR HOSPITAL

One single hour........................ $1.50

For each of two or more consecutive hours $1.00

A charge of one-half day is made when in conjunction with one or more days.

Pictured is a rate card for registered nurses, as approved by the A. Barton Hepburn Hospital Alumnae Association.

Four

Construction from 1902 to 1975

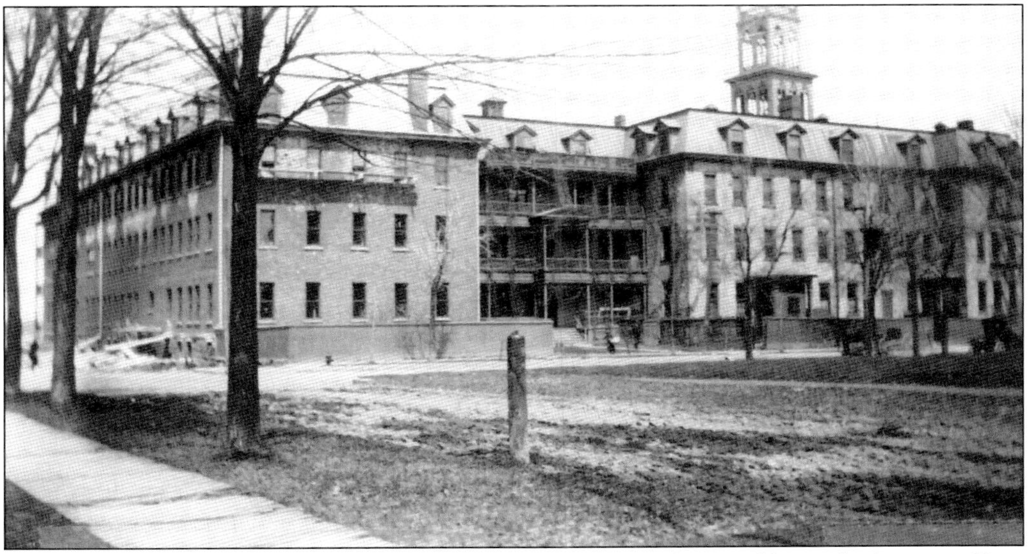

This is the original Ogdensburg City Hospital and Orphan Asylum Building, which was on King Street, across from the current hospital. The right-hand portion of the building is the addition that was added to the original Ford Mansion to accommodate the hospital in 1885. In 1902, when the hospital moved across the street to the new building, an orphanage and home for the elderly remained in these original buildings. In 1907, the orphanage and home for the elderly incorporated an addition that is shown on the west (left) side of the building.

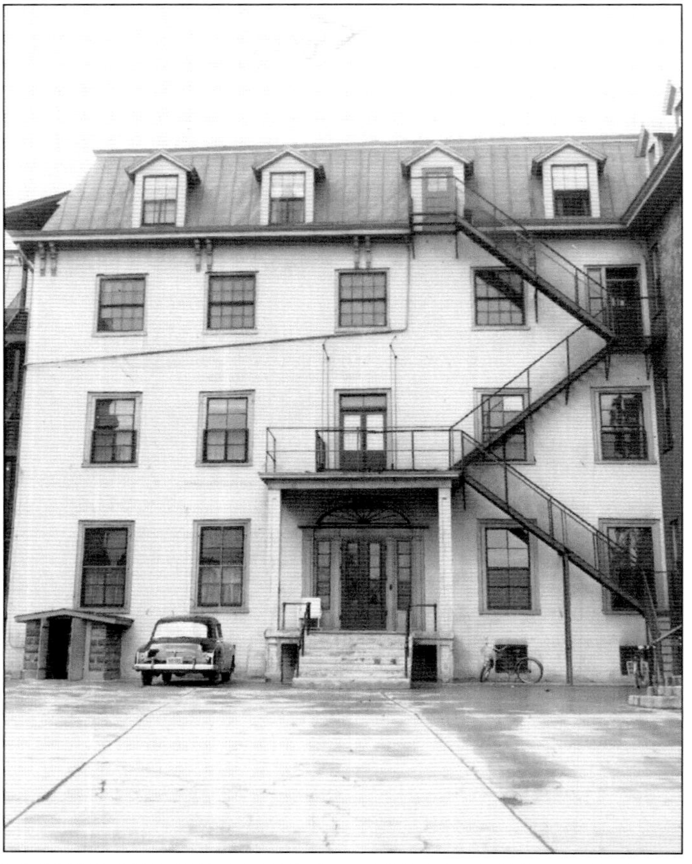

This is the 1907 western addition to the old Ford Mansion on King Street prior to its demolition in the 1960s.

A new, 60-bed hospital was built across the street from the Ford Mansion in 1902 to meet the special needs of the sick. George Hall, the mayor of Ogdensburg at the time, paid half the cost to complete the hospital building project. This is a picture of the 1902 building facing King Street. All the way up in the left-hand corner of the building, through the tall windows, are the operating rooms. The first floor was used for offices, and on the second floor were private rooms.

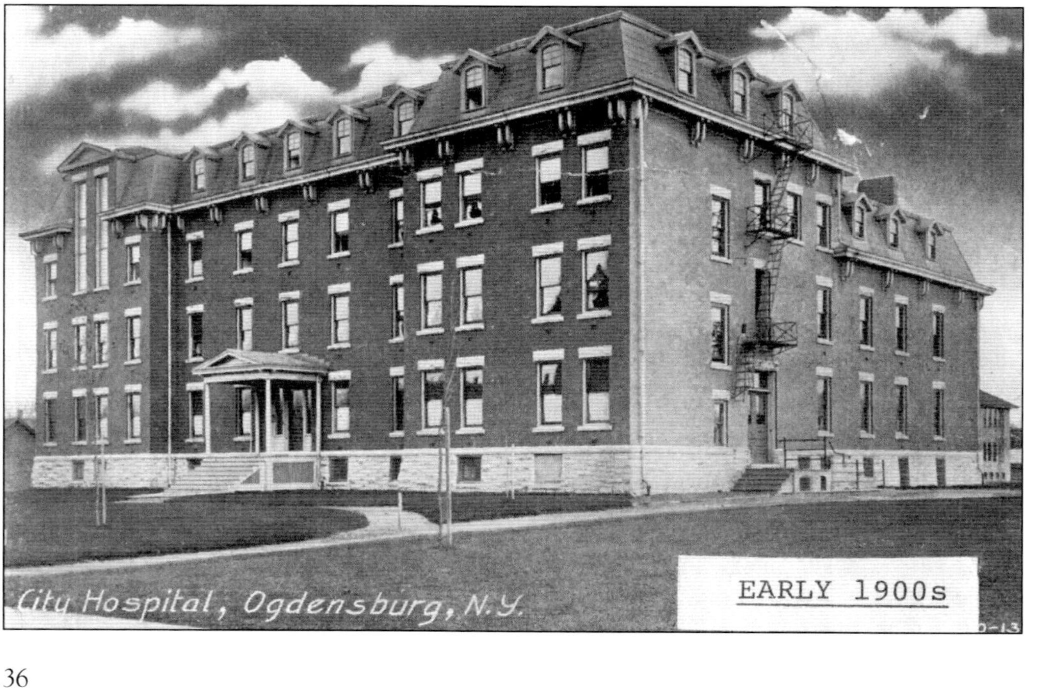

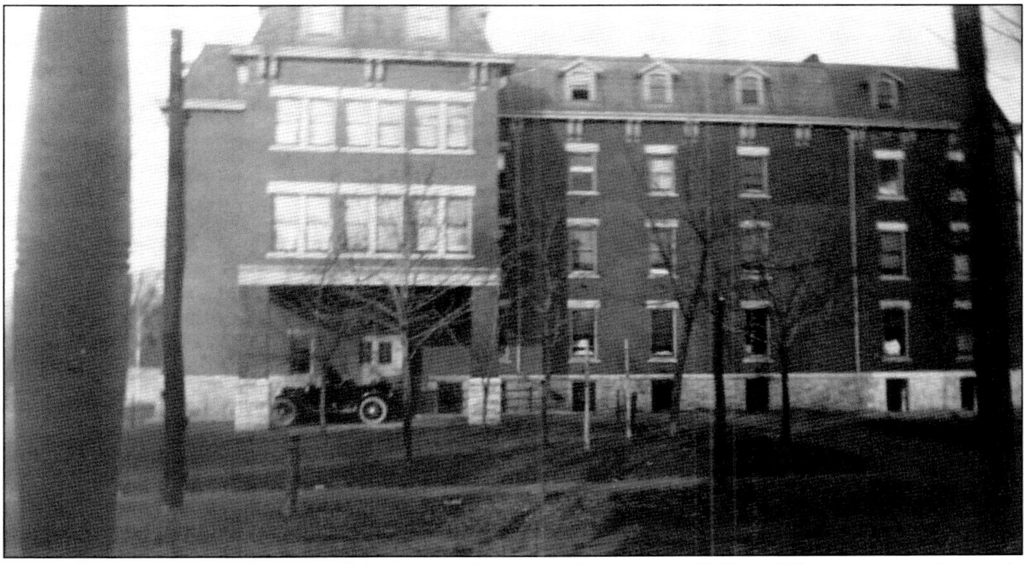

The solarium and south wing of the hospital were added to the 1902 building later in the early 1900s. The wing later housed the emergency entrance and survived the construction of the 1960 building when the rest of the 1902 building was razed. This wing was finally removed to make way for the 1970s addition, which now houses the emergency department, the intensive care unit, and other departments.

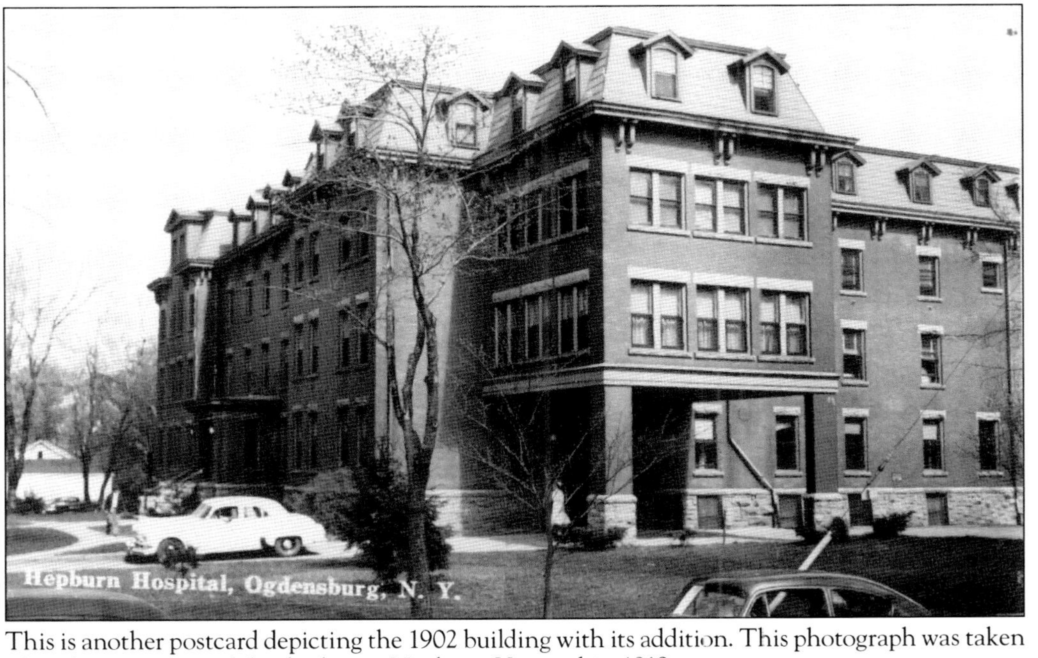

This is another postcard depicting the 1902 building with its addition. This photograph was taken after the renaming of the facility to Hepburn Hospital in 1918.

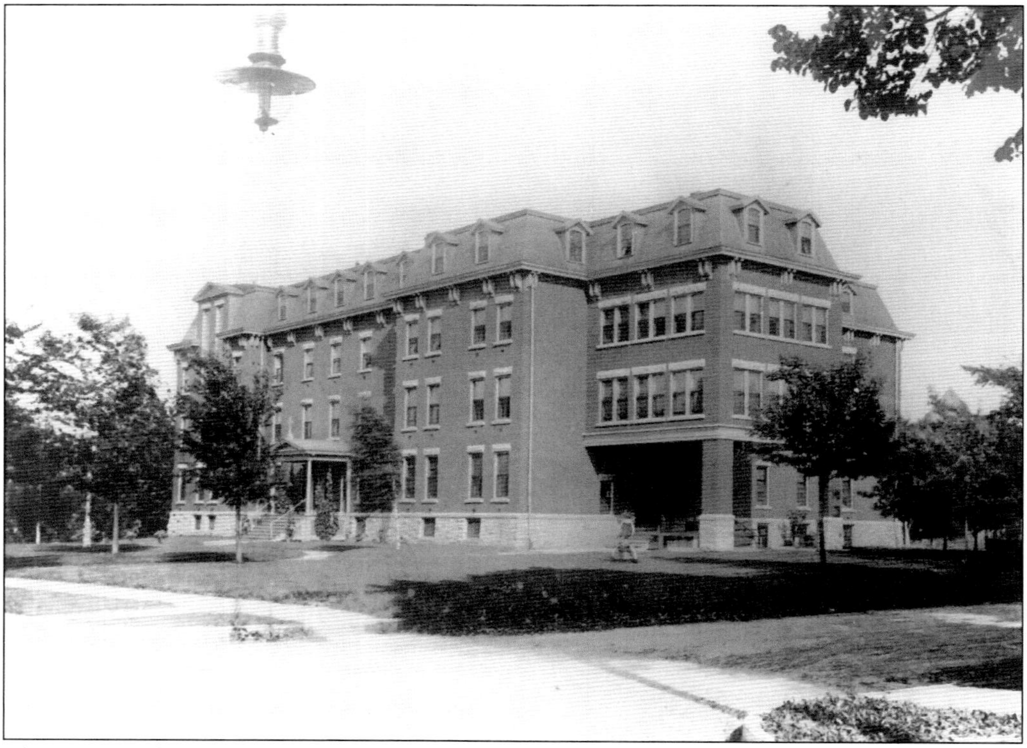

This picture also shows the 1902 building with the west-side addition and porte-cochère. The second floor above the porte-cochère was a sunporch, and the third floor was the location of the chapel.

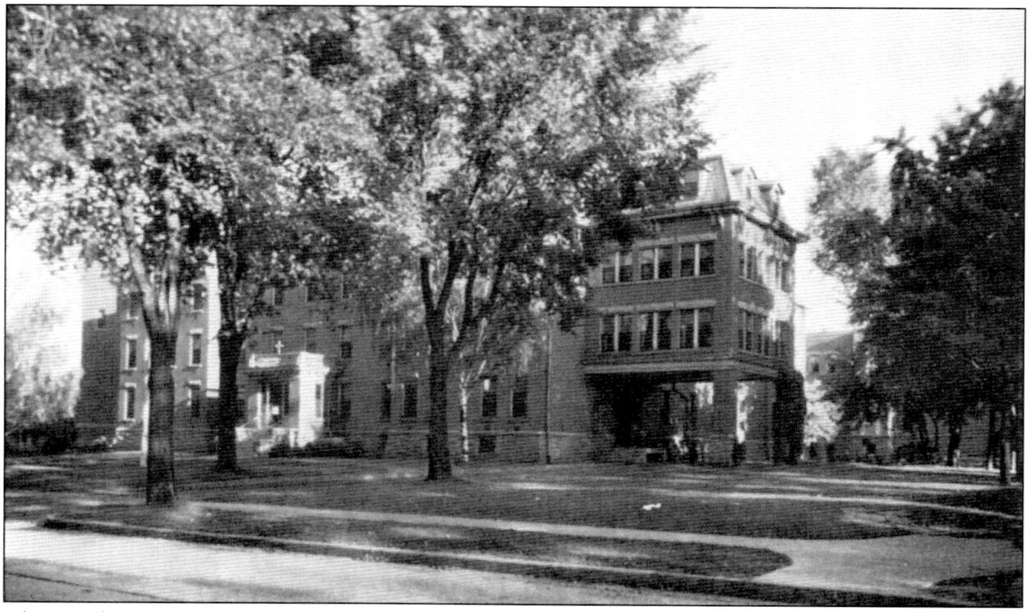

This is a later picture of the 1902 building with the west-wing addition, now surrounded by more mature trees. In the background, on the right, part of the nurses' residence is visible.

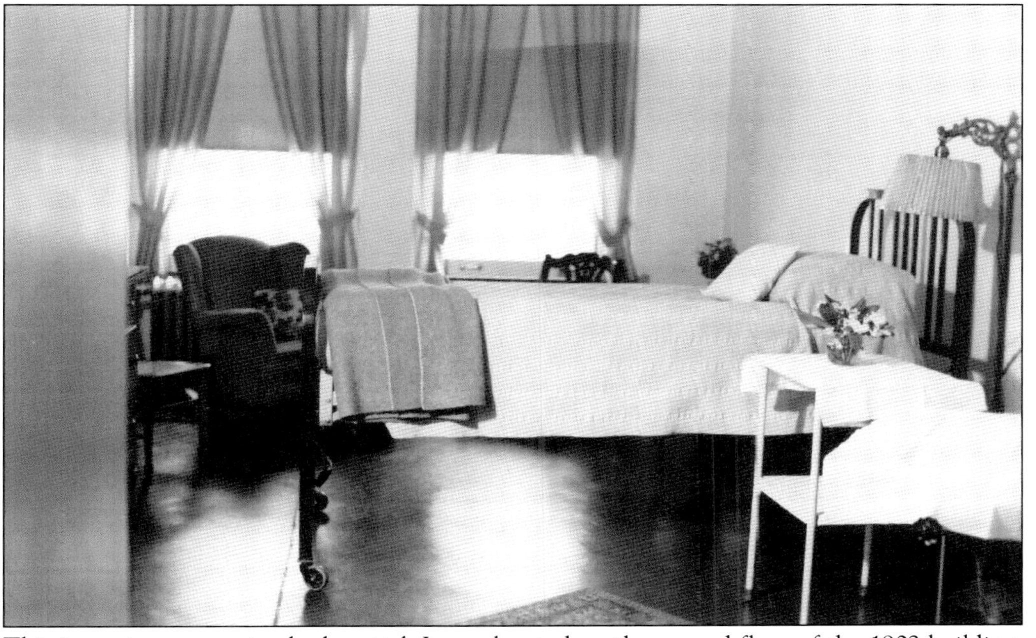

This is a private room in the hospital. It was located on the second floor of the 1902 building. The rooms were decorated to enhance the comfort of the patient in the attempt to provide a more homelike environment. In most of today's hospitals, rugs, draperies, and upholstered furniture would not be found because of concerns about infection control and safety.

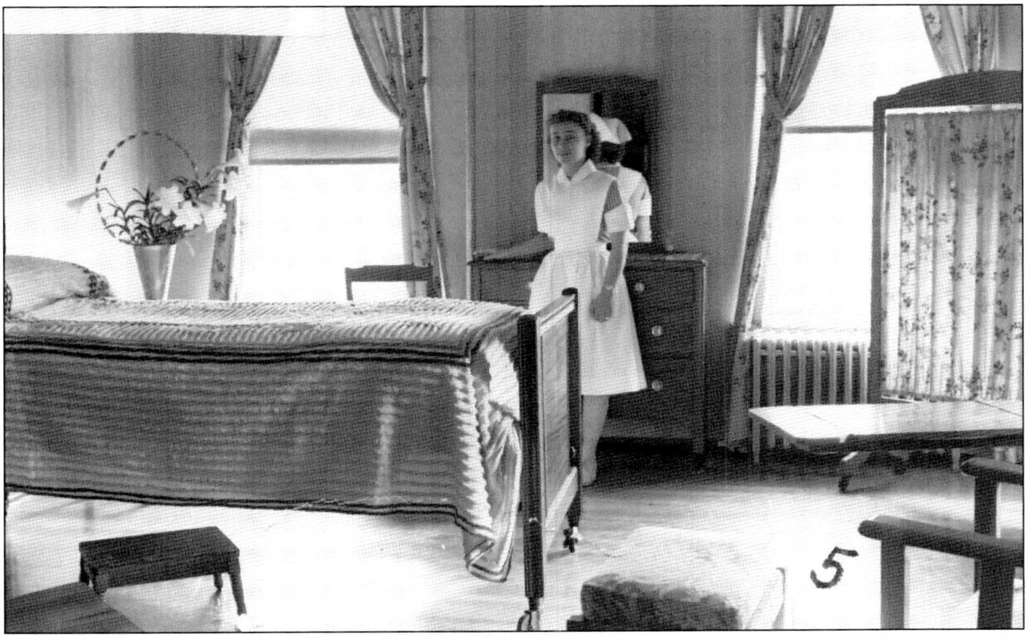

An unidentified nurse poses in a private room. Again, the environment is homey and comfortable. It was not uncommon for patients to have extended stays in the hospital in those days, whereas today's patients have shorter recovery times. There is a screen in the right side of the room to provide privacy for the patient when changing.

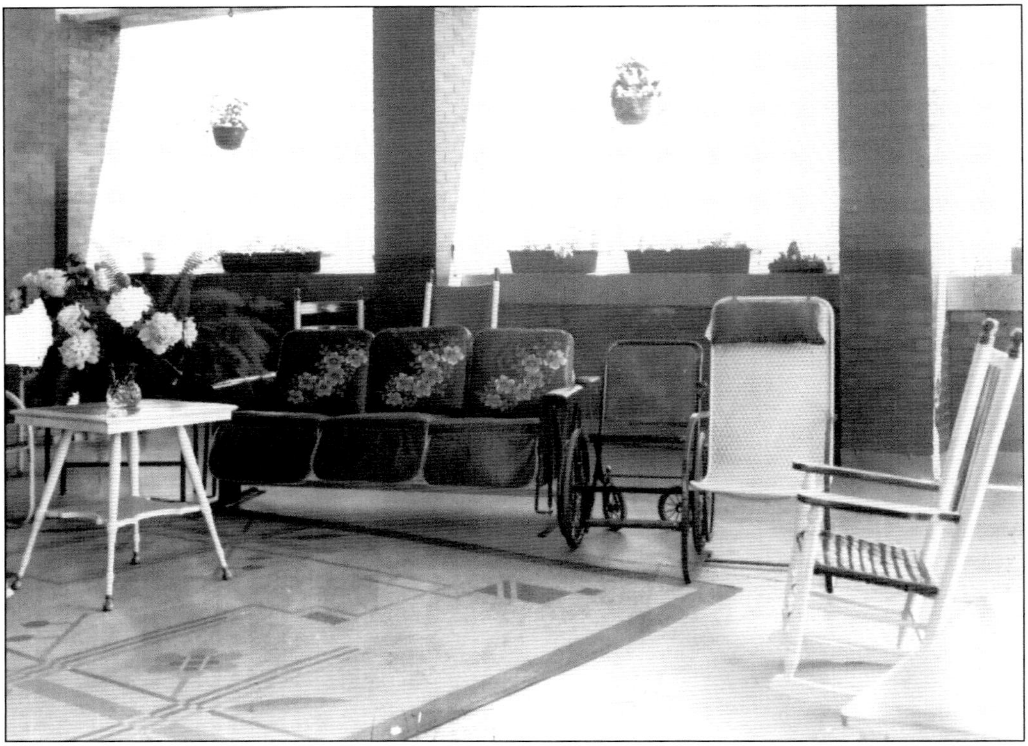

This is a photograph of the roof of the 1918 wing of the hospital. This space was used as a place for patients to relax and get fresh air.

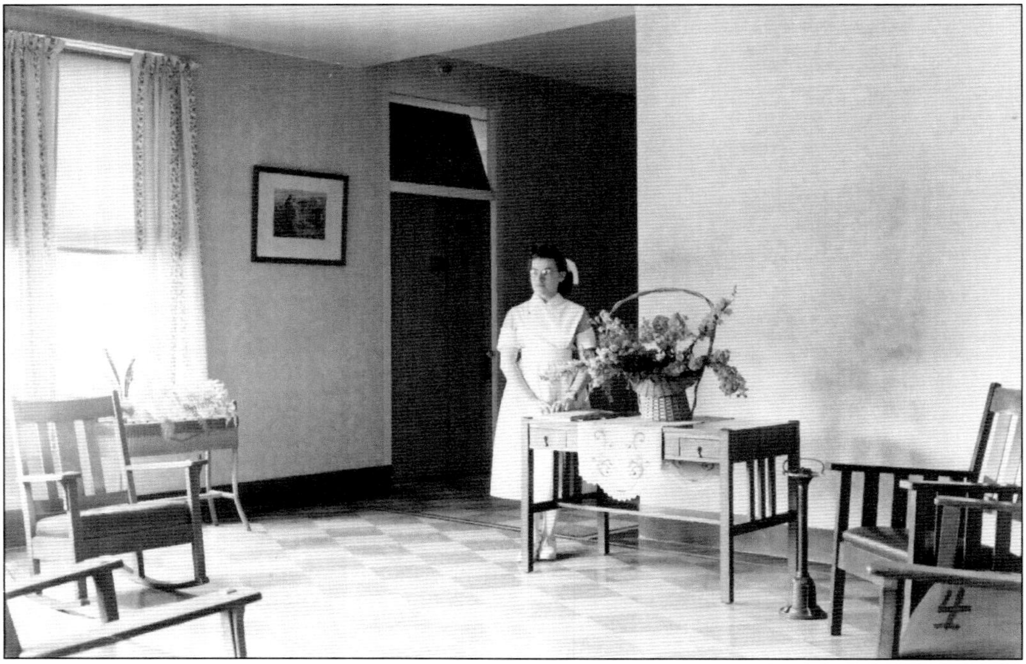

An unidentified nurse stands in the solarium.

This image of an operating room is perhaps from the 1920s.

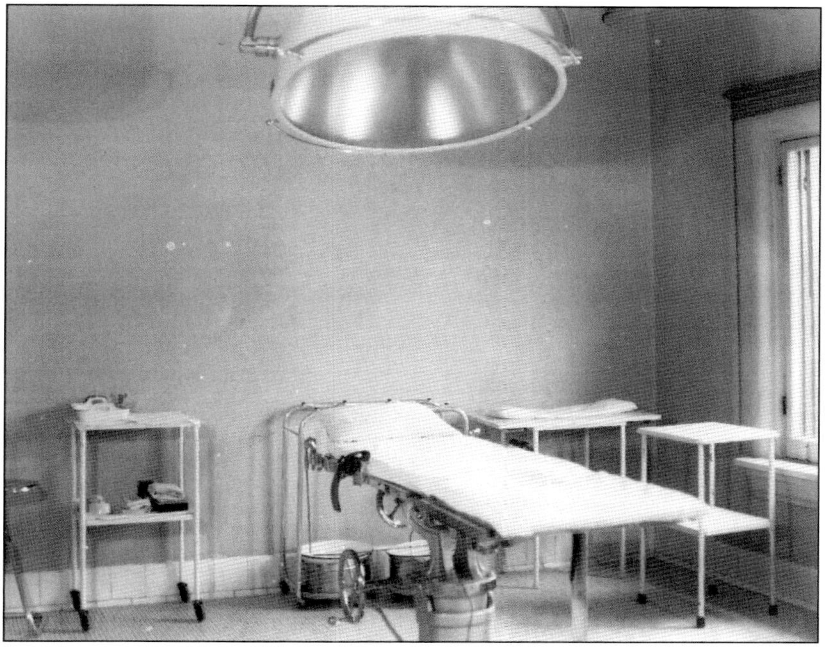

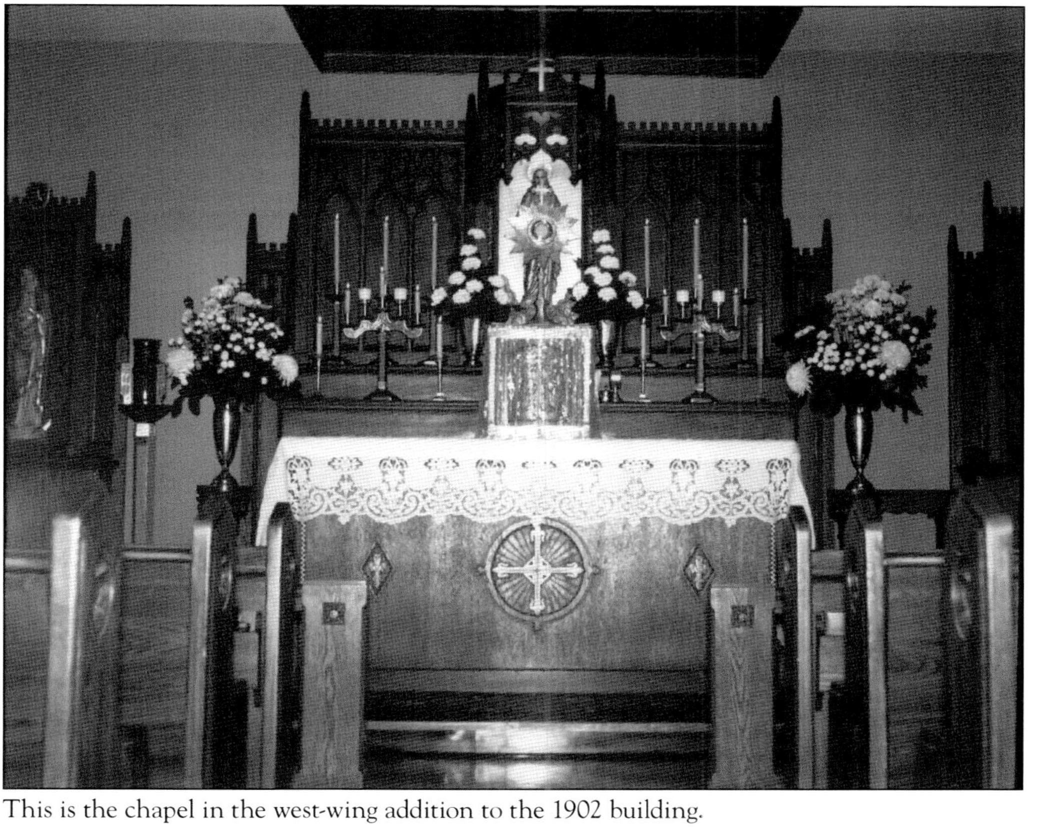

This is the chapel in the west-wing addition to the 1902 building.

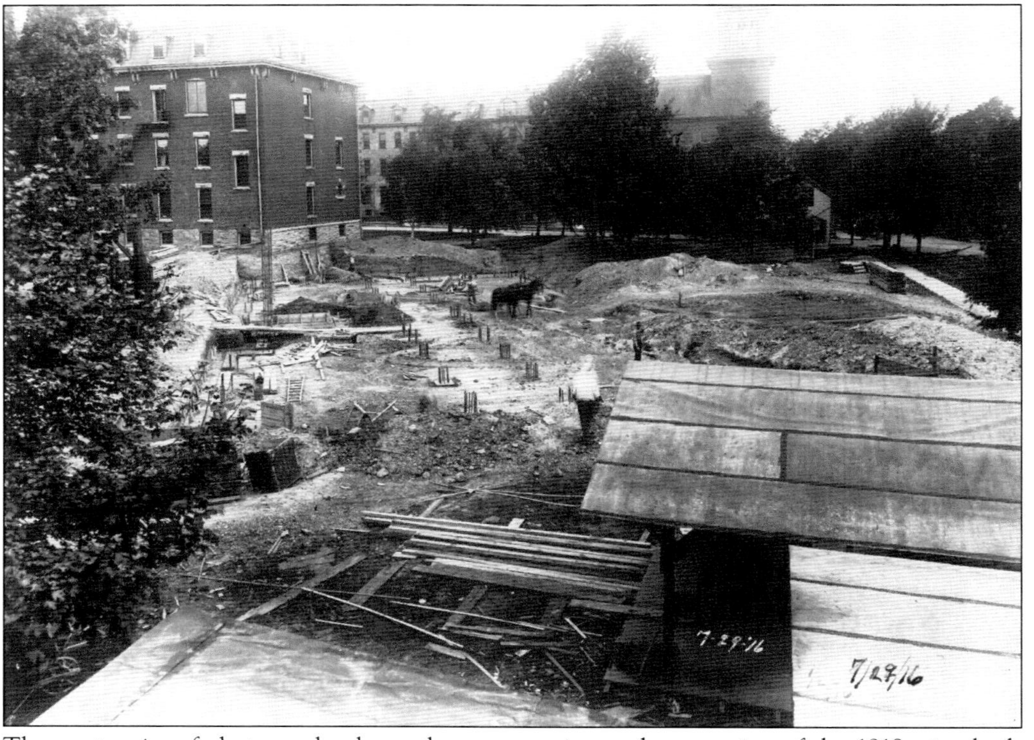

The next series of photographs shows the construction and progression of the 1918 wing built on the east side of hospital. Construction began in 1916. This photograph is from July 29, 1916, when crews began preparing the land for foundation. Horses are being used for the movement of heavy items.

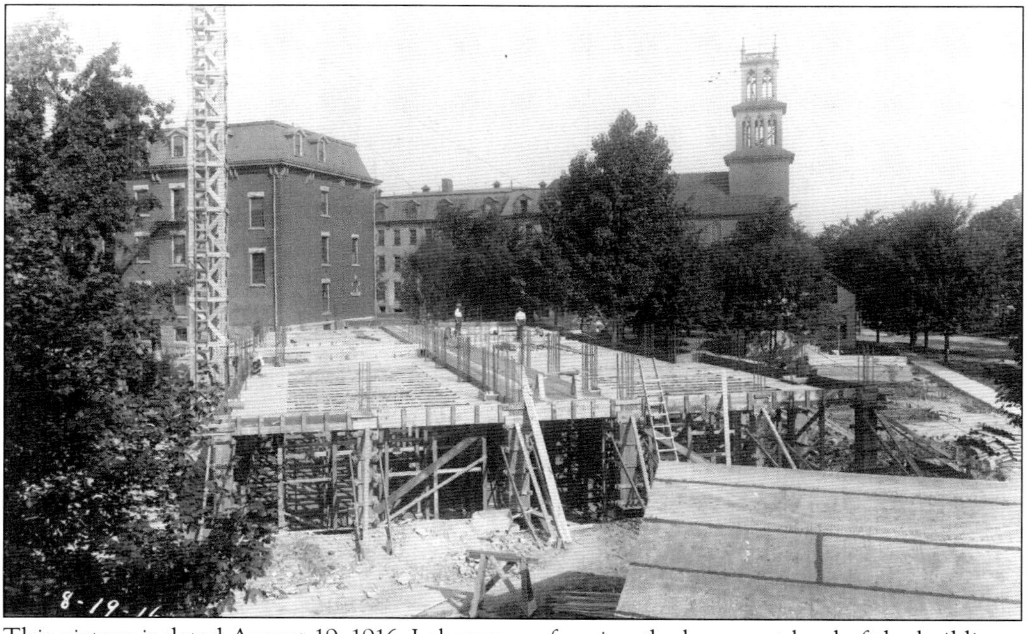

This picture is dated August 19, 1916. Laborers are framing the basement level of the building.

This picture is dated September 16, 1916, and shows that the framing of the first and second floors of the building is in progress.

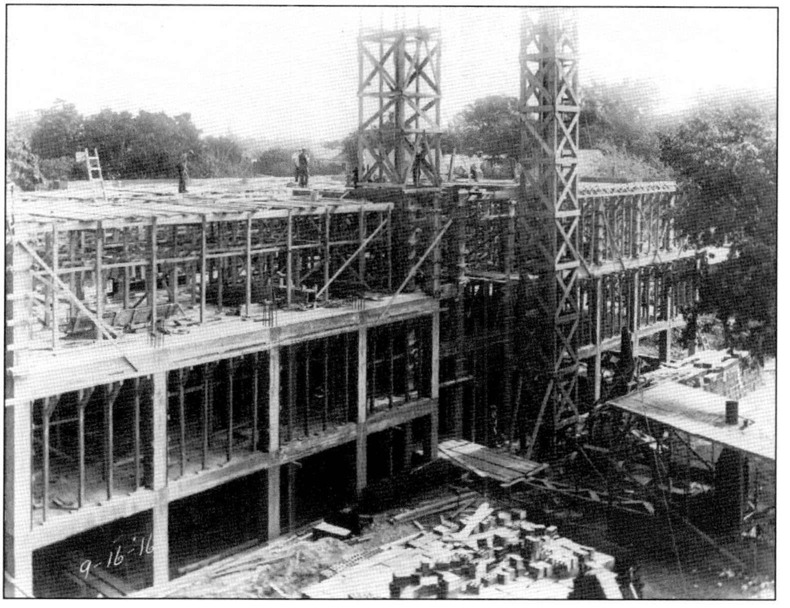

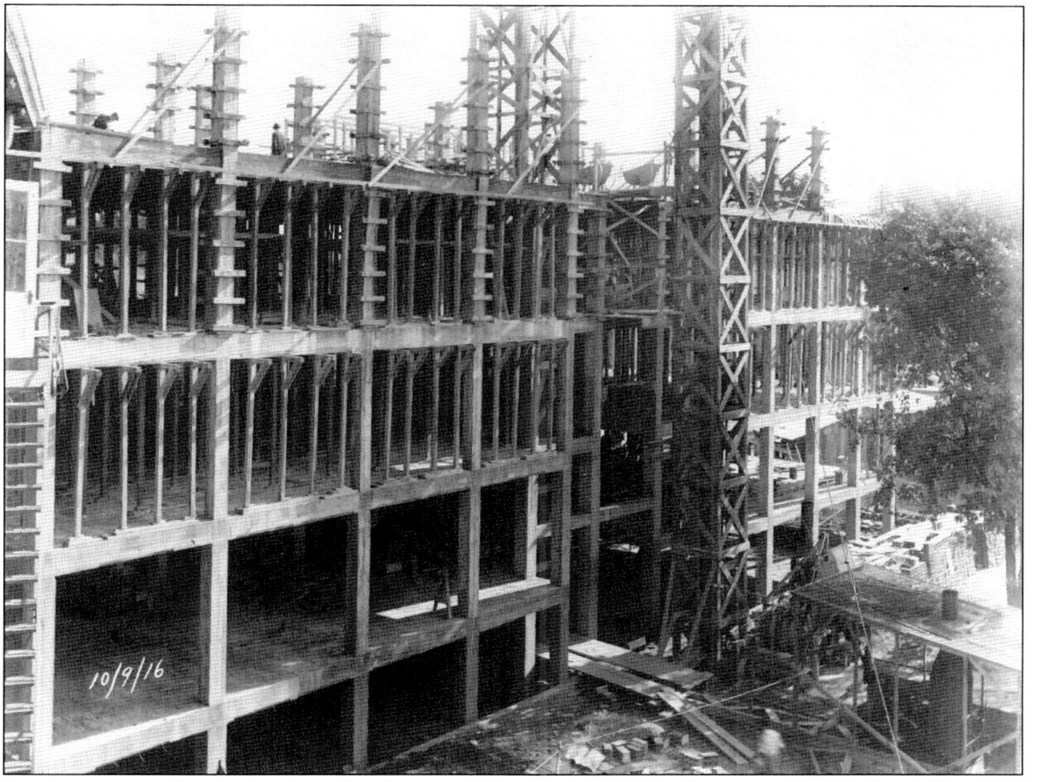

In this image dated October 9, 1916, workers are framing the second and third floors of the building.

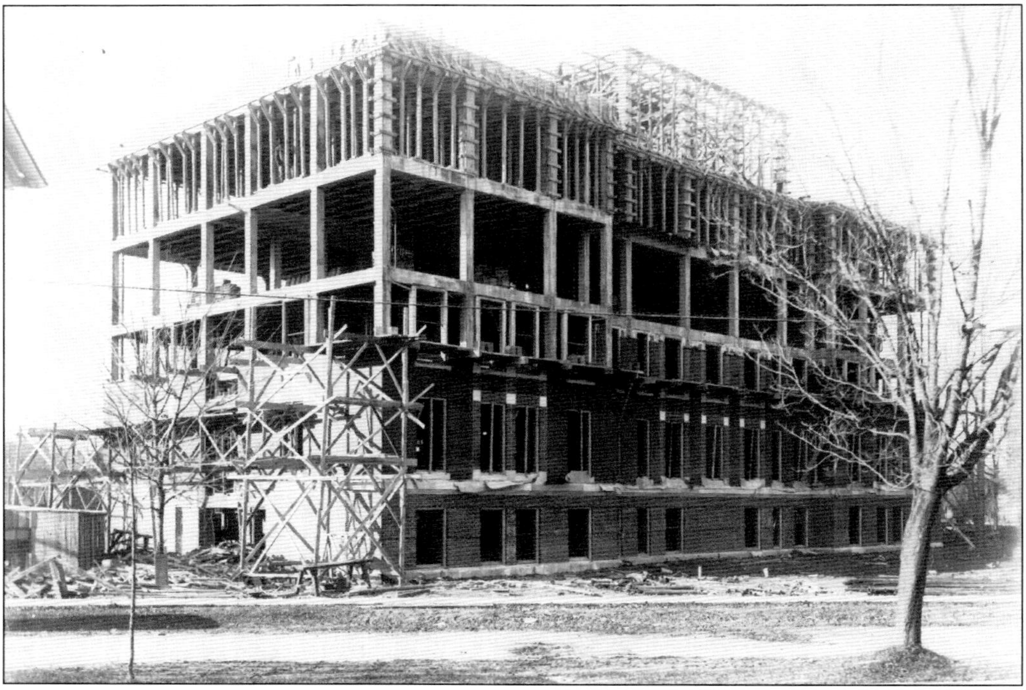

In this picture dated November 11, 1916, the basement level is enclosed, and work is continuing on the first and second floors.

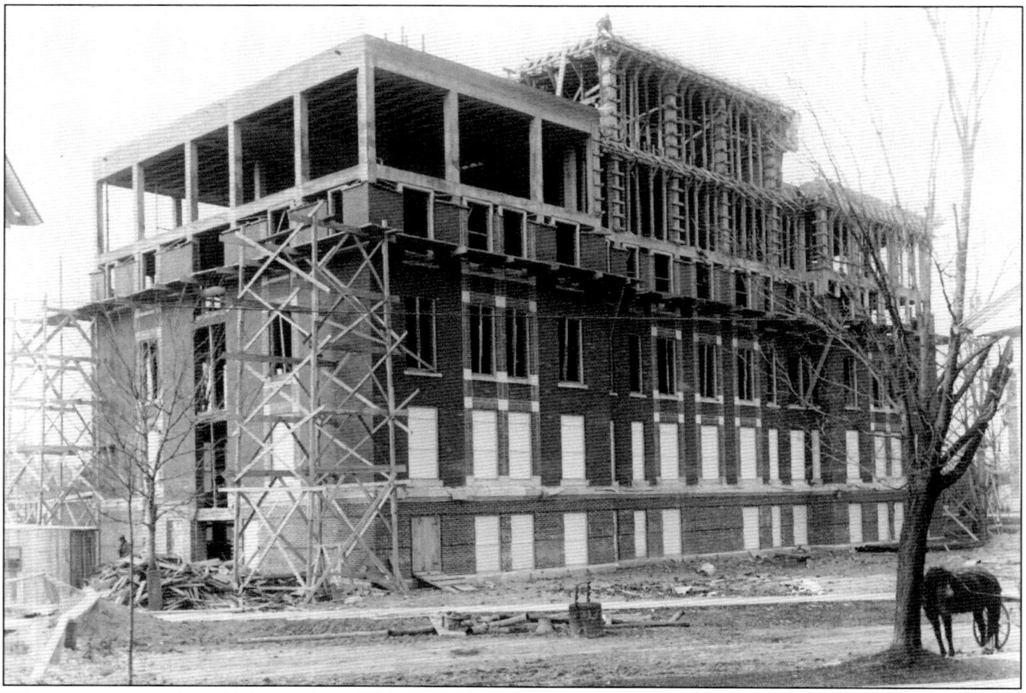

This picture is dated November 25, 1916. Here, construction workers are continuing with the brickwork and finishing the enclosure of the third floor.

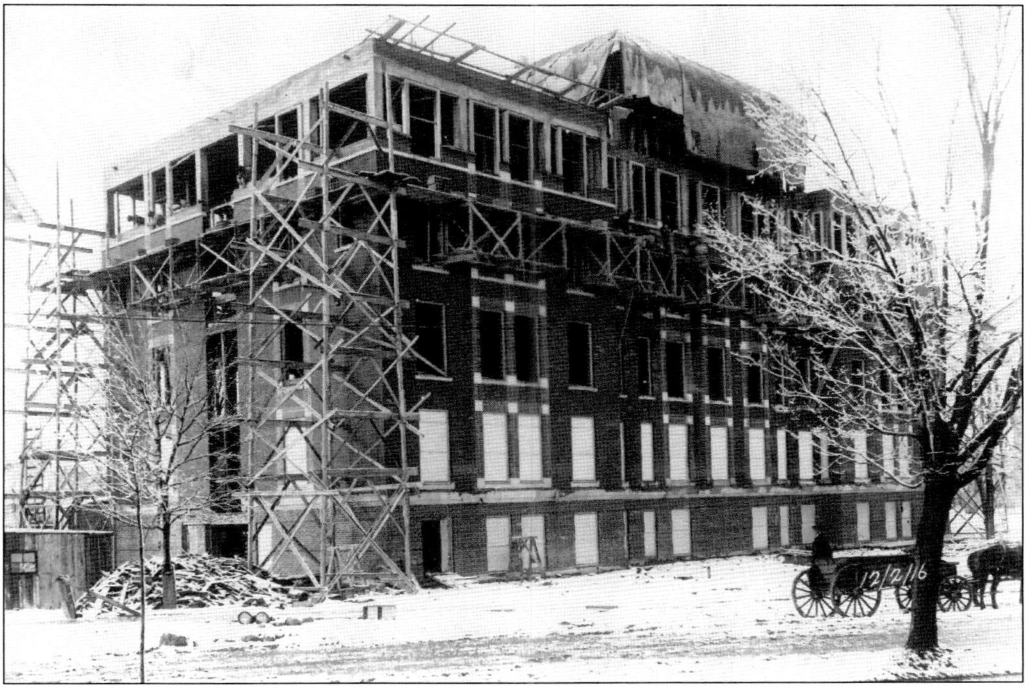

There is snow on the ground as workers rush to enclose the fourth floor in this December 2, 1916, photograph.

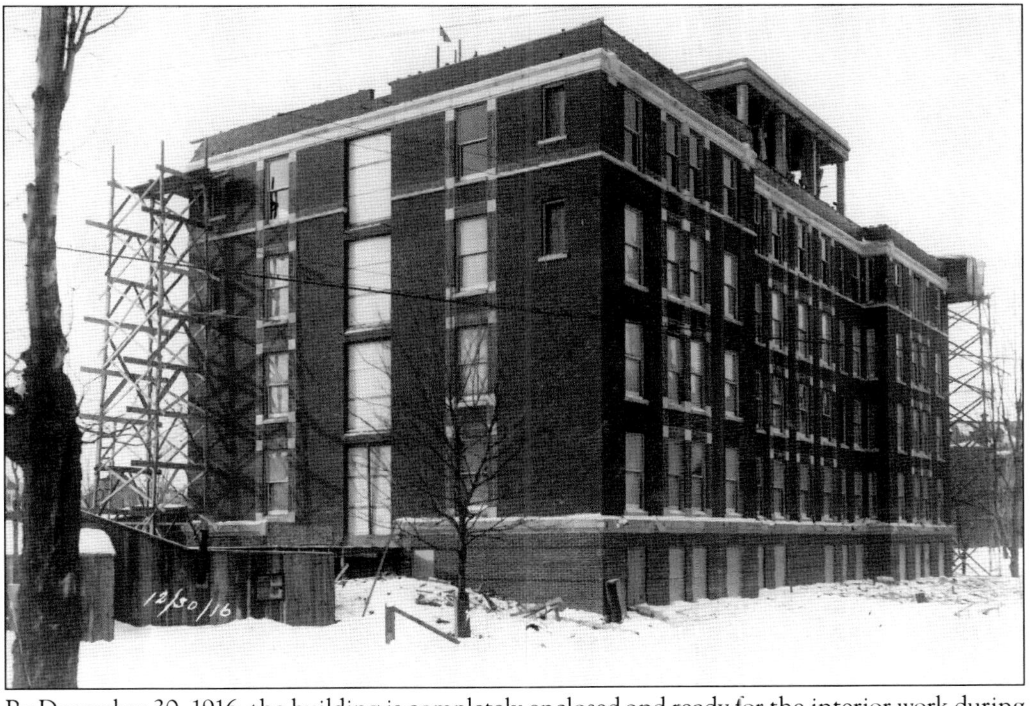

By December 30, 1916, the building is completely enclosed and ready for the interior work during the winter.

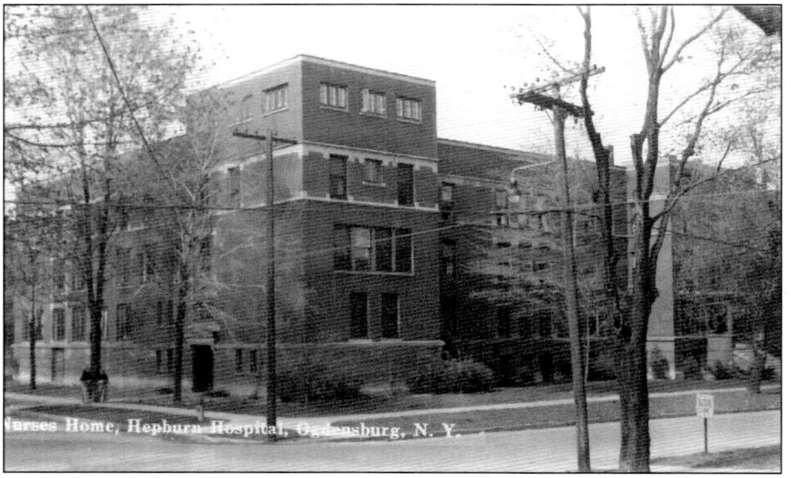

This is another postcard depicting the nurses' home. This is at the corner of Mansion and Rensselaer Avenues.

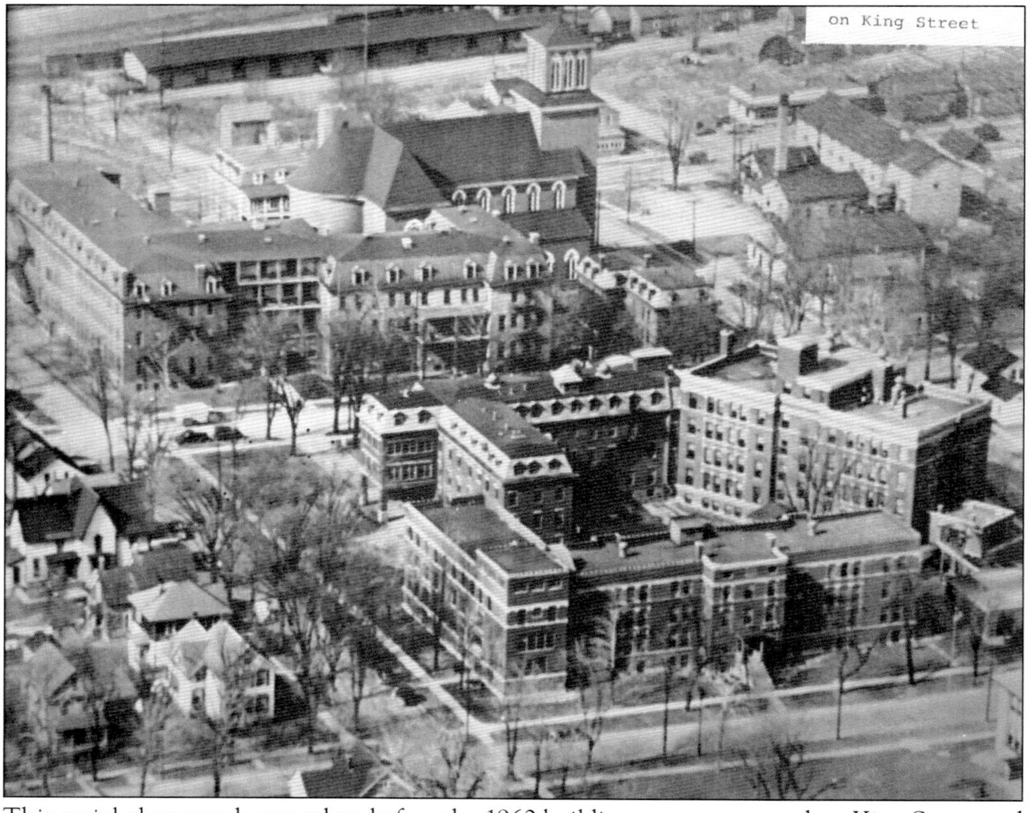

This aerial photograph was taken before the 1960 building was constructed on King Street and before the old Ford Mansion building was demolished. The back of the 1902 building is visible with its west-wing addition. To the right, the 1918 east-wing addition is visible. In the foreground is the nurses' home building, located on the corner of Mansion and Rensselaer Avenues. Also pictured is the 1932 addition to the nurses' home, which included an auditorium on the first floor, faculty offices, a library, classrooms, 17 additional sleeping rooms for students, and a large recreational sundeck.

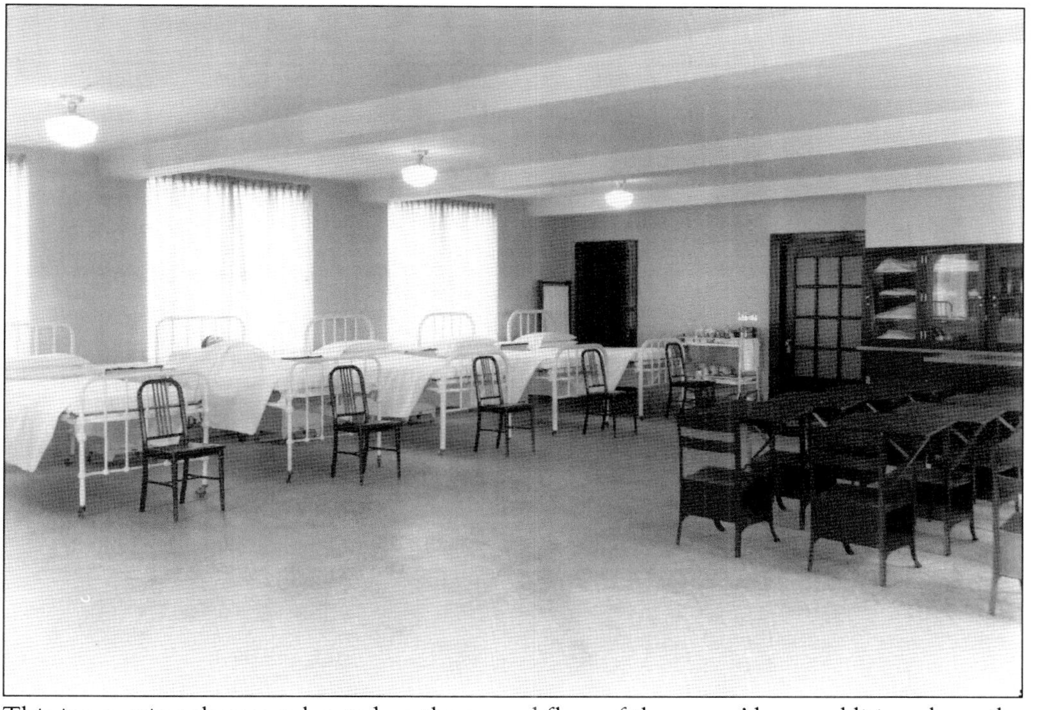

This is a nursing classroom located on the second floor of the nurses' home addition above the auditorium. The hospital beds on the left-hand side of the classroom are for students to practice their nursing skills.

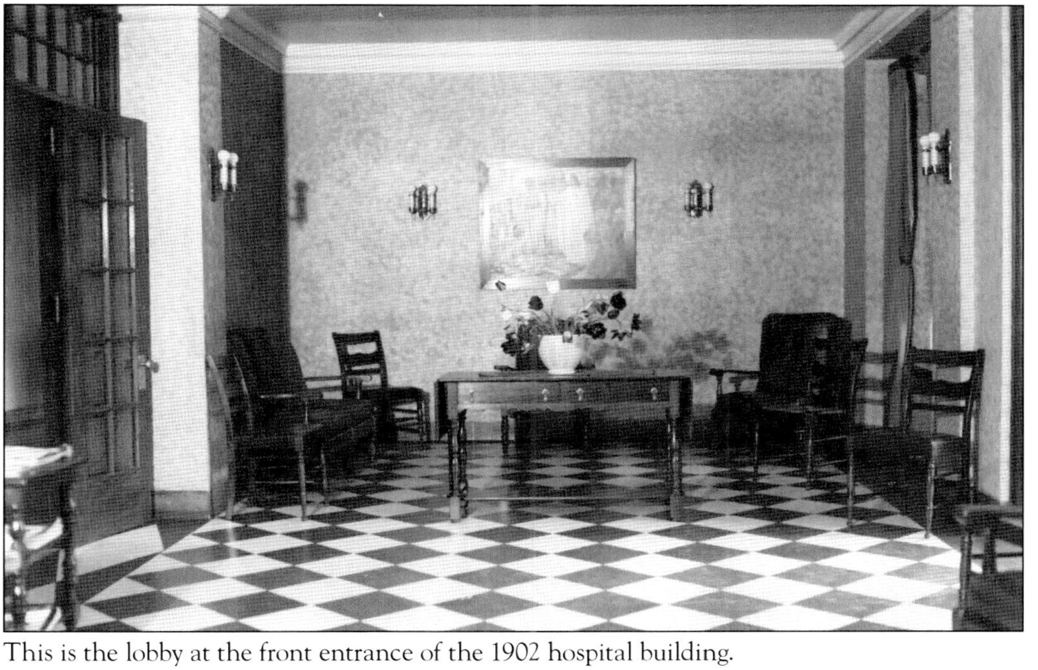

This is the lobby at the front entrance of the 1902 hospital building.

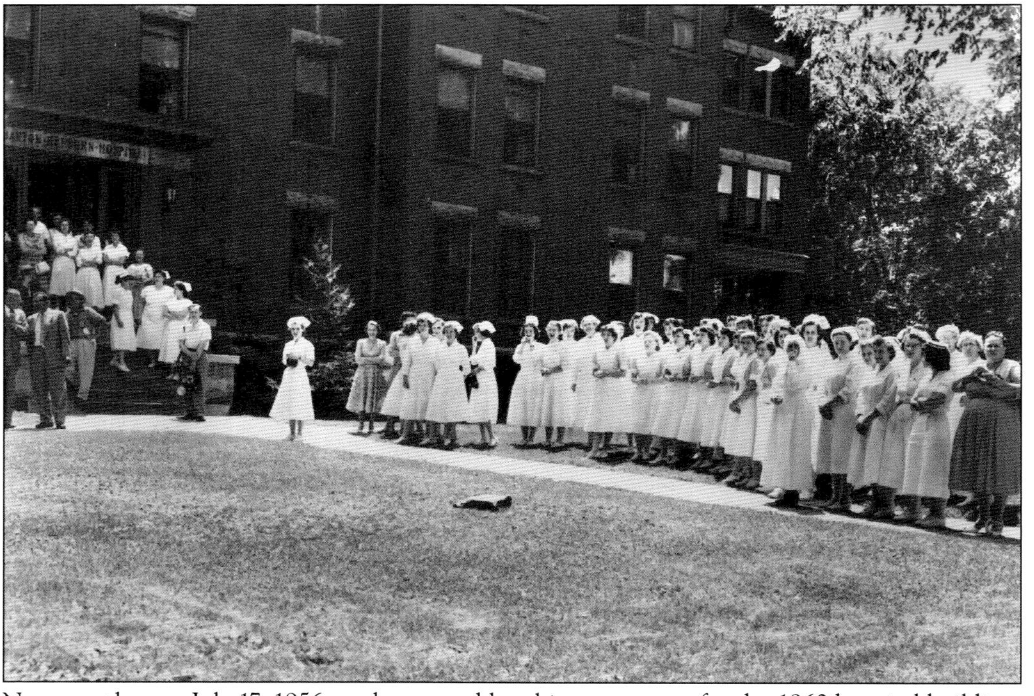

Nurses gather on July 17, 1956, at the ground-breaking ceremony for the 1960 hospital building, erected in front of the 1902 building on King Street.

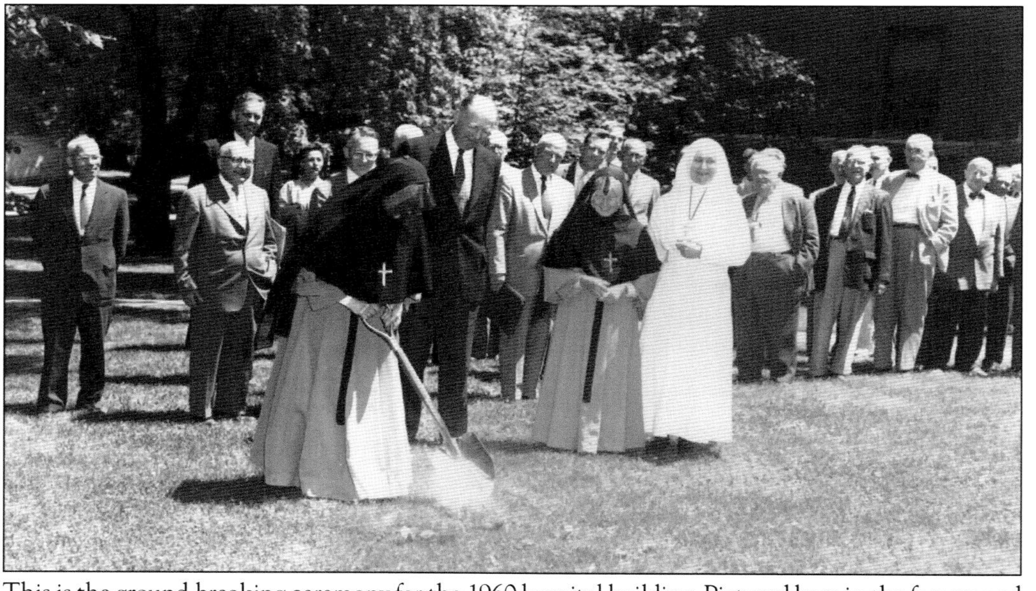

This is the ground-breaking ceremony for the 1960 hospital building. Pictured here in the foreground are, from left to right, Sisters Mary Monica, Irene Marie Murphy, and Martin Maloney, of the Sacred Heart. Some of those in the background are Mayer Sperling, Dr. Ernest Sostheim Sr., Edmund L. Shea, Dr. Edward Whalen, Dr. James J. Barry, and Dr. Fred Clark. Sr. Mary Monica served as the administrator from 1927 to 1935, from 1938 to 1944, and from 1952 to 1963. She was also a graduate of the A. Barton Hepburn Hospital School of Nursing, class of 1919.

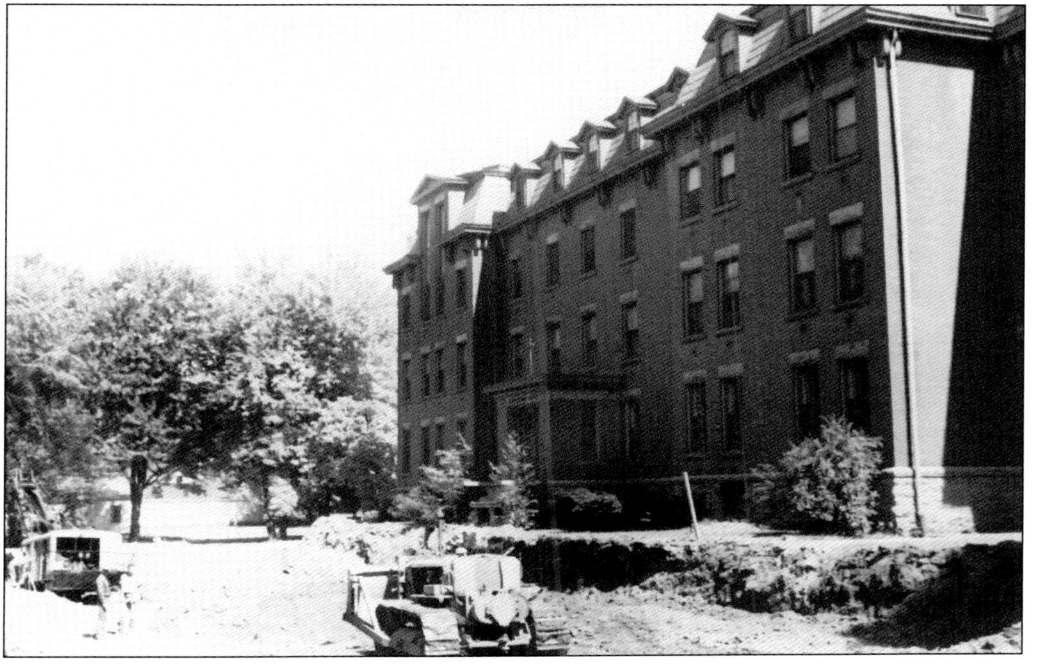

Workers prepare the ground for the foundation of the new hospital building being constructed on King Street.

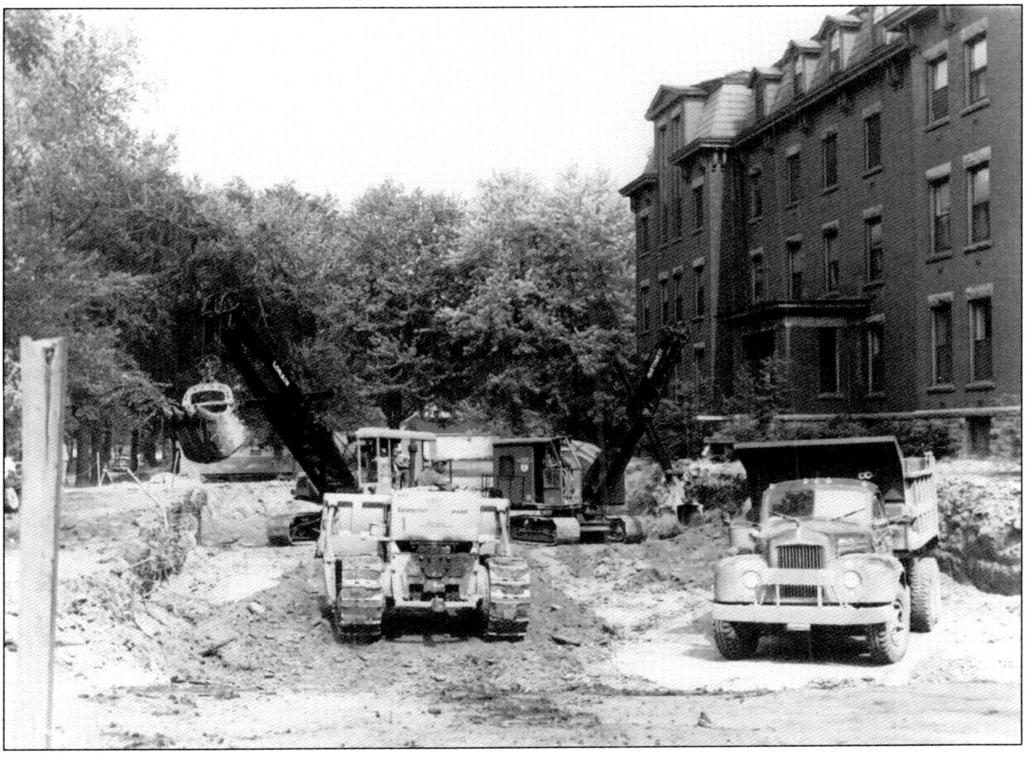

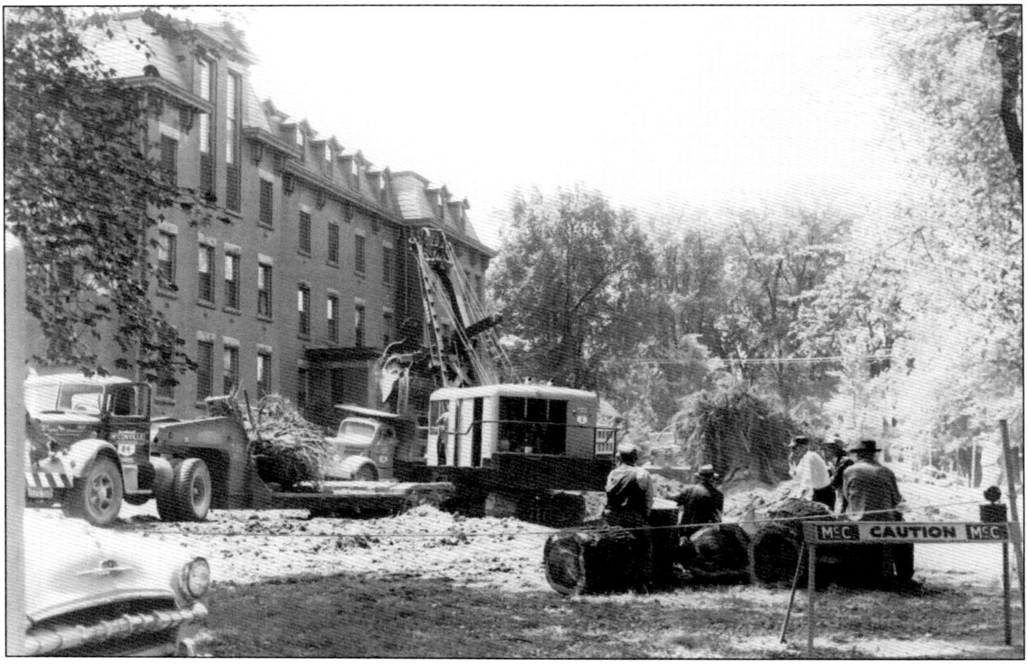

This photograph shows further progress on preparing for the construction of the building on King Street. It looks as if workers have removed the portico on the right to make way for the new building.

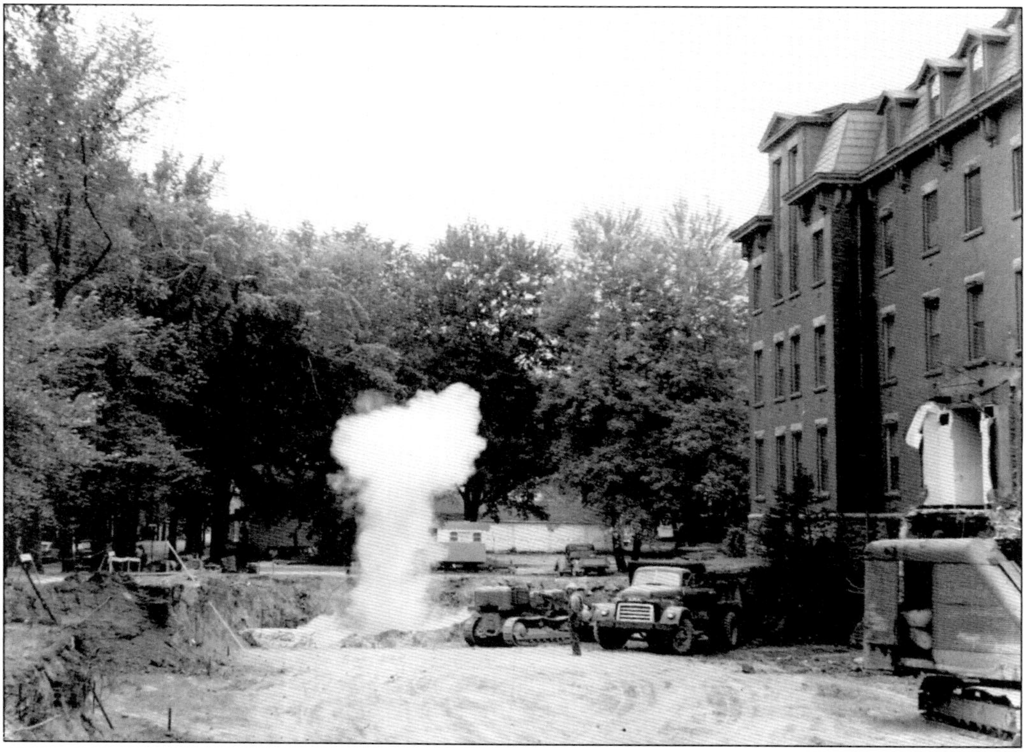

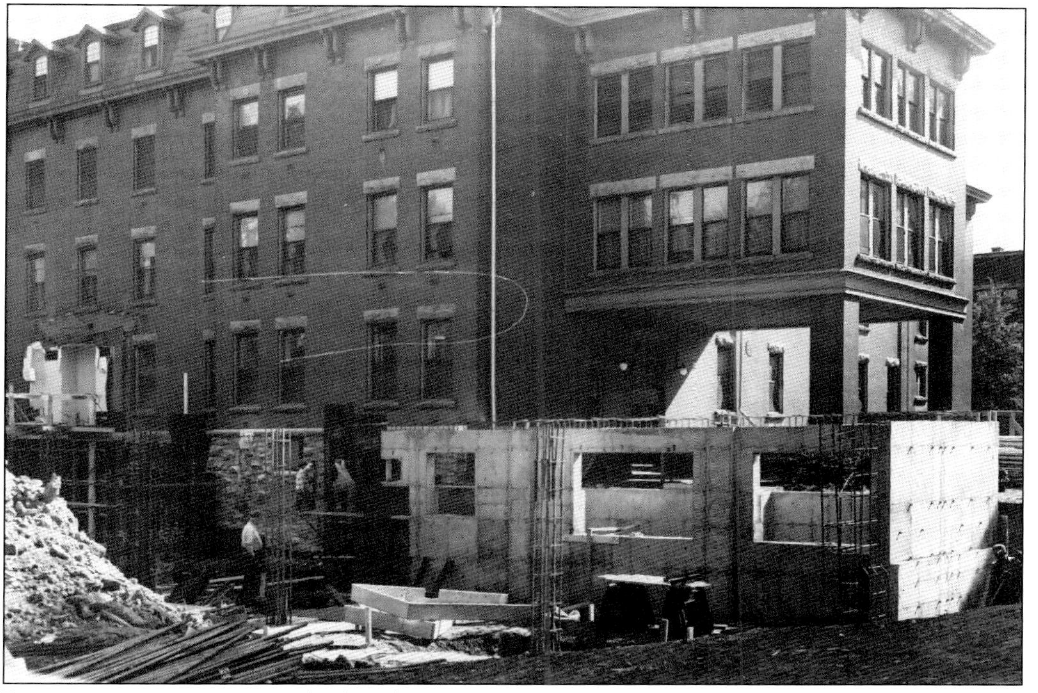

Beginning construction on the foundation for the new building on King Street is pictured above. Below, the new hospital building begins to replace the 1902 structure, and the 1918 wing (left) is being renovated.

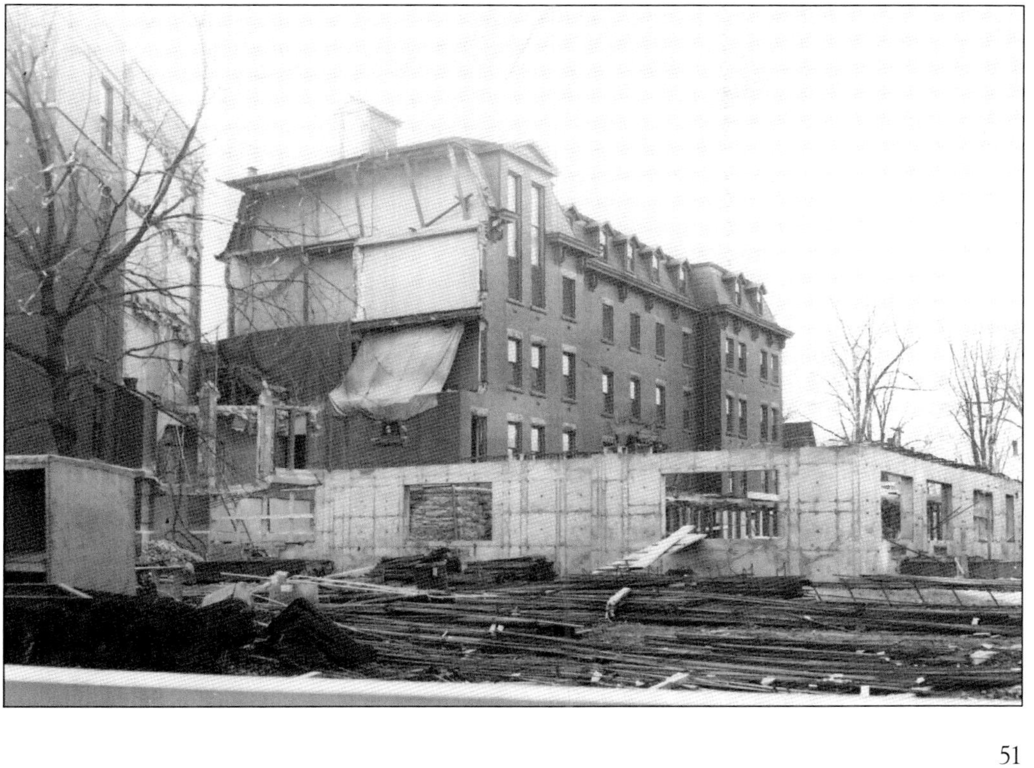

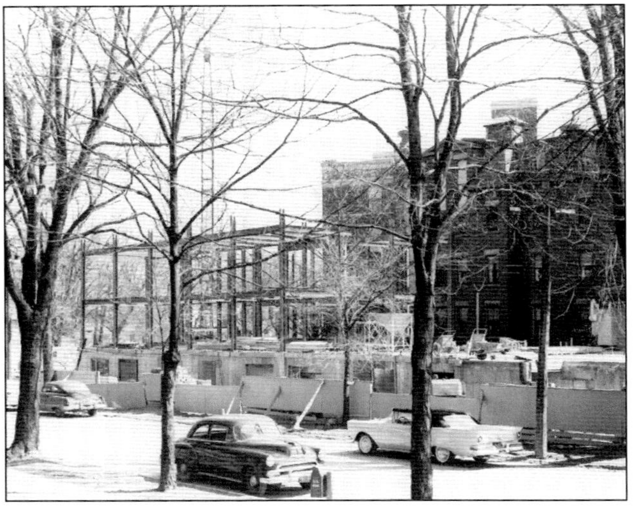

This picture shows the completed foundation of the 1960 building and the beginning of the framing process for the first and second floors. The community raised nearly $600,000 of the total cost of $2 million.

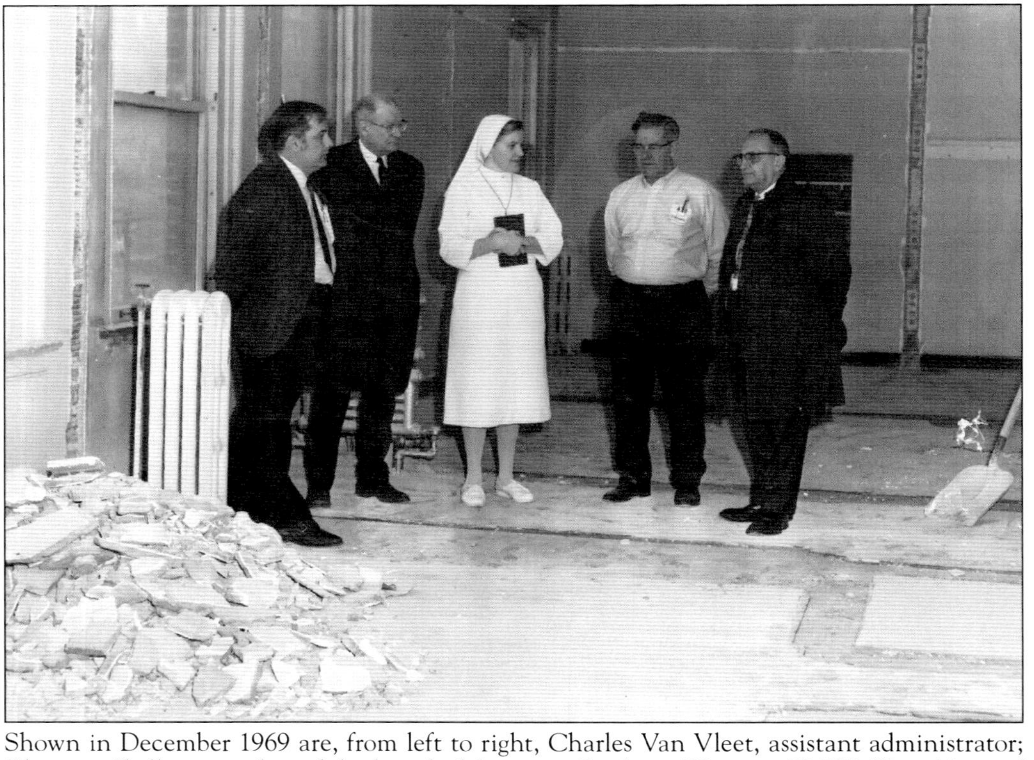

Shown in December 1969 are, from left to right, Charles Van Vleet, assistant administrator; Clarence Skelly, a member of the board of directors; Sr. Anne Therese, GNSH (Grey Nuns of the Sacred Heart), administrator; Lawrence Rapin, maintenance superintendent; and Frank Murray, a member of the board of directors. They are discussing renovations to the old nurses' residence shortly after the school closed in 1968. The walls that separated individual student rooms were removed, and construction was begun to create offices for physicians. Glen Tusler was construction superintendent for this project. Bruce Tusler, his son, also worked on the project as a union laborer. Sr. Anne Therese was the administrator at the hospital from 1963 until 1976. (Courtesy of Bruce Tusler.)

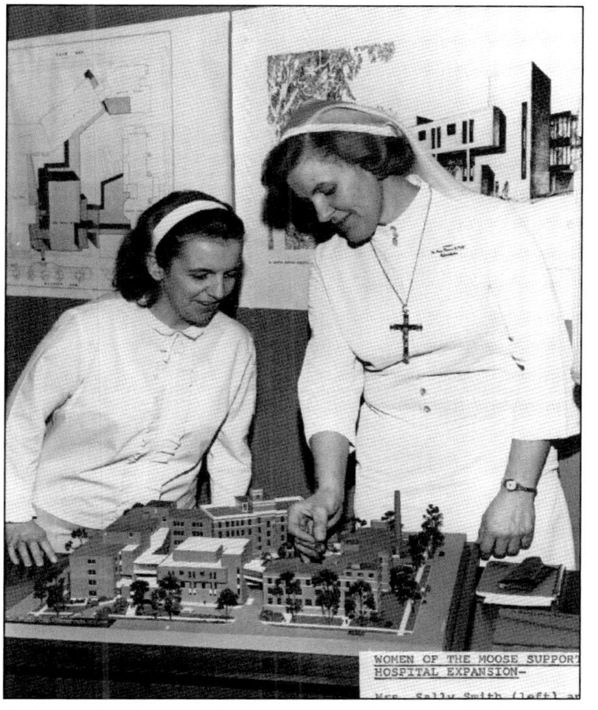

This is a c. 1972 photograph of Sally Smith (left), of the Women of the Moose, and Sr. Anne Therese looking at the model of the planned west-wing hospital expansion. The model was on display in the lobby of the hospital and available for everyone to see. The project was estimated to cost $3.2 million.

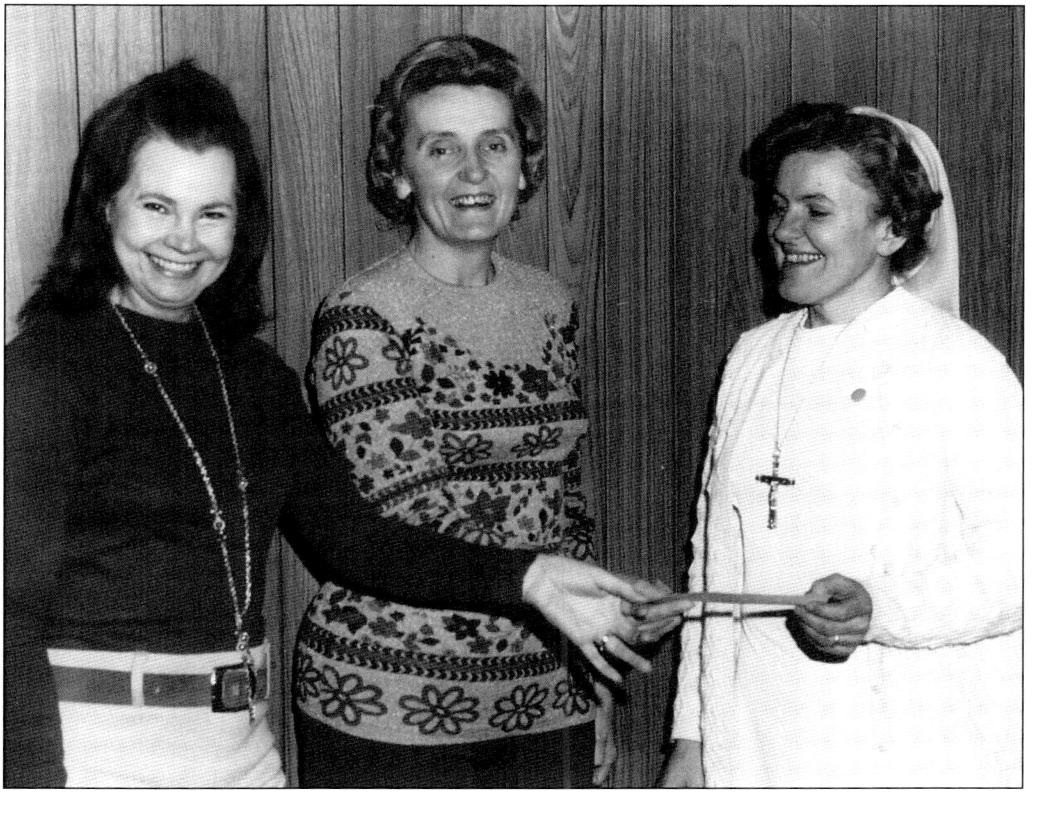

In January 1974, the City Guild, the predecessor of the current hospital auxiliary, made its final pledge payment for the west-wing project. In this picture are Judy Velocchi (left), president of the guild; Helen Ellis (center), past president of the guild; and Sr. Anne Therese, administrator. Later, in 1987, the City Guild would change its name to the A. Barton Hepburn Hospital Auxiliary.

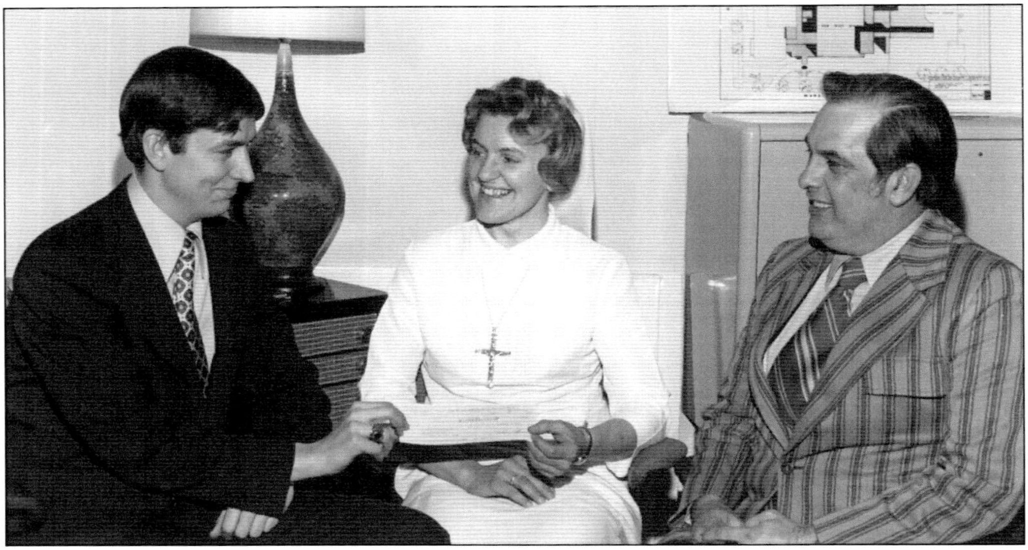

On February 19, 1973, the St. Lawrence National Bank presented a $1,500 check to Sr. Anne Therese, administrator (center). Pictured with the sister are James Wears (left), loan officer of the Ogdensburg branch of the bank; and Charles Van Vleet, assistant administrator.

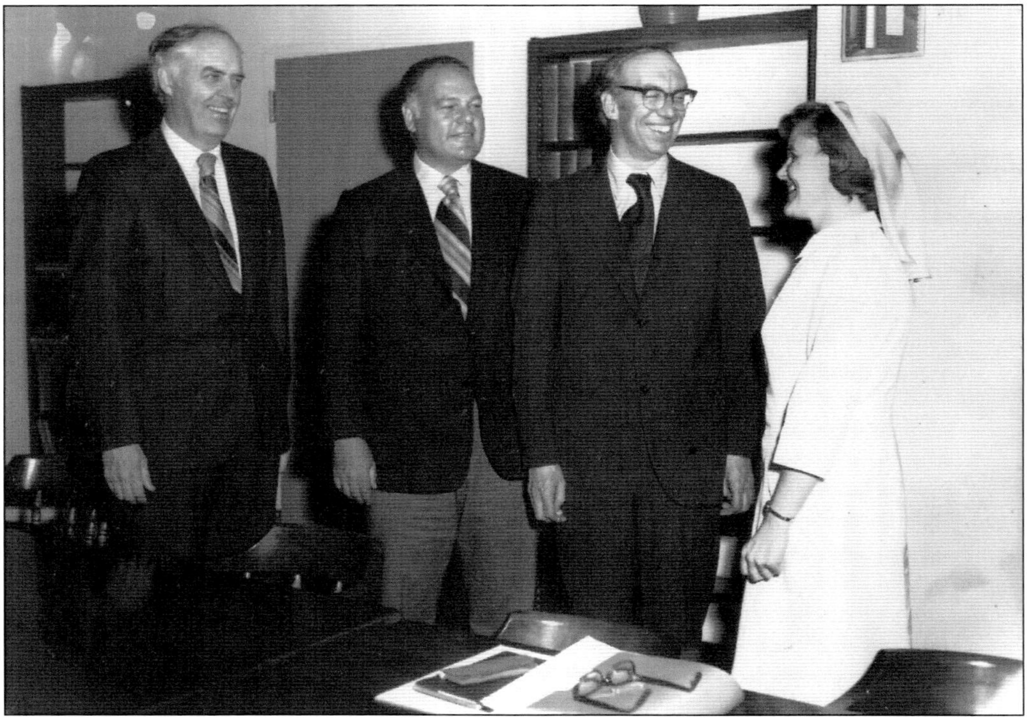

On March 26, 1972, Sen. H. Douglas Barclay visited Hepburn in an effort to get the hospital a higher priority loan with the State of New York for the west-wing expansion project. Pictured from left to right are Sen. Edmund L. Shea, Frank A. Augsbury Jr., Sen. H. Douglas Barclay, and Sr. Anne Therese, administrator. Augsbury was chairman of the hospital board of directors from 1966 to 1977.

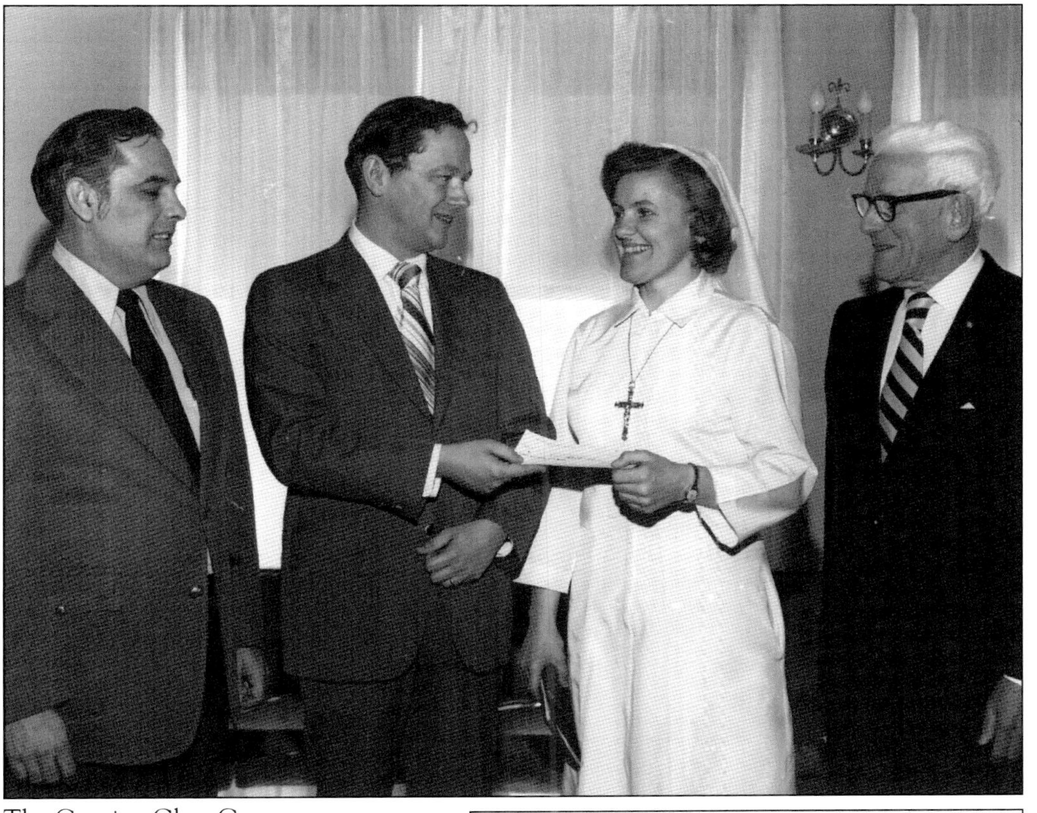

The Corning Glass Company presents $2,500. From the left are Charles Van Vleet, assistant administrator; Richard P. Davis, facilities manager of Canton branch of Corning Glass; Sr. Anne Therese, administrator; and Wayne Lowe, chairman of the building committee.

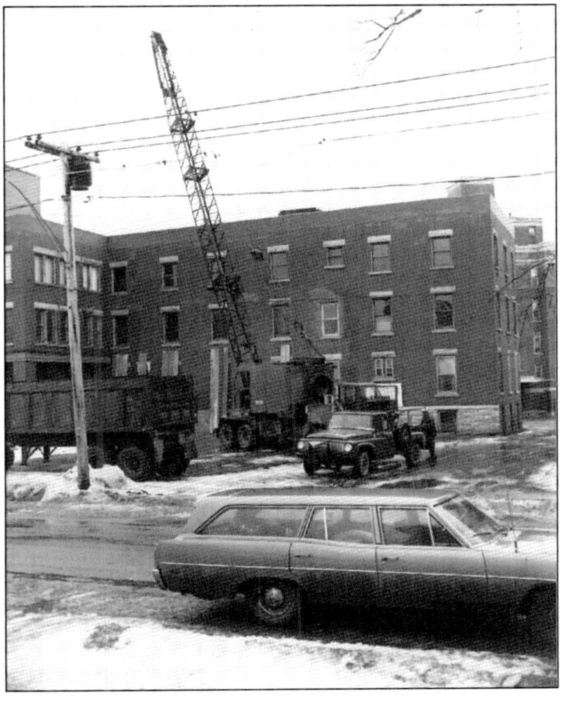

Pictured here is the old, 1907 west-wing addition to the 1902 building. This section survived the demolition of the 1902 structure. In this image, the Visconti construction crew, from Syracuse, is razing it to make way for the new west-wing project. Demolition began on March 11, 1973.

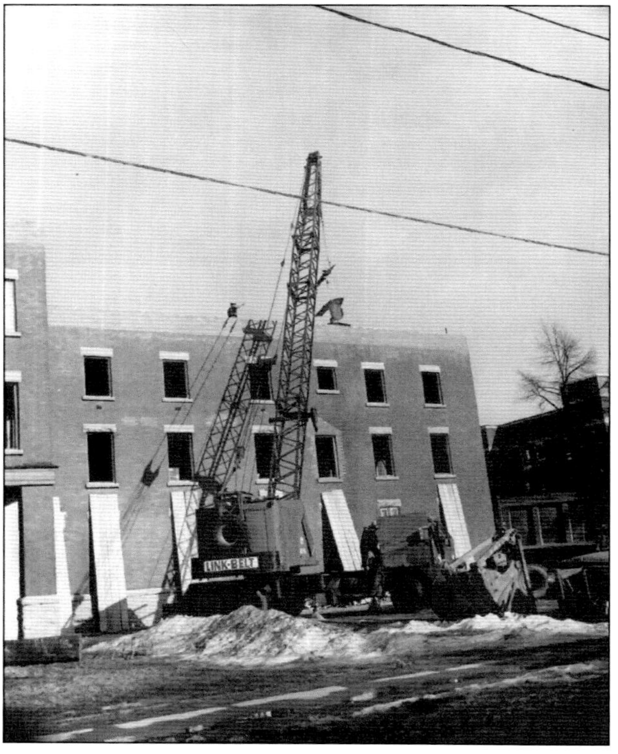

This is another picture of the beginning of the demolition of the 1907 wing on March 11, 1973.

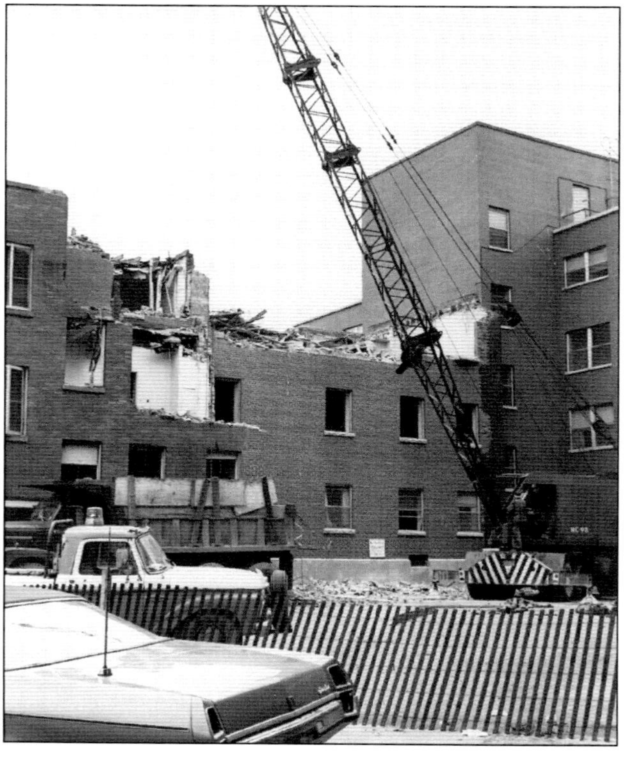

This is a view of the demolition of the 1907 building as seen from the courtyard on March 14, 1973.

This is another courtyard perspective of the demolition of the 1907 building. The photograph was taken on March 14, 1973.

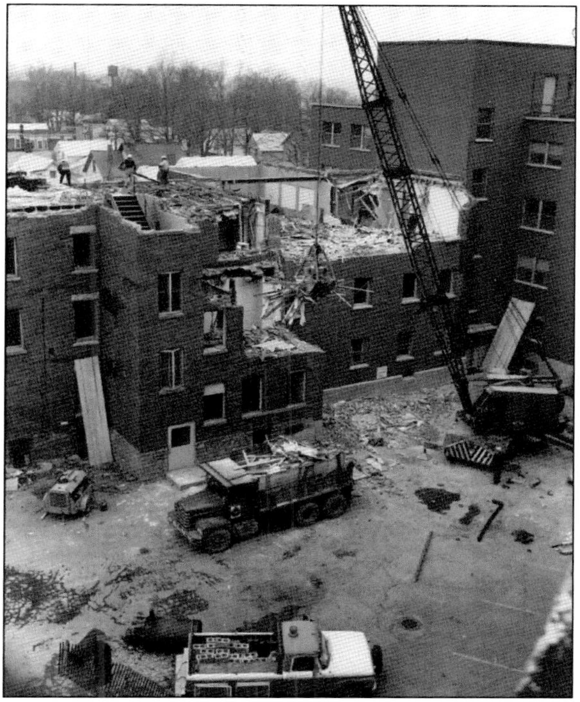

This is a picture taken after the demolition of the 1907 west wing and just before construction began on the new west-wing project.

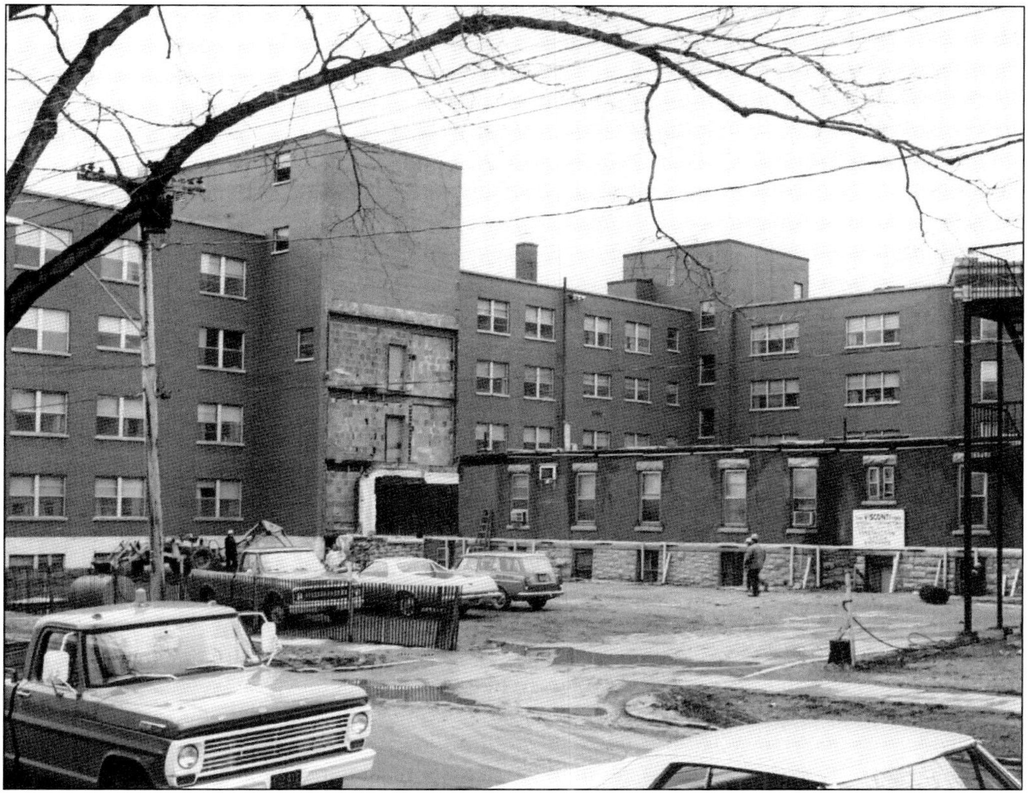

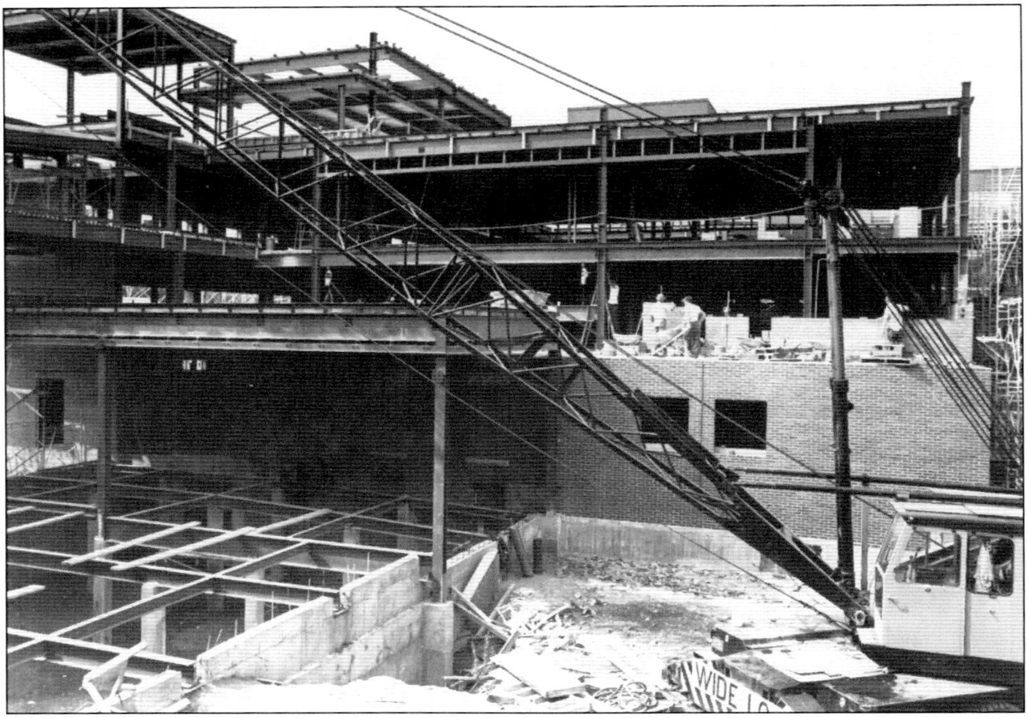

Shown here, construction on the new west wing has begun in September 1973. This picture was taken from the courtyard. Below, more progress has taken place on the construction of the new west wing in 1973.

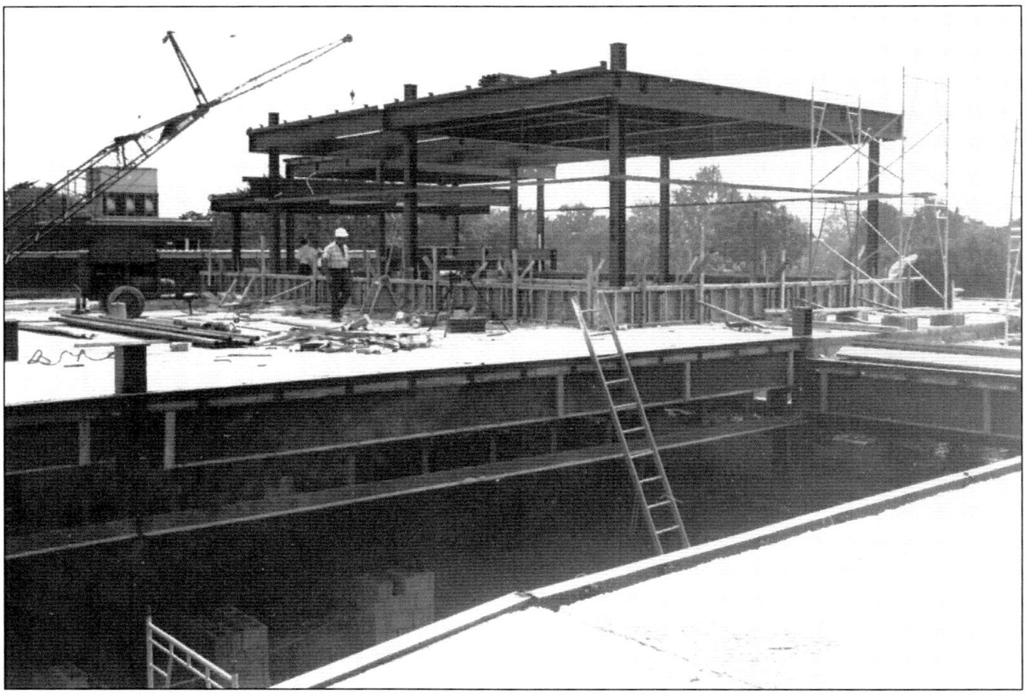

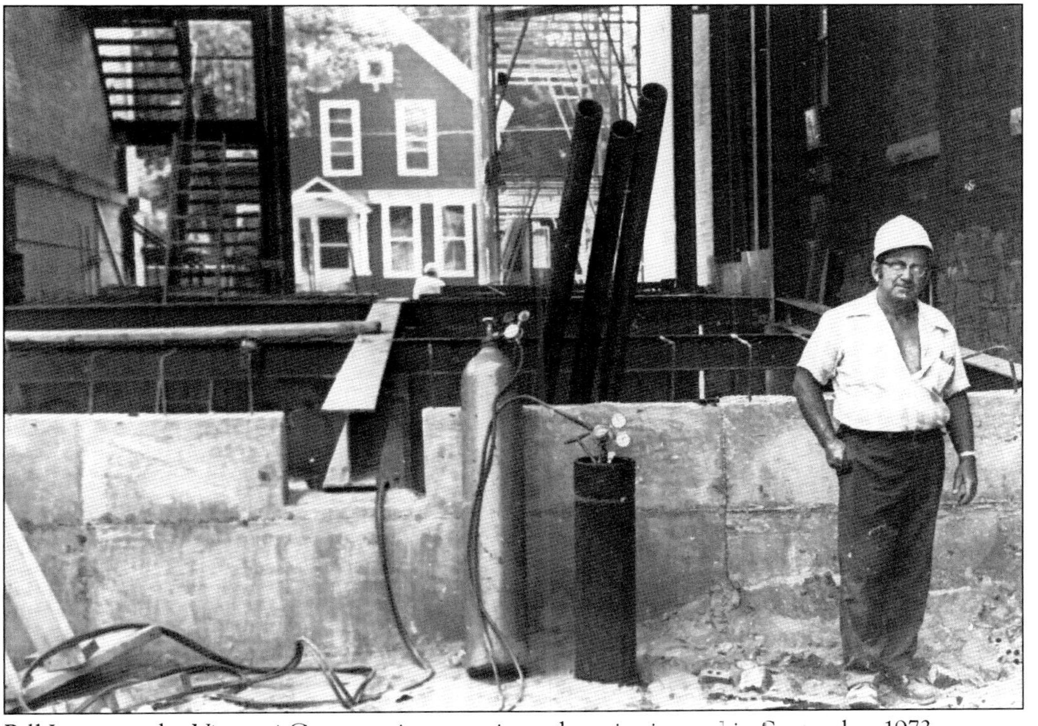

Bill Limoges, the Visconti Construction superintendent, is pictured in September 1973.

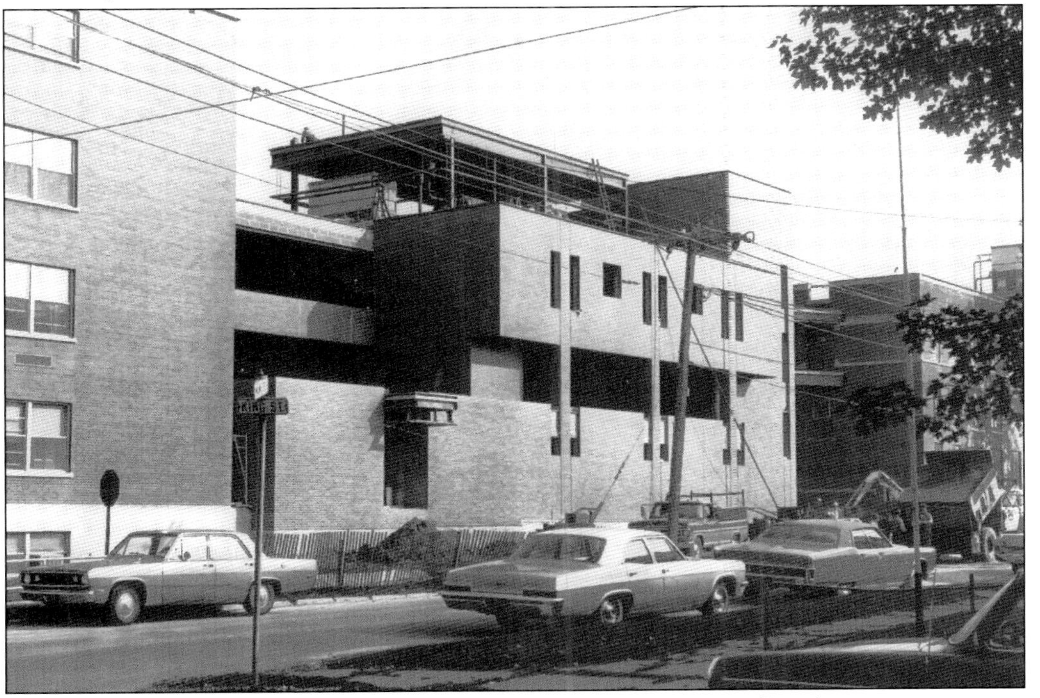

This Mansion Avenue view of the new west wing shows that it is still under construction on October 16, 1973.

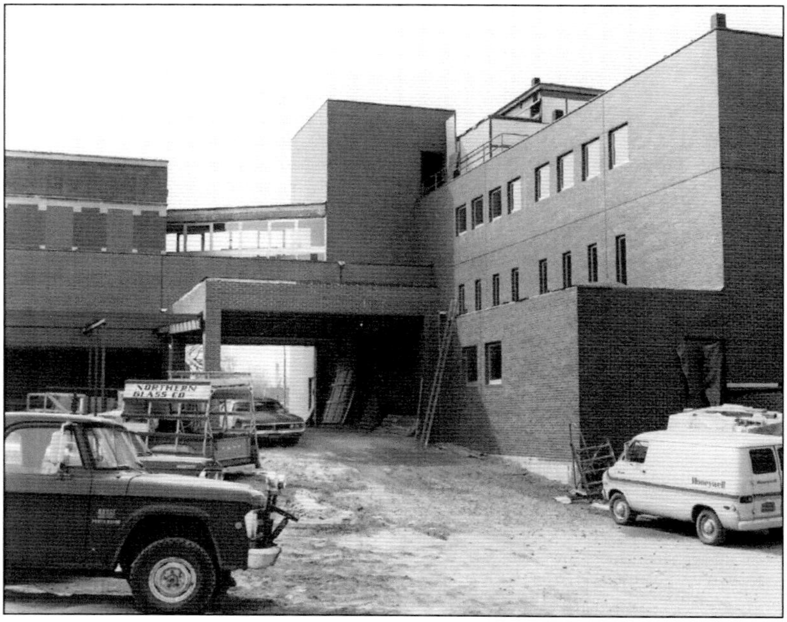

This picture of the new ground-level emergency room entrance with its overhead protection against the weather was taken from inside the courtyard in March 1974. The construction project was 65 percent complete at this point.

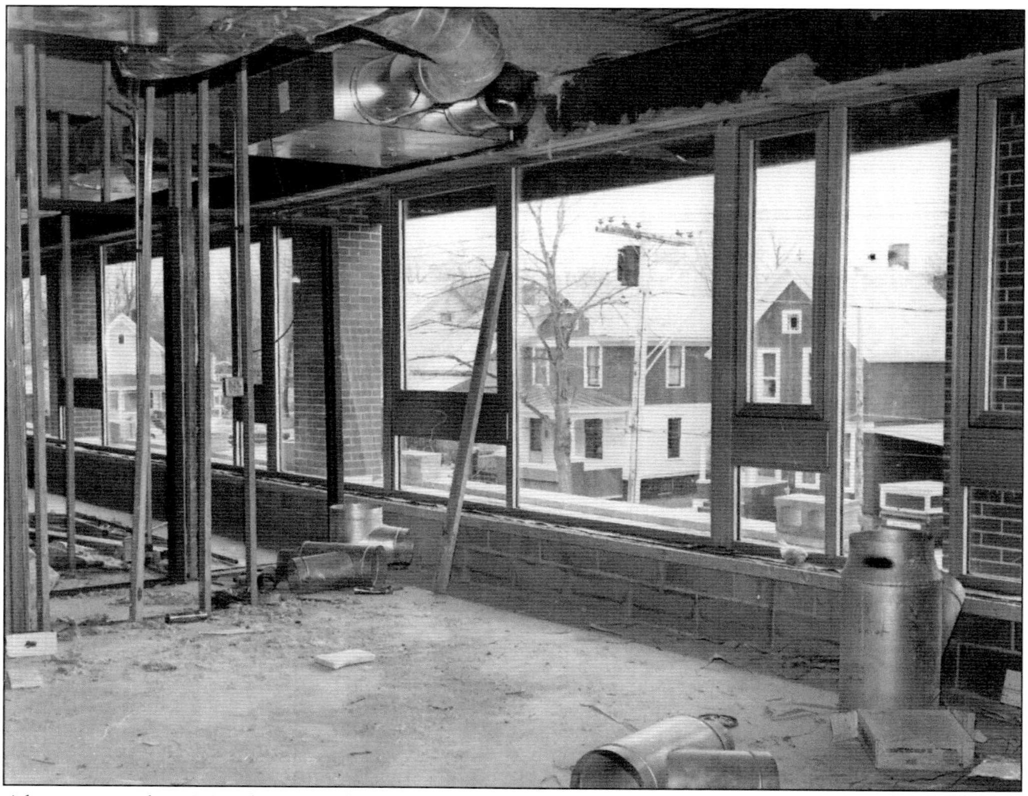

Also pictured in March 1974, this is the second floor of the new wing. It was designated for the administrative suite of offices, the nursing service department, physical therapy, and a meditation room.

In another picture from March 1974, this courtyard scene features the site of the new laundry department, located in the basement. A new passageway was to be used in transporting patients to and from x-ray, surgery, intensive and coronary care, and so on. The laboratory department was also accommodated with expanded facilities in the basement area.

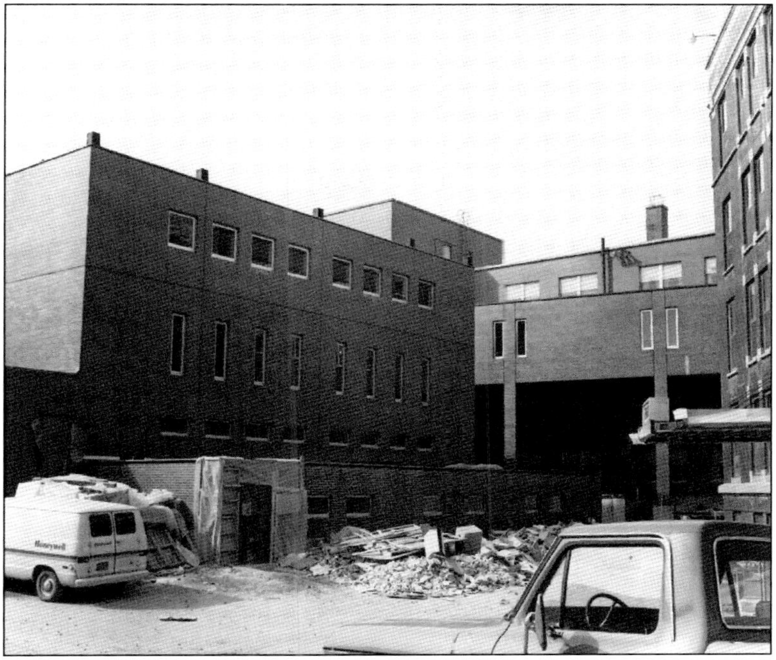

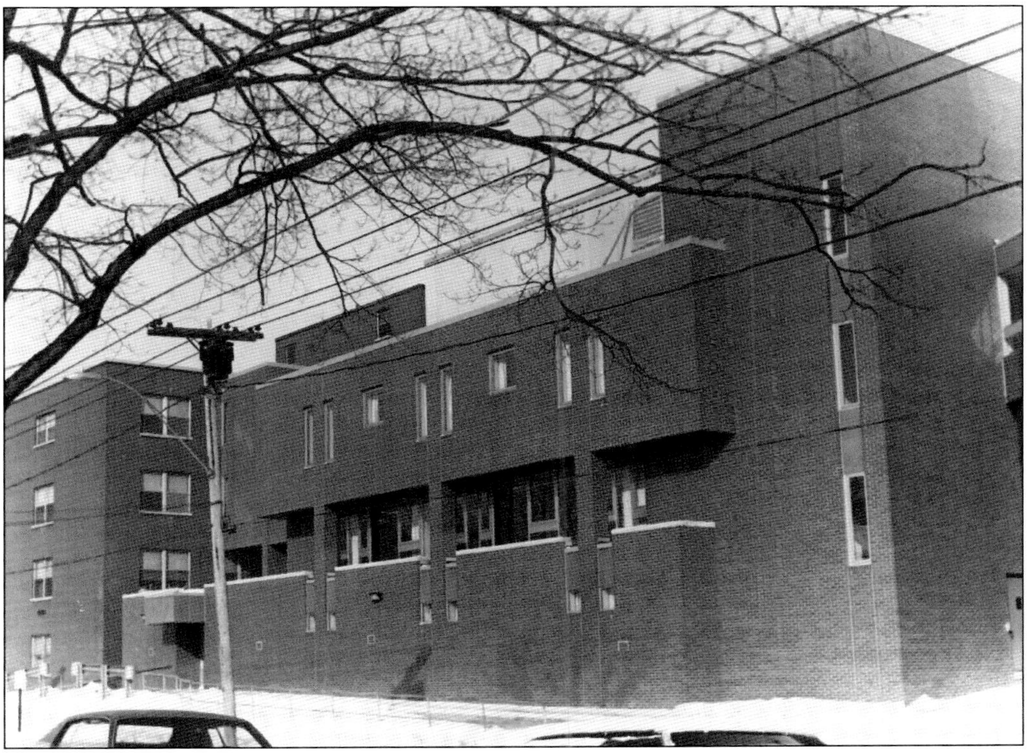

Pictured here is the 1975 west-wing project, completed and providing space for the emergency room, radiology, intensive care, and renal dialysis. Over $1 million of the $3.2 million cost was raised locally.

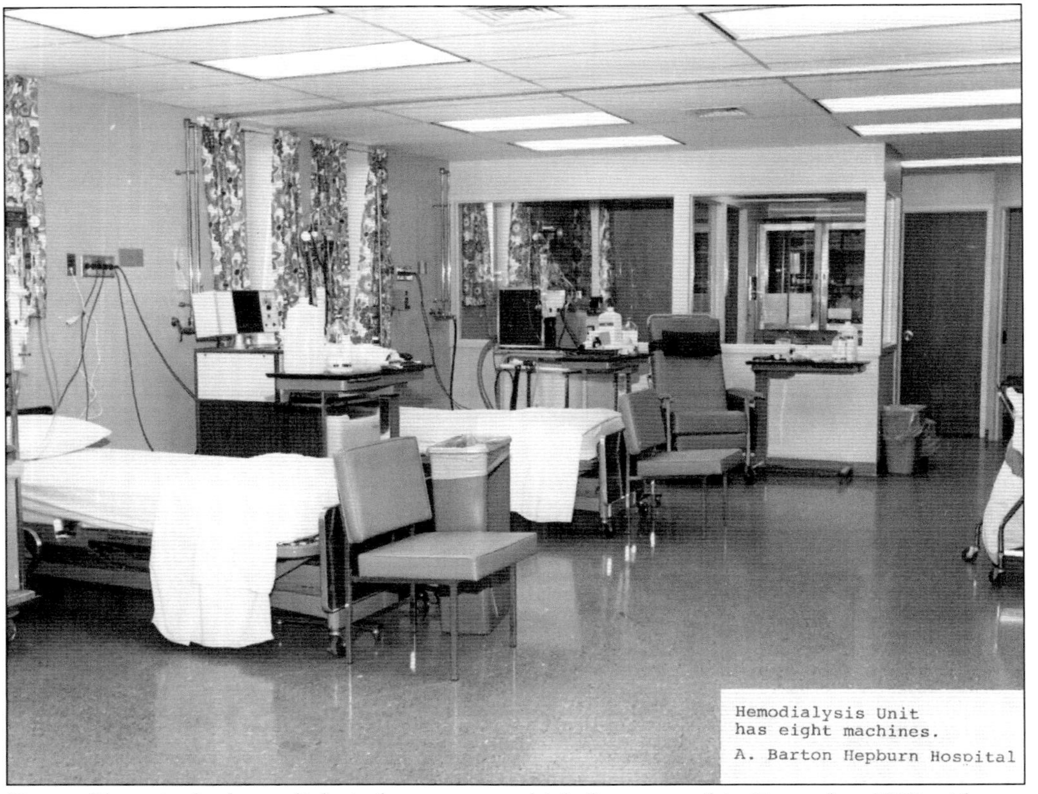

Pictured here is the hemodialysis department, which first opened in December 1968 with one "artificial kidney" machine. The department, located in the newly constructed west wing, had three units in operation daily when it opened. It was the only hemodialysis center north of Syracuse.

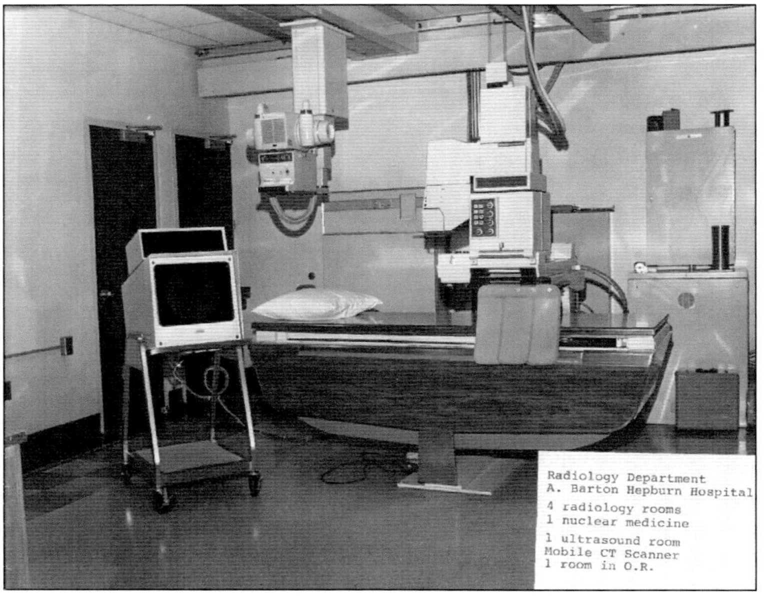

This picture shows the radiology department in the new west wing in February 1976. Radiology conducted 15,424 tests in 1975, an increase of 116 percent over the previous 10 years, creating the necessity for a new diagnostic room and expanded quarters.

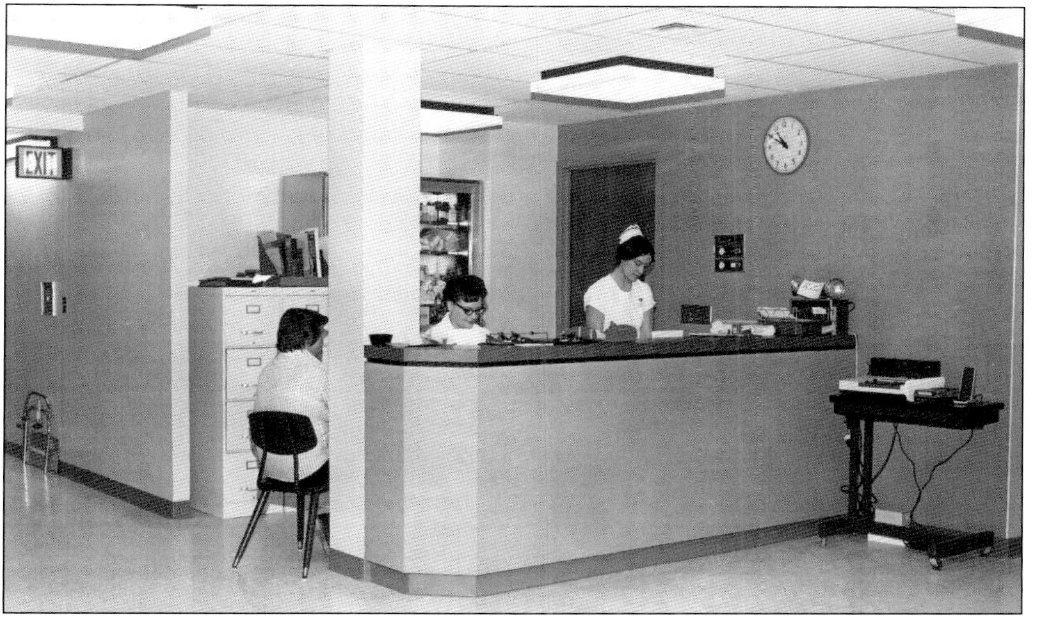

This picture of the nurses' station in the new facility, located directly inside the new emergency entrance, is from April 1975. The new radiology department was right around the corner from the station.

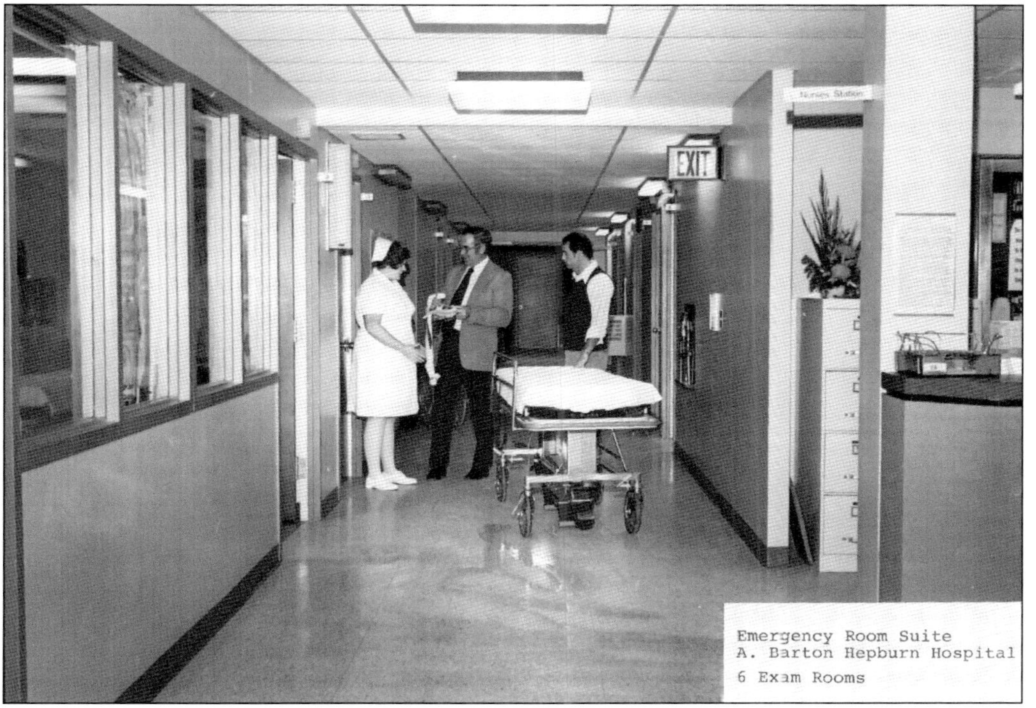

This is another view of the new emergency room suite. It had six exam rooms. Pictured here are, from left to right, Amy Hazelton, Al Winney, and Dr. Hugh Inness-Brown. Dr. Inness-Brown was a general surgeon at the hospital from 1969 to 1988.

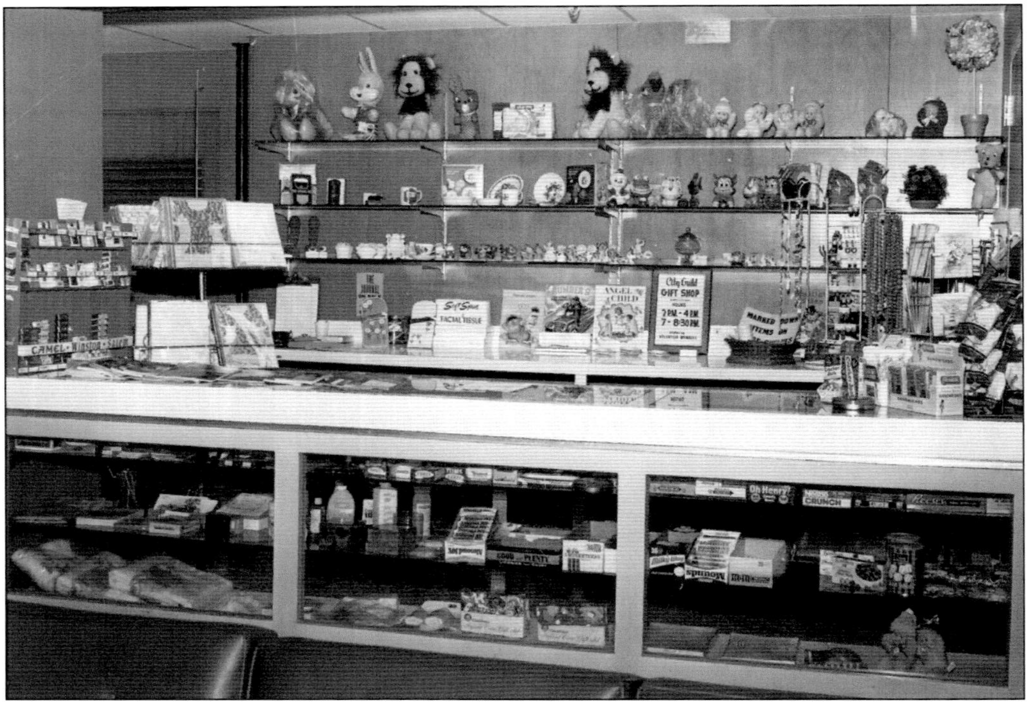

Above, the City Guild gift shop is pictured in 1975. Below, the gift shop is shown in May 1969. Pictured from left to right are Mrs. George Bench, a member of the City Guild; Helen Fields, president of City Guild; and customer Frances Van Horne.

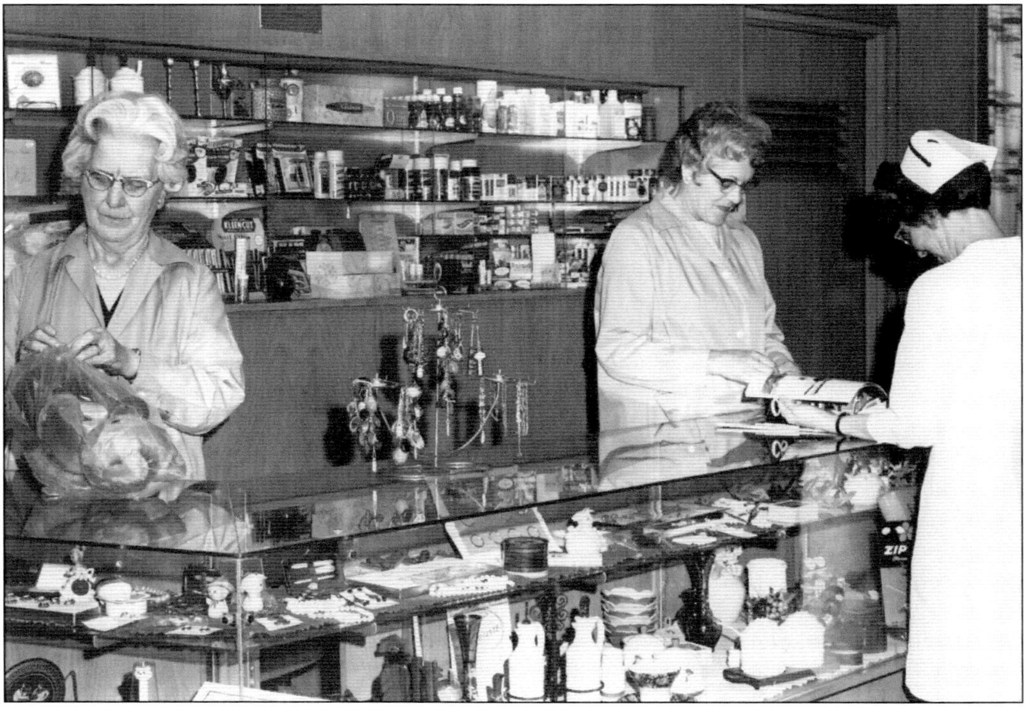

Five

Patient Care

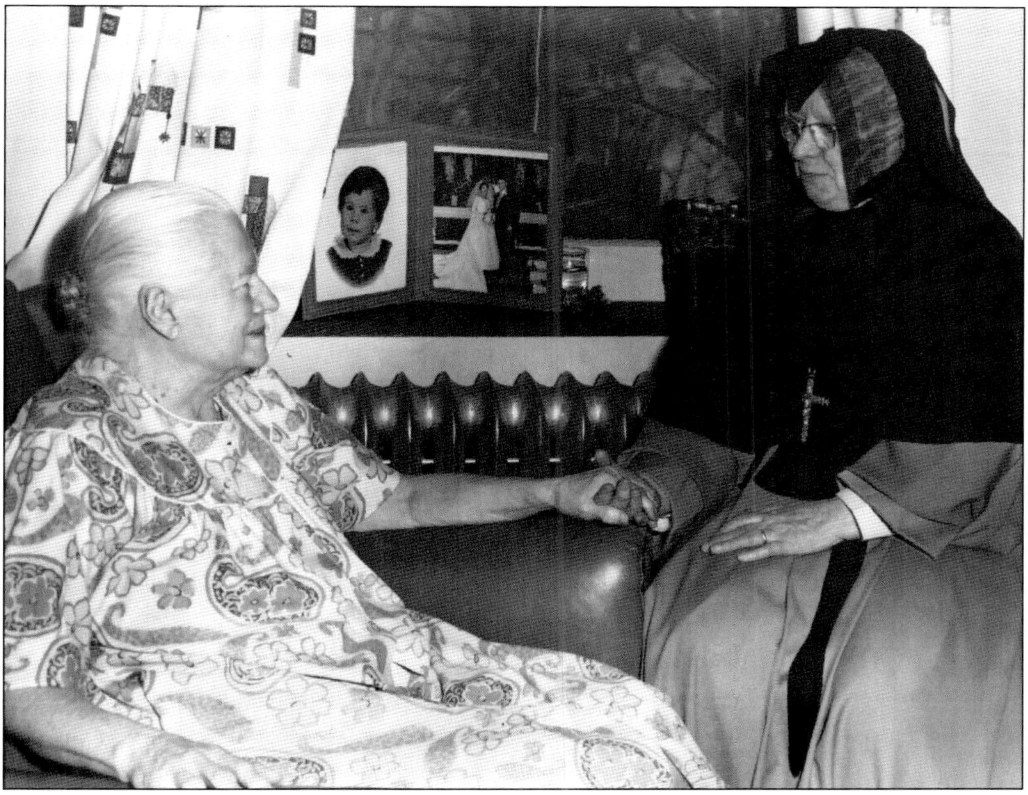

Sr. Mary Patricia holds the hand of May Stout to comfort her in the chronic care unit in 1965.

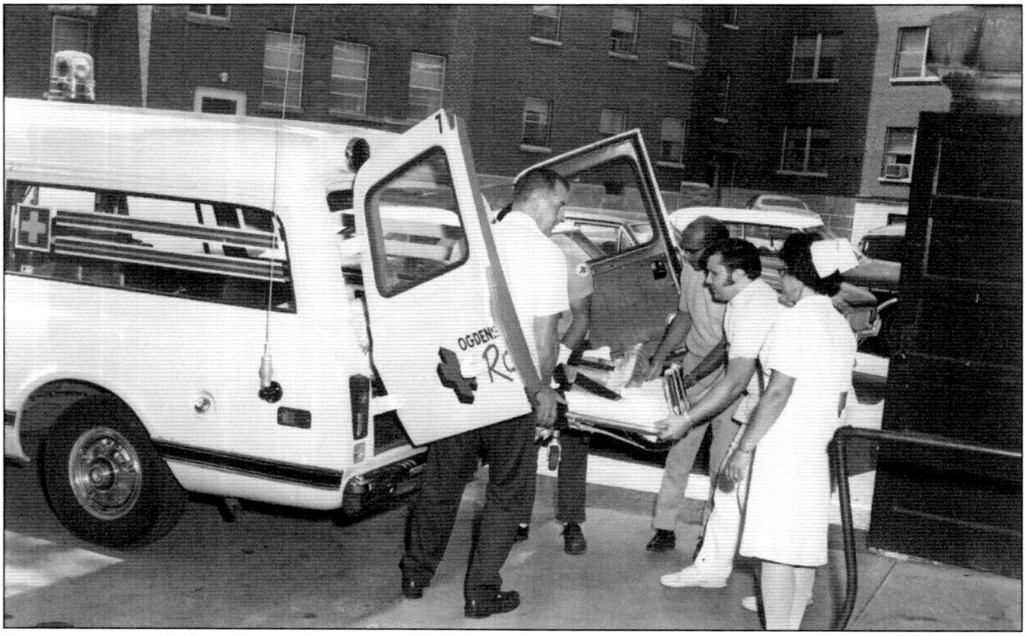

In a picture titled "Their job is never done," the Ogdensburg Rescue Squad delivers a patient to the emergency room entrance in 1969. Dr. Bansi Bazaz (left), David Delarge (center), and an unidentified nurse receive the patient. Dr. Bazaz continues today as a member of the active medical staff in medicine and cardiology.

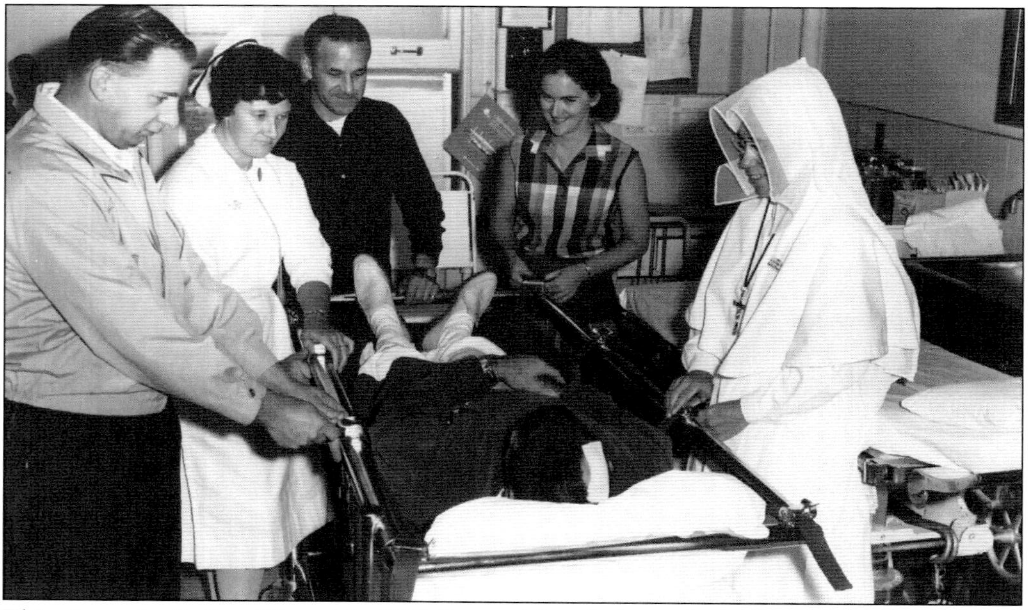

This picture is of a Surgilift unit in 1964. Pictured from left to right are Ray LaFlair, rescue squad volunteer; Joan Reed, head nurse; Cam Gates, president of the rescue squad; Frances Ann Pagano, City Guild representative; Sr. Saint Patricia, assistant director of nursing service; and Paul Grall, a patient (center). They are demonstrating the use of the new Surgilift, which is thought to have been a gift from the City Guild.

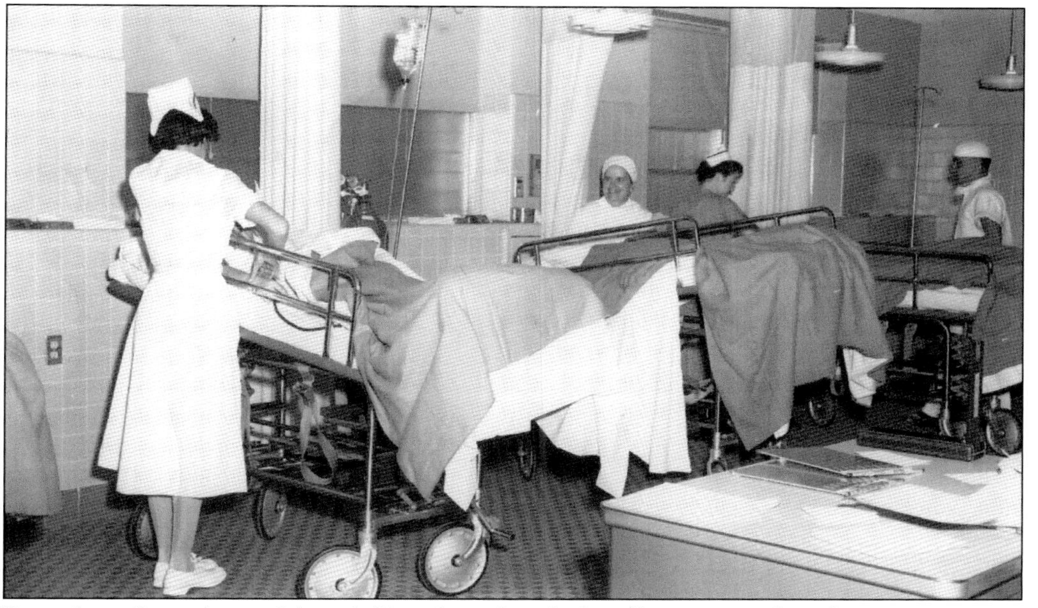

Bernadette Sovie (second from left) and unidentified staff are pictured in the recovery room in 1964.

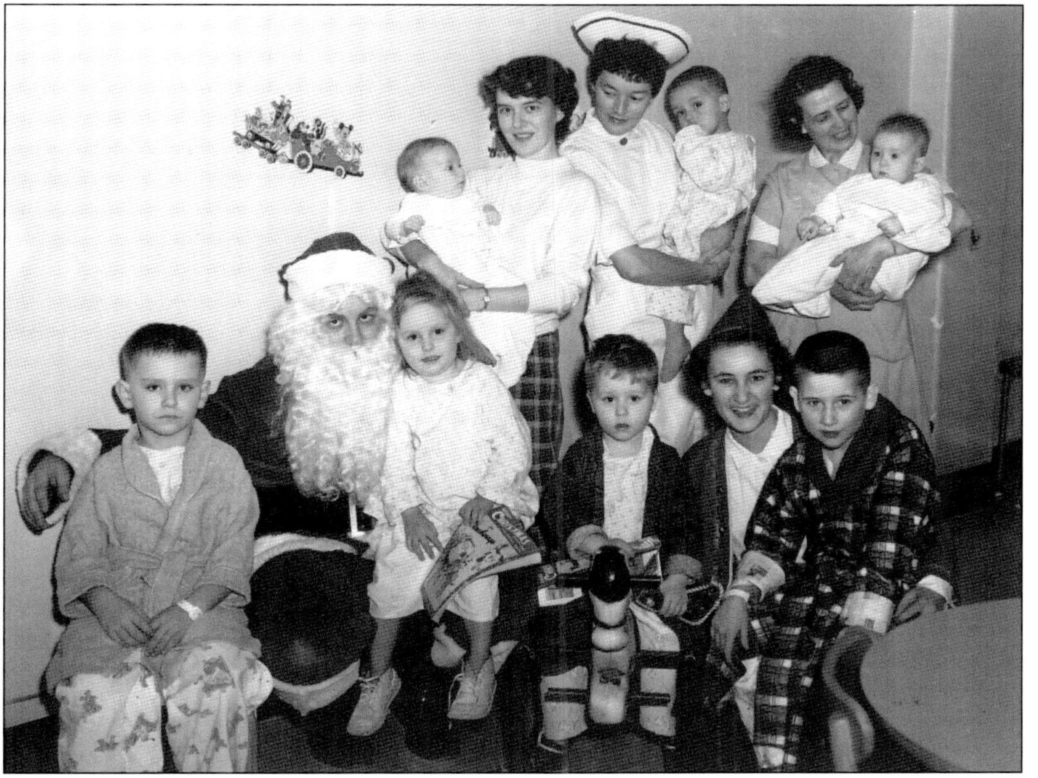

Staff and patients in the pediatrics unit celebrate Christmas with a visit from Santa Claus. This photograph is believed to have been taken in the 1960s.

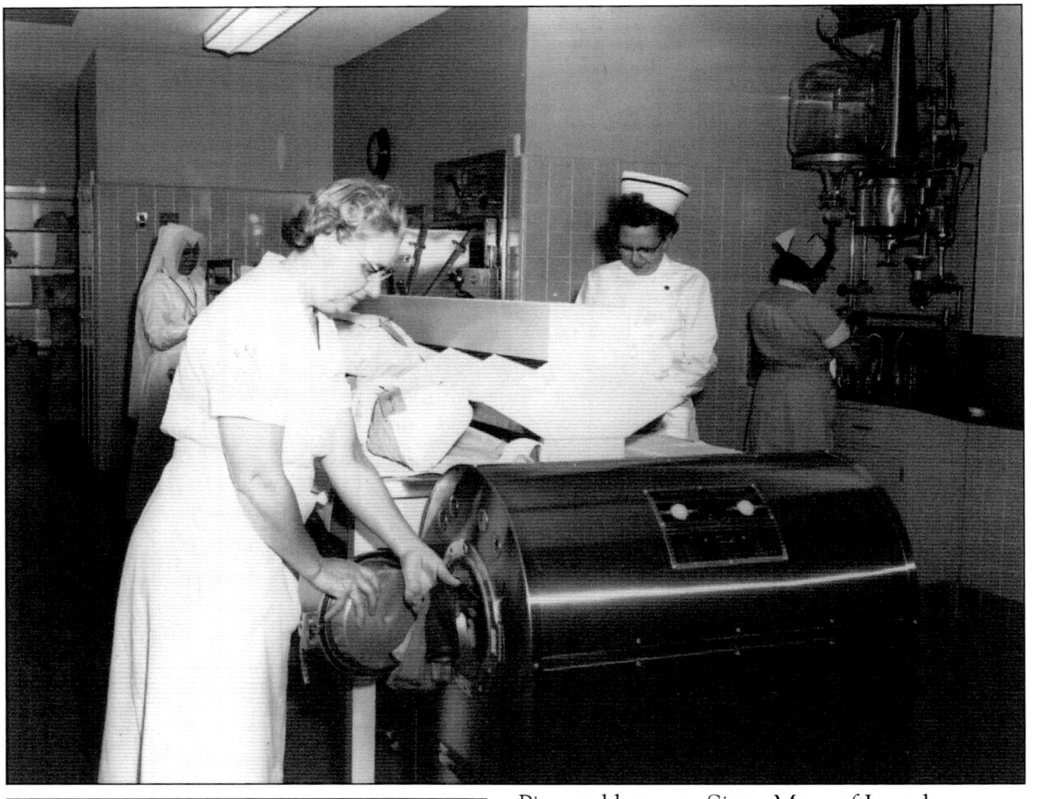

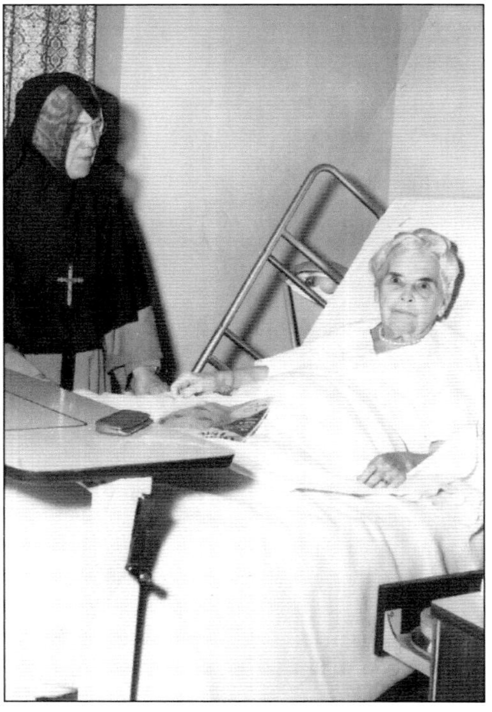

Pictured here are Sister Mary of Lourdes, Blanche Lapine, Mary Thompson, and Elizabeth Martin cleaning and sterilizing medical instruments in the central supply sterilization department. Sister Mary of Lourdes worked at Hepburn Hospital for 44 years, and for the last two years, she was on the nursing staff in the extended care facility. She retired in 1972.

Sr. Mary Monica, hospital administrator from 1927 to 1935, 1938 to 1944, and 1952 to 1963, visits with Hattie Lovejoy in her hospital room.

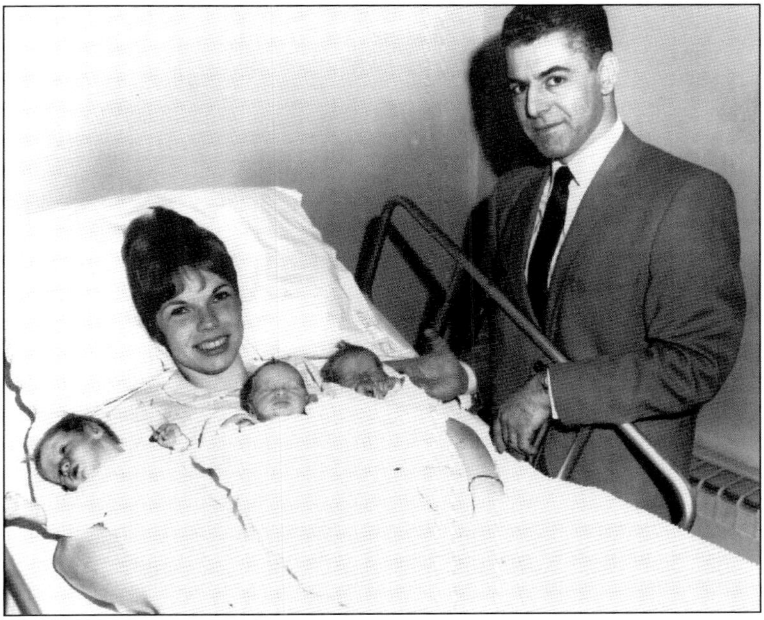

Dr. M. Kouyoumdjian (right) delivered triplets at Hepburn Hospital. Judy Longshore holds her three new baby girls, named Amy, Bridget, and Heidi, on January 3, 1970. Dr. Kouyoumdjian, obstetrician, served on the medical staff at Hepburn from 1967 until 1987.

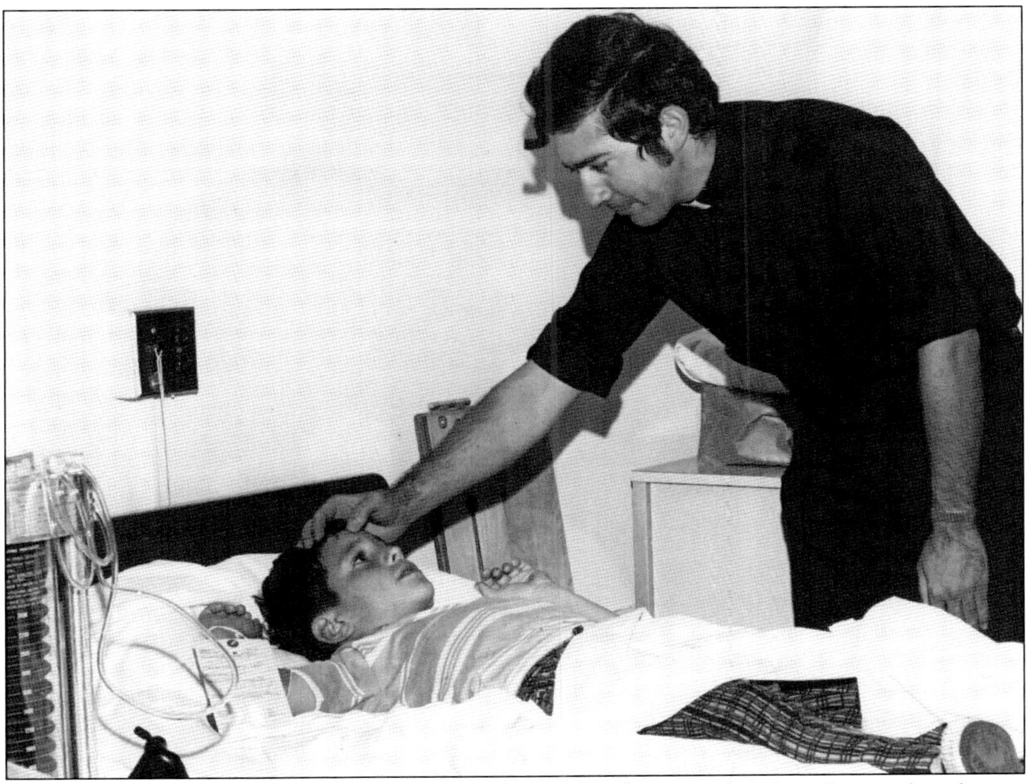

On July 27, 1972, Rev. Joseph Falletta, of Notre Dame Church, was on hand tending to the religious needs of members of his congregation. The boy is unidentified.

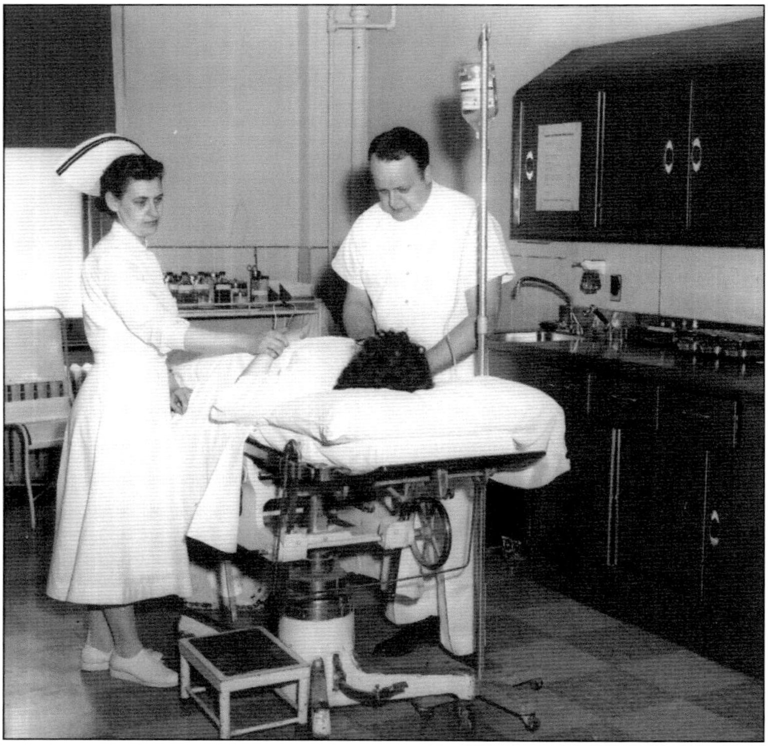

Dr. Robert Lonngren and Alice Sears, first-floor nursing and emergency department supervisor, treat a patient.

On July 27, 1972, the staff performs a disaster drill. Mary Beauchamp is the nurse second from right in the picture.

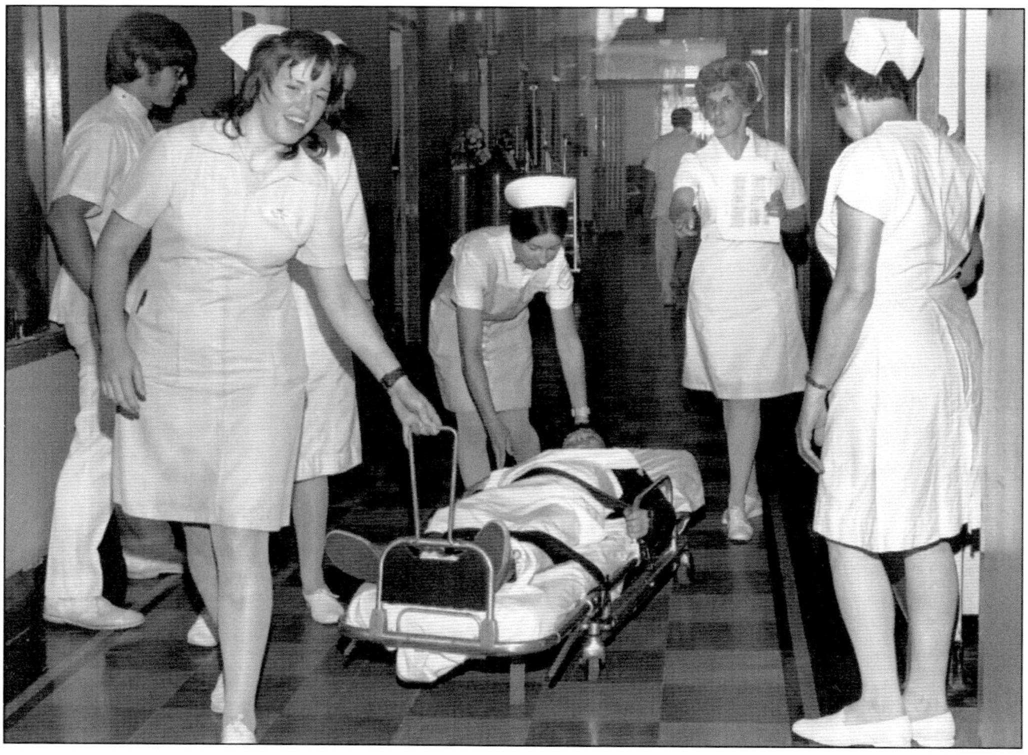

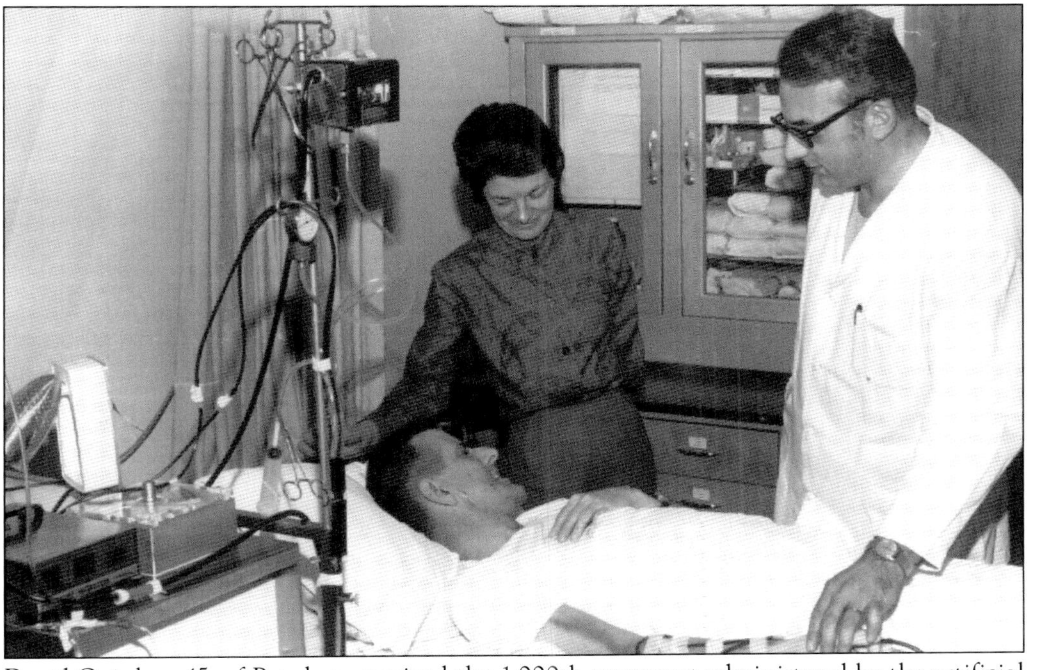

David Quinlan, 45, of Potsdam, received the 1,000th treatment administered by the artificial kidney in the hemodialysis unit on Wednesday, November 24, 1971. His wife, Sally (pictured), administered the treatment under the supervision of Dr. John R. Bongiovanni, urologoist and surgeon. Dr. Bongiovanni brought hemodialysis to the North Country in 1968, before even most urban hospitals had it. As of 1971, there were two machines in use daily. Dr. Bongiovanni served on the medical staff from 1964 until 1984.

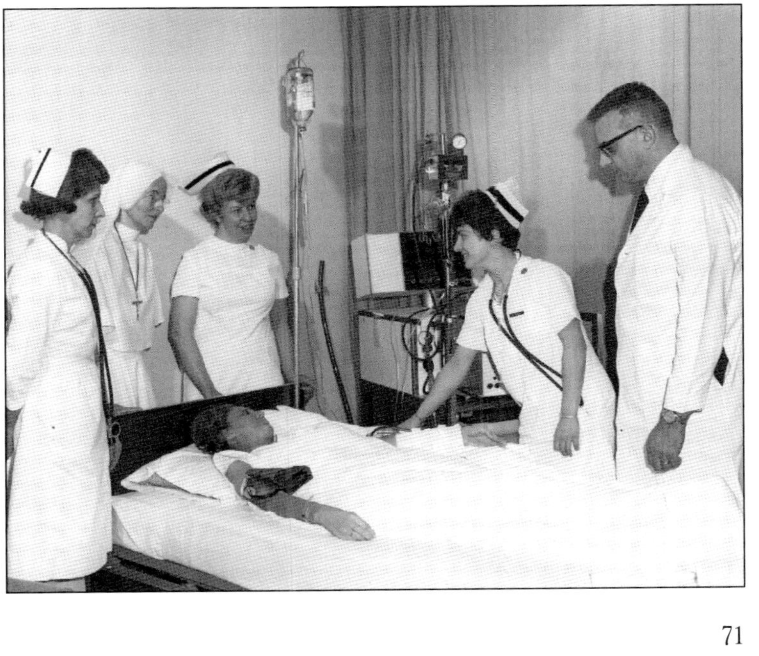

From left to right, Mary Beauchamp, Sr. Mary Gemma, Gail Bongiovanni, an unidentified nurse, and Dr. John R. Bongiovanni tend to a hemodialysis patient.

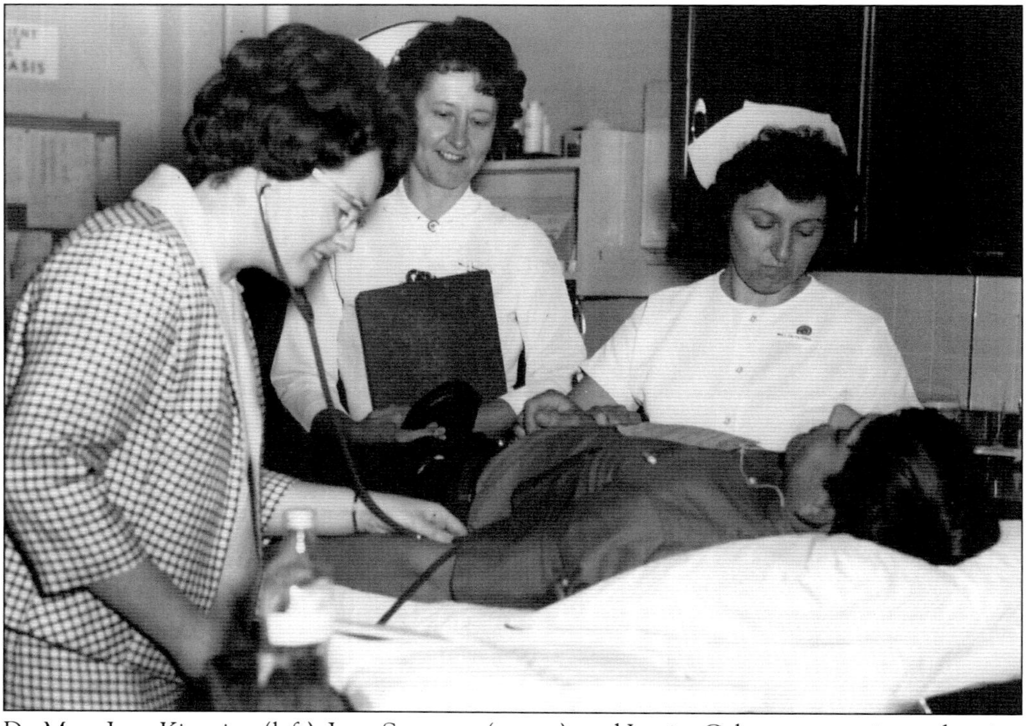

Dr. Mary Jane Kinosian (left), Joan Swanson (center), and Louisa Calcaterra are pictured caring for a patient.

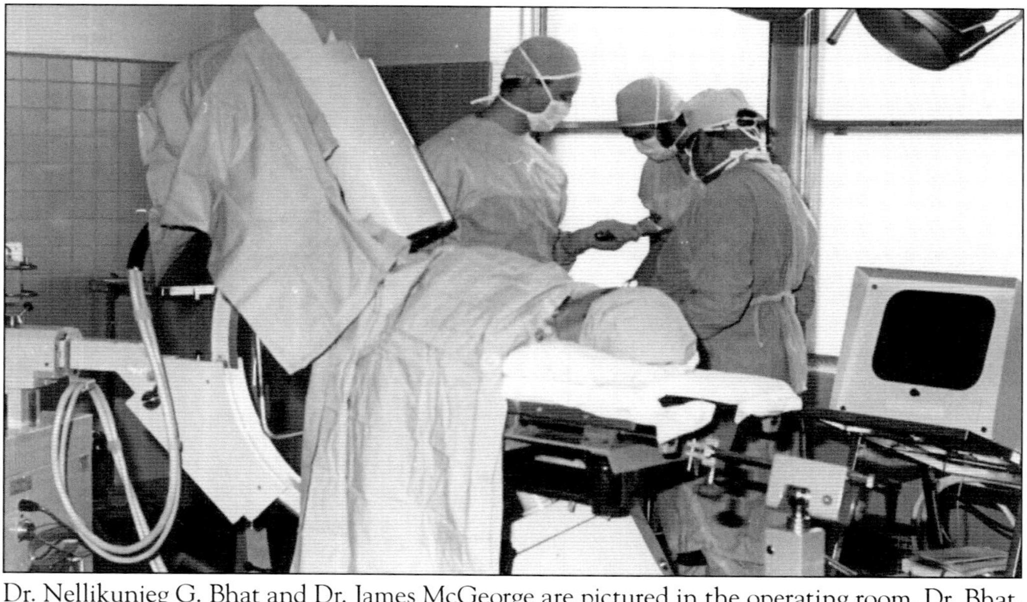

Dr. Nellikunjeg G. Bhat and Dr. James McGeorge are pictured in the operating room. Dr. Bhat, an orthopedic surgeon, first joined the Hepburn Hospital Medical Staff in October 1973. He was the first to perform many operations at Hepburn Hospital, such as hip replacement, total replacement of the knee, and silastic toe prosthesis. Dr. McGeorge was also an orthopedic surgeon at the hospital from 1983 until 1989.

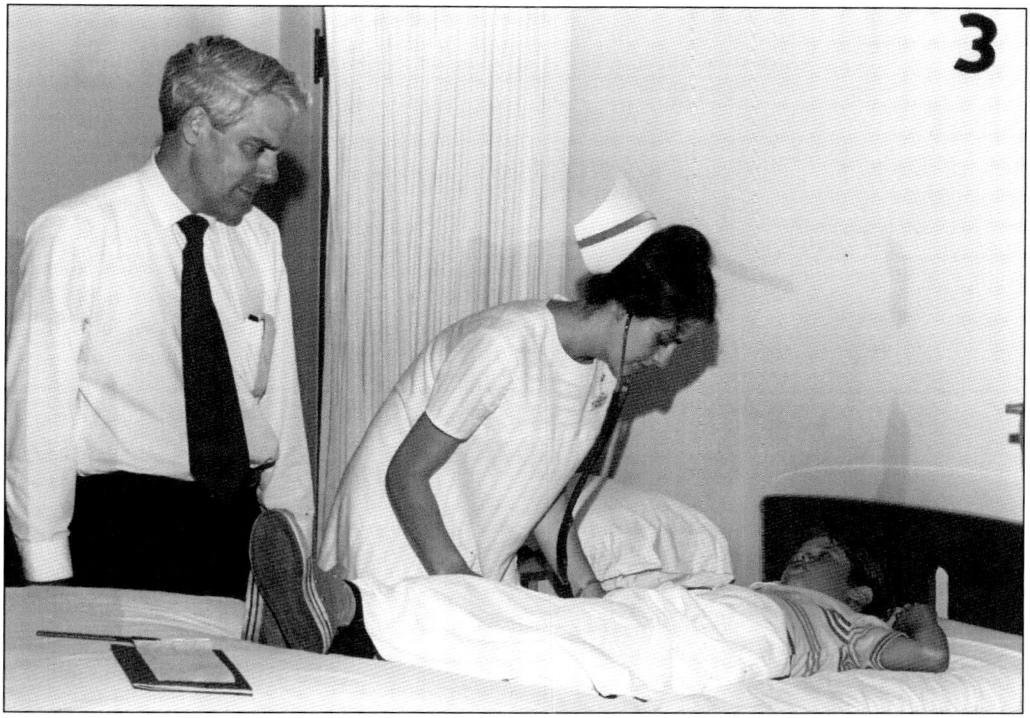

On July 27, 1972, Dr. Berwyn H. Woodman and Sue Bouchard show concern as they check the blood pressure of a pediatric patient. Dr. Woodman, a surgeon, was on the medical staff at Hepburn Hospital from 1966 until 1992.

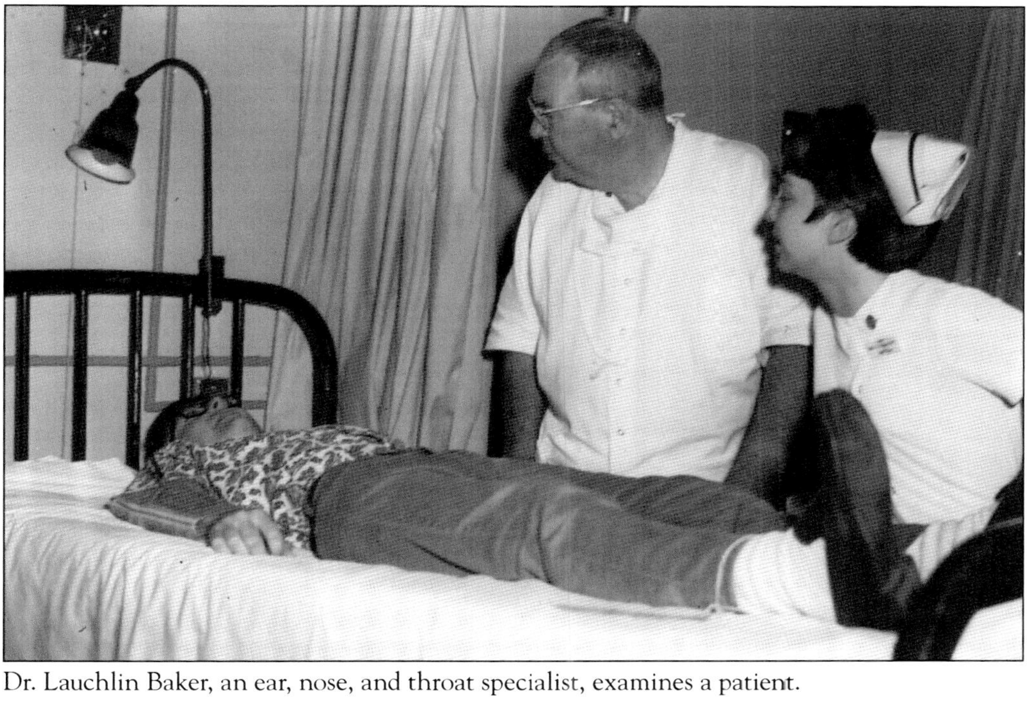

Dr. Lauchlin Baker, an ear, nose, and throat specialist, examines a patient.

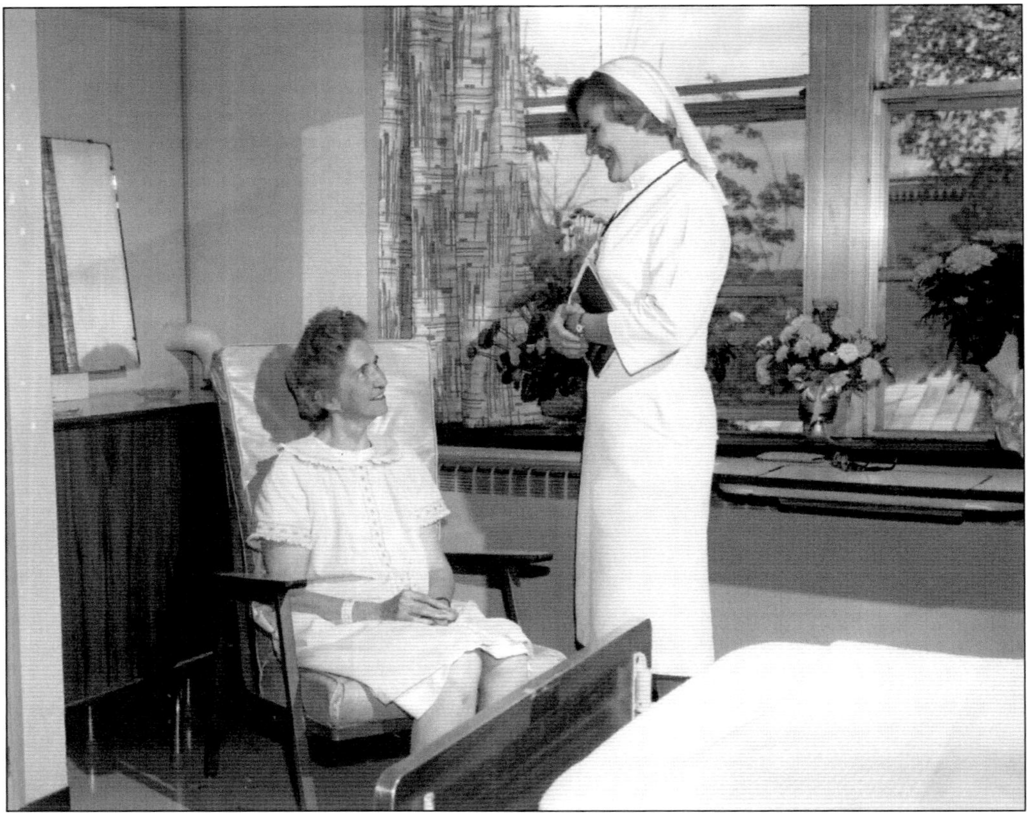

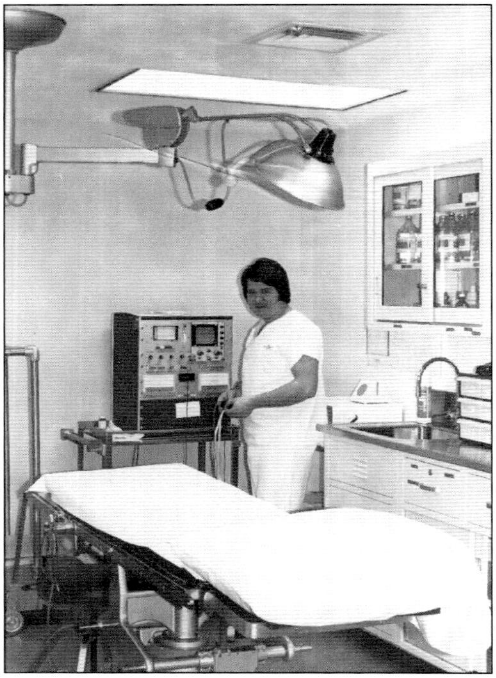

Above, Sr. Anne Therese visits with an unidentified patient. In the picture on the left is David Delarge, manager of the emergency department.

Minnie Knowlton, of Gouverneur, meets with Dr. Robert Hentschel (right), surgeon, and Dr. Bansi Bazaz, internist, one week following the operation she underwent for the insertion of a permanent pacemaker (implantable pulse generator). This was the first permanent pacemaker operation at Hepburn Hospital, performed on Saturday, July 14, 1969, by Dr. Hentschel, assisted by Dr. David DePue, chief surgeon. Dr. Bazaz and Dr. Federico Loinaz were the attending internists. Dr. Loinaz joined the medical staff in 1971, and Dr. Hentschel joined in 1969. Both are still active members of the medical staff today. Dr. DePue, a general surgeon, was on the medical staff from 1948 until 1983.

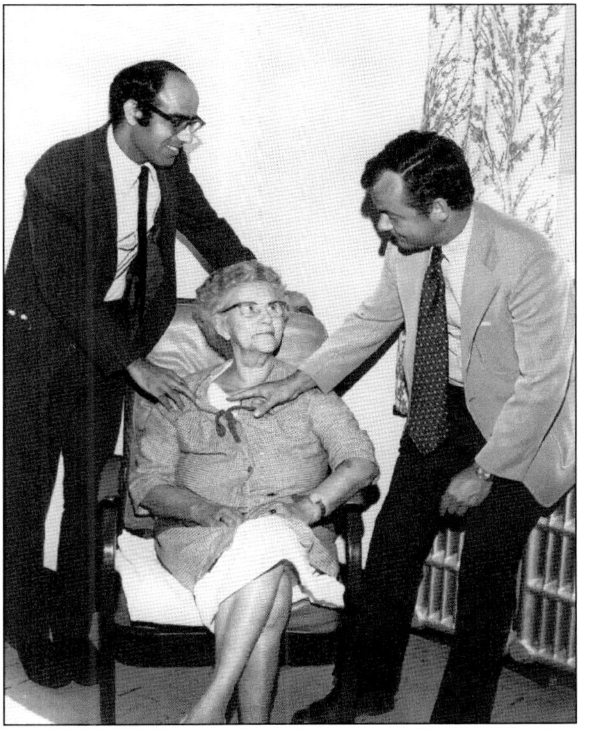

Dr. Berwyn Woodman stands at the door of the ambulance during a disaster drill on July 27, 1972.

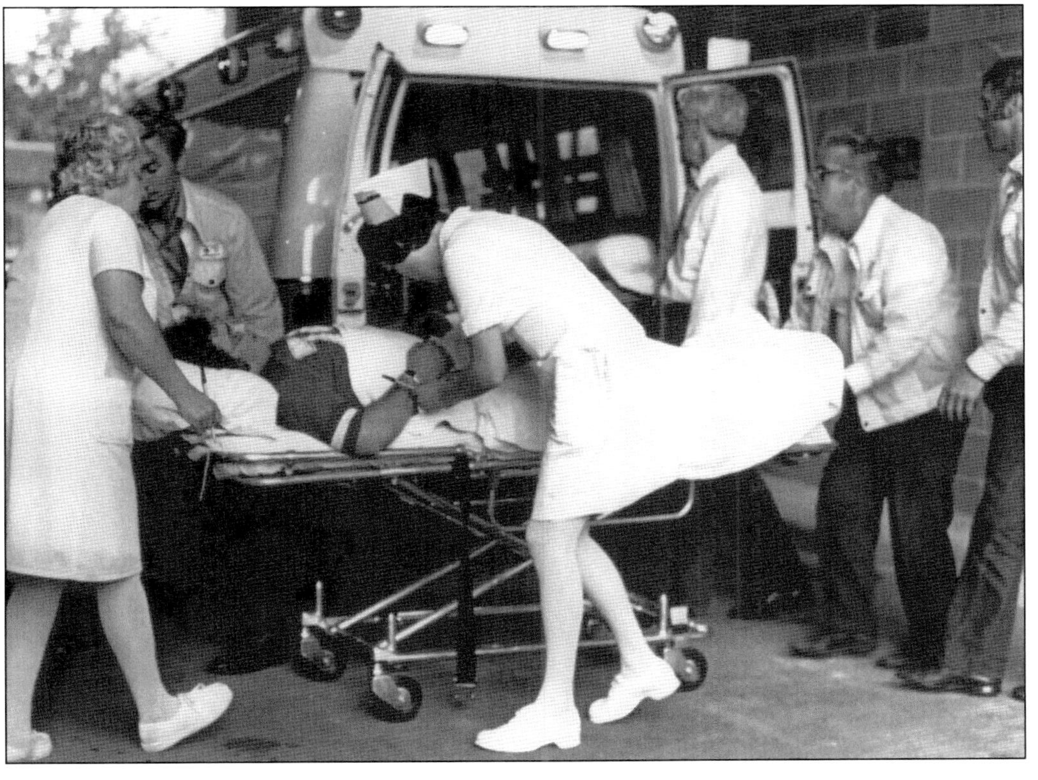

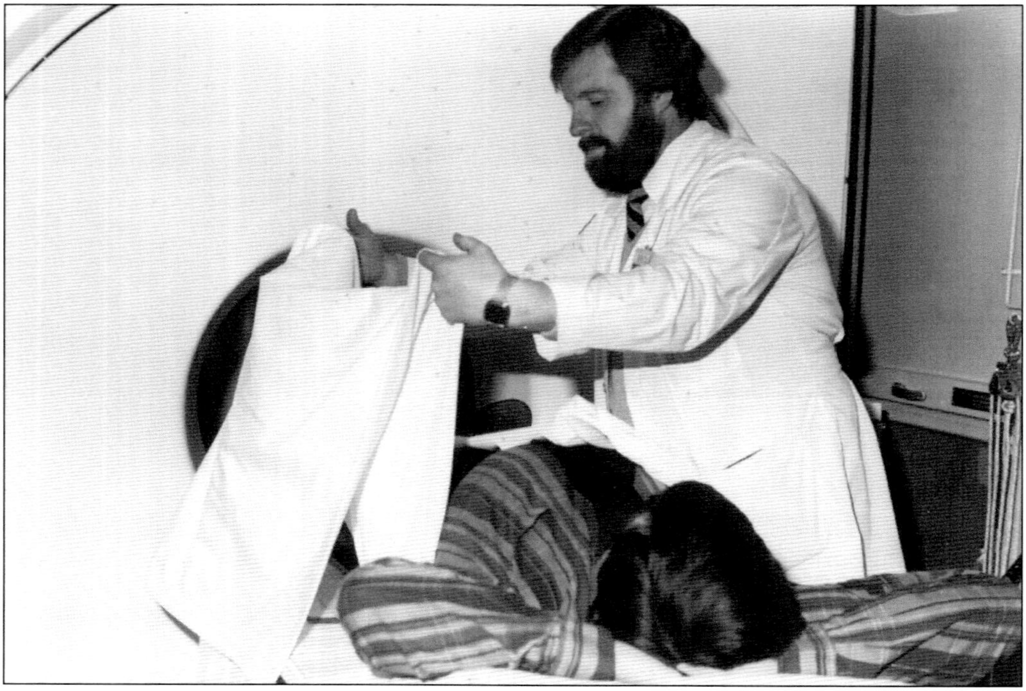

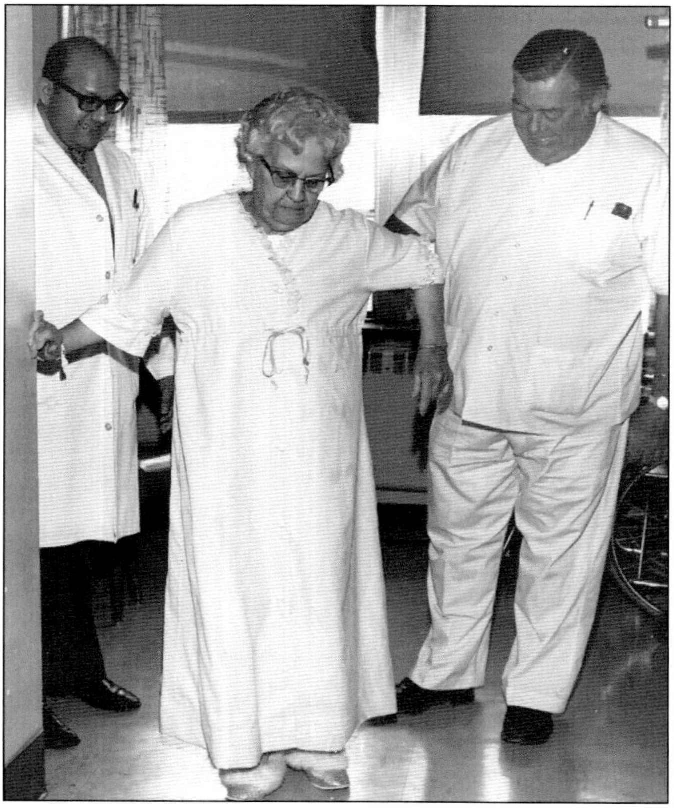

This is believed to be an early CAT scan performed at the hospital. The first CAT scans at the hospital were done in a mobile unit in the 1980s.

The first total hip replacement operation ever performed at Hepburn Hospital took place on May 3, 1974. Suffering with arthritis, Ella Barkley, of Rensselaer Falls, New York, underwent the surgical procedure performed by Dr. David DePue, surgeon, and Dr. Nellikunjeg G. Bhat, orthopedist. In this picture, Barkley demonstrates her ability to walk alone for the first time in nine months.

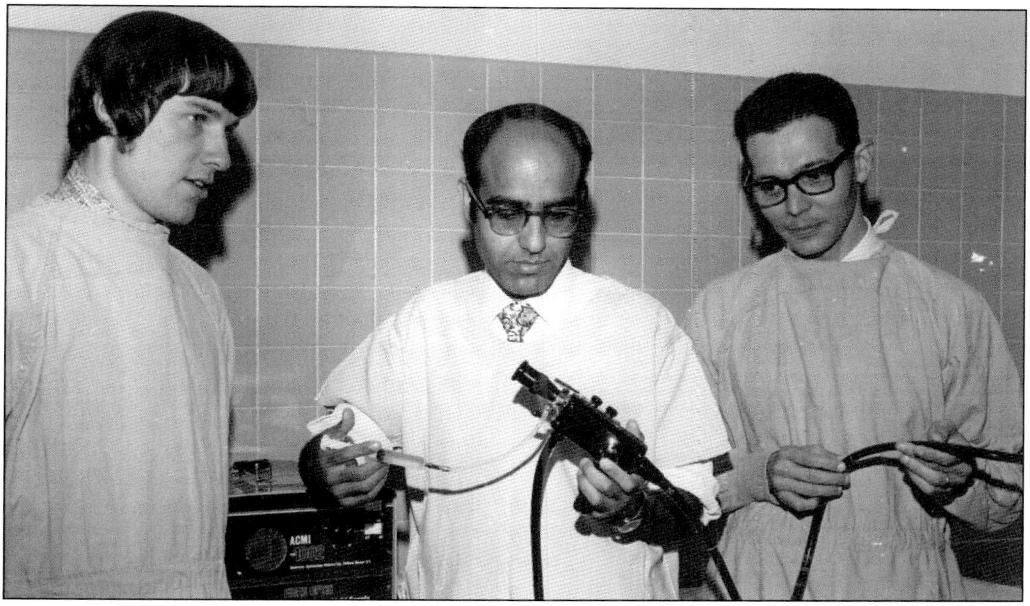

Medical student Robert Rogers (left), Dr. Bansi Bazaz (center), and Dr. Federico Loinaz are testing the new fiber-optic panendoscope installed in the operating room in 1973. The new instrument enables the internist to do a simple procedure called a gastroscopy. Gastroscopy can be used for visualizing lesions, taking biopsies of suspicious lesions, and taking pictures of visualized fields. It consists of a flexible tube of thousands of coated glass fibers.

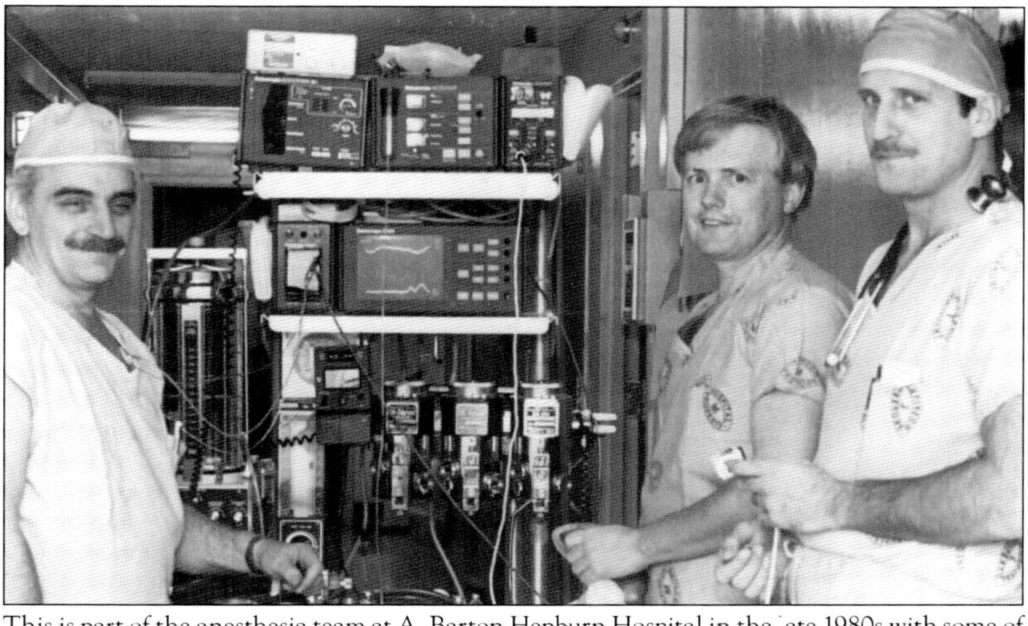

This is part of the anesthesia team at A. Barton Hepburn Hospital in the late 1980s with some of the equipment that provided constant monitoring of patients who had been anesthetized. From left to right are Robert LaRock, a certified registered nurse anesthetist, and anesthesiologists Dr. Jeffrey Doyle and Dr. David Bowman. Dr. Doyle joined the medical staff in February 1977 and continues as an active member today. Dr. Bowman was on the medical staff from 1987 until 1990.

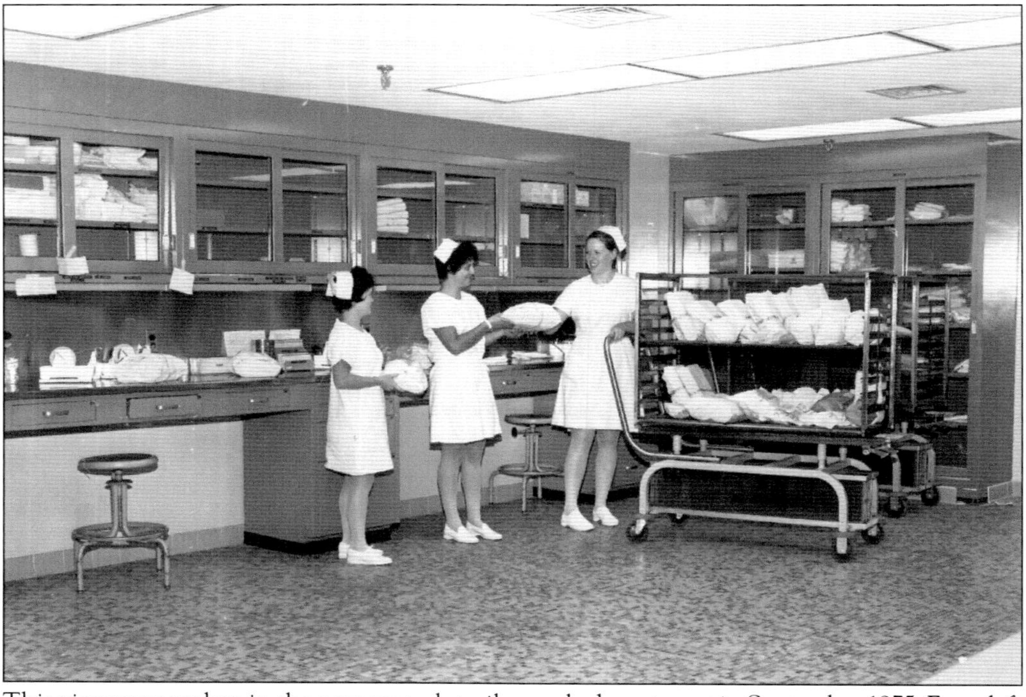

This picture was taken in the new central sterile supply department in September 1975. From left to right are Gloria Gilbert, Carol Knable, and Joanne Guasconi.

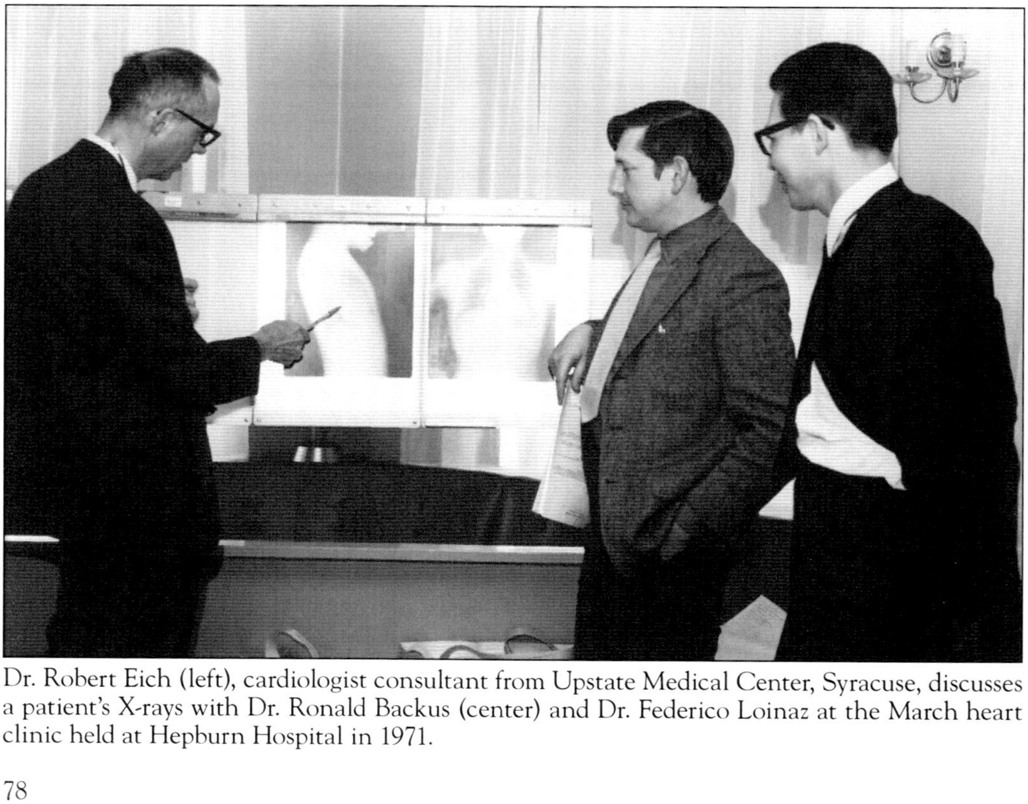

Dr. Robert Eich (left), cardiologist consultant from Upstate Medical Center, Syracuse, discusses a patient's X-rays with Dr. Ronald Backus (center) and Dr. Federico Loinaz at the March heart clinic held at Hepburn Hospital in 1971.

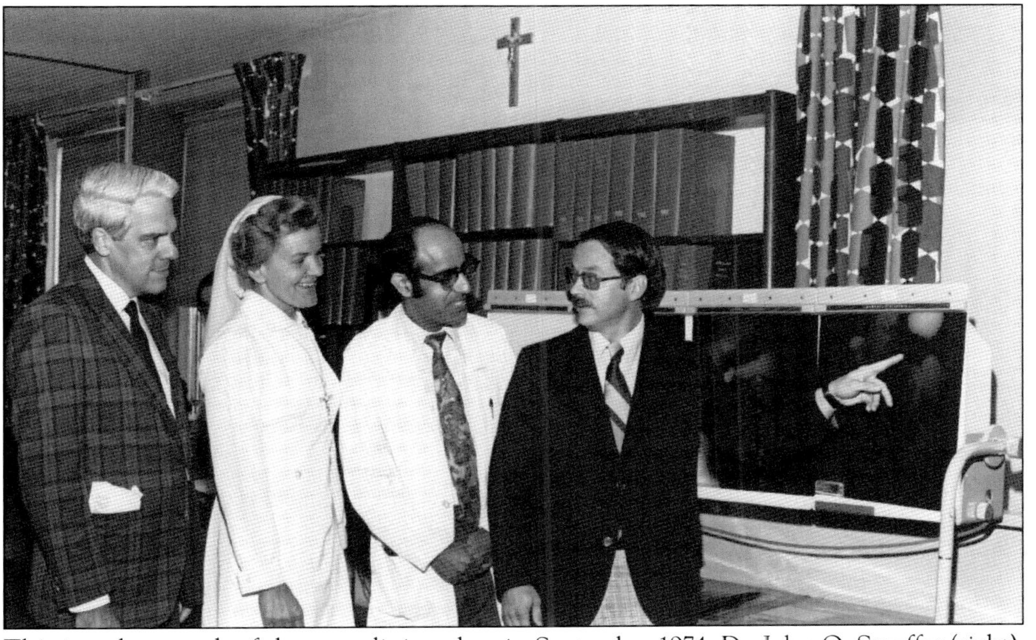

This is a photograph of the new clinic, taken in September 1974. Dr. John Q. Stauffer (right), a specialist in gastroenterology in Syracuse, conducts his first monthly gastroenterology clinic at Hepburn Hospital. Dr. Stauffer discusses a case with surgeon Dr. Berwyn Woodman (left), administrator Sr. Anne Therese, GNSH, and Dr. Bansi Bazaz, internal medicine.

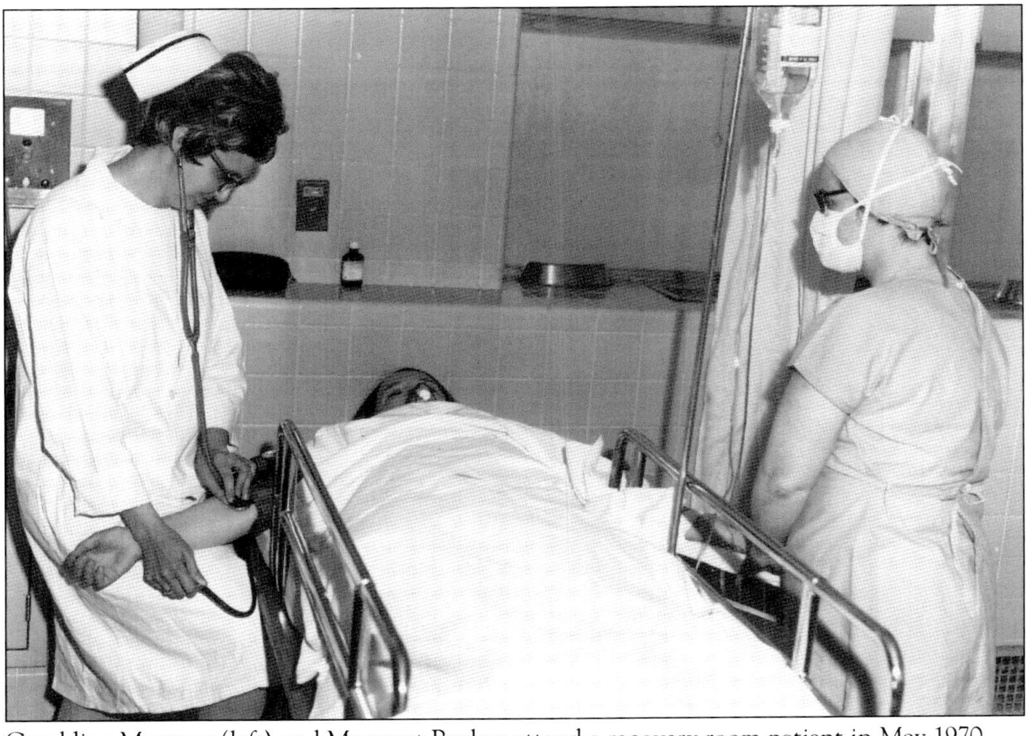

Geraldine Montroy (left) and Margaret Backus attend a recovery room patient in May 1970.

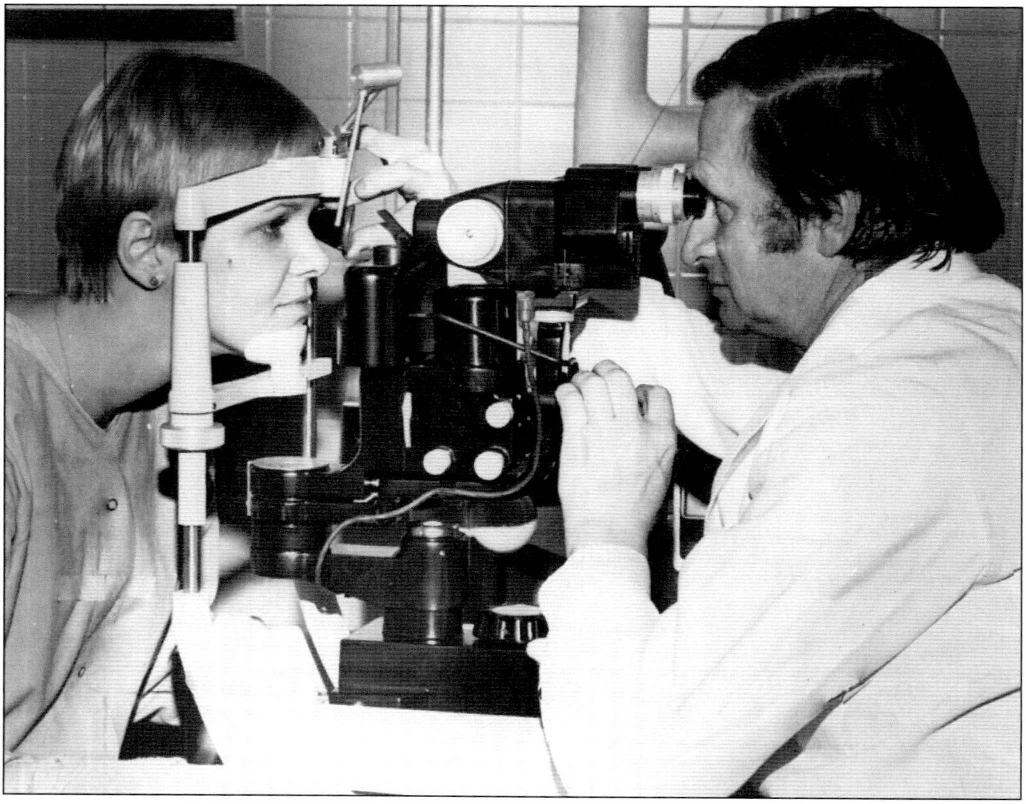

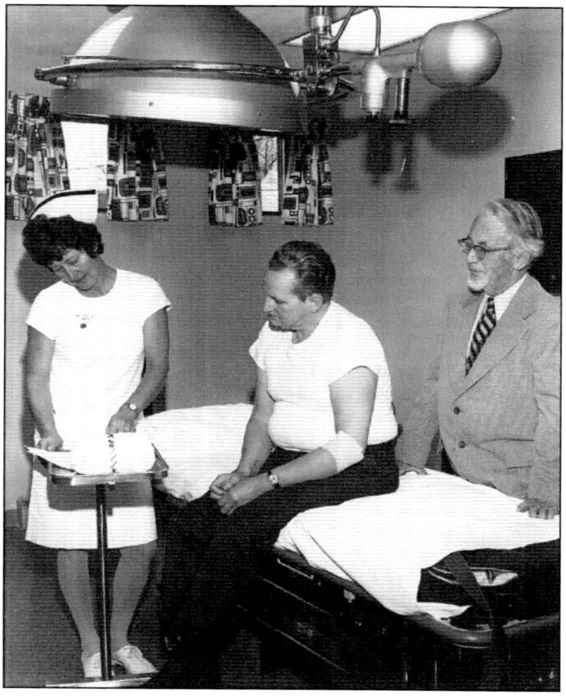

Dr. Jerry Jacobson, an ophthalmologist, demonstrates the use of a laser beam with volunteer patient Susan Walff in March 1972. In 1974, Dr. Jacobson performed the first corneal transplant at Hepburn Hospital. Before the procedure, he worked with the local Lions Club to identify an eye donor for his patient.

Dr. Edward Whalen listens as Joan Swanson explains treatment and orders to a patient. Alton Whittaker, of Balmat, New York, was treated in one of the rooms in the new emergency room facility that opened in April 1975.

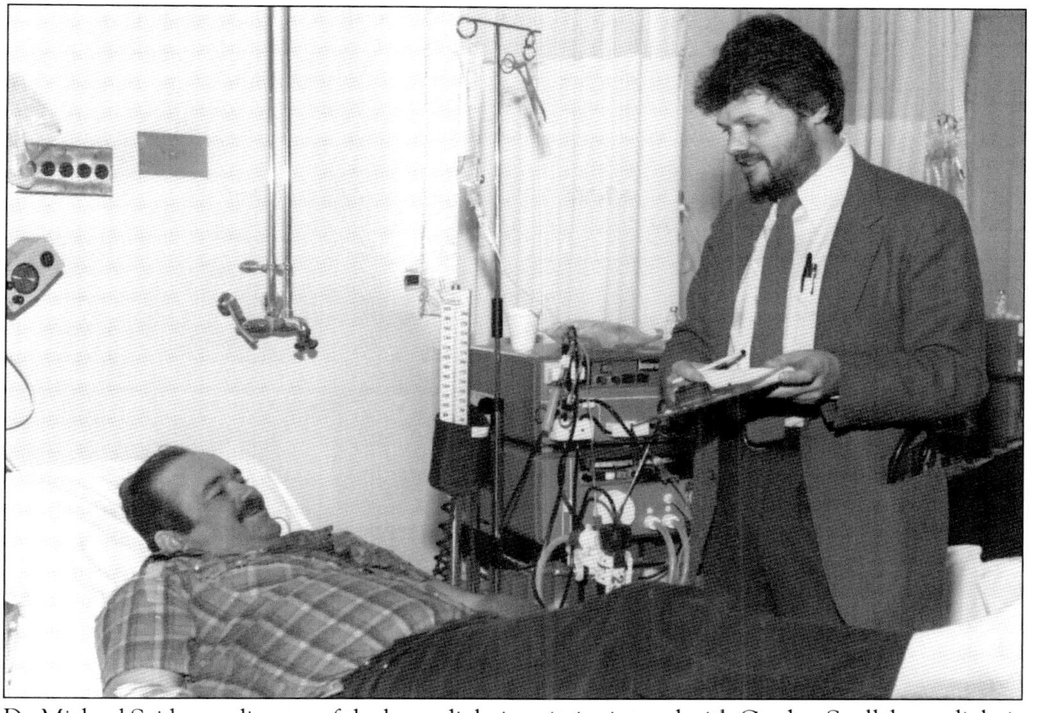

Dr. Michael Seidman, director of the hemodialysis unit, is pictured with Gordon Snell, hemodialysis patient. Dr. Seidman specialized in the treatment of kidney disease at Downstate Medical Center–Kings County Hospital, Brooklyn. He graduated from Boston University and trained in internal medicine at Montefiore Hospital in the Bronx. Dr. Seidman joined the Hepburn Hospital medical staff in 1983 and remains an active member today.

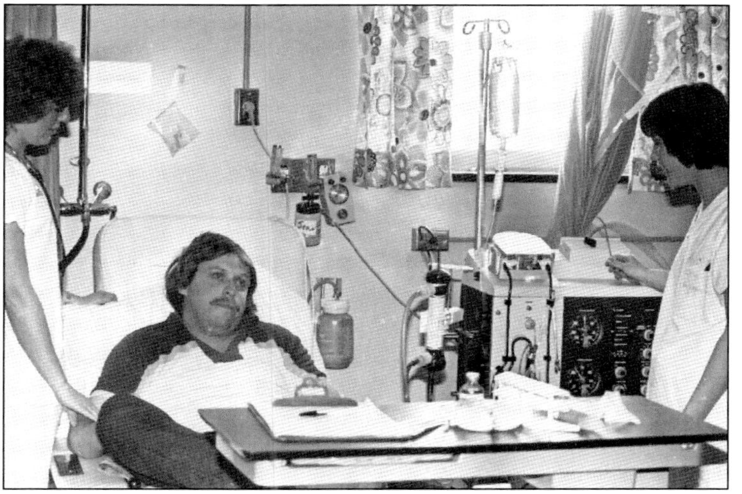

Kandy Simmons (left) and Chris Wright administer hemodialysis treatment to patient Daryl Greenfield in May 1983.

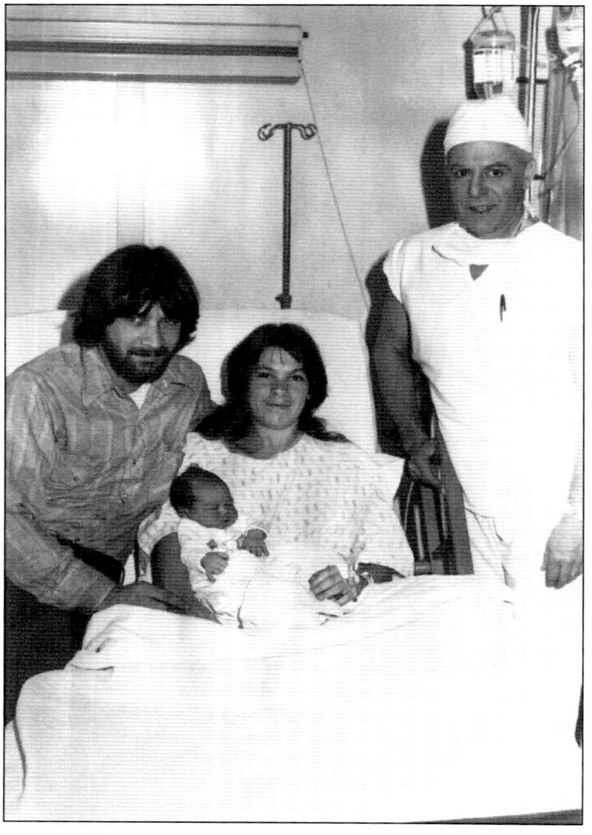

Pictured here is Ogdensburg's first baby of 1985, Donald Cresson Gilbo Jr. Donald Jr. was born at A. Barton Hepburn Hospital at 1:57 p.m. on New Year's Day and is the son of Ellen Meunier and Donald Gilbo. Dr. Meguerdich Kouyoumdjian (pictured) delivered the baby. Dr. Kouyoumdjian served on the medical staff from 1967 to 1987.

Colleen Ross (left) and Nancy Stacey, nurse manager of obstetrics, prepare a birthing room on November 18, 1985.

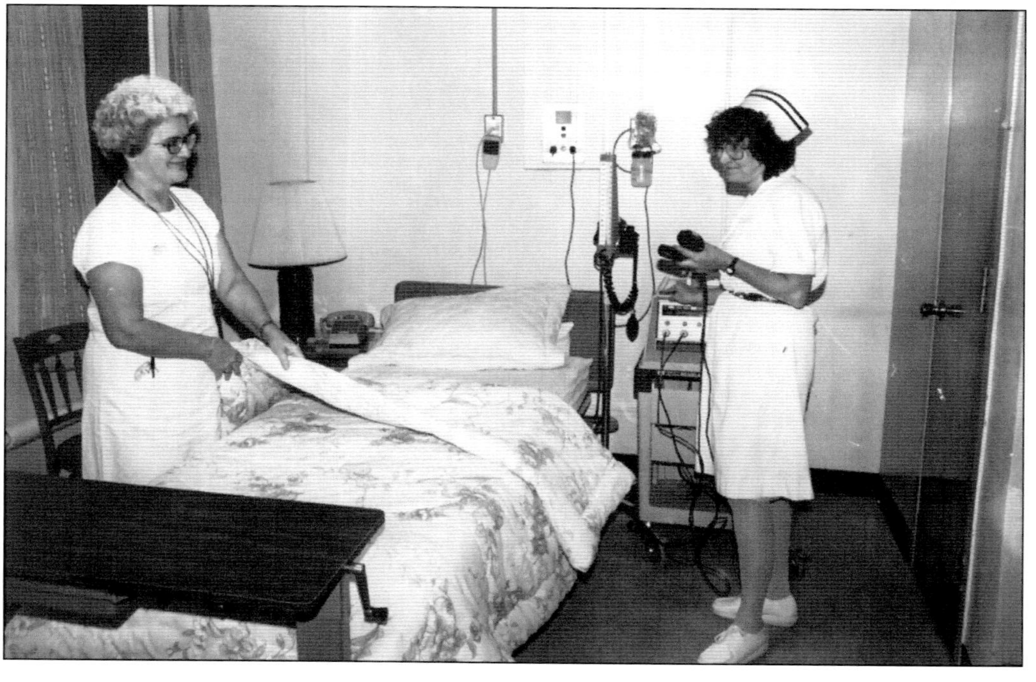

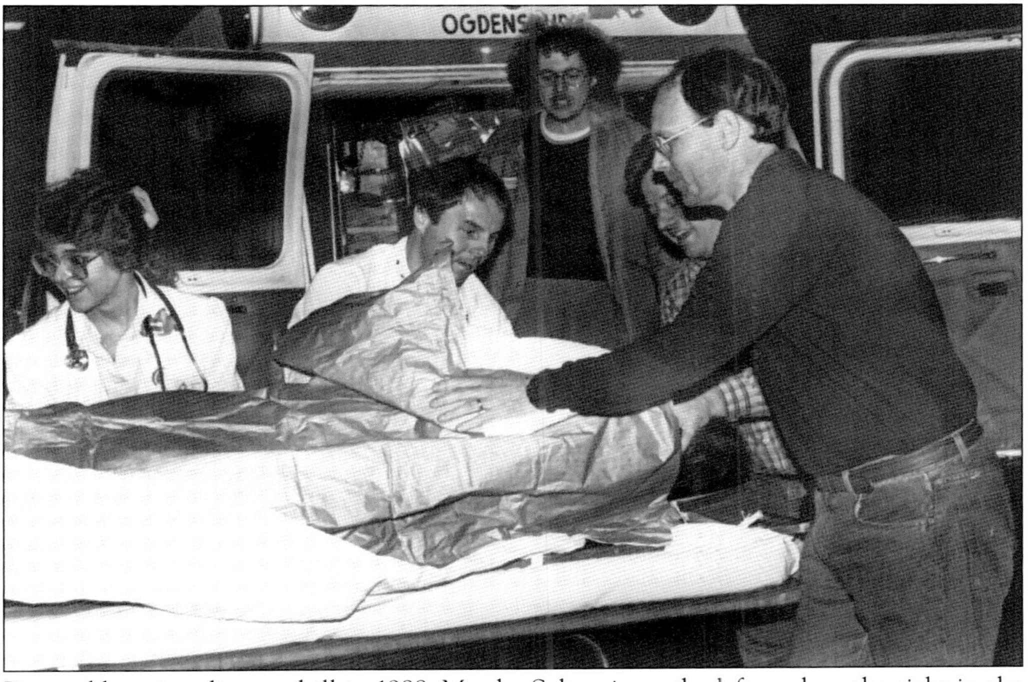

Pictured here is a disaster drill in 1988. Marsha Salton is on the left, and on the right in the foreground is Don Lewis, president and CEO. Lewis started at Hepburn in December 1986 and left in August 1997.

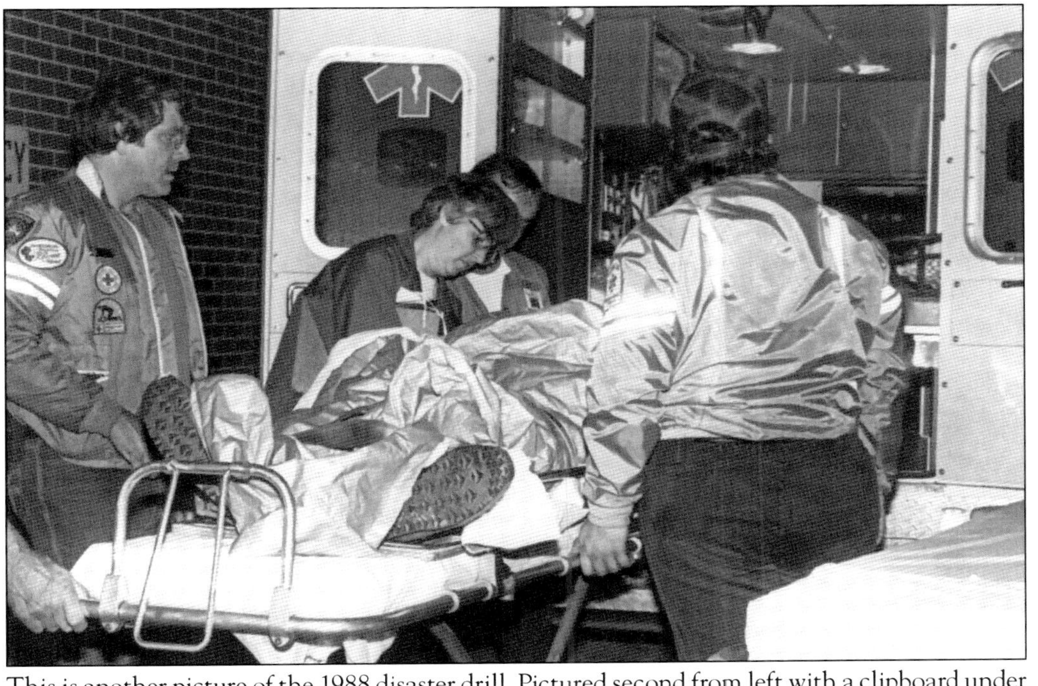

This is another picture of the 1988 disaster drill. Pictured second from left with a clipboard under her arm is Sandy Lyons. The other people are unidentified.

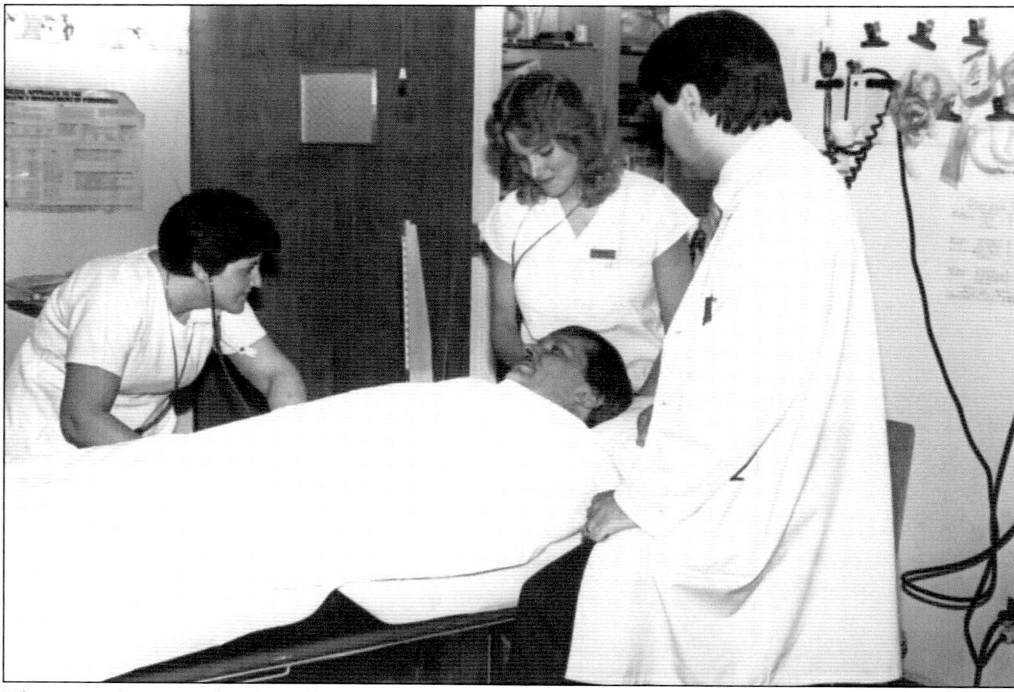

This is a photograph of Linda Calcaterra (left), Kathy Pike (center), and Rod Roca tending to Glenn Allen, a staff member posing as a patient in the emergency room.

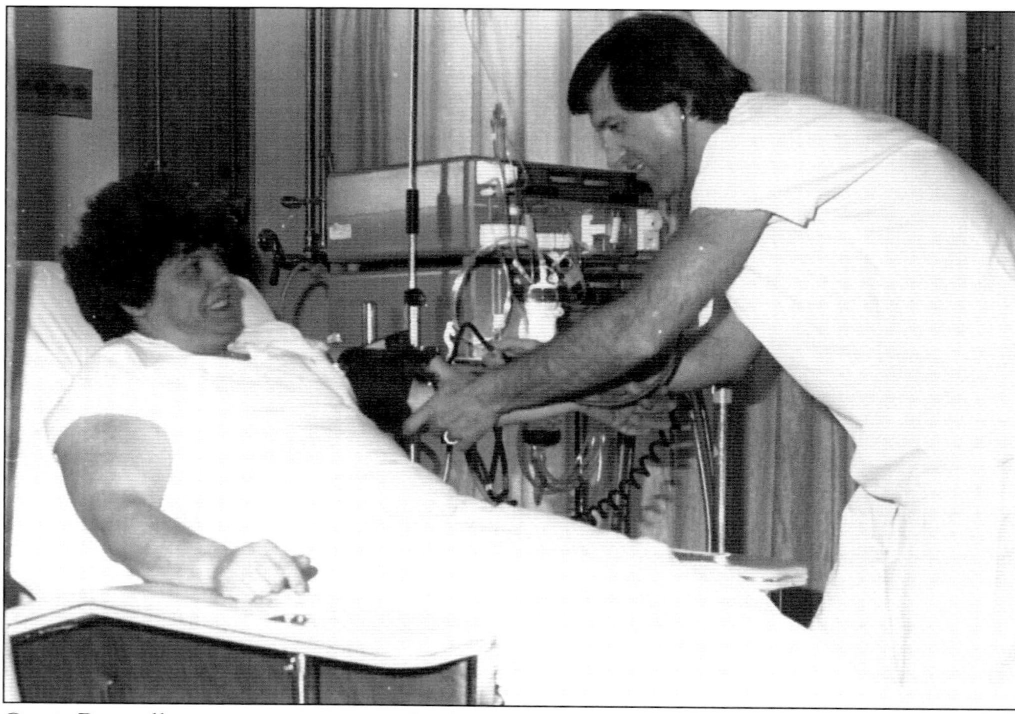

Cassie Donnelly poses as a patient with Thomas Mahoney.

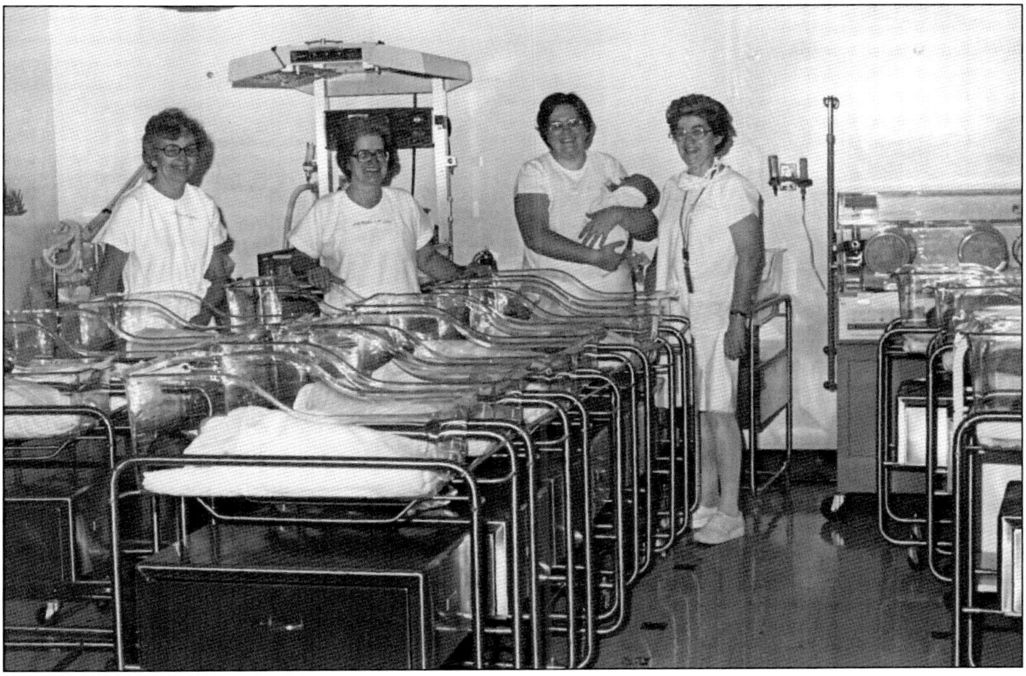

On November 17, 1981, this picture was taken to mark the occasion of 19 newborns at Hepburn Hospital. Pictured are, from left to right, Phyllis Powers, Colleen Ross, Alice Hunter, and Eileen Holleran.

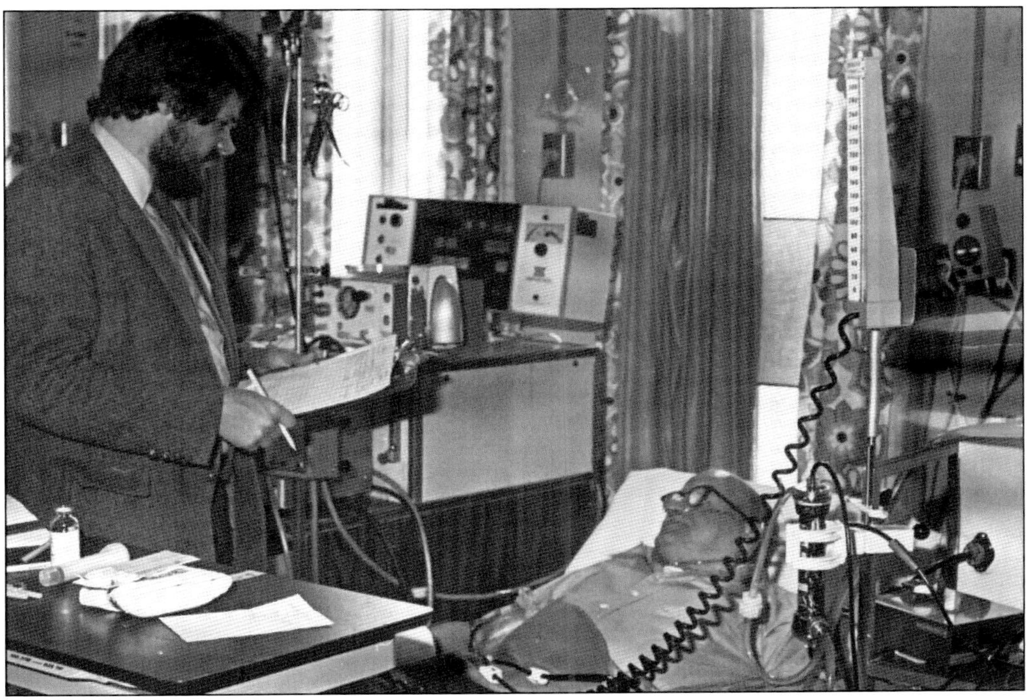

Dr. Michael Seidman, director of the hemodialysis unit, makes his rounds in 1984.

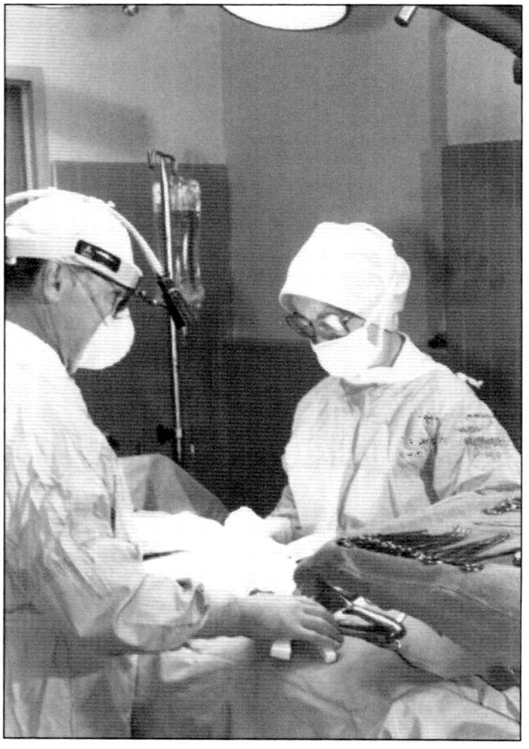

Dr. Hentschel performs surgery with Colleen Lago, nurse manager of the operating room.

Dr. Ali Gharagozloo, a radiologist, reads X-rays. Dr. Gharagozloo joined the medical staff in November 1996.

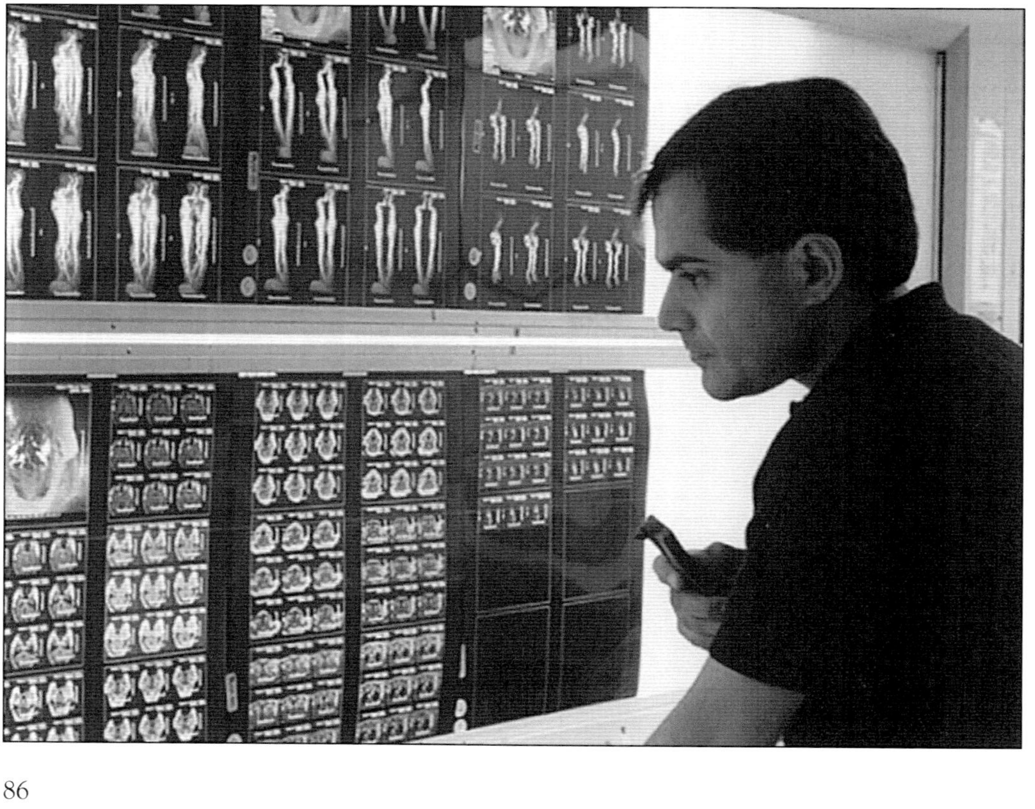

Six

Life in the Hospital

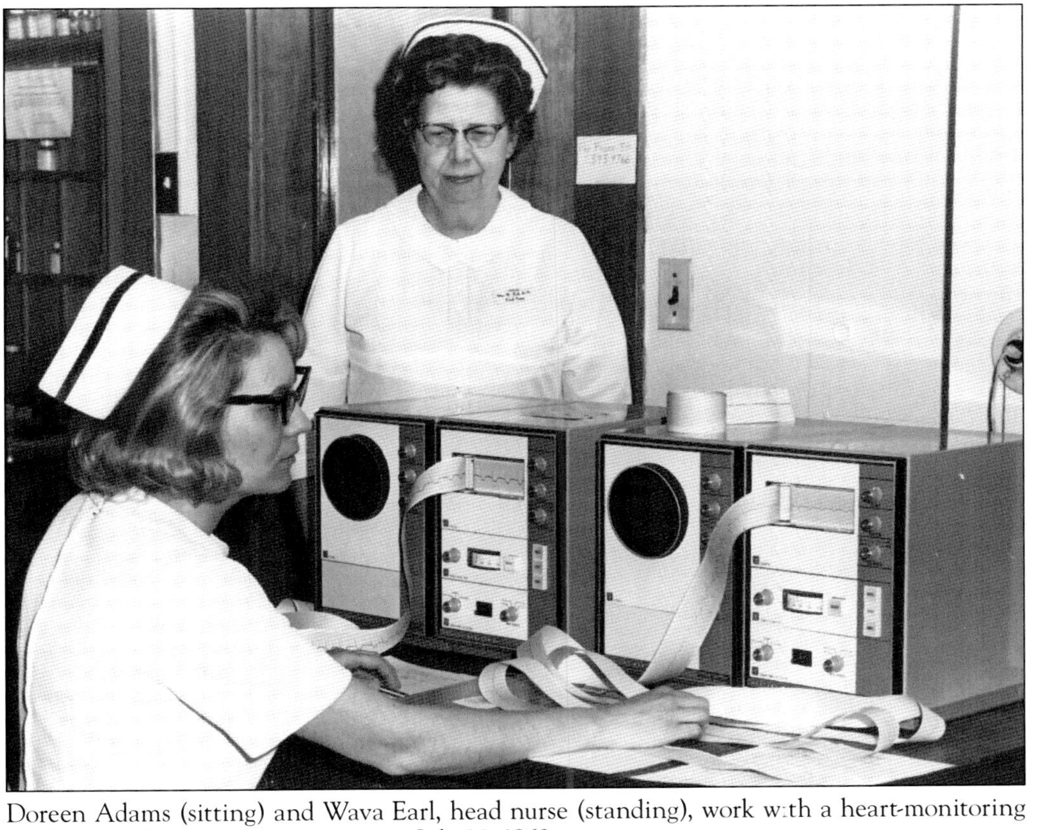

Doreen Adams (sitting) and Wava Earl, head nurse (standing), work with a heart-monitoring machine in the coronary care unit on July 14, 1969.

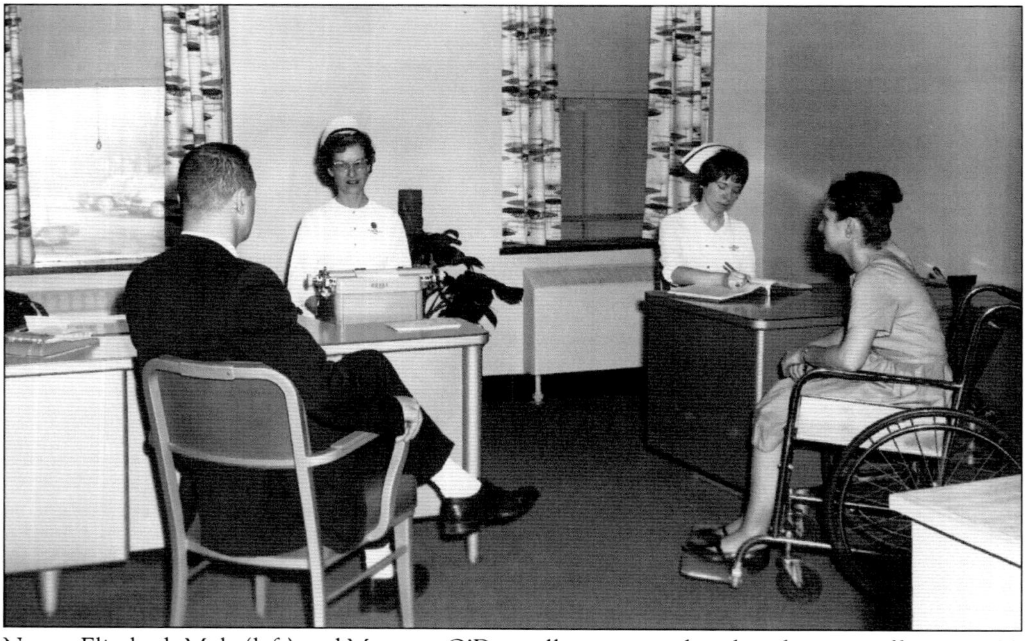

Nurses Elizabeth Male (left) and Maureen O'Donnell are pictured in the admitting office in 1966. The two nurses had the prime responsibility of assisting the more than 6,300 patients admitted annually to the hospital at that time. Volunteer patients with their backs to the picture are Leonard Berard, hospital purchasing agent, and Carol Lesperance, insurance clerk.

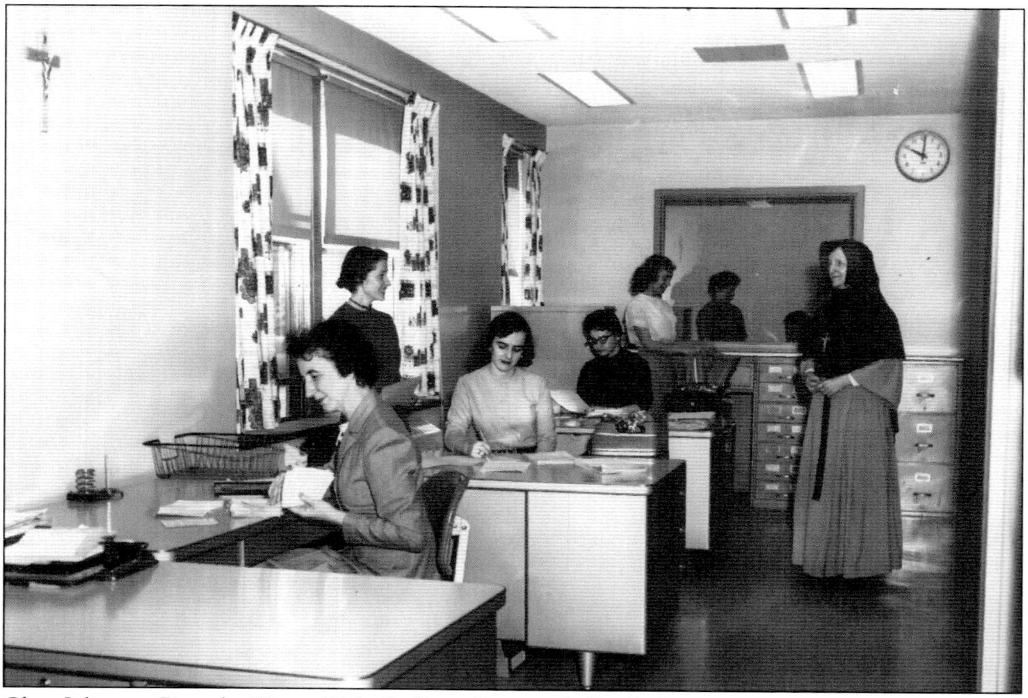

Clare Johnson, Dorothy Kieger, Tisha LaRose, Suzanne LaRock, Sonya Souie, Pauline Phelps, Rozelle Bedond, and Sr. Mary Clement are pictured in the administrative office at Hepburn Hospital.

Joseph Gebo, executive housekeeper, and Lincoln Aldridge, an industrial engineer, are talking over a product that is used for cleaning.

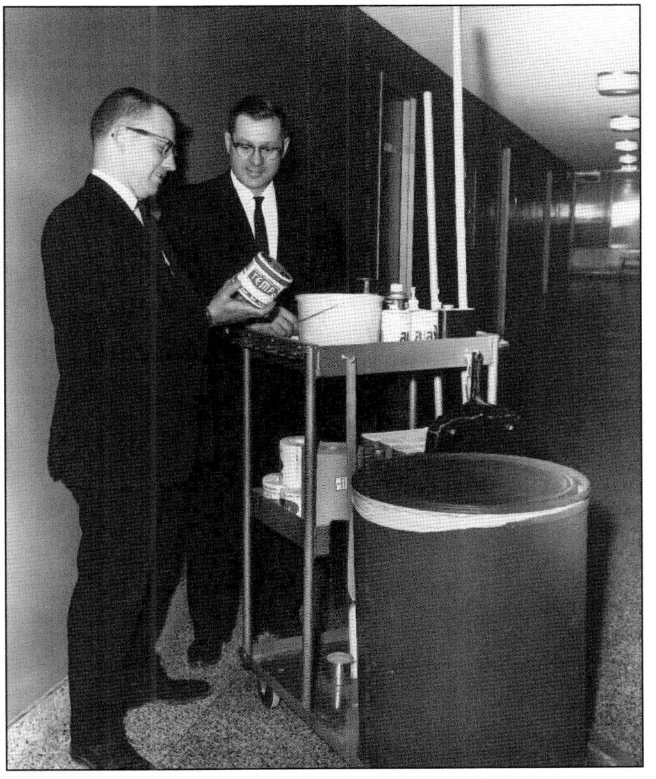

Pictured is Sr. Mary Brennan, director of nursing service. Sr. Mary Brennan worked at the hospital from 1966 to 1989. (Courtesy of Aggie Lightfoot.)

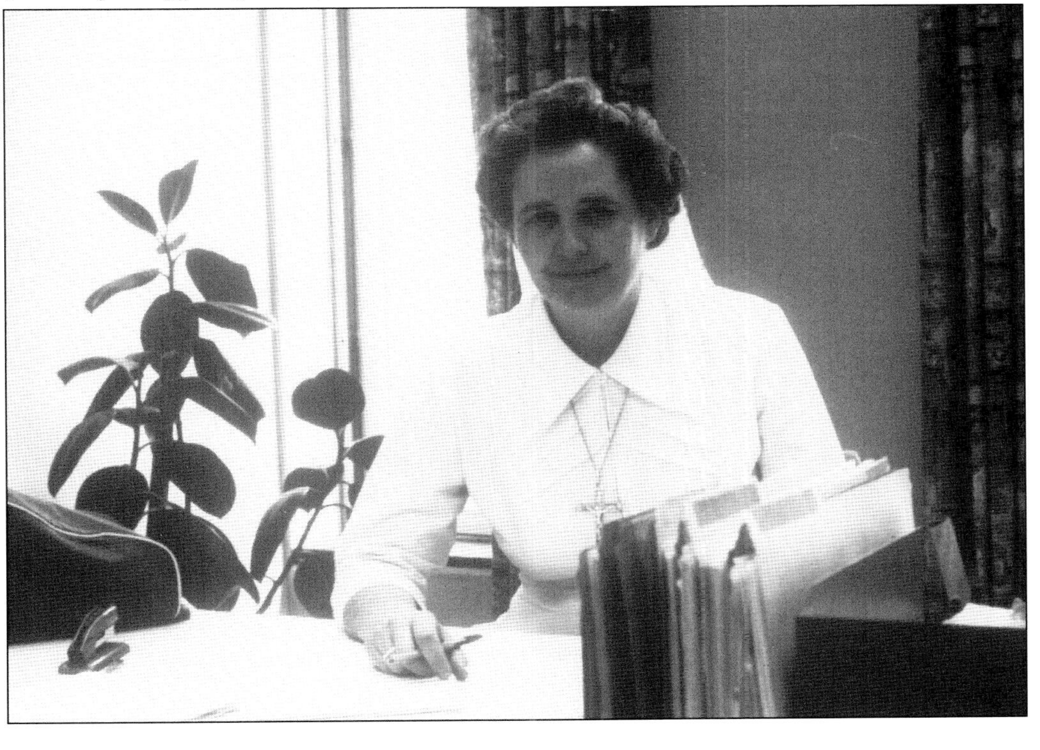

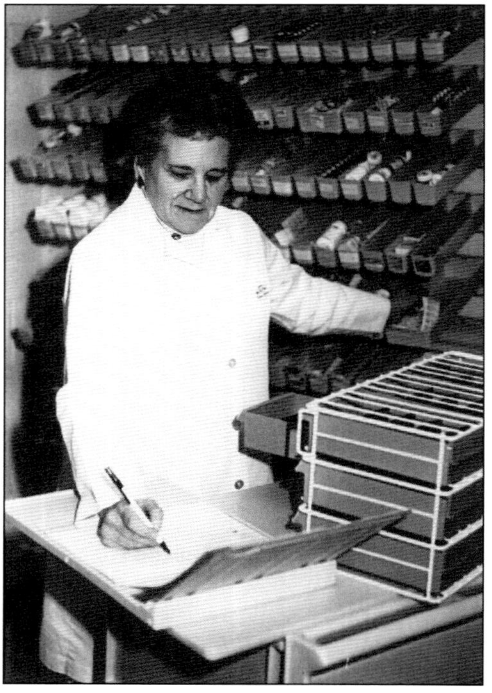

Joan Flood, a pharmacy technician, is pictured here dispensing medication.

Candy stripers are being recognized by Sr. Anne Therese in 1967. Receiving pins for hours of service are, from left to right, Christine Montroy, Elizabeth Brown, and Lynn Rishe. Also pictured is Mrs. Edwin Mitchell, who was chair of the candy striper program.

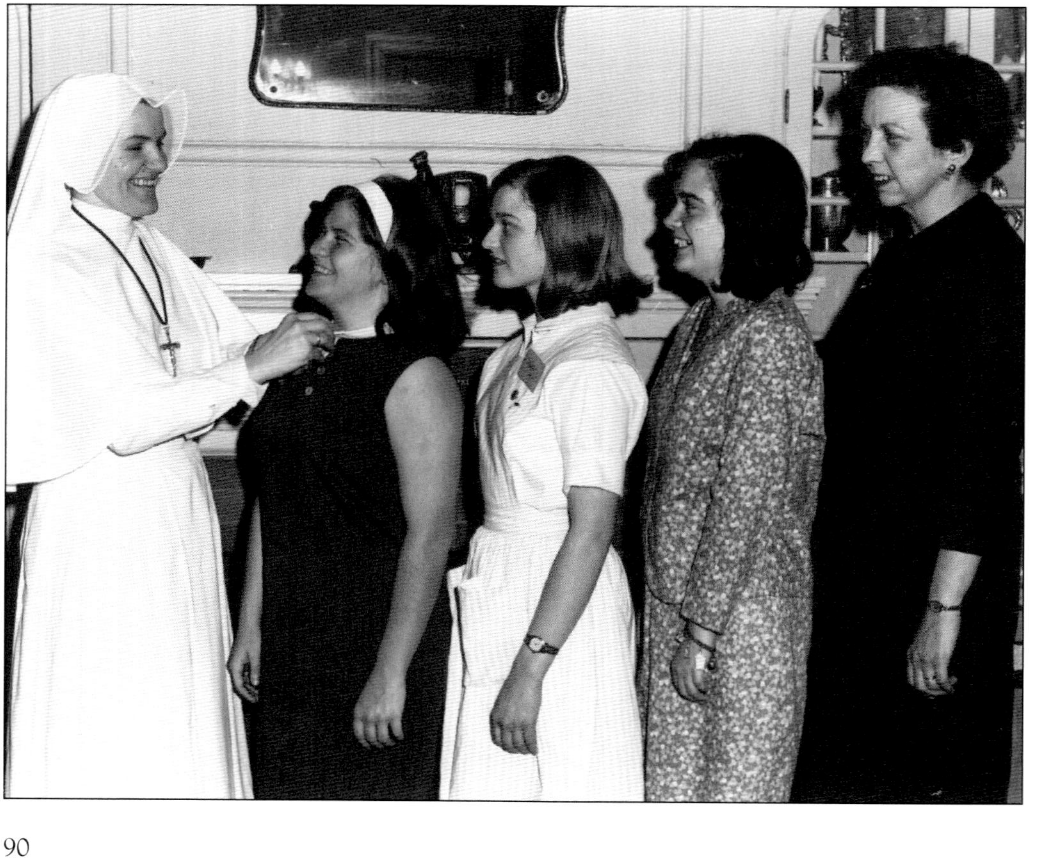

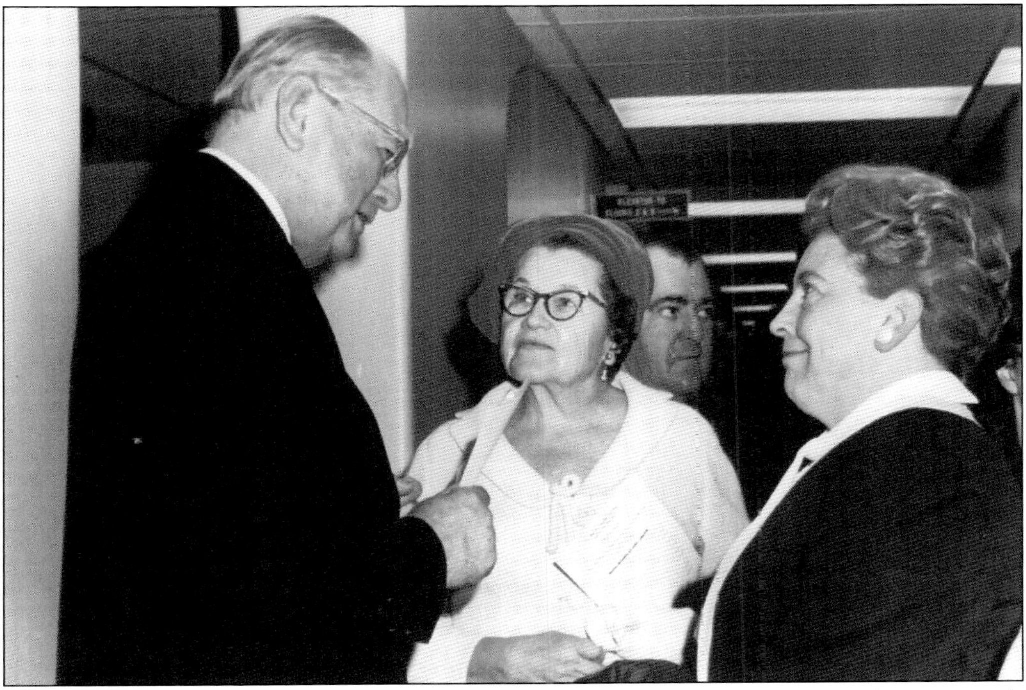

Dr. Stuart Winning (left) and Ruth Brown Warren (center) are pictured here in the 1960s with an unidentified woman. Dr. Winning was chief of surgery from 1950 to 1970.

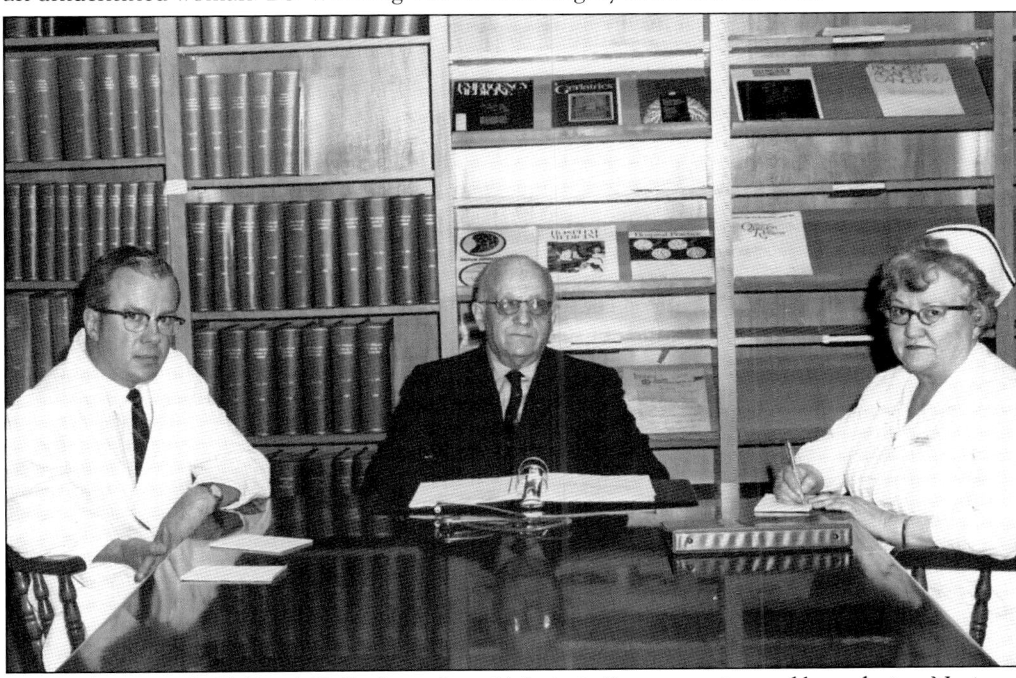

Dr. Hugh Frame (left), Dr. A.D. Redmond, and Marjorie Boyer are pictured here during National Hospital Week in May 1969. Dr. Frame came to Hepburn in 1962 and served as pathologist until 1991.

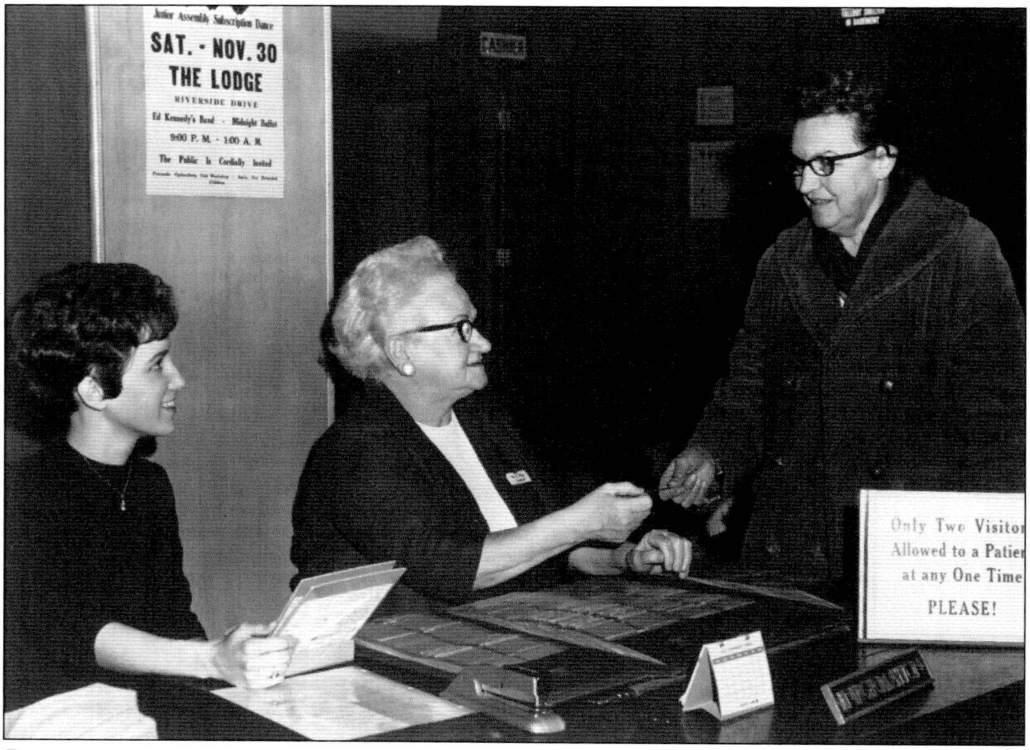

Receptionists Diane Streeter (left) and Genevieve Phelps greet visitor Beatrice Skelly in November 1968.

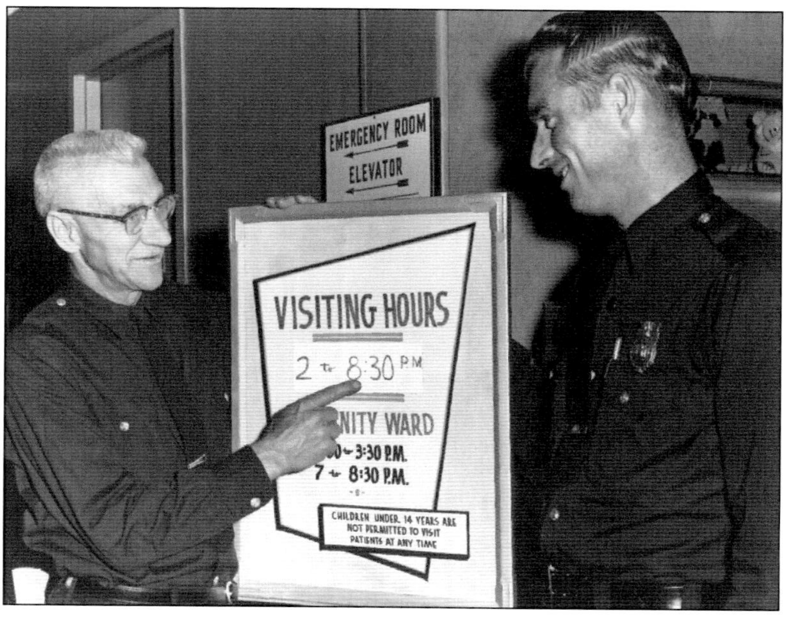

William Amo and Mike Kelly were security officers at Hepburn Hospital. They are pictured on October 1, 1964, with a sign listing the visiting hours at the hospital.

Mrs. John Douglas and Mrs. Douglas Fisher pose with the City Guild cart in May 1969.

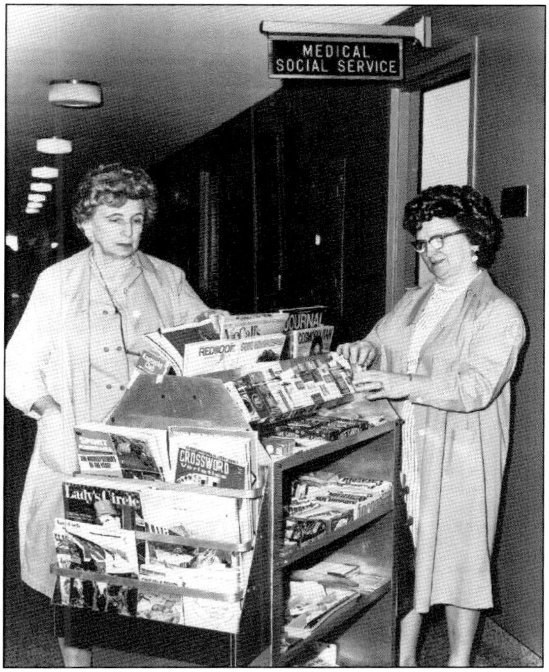

Edgar J. Martin (left), Sr. Mary Frances, and Dorajean Kenyon Martin are caught having a conversation. Sr. Mary Frances was the director of the School of Nursing from 1958 to 1968.

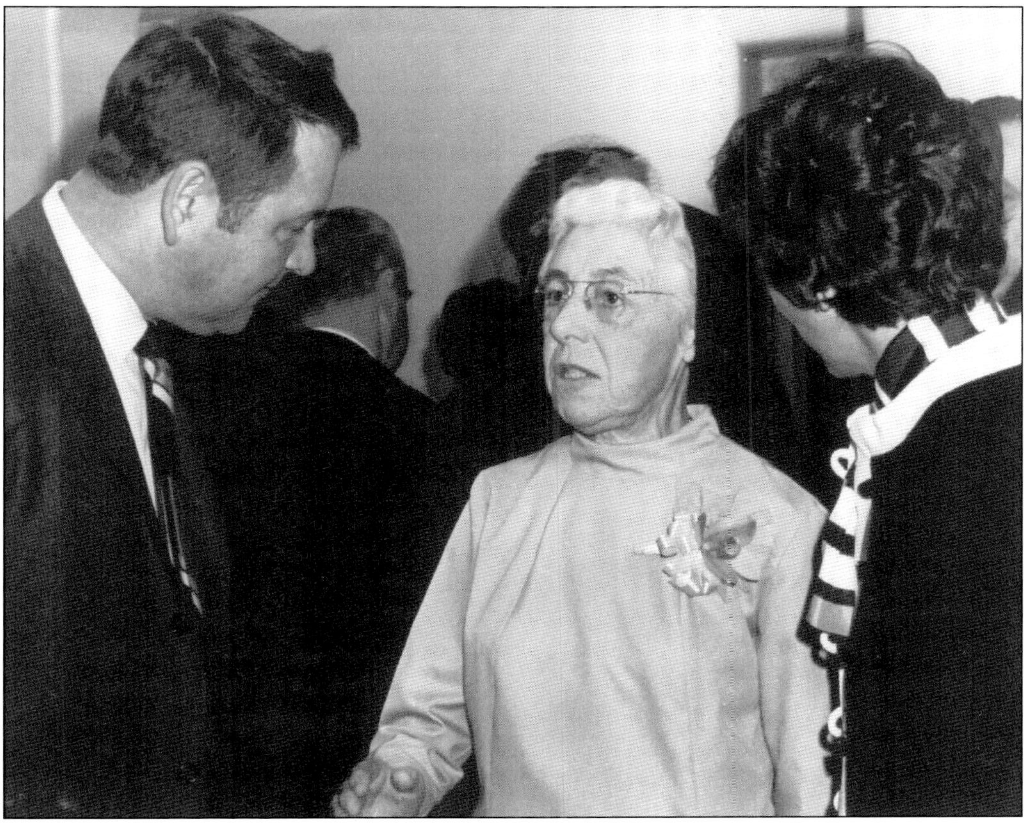

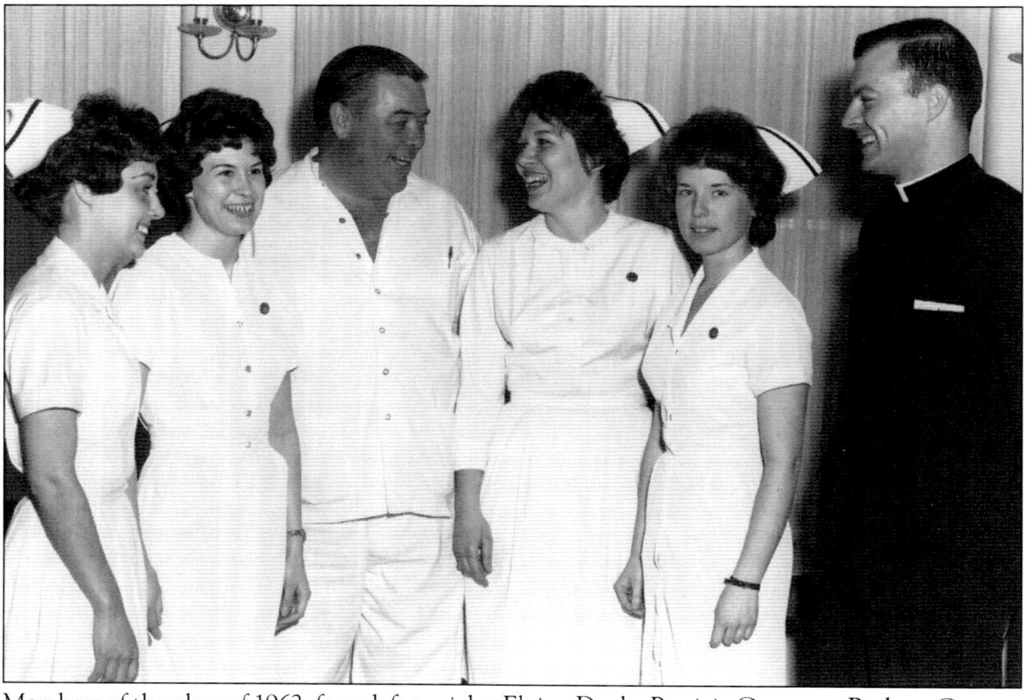

Members of the class of 1962, from left to right, Elaine Doyle, Patricia Cameron, Barbara Greene, and Maureen Regan, are pictured here with Dr. David DePue and Father Gagnier.

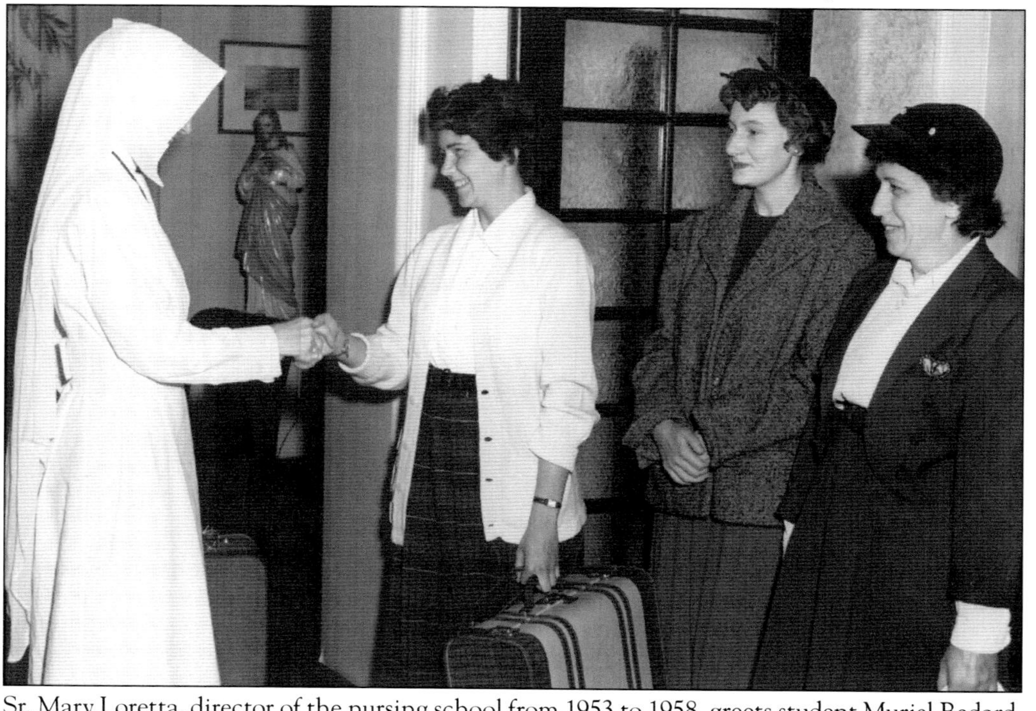

Sr. Mary Loretta, director of the nursing school from 1953 to 1958, greets student Muriel Bedard, a member of the class of 1958. Also pictured is Regina Rapin, a nurse, on the far right.

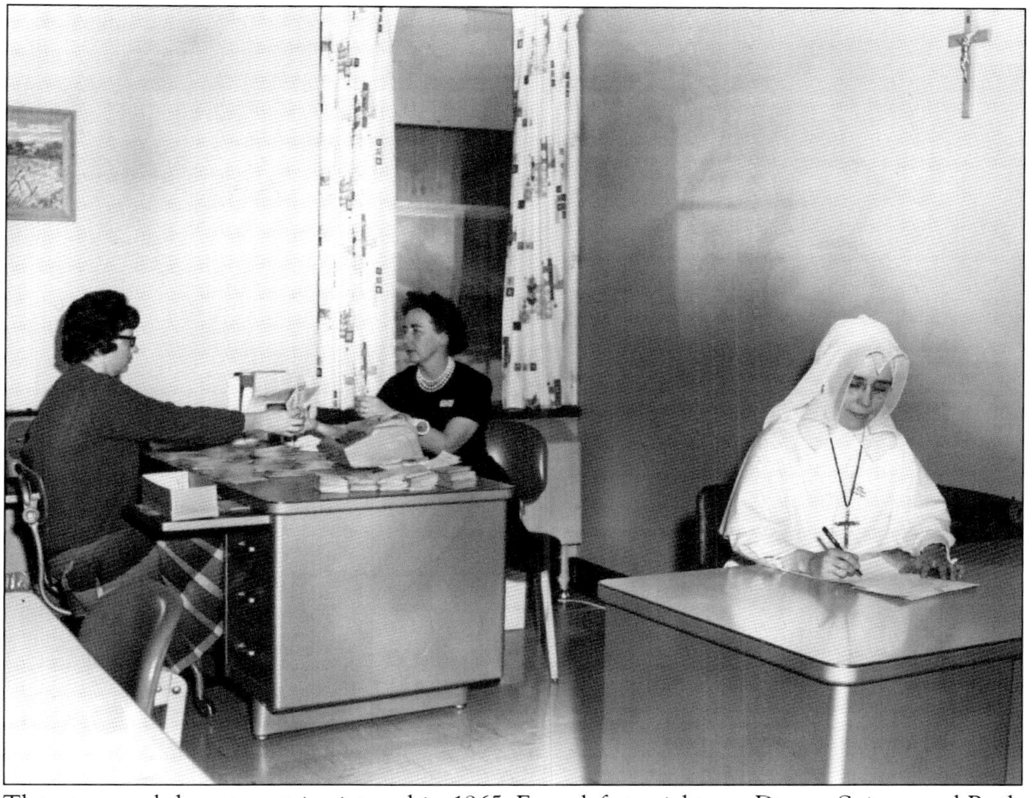

The personnel department is pictured in 1965. From left to right are Donna Sojean and Ruth Murphy, secretaries, and Sr. Saint Patricia, personnel director.

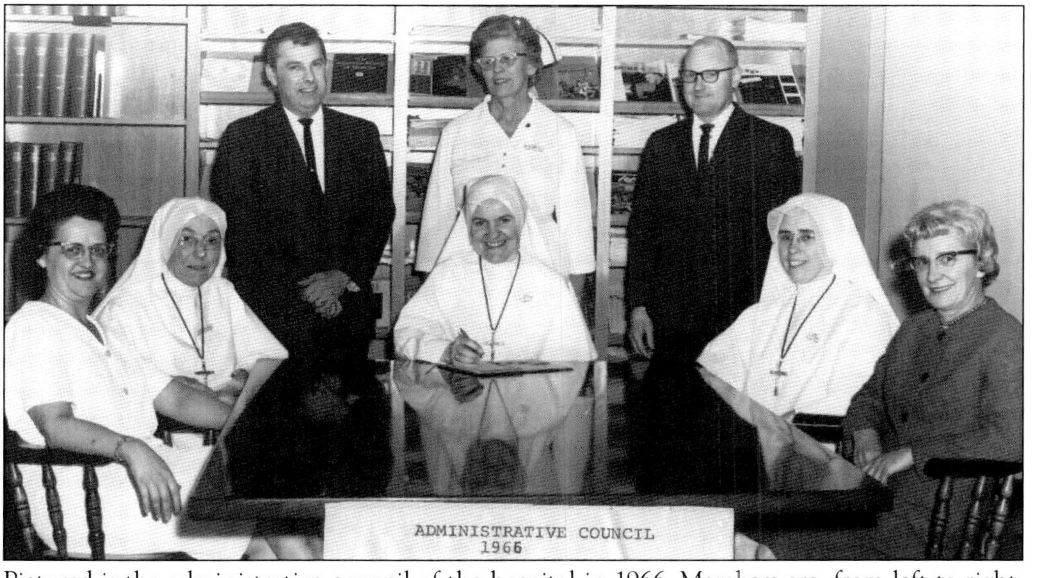

Pictured is the administrative council of the hospital in 1966. Members are, from left to right, (sitting) Caroline Fayette, Sr. Mary Frances, Sr. Anne Therese, Sr. Saint Patricia, and Catherine McCarthy; (standing) Charles Van Vleet, Mary McCabe, and Kenneth Marshall.

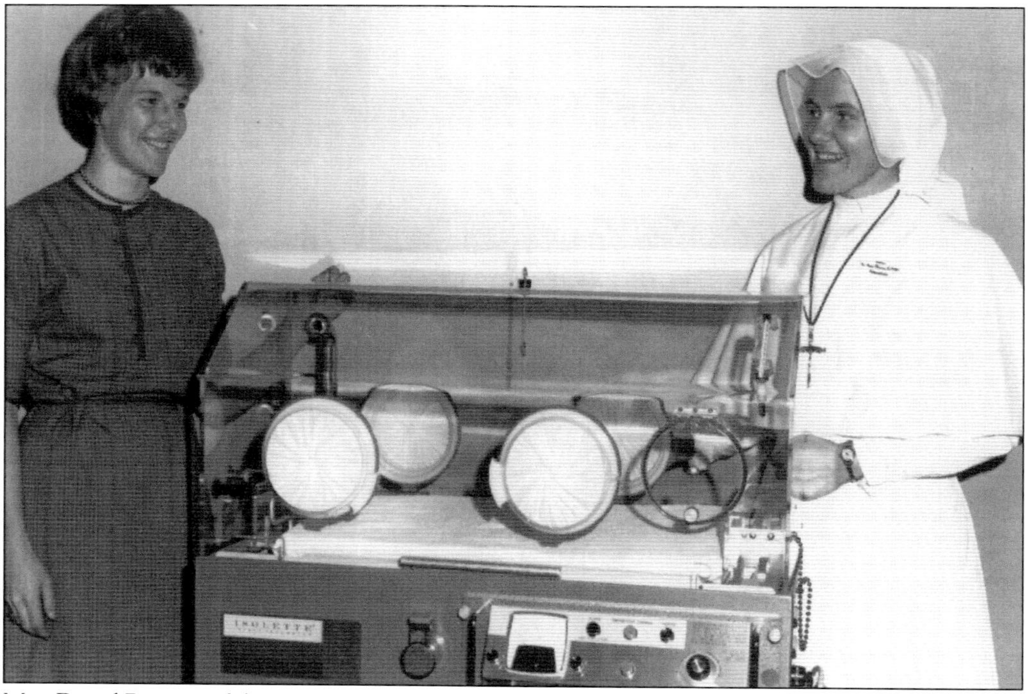

Mrs. David Breton, of the City Guild, officially presents this Isolette to Sr. Anne Therese, hospital administrator, in 1966. Pictured below are Sr. Mary Monica (left) and Sr. Mary Clement.

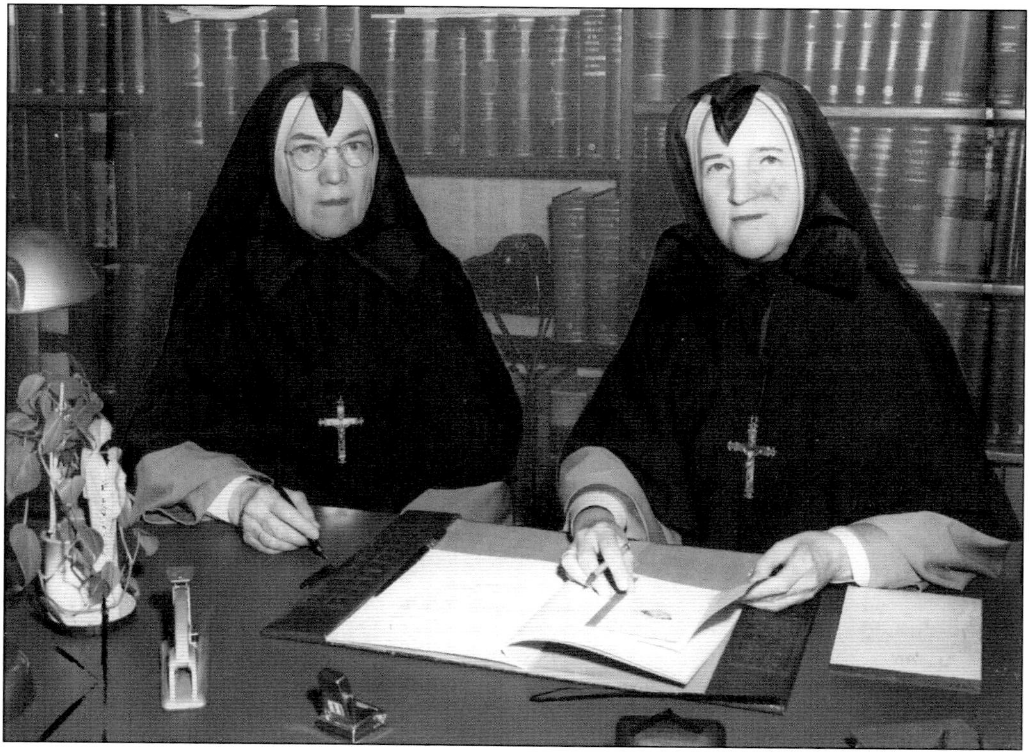

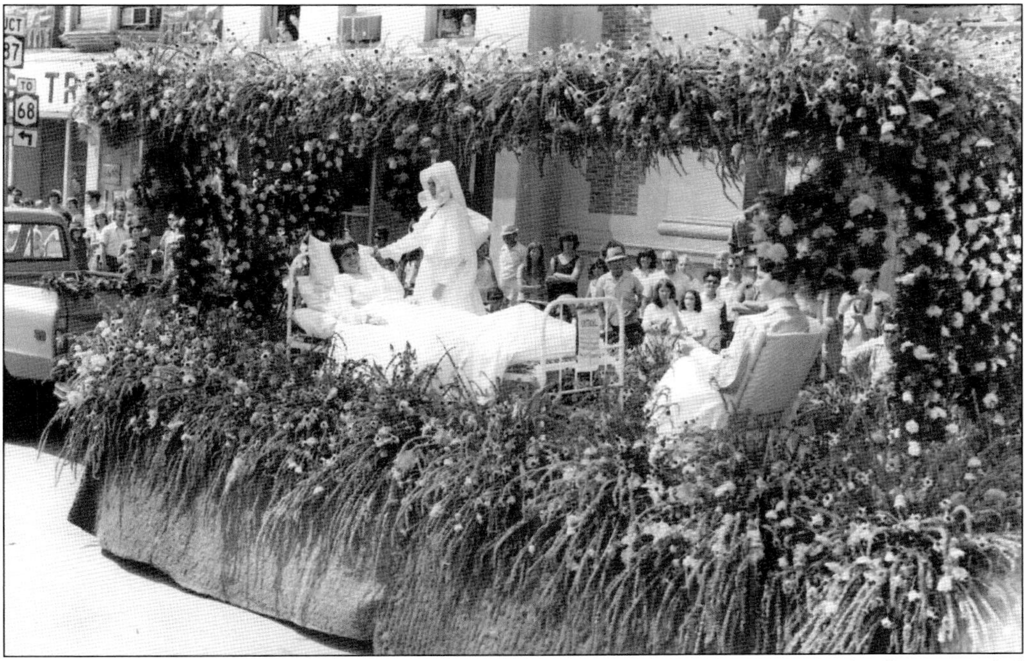

The Hepburn Hospital float is pictured in the Seaway Festival Parade in 1973. The float, entitled "I Never Promised You a Rose Garden," won first runner-up in the contest. Pictured on the float are Sr. Joan McElwain (standing), Sr. Janet Fallon (seated), and, posing as the patient, Ann Beauchamp (in bed).

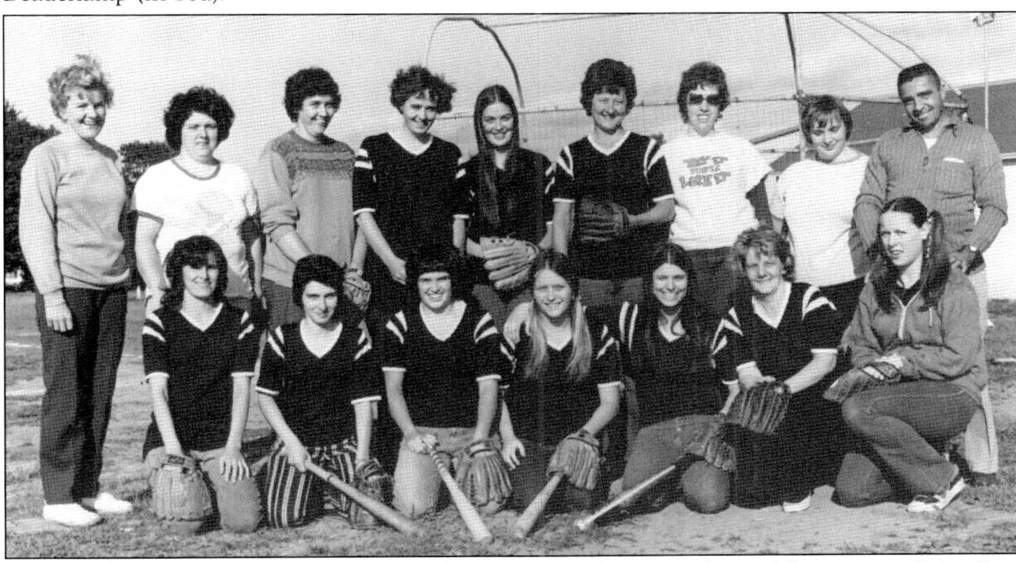

The Hepburn ladies softball team poses in September 1974. Members of the team include, from left to right, (first row) Sheila Morley, Sr. Joan McElwain, Kathy Farley, Joan Doboze, Mary Cobb, Dorothy Durant, and Joanne Guascone; (second row) administrator Sr. Anne Therese, Cassie Stark, Edna Norton, director of nursing service Sr. Mary Brennan, Debbie DePue, Joan Swanson, secretary Carol Sharlow, and manager of the team Norman LeBoeuf. Absent from the photograph are Joan Reed and Kathy Lewis.

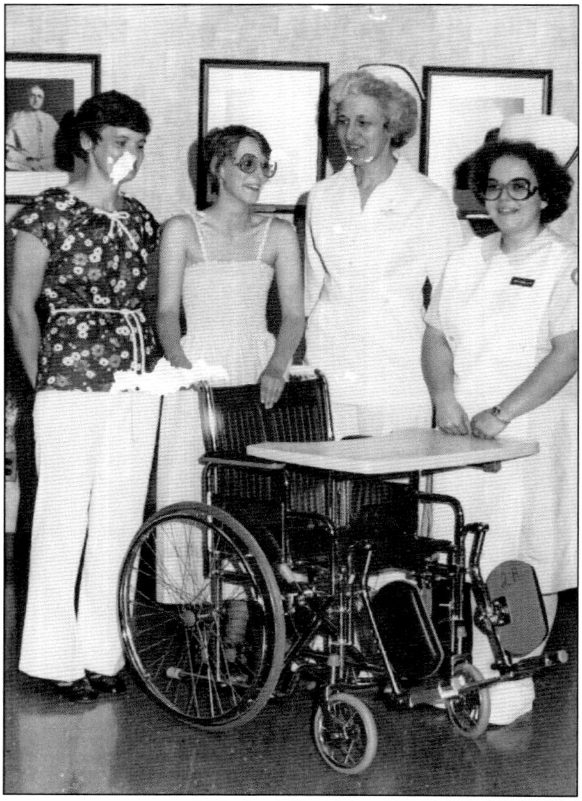

In June 1977, Trudy Shaver (left) and Evelyn Wells (second from left), members of Women of the Moose, presented a wheelchair to June Cassidy (third from left) and Emily McGill (right), St. Lawrence Psychiatric Nursing Center students.

In June 1978, Hepburn Hospital purchased new Teletrace equipment for monitoring pacemakers. Pictured are Dr. Warren Heller (seated) and Cindy Deloney, nurse manager of the intensive care unit. Dr. Heller was a cardiologist and was director of the coronary care unit at Hepburn Hospital. Dr. Heller worked at the hospital from 1951 until 1986.

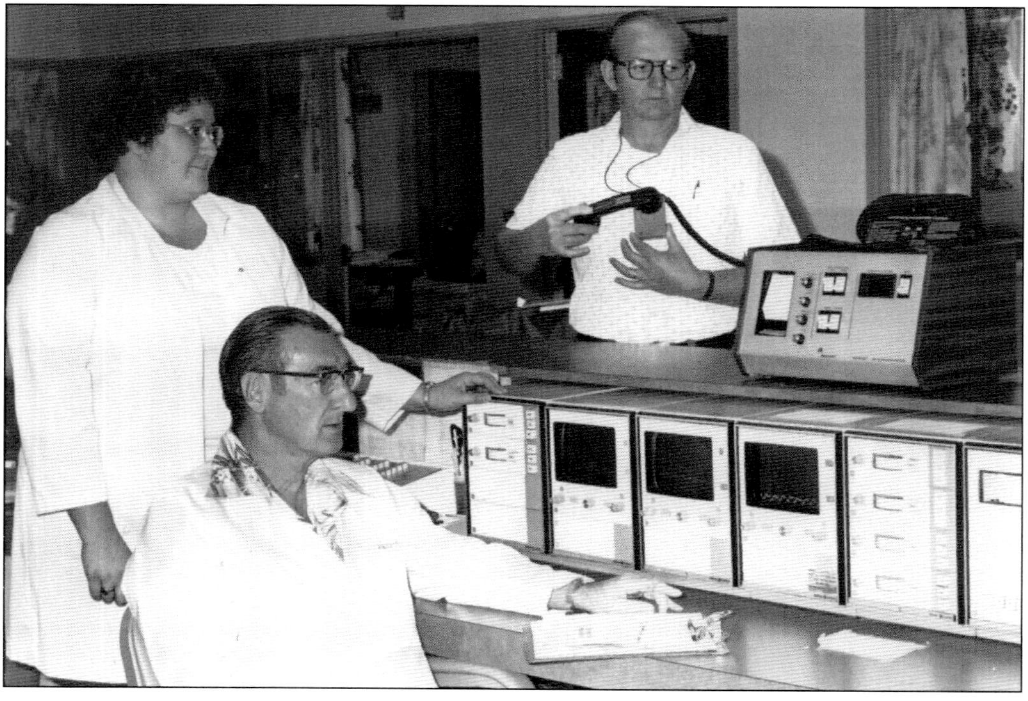

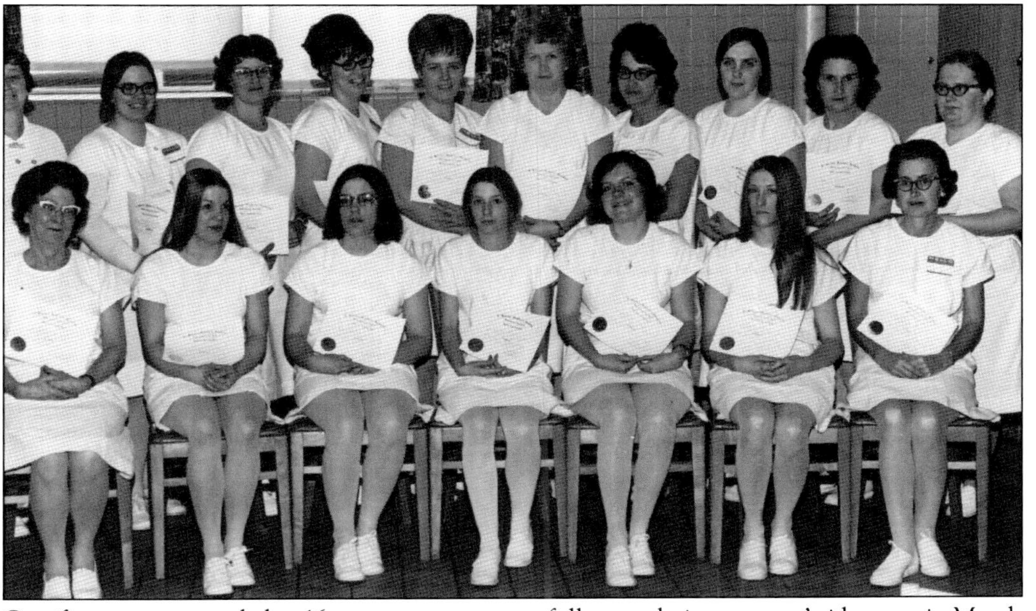

Certificates were awarded to 16 women upon successfully completing a nurses' aid course in March 1974. Pictured from left to right are (first row) Marion Long, Theresa Flack, Nancy LeFleur, Cindy Lylow, Mary Woodman, Marilyn Silmser, and Eleanor Drummond; (second row) instructor Rita Hess, Maureen Downing, Marlene Kiah, Linda Carroll, Martha Mashaw, Jean Thornhill, Lynn Travis, Janette Sawyer, Margaret Scott, and Catherine Dishaw.

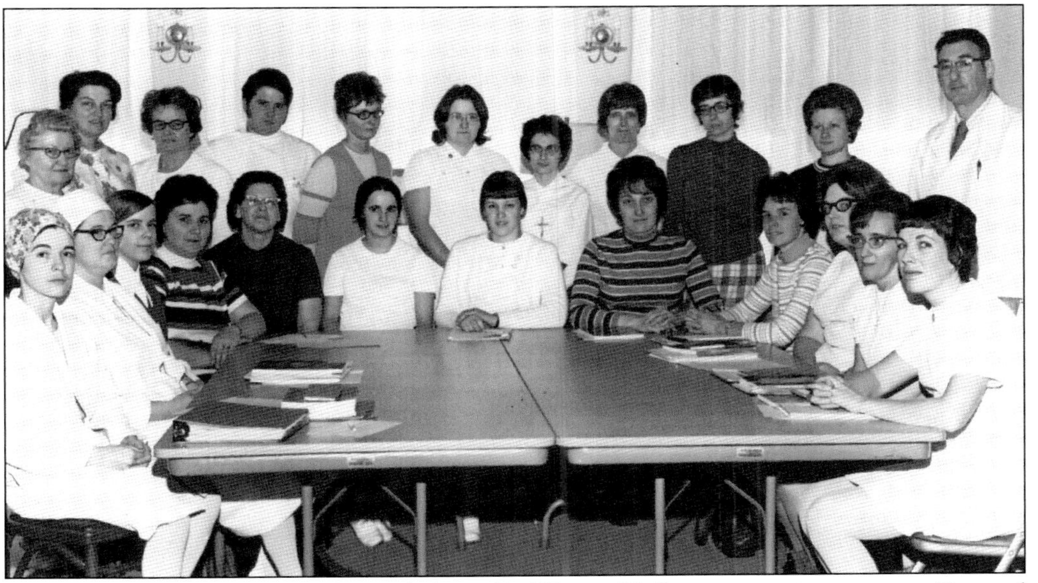

This is a training session given by cardiologist Dr. Warren Heller on intensive coronary. Pictured from left to right are (seated) Colleen Lago, Sr. Marie Jerome, Sally Lilley, Patricia Montroy, Alice Carroll, Sandra Fortin, Melanie Kring, Linda Aubertine, Christine Wentworth, Clair Carswell, Phyllis Hamilton, and Joanne McCabe; (standing) Marjorie Boyer, Carmen Mussen, Joyce Mallette, David Delarge, Sally Kelly, Cynthia Shannon, Sr. Joan McElwain, Carolyn Haines, Patricia Jackson, Linda Richardson, and Dr. Warren Heller.

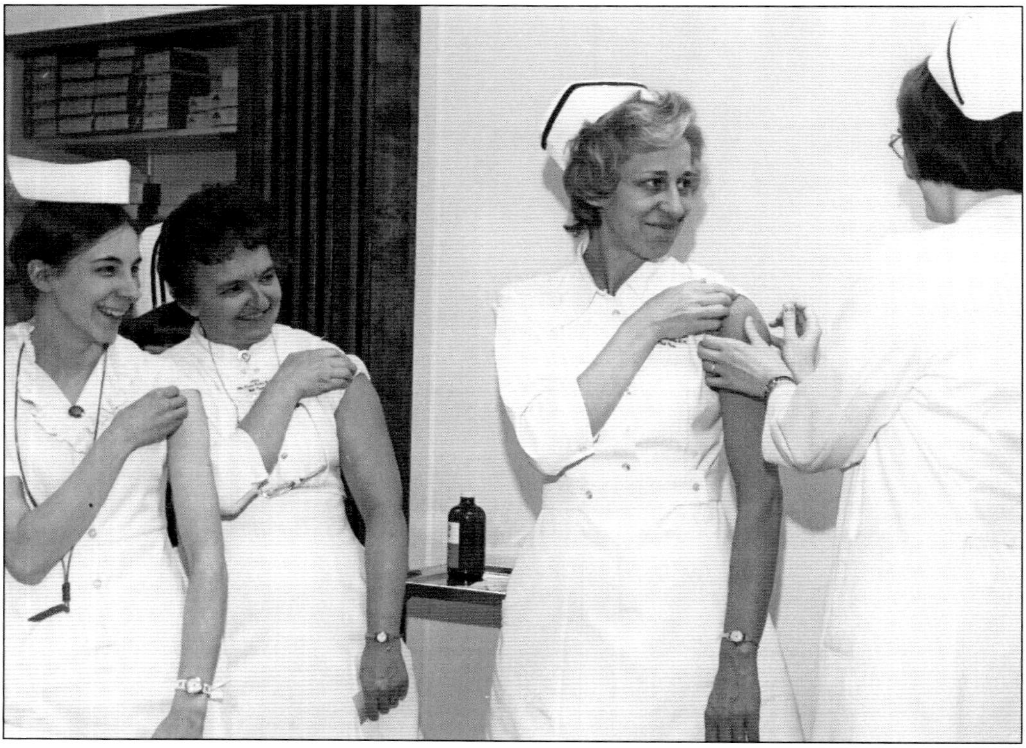

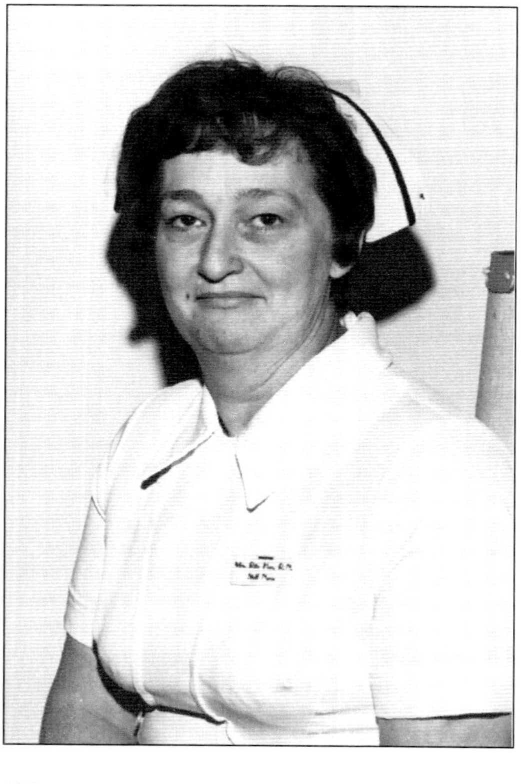

In April 1975, employees line up to receive a smallpox vaccine. The New York State Department of Health required this immunization for hospital employees. Pictured from left to right are Carol Moshier, Harriet Barley, and June Cassidy, head nurse on 2-A. Sr. Julia Lanigan administers the shots to this group.

Rita Hess graduated from the nursing school in 1953. She worked on the first floor of the hospital following her graduation. For three years, she taught the licensed practical nursing program at the hospital. In 1971, she went to work in the recovery room, and in 1973, she was appointed as assistant in in-service education.

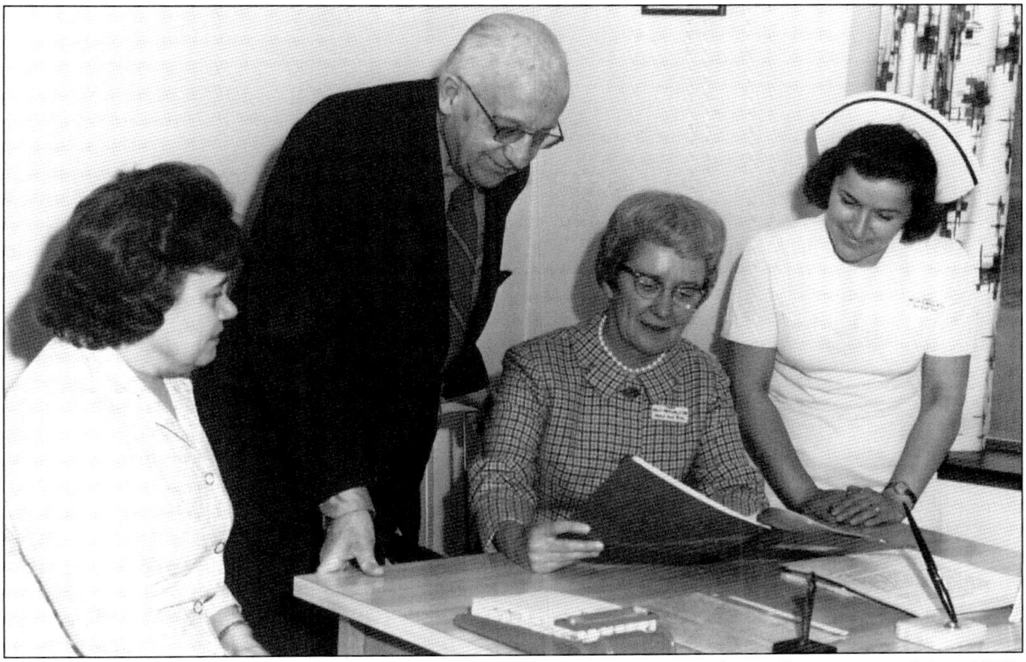

Dr. A.D. Redmond is pictured with members of the department of social service in May 1970. They are, from left to right, secretary Anne Wicks, certified social worker Catherine McCarthy, and Norma Callahan.

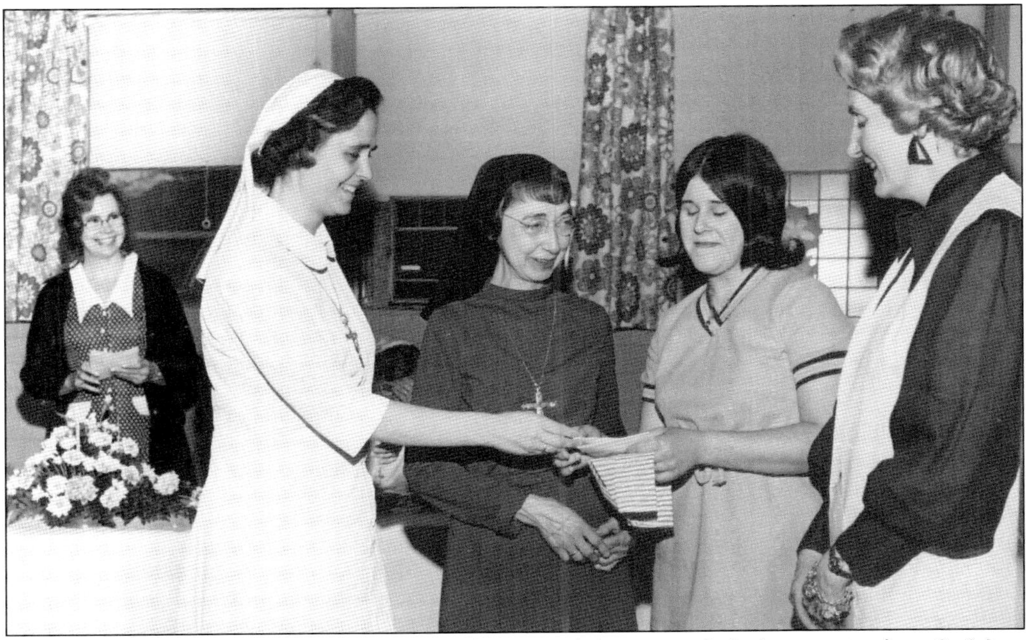

On May 17, 1973, candy striper Marilee Kinch received three awards for her service from Sr. Mary Brennan, director of nursing service. Pictured are Judy Velocchi (standing at table), president of the City Guild; Sr. Mary Brennan; Sr. Mary Loretta, director of volunteer services; Kinch; and Helen Ellis, chairman of the candy striper program.

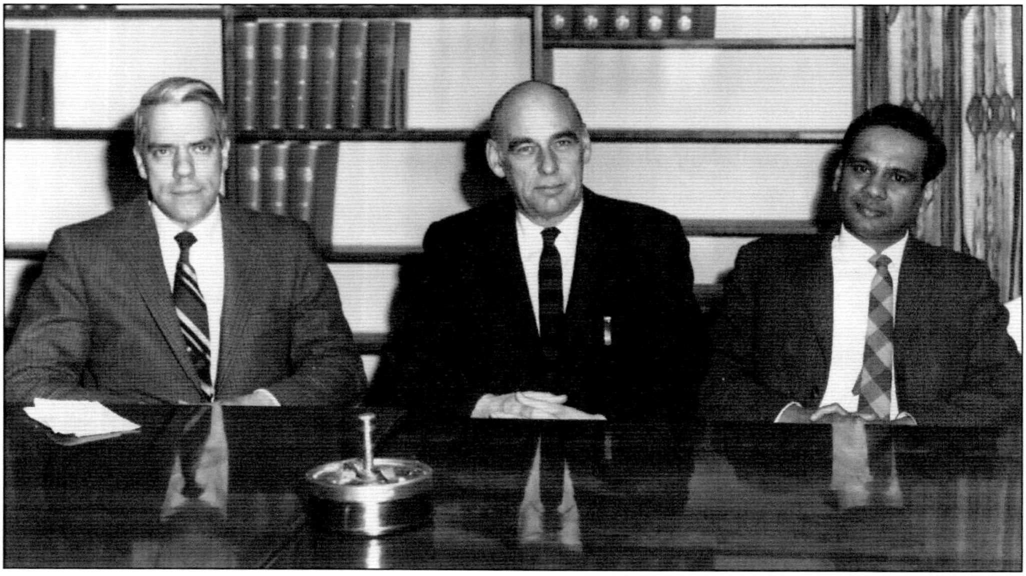

Pictured here in 1970 are, from left to right, Dr. Berwyn Woodman, surgeon; Dr. Carl Alverson, general practitioner; and Dr. Ravinder N. Agarwal, ear, nose, and throat physician. Dr. Alverson joined the medical staff in 1946, and Dr. Agarwal started in 1967.

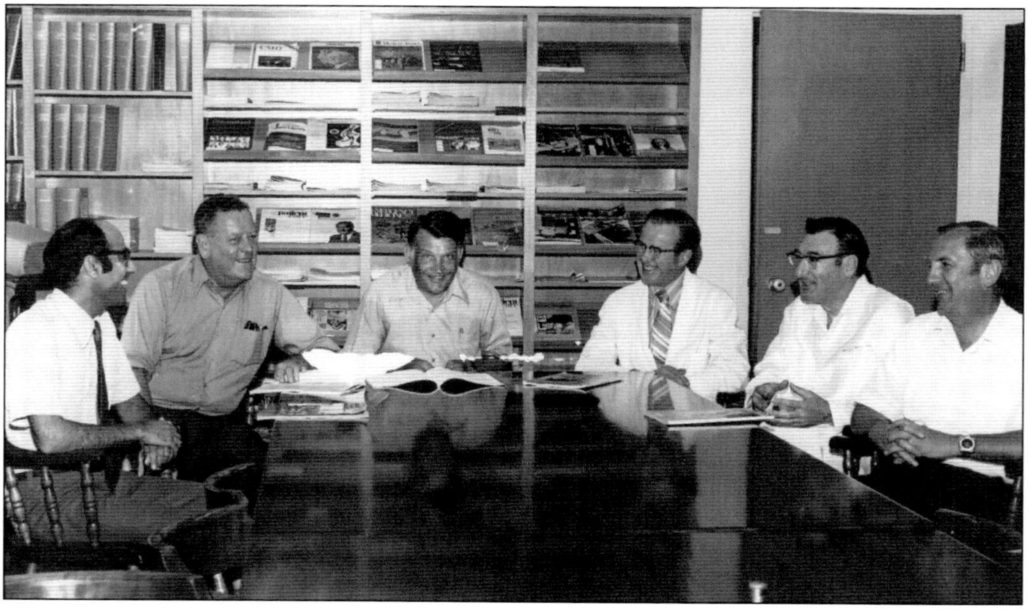

In 1973, at the annual meeting of the medical staff held in June, the following officers, pictured from left to right, were elected to serve for two years: Dr. Bansi Bazaz, chief of internal medicine; Dr. James J. Barry, chief of radiology; Dr. Bernard Musselman, chief of pediatrics; Dr. Hugh Frame, chief of pathology; Dr. Warren Heller, chief of medicine; and Dr. Joseph R. Brandy, chief of obstetrics and gynecology. On duty in the operating room (and therefore not present) at the time the picture was taken were Dr. David DePue, chief of surgery; and Dr. Paul Campanella, chief of anesthesiology. Dr. Musselman served at the hospital from 1963 until 1990, and Dr. Campanella from 1946 until 1977.

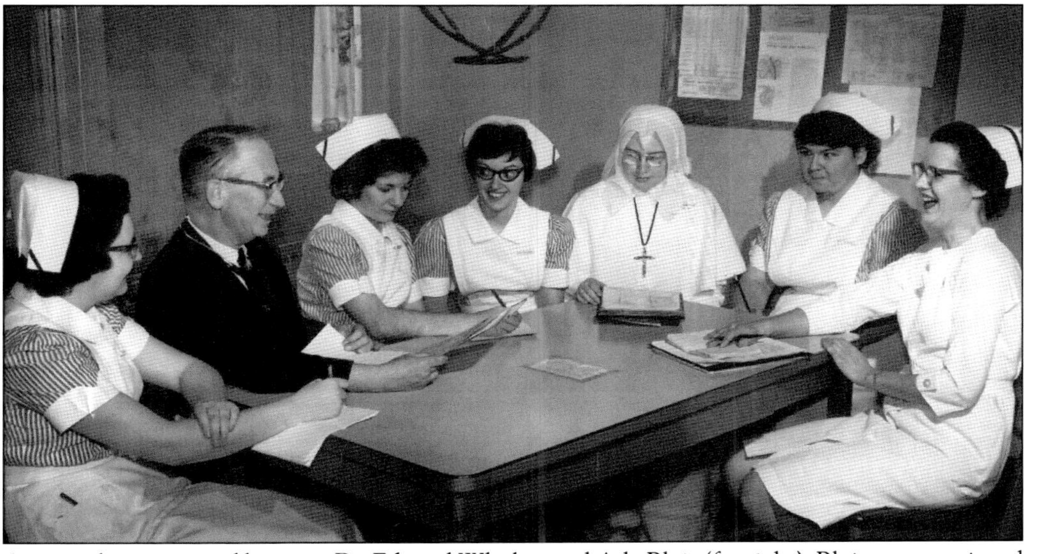

Among those pictured here are Dr. Edward Whalen and Ada Blair (far right). Blair was appointed in-service education coordinator in 1966. She was also a 1943 graduate of the A. Barton School of Nursing.

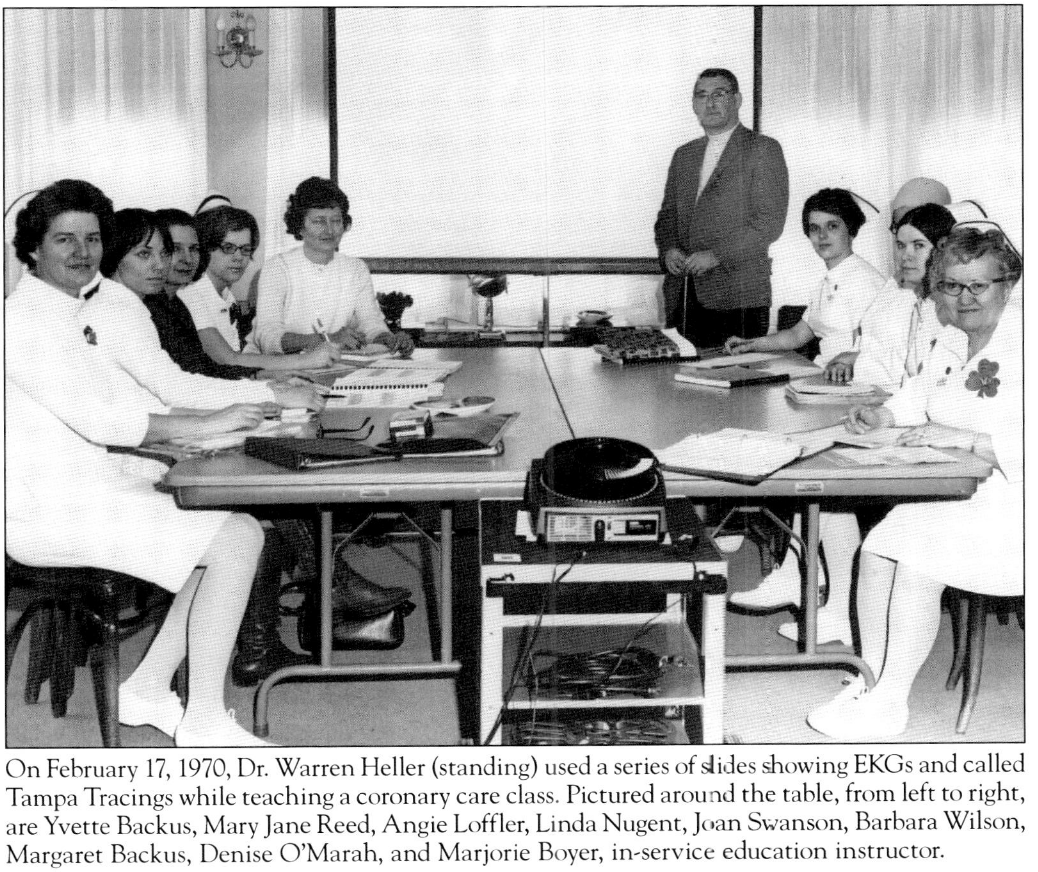

On February 17, 1970, Dr. Warren Heller (standing) used a series of slides showing EKGs and called Tampa Tracings while teaching a coronary care class. Pictured around the table, from left to right, are Yvette Backus, Mary Jane Reed, Angie Loffler, Linda Nugent, Joan Swanson, Barbara Wilson, Margaret Backus, Denise O'Marah, and Marjorie Boyer, in-service education instructor.

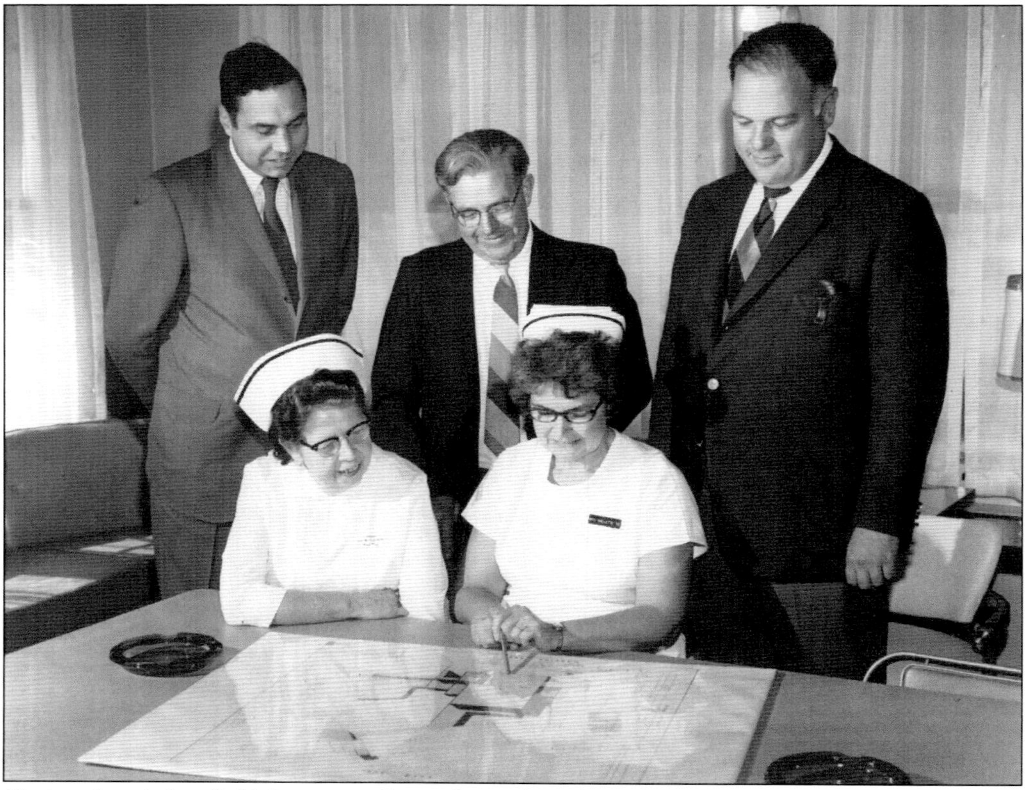

Christopher Acker (left), Lawrence Rapin (center), and Frank Augsbury, all longtime members of the hospital board of directors, pose with nurses Wava Earl (left) and Joyce Mallette to review what is believed to be the architectural drawing of the new west-wing project in the early 1970s.

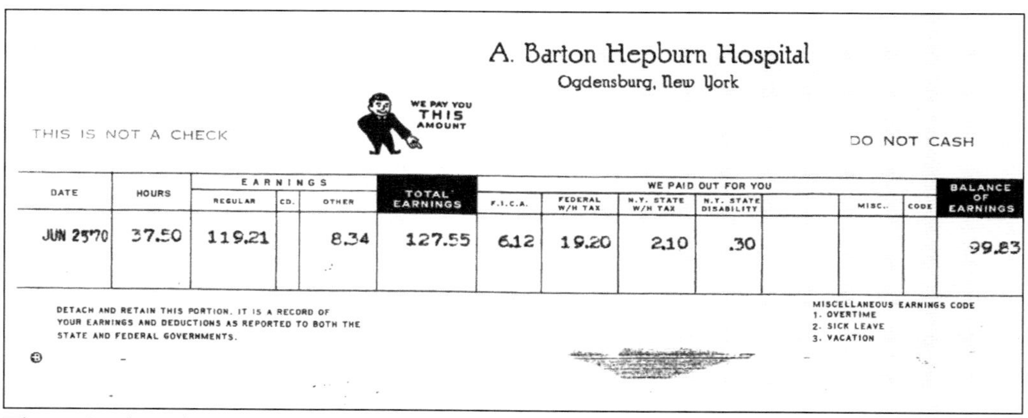

A. Barton Hepburn Hospital
Ogdensburg, New York

WE PAY YOU THIS AMOUNT

THIS IS NOT A CHECK

DO NOT CASH

DATE	HOURS	EARNINGS REGULAR	CD.	OTHER	TOTAL EARNINGS	WE PAID OUT FOR YOU F.I.C.A.	FEDERAL W/H TAX	N.Y. STATE W/H TAX	N.Y. STATE DISABILITY		MISC.	CODE	BALANCE OF EARNINGS
JUN 25'70	37.50	119.21		8.34	127.55	6.12	19.20	2.10	.30				99.83

DETACH AND RETAIN THIS PORTION. IT IS A RECORD OF YOUR EARNINGS AND DEDUCTIONS AS REPORTED TO BOTH THE STATE AND FEDERAL GOVERNMENTS.

MISCELLANEOUS EARNINGS CODE
1. OVERTIME
2. SICK LEAVE
3. VACATION

This is Cindy Deloney's first hospital pay stub from 1970. Deloney would eventually become nurse manager of the intensive care unit. This pay stub was contributed by Jennifer Shaver, current nurse manager of the intensive care unit at Claxton-Hepburn Medical Center.

"Nancy" Margaret Murphy impersonates Nancy Sinatra, singing "These Boots are Made for Walking" at the employee recognition dinner in 1973. Serving as toastmistress is Joyce Mallette.

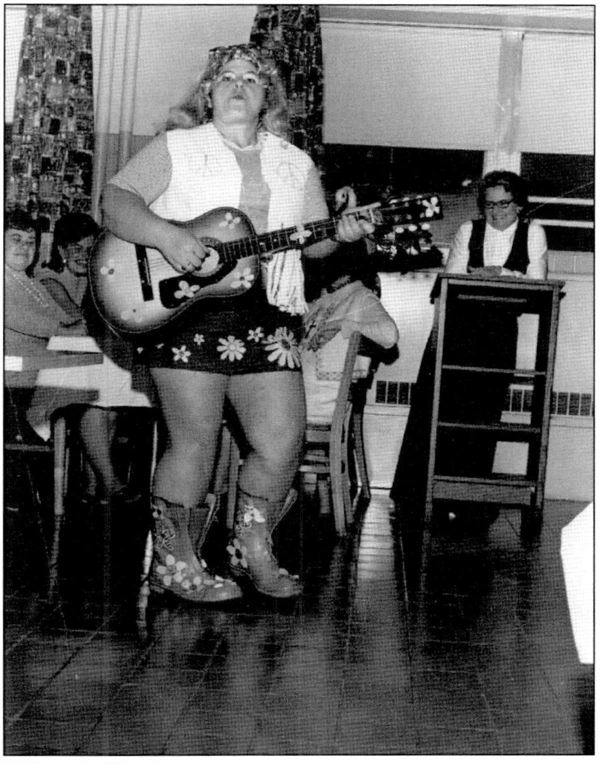

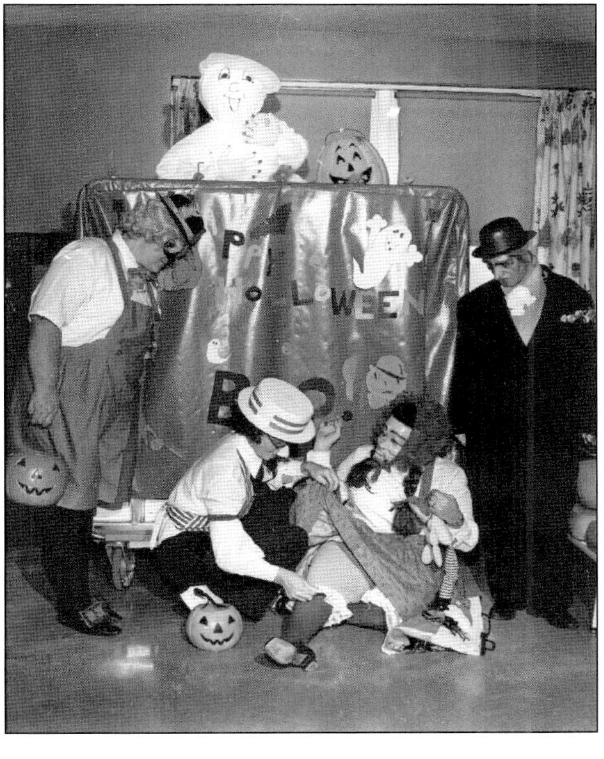

This is a photograph of the extended care facility, taken on Halloween in 1973. The staff dressed up to entertain residents. The masqueraders include head nurse Regina Rapin, Pauline Guslaw, Doris McCarthy, Evelyn Breen, Rachael Harrison, Barbara Peters, Virgir Flansberg, Carol Mosier, and Joan Kennedy.

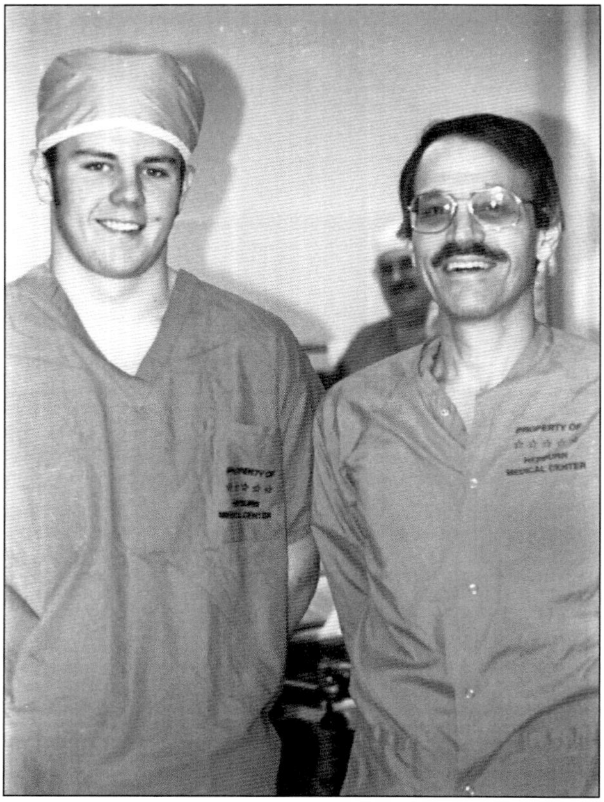

This is a picture of Dr. Ben Handelsman (right) with an unidentified medical student. Dr. Handelsman joined the medical staff in September 1989.

These pharmacy technicians have recently passed an exam on intravenous admixture, given by the Pharmacist Consultation Services/Academy of Pharmacy Technical Skills. The exam followed a six-week course covering topics such as mixing and storing intravenous solutions, routes of drug administration, quality assurance, and other pharmaceutical procedures. Pictured are Beverly Green (left), Angela Morley (center), and Joan Flood.

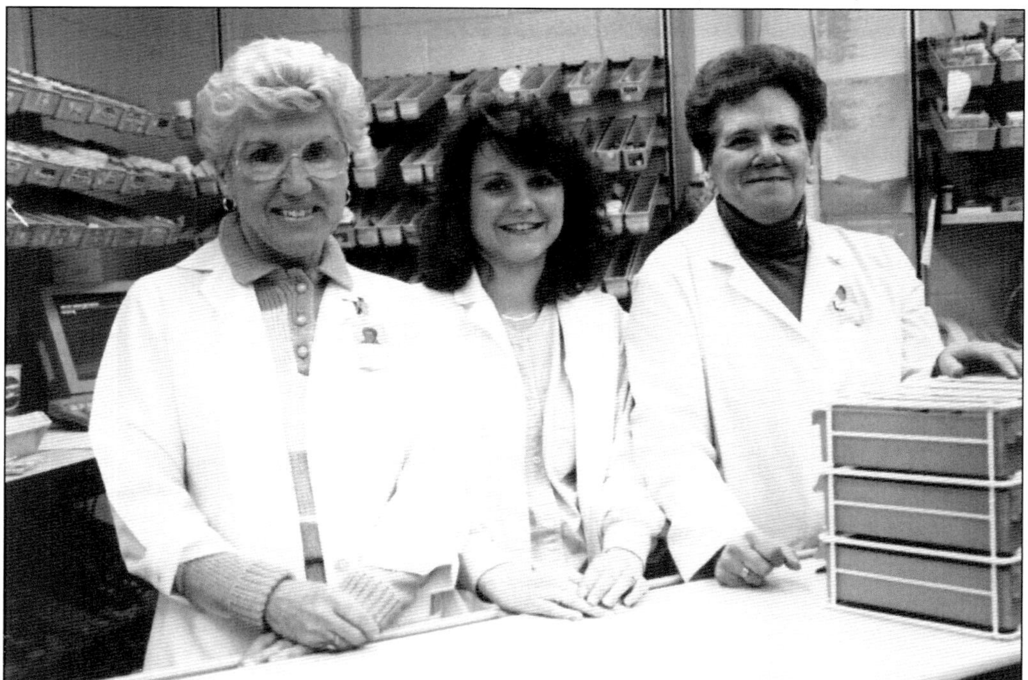

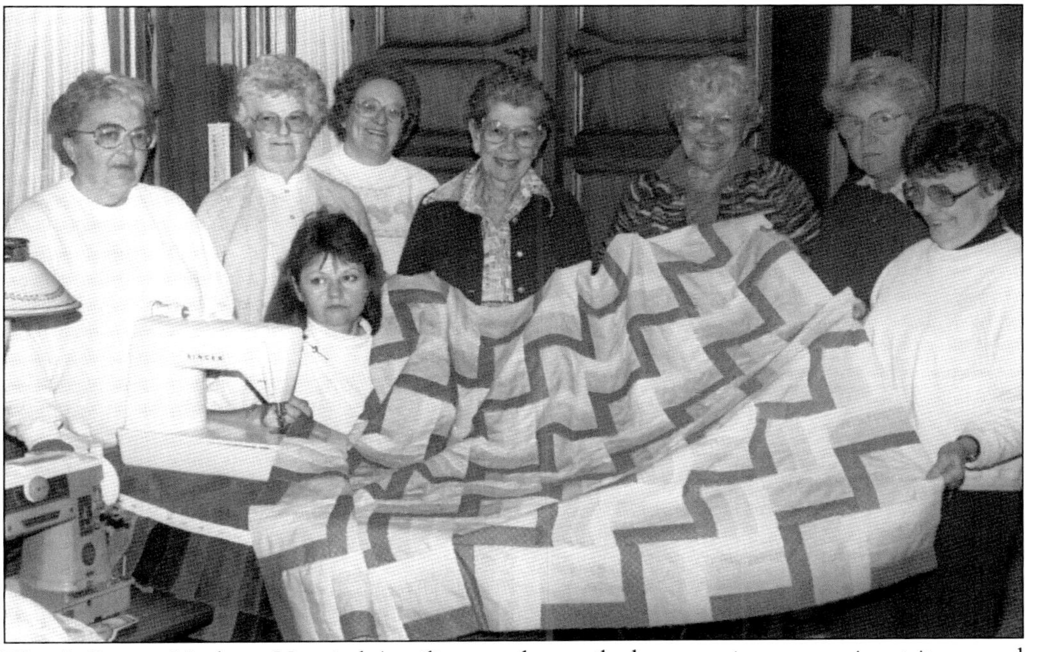

The A. Barton Hepburn Hospital Auxiliary made a quilt that was given as a prize at its annual holly berry sale. Shown sitting in front is Marita Lewis. Standing are, from left to right, Mary Katherine Hackett, Mary Thompson, Evelyn Cardinal, Lucienne LeBeau, Willie Dobisky, Vivian Cordwell, and Toni Lavigne.

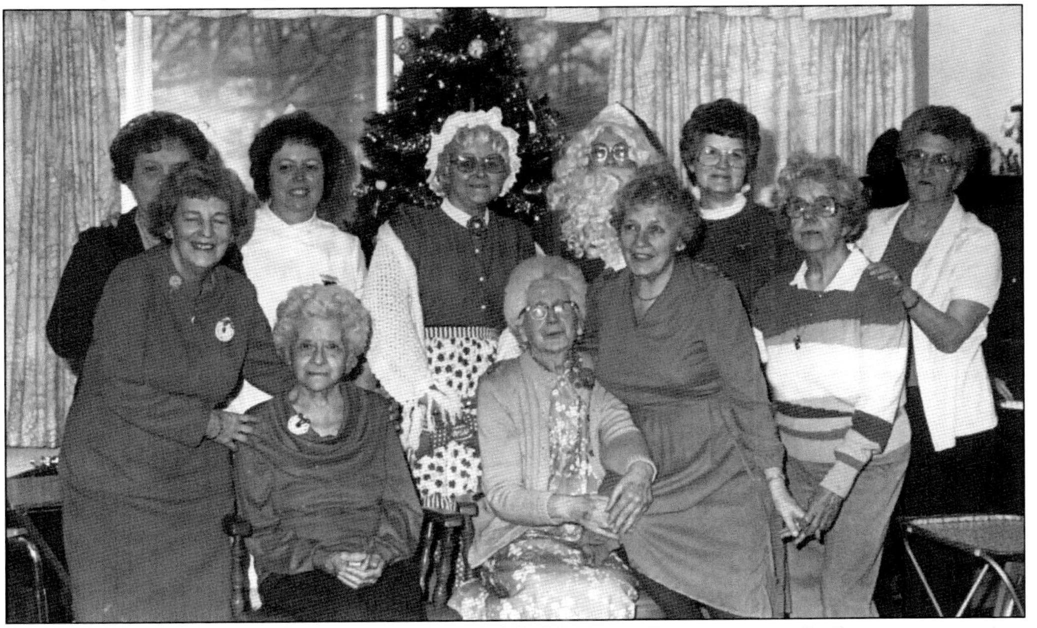

Members of the Ogdensburg Women's City Club held a party for patients in the long-term nursing unit at the hospital. Shown from left are (first row) Helen Dana, Mary Major, Ottomae Soucy, Regina Rapin, and Irene Lalonde; (second row) Mary Sovie, president of the City Club Joan Kennedy, Mr. and Mrs. Santa Claus (both unidentified), Betty Spooner, and Audrey Bouchard.

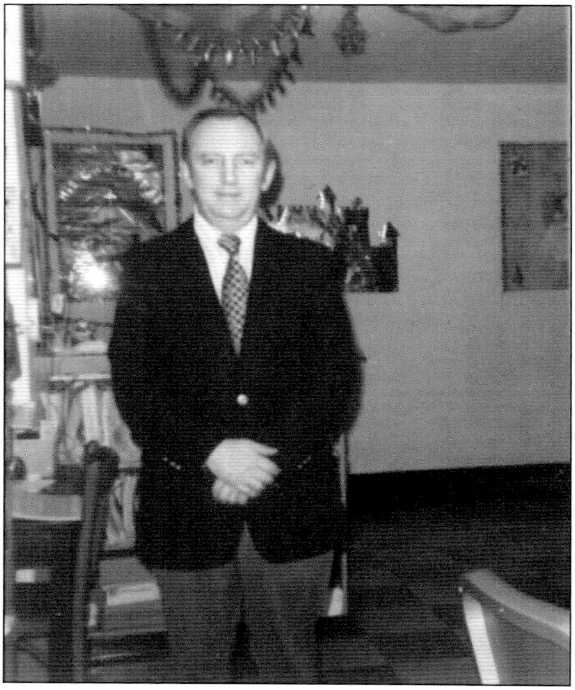

Dr. Joseph R. Brandy, obstetrician, joined the medical staff in 1960. He passed away tragically in a plane crash with his wife and son in 1990.

In November 1985, the hospital held a centennial-celebration dress-up day. Pictured from left to right are (first row) Rose Mary Demers, Sr. JoAnne Marie Hanlon, and Marlene Kotz; (second row) Jane Jackson, Elizabeth Wright, Greg McAdam, and Michelle Snye.

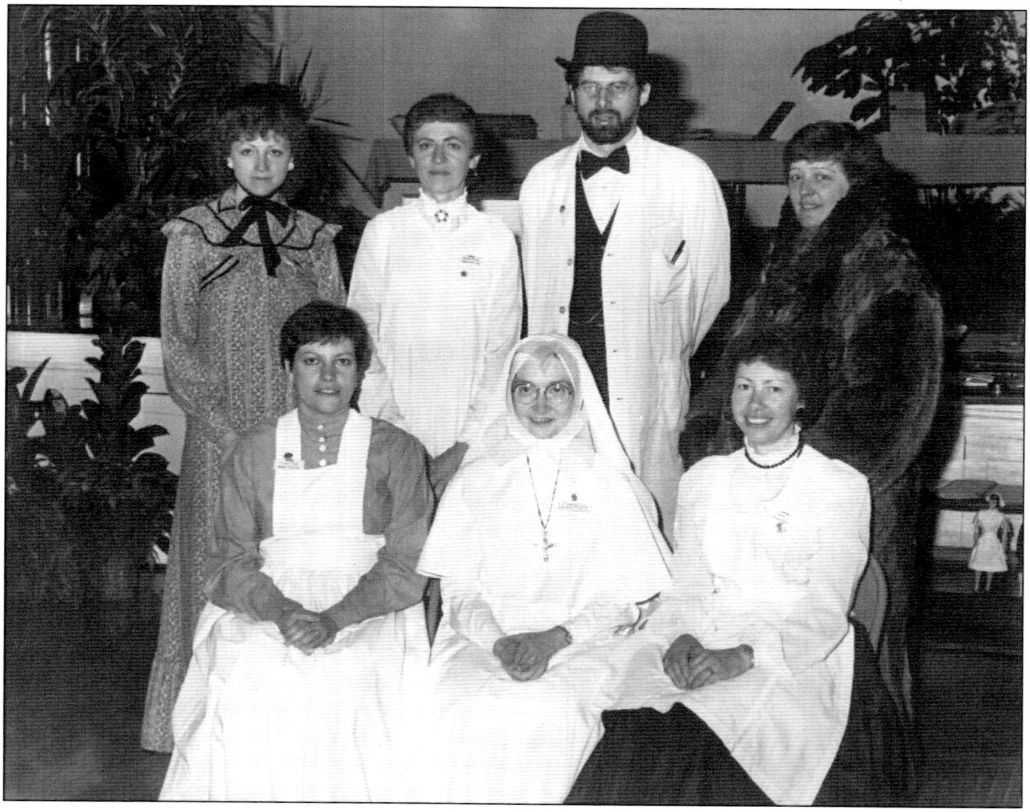

Seven

DR. E. GARFIELD CLAXTON

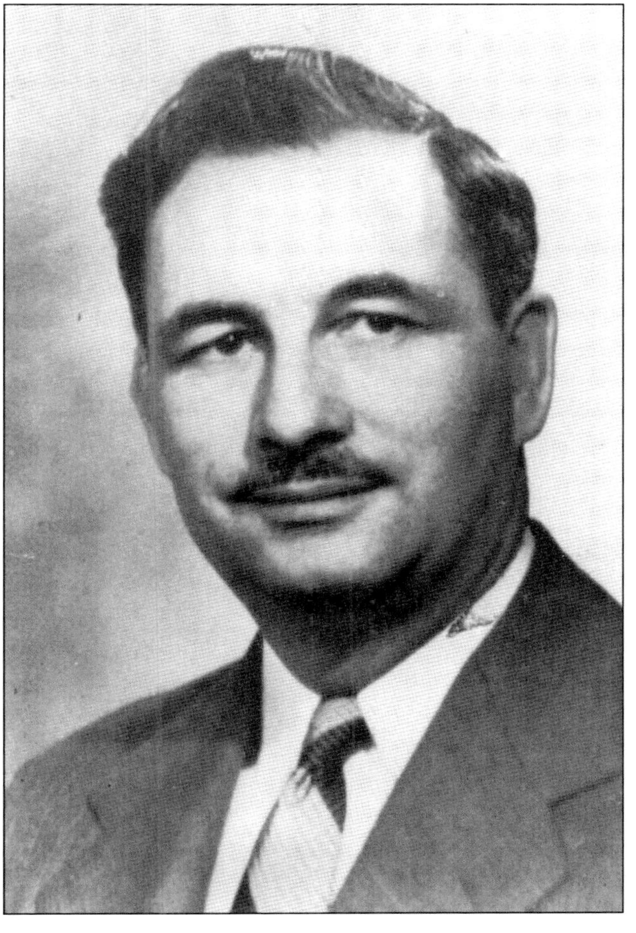

Dr. E. Garfield Claxton was born in Ottawa and began his obstetrics practice in Ogdensburg, New York, in 1932. He delivered more than 10,000 babies before his retirement in 1963. He and his wife, Ruth, adopted a son named John E. Claxton. Sadly, John passed away at a young age. This tragedy prompted a large gift to the hospital in the 1970s to fund construction of the Claxton Emergency Department and Outpatient Services in John's memory. In the late 1990s, another large gift from Dr. Claxton funded the Connection for Women, which encompassed the birth center, the perinatal clinic, women's medical imaging, and women's health education. In 2000, Dr. Claxton committed to a transformational $7.5 million gift to the hospital, which provided $4.5 million to establish an endowment fund, and $3 million for future construction projects. Altogether, Dr. Claxton's giving totaled over $8 million.

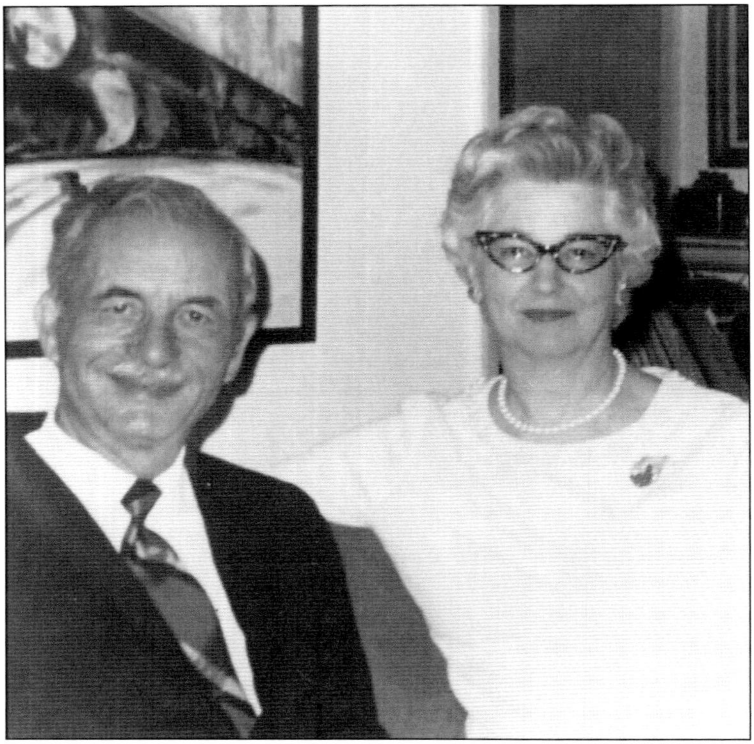

Dr. E. Garfield Claxton and his first wife, Ruth Claxton, are pictured in December 1969. The Claxtons were also generous benefactors to a number of other charities in Ogdensburg, including the First Presbyterian Church, United Helpers, the Boys and Girls Club, and the Frederick Remington Art Museum.

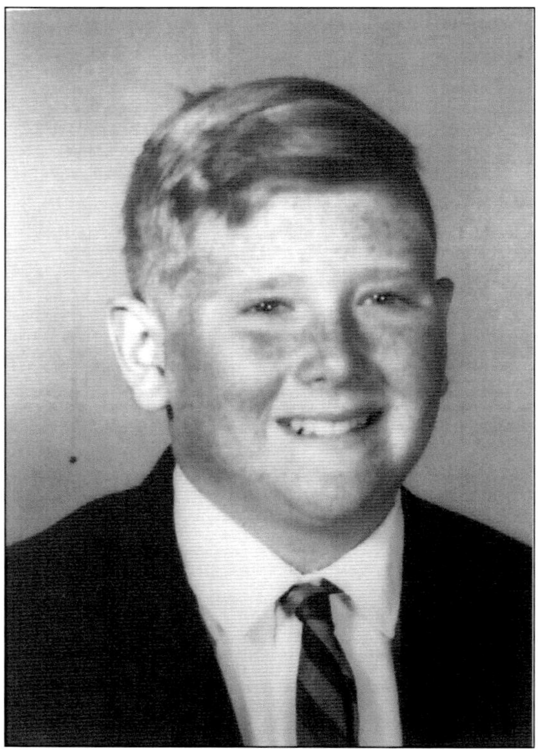

This is a photograph of John E. Claxton, son of Dr. Claxton and his first wife, Ruth Claxton. John passed away tragically as a teenager.

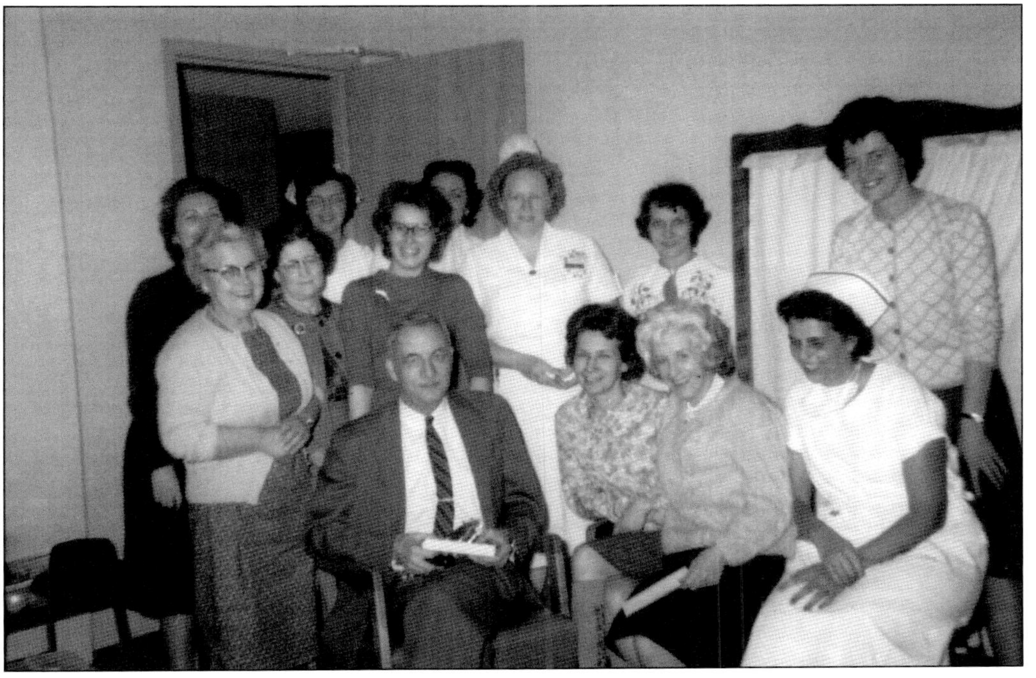

This is a photograph of Dr. Claxton's retirement party at the hospital in 1963. (Courtesy of Angie Loffler.)

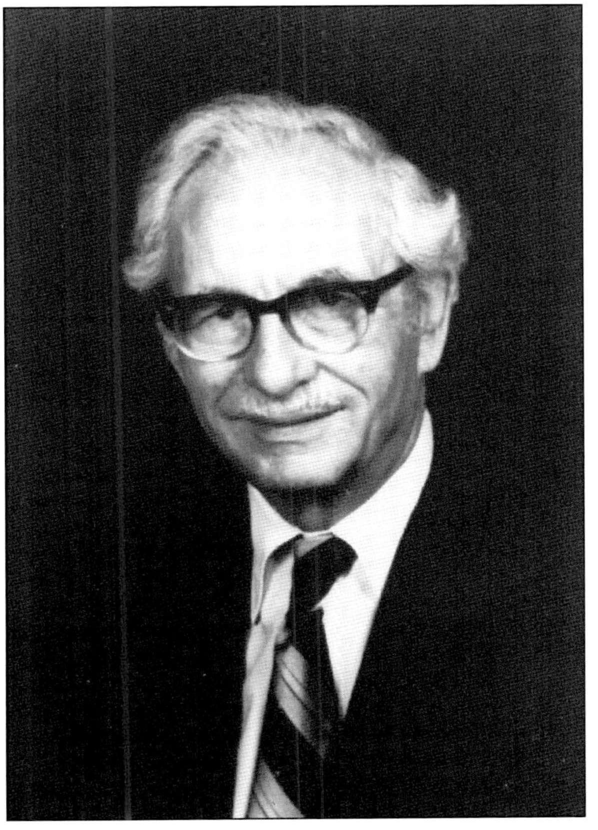

Dr. E. Garfield Claxton moved to Florida in 1964 with his first wife, Ruth. Ruth developed an illness in Florida and passed away in 1984. After Ruth's passing, Dr. Claxton married widow Helena Laidlaw Livermore. Helena Laidlaw grew up in Canton and graduated from St. Lawrence University in 1927. Her first husband, Merle Livermore, was a teacher at Ogdensburg Free Academy.

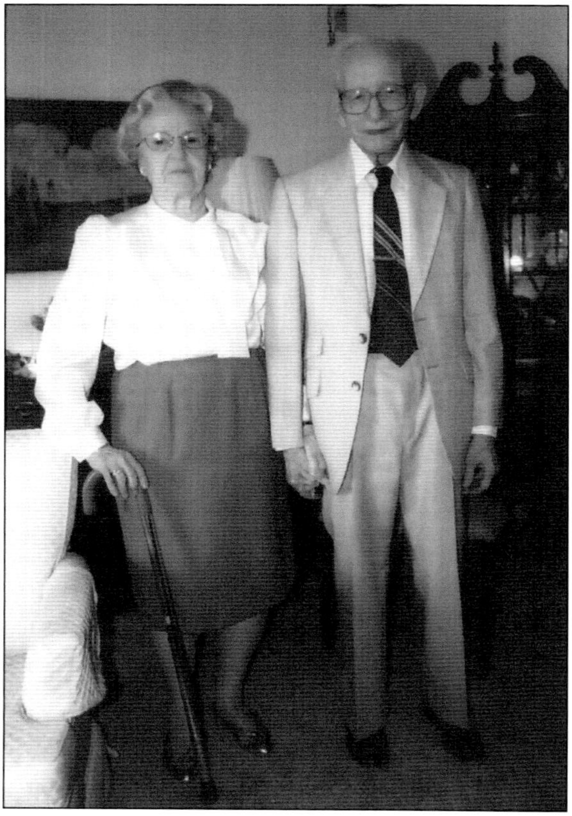

Dr. E. Garfield Claxton and his second wife, Helena, are pictured on the occasion of a visit by members of the hospital administration and board members to Florida to celebrate the Claxtons' extraordinary gift. Dr. Claxton passed away in 2002, but Helena continues to live in their home in Florida.

Rev. Thomas Patterson (far left), chairman of the hospital board, presents a special plaque to Helena Claxton, commemorating their gift. Dr. E. Garfield Claxton receives a key to the city and special citation from Mayor William Nelson (second from right). At right, Lorraine Kabot, president and CEO, is holding a plaque recognizing Dr. Claxton's many years of service.

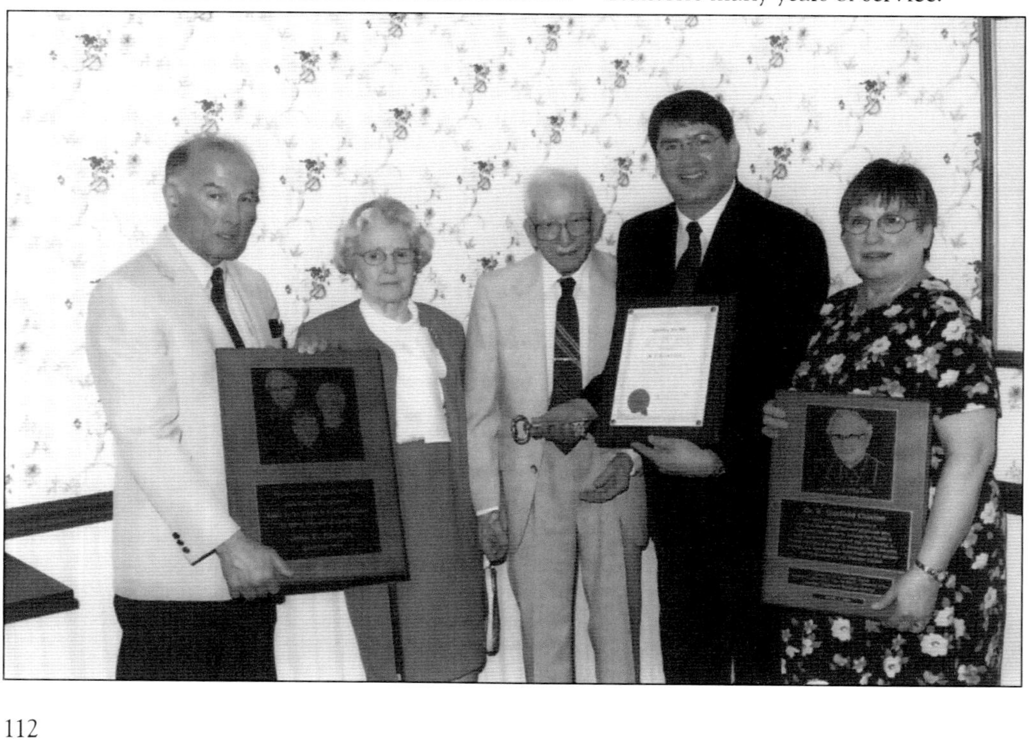

Eight

Expansion and New Services

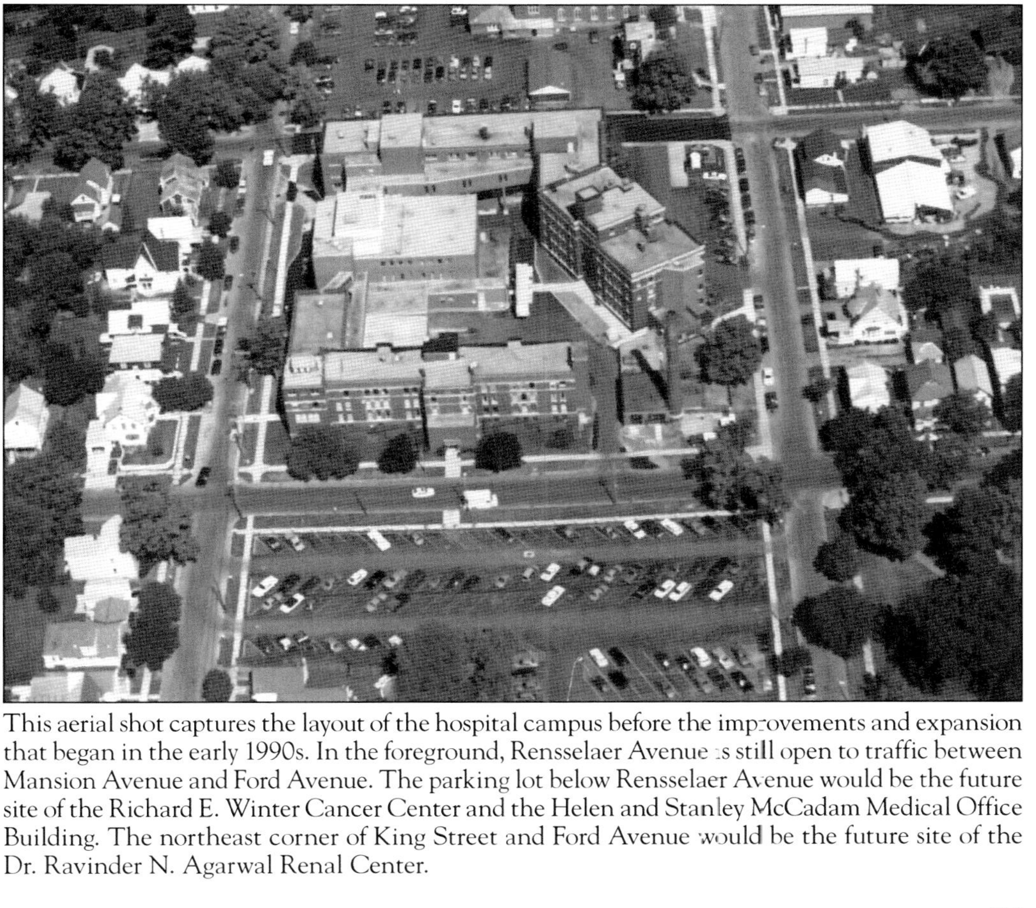

This aerial shot captures the layout of the hospital campus before the improvements and expansion that began in the early 1990s. In the foreground, Rensselaer Avenue is still open to traffic between Mansion Avenue and Ford Avenue. The parking lot below Rensselaer Avenue would be the future site of the Richard E. Winter Cancer Center and the Helen and Stanley McCadam Medical Office Building. The northeast corner of King Street and Ford Avenue would be the future site of the Dr. Ravinder N. Agarwal Renal Center.

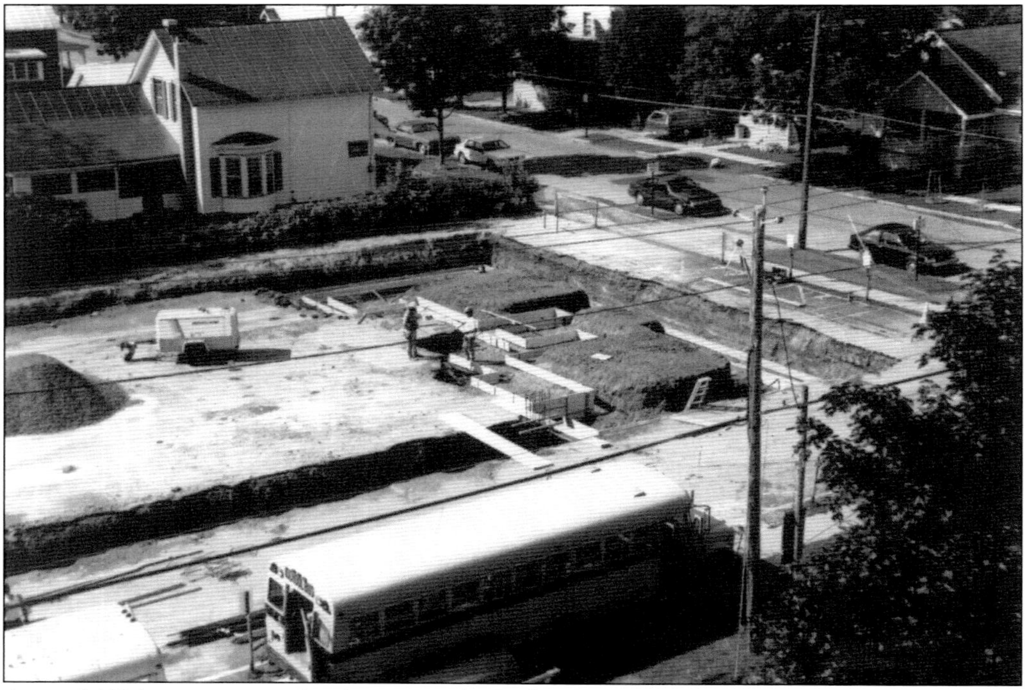

Around 1994, construction has begun on the Richard E. Winter Cancer Center.

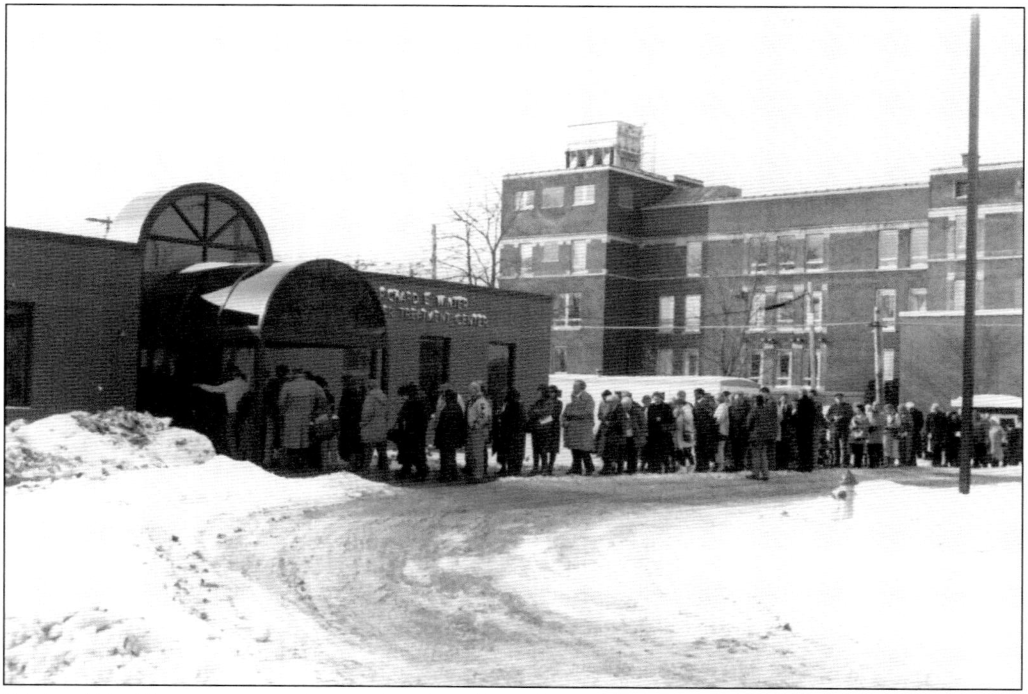

Richard E. Winter stepped forward with a $1 million gift to the Modernization Campaign to build St. Lawrence County's first cancer treatment center. In this picture, community members file into the new facility during its dedication in 1994.

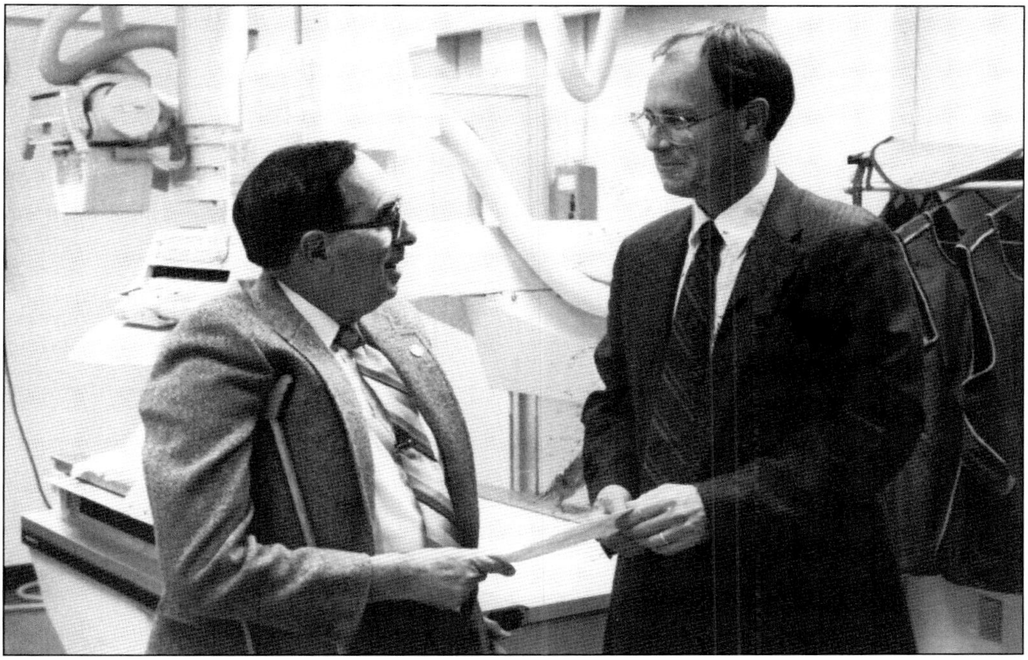

Abe Rothenberg (left), the first chairman of the foundation board, presents a check from the foundation to Don Lewis, president and CEO of Hepburn Hospital. Don Lewis served as the president and CEO of the medical center from 1986 until 1997.

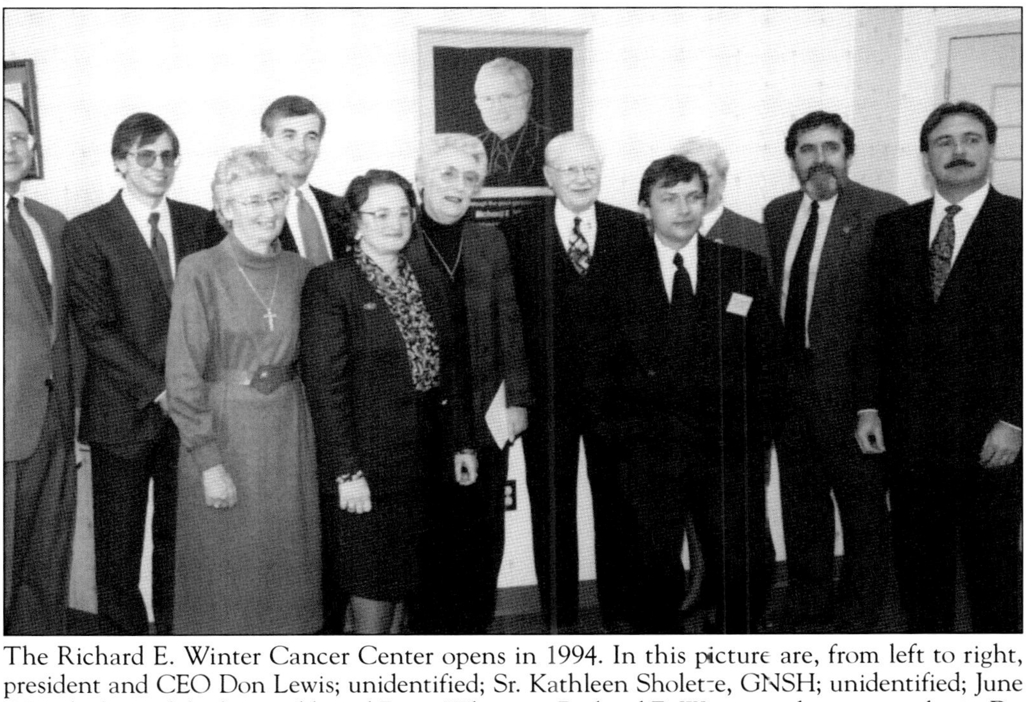

The Richard E. Winter Cancer Center opens in 1994. In this picture are, from left to right, president and CEO Don Lewis; unidentified; Sr. Kathleen Sholette, GNSH; unidentified; June O'Neil; chair of the hospital board Doris Wheaton; Richard E. Winter; radiation oncologist Dr. Allen Bradshaw; unidentified; mayor Dick Lockwood; and Dr. Christopher Williams.

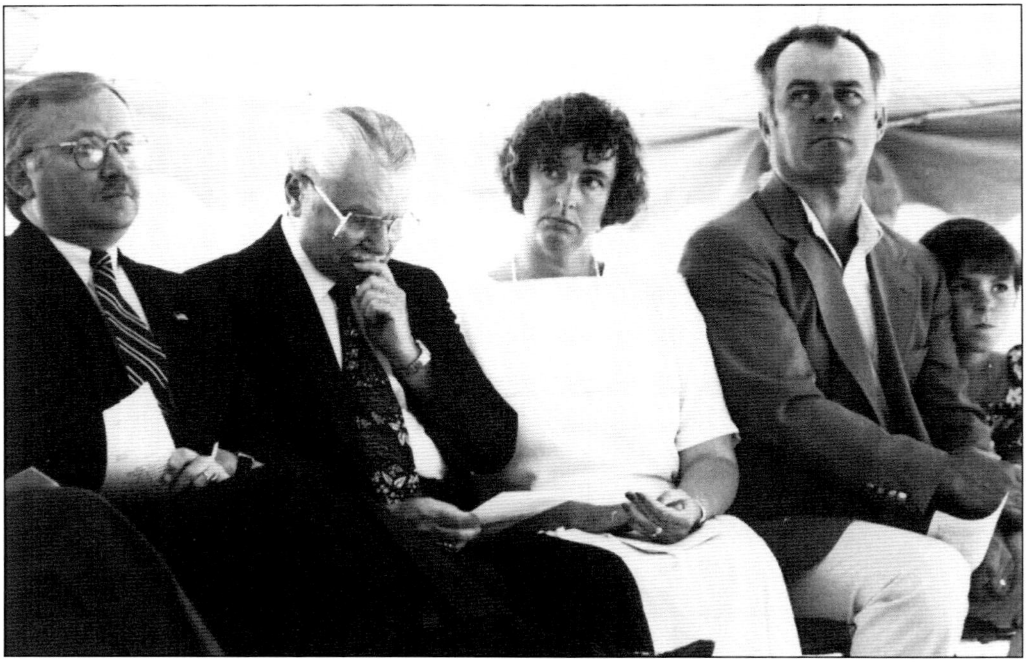

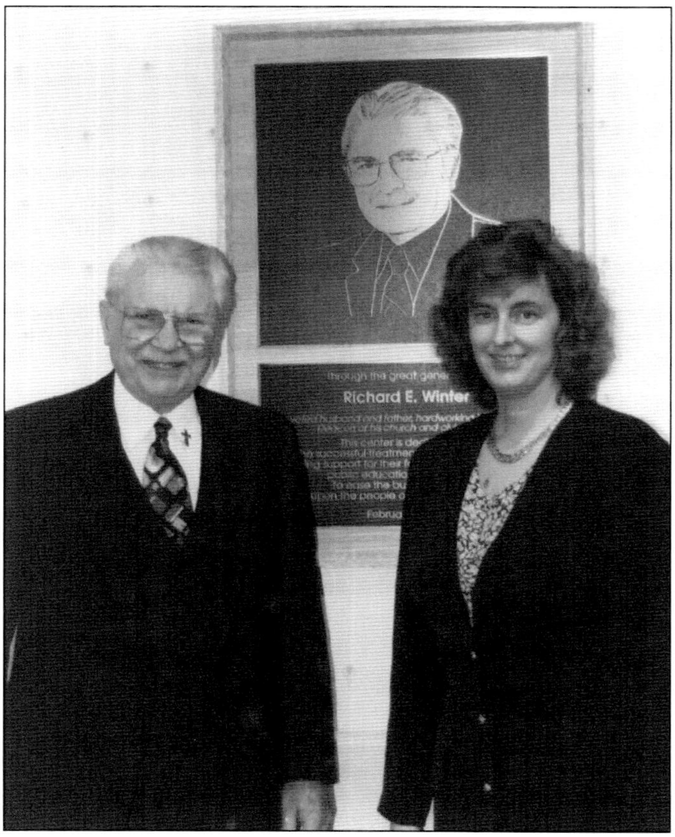

From left to right, Sen. Jim Wright, Richard E. Winter, Bonnie Winter Wright (daughter of Richard E. Winter), Richard Wright (son-in-law of Richard E. Winter), and Shannon Wright (granddaughter of Richard E. Winter) attend the ground-breaking ceremony of the new Richard E. Winter Cancer Center.

Richard E. Winter poses with his daughter Bonnie Winter Wright in front of the plaque commemorating his gift in the new cancer center.

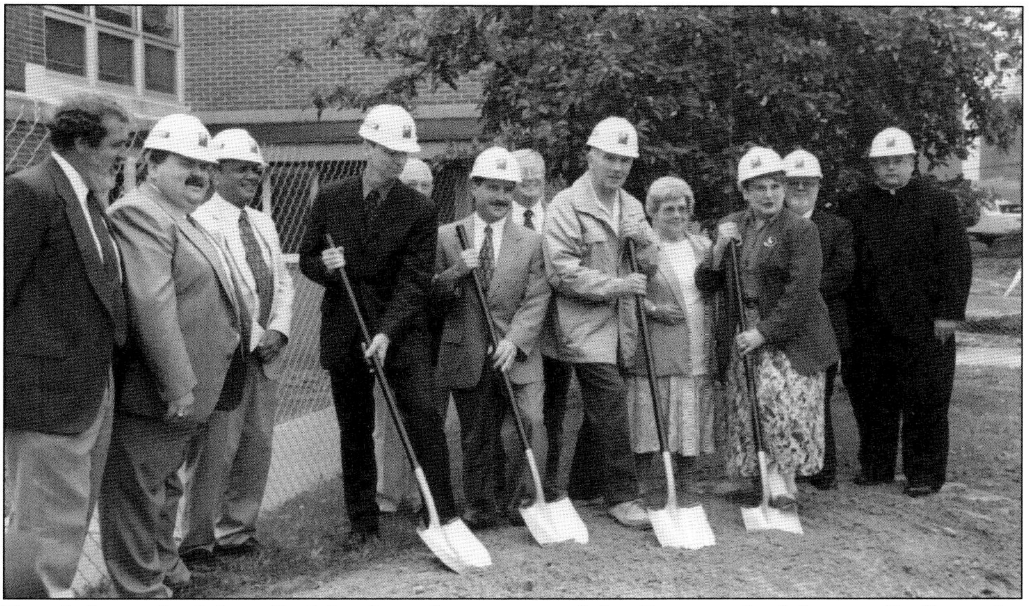

From left to right, Mayor Dick Lockwood; accountant John Gray; medical director Dr. Ravinder N. Agarwal; Dr. Denys Beauvais; medical center board members Phillip Cosmo and Rev. Thomas Patterson; Sr. Mary Teresa LaBrake, GNSH; president and CEO Lorraine Kabot; Msgr. Harry K. Snow; and Rev. Walter Smith participate in a ground-breaking ceremony for the new Helen and Stanley McCadam Medical Office Building, to be adjacent and connected to the Richard E. Winter Cancer Center.

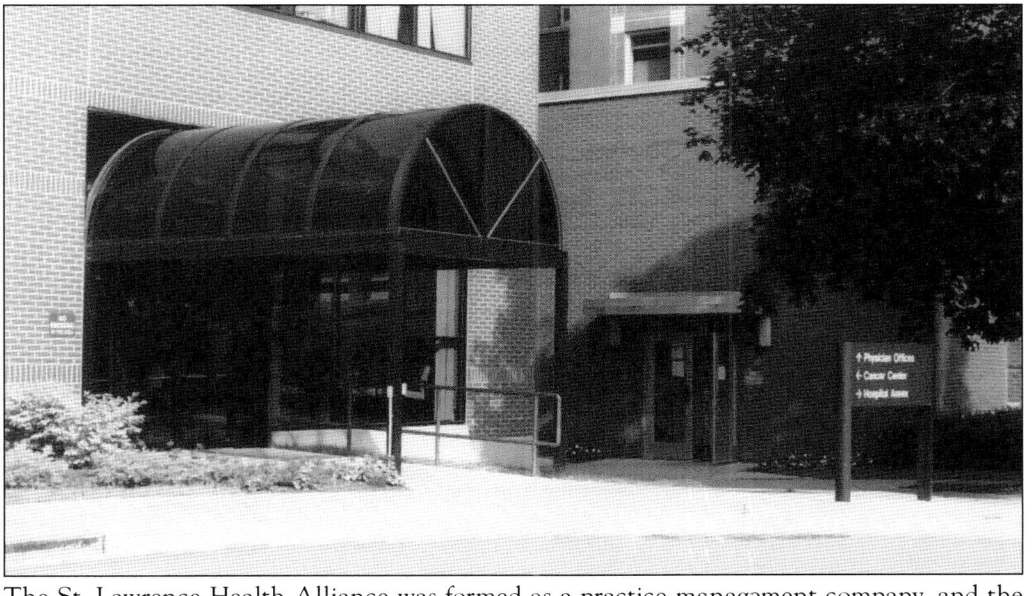

The St. Lawrence Health Alliance was formed as a practice management company, and the Helen and Stanley McCadam Medical Office Building opened in August 1995. Also in 1995, the hospital was renamed Hepburn Medical Center in recognition of its growing prominence as a regional health care provider, and Lyon Place, in front of the medical office building and cancer center, was dedicated in honor of benefactor Helen Griffin Lyon.

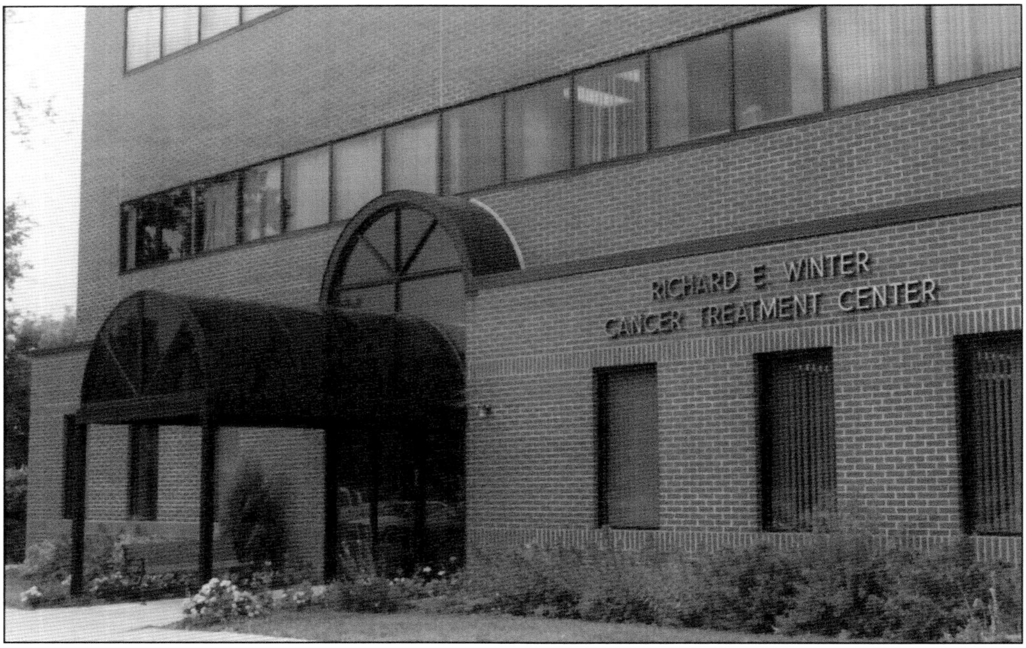

The Richard E. Winter Cancer Center is pictured in 1995 after construction is completed on the Helen and Stanley McCadam Medical Office Building, which was erected next to and over the cancer center.

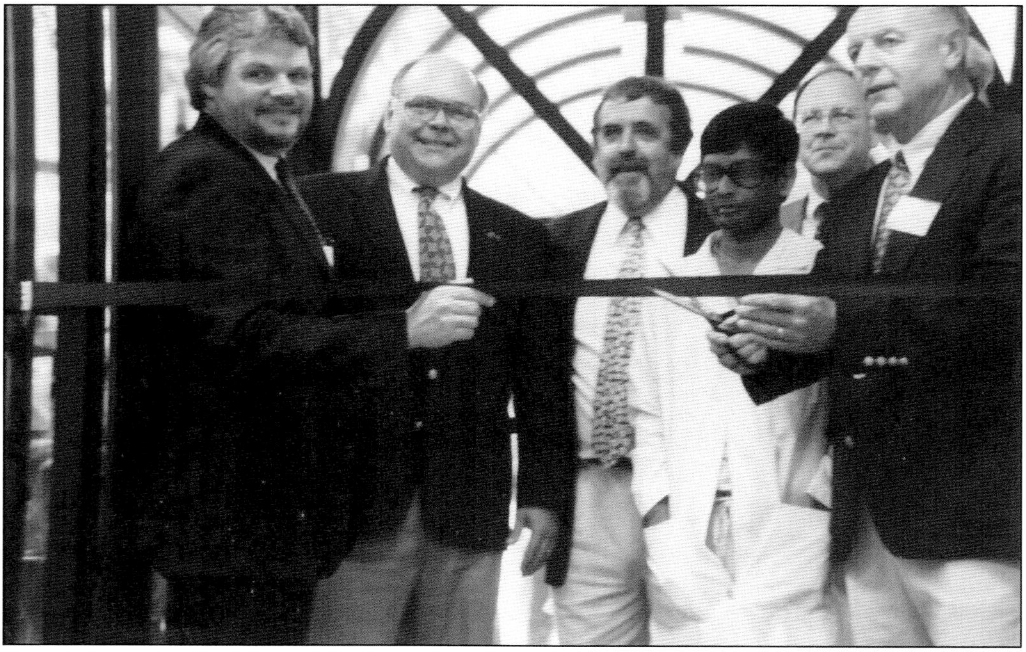
From left to right, Dr. Michael Seidman, board member Joseph Tracy, Mayor Dick Lockwood, Dr. Prasad Yitta (surgeon), president and CEO Don Lewis, and board member William Plimpton cut the ribbon on the new Helen and Stanley McCadam Medical Office Building.

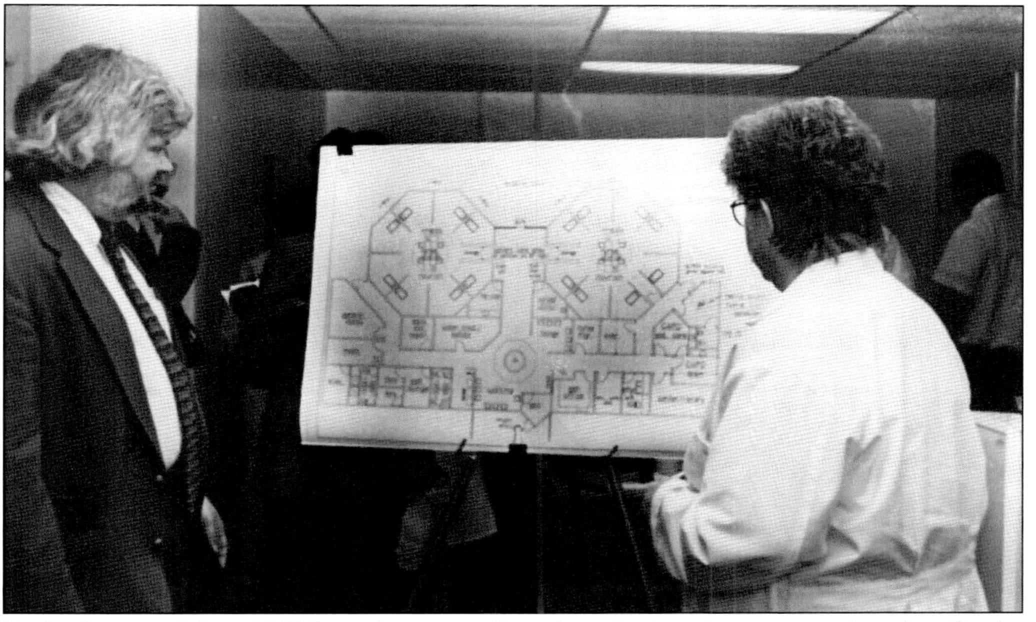

Dr. Seidman and Ann McRoberts (manager of renal services) review construction plans for the renal center.

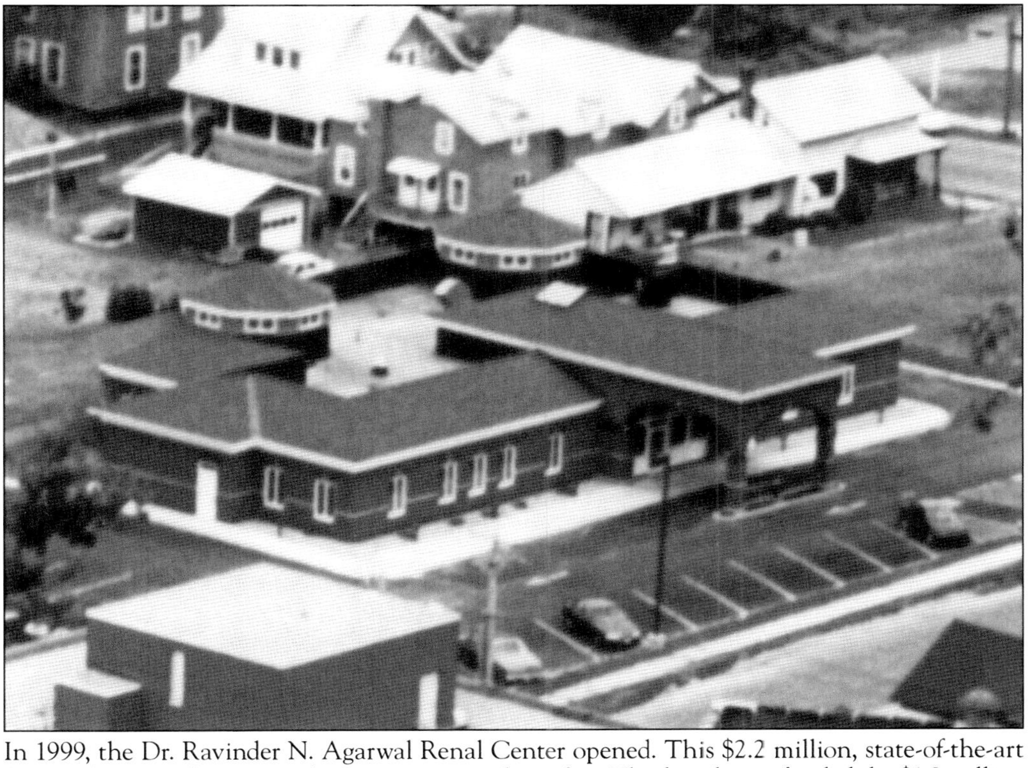

In 1999, the Dr. Ravinder N. Agarwal Renal Center opened. This $2.2 million, state-of-the-art facility dramatically improved patient access and comfort. The foundation funded the $1.8 million cost of construction and raised over $1.1 million from the community.

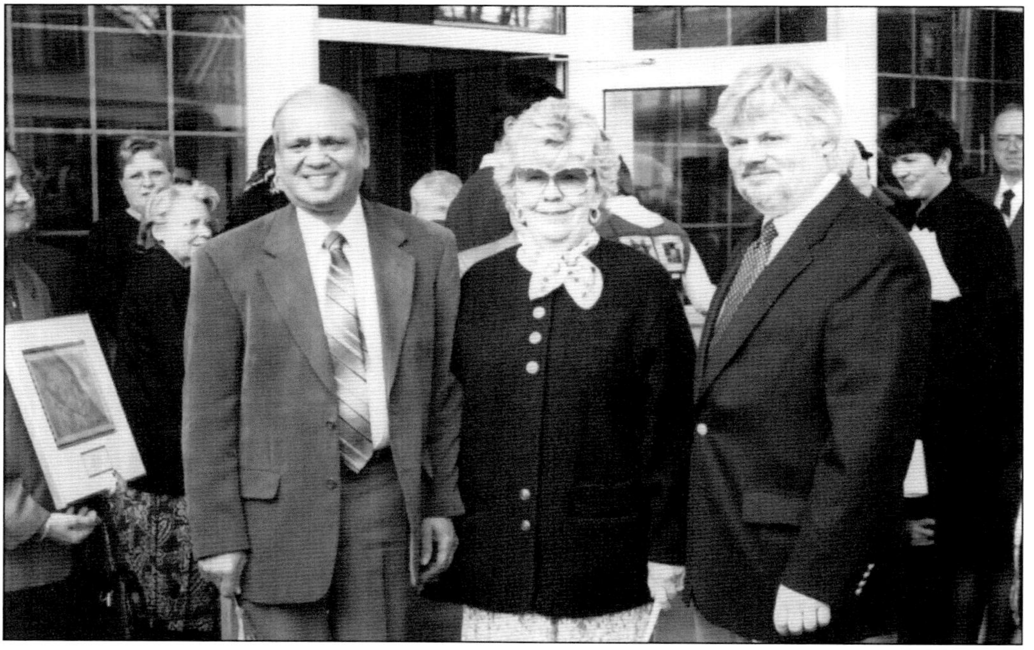

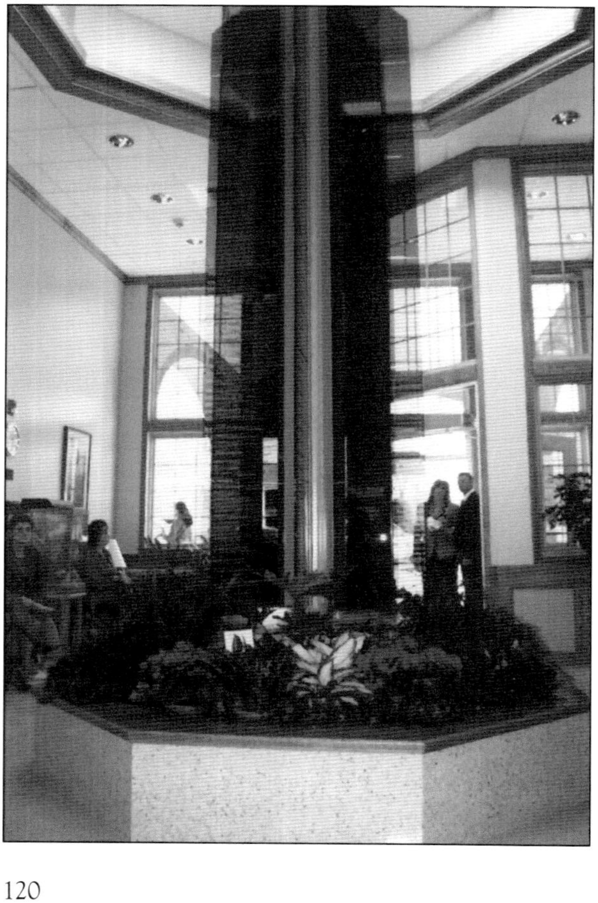

Pictured at the dedication ceremony of the renal center are donor Dr. Ravinder N. Agarwal (left); Gail Bongiovanni, widow of Dr. John R. Bongiovanni, who first brought hemodialysis to the hospital; and Dr. Michael Seidman, director of renal services.

This interior photograph shows the lobby of the new Dr. Ravinder N. Agarwal Renal Center.

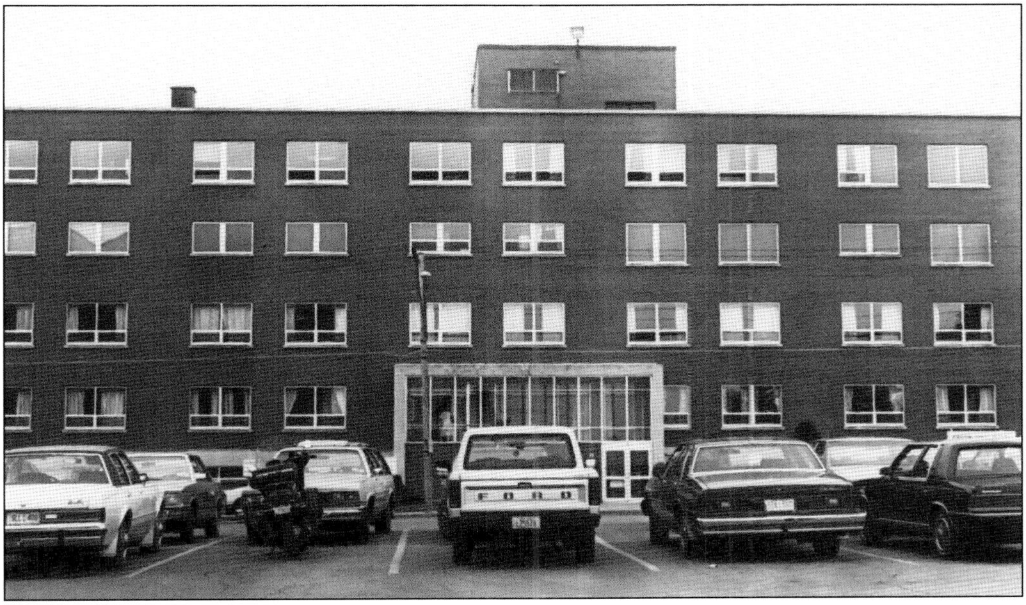

This exterior shot of the medical center captures the entrance before the improvements were made to it and the lobby in 2000.

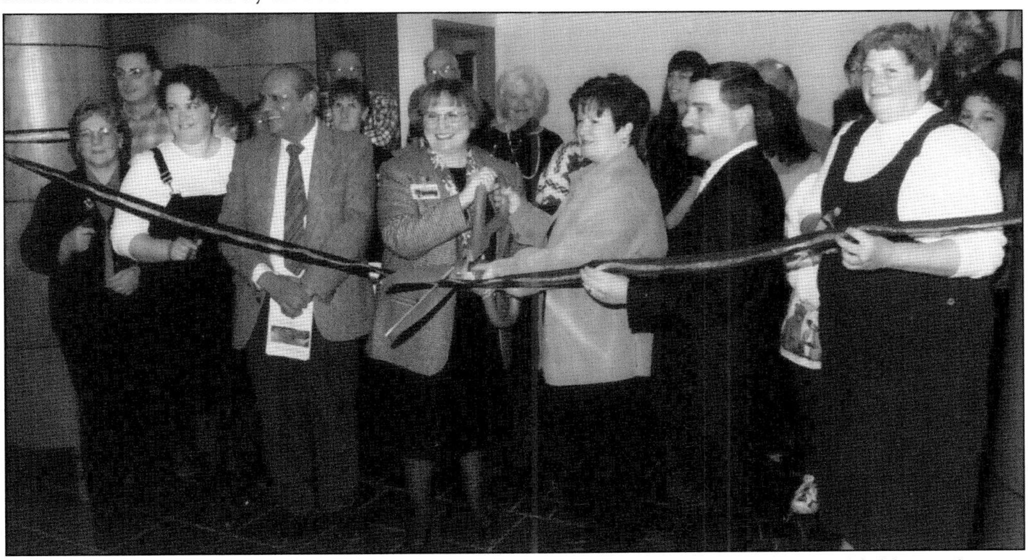

In 2000, the medical center celebrated the opening of a new main entrance and lobby, cafeteria, and cardiology, physical therapy and cardiopulmonary rehabilitation, medical-surgical, pharmacy, chapel, and radiology facilities. At the dedication ceremony, the renaming of the medical center is announced in honor of Dr. E. Garfield Claxton, whose lifetime contribution of $7.5 million is acknowledged as the largest charitable gift by a living donor in North Country history. Of this amount, $4.5 million is earmarked for endowment and the balance dedicated to future capital improvements. Pictured in the first row are, from left to right, Christine Caroll, Karen Peck, Dr. Ravinder Agarwal (medical director), Lorraine Kabot (president and CEO), Darlene Lynch, Phil Cosmo, and Charlotte Paro. Among those in the back are Ken LaRock, Debbie King, Joanne Garno, and Ramona Kennedy.

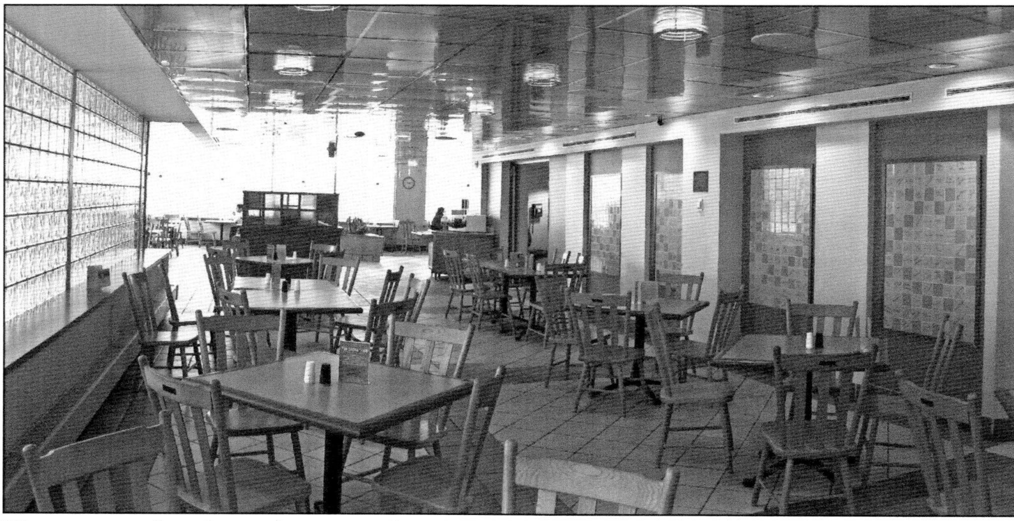

This interior shot shows the new cafeteria.

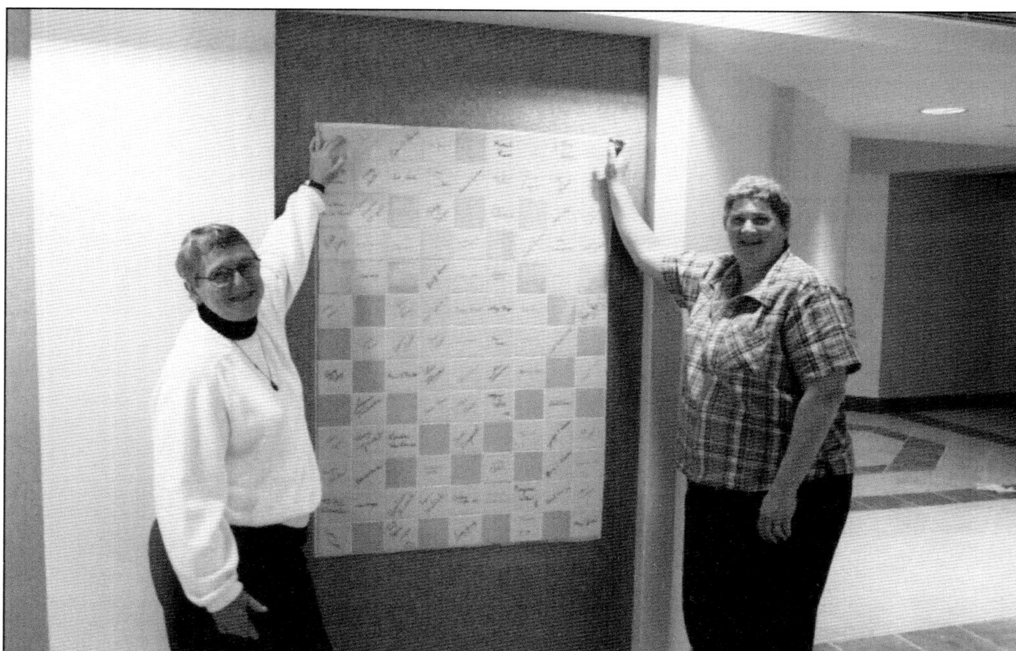

Rita Hess (left) and Charlotte Paro, members of the Hepburn Employees Always Reaching for Tomorrow (HEART) Committee, pose for a picture in front of tile work in the new cafeteria. Employee donors to the cafeteria project were recognized through an opportunity to have their signature on a tile. The HEART Committee was founded in early 1993. The group rallies financial support for the hospital from employees through events and activities. Hess was the first chair of the group and was followed in that role by Paro.

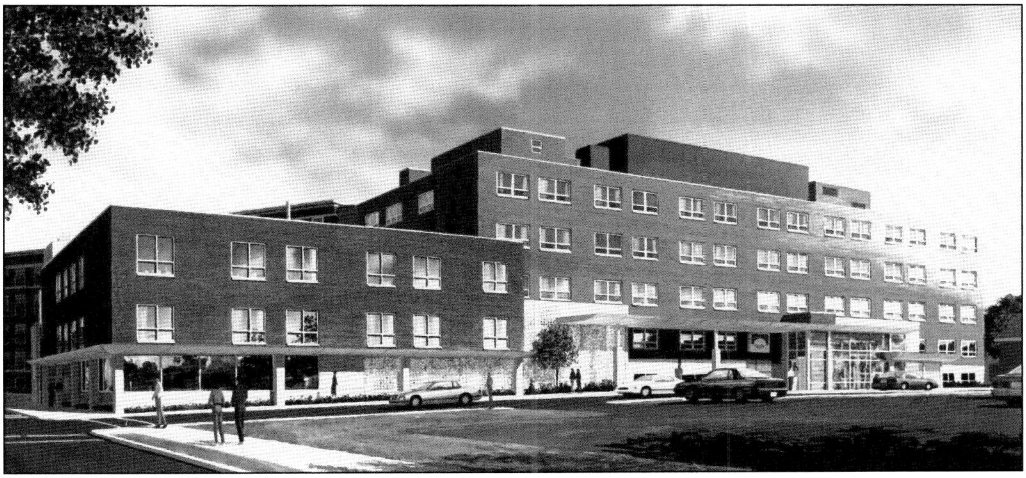

This sketch of the front of Claxton-Hepburn Medical Center shows the view from King Street after the addition and improvements were completed in 2000.

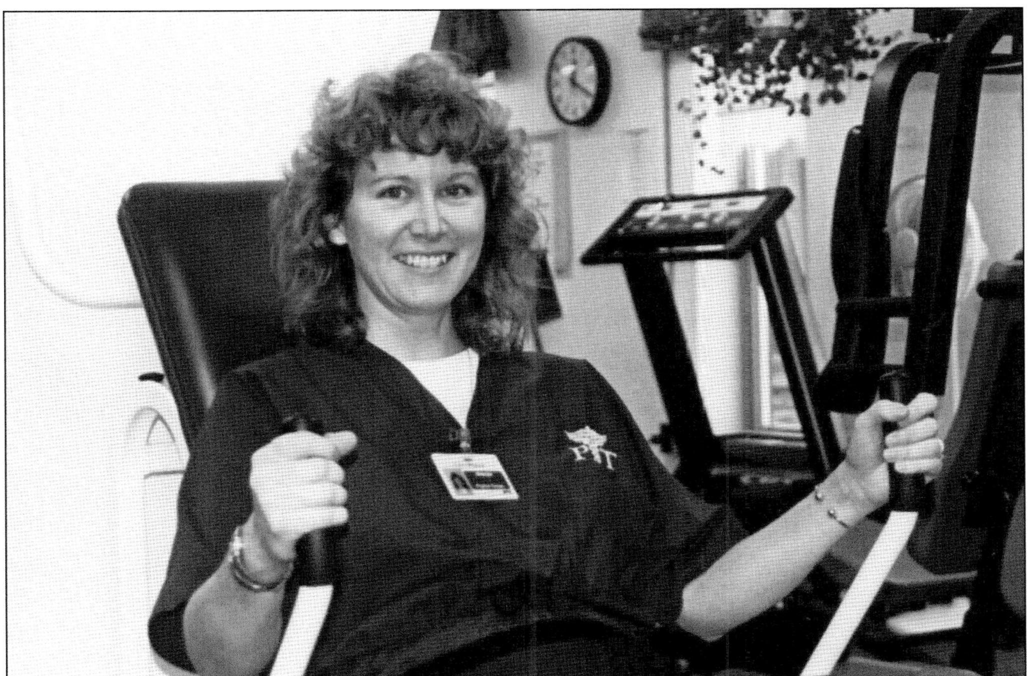

Cinci Weaver, manager of the physical therapy department, poses in the new facility while demonstrating the use of new equipment.

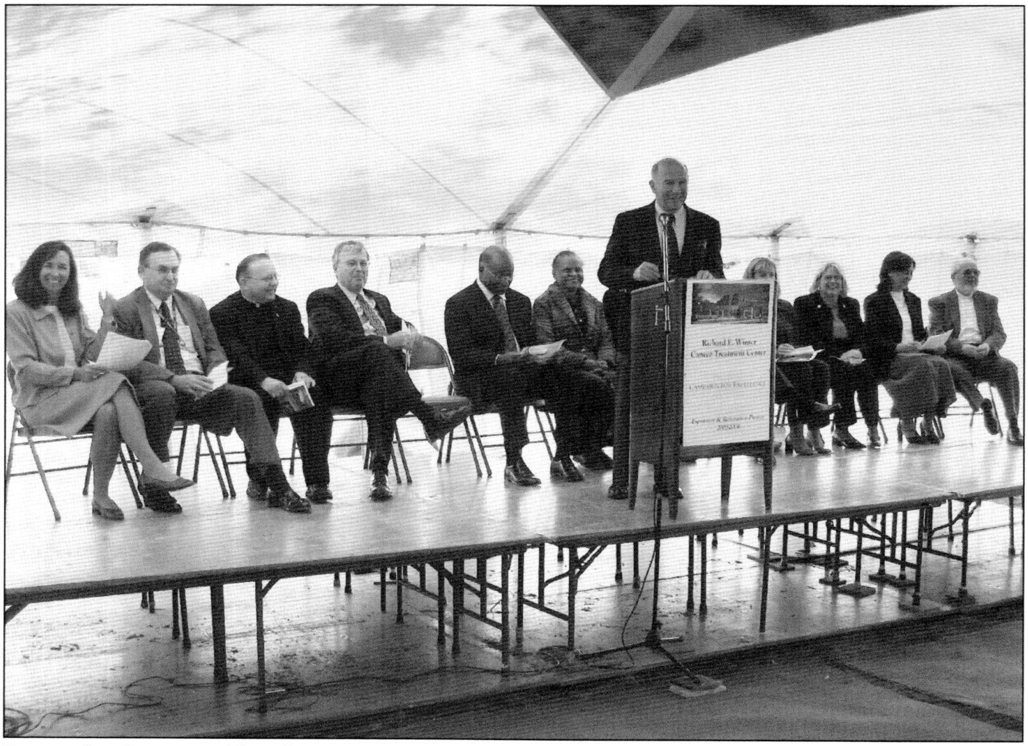

Pictured is the ground-breaking ceremony for an addition to the Richard E. Winter Cancer Center, which commenced in 2004. The new project added space for chemotherapy infusion treatments and a new relaxation garden. The Reverend Thomas Patterson delivers a speech on the occasion, with Maureen Missert, Richard Krasnauskas (president and CEO), Fr. James Shurtleff, Robert McNeil, Dr. Max Laguerre, Dr. Lucille Alston, Bonnie Wright, two unidentified women, and Rev. Walter Smith behind him on the stage.

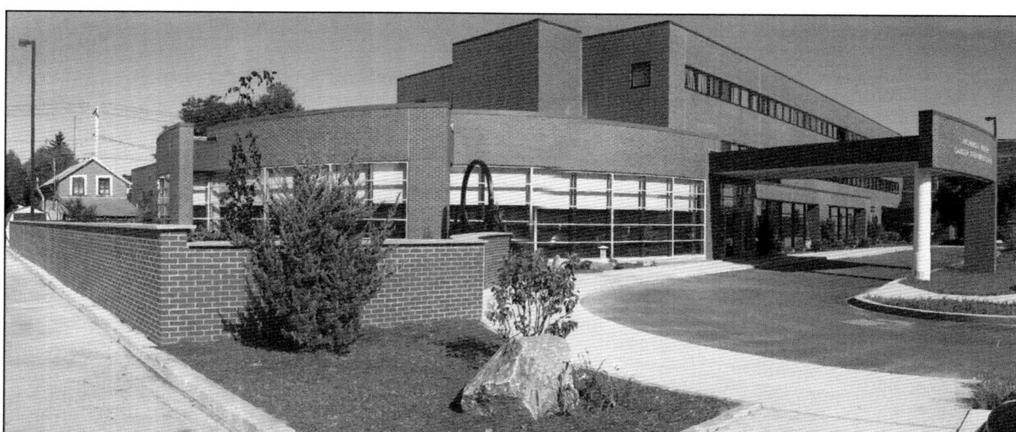

This is a picture of the Richard E. Winter Cancer Center with the new infusion treatment space, the new covered drive-through entrance, and the Barbara Cuthbert Welch relaxation garden.

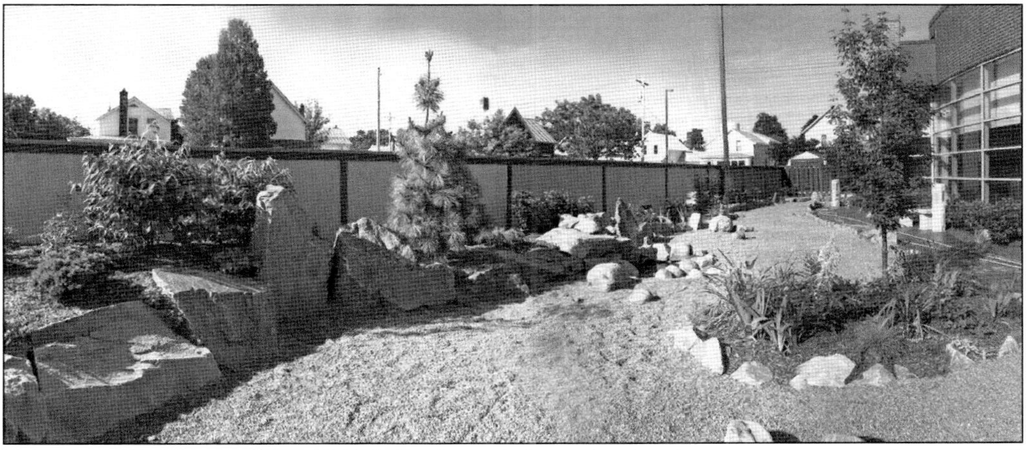

In 2005, the Barbara Cuthbert Welch Garden is dedicated to "mediation, reflection and enjoyment" of patients, visitors, and staff, adding a new dimension to the healing environment of the Richard E. Winter Cancer Center.

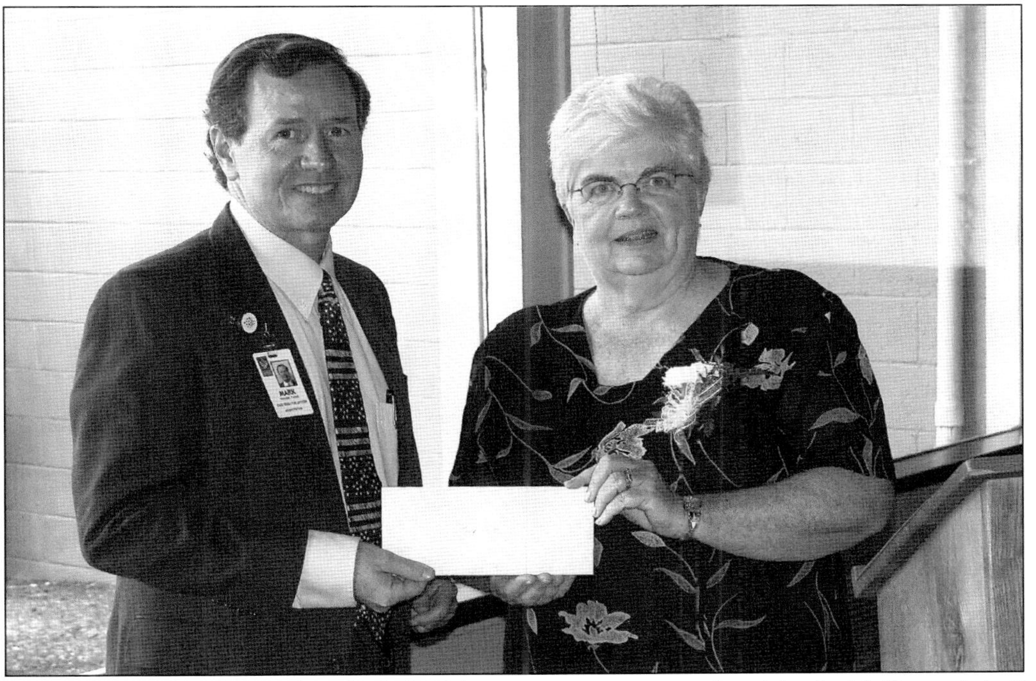

In this picture, president and CEO Mark Webster accepts a payment from Martha McKee on behalf of the Claxton-Hepburn Medical Center Auxiliary. She was the auxiliary's president in 2006. The auxiliary committed $200,000 for the Building Our Future Together campaign for the new ambulatory surgery, radiology, mental health, and obstetrics areas of the hospital. The auxiliary, formerly known as the City Guild, has been tremendously successful raising money for the hospital through various events and profits from its gift shop at the main entrance of the hospital.

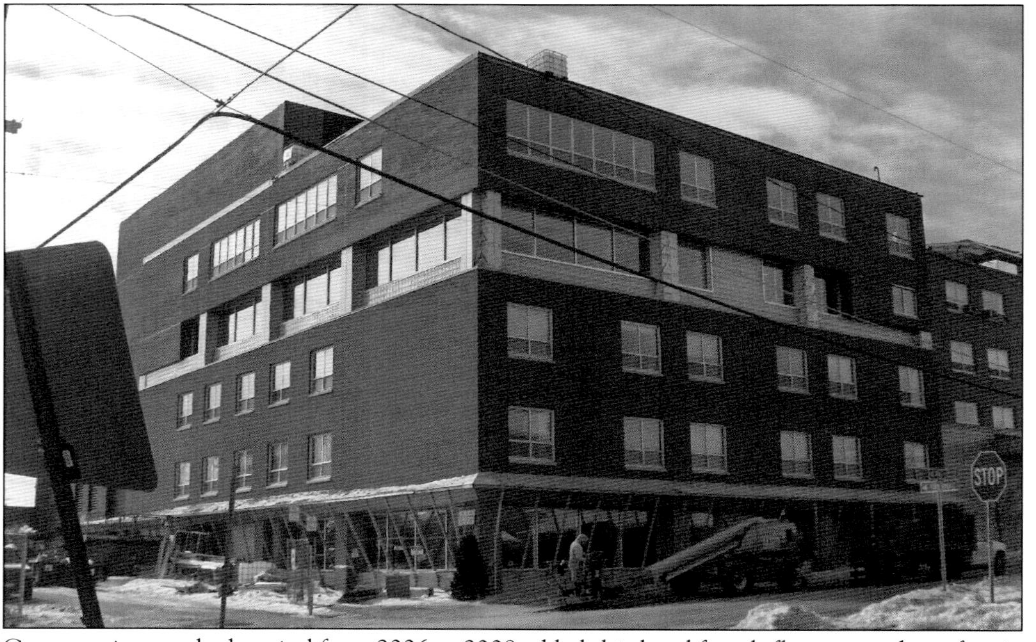

Construction on the hospital from 2006 to 2008 added third and fourth floors over the cafeteria and physical therapy areas. The third floor houses a new mental health center, and the fourth floor is a new obstetrics department.

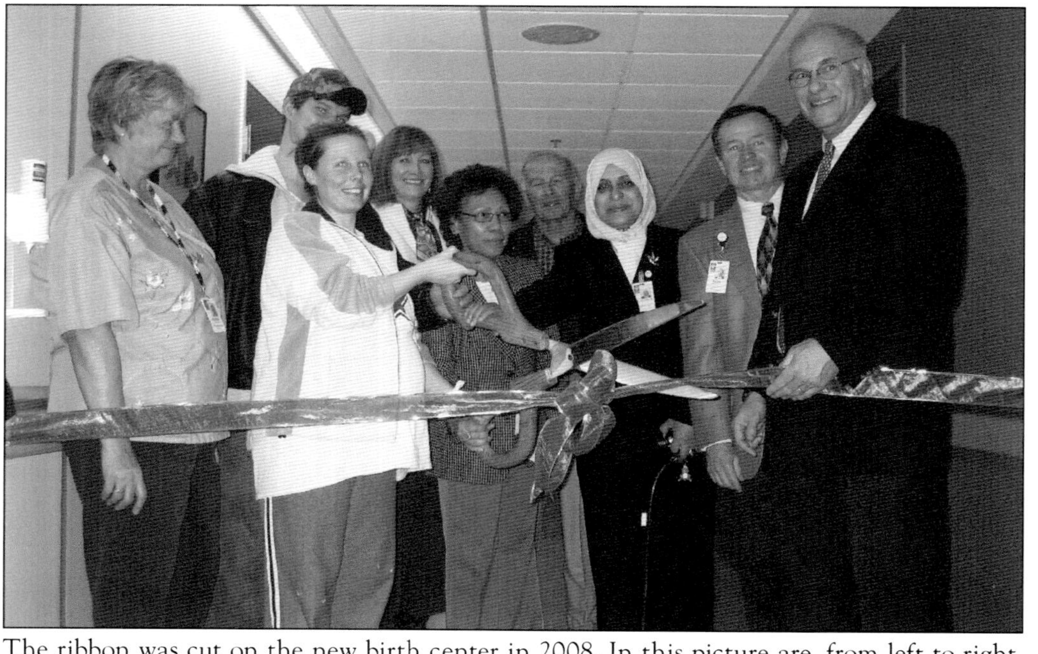

The ribbon was cut on the new birth center in 2008. In this picture are, from left to right, manager of the department Gloria Hoogenraad, an unidentified expectant mother and her partner, campaign cochair Dr. Patti Mahoney, pediatrician Dr. Imelda Abear, board member Rev. Thomas Patterson, pediatrician Dr. Azza Aboo-deeb, president and CEO Mark Webster, and board chair Russell Strait.

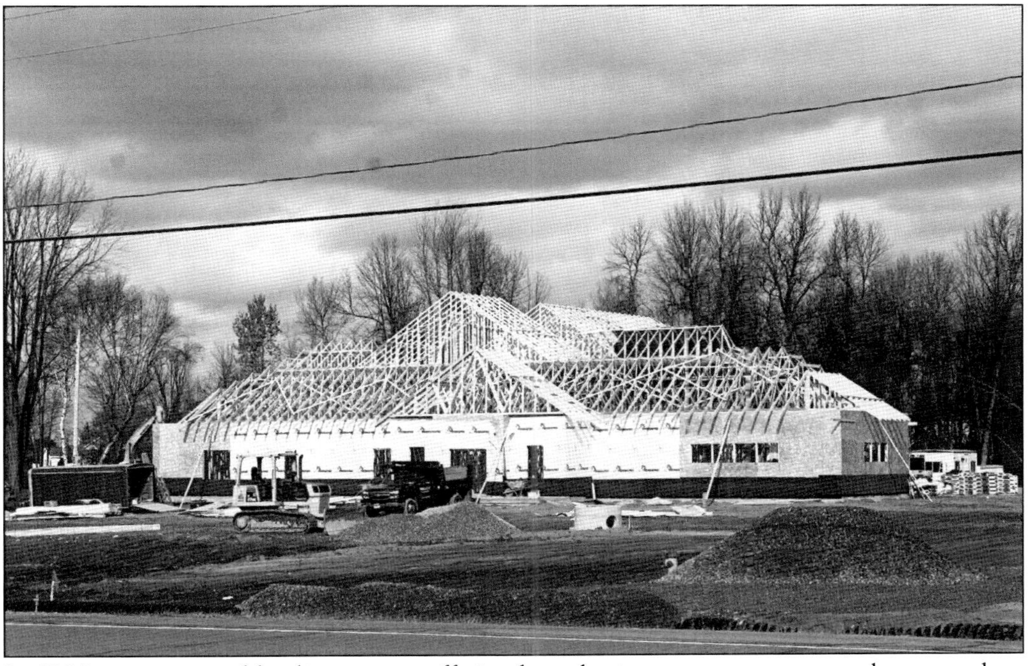

In 2008, a new wound healing center, offering hyperbaric oxygen treatments, also opened on Ford Street Extension. The wound healing center is located in a brand-new building that also houses a primary care clinic and the aquatic therapy program. The building was constructed by Richard Maginn, president and CEO of Heritage Homes.

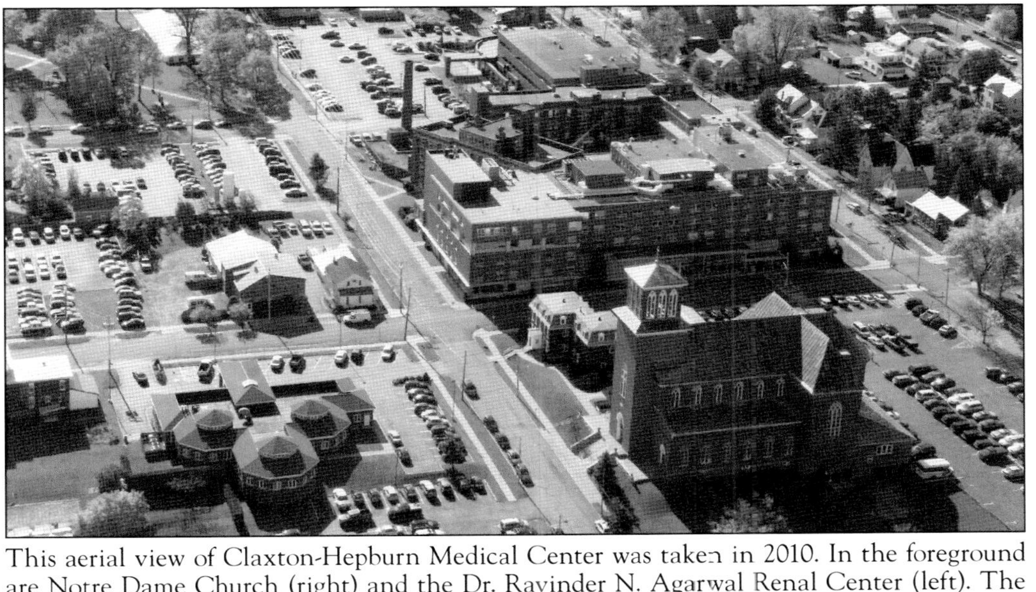

This aerial view of Claxton-Hepburn Medical Center was taken in 2010. In the foreground are Notre Dame Church (right) and the Dr. Ravinder N. Agarwal Renal Center (left). The main hospital building on King Street is shown with its new entrance, completed in 2000, and the expansion on the left-hand side on the third and fourth floors, completed in 2008. In the background, the Richard E. Winter Cancer Center and Helen and Stanley McCadam Medical Office Building are visible.